Contents

PART III THE POLITICS WITHIN

PART IV LOCAL STRUGGLES, GLOBAL IMPACTS

Acknowledgements

Ashgate would like to thank our researchers and the contributing authors who provided copies, along with the following for their permission to reprint copyright material:-

African Studies Center for the essay: Albert Grundlingh (2004), '"Rocking the Boat" in South Africa? Voëlvry Music and Afrikaans Anti-Apartheid Social Protest in the 1980s', *The International Journal of African Historical Studies*, **37**, pp. 483–514.

Camden House for the essay: David Robb (2007), 'Mühsam, Brecht, Eisler, and the Twentieth-Century Revolutionary Heritage', in David Robb (ed.), *Protest Song in East and West Germany since the 1960s*, Rochester, NY: Camden House, pp. 35–66.

Faber and Faber for the essay: Robin Denselow (1989), 'Feed the World, Free the World ...', in *When the Music's Over: The Story of Political Pop*, London: Faber and Faber, pp. 233–61.

Mosaic, a Journal for Interdisciplinary Study of Literature for the essay: Jennifer Gerstel (1999), 'Irony, Deception, and Political Culture in the Works of Dmitri Shostakovich', *Mosaic, a Journal for Interdisciplinary Study of Literature*, **32**, pp. 35–51. Copyright © 1999 *Mosaic*.

Oxford University Press for the essays: Yayoi Uno Everett (2009), '"Scream Against the Sky": Japanese Avant-Garde Music in the Sixties', in Robert Adlington (ed.), *Sound Commitments: Avant-Garde Music and the Sixties*, Oxford: Oxford University Press, pp. 187–208. By permission of Oxford University Press, Inc.; Timothy D. Taylor (1998), 'Moving in Decency: The Music and Radical Politics of Cornelius Cardew', *Music and Letters*, **79**, pp. 555–76.

Princeton University Press for the essay: Anna Caraveli (1986), 'The Bitter Wounding: The Lament as Social Protest in Rural Greece', in Jill Dubisch (ed.), *Gender and Power in Rural Greece*, Princeton: Princeton University Press, pp. 169–94. Reprinted by permission of Princeton University Press.

Random House and Mark LeVine for the essay: Mark LeVine (2008), 'Iran: "Like a Flower Growing in the Middle of the Desert"', in *Heavy Metal Islam: Rock, Resistance, and the Struggle for the Soul of Islam*, New York: Three Rivers Press, pp. 172–211. Copyright © 2008 by Mark LeVine. Used by permission of Three Rivers Press, a division of Random House, Inc.

Sage Publications for the essays: Light Carruyo (2005), 'La Gaita Zuliana: Music and the Politics of Protest in Venezuela', *Latin American Perspectives*, **32**, pp. 98–111. Copyright © 2005 Latin American Perspectives; José Arturo Saavedra Casco (2006), 'The Language of the Young People: Rap, Urban Culture and Protest in Tanzania', *Journal of Asian and African Studies*, **43**, pp. 229–48. Copyright © 2006 Sage Publications.

Publisher's Note:

The material in this volume has been reproduced using the facsimile method. This means we can retain the original pagination to facilitate easy and correct citation of the original essays. It also explains the variety of typefaces, page layouts and numbering.

Series Preface

One doesn't need to be a prime minister or president to appreciate that politics – understood here in its broadest sense as a multifaceted process through which individuals or groups are persuaded or coerced to a particular course of action or point of view – is a fluid construct. Similarly, one doesn't need to be Beethoven or Bono to grasp the idea that music as a vehicle for social interaction cannot avoid being caught up in that process. Music has long been used and abused, claimed and disowned, for propaganda purposes, as a vehicle for protest, as a means of articulating national, racial and sexual identities, and in the name of religious, courtly, party political, and commercial imperatives.

This four volume series surveys the horizon of scholarly enquiry into the intersection of music – art and vernacular, Western and non-Western – and politics. It does so according to four broad, occasionally overlapping themes: patronage (by governments, religious and aristocratic courts, and commercial interests); ideology (political, nationalist and points in between); protest (in Western and non-Western societies, and encompassing political, racial, gender and environmental causes); and identity (gender and sexuality, race, and social stratification).

While the introductions and content of the respective volumes speak for themselves, it remains here to point out that in the area of music and politics what Ian Biddle in his introduction rightly describes as the 'genteel' discipline of musicology has emerged finally from the shadow of its doctrinaire, chauvinist (in all senses of the word) Musikwissenschaft origins. The readings span the discipline's journey to that end, and do so in a way that captures the sheer intellectual vitality and social relevance of inquiries into the convergence of two phenomena that touch us all in some way, shape, or form: music and politics.

MARK CARROLL
University of Adelaide

Introduction

Protest: the term dissolves into ambiguity. It encompasses, variously, myriad contentions, a legion of grievances and countless dissentions; it explains and it obscures. This, nonetheless, is a book with that vexing term at its core. Given the complexity of the subjects addressed in this volume, perhaps the most suitable place to begin is with the proviso that the music of protest is made rebellious or political by the meanings the audience imbues it with. Always socially produced, music is *made* political or revolutionary. Contextually defined, often tactical in its immediacy, and antithetical in its challenge to the status quo, music obtains its meaning and effect from the social milieu in which it is produced, disseminated and interpreted. In short, music never 'is', rather it becomes.

One of the most illuminating examples of the realization of meaning in protest music can be found in the example of the legendary English band The Clash, whose star by the mid-1970s was rapidly rising. After the riots at the Notting Hill Carnival in 1976, which the members of The Clash attended, and where inner-city black youth clashed with some rather heavy-handed policing, the band introduced two songs of especially contentious interpretation. The first, '1977', which was not released on album until the 1994 collection *Super Black Market Clash*, included references to 'knives in West 11' and 'sten guns in Knightsbridge'. Having fielded criticism that The Clash were imagining themselves as some kind of urban guerrilla outfit about to overthrow western civilization, song writer and lead singer Joe Strummer explained his intentions when he wrote the song: 'I imagined sten guns in Knightsbridge pointed at *me*. But people took it to mean that WE had them and we were pointing them at other people,' he continued. 'This was a song written about the future. I thought the future was going to do us in' (quoted in Gray, 2001, p. 158). Whatever auguries Strummer alluded to here and in similar statements of this nature, at the time he was articulating these visions the kind of heightened, politicized music with which The Clash became associated was in its infancy in the UK. For all the transparency of political vision with which The Clash has become associated, it should also be beyond doubt that the political implications of The Clash's work required a period of incubation before it could be properly assessed.

Similar confusion that arose over '1977' existed around 'White Riot', perhaps The Clash's signature tune, which appeared on the band's eponymous debut album, *The Clash*, in 1977. Even if we make allowances for the fact that culturally and politically the 1970s now looks like a period of transition, the fact that 'White Riot' was initially regarded with great suspicion is hardly surprising. Coming as it did less than a year after the trouble at Notting Hill, the fact that the band was calling for a riot – and a *white* one at that – seemed especially worrying. Strummer explained that the song was actually a call for young white men to wake up and challenge a life of passive acceptance. Yet in the politically charged atmosphere of mid-1970s Britain, with the National Front gaining political ground and artists like David Bowie making pro-Fascist statements and Eric Clapton outright racist ones, it was easy enough to confuse the song's direction and aim. Only with the passing of time did 'White Riot' become a fundamental part of the protest capital upon which so much of The Clash's reputation rests.

In a way, then, the argument that Strummer offered, that apathy is the enemy of progress, suggests that protest music is about more – much more – than we might first concede. All-encompassing statements that purport to delineate the parameters of protest music should be treated with suspicion. In this context, the shortcomings of statements such as Greil Marcus's (1994, p. 367) contention that 'to make true political music, you have to say what decent people don't want to hear' are useful not as distinctions over what does and does not constitute possible protest music – they are far too narrow and dichotomous for that – but as a means of illuminating both how difficult the concept of protest music is as well as the extent to which scholarship around the subject is becoming increasingly sophisticated. Those who conceive protest music in terms of such blatant polarization hear it through a limited register; more worryingly still, it suggests a limited vision of protest music conceived around antithesis – an idea that has proven especially resonant. In the same way that the intricacies and complexities of contemporary society, the competing ideologies and contested social visions, demand analysis able to embrace its ambivalences, contradictions and difficulties, so protest music requires an approach able to contain its complexities. This is more than an argument against simplicity: self-evidently it is possible to tell people what they want to hear and still affect a form of protest just as it is possible to tell them what they don't want to hear and fail to strike the right protestatory chord as the audience fails to comprehend what it is hearing. An example of the former is the work of Soviet composer Dmitri Shostakovich, whose music had to please the Stalinist regime or the consequences would likely be severe. To this end, the surface of Shostakovich's music appears to endorse the familiar themes that led to artists championing Russian history and culture as 'the sole inspiration for all artistic endeavors' (Gerstel, Chapter 7, p. 154). Yet this ostensible acquiescence belied music that was able to lie and tell the truth at the same time, for Shostakovich's music is marked by irony and deception, not least in the *Tenth Symphony* (1953), which is resplendent with an anger and disgust made more poignant when conceived of in the light of the paralysis synonymous with political life under totalitarianism.

From the perspective of popular music, a more approachable example of the difficulties that surround definitive pronouncements as to what protest is or is not can be found in the work of Bruce Springsteen one of America's most celebrated artists. Had all of his audience understood it, Springsteen's 'Born in the USA' (1984), collected on the same-titled album, would have told many of them something that they did not want to hear. The song, which is as dark as anything on his previous album *Nebraska* (1982), and which, astonishingly, was co-opted as an election-year campaign track by Ronald Reagan, is actually a meditation on an unemployed Vietnam veteran and his growing disillusionment with the United States. Yet I recall informing a disbelieving group of final year university students that 'Born in the USA' was not quite the anthemic nationalistic song they had assumed.

That these students were not alone in their mistaken assumptions about Springsteen's controversial song underscores the ubiquitous presence of difficulties, ambiguities and tensions that make music so exciting. At the same time, we would do well to be mindful of the kind of 'consumptive escapism' to use Simon Frith's term, that implicitly questions the sincerity of protest. For all that we can be certain that music has nourished the seeds of liberty on countless occasions. The importance, for instance, of Lou Reed and the Velvet Underground to former Czech President Václav Havel, the Charter 77 movement, and ultimately to human rights and independence in the Czech Republic, only became clear in Havel's iconic 1978 essay 'The Power of the Powerless'. In that account, Havel revealed that a key aspect of the launch of Charter 77 was the trial and imprisonment of the group, the Plastic People of the Universe. 'Everyone understood,' Havel (1978) noted,

> that an attack on the Czech musical underground was an attack on an elementary and important thing, something that in fact bound everyone together: it was an attack on the very notion of 'living within the truth,' on the real aims of life.

Conclusions such as these afford a deeper, more profound insight into the power of music than do gestures towards vague notions that, say, music 'mobilizes'. In fact, amid the carefully orchestrated demonstrations of loyalty that were quotidian events in the Eastern Bloc, the importance of the roles music played is still being uncovered. According to Russian music critic Artemy Troitsky (1988, p. 6), 'in those deceitful days, [music] was the only way for millions of kids to identify with the truth and to learn about State hypocrisy and corruption'. Such claims on behalf of music are by no means excessive. Music, as former Latvian President Vaira Vike-Freiberga (2011, p. xiv) put it, 'may open cracks even in iron curtains'.

Whatever the colour or texture of the revolution, the transformative power of music remains one of its most enduring features. Invariably, the musical articulation of grievance and hardship hardens into protest even under the most austere and threatening regimes. In the mid-1970s, during Argentina's Dirty War, a state-sponsored period of violence during which people simply disappeared without trace, it was music around which the kernel of protest began to cohere. The terror that random disappearance was meant to foster – and the goal, according to junta leader Jorge Videla, was the 'profound transformation of consciousness' – drove young people towards resistance rather than the servile acceptance the junta expected. Thus concerts became a site of solidarity and collective struggle where the audience would frequently chant anti-government slogans. Under such conditions, the identity of interests of the concertgoers is defined by the distinction between them and the government; music provides the platform for the distinction just as it nourishes it.

The annals of persecution, then, long and violent, provoke protest. Music is the articulation of that protest; it speaks its opposition. In the rhetoric of democracy, most are silenced or forgotten, and the inarticulate leave few records. But records there are and it is the goal of this book to tease out those traces, the faint lines of dissent where the mark of protest can be discerned. In this respect, this book is at the vanguard of a growing body of scholarship on the importance of music and protest. Recent important contributions to the field include Ian Peddie's *The Resisting Muse: Popular Music and Social Protests* (2006), as well as the two volumes from the same editor, *Popular Music and Human Rights, Volume I: British and American Music* and *Popular Music and Human Rights, Volume II: World Music* (2011a, 2011b). Four of the essays in this book are taken from the latter volume. Regrettably, space mitigates against the inclusion of any of the essays from Daniel Fischlin and Ajay Heble's *Rebel Musics: Human Rights, Resistant Sounds, and the Politics of Music Making* (2003), or, more broadly, Ron Eyerman and Andrew Jamison's (1998) study *Music and Social Movements: Mobilizing Traditions in the Twentieth Century*, both of which include admirable scholarship. Chapters in the opening part of the book, 'The Social Discourses of Music,' include pieces on Venezuela, benefit concerts, 1960s Japanese avant-garde music, revolutionary music in Central America, Rastafarian protests music, as well as work on early twentieth-century music halls and working-class identity. 'Resistance, Struggle, and Conflict', the second part of the volume, includes work on Shostakovich, music in Iran, political music in the former Yugoslavia, songs of protest in Israel, and an essay on the radical composer Cornelius Cardew. 'The Politics Within', the title of Part III, includes chapters on rap and protest in Tanzania, anti-apartheid music in South Africa, pre-war German cabaret music and its revolutionary legacy, as well as an essay on rock music in Soviet Ukraine. The final part of the book, 'Local Struggles, Global Impacts', includes work on women and protest in the Americas, rap in Indonesia, Greek lament, Aboriginal human rights, environmental protest, protest in French Arab music, and indigenous protest in Hawaii as well as a chapter on the Tiananmen Square uprising in China in 1989.

The Social Discourses of Music

Part I, 'The Social Discourses of Music', includes work that examines some of the key elements that embrace lived experience and the political uses of music. Light Carruyo's discussion of Venezuela's *gaita* music, a fusion of African, Indigenous and Spanish influences, illuminates how locally performed music can become a significant tool of social protest (Chapter 1). More specifically, the gaitas under discussion here use communal historical memory, local experience and regional symbols to create a sense of community and solidarity in the face of perceived injustice. With a focus largely on the period between 1989 and 1996, during the presidencies of Carlos Andrés Peréz and Rafael Caldera, the author addresses how gaitas use shared symbols such as God, the promise of change, and a collective 'we' to maintain a sense of patriotism at the same time as they engage a critique of state and society. Interpreting the interplay between the local and the national, between macro-economic policy and lived experience, means that gaitas are an important means through which identity, community and protest can be understood.

Robin Denselow's *When the Music's Over: The Story of Political Pop* is as relevant now as when it first appeared in 1989. The chapter from that study included here, 'Feed the World, Free the World ...' (Chapter 2), brings together benefit concerts and the emerging sense of political legitimacy popular music garnered in the 1970s and 1980s, particularly from its association with various causes. Beginning with the little-known story of 1970s American singer Harry Chapin, who has good claim to be one of the earliest pop musicians to mobilize his fellow artists against world hunger, the chapter covers the rise of the Chapin and civil rights veteran Bill Ayres inspired 'World Hunger Year' (WHY), an initiative that took its lead, in part, from George Harrison and Ravi Shankar's Concert For Bangladesh (1971) as well as Chapin's own concerns over starvation in the southern Sahara. Denselow charts the rise of Chapin/Ayres benefit events and the subsequent politicization of music, from Live Aid (1985) to Hands Across America (1986) and beyond. The subsequent internationalization of pop music, underpinned by political roots that stretched across the world, exemplified the marriage between politics and pop. In large part, too, the development of popular music these political alliances signalled took the genre from a rebel teenage music of the 1950s and legitimized it as the kind of anti-establishment political force it was to become in the 1980s.

The internationalization of popular music was underway at least as early as the end of the Second World War. Yayoi Uno Everett's study of Japanese music in the 1960s (Chapter 3) examines the importation of the European concept of 'avant-garde', especially its discursive trajectories, in combination with the political sphere after the 1951 military partnership with the United States. Central to Everett's analysis is Tokyo's Sôgetsu Center for the Arts, which functioned as a locus where questions about post-war, post-atomic Japanese cultural identity met avant-garde ideas. During the 'protest years' (the security treaty with the USA was renewed in 1960), the political thrust of the avant-garde challenged audiences to assess the meaning of a work in its social context, suggesting that the avant-garde itself functioned as a harbinger of social and political enlightenment. These initiatives crystallized around a series of concerts, events and 'happenings' all of which pointed to the exploration of selfhood where cultural resonances captured the post-war Japanese zeitgeist.

The sociopolitical possibilities that music offers are the keystone of Fred Judson's chapter on Central American revolutionary music (Chapter 4). Proceeding from the Marx-inspired argument that Central American revolutionary music is comprised of a set of social discourses specific to the circumstances of the 1970s and 1980s, Judson contends that the music in question must be analysed in terms of political economy, political culture and cultural studies. Using this theoretical framework, the author reads Central American revolutionary music through a clutch of interrelated themes such as anti-imperialism, internationalism, solidarity with comparable struggles, martyrology and the 'realm of the future', with its associate hope of the revolutionary society to come.

In ways reminiscent of Judson's focus on music as a form of social discourse for 'el pueblo', or, the people, Stephen A. King's 'Ska and the Roots of Rastafarian Musical Protest' (Chapter 5) illuminates how black American music and the Rastafarian 'language of protest' influenced the rise of Ska music. This 'creolization' of genres produced a music that exploited the tensions inherent to Jamaican society, not least in its dissent against repression, intolerance and discrimination. In terms of its social commentary, too, the rise of Ska was especially prescient: its concern with Jamaica's poor was portentous enough to lead The Wailers in 1963 to suggest that people should 'simmer down', a song that probably emerged as a result of the 'Holy Thursday Rampage' of Rastafarians at Montego Bay. Ultimately, though Ska's political concerns can be easily missed in favour of its 'happy, almost optimistic sound', the author concludes that Ska was an important part of the evolution of Jamaican popular music and protest.

Ian Peddie's premise, that the English music halls were purged of class antagonism and political agitation by the turn of the twentieth century, and that the working classes were given back a sanitized, de-politicized image of themselves with which they were invited to identify, underscores the importance of music as a crucial battleground for sociopolitical ideologies (Chapter 6). Beginning with Daisy Hill's politically charged, didactic lyric, 'it's nice to be common sometimes', the author asserts that the reconfiguring of the image of the working class from one of political agitation to obedient acquiescence involved big capital's realization that the music hall offered a fiscal opportunity as well as the means through which established hierarchy could be maintained. Hence the promotion of London music hall stars, especially those like Albert Chevalier, whose act served transparently ideological goals, over the radicalism of provincial artists, was a didactic rather than an aesthetic choice. The goal, Peddie argues, was the reinforcement of prevailing hierarchy and the reassertion of station and rank via an ideological platform bent upon reinforcing social distinctions 'contingent upon the acceptance of one's "lot" or "place"' (p. 146).

Resistance, Struggle and Conflict

The second part of the book, 'Resistance, Struggle and Conflict', includes material produced under some of the most repressive regimes in history. Jennifer Gerstel's study of irony, deception and political culture in the work of Soviet composer Dmitri Shostakovich (1906–75) advances the notion of irony as disguise and communication (Chapter 7). Important here is the extent to which the opacity of Shostakovich's work resists formal analysis. Hence given the savagery of Stalinist reprisals, irony also functions as a survival tactic in the composer's work. Denounced in *Pravda* as early as 1936, the same year as Stalin's Great Terror began, Shostakovich's initially successful opera *Lady Macbeth of the Mtsensk District* (1934) provided the spurious ammunition critics used to attack the composer who had simply fallen out of favour. In light of these warnings, personal safety dictated that the composer mothball his *Fourth Symphony* in favour of 'suggestions' that he write music reflecting the glory of Stalin. In a society where everything was political, including the personal, the relentless pressure to conform compelled Shostakovich to adopt increasingly complex forms of irony. Examples of how the composer was able to 'give voice to truths' (p. 160) include the *Tenth Symphony* (1953), where his musical characterization of Stalin, encompassed in the second movement, blends emotion, anger and disgust with a 'frenetic surface activity and underlying tonal paralysis' (p. 160). And it is this masterful use of deceptive irony that enabled the composer to declare with complete sincerity, 'I never lie in music' (p. 166).

Mark LeVine's study of heavy metal in Iran (Chapter 8) confirms the importance of the genre in the Middle East. Beginning with the rise in popularity of heavy metal, which the author suggests occurred near the end of the Iran–Iraq war in the late 1980s, metal grew as the revolutionary fervour that surrounded Ayatollah Khomeini began to dim. For those fans who exchanged cassettes of heavy metal bands, the music became life affirming, a 'flower growing in the middle of the desert' (p. 185) of political repression. In a country where, as one musician puts it, 'when you breathe ... it's political' (p. 193), metal, and later rap, are a means through which individual assertion can be exercised. With so many bands denied the opportunity of live performance, which, in a memorable phrase is described as 'like walking without legs' (p. 190), LeVine argues that it is hope in all its guises that fuels much of the underground music in Iran.

While the cultural contestation of the production and dissemination of music involves an assertion of identity, the search for selfhood, so often a significant text in popular music, is compounded in time of war. Rajko Muršič's study of human rights in the former Yugoslavia (Chapter 9) uses music to chart the dissolution of the erstwhile communist federation and the subsequent rise of the independent republics that replaced it. In exploring the violence of much of the music at the time the Yugoslav state began to crumble, Muršič examines the rise of extremists such as Thompson – named after the machine gun – and how his brand of 'pop-nationalism' incorporated a Fascist element into existing anxieties over the idea of nationhood. Post-Thompson, the rise of 'Turbofolk', an amalgamation of love songs and older folk tunes, provided a counterweight to some of the edgier expressions of nationalism that arguably have never been completely eradicated from music in the area. Yet it is the rise of independent republics that has illuminated the uneasy position that music continues to occupy in the region. Certainly music has been a unifying force in that it has broken down some nationalist barriers, though at the same time for some musicians it is still a medium expressive of a rather narrow nationalism. Perhaps the complex nature of music in the former Yugoslavia is best summed up by contemplating one journalist's conclusion that 'rock was absolutely never a real force here' with the many Serbs who believe that 'Milošević was brought down by rock and roll' (p. 221).

Scott Streiner's analysis of protest in Israeli popular music (Chapter 10) examines left-wing dissent over the Israeli government's security and peace policies. Given that Israel has been a site of significant conflict since its establishment in 1948, the fact that peace and security concerns have dominated politics is hardly surprising; neither is it surprising that Israelis have come to regard a kind of organized cohesion as essential to security. In this climate, where unanimity was essential to survival, it is not surprising to discover that there were few voices of dissent between 1948 and 1970. Incrementally, however, the underlying currents driven by the slow erosion of solidarity which had been historically cohered around the Diaspora experience began to have an increasing influence on Israeli society. As that solidarity receded, and Israelis began to see themselves in ways other than as an embattled minority, in the 1970s and, particularly, around the time of the Lebanon War in 1982–83, more and more protest music began to appear. Little by little protest music began to gain a sense of legitimacy, though as Streiner argues, rather than emerging from any definitive sense of evolution Israeli protest music often appears piecemeal, as a response to a series of powerful events.

The mysterious death of the enigmatic composer Cornelius Cardew (1936–81), who was killed by a hit and run driver who was never found, robbed the hard left of one of its most intriguing voices. Weaving biography, politics and music together, Timothy D. Taylor examines Cardew's ideological conversion, from a central figure in the 1960s musical avant-garde in England to his later Marxist-Leninist-Maoist position (Chapter 11). Cardew's alienation from the European avant-garde, Taylor argues, began when he co-founded the Scratch Orchestra, a project designed to encourage amateur musicians. After following this with *The Great Learning*, a Confucius-inspired experimental piece, Cardew moved to the left, declaring in the notes to *Piano Album* (1973) that he had 'developed a dialectical materialist conception which sees art as the reflection of society' (p. 257). This synthesis of Cardew's outlook defined his future composition just as surely as it ensured his marginalization. While Cardew's legacy, as recondite as it is engrossing, remains to be decided, what is certain is that he made a significant contribution to protest music.

The Politics Within

Part III, 'The Politics Within' begins with two chapters with an African theme, namely an essay on Tanzanian rap and one on South African Voëlvry music. Rounding out the part is a chapter on the enduring legacy of 1930s German protest music and a fascinating study of protest music in the Ukrainian city of Dniepropetrovsk immediately prior to the fall of the Soviet Union. José Arturo Saavedra Casco's 'The Language of the Young People: Rap, Urban Culture and Protest in Tanzania' (Chapter 12) examines the political content of Tanzanaian hip-hop and its impact on the country. After a discussion of the origins and development of hip-hop in Tanzania, the author considers the influence Swahili poetry has exerted on hip-hop, among which are competition among composers, a mutual consensus between artist and audience as to the appropriate use of poetry, the use of poetry to express social concerns, and the improvisation of verses. Using the rappers Professor Jay and Wagosi wa Kaya as his guides, Saavedra Casco concludes that there is significant 'commitment to express popular non-conformity with the current political, social and economic situation of Tanzania' (p. 289).

The means through which Afrikaans anti-apartheid music emerged, as well as its impact, is at the centre of Albert Grundlingh's study (Chapter 13). Grundlingh suggests that in the 1980s a significant feature of anti-apartheid struggle crystallized around the so-called 'Voëlvry' music, a term which meant both free as a bird and outlawed – the double meaning was intentional. With the Gereformeerde (Reformed) Blues Band as its headline act – its name a satire on the Dutch Reformed Church – Voëlvry musicians toured the country with a clear anti-apartheid message. In the 'shackled Afrikaans cultural and political world' (p. 295) the Voëlvry message was regarded as threatening for reasons beyond the fact that it challenged the prevailing status quo or that it rejected aspects of Afrikaaner identity. Despite the fact that this oppositional movement arrived twenty years after similar antithetical music heard in the West in the 1960s, Grundlingh nonetheless concludes that musical protest and resistance has a long tradition in South Africa. The re-emergence of this tradition in the 1980s, along with the resurgence of opposition to apartheid, allowed Voëlvry to 'rock the boat, but more gently than has often been assumed' (p. 320).

The importance of legacies, of what we might call the 'precedent of protest', is, of course, important to all of the chapters in this part. David Robb's exploration of the revolutionary heritage in twentieth-century German music (Chapter 14) makes the case for the critical influence of the work of Erich Mühsam, Bertolt Brecht and Hanns Eisler on the Liedermacher (singer-songwriter) from the 1960s up to the 1990s. Examining this legacy through topics such as utopia and defeat, the grotesque, montage technique, agitprop and so on allows the author to establish that political song from the 1960s onward was heavily informed by the number of protest songs that emerged between 1900 and 1930. Perhaps in the same ways that the political content of early twentieth-century song appealed to the Liedermacher, in terms of form and technique this earlier period of musical protest introduced the kind of groundbreaking innovation that was also appropriated by later musicians both in East and West Germany.

Looking eastward from West Germany, towards the Soviet Union during the 1970s and 1980s, reveals the extent of Politburo fears over the cultural influence exerted by Western music on Soviet youth. Sergei Zhuk's study of what Soviet authorities called 'Fascist music' (Chapter 15) illuminates dichotomies that are invariably either comedic or dreadful. Of the former, examples abound: the arrest and detention of Ukranian youth for listening to Western music and thereby implicitly endorsing the Western lifestyle, the confiscation of tapes and other music and relentless harassment. Notwithstanding these unpalatable truths, amid the crusade to eliminate what Andropov called 'ideological pollution' were moments of unplanned hilarity. One can only laugh at the denigration of British band 10cc, for instance, whose name was misinterpreted as 'Ten SS', which recalled Hitler's secret police, as dangerous because of their 'hellish anti-human imagery' (p. 362). Appalling to Soviet censors though 10cc's 'Reds Under My Bed' was, Pink Floyd's 1983 album *The Final Cut*, with its criticism of Soviet imperialism in 'Mr. Brezhnev and the Party' (p. 363), induced apoplexy. Yet as these and other example serve to indicate, Soviet paranoia only amplified the absence of human rights and self-determination in the country. For those Ukrainians who considered Soviet culture as conservative and backward, Western popular music held an almost magnetic appeal. Equally, as Zhuk points out, to those living in Soviet Ukraine the appeal of Western popular music, with its implications of some form of individual identity allied to its promise of human rights, was inextricably bound to notions of freedom.

Local Struggles, Global Impacts

The final part, 'Local Struggles, Global Impacts', begins with Sheila Whiteley's consideration of women and human rights (Chapter 16). With millions of women living in conditions of abject deprivation, the author implies that statutes of rights all too often fail to anticipate the contentious and fractured ways in which women experience autonomy. When conceived of in relation to women, then, the principle that lies behind the Universal Declaration of Human Rights charter, that '[e]veryone has the right to freedom of opinion and expression' (p. 376) is highly problematic as the silencing of women from so-called religious, political or sexual motivations remains an indelible part of our world. As she builds her discussion around Joni Mitchell and the Magdalene Laundries, and, more generally, songs that address domestic violence towards women, Whiteley examines prescribed gender roles and how the subjugation of women confirms that the personal is political. To this end, popular music offers a 'vision of possibility' (p. 385) that may be able to address the silent oppression under which all too many women suffer.

The rise of rap among Indonesia's myriad musical genres is the subject of Michael Bodden's chapter (Chapter 17). The author's discussion turns on the argument of how and when aspects of global commercial culture may be deployed in local struggles. Conceived of in this way, such genres serve as 'weapons of social protest and/or as expressions of a desire to create a new social space or even identity' (p. 389) that differ from the prescribed norms. Given that successive Indonesian governments have attempted to exert control over all aspects of society, the appeal of appropriating genres that carve out new spaces or challenge the prevailing ideology is clear. Indonesia's 'guided democracy' (p. 391), which incorporates attempts to control social discourse and behaviour, includes the kind of rules for social contact that Indonesian rappers quickly seized upon. Rappers like Iwa-K sing of a servile society populated by the obsequious who will not or cannot show concern for their fellow citizens. These concerns for one's fellow citizens are extended to the poor, whom the author shows are an important feature of Indonesian rap's sociopolitical protest. In the face of the limited democracy in the country, rap in Indonesia has become a medium of populist expression, one that in all its guises illuminates the iniquities of an authoritarian regime.

Anna Caraveli's enquiry into the lament as social protest (Chapter 18) originated from fieldwork in Epiros in Greece and the village of Dzermiades on Crete. The historical connection between lament poetry and expressions of grievance emerges in a variety of lamentations many of which permit the focus of the song to shift from the deceased to the mourner. This crucial movement admits myriad forms of social protest often played out in the subtlest of ways. With widowhood and emigration considered metaphorical extensions of death in Greek folk tradition, for example, laments about the loss of a partner turn to the loss of social status suffered by Greek widows. In like manner, Caraveli points out that ritual laments can appropriate the voice of the 'weak, marginal, or downtrodden' (p. 429), which considerably extends the possibilities of protest. This critical perspective opens an avenue of enquiry from which the author notes lamentations against the church, against the failures of modern medicine, and against war. Necessarily formulaic in style, these songs of loss nonetheless allow for improvisation as the singer assumes the role of an agent of change. That many women believe that these laments offer the possibility of connection with the dead only enriches the communicative aspect of this most intriguing of forms.

In some ways the pain expressed in rural Greek laments is evocative of indigenous attempts to secure equality. And there are few more troubling attempts to secure rights and some form of self-determination than the agonized example of the Australian Aborigine. Aaron Corn documents this struggle for justice over the last fifty years and how it is represented in the work of Aboriginal artists (Chapter 19). Around the time of the abolition of the White Australia Policy in 1975, Aboriginal elders began to agitate for an independent national network of Indigenous arts co-operatives which led to the creation of a national non-profit body designed to protect the interests of Indigenous artists. Not only did the subsequent establishment of the Aboriginal Artists Agency in 1976 promote Indigenous art, but it also represented Indigenous bands. Slowly, these bands began to receive the kind of exposure crucial to their attempts to reveal the worrying levels of inequality in Australia, which were underpinned by institutionalized racism, social exclusion and state oppression. As the author makes clear, many of the heart-rending songs are steps on the road to something that has still to be achieved: a reconciled Australia.

The topicality of David Ingram's chapter (Chapter 20) on Pete Seeger's environmental protests reveals how far ahead of his time this great folk singer was. In his 1966 album *God Bless the Grass*, Seeger addresses environmental concerns through the tradition of proletarian realism. For an artist as committed to causes as Seeger, environmentalist advocacy was a natural extension of his Civil Rights concerns. Seeger's dedication to environmentalist concerns was part of a lifelong activism; his Clearwater project, established in 1969 and still in operation today, is a non-profit organization dedicated to protecting natural resources. In 'My Dirty Stream' he sings of pollution in the Hudson River; in 'The Faucets Are Dripping' Seeger pointed to wasted water and the culpability of absentee landlords. As surprising as it now appears, Seeger's environmentalist message was, however, undermined somewhat by the now infamous Newport Festival in 1965, where Bob Dylan wore a leather jacket, plugged in his guitar, and played rock. This 'new' rock, Ingram contends, made Seeger's more traditional approach seem slightly conservative though by 1967 Dylan had returned to the acoustic fold. Despite the continued rise of rock, Seeger's approach and his message endured just as it has inspired countless musicians over the last forty years. Today, it may be more important than ever.

Barbara Lebrun's discussion of *rock métis*, a fusion of rock with instruments, rhythms and languages drawn from non-Western genres, (Chapter 21), concentrates on its performance by North African Arab musicians in contemporary France. The early radicalism of this relatively new genre has, however, been compromised by its success as a branch of so-called world music; Lebrun connects this sense of world music as an unhelpful ambiguity with the rise of *métissage*, which refers to cultural and ethnic mixing without recourse to the word 'ethnicity'. Not surprisingly given the ethnic identities of so many *rock métis* artists, critics have been swift to point out the challenge the genre poses to French ideals of Republicanism, which are contingent on the idea that the nation is 'one and indivisible' and that all individuals must be integrated within it. In fact, *rock métis* contains a hybridity that announces challenges to mainstream identities, to the dominance of white and Western in French music, and to the rise of right-wing politics exemplified by the Front National. All of these concerns converge to raise important questions about post-colonial France, its politics and its identity, in addition to the complexities that surround assimilationism.

In varying ways aspects of assimilationism are at the core of social protest music in Hawaii. Though social protest has always been a feature of Hawaiian music, much of it has been hidden from outsiders. Beginning with Indigenous musical protests against the signing of the annexation of Hawaii to the United States in 1893, George H. Lewis's 'Don' Go Down Waikiki: Social Protest and Popular Music in Hawaii' (Chapter 22) draws a clear distinction between native music and the invention of a commercial Hawaiian music. The former, heavily influenced by the kaona style, which effectively disguised the meaning of the song, is at the heart of Hawaiian culture. The commercialization of Hawaiian music, on the other hand, with its implicit subtext of 'happy-go-lucky' musicians, was mistakenly perceived as representative of Hawaiian society and culture. Though this 'Hawaiian Sound' flourished from the 1930s and on into the 1950s, by the 1970s and 1980s a more politically aware, culturally representative music emerged. As a result of domestic initiatives to produce more representative and authentic sounds, music celebrating Hawaiian ethnicity began to appear, as did songs deeply critical of tourism and the damage it has allegedly done to Hawaiian culture and society. The return of a more politically aware music, Lewis argues, heralded a broad movement towards social solidarity that fostered a musically nurtured spirit of self-identity and pride in Hawaiians.

Over two decades after the momentous events in Beijing's Tiananmen Square, the images remembered, the singing and chanting, the banners, Wang Weilin's lone confrontation of a line of tanks, are still as powerful as they ever were. Valerie Samson, a student at the Central Conservatory of Music in Beijing when the protests began, addresses the roles music played in the demonstrations (Chapter 23): music aided the mobilization, solidarity and order of protesters; it provided a rallying point for morale, it channelled energy, it helped allay fears and doubts, it provided a means through which patriotic songs could be aired. So important was music that the author suggests it played a significant role in every aspect of the demonstrations. The sense of a collective consciousness that singing and playing offered was legitimized by the contextual items that strengthened the cultural authority of the protesters. The Goddess of Democracy statue, for example, a 10 metre high plaster statue of a woman holding a torch became an important symbol. In addition to the intimations towards liberty and democracy that the statue implied, collective performances at the statue's base indicated a desire for solidarity while the variety of music played and sung suggested self-validation regardless of political orientation. In fact, the ubiquity of music during the demonstrations ensured that 'the struggle for control of the sound-space at Tiananmen Square' (p. 519) was synonymous with the struggle for political control.

'Music doesn't lie', Jimi Hendrix once allegedly said. 'If there is something to be changed in this world, then it can only happen through music.' As an assertion of hope against the oppressive regimes, ideologies, and systems that appear, sometimes murkily, sometimes openly, in various chapters of this volume, Hendrix's words offer much consolation. So many of those oppressive regimes, in fact, were strongly met with the vitality and passion of protest music; they had to be, for many an authoritative regime has embraced Plato's contention that 'any musical innovation is full of danger to the whole State' (1892, p. 112). Those who conceive of music as a threat – and there are many that do – are arguably those with something to hide. Yet it is an inescapable fact that one of the most abiding reasons for the continuation of protest music is the presence of inequality. The examples discussed here serve to remind us that for all its complexity what drives the music of protest has changed little over many years. Opposition to the unrepresentative or usurping government, the illegitimate ruler or the oppressive system as much as hostility to the totalitarian, the tyrant, the demagogue: these are the common threads and abiding virtues of protest music over many centuries.

References

Eyerman, Ron and Jamison, Andrew (1998), *Music and Social Movements: Mobilizing Traditions in the Twentieth Century*, New York: Cambridge University Press.

Fischlin, Daniel and Heble, Ajay (eds) (2003), *Rebel Musics: Human Rights, Resistant Sounds, and the Politics of Music Making*, Montreal: Black Rose Books.

Gray, Marcus (2001), *The Clash: The Return of the Last Gang in Town*, London: Helter Skelter.

Havel, Václav (1978), 'The Power of the Powerless', *The American Dissident*, at: www.theamericandissident. org/CriticalEssays/Havel.htm (accessed 12 December 2011).

Marcus, Greil (1994), *Ranters & Crowd Pleasers: Punk in Pop Music, 1977–92*, New York: Anchor.

Peddie, Ian (ed.) (2006), *The Resisting Muse: Popular Music and Social Protests*, Aldershot: Ashgate.

Peddie, Ian (ed.) (2011a), *Popular Music and Human Rights, Volume I: British and American Music*, Farnham: Ashgate.

Peddie, Ian (ed.) (2011b), *Popular Music and Human Rights, Volume II: World Music*, Farnham: Ashgate.

Plato, trans. Benjamin Jowett (1892), *The Dialogues of Plato, Volume III: Republic, Timaeus, Critius*, London: Macillan.

Troitsky, Artemy (1988), *Back in the USSR: The True Story of Rock in Russia*, London: Faber.

Vike-Freiberga, Vaira (2011), 'Foreword', in Ian Peddie (ed.), *Popular Music and Human Rights, Volume II: World Music*, Farnham: Ashgate, pp. xiii–xiv.

Part I
The Social Discourses of Music

[1]

La Gaita Zuliana

Music and the Politics of Protest in Venezuela

by
Light Carruyo

The regional form of Venezuelan popular music called *gaita* began as improvised songs created collectively at neighborhood gatherings in the state of Zulia (Hernández Oquendo, 1991). Gaita is a fusion of African, indigenous, and Spanish instrumentation and rhythms (Matos Romero, 1968; Arrieta, 1984). While gaitas are most widely heard around Christmas, from the day of the Virgen de Chiquinquira in November through December, these festive songs invoke a multitude of themes, including religion, community, history, and political protest. It may seem contradictory that holiday music should also be protest music, but many people I interviewed suggested that this was because the music emerged from working-class neighborhoods and was spontaneous, improvised, and thus reflective of the diverse concerns of a community at any given moment. Since the 1950s gaita has moved from the neighborhood to the recording studio, has incorporated a variety of international beats, melodies, and instruments, and has been marketed and embraced by Venezuelans beyond the state of Zulia (Barboza de la Torre, 1968). While gaita production and consumption have changed dramatically, the music continues to draw on historical memory, local lived experience, and regional symbols to create a sense of community and collective opposition to perceived injustice. The subjects of gaitas are wide-ranging and conjunctural; themes include politics, family, religion, and environmental concerns. In other words, this music is focused not exclusively on protest but on lived experience. Although gaitas may include references to Nueva Canción artists such as Alí Primera and there are examples of intertextual referencing between gaitas and Nueva Canción, gaitas are more comparable to other regional folk music than to explicitly leftist music. This article, however, focuses on the significance of gaitas as a tool for popular protest

Light Carruyo is an assistant professor of sociology at Vassar College. She is currently working on a book that addresses the gendered and racial dimensions of economic development and nation building in the Dominican Republic. She acknowledges the helpful feedback of John Foran, Tim Harding, Kum-Kum Bhavnani, Peter Chua, Susana Peña, and the *Latin American Perspectives* reviewers, as well as the artists, fans, scholars, and DJs in Maracaibo.

between 1989 and 1996, during the presidencies of Carlos Andrés Pérez and Rafael Caldera. This was a time when popular opposition to political party politics and neoliberal reform was on the rise throughout the nation. The nation was ready for a change, and examination of this dialogue between culture and politics may well provide insight into Hugo Chávez's rise to power.

POLITICS AND CULTURE IN LATIN AMERICA

Recent work on culture in Latin America has attempted to understand the importance of civil society and place new value on culture as a process not merely reflective of material conditions but also constitutive of social formations and identities (Mallon, 1994; Beverley, Oviedo, and Aronna, 1995; García Canclini, 1995; Vandegrift, 1998). The ways in which culture has been used by those in power to maintain and perpetuate their control are discussed in several recent collections of essays on Latin America (cf. Beezley, Martin, and French, 1994). However, as Raymond Williams points out, "no mode of production and therefore no dominant culture in reality includes or exhausts all human practice, human energy, and human intention" (1977: 125). While culture has been used to validate oppressive relations, it is simultaneously a space in which domination is contested and oppositional meanings are created. Ana María Alonso (1992) points out that if hegemony is historical and contingent, then domination over the "masses" is never achieved; in fact, there is always space in which struggles of resistance can emerge.

Scholars interested in issues from revolution to resistance to nationalism have stressed the importance of everyday sense-making to maintaining and challenging oppressive systems. My analysis of gaitas integrates the concept of the "imagined community" (Anderson, 1983) with theories of opposition that posit both the political uses of culture and the tactical possibilities it provides (Sandoval, 1991; Lipsitz, 1994) to argue that gaitas both emerge from and help create an imagined oppositional community. In other words, gaitas invoke regional symbols and shared experiences to create a sense of community, and it is in this collective that they ground their discontent. John Foran (1997) has referred to the sentiments that create this community as "political cultures of opposition." The people's deep dissatisfaction with the government and the material conditions in which they find themselves are discursively interwoven with their shared love for their region and for their nation. However, as in Anderson's imagined community, the community created and reflected by gaitas is experienced as "real" on one level, but it is fraught with inequalities and differences that are sometimes blurred for the sake of a Zulian and Venezuelan "we."[1] Additionally, while gaitas have grown from "tangible" communities in the sense that they included ties of kinship, daily interactions, and geographic proximity, they now speak to larger and geographically dispersed ones. Recorded gaitas facilitate these links and have developed specific ways of creating them—universalizing content, incorporating new forms, and building bridges between the studio and the street (Carruyo, 2002).

This article is based on a sample of 103 gaitas recorded between 1989 and 1996 and interviews with DJs, musicians, and listeners in Maracaibo conducted in 1996. Maracaibo, the capital of the state of Zulia, is the most significant oil-producing region in Venezuela. Many protest gaitas are grounded in the outrage felt by residents over the amount of labor and wealth that they provide the country without seeing the benefits in their own lives. However, the data indicate that local opposition has in many ways been translated into national opposition; a coalitional cultural politics has emerged from the songs and artists of this historical moment. Recorded and commercially distributed gaitas move strategically between local and national, creating a cross-regional solidarity among Venezuelans. This article seeks to understand this movement and the dialogue between the songs, popular consciousness, and Venezuelan political and economic policy.

HISTORICAL MEMORY, *ZULIANIDAD*, AND POPULAR PROTEST

To understand the significance of protest gaitas it is necessary to understand gaitas as intimately linked to a sense of regional history, identity, and pride. According to the composer, DJ, and student of gaitas Arnoldo Hernández Oquendo,

> A gaita—understood as the gaita that we cultivated, at least in my generation (I am a 62-year-old man) or my grandparents' generation, which was the folk gaita—is a typical regional song. It was made up of a chorus of six lines that alternated with a four-line verse. The chorus could be on any theme, and the verses were improvised and had absolutely nothing to do with the chorus. The instrumentation that was used for that gaita was the *furro* [a percussion instrument], the *cuatro* (a small four-stringed guitar), the *charrasca* (a ridged gourd), and the *maraca*.[2] Eventually the tambora, clarinet, a spoon, and a coconut grater or a soda bottle were added. Each person joined in harmony with the basic instrumentation.

The history of gaita is inextricably linked with his biography. He emphasizes that the music was a collaboration of the community, which was responsible

for the improvisation of each verse as well as for the instrumentation. It was
created collectively and spontaneously, always reflecting concerns of the
community. Younger people also discussed the importance of gaitas in passing knowledge from generation to generation. Amarily, a 26-year-old native
of San Francisco, refers to her favorite gaitas as "documentaries":

> They are very pretty—they are like documentaries, they explain things that are
> happening in your region, everything that's going on, and so you are learning—
> I mean, I had no idea what had happened with the bridge when it collapsed!
> And through that song ["El Ferry"], I began to—OK, it was knocked down by
> an oil barge, and so they started up the ferry that had been abandoned, and that's
> when people started to use it again. They used it until they fixed the bridge and
> started to use the bridge again. These are histories. People listen to them and
> they know that that happened in Maracaibo, so more or less you go piecing
> together the things that are happening in the birthplace of gaitas. There are
> other songs just like "The Ferry." So those things really happened. I mean, you
> ask your grandfather or your uncle and they say, "That really happened." So
> they are like documentaries, Those are the types of gaitas that I like. They tell
> you what has been happening in Maracaibo—not the bad stuff, not like the pro-
> tests, "There is hunger. There is misery," you already know that, why are they
> going to keep reminding us? Why not remember the nice things? That's what
> stimulates you, see?

Amarily reconfirms that the events "really happened" with older members of
her family, creating an intergenerational continuity that links subjects to a
sense of history. She sees gaitas as a way of learning about the parts of the history of her city that might not be talked about otherwise. For Amarily, gaitas
both document the past and distract her from a present in which "hunger and
misery" are in the foreground of lived experience.

The importance of gaitas as keepers of history and tradition is brought to
light in many of the songs. They are, in fact, popularly understood as symbols
of tradition, signified as such through key words such as "tradition," "typical," "original," "folklore," and "authentic" that frequently appear in the lyrics. They position themselves as keepers of local history and promoters of
regional pride with their use of regional symbols (the lake, the bridge, the
heat), regional religious figures, local heroes and heroines, and everyday
people from the street vendor to the widow down the block. Even everyday
items and happenings in the region are celebrated and made cause for solidarity as in Elías Hernandez's 1996 "Total Zulianidad": "Everything native here
comes with a first-rate seal / flip-flops made in El Moján / and the heat of the
city / an iguana from La Cañada / even our identity / the street-wise cleverness
of total Zulianness (*zulianidad*)." Here various rural and urban townships are
brought together, and the items that they produce and their very identity are

hailed as "first-rate." By invoking a shared sense of history, regional identity, and pride, a Zulian "we" can be imagined. This "we" that serves as author, subject, and audience to the messages in gaitas is often simply referred to as "the people" (*el pueblo*).

The songs also draw on the lived experiences of Zulians—local people, places, and everyday happenings. In the everyday, the provision of basic needs is fundamental, and therefore gaita lyrics include discussion of food, utilities, and transportation. These everyday activities and basic needs link people to the government; the effects of policy are understood through their impact on the lived experience of Zulians. The importance of drawing on lived experiences and shared meaning to create an imagined oppositional community then becomes evident.

Zulians have a sense of themselves as exploited, marginal, and deprived within Venezuelan society. While their oil and labor in the oil industry are responsible for the economic prosperity of the country, they have been robbed of their "fair share" of the profits. The themes in my sample of gaitas suggest that because of the deteriorating standards of living in the country, this sense of Zulian marginality increasingly coexists with cross-regional themes of opposition. While many regions have their own songs, local expressions, and traditions, José, a native San Franciscan, pointed out to me that as far as protest goes, gaitas are at the forefront. After making this claim he himself seemed to have a revelation: "I mean, maybe that's why—because the people of Maracaibo are such complainers [LC laughs]. Yeah, yeah [JV laughs] I had never thought of that, I'm just thinking of it now." His suggestion is that Zulianness is partially constructed around protest—about the heat, the traffic, or the political elite—and this influences the type of music produced regionally and makes protest an integral part of regional self-identification. In other words, political awareness becomes as "second-nature" as complaints about the heat. Yet beyond complaints about the heat or the traffic, the songs point to a precise understanding of the ways in which national government and policy decisions are experienced on a day-to-day basis. While the songs are shaped by Zulianness, they in turn influence the ways in which Zulians understand politics and interpret their experiences politically.

THE CULTURE OF "LA GREY ZULIANA"

Ricardo Aguirre's "La grey zuliana" (The Zulian Congregation) historically locates protest gaitas as an important aspect of Zulian self-identification. Recorded in 1968, it establishes the notion of Maracaibo's people as exploited in the Venezuelan economy. Despite the fact that revenues from oil are made possible through Zulian labor and resources, Zulians have not seen this wealth trickle down to their state, much less to the working class. The song brings this concern to the airwaves and points to a great irony: the state that contains the oil has inadequate roads: "Mother, if the government / doesn't help the Zulian people / you'll have to interfere / and send them to hell . . . Maracaibo has given so much / that it should have roads paved / with golden coins of song . . . They used up all the money / and started to laugh / but that can backfire . . . Your people ask you / mother that you help / and give them fortune / with a great deal of love they demand it."

The interviews I conducted indicate that Zulians understand themselves as having been cheated out of their fair share of the wealth generated by the oil industry. Moreover, nearly all of the people I interviewed indicated that "La grey" is the most memorable gaita of all time, "the anthem of Zulia and of all gaitas."[3] This adoption of "La grey" as both an anthem and a reference point is indicative of its influence on Zulian understanding of self, region, and national politics. While the song is a reference point in many ways, it is in no way static or trapped in its own historical context; rather, it is constantly given new life and meanings by those who invoke it.

"La grey zuliana," constructs a Catholic regional community that looks to the Virgen de Chiquinquira for guidance and protection against an unjust state. The song appears to have helped shape regional thought around a sense of marginality and opposition to the state. It unifies Zulians because it calls on common identity, regional symbols, and a sense of place—a cross-class sense of marginality is critical to the imagining of such a community. In other words, by focusing on regional commonalties rather than internal differences or inequality, it builds an imagined cohesiveness among Zulians. Antonio, a San Francisco tire salesman, discusses its significance:

> Ricardo Aguirre is the most memorable performer of all of gaita history, and that gaita relays the feelings of Zulians, seeing that we produce more than 80 percent of the revenue at the national level (we are talking about oil revenues here) and we receive less than anyone. That gaita says that Maracaibo should have roads made of gold, and all of that is to show that there is so much wealth here and we see so little of it . . . and that gaita, still in history, the things it says, that it makes known, they haven't stopped happening. And we live in almost the same situation, we continue to produce 80 percent of the revenue and we're still in the same boat.

Antonio takes up the discussion of the Zulian "fair share" and makes an argument for the salience of the song's message in the present. He repeatedly uses a notion of a Zulian "we," indicating his understanding of a community that stands together as a united front.

The echo of "La grey" is audible in recent recorded gaitas. A former gaitero speaks of an Abédnego "Neguito" Borjas 1996 gaita called "Corona de tunas" (Crown of Thorns): "The expression says it all. . . . How can it be possible that, being—Cabimas is the heavyweight in oil production, the biggest treasure that Venezuela has is oil and it comes from Cabimas—how is it possible that, being that rich, it does not have streets, at least some decent streets, you know? That's what the gaita is talking about, see?" Here politics is understood through lived experience—the condition of the roads is seen as a direct result of policy that neglects the needs of Zulia. His comment that the "expression says it all" reflects the feeling of many people that gaitas put into words what they feel but are unable to articulate. Nearly every subject I interviewed broke into song during our interview to illustrate a particular point. For instance, referencing "Dr. Caldera," Mercedes said, "I like it because it tells it like it is to the President of the Republic." She suggested that gaitas expose the "truth" about the material conditions of the people. But in "telling it like it is" gaitas both expose truth and participate in the creation of truth. Of course, this is not a one-way relationship; in fact, part of what makes it work is that often the language and the stories told by gaitas have been borrowed from "the word on the street."

"EL PAQUETAZO"

While the fair-share theme remained central to the gaitas that were popular between 1989 and 1996, they were increasingly interlaced with a broader sense of Venezuelan people's desperation and lack of confidence in the state. Materially based, the critiques in the sample focus on the effects of the 1989 structural-adjustment measures adopted by President Carlos Andrés Pérez and the perceived corruption and inefficiency of the political elite. Although the critiques are biting, straightforward, and at times directed at individuals, they are presented as rooted in patriotism and love of God. This tension is critical to the power of gaitas: the songs draw oppositional strength precisely from the combination of concepts—patriotism, nationalism, religion—that have historically been used against the people.[4] While the government might suggest that love of the country can be measured by how much is sacrificed to increase the gross national product, the people argue that the quality of life of the average Venezuelan worker is a more suitable indicator. For gaitas love for the country includes concern for the survival of its people and resources, and therefore the government, held responsible for the poor quality of life, becomes the enemy. Neguito Borjas's 1990 song "El paquetazo" explicitly connects hunger, corruption, and the 1989 reform measures. While Carlos Andrés Pérez referred to his 1989 "macroeconomic stabilization plan"as the Great Turnaround, the Venezuelan populace referred to it as "el paquete," a popular expression meaning "a problematic, cumbersome situation" and used to refer to structural-adjustment programs throughout Latin America (Naím, 1993). The first is as follows: "For the first time in history / we see that in a country / they make the masses suffer / to pay for what others steal . . . By means of mega-packages / this government punishes / the pockets and bellies / of the Venezuelan people." This verse immediately links people's suffering to the corruption of the government; politicians are perceived as stealing the fruits of Zulian / Venezuelan labor for their personal gain, and the loans and austerity measures that they adopt are seen as a way to pay the debt that corruption has created. In the fifth line, the phrase *a fuerza de* (by means of) might normally be followed by a word such as *golpazos* (hard-hitting blows), but here the word is *paquetazos* (hard-hitting structural-adjustment packages), indicating the violently negative effects of the measures on the lives of most Venezuelans. This song exemplifies the continued influence of communities on the production of gaitas: people develop a language for talking about economic policy, and this language is absorbed and reflected by each new song. Although this relationship may seem linear, it is in reality much more nuanced and complex when looked at in its historical context. Other music, policy, and "street talk" have preceded and surround it. It must be understood as part of an oppositional conversation that can take on national significance.

The second verse moves into an in-depth critique: "The government pays no attention / and I don't think they care / that these days transportation / costs an arm and a leg . . . Medicine, hospitals / housing, food / light, water, and gasoline / the cause of all our problems." Here the song calls attention to the specific sacrifices that are expected of most Venezuelans because of specific policies such as the elimination of subsidies and price controls on staple food items. The liberalization of the economy led to an overnight increase in the cost of electricity, water, gas, public transportation, and telephone services, which have since been privatized (Naím, 1993). The final sentence refers to gasoline as the "cause of our problems," perceptively pointing to the fact that oil, despite being one of the major resources of Venezuela, has been a mixed blessing for Zulians. Many Zulians associate oil with the exploitation of land and workers, lack of their fair share of the profits, and ever-present political and economic instability.

While the verses of "El paquetazo" cross regional boundaries and attempt to speak to and with the voice of an imagined national populace, the first line of the chorus, "¡Ay, qué machete, qué original!" ("Oh, how cool, how original!") weaves the song back into Zulia through its use of a popular regional expression. "Machete," a regional term meaning "cool," marks the song as regionally produced. By drawing on colloquial language and instrumentation the song, though directed at Venezuelans in general, speaks to a Zulian sense of shared regional identity. This is one of the strategies that is used to negotiate the regional and national tensions that have emerged as gaita has crossed musical and geographical boundaries.

"UN OJO DIMOS"

Like "El paquetazo," Borjas's "Un ojo dimos," released the previous year (1989), draws on the image of the sacrifice of the people (sacrificing an eye), and the effects of structural adjustment but in this case cleverly playing with a double meaning. "Un ojo dimos" said quickly sounds like the Venezuelan pronunciation of "Nos jodimos,"[5] loosely translated as "We're screwed." One of the song's verses follows: "We gave an eye so that he would / give the people a better life / implementing a set of measures / that only come out well for him . . . We gave an eye for you, mister / because we believed in your promises / and now both rich and poor pray / because we are all worse off." Speaking directly to President Pérez and using the informal *tú*, this song laments the sacrifices that the people made to elect him to office and accuses the president of implementing reforms that benefit only the political elite. Tellingly, this song was censored in Caracas the year it was released for fear that it would encourage manifestations of public unrest that had been occurring in the capital since the beginning of Pérez's presidency. Yet according to Alberto Silva Narváez, the director of the band that performed "Un ojo dimos" (Barrio Obrero), Pérez's response was simply, "Oh, those *Maracuchos* are really something!" (Hernandez Oquendo, 1991: 191)—dismissing the protest as a quirk of a regional population when in fact the discontent was widespread. Father Vilchez, a local parish leader and director of a community-based youth gaita band, recalled a gaita that jokingly suggested that even the rich would protest if the cost of bread continued to rise: "If bread stays at three cents / Even the rich will protest / Because they'll want to eat bread." With the suggestion that both rich and poor are suffering the effects of this policy, "Un ojo dimos" establishes cross-class links through religion and thus calls up the notion of the unified "congregation" that I have mentioned. This oppositional community is not uniquely Zulian but spans regional boundaries, broadening the imagined oppositional community into a national one. As in many popular protest gaitas, Catholic faith and prayer are presented as a form of resistance and community building, though not in the sense of accepting one's lot quietly. In other words, prayer exists alongside fragmented analysis of the economic and political material conditions. For instance, in gaitas individuals such as corrupt public officials are often blamed without explicit critique of structural issues.

Both "Un ojo dimos" and "El paquetazo" explicitly address the debt crisis and structural adjustment and highlight the corruption of the political elite, especially Pérez, who was seen at the time as responsible for the difficult living conditions faced by Venezuelans. It is not surprising that Pérez was forced to resign and face corruption charges in a trial that at least in part confirmed the links that the public had made between hunger and corruption. The mistrust of politicians was drawn on by Rafael Caldera in 1993 in his campaign for the presidency on a platform emphasizing that the economic problems Venezuela faced were the result of government and business elite corruption (Perry and Bailey, 1994). Thus the language of "elite corruption" that had been made oppositional on the streets and in music was effectively incorporated into hegemonic party politics and given an entirely new meaning.

"ESCUCHE DR. CALDERA"

Borjas's popular gaita "Dr. Caldera" was released in 1996, three years into Caldera's presidency. While all three of the protest gaitas discussed thus far are explicitly critical of the government, "Dr. Caldera" shows a shift in tone: "Listen Dr. Caldera it's the people who are speaking to you / badly hurt and asking how long are they to be condemned / I am only a messenger who gathers the suffering / the rage, anguish, and lament of the land that we love." First, the president is addressed as *Ud.*, a pronoun typically used to indicate both formality and respect. Whereas "Un ojo dimos" addressed Carlos Andrés Pérez informally, involved clever insults, and played with what might be seen as vulgar language, here Caldera is not only formally addressed but referred to as "Dr." (a title used to address individuals, even if they are not doctors, to show respect or to flatter). This tactic enables the singer to construct a "humble" population suffering as a result of the decisions made by his administration. In this case, the singer disclaims any accountability, suggesting that he is only a messenger representing the people and expressing a widely accepted "truth." The initial encounter between the people and the president here is one of respect and pain rather than outrage—though anger is later mentioned. In an informal conversation Nestor, a Maracaibo taxi driver, pointed out that when Borjas sings the song on TV he "has a mischievous look on his face." In other words, the words themselves are respectful but both delivery and reception are loaded with a cynicism that changes their meaning. Thus, direct accusations of government corruption are replaced by manipulation of the language of humility and respect as oppositional tools.

Critical to this verse and to many protest gaitas is the grounding of the protest in the people's love of the country. Those who protest are not traitors to the country; it is precisely their love for Venezuela that drives them to protest the corruption of politicians and the mismanagement of national resources.

"UN REVERÓN PARA EL PUEBLO"

While the Venezuelan state is held accountable in many gaitas, it is not seen as isolated from the global economy. Wolfgang Romero and Leandro Zuleta's 1994 gaita "Un Reverón para el pueblo" (A Reverón for the people) points to the role of the United States in the economic troubles Venezuela is facing. This musical plea exhumes the Venezuelan artist Armando Reverón to do a painting of Venezuela, making an important connection between politics, art, and the possibilities for expressions of resistance. Verse by verse, the singer gives detailed instructions as to what Reverón should place on the canvas: "On your canvas Reverón / insinuate in the distance / a northern galaxy / in tricolor sand . . . Please draw the dollar / and if it floats / paint the boot of our liberator on top of it."

While the song is directed to all of Venezuela, it is sung to the painter in regional colloquial Spanish, using *vos* commands. Thus the lyrics produce a sense of Zulianness while attempting to build alliances that span the geographical and symbolic borders of the region. The singer asks that the United States be "insinuated in the distance," suggesting the power held by the United States over the lives of Venezuelans. Yet resistance to that power is also called for, as the singer demands that the floating dollar (a reference to the instability of Venezuelan currency) be held down by the boot of Simón Bolívar. Again, the reference to Bolívar clearly places the protest in the framework of patriotism. The government at that time did not escape complicity because it did not show the strength to stand up to the "northern galaxy" as Bolívar presumably would have. The reference to his boot in particular is significant because it denotes the masculine strength and militarism that some perceive as the solution to the lack of leadership in the country. This is an indisputably patriarchal vision of leadership that is woven into the themes of resistance in many gaitas. However, given the time period, this reference to Bolívar takes on new meaning. Hugo Chávez, since the coup attempt he led in 1992, had become a figure of resistance who invoked both the spirit and the name of Bolívar. Moreover, he embodied the militaristic strongman who would stand up to the "northern galaxy."

CONCLUSION

By rooting the protests in patriotism, love of God and La Vírgen, and a sense of a unified "we," "El paquetazo," "Un ojo dimos," "Dr. Caldera," and "Un Reverón para el pueblo" carry off critiques of the state and economic policy while conveying a sense of justice and community. By discussing politics as personal and intimately tied to the lived experiences of Zulians and Venezuelans, gaitas bridge the divide between macroeconomic policy making and the day-to-day struggle. This makes them a critical site in which to understand identity, community, and popular protest. Inseparable from Zulianness, gaitas are a way in which people make sense of politics and battle over meanings.

While the songs protest the national economic situation, they do so in a way that combines humor, sarcasm, and a familiar danceable beat. Their seemingly contradictory edgy critiques and marketability exemplify what George Lipsitz (1997) has called the power to both soothe and subvert. While they constantly engage a tradition and history of regional identity and meaning-making, they speak to the demands of the moment and the market through a clever weaving of regional and national oppositional themes. Since the reform measures have meant increasing instability and inflation for Venezuelans across the board, the fair-share theme is accompanied by the concerns of the country as a whole. There is an important dialectical relationship between the production and consumption of gaitas on a national scale. In the years between 1989 and 1996 when these data were collected, the increasing discontent of Venezuelans and the more widespread use of non-region-specific instrumentation and musical styles combined to increase the national appeal of gaitas. This in turn has prompted cross-regional marketing and encouraged further hybridization of the music as Zulians and others fuse gaitas with other musical styles. The genius of gaitas is in not only moving between and among regional and national alliances, religious and political discourses, and commercial and folk identifications but using these to help create an imagined oppositional community.

Zulians are not observers of politics but active participants in discursive and material contestation. The protest is cleverly entangled with holiday celebrations and festive beats and melodies that bring a sense of joy and the comfort of community to the listeners. Resistance is not solely about drawing attention to the problems of the people; it is balanced with building a sense of pride, cohesiveness, and happiness. Protest gaitas are effective and popular because their critiques of national politics root themselves in community identity, history, and pride.

NOTES

1. In 2002 the commercial protests (several written by the same composers who protested neoliberal reform in this sample) were directed at Chávez despite the seemingly widespread support he had among poor and working-class Venezuelans. While outside the scope of this article, this raises questions about the politics of the song writers, the marketing of gaitas (for instance, whom do they claim to speak for, and who is the intended audience?), and perhaps whether Chavez's commitment to structural changes has directly improved the quality of life of most Venezuelans.

2. I am not implying, however, that these songs are in some way creating a utopian unity across class, race, and gender. In fact, they erase differences by suggesting that "we are all in the same boat." Challenges to race and gender conflicts are conspicuously absent from the sample of songs that I have collected. While the worker is considered to occupy a marginal position in Zulia, the absence of any discussion of the indigenous population in the region is indicative of the avoidance of open discussions of race inequality in a "racial democracy." In fact, discussions of indigenous presence in the sample are limited to romanticized references to the Guajiro population rather than critical discussions of contemporary racism.

3. Many of the subjects I interviewed discussed gaitas as the "regional anthem." This phrase belongs to Alfredo, a radio show chronologist and gaita historian.

4. Cardoso, Enrique, and Faletto (1971: 132) have discussed the ways in which nationalism and populism have been used to create mass support for modernization projects that do not benefit the people. However, Hall (1993: 354) uses Ernesto Laclau's phrase "Nationalism has no necessary belongingness" in his discussion to emphasize that it is "capable of being inflected to very different political positions at different historical moments and its character depends very much on the other traditions, discourses and forces with which it is articulated."

5. Spoken Venezuelan Spanish tends to omit the final *s*.

REFERENCES

Alonso, Ana María
    1992 "Gender, power, and historical memory: discourses of Serrano resistance," in Judith
    Butler and Joan W. Scott (eds.), *Feminists Theorize the Political*. New York: Routledge.
Anderson, Benedict
    1983 *Imagined Communities*. New York: Verso.
Arrieta Abreu, Francisco
    1984 *Las gaitas del Zulia*. Maracaibo: Refolit C.A.
Barboza de la Torre, Pedro A.
    1968 "Evolución y degeneración de un cantar popular venezolano en una era de cambios."
    Revista de la Universidad del Zulia 11 (42–43): 64–72.

Beezley, William H., Cheryl English Martin, and William E. French (eds.)
    1994 *Rituals of Rule, Rituals of Resistance*. Wilmington: Scholarly Resources.
Beverley, John, José Oviedo, and Michael Aronna (eds.)
    1995 *The Postmodernism Debate in Latin America*. Durham: Duke University Press.
Cardoso, Fernando Enrique and Enzo Faletto
    1971 *Dependency and Development in Latin America*. Translated by Marjory Mattingly
    Urquidi. Los Angeles: University of California Press.
Carruyo, Light
    2002 "La gaita ¡Que suene a gaita! Venezuelan regional music at the crossroads of authentic-
    ity." *Studies in Latin American Popular Culture* 21.
Foran, John
    1997 "Discourses and social forces: the role of culture and cultural studies in understanding
    revolutions," in John Foran (ed.), *Theorizing Revolutions: New Approaches from Across the
    Disciplines*. London: Routledge.
García Canclini, Néstor
    1995 *Hybrid Cultures: Strategies for Entering and Leaving Modernity*. Minneapolis: Uni-
    versity of Minnesota Press.
Hall, Stuart
    1993 "Culture, community, nation." *Cultural Studies* 17: 349–363.
Hernández Oquendo, Arnoldo
    1991 *Memoria y cuenta de la gaita zuliana y algo más*. Maracaibo: n.p.
Lipsitz, George
    1994 *Dangerous Crossroads*. New York: Verso.
    1997 Panel discussion on Music and Social Movements, Santa Barbara, CA.
Mallon, Florencia E.
    1994 "The promise and dilemma of subaltern studies: perspectives from Latin American his-
    tory." *Latin American Historical Review* 99 (5): 14–93.
Matos Romero, Manuel
    1968 *La gaita zuliana*. Maracaibo: Tipografía Cervantes.
Naím, Moisés
    1993 "The launching of radical policy changes, 1989–1991," in Joseph S. Tulchin with Gary
    Bland (eds.), *Venezuela in the Wake of Radical Reform*. Boulder: Lynne Rienner.
Perry, William, and Norman A. Bailey
    1994 *Venezuela 1994: Challenges for the Caldera administration*. Washington, DC: Center
    for Strategic and International Studies.
Sandoval, Chela
    1991 "U.S. Third World feminism: the theory and method of oppositional consciousness in
    the postmodern world." *Genders* 10 (Spring): 1–24.
Vandegrift, Darcie
    1998 "Reading resistance to imagine change: Bribri women and international development
    in Costa Rica." MS.
Williams, Raymond
    1977 *Marxism and Literature*. Oxford and New York: Oxford University Press.

[2]

Feed the World, Free the World . . .

Robin Denselow

Bill Ayres sits in a little office seven floors up above one section of New York's Broadway where the neon lights don't shine too brightly. Around the one-time Catholic priest are piles of the *Food Monitor* magazine with which he is trying to educate the USA on the problems and politics of hunger, both in the Third World and in the USA. It is not an easy task, and he admits that, 'Cash is tight', even though he's been helped by benefit shows such as that by Pete Seeger.

His campaign has never hit the headlines like Live Aid, though in its way it is almost as impressive. For Ayres, a veteran of the civil rights and anti-Vietnam campaigns, has been doing this work for over a decade, and says he'll keep going for the rest of his life. In the process, he's continuing the ideals of a seventies star who claimed, with some justification, to have more political sway than anyone else in the American music business.

The singer was Harry Chapin, the folk-rock balladeer, famous for story-songs like 'Sniper' and 'W.O.L.D.', who died in a car crash in July 1981. He had first met his 'friend and partner', the then 'rock priest' Father Bill Ayres, in 1973 when Chapin appeared as a guest on his rock-and-religion chat show, *On This Rock*. At the time, Ayres was much concerned at the drought and mass starvation in the Sahel region, south of the Sahara, and suggested that Chapin should help him to organize the first-ever food benefit show for Africa, much along the lines of George Harrison's extravaganza for Bangladesh.

Chapin agreed, though he was hardly a well-established star (it was only a year since he had notched up his first hit, 'Taxi'), and had no experience of any such event. The duo met the US Ambassador to the UN, who agreed to help if they would accept the team who had organized the entertainment for Nixon's second inaugural celebrations to oversee the project. They, in turn, planned to go one better than the Bangladesh show by staging a Beatles reunion. Needless to say, the whole idea collapsed.

It was an embarrassing start, but Chapin and Ayres kept studying, and worrying about world hunger, and decided to change their approach. The Sahel benefit, they decided, would have been an example of 'event psychosis', the idea that one major event will appear to solve a particular problem so that the public will feel they don't have to worry about it again, and can move on to worry about something else. 'We decided', said Ayres, 'that hunger could be solved not through an event but only through a process.' He and Chapin dedicated themselves to that process, for life, and in 1975 they founded World Hunger Year (WHY). Its name gave him an excuse to do what he was best at – incessant lobbying. 'What year is World Hunger Year?' he'd been asked. 'Every year is World Hunger Year until we end hunger.' And with that he would launch into a barrage of theories and statistics that would eventually impress even the President of the USA.

Harry Chapin was not so much a sixties idealist adrift in the seventies as a folk-scene idealist who had drifted into the rock camp. The son of a jazz drummer who had played in the Tommy Dorsey and Woody Herman bands, he performed in the Greenwich Village clubs in the sixties, then turned his attention to documentary film-making, winning an academy award nomination for his boxing film, *Legendary Champions*. In the early seventies he became a full-time musician, and by now his songs had developed the narrative line, and the sense of place, detail and atmosphere, of a strong, realistic movie. He notched up four hit singles (including the American number one, 'Cat's In The Cradle', in 1974), and was a prolific writer, who built up a large and faithful live audience for his musical stories about depressed waitresses, disc-jockeys or taxi-drivers.

Chapin gave multi-media shows, or used a 'soft rock' backing group, but the performers he most admired were from an earlier folk scene. His heroes were Pete Seeger ('I'd love to have his qualities, he's approaching sainthood,' he told me in 1977), and Phil Ochs, the subject of his song 'The Parade's Still Passing By'.

Chapin didn't think much of the seventies' pop, or what had happened to the sixties' heroes. In the autumn of 1977, sitting in a record company office in London before a show, he complained, 'At various times, music has been the conscience, and in 1967 it was the lifestyle. Now, it's like junk food. You lose the nutritional value if you belch.' He complained at the fate of the sixties rebels, and their lack of staying power: 'They are now evangelists or selling real estate. They marched twice and complained they didn't change the world.' As for the surviving rock idols, he considered that 'Bob Hope and Frank Sinatra probably do more benefits for people than the Rolling Stones. I don't know the last anti-establishment cause they were involved in.'

His own approach was rather different, for over half of the concerts he gave were benefits. 'I do a hundred benefits a year', he claimed, 'and only Arlo Guthrie and Pete Seeger are in the same ballpark – but I don't see myself as a folkie.' Bill Ayres estimated that Chapin raised $350,000 a year to fight world hunger.

'And not one dollar goes to a starving child!' Chapin would exclaim, with a delighted theatrical flourish, and when there was the expected murmur of disapproval or confusion from the audience, he would launch into one of his favourite arguments. If a George Harrison-style Bangladesh show was held every day for a year (and the money actually rescued from the taxman), then it might raise $730 million – enough to give just $1.50 to every starving person in the world. Chapin claimed that if he was in charge of that money he could increase its impact 'a thousandfold', by spending it on lobbying, education and the media. He wanted to encourage Third World self-sufficiency, and change US aid and foreign policy 'because we deal with some of the most regressive countries in the world'.

Chapin and Ayres were persistent. They held 'radiothons', at which a radio station was taken over for twenty-four hours, while experts and local pressure groups talked about hunger abroad, or in the USA. It was hoped that rock audiences, who never thought about such problems, would be educated, and activated, in the process. WHY also started its magazines, and set up a 'hotline' in New York City, so that the needy could ring in to check on food programmes.

Chapin's most impressive work was in using the established political system. Right from the start, he gave benefit shows to raise money for the campaigns of would-be congressmen and senators of whom he approved, including Gary Hart. He didn't mind if they were Republicans or Democrats, as long as they were 'good on food and hunger issues'. Once they were in power, the politicians found there was a price to pay; Chapin started lobbying for the creation of a presidential commission on world hunger.

Thanks largely to his remarkable energy, and his ability to talk persuasively non-stop for hours, the proposal passed through both Houses, and ended up on President Carter's desk. In February 1978, Chapin flew to Washington from Canada after a concert, and drove to the White House. He repeated his arguments to the President, who by now (thanks to Chapin) had even been lobbied by his daughter Amy. The Commission was created. The consumer activist Ralph Nader said it was the most impressive lobbying effort by an outsider he had ever seen.

It was a personal triumph, but also a sign of what a musician could achieve in the USA in the Carter era. The President clearly wanted to develop the pop image that he had acquired through the early help of the Allman Brothers, and as the 1980 elections approached he tried to win other influential entertainers to his camp. He wanted to have his photo taken with Stevie Wonder, and when the singer refused, his aides phoned Wonder's office with an extraordinary invitation to join the President's Energy Committee. According to Wonder's former aide, Keith Harris, it didn't seem to matter that the singer was no expert in the field (though he had supported anti-nuclear campaigns). It was stressed that the Committee would only have to meet twice a year. Wonder again declined.

Harry Chapin's approach to Washington was very different. There was no question of his being used by the system; if anything he was determined that it should be the other way round. He was appointed to the new Commission On World Hunger, and over the next two years he never missed a meeting, even though it often meant flying in to the capital after a concert the night before.

It wasn't an easy task, because he disagreed with the views of many of the other members. There were those who somehow argued that the problem of hunger could be dealt with 'without addressing the problems of poverty', and it took a major battle before Chapin persuaded them to concede that 'people are hungry because they are poor', in the Commission's report.

Chapin, and a few allies, disagreed with much of the report, and expressed their views in an appendix. It must have been tragic for the singer to write about the findings of a commission that he had created that, 'The most glaring issue not addressed is the most important – the interrelationships between our economic and governmental policies and hunger', or 'Food aid from the United States often has undermined commodity prices in developing nations, thus creating a disincentive to local production.'

The list of Chapin's views that were not shared by other members of the Commission covers several pages, and shows that they didn't even begin to consider some of the ideas that he considered fundamental. According to his widow, Sandy, who had first suggested the idea of the Commission, Harry had 'mixed feelings about the Commission because it was hiding as much as it was recognizing'. And as for President Carter, 'Harry thought he vacillated a lot.'

But at least the President had agreed that the Commission should come into existence, at least it had met, and produced recommendations that both the President, and the American public, could consider. What was needed next was some action, but that never came, for the simple reason that President Carter lost his job. Ronald Reagan did not show the same interest in the ideas of liberal-minded pop stars or in world hunger.

Harry Chapin had every reason to be depressed during the last year of his life. The Commission was finished, and every candidate he had recently supported through fund-raising shows – both Democrats and Republicans who were 'good on hunger' – had been defeated. According to Sandy Chapin, her husband had 'anticipated everything that would happen', once Reagan became President, but he kept going. He hadn't managed to change the world, so he tried to change his own neighbourhood, helping campaigns like the local Food Bank (a scheme, later publicized by Bruce Springsteen, to collect food that manufacturers plan to throw away, and redistribute it to welfare groups).

Chapin, like Britain's Red Wedgers, tried to effect change by using his skills as a pop star to raise money, and then working within the established political system. After 1980, it was clear that he had failed in the short term, but he was also planning a long-term campaign.

At the end of every show, Chapin startled his audience by coming out to meet them in the theatre foyer, and encouraging them to buy magazines or T-shirts to promote WHY. Once Reagan had become President, Chapin began planning to use this devoted audience in a different way. Just before his death, he ordered the printing of 'sign-up cards', to be filled in by fans who wanted to get on to his mailing lists. Fifty thousand such cards are piled up in the basement of Chapin's elegant shoreside house in Huntington Bay, Long Island, where Sandy still lives. His plan, she says, was to build up a constituency, keeping in touch with his followers by using these cards. He had hopes of running for the Democrats as senator in New York State (a role later offered to Harry Belafonte, which Belafonte refused). According to Sandy, her husband 'also talked about running for President – and I don't think it was out of the realm of possibilities'.

Any such hopes seemed a long, long way off on 16 July 1981, the day when the thirty-eight-year-old singer and would-be politician was killed on the Long Island Expressway. 'He must have been depressed when he died,' said Sandy. 'There weren't the days in the year to deliver what he'd committed himself to. Husbands and wives are supposed to know what each other think, but he was always very positive, he'd say, "Onwards and upwards", and "No problem." But I'd say that in a private part of him he really hurt.'

Chapin, the singer who believed in the American system, learned how to lobby Congress, and tried to make Washington work for him, was honoured in a quite extraordinary way once he was dead. Nine senators and thirty congressmen paid tribute to him on the floor of Congress. In May 1986, two congressmen and two senators (including Robert Dole), wrote to the President's assistant at the White House. They 'respectfully requested' a signing ceremony for bill HR 1207, which had passed both the House and Senate the previous week, and called for a gold medal to be awarded to the family of Harry Chapin, 'in recognition of his extra-ordinary efforts to eliminate world hunger', and for 'raising money to fight world hunger before it was fashionable'.

It was one of the final ironies of Chapin's career that his widow should be awarded a Congressional Gold Medal by the President of the USA whose election victory had meant the defeat of so many of the singer's hopes and plans. 'I'm not comfortable,' said Sandy. 'It's one of the things I have to live with.'

When Harry Chapin died, there wasn't much to be seen for all the years of work he had put in, and all the millions of self-earned dollars that he had spent or handed out. His achievements hadn't been instantly spectacular, putting it mildly, but he had made tens of thousands of Americans and Europeans at least think about world hunger, and some of those who worked with him didn't give up. Bill Ayres was still slogging away with WHY, and his former manager, Ken Kragen, was acting most unlike a typical rock 'n' roll businessman.

Kragen had become the highly successful manager of stars like Lionel Richie and Kenny Rogers, and he persuaded his multi-millionaire middle-of-the-road country-rocker client that he should put aside $1 million, over ten years, to finance the World Hunger Media Awards – a prize for the best reporting on hunger issues. Kragen came up with more schemes to keep the hunger issue alive, which varied wildly between good works and good PR. When Bob Geldof first set the Live Aid bandwagon in motion by getting his British rock star chums to record 'Do They Know It's Christmas?', it was Kragen who contacted Geldof to discuss the possibility of an equivalent American record to raise money for the famine in Africa, Kragen who got together with Harry Belafonte to discuss how such a record could actually be made, and Kragen's client Lionel Richie who co-wrote the resulting best-seller, 'We Are The World', with Michael Jackson.

A year after Geldof's extraordinary triumph with Live Aid, Kragen was responsible for another vast-scale hunger-related media spectacular that was far less successful as a fund-raiser, and decidedly dubious as a political event. Hands Across America was an attempt to get over 5 million Americans to join hands in a human chain that would stretch from New York to Los Angeles. Each would donate at least $10, and it was hoped that around $100 million would be raised for the USA's hungry and homeless.

'This one's for you, Harry Chapin!' announced Kragen at the start of the brief event, on 25 May 1986, but Chapin would surely have been furious at what happened. There were lengthy gaps in the route, and over half the money that was raised was paid out in expenses and salaries, leaving only around $12 million for the homeless. Watching the crowds holding hands in Trenton, New Jersey, it seemed like a classic case of 'event psychosis'. The mood was cheerful and patriotic, there was much waving of American flags, and massed choruses of 'We Are The World', 'America The Beautiful', and a rather less impressive pop song specially written for the occasion. What was lacking was any feeling of anger or shame that hunger and homelessness should exist in the world's richest nation, or that the administration had in any way failed by helping to cause such misery or allowing it to continue. Chapin would surely have demanded a political event, but Hands Across America became exactly the opposite.

For a start, the event was 'sponsored' by corporations like Coca-Cola, McDonald's and Safeway supermarkets, who all make millions out of feeding the USA, and whose involvement could well give the impression that the hunger issue could be solved by being privatized, and taken out of the political arena. Stranger still was the involvement of President Reagan. Soon before the event he had said that hunger in the USA was the result of 'lack of knowledge' by the poor about where and how to get help – and this at a time when agencies like the Washington Food Research Action Center were blaming the new poverty on cuts in social assistance, increased taxation for lower-paid workers, or tougher eligibility requirements for food stamps.

President Reagan was responsible, and yet Reagan decided to join the Hands Across America line. 'Terrific,' said Kragen, but Bill Ayres, who was acting as co-host of the event, on radio, was not so happy. He tried to point out the contradictions by comparing military spending with the comparatively tiny amount spent on food nutrition programmes, but once Reagan appeared, his listeners may have missed the point. 'Reagan could claim credit for this day, and for the amount of hungry people we have,' he said later, 'because he's been cutting back on food stamps and child nutrition programmes. We wanted to trap him, and make him appreciate the problem. But when I saw him singing the songs . . .'

Hands Across America was held on the Sunday before the UN General Assembly's debate on long-term relief and development policy in Africa, and coincided with a worldwide event organized by the Live Aid team. Bob Geldof planned to whip up publicity for the UN debate, as well as raise more money to combat the famine in Africa, through Sport Aid and Race against Time. Unlike Hands Across America, this was a brilliant success; it involved the participation of over 20 million people, running in seventy-eight countries. The event raised $35 million, and the overheads were kept low. It would have been even more successful if the American event starring Ronald Reagan hadn't taken place at the same time, with the result that the American media virtually ignored the Race against Time.

Geldof was remarkably sanguine about the whole affair. He said he didn't want confusion between the issues of African famine and hunger in the USA, he supported Hands Across America, and he even helped in their advertising. But he had one major criticism – he was furious that the President had been allowed to take part. 'It was an ideal opportunity to make a massive political lobby,' said Geldof, 'but they shouldn't have let Reagan join, because that man is the one man who can get up at night, and sign a paper that will eradicate a lot of the problems of homelessness in

America. He was very clever. It negated the political effect, allowing him to join the line.'

Chapin would have been dismayed by that, but he would have been impressed by one Hands Across America spin–off: $100,000 that was raised was set aside for a coalition of different groups, including WHY, to campaign during the 1988 presidential campaign, to make sure that the issues of hunger and homelessness in the USA were not forgotten. It was ironic, putting it mildly, that President Reagan and his family and staff had contributed towards that.

If Chapin had been alive in the years when hunger did actually 'become fashionable', thanks largely to Geldof's remarkable efforts, it seems he would have had mixed feelings about what was going on. He would have been delighted that so many big–name rock stars had come out of their cocoons after the indulgent seventies, but disappointed that so few followed up their work as 'do–gooders' (an enjoyable and important indulgence of stars throughout the ages) with more controversial and less socially acceptable political action.

Chapin used to fantasize about a meeting between his 'three gods', Che Guevara, Elvis Presley and Bob Dylan (he once wrote a screenplay about a meeting between 'the pure revolutionary, the commercial public hero, and the man wavering between the two'). Another intriguing discussion, and one that would surely have happened if only he had lived, would have been between himself and the stars at the 'We Are The World' recording session. Chapin talking politics and pop with Bruce Springsteen, Stevie Wonder and Geldof – now that would have been well worth hearing.

Springsteen, the best big stadium rock performer of his generation, has been regarded as a blue–collar god throughout most of the eighties, and Chapin would doubtless have been much impressed with his grassroots support for the Food Bank movement. The admiration would presumably have been mutual (after all, Springsteen dedicated songs to Chapin after he died, and made a $10,000 contribution to WHY). What Chapin might have questioned was just how far the Boss's political actions or interests really extended, and what he really believes in.

Springsteen has donated large sums to the hunger movement, and other blue–collar good works, he has turned out for MUSE and Sun City, and has hinted at greater political interest and involvement through his songs and on–stage speeches. He hasn't, as yet, followed up with much action to show just what he is trying to achieve, other than a romantic notion of support for the blue–collar under–dog. As Bill Ayres put it, 'Harry would have loved what Springsteen is doing, but he was more overtly political. Bruce has got to make the decision, somewhere in the next year or two, as to how political he's going to get. Because if you're going to deal with these issues, you're going to get political.'

Springsteen seemed happiest dealing with hunger as a straightforward humanitarian issue, and on this level, at least, he made an impact. In Newark, just south of New York City, there is an industrial wasteland known as the 'ironbound' area, because it is surrounded by railroad tracks. Here, there is a large food warehouse that boasts its own truck, and a picture of Springsteen on the wall. This is a Food Bank. There are shelves of macaroni, baby food, crackers and salad dressing, and freezers filled with fish or ice-cream. Some of it has damaged packaging, some has packaging that the manufacturers have decided to change, and some is simply the result of overproduction. It is an extraordinary display of big corporation waste in a land of plenty and starvation.

Kathleen DiChiara, who runs the bank, is responsible for finding such food and overseeing its transfer to a selection of 500 different hunger groups in New Jersey and surrounding states. It helps to feed around 50,000 people, in an area where 'maybe one in seven don't get enough to eat at some time during the month'. An operation like that needs finance, and Springsteen has helped. According to DiChiara he made a sizeable, unpublicized donation, plugged the Food Bank when he gave concerts in neighbouring stadiums, and suggested to *Rolling Stone* that they should give money to it, rather than provide the Boss with a car, when he received one of the magazine's awards. Springsteen made similar hefty donations, and speeches about Food Banks, right across the USA.

Because of Springsteen, Food Banks suddenly received a lot of attention. Teenagers and even children started sending in letters and money, and DiChiara found that she suddenly had support from 'an audience that wasn't listening in traditional places, like the church or school'. His initiative also inspired a group of fellow Jersey musicians, including some of the E-Street Band, to record the pompously titled Jersey Artists for Mankind's (JAM) offering to the 1986 charity stakes, 'We Got The Love' (with proceeds donated to the Food Bank network). The Boss played guitar on the record, but didn't turn up at the Food Bank for the video shoot. He apparently felt that he was being used: the song was released on Arista rather than CBS, and they were wisely trying to exploit his involvement as much as they could.

The song was 'partly inspired' by Lee Mrowicki, who for ten years has been the DJ at the Stone Pony music bar in Asbury Park, the run-down New Jersey seaside resort where Bruce started out. When Springsteen began his support campaign for Food Banks, Lee says he told him, 'You'll cause political unrest.' 'Yeah,' the Boss allegedly replied, 'that's the point of it.' As a result of that conversation, says Lee, the JAM team inserted the line 'We got the power' into their song.

It was all very admirable, but political power, let alone political unrest, just didn't seem to be part of the Springsteen plan. He has reportedly spent $1 million on good works (an impressive sum, but a mere fraction of what Chapin had given away, as a proportion of earnings), and the recipients of his generosity have ranged from American unions to the Northumberland and Durham Miners Support Group in Britain (an involvement in the miners' strike that won him some startled admiration from the Left).

Lee has watched Springsteen's rise from the Stone Pony to superstardom with awe. 'Most people nowadays think he's God,' said the DJ, who still works in the sweaty club across the road from the bleak Asbury Park boardwalks. 'He's got power, but he knows he mustn't abuse it, which is why, most of the time, he fades into the background.' When he has used that power, the result hasn't always been a success. Just up the road from Asbury Park is Springsteen's hometown of Freehold, New Jersey, where one of the local factories belongs to the 3M, the Minnesota Mining and Manufacturing Company, who make professional recording tape. The company decided to close the plant, and lay off over 300 workers, in a scenario that could have come from one of Springsteen's blue-collar laments.

In Freehold, the workers didn't go along with blind acceptance that 'there ain't been much work on account of the economy'. The Oil, Chemical and Atomic Workers Union Local 8–760 decided to fight back, and wrote to various artists, like Springsteen, who might use 3M tape, and be concerned at the closure. Springsteen was one of those who replied – along with the cast of Hill Street Blues, Willie Nelson, The Blasters, John Cougar Mellancamp, and others. An advertisement signed by some of these later appeared in the national press, asking 3M – in the most friendly fashion – to reconsider their decision, 'and come up with a humane programme that will keep those jobs and those workers in Freehold'. As the campaign started up, Springsteen returned to the Stone Pony, in January 1986, to play a Hometowns Against Shutdowns benefit for the workers, and made a donation to the union.

It could have been an extraordinary campaign, especially as it began to take on international dimensions. A month after Springsteen's little concert, 3M's black workers in South Africa, who surely have problems that are even more serious than redundancy in Freehold, staged a four-hour strike 'in support of the Freehold workers'. 'And that', said Local 8–760 President, Stanley Fischer, 'has never happened before in the modern age.'

The South African connection continued, as a 3M union leader was invited to visit the USA – only to be jailed on his return. Meanwhile, much of the plant was closed, and 383 men lost their jobs. Springsteen donated another $25,000 to help unemployed workers' projects, but a year later, 60 per cent were still out of work. The rather genteel campaign faded away.

Springsteen had at least done something – far more, it could be argued, than an earlier set of very rich rockers like the Rolling Stones – but the Stones didn't lecture their audience on politics, they didn't fill their songs with images of blue-collar suffering, and they never ended their shows with the stirring cry, 'Let freedom ring – but remember, you gotta fight for it.'

What Springsteen didn't do was scream, yell, go out on a limb, or get angry at what was going on. He acted like a character from his songs, for Springsteen's heroes accept their fate – even if it drives them to murder, as in 'Johnny 99'. They are portrayed as noble, hopeless victims of forces that are beyond their control. It is this attitude, surely, that explains why the Boss's glorious, stirring rock songs that honour the American working man have appealed to the Right just as much as the Left. Springsteen's heart may or may not still be with the rebels when he sings Woody Guthrie's 'This Land Is Your Land', and announces that it was written as 'an angry song, an answer to Irving Berlin's "God Bless America" '. We don't know, because he doesn't go on to explain the cause of Guthrie's anger, or his politics.

This vagueness has meant that songs can have different messages for different people. Bono, who has suffered the same fate at times, recalls his horror at watching an American bar-room crowd standing to attention when 'We Are The World' was played, and at the way audiences were reacting 'with fists in the air and hands on their heart' to Springsteen's 'Born In The USA'. 'I know Bruce Springsteen finds this a quite terrifying thought,' said Bono, 'a song written about Vietnam, and America's role in the destruction of another country and culture, and people are seeing that again as a national anthem.'

'Born In The USA' was taken up as an anthem by another group whom Springsteen had helped, the Vietnam Veterans. It was ironic, then, that on the other side of the world, the musical champion of another group of Vietnam Vets should emerge as one of Springsteen's critics. Redgum was one of Australia's leading political bands in the early eighties, and they even knocked Michael Jackson off the top of the Australian charts with their carefully researched tribute to Australian Vietnam Vets, 'I Was Only 19'. John Schumann, who wrote it, was not impressed by his rather more successful US counterpart – at least as a political singer. For him, Springsteen was suspicious 'because he never puts his arse on the line. He hints at problems, but there's no anger in his songs. His depiction of the working-class struggle is a folksy, romantic one, with no acknowledgement of exploitation, division or oppression. He could be a very powerful voice, but when both Reagan and Mondale can court him, now that disturbs me!'

The rival endorsements, at the height of the 1984 presidential campaign, clearly worried Springsteen as well. First there was Reagan, speaking in New Jersey, and announcing, 'America's future rests in a

thousand dreams inside your hearts. It rests in the message of hope in
songs of a man so many young Americans admire: New Jersey's own
Bruce Springsteen. And helping you make those dreams come true is
what this job of mine is all about.' Springsteen quickly distanced himself
from such remarks, to the delight of the Democrats. Just over a week later
Walter Mondale tried to claim the Springsteen endorsement – again
without the Boss's approval.

It was an amusing diversion in an election campaign, and a sign of what
can happen if you write political songs without having made your
position absolutely clear. A Washington veteran like Chapin may not
have had such fame, but, then, he would never have had such problems.

If he had been asked to choose the one performer at the recording of
'We Are The World' whom he regarded as the best musical politician,
then I suspect that the award wouldn't have gone to Springsteen, but to
the man who also happened to be the greatest musician in the studio –
Stevie Wonder. He, after all, had carried on the great black traditions of
social comment in his songs, keeping the spirit of Marvin Gaye and the
early Curtis Mayfield alive in the eighties, and had also achieved
something more concrete, in MLK Day. To be a successful lobbyist and a
musical genius (if a somewhat slushy one at times) is no mean feat.

Also in the studio, along with such politically important, and sometime
politically important, figures as Harry Belafonte and Bob Dylan, there
was Bob Geldof. What would Chapin have made of the passionate and
scruffy Irish motor-mouth? Obviously, he would have shared the world's
admiration of a man who had, for a while at least, succeeded in the task to
which he had devoted his life – making rock audiences aware of the
problems of world hunger.

But while Chapin was 'committed for life', Geldof's campaign ran for
just two years, because he was determined from the start that Band Aid or
Live Aid shouldn't become an 'institution'. He started off, as a struggling
pop star, persuading his more famous friends to put together a charity
record, as a reaction to the horrors of African famine that he saw on his
television screen. He ended up by organizing the most spectacular global
pop show and fund-raising event in history, and then touring the world,
supervising aid programmes and lecturing world leaders. He was largely
responsible for $140 million worth of aid contributions, and for the
progressive way in which much of that money was spent. And at the end
of all that, he tried to go back to being a pop star, with only limited
success.

It was an extraordinary story that left many unanswered questions.
Geldof insisted that his campaign was humanitarian, and not political,
because 'famine is above politics' (as he furiously announced to a
squabbling group of Euro MPs). But though he succeeded in keeping his
campaign out of party politics, his own experiences soon showed him that

politics and famine are very closely linked. By the end of his deliberately brief career as musical conscience to the world, he was also talking of having a 'constituency' of those millions who watched the fund-raising concerts on television, ran in Sport Aid, and supported his ideas. He felt he had a responsibility in 'using this constituency to generate political change'. Chapin would have approved of that, and of the furious attacks that Geldof made at the European Parliament or the UN in New York. Knowing that change normally involves long-term campaigning, he might have questioned why Geldof should rightly demand such change, but then turn his back on his achievement and involvement and concentrate on trying to be a pop star.

In the broadest sense, at least, Live Aid was political even before Geldof started asking Mrs Thatcher about the over-production of butter, lecturing Europeans about the EEC food surpluses, or the West, and the Russians, at the UN. Geldof told the UN that Live Aid had reached 'two billion people'. Any television programme that reaches an audience like that, and which by its very nature questions the distribution of wealth on the planet (even if through such soft, if effective devices as a Cars video), will stimulate a debate and become a political event. The concert raised other political questions that Geldof doesn't seem to have expected. He wanted the world's top artists to appear at the two overlapping concerts at Wembley and Philadelphia, so that the world-wide audience would not get bored for a second, not switch off, and not stop sending in money. All very admirable, but he didn't just go for big stars, but big white stars. Two years after the event, there were still black British musicians who felt insulted at the lack of black musicians at Wembley (Sade was one obvious exception), particularly as Ethiopia is a spiritual homeland for many of them.

In his autobiography, Geldof hit back furiously at such charges, pointing out – rightly, I'm sure – that he just wanted to raise money, that he's obviously no racist, and that 'there aren't any world famous million-selling reggae bands', particularly in Britain. But the brief inclusion of Eddy Grant, Junior Giscombe, Imagination or even Hot Chocolate would have balanced Wembley's almost all-white image, and might have improved the show's uneven musical quality.

In America there were no such complaints, though some surprise that Springsteen didn't show up, and some confusion as to why Stevie Wonder didn't appear. It has been suggested that it was because Wonder felt he was being asked as a token black, but when asked, he simply replied, 'I don't have to do everything that there is. It was my desire to stay at home, so I did.'

The only embarrassment in Philadelphia came from a veteran white singer of uncertain political conviction – Bob Dylan. He was introduced by Jack Nicholson as 'the transcendent Bob Dylan', and played three decidedly ragged acoustic oldies, including 'Blowin' In The Wind', with uneven assistance from Ron Wood and Keith Richard. He then suggested that some of the money that had been raised for Africa, 'maybe two or three million', could be used to 'pay off the mortgages on some of the farms that some of the farmers here owe to the bank'. It was a comment that led to 'Farm Aid', and reminded the USA that there was also poverty at home, but the timing was terrible. This, after all, was one occasion when the USA was being asked to think of people beyond her borders.

Live Aid brought considerable publicity and commercial success to many of the bands who took part, and brought Geldof a quite extraordinary power and responsibility. When he started out, he was planning a simple charity, handing over food or money. Such good works tend to be non-controversial, because they accept the status quo, and don't attempt to tackle the root cause of the problem. Charity on this level can be seen as favouring the Right, because responsibility for tackling social ills is taken away from the state, and placed in the hands of the individual, or voluntary organizations. The Victorian era was a time of appalling social ills, and the Victorians were very charity conscious.

Inevitably, then, there was suspicion of Live Aid from the British Left, for it came at a time when Mrs Thatcher had talked approvingly of 'Victorian values'. The *New Socialist* complained,

> In a period where the very ethos of a planned, socialized and welfarized society is running down – *being* run down – and the individual-in-the-market is the intended locus of all social organization, a happy story where an individual can be seen to put the world to rights is of tremendous ideological value. Value, that is, to an interest group which depends on fostering Victorian charity and free-market fantasies.

To which Geldof would doubtless have replied, as he did when he met any obstacles or critics, 'But people are dying. Just look at the TV. I don't want another dead child in my living room.' Once he started dealing with the vast amounts of donations that poured in, he was inevitably involved in a crash course in food aid politics, the realities of the African scene, the problems of debt, and an understanding of the strings often attached to aid offers from West or East, and the amounts Africa spends, and is encouraged to spend, on armaments.

All this, and a lot of expert advice, helped to formulate Band Aid's policies of holding much of the money back, and spending it carefully to encourage long-term development and rehabilitation programmes, rather than simply emergency relief (which, of course, was also badly needed). The results were projects, right across Africa, that ranged from tree-planting to vaccination programmes, and the aim, by the end, was to Africanize the schemes, so that local people made the decisions rather than relying on outside help. This, clearly, was very different from 'Victorian charity', and so was the way in which he used the event to embarrass governments into action.

Geldof's transformation, in the months after Live Aid, was remarkable. He lectured and cajoled world leaders, railed at the iniquities of Third World debt, arms sales and the aid system, and developed an instant and privileged political education by meeting everyone from the starving peasants of Africa to George Bush and the future British monarch. Because he had no long-term political career to worry about, the scruffy pop singer in his yellow sneakers could say what he wanted, and because of his insistence, world leaders had to listen. In October 1985 he returned from a tour of the famine areas of Africa, and startled the European Parliament in Strasbourg with a vicious attack on 'the crowning idiocy' of the over-production caused by the Common Agricultural Policy (CAP), and he attacked EEC bureaucracy by announcing, 'This place needs a laxative.'

It was an extraordinary and effective blitz of a campaign, and it climaxed in May the following year, in New York. The UN General Assembly was holding a Special Session on Africa, to discuss famine and relief, and Geldof organized Sport Aid, the biggest sporting event in history, both to raise money and pressurize the UN into action.

He wasn't too pleased at what went on. At a press conference at the UN's New York headquarters on 29 May, he called the session a 'farce' because it only lasted four days, and while he applauded plans for a moratorium on African debt, he insisted that the UN had 'missed the mark' by not dealing with the effect of Western agricultural policies on Africa, or the effect of arms sales. He attacked both the Russians ('cynical and laughable'), and the Americans (George Schultz was 'simplistic and nonsensical'), and announced that, 'Africans themselves come out with very little credit.' And who was he speaking for? Geldof said that 'after last Sunday, 30 million people around the world who physically took part in Sport Aid are not going to be satisfied'.

The UN was dealt with in typical Geldof style. 'If only they could grow up in this place for once in their fucking lives, and talk about it seriously! Who do these people purport to represent? They certainly don't represent the 30 million who got out on the streets, nor the two billion people who watched one hot summer's day last year!' These unseen masses, half the world population, were, he said, a 'political constituency', and yet at the end of the press conference Geldof could be heard to mutter, 'This is it for me . . . there's nothing else I can do . . .'

Within the rules he had set himself, he was absolutely right. He didn't want Live Aid to become an institution, so he made his extraordinary contribution, and got out. As for his 'political constituency', they were left without a leader or a figure-head, assuming that they actually existed as a political force, rather than simply being well-meaning pop fans who

were touched by the horror of the cause and the emotion of the whole
event.

It seems wrong and ridiculous to criticize Geldof, for he was true to his
beliefs, and achieved more than most mere mortals. But watching that
press conference, and then listening to his rather ordinary solo LP when it
appeared a few months later, it seemed that an awful lot had been lost, or
wasted. It only seemed right that he should return to the famine areas of
Africa in 1987.

The ripples from Live Aid spread right across the pop spectrum. That
musicians could raise such vast sums, and have such an effect, enthused
and encouraged those attempting more directly political campaigns
through music, with Red Wedge, CND or AAA. It also caused a series of
quite different effects. Live Aid helped to make pop music – the 'rebel'
music of previous eras – seem even more respectable, as politicians and
pillars of the establishment fell over themselves to heap praise on Geldof,
who was awarded an honorary knighthood in Britain (he is an Irish
citizen), and nominated, though unsuccessfully, for the Nobel Peace
Prize.

It also, indirectly, helped in the growing feeling that Western pop was
now an international style and therefore should have international
concerns – and this despite the sad lack of Third World performers among
the superstars at Wembley or Philadelphia.

The immediate effect was a wild proliferation of good-cause concerts.
In the USA, Dylan's comments on the plight of farmers led to Farm Aid,
organized by Willie Nelson and featuring an impressive line-up including
Dylan and Neil Young. In Britain, over the following year, the events
ranged from Pete Townshend's anti-heroin campaign to a large-scale
Midlands charity show for a Birmingham children's hospital, organized
by Conservative supporter Bev Bevan of the Electric Light Orchestra, to
concerts for the environmental group Greenpeace.

At any other time, a week-long series of shows at the Albert Hall would
have been considered a major event, especially as the money being raised
was for campaigns against the nuclear contamination of the Irish Sea and
French nuclear testing in the Pacific, and as the French had blown up the
Greenpeace ship the *Rainbow Warrior* in New Zealand. In post-Live Aid
Britain, such events now seemed so predictable that they were almost
overlooked.

Charity events had become part of the pop calendar, and the charity
that benefited the most was the one that proved just how close certain
well-established performers and the establishment had now become. The
most distinguished spectators at Live Aid were the Prince and Princess of
Wales, the latter Britain's best-publicized pop fan. The Prince had first
attended a rock concert in 1982, when Status Quo performed in

Birmingham, to raise money for his own charity, the Prince's Trust. This had been started in 1976, as a way of helping disadvantaged young people, but had a low budget of around £30,000 a year, provided by private individuals, business, or the Prince himself. That changed, dramatically, when the Trust became involved with pop music.

The Quo show was followed by a Prince's Trust Rock Gala (starring such heavyweights as Phil Collins, Robert Plant, Pete Townshend and Ian Anderson), and from then on the Trust shows became regular events, with royalty always in attendance. Some events were simply scheduled concerts by major acts like Dire Straits, the Eurythmics or Genesis, and others were specially arranged galas. The events in 1986 and 1987 were recorded and filmed, and by now 75 per cent of the Trust's income of well over £1 million a year was coming from pop music, mostly through television and video deals. The events started before Live Aid, but the post-Live Aid mood provided an enormous encouragement. Many famous artists often have a dull time, cocooned from the real world, when they are on tour, and have few opportunities to meet each other casually and perform together.

The participants in Live Aid clearly enjoyed themselves (more so in Britain than in the USA, where it was a more competitive affair), and the Prince's Trust shows had the same sort of atmosphere. Elton John, who appeared on both the Trust's live LPs, said the shows had another appeal. 'With a lot of charities you're dubious where the money goes – like the Bangladesh show – and you can see a rat a mile off. But with this, you can enjoy yourself and not worry . . .' As for the proceeds, they are handed out through a series of fifty-four local committees across Britain. Every year, between 3,000 and 5,000 young people, aged between fourteen and twenty-five, are given grants of up to £300 'to help them help themselves'. Money has been paid out for a football kit, electric guitars, and a bike for a girl who couldn't afford bus fares and wanted to go out looking for work.

Is this old-fashioned Victorian charity? A future king who is trying to help is preferable to one who does nothing, though, as his office admits, 'This is just a drop in the ocean, but it's better to help a few thousand than help none.'

The post-Live Aid mood spread beyond the West, and it even affected the USSR, from where the band Autograph took part, playing over a satellite link from Moscow, and where a new General Secretary of the Communist Party had taken office just a few months earlier. At fifty-four, Mikhail Gorbachev was the youngest Soviet leader since Stalin, with a thankfully different approach, as he proved early the next year when he addressed the Party Congress with a scathing attack on corruption and inefficiency. It was the beginning of a new phase of openness (*glasnost*) and the policy was soon put to the test. The USSR (and much of East and West Europe) experienced the worst nuclear accident in history, an explosion at the Chernobyl nuclear power station that led to more long-term radiation being emitted into the earth's atmosphere than from any previous nuclear disaster.

One result was a special Live Aid–style charity concert, that was held in Moscow to encourage contributions to the disaster fund. It was a reminder that the USSR had its rock stars too, though they hadn't had an easy time in a country where pop music and jazz were traditionally seen as signs of decadent Western culture (in the twenties, there was even a Soviet slogan 'Today He Plays Jazz, Tomorrow He Betrays His Country').

The situation had changed, a little, by the time Gorbachev took over, with some 'official' bands like Autograph signed to the State record label, Melodiya, while others, who refused to conform to officially approved styles, had to eke out a living, taking other jobs, and playing at impromptu shows whenever they got the chance, their shows advertised only by word of mouth. In the new era, their situation began to improve, and bands like Popular Mechanics found life easier under a leader who actually signed international deals involving pop music.

In the summer of 1987, the thaw in East–West relations could be judged from events on the pop circuit. The Soviet band Dialogue appeared in London, as the West began to take an interest in Soviet pop. Meanwhile Billy Joel became the latest in a series of Western rockers to visit the USSR, his six shows resulting from the US/Soviet cultural exchange agreement signed during the Reagan/Gorbachev summit two years previously. Joel was particularly successful with the Beatles classic, 'Back In The USSR'.

In East Europe, too, pop music was now a barometer of political change, though the outlook was not always favourable. Great powers have traditionally greeted each other, and shown symbolic signs of friendship and respect by allowing the visits of naval fleets. In the eighties, it seemed that pop musicians were assuming that role.

One sign of the new mood was the remarkable event staged at the People's Stadium, in Budapest on 27 July 1986. Stomping up and down across the stage in front of the 80,000-strong crowd came a twenty-piece women's dance group, dressed in full national costume, and belting out an odd but lively version of 'Honky Tonk Women'. They were the opening act at the largest pop show ever held in East Europe, at which the main attraction was Queen (who had now apologized for playing at Sun City two years earlier).

On stage, Queen went through their standard big stadium ritual, enlivened by the spectacle of Freddie Mercury prancing down a cat-walk draped in British and Hungarian flags, in the shadow of a pavilion that was ordered by Stalin. Down in the crowd, before the show started, the event had led to an intriguing discussion. A group of teenagers, dressed in

the dark-green uniforms of the Communist youth organization, the
Young Guard, were debating Communism, pop music and censorship.
The younger of the teenage guards argued that they didn't like the present
state control of the record industry, they didn't like censorship, and they
wanted the music scene opened up. They were particularly concerned at
the jailing of local punk bands like CPG and ETA, whose lyrics include
such lines as 'Hitler and Stalin all wanted too much. I don't need that. I
need anarchy and the beach.'

Their elders (who eventually suggested to my translator that the
discussion had gone on long enough) argued that such punks were
dangerous, that there had to be limits within a socialist society, and that
unbridled punkdom could 'lead to another 1956'. That, of course, was the
year when Russian tanks rolled in to put down what is officially described
as a 'counter revolution'.

Pop music hadn't made this debate possible, but pop was now being
used as a yardstick by which freedom of expression was judged.
Elsewhere in East Europe, pop music could be used as a gauge of youth
attitudes. Poland developed its own lively home-grown music scene (and
an attachment to veteran punks like the Stranglers), while in East Berlin
there were riots alongside the Berlin wall as young fans tried to hear a
Bowie concert taking place – somewhat irresponsibly – just a few
hundred yards away in the West.

In East Germany, pop music was also being used by the authorities as
entertainment and propaganda, and even as a way of signalling diplomatic
changes to the West. East Germany holds its own annual political song
festivals, or musical peace festivals, at which performers from all over the
Eastern bloc, and a few sympathizers or potential sympathizers from the
West, gather to perform under such slogans as 'Peace and Solidarity with
the World'.

The main musical event at one such concert, in October 1983, also
signalled a major political change. It involved the appearance of Udo
Lindenberg, the outspoken and highly political West German singer, a
supporter of the Green Party who later tried to upset the cosy atmosphere
of Live Aid by talking about the politics of aid, and comparing the money
needed in Ethiopia with the defence spending of East and West. For
years, he had taunted the East German leadership from across the border,
and in his song 'Special Train To Pankow' he had asked to be allowed to
sing in the 'workers' and peasants' state', and had satirized the East
German leader, Erich Honecker, by suggesting that he might be a closet
rocker.

Those are the sort of suggestions that land East German bands in jail, so
his followers in East Germany were amazed when he was suddenly invited
in, to sing for his screaming and sobbing fans, and the sober-suited party
officials, and appear alongside Russian and Czech singers, and Harry

Belafonte, at a 'peace' gala. Lindenberg delighted the East Germans with his comments on disarmament, and developed a 'special relationship with Honecker', the man who had supervised the building of the Berlin wall.

The pop singer's visit was seen as marking the start of a new era in East–West German relationships, an era in which it was possible for Honecker to visit West Germany for the first time. During his visit, four years later in September 1987, the East German leader visited the now-rebuilt house in Wuppertal where Karl Marx's collaborator Friedrich Engels was born. Waiting outside for 'Honny' was Udo Lindenberg. The unlikely duo held a brief, but much publicized conversation in front of the inevitable television cameras.

Not all Western singers who appeared at the East German festivals felt they had achieved so much. In 1986, the line-up included Leon Rosselson, Billy Bragg, the ANC band Amandla, Russian rock bands, and Pete Seeger, who sang 'We Shall Overcome' and 'Where Have All The Flowers Gone?'. Rosselson, the furious critic of politicians in Britain and the USA, was not impressed. 'I felt out of it. My job is to challenge people and provoke people, and their attitude was that there are no problems – not even about nuclear power or feminism. There were a lot of things they thought it too dangerous to face up to. I didn't see the point of singing generalized songs in favour of peace which absolutely everyone was going to agree with.'

Billy Bragg, who has since paid several visits to Russia and East Europe, didn't mind being used by politicians, because the experience was worth it. 'Pop having no frontiers has a role to play in international communications that don't go through the ruling political parties,' said Bragg. 'The process of exchanging ideas has got to begin somewhere.'

For him, at least, concerts in the Eastern bloc were important not just because of the music but because of the discussions with the audience that were arranged to take place afterwards. A 'socialist' singer was forced to rethink what he meant by the word when he visited 'socialist' countries as different as East Germany, Hungary, the USSR and Nicaragua, and when he found that audiences in East Europe accused him of 'spouting the Government line' when he talked about peace initiatives. He found that he was getting more applause when he announced that 'Ideology is important, but people and their happiness are even more important.'

Bragg's travels may have left him 'as confused about politics as I've ever been', but his forays in East Europe could only help the process of *glasnost*. A pop singer who had been arrested for cutting the fence at a nuclear base learned how musicians elsewhere could really suffer for their beliefs, and their art. 'In Russia,' said Bragg, 'you can get arrested for doing a gig, and in East Germany you can get arrested for just going to one. You can't just go over there to play, then walk away.'

In Czechoslovakia the situation was worse. There, in September 1986, the leading members of the voluntary youth organization, the jazz section of the Union of Musicians, were raided by the State security police and arrested, charged with 'illicit trading'. The section, which had 7,000 members and links with the Charter 77 opposition, had been under attack for the previous two years, after a bureaucratic error had apparently given the group far greater autonomy than the authorities had intended. Because of this slip-up, the jazz section was also able to publish its own uncensored magazines and paperbacks, and they brought out books on John Lennon, on rock 'n' roll history, and on African music – all apparently subjects of which the Czech authorities didn't approve.

The arrest of the jazz musicians led to protest concerts in the West, and perhaps because of this pressure, some were released, and others given shorter jail sentences than expected. In March 1986, as the Chairman of the jazz section, Karel Srp, was taken away from a Prague court to begin a sixteen-month prison sentence, the crowd outside began to sing Lennon's 'Give Peace A Chance'.

The new internationalism of pop was reflected in the music. The rock 'n' roll era was over thirty years old by the late eighties, and was beginning to show its age. The music had progressed through white rock and folk styles, black soul, blues, reggae and funk, along with revivals and permutations of all of them, and was still looking for fresh new noises. Global styles provided one answer, and the new music scene began to include artists from Africa, from Latin America, and even from East Europe. The spread of 'world music' was helped by Peter Gabriel and the WOMAD movement, who since 1982 have brought non-Western musicians to Britain, and released their records, and it was also encouraged (until its demise) by the musical policies of the GLC.

In the USA, the new mixture of African, Latin and Caribbean styles even led to a new global fusion movement, 'World Beat', promoted by San Francisco musician Dan Del Santo, and other Bay area bands who mixed these styles together and added a radical line in lyrics. All of this affected the politics of pop. Musicians found, as Phil Ochs had nearly two decades earlier, that there were political singers right across the world, even in ignored corners of the English-speaking world.

This was a climate in which, at long last, it seemed possible that the great Canadian singer Bruce Cockburn might win greater recognition for his increasingly angry, varied and complex songs that have mixed rock and folk styles with 'music from all over the world'. He started writing political protest songs in the mid-seventies, dealing largely with his country's large southern neighbour, but in the eighties he has been looking even further south, to Central and South America. His visits to Nicaragua, inspired by the poetry of the Nicaraguan Minister of Culture,

Father Ernesto Cardenal, changed both his musical styles and his lyrics, as shown by furious songs of a Christian pacifist-who-can't-stand-it like 'If I Had A Rocket Launcher'. He has followed up his pro-Nicaragua, anti-Contra stance by actively supporting the Sanctuary movement, the network of American churches and safe houses that harbour 'illegal' Salvadoran and Guatemalan refugees. The Reagan administration claims that such people cannot be genuine political refugees, as they are fleeing from regimes that the US supports.

In Central America, another political singer was helped by the new climate. Ruben Blades, from Panama, is a lawyer in his late thirties, and a major star right across the Spanish-speaking Americas, where he is renowned for his highly contemporary blend of salsa, the music of Puerto Rico, Cuba, and the Latin clubs of New York. He is also a man with a carefully thought out mission. He aims to use his music and fame as a device to change the way in which the USA thinks of Latin America, and then return to Panama to play an active role in politics. It is no far-fetched 'cross-over dream', for he has two law degrees (one from Harvard), and has rapidly developed his career as a film star as well as a musician.

Blades' politics were born of experience. He grew up in the canal zone, an avid fan of American rock 'n' roll, which he imitated, without understanding the words, and he thought of the USA as 'the people we idolized, the best in the world'. That changed in 1964, when there were riots in Panama, 'because we were demanding to have the Panamanian flag flying alongside the US flag', and American residents disagreed. US forces were sent in, and twenty-one people died. It was, said Blades, 'a tremendous shock – all of a sudden the army that defeated the Nazis was also kicking us'. It had the effect of making him study the history of his country, 'and without becoming a lunatic-fringe anti-US person I started to educate myself, and deal with things according to the facts'.

Since the mid-seventies, Blades has been based in New York, playing in bands, and trying to develop salsa into an international style, keeping all the percussion but using synthesizers instead of brass. In the process, he has actually broken through to English-speaking pop audiences, who appreciate good raw, rhythmic dance music, and he makes sure that he explains the Spanish lyrics of his often political songs, such as 'Father Antonio And The Altar Boy, Andres', his song about the murder in 1980 of El Salvador's Archbishop Romero, and 'Muevete', a stirring piece about 'finishing off evil' from South Africa to the Caribbean, and 'Tiburon' ('The Shark'), a song critical of American foreign policy. Songs like these infuriated the Cuban exiles in Miama, who have refused to play Blades' records on the local Spanish-speaking radio stations. 'It's interesting', he said, 'that these are the people who say they had to leave Cuba because they couldn't say what they wanted when they were there.'

Blades performed on the *Sun City* LP, but he uses his own work to try to attack something less tangible than apartheid. He is, he says, trying to break down the stereotype of Latins as being 'Mexicans with big hats sleeping next to a cactus, or drug dealers, or people who have revolutions every two minutes', and he is using the cinema to get the new image across. Alongside his acting career, Blades has planned to win an even bigger market for salsa by recording songs in English, with help from an array of leading songwriters. Once he has achieved all that, the master plan involves a return to Panama to build up a local organization and study local issues. It has been rumoured that Blades plans to be President, but he now says his initial plans are more limited, 'to set up as an independent and shoot for mayor of Panama City'. It is not a completely crazy idea in a small young country with its share of discredited politicians: one television survey showed that nineteen out of twenty people in Panama would vote for him.

Elsewhere across the world, other political singers who might have operated in isolation now found themselves part of a very loosely defined movement that spread from the Americans and Europe to Australia and Africa. The Australian music scene had been dominated by American pop until the mid-seventies, when Gough Whitlam introduced the Canadian idea of a quota of local music being played on the radio. The country needed its own pop culture, and the band who tackled the problem most seriously were the outfit who backed Australia's Vietnam Vets, and complained that Springsteen's lyrics weren't tough enough.

Redgum were special because they set out, from scratch, to perform political songs, and became best-selling pop stars in the process. John Schumann, Michael Atkinson and Verity Truman were all students at Flinders University, Adelaide, where they were taking a politics and art course for philosophy students, under the tutelage of Professor Brian Medlin, who had become something of a cult hero for leading anti-Vietnam war demonstrations in South Australia, and getting beaten up by the police while doing so.

Medlin suggested that his students should discuss what was 'progress-ive music', and after they had dug through their record collections, picking out copies of Neil Young's 'Southern Man' and the like, they decided to write their own songs, to entertain the other students. They tried to sing in Australian accents, rather than ape American styles, and follow Medlin's advice that songs (or philosophy) should always be intelligible to 'any man in a bar'. Redgum became a cult success on the Australian campuses, thanks to songs like 'If You Don't Fight You Lose', which dealt with the closure of a local General Motors factory, and topped the Australian charts in 1983 with their Vietnam song, 'I Was Only 19'. A piece of condensed musical journalism, written after Schumann had spent hours talking to a wounded veteran, who for a decade had refused to discuss his experience with anyone, the song was used to raise money for the Australian Vietnam Veterans Association.

Other Redgum songs might not have met the Vets' approval. Their 1985 song, 'The Drover's Dog', was an attack on the Labour Prime Minister Bob Hawke, which accused him of being the 'dog' of the Americans, because (unlike the new Labour Party leadership in New Zealand) he allowed American nuclear weapons in the country. Nuclear disarmament had become a major issue in Australia, with 300,000 demonstrators taking part in the Palm Sunday rallies in 1985, and the new Australian pop reflected what was going on.

The most prominent anti-nuclear band, the hard-rock Midnight Oil, was led by the remarkable-looking Peter Garrett, a tall ex-lawyer with a shaved head, who emerged as the figure-head of the Nuclear Disarmament Party (NDP). Garrett stood for the Senate in New South Wales in the 1984 elections, and though he didn't get in he managed to whip up an enormous amount of publicity, and was credited with the party winning one Senate seat elsewhere in the country. Midnight Oil songs like 'US Forces' clearly reflected what many, if not all, Australians were thinking.

In Africa, meanwhile, the musical politicians were not solely concerned with the horrors of apartheid, or the effect that South Africa was having on its neighbours like Zimbabwe and Mozambique. Black Africa has its political repression too, and musicians who speak out against it may well find themselves in trouble with the authorities. Fela Kuti, the Nigerian superstar known for a while as Prisoner E1106, became black Africa's best-known example.

Kuti began using music as a political force back in the sixties. He studied jazz in London, developed his political views after meeting black power leaders in the USA, and in Nigeria he began to build up his massive reputation as an unexpected musical and political force. He developed a new style, Afro-Beat, in which songs can last forty minutes and involve elements of African chanting and rhythms along with brassy big band jazz and his own keyboard and saxophone solos. His targets were the Nigerian authorities, whether military or civilian. He attacked government corruption, army brutality, and multi-national corporations in songs like 'VIP, Vagabonds In Power', or 'ITT, International Thief Thief', and caused further trouble when he declared that the compound around his Lagos club, the Shrine, was an independent state, the Kalakuta Republic. In 1977, when the military were in power, there was a full-scale army attack on Kalakuta, and Kuti's mother was killed in the assault. When the army handed back power to the civilians, Kuti handed them a replica of her coffin.

The new civilian regime didn't treat him much better. He founded his own political party, the Movement of the People, announcing that he aimed to be President, and that 'music is the weapon of the future'. His political philosophy appeared to be a post-Nkrumah blend of Pan-Africanism and 'progressive African socialism', mixed with outspoken views on the role of women that proved an embarrassment to the GLC when they sponsored his shows in London, Kuti, who once married all of his twenty-seven girl singers in one day, considered that, 'Women's Liberation can never happen in Africa. Women can hold high positions, but at home the man is boss.'

The civilian government liked his attacks no more than the military had, and in 1981 he claimed that there had been an attempt to kill him, when he was arrested on an armed robbery charge. When the soldiers returned to power two years later, it was clear that there would be even more trouble.

In September 1984, during the Buhari military regime, the most controversial musician in Africa was arrested at Lagos airport, just as he was setting out for a major American tour. It was claimed that he was illegally attempting to export £1,600 in foreign currency, though he says this was money he had just earned, quite legally, abroad. He drew the inevitable conclusion that, 'They didn't want me to go to the US to play. They wanted to deal with me in a special way. They have dealt with me violently, and now they wanted to deal with my mind.' He was jailed for nearly four years, and kept in prison even when the military government of Major-General Babangida took over, promoting Kuti's elder brother to Health Minister.

All over the world, there were campaigns for the release of a musician who was judged by the human rights group Amnesty International to be a political detainee. Musicians like Hugh Masekela were involved, and so was Dan Del Santo, who recorded 'Free Fela'. Eventually, he was set free in April 1986, after allegations (later disputed) that he had been visited by the judge who sentenced him, who said he had been acting under government pressure. In London, soon after his release, he sat in a luxury hotel wearing only underpants and a chain round his neck, surrounded by smartly dressed women. He said that he had made some decisions in prison. He decided that marriage didn't suit him, and (rather less realistically) that he was definitely going to be President. 'It's possible they will call me to the presidency by popular demand,' he claimed in typically extravagant style. 'I'm sure I will be President. There's no leader who can help the country now, except myself.'

One of Kuti's first acts after he was released was to fly to the USA, to take part in the spectacular finale of Amnesty International's Conspiracy of Hope tour, along with Peter Gabriel, Jackson Browne, and other major acts who were raising money and support for the organization. It was equally appropriate that Kuti should join forces on stage with that other Third World superstar with political aspirations, Ruben Blades.

Amnesty's tour was the major musical–political event in the USA during the year, and it succeeded because the organization's aims perfectly fitted the new mood in political pop. Live Aid had pioneered co-operation between megastars, and this was now broadened to incorporate pop's new internationalism, to bring world attention to a series of campaigns that appeared to be far more directly political than hunger. What's more, Amnesty could claim to be more than a single-issue campaign like CND, because it could draw support from those fighting against the death penalty, or torture, or religious and political persecution in different parts of the world.

This voluntarily funded, non-sectarian organization was started in 1961, to defend freedom of speech, opinion, and religion around the world, and campaign for human rights, the release of 'prisoners of conscience' with peacefully held beliefs, and document and publicize cases of political imprisonment and torture. Governments around the world were reminded of the UN Universal Declaration of Human Rights, and persuaded to live up to their commitments. The movement spread to seventy-five countries, but Amnesty tended to be a fairly middle-class, academic concern until its involvement with the pop world.

Amnesty's first brush with pop culture came with *The Secret Policeman's Ball* shows in London in 1979 and 1981, starring Pete Townshend, Sting, Phil Collins, Bob Geldof, and the *Monty Python* team. Then there was a pause until the organization were approached by the Scottish band Simple Minds, in the aftermath of Live Aid. Jim Kerr and the group wanted to give Amnesty the proceeds from three shows on their 1986 World Tour. They held press conferences in the USA and Britain, invited Amnesty workers along to hand out leaflets, and on stage they began to dedicate their song 'Ghost Dancing' to the organization. Audiences were reminded of specific Amnesty campaigns to free political prisoners from Africa to El Salvador and the USSR, and were encouraged to send money and join up. They did so, in their hundreds.

Nineteen eighty-six was the twenty-fifth anniversary of Amnesty International, and the American branch followed the Simple Minds shows with a week-long anniversary tour that travelled from San Francisco to New York, where the just-released Fela Kuti joined the finale. Others who took part in Conspiracy of Hope shows included U2, Tom Petty, Lou Reed, Sting (together with a specially reformed Police), Joan Baez and Bob Dylan (singing 'I Shall Be Released'). Bruce Springsteen, who hadn't turned out for Live Aid, didn't want to perform for Amnesty either. 'He's not into broad issues, he's into community issues,' Bono explained.

The Boss's absence didn't matter, for the tour was remarkable anyway, both for the effect that it had on the artists and for the way it helped to transform Amnesty. Bono had been worried about the event before it started, for he felt that after Live Aid 'there's a danger it becomes a yawn'. When the tour was over, he was talking as if it had transformed U2, and the USA.

A year later, during the *Joshua Tree* tour, U2 were rightly regarded as the biggest and best rock band in the world. Bono saw their new success as part of a wider phenomenon that had started with Amnesty. Sitting in a hotel room in Connecticut, he looked back at what had happened. 'It was quite amazing, with all those people playing on stage, but the effect has been a real reawakening in America, a backlash against Reagan's Right and the moral majority. Amnesty have doubled their membership in the United States since that tour. The Amnesty tour was a turning point.'

As at Live Aid, the artists could get together, enjoy themselves, and attempt to escape from their egos, minders and managers. This tour was different, though, because it was more directly political, and the back-stage discussions involved a decidedly non rock 'n' roll set. Through Jackson Browne, Bono met lawyers who had studied the Karen Silkwood case and were now investigating the way in which the Contras were getting their money. He met others involved with the Sanctuary movement, or co-operatives in Nicaragua and El Salvador, and while in San Francisco he was invited on a tour of the Latin Quarter, the part of the city most tourists don't see. Along with Lou Reed, he was taken down 'barmy alley', where 'for seventy yards, the houses, wood, glass and drainpipes are covered in the most incredible anti-American murals you've ever seen. There's America as a snake, or America as a wave, engulfing Central America – the most luminous graffiti I've seen.'

They ended up in the workshop of a Chilean artist, Reme Castro, who was reluctant to talk to them until he discovered that they were part of the Amnesty tour. 'And then his eyes lit up, and he said Amnesty had saved his life. He'd been a political prisoner in Chile, and he was held in the stadium with Victor Jara when Jara had his fingers torn off. And he'd been tortured too . . .'

After that, Bono started on a trail that ended, inevitably, in Central America. In August, he visited Nicaragua and El Salvador ('just to root around and see for myself'), and met the Nicaraguan Culture Minister, Cardenal, whose writings had influenced Bruce Cockburn. In Salvador he noted 'the malevolence of the troops and police towards the people, and the fear', and he spent a day with the group set up by the late Archbishop Romero (who Ruben Blades sings about) for those whose children had been taken by the authorities. This visit led to the two most political songs on *The Joshua Tree*, 'Bullet The Blue Sky' and 'Mothers Of The Disappeared'.

In 1987, when the band triumphantly toured the USA, after the album had been released, Bono could look down from the stage and see what the effect had been. The halls were filled with Amnesty banners, or slogans calling for the release of political prisoners, the ending of apartheid, or praising that hero of earlier U2 songs, Martin Luther King. Rock fans are traditionally keen to imitate their idols, or demonstrate symbols of their affection (like the infuriating Beastie Boys set, who steal Volkswagen badges) but this seemed to go far further. 'We're not pointing them in any particular direction,' said Bono. 'There's no handbook that goes with it.'

He seemed genuinely bemused that the band's followers were starting their own fan clubs, which encompassed anything that seemed to be part of this new movement, whether it was digging out old Clash records, or helping Amnesty letterwriting campaigns on behalf of particular prisoners. Once again, he insisted, 'We're not a political band,' then added, 'but politics is a part of it.'

The view from the stage must have been exhilarating, and Bono insisted that it was a reflection of what was happening in the USA. 'When we first came here five years ago, there was this incredible entrenchment, and a broken spirit, made up for by an arrogance and a right-wing prevalence through the colleges and schools, and a feeling not just that rock 'n' roll couldn't change anything but that the individual couldn't change anything. But now there is a turning of the tides.'

The band's actions became political, whether they liked it or not. At the start of the tour, when they played in Arizona, they found themselves at the centre of a controversy because the State was refusing to honour MLK Day. There were stories that Stevie Wonder had asked U2 not to perform there, as a protest, but Bono says they checked with Coretta King and black rights groups, who asked them to go ahead. They did perform 'and caused a stink, with all the media present'. Bono claims that it was as a result of this that New Mexico, which was also considering repealing MLK Day, now decided publicly to endorse the holiday.

Amnesty International was undergoing a rapid change. Membership was soaring, and the staff tried to work out ways of mobilizing their new young supporters, and involve them in campaigns. In Britain, where Amnesty members were invited to hand out leaflets at U2 and Peter Gabriel shows, Director Pat Duffy claimed, 'We're going to be the biggest non-governmental active membership organization in the country, and even outstrip CND . . . thanks to the intervention of very famous, popular people, and their fans.'

Duffy had spent much of his life publicizing the plight of political prisoners, and trying to raise money to finance such work, but now found that he suddenly had to learn the skills of a record company A and R man and lawyer. In the US, there had been one major disappointment on the Conspiracy of Hope tour: the organization had lost out on money and publicity by failing to get all the necessary clearances from record companies and publishers to film the final concert. In Britain, too, Amnesty learned the hard way about the perils of pop. A twenty-fifth anniversary LP was planned, which contained such excellent material as a new Sting song (a version of the Billie Holiday classic 'Strange Fruit'), along with tracks by such as Peter Gabriel and Steve Winwood.

The LP was also supposed to include two brand-new tracks from U2 – their versions of 'Maggie's Farm' and 'Help' – that would guarantee massive sales. But because the LP was titled *The Conspiracy Of Hope*, they felt it should reflect the bands who had taken part on the American tour, and include their new friends Lou Reed and Jackson Browne, so they kept those tracks back.

Amnesty kept their vital pop connection going, releasing a third *Policeman's Ball* set (with Mark Knopfler playing with Chet Atkins, Gabriel with the African star Youssou N'Dour, and Kate Bush with Pink Floyd), and even set up an Amnesty Records and a music publishing company, just to show how neatly the marriage of pop and politics can be cemented.

All of this could be seen as part of a gradual, triumphant development. Pop music, the rebel teenage music of the fifties, and the heady, manic protest music of the sixties, had survived through the commercial seventies, and settled down as a vital, if unpredictable, force within more establishment politics in the eighties. In the process it had helped a variety of often interrelated causes, and helped break down the ridiculous distinctions between pop, rock, and folk. That is the hopeful view of what has been going on – that progress really has been made, even in a world where Lennon's 'Revolution' is used to advertise jogging shoes.

Alas, life is rarely as straightforward or pleasant as it should be. In the post-Live Aid era, just as pop seemed to have become more respectable and responsible than ever, and when the music once again seemed to be gaining ground as a channel for political views, the old spectre of censorship began to reappear. Both right-wing politicians and right-wing fundamentalist Christian groups used the final years of the Reagan era to renew the attacks that had been made on the music two and three decades earlier. They were helped by elements within the record industry, who clearly felt that protest and political pop were all very well so long as they didn't cause controversy that might affect sales.

[3]

"Scream against the Sky"

Japanese Avant-garde Music in the Sixties

Yayoi Uno Everett

In September 1994, the Guggenheim Museum in New York City hosted a retrospective exhibition of Japanese avant-garde art since 1945, titled "Scream against the Sky" after Yoko Ono's conceptual piece of the same name. The catalog of works from this exhibition displays numerous paintings and sculptures that capture the explosive and confrontational spirit of the Anpo Movement in the early 1960s, which was marked by large-scale protests and riots against the renewal of the U.S.-Japan Security Treaty (the "Nichibei Anzenhoshô Jôyaku" or "Anpo" for short). This period gave birth to a rich legacy of artistic and musical avant-garde creativity. This essay examines the interrelation of the discursive trajectories of the postwar avant-garde with the political sphere, focusing on the developments in avant-garde music at the Sôgetsu Center for the Arts in Tokyo during the early sixties, and their ramifications in the following decades.

On September 8, 1951, Japan entered a military partnership with the United States, which spurred political controversy throughout the decade. As the Security Treaty gave the United States the right to station troops in Japan (Article I) and prohibited Japan from giving bases to a third power without U.S. consent, it instilled fear in the minds of many that Japan would soon become a military base in the expanding cold war.[1] Against the conservative Liberal Democratic Party (LDP) which sided with the U.S., the Japan Socialist Party (JSP), Communist Party (JCP), and progressive intellectuals relentlessly opposed these measures through staging protests and demonstrations.[2] Under the umbrella of the JCP, a nationwide student organization called Zengakuren (All-Japan Federation of Students' Self-Governing Associations) gathered force to oppose any compromise to Article IX of the postwar constitution, which prohibited Japan from rearmament; much of their protests revolved around nuclear testing, which proved to be one of the key issues of negotiation when the treaty was revisited in the late fifties.[3]

During the three-year period (1957–60) of Nobusuke Kishi's term as prime minister, the political parties focused on the treaty revision issues, united under the belief that Japan must regain a leading role in world affairs by ceasing its relationship with the dominant U.S. power. In the process, other vital matters such as the JSP's proposal to renounce nuclear weapons, the Vietnam reparations bill, the fisheries agreement with the Soviet Union, and relations with China, became entangled in the controversy over the treaty renewal.[4] In January 1960, despite the continuing disputes among the parties, Kishi announced the renewal of the treaty with certain provisions; this announcement, in turn, ignited massive protests, demonstrations, and strikes and culminated in a national crisis over the course of the next six months. Due to the large-scale revolts led by the socialist parties and Zengakuren in May and June of this year, President Eisenhower's visit to Japan was effectively annulled and Kishi was forced to resign from his post.

The artists and intellectuals who participated in these cultural and political movements were disillusioned with postwar Japanese democratic institutions and demanded a clear break from the "Old Left"—meaning the JCP, which lost popularity with the public after 1952. In challenging the authorities, an artistic revolution also emerged, manifesting itself in junk art, underground theater (Angura), New Wave cinema, Ankoku Butoh,[5] Happenings, and Fluxus. David Goodman describes the state of the "dual alienation" experienced by students and young artists as follows:

> The artists of the sixties generation were educated in the period of extraordinary freedom that the chaos of the immediate post-war period brought, and this accounts in part for a common belief that anarchy is conducive to creativity. Alienated by their own culture, they shared a certain psychological distance from it that empowered them to undertake some of the most trenchant examinations of Japaneseness ever attempted. Greatly influenced by American culture, they were at the same time alienated by the United States, which was occupying their country, testing and stockpiling nuclear weapons, and fighting an unpopular war in Vietnam.[6]

What did it mean to be "Japanese" for the youths who faced the task of rebuilding their cultural identity from the charred ruins of post-atomic history? How did the aesthetic goals and praxis of the postwar musical avant-garde relate to pre-war Japanese and European avant-garde antecedents? In order to answer these questions, this essay explores the developments that took place at the Sôgetsu Center for the Arts in

Tokyo between 1960 and 1964, and the contributions made by John Cage, Toshi Ichiyanagi, Yûji Takahashi, and Yoko Ono to the formation of the radical avant-garde. The first phase of development in avant-garde music in the early 1950s was heavily influenced by European modernist idioms (serialism, musique concrète). The 1960s brought the advent of experimental approaches to performance: moving beyond the formality of concert music, composers and musicians came together to present multimedia events, Happenings, Events, conceptual art, and group improvisations. By focusing on the critical developments that took place at the Sôgetsu Center, I hope to offer an understanding of the musical avant-garde in relation to the changing sociopolitical milieu of postwar Japan.

The Japanese Avant-garde

In concept and praxis, "avant-garde" (*zen-ei* in Japanese) is a term imported from the West, which acquired different forms in the course of the twentieth century. It was initially attributed to the iconoclastic activities and experimentation undertaken by the so-called Mavo group of visual artists during the Taishô period (1912–26), who responded to the social unrest of the 1920s by revolutionizing artistic practice.[7] Influenced by futurist, expressionist, and cubist art forms, the Mavo artists explored anarchistic and constructivist ideologies by disavowing both mimetic reproduction and romantic subjectivity. Depicting events that accorded with a Marxist political agenda, their work contributed to the proletarian movement in the arts, and garnered considerable support from the working class. However, due to increased governmental censorship, the group was forced to disband by 1928.[8] Historically, their activities can be interpreted as a rebellion against the "modernizing" agenda of the post-Meiji era government, which lay emphasis upon rationality, order, and collective conformity. This modernization ushered in not only the rise of mass society and cosmopolitanism but also authoritarianism. Between the early 1930s and the end of the Second World War, political activists were arrested, tortured, and imprisoned, and left-wing artistic and musical associations (such as the Proletarian Musical League) were forced to disband in a period of brutal repression.

After the Second World War, a renewed focus on individual autonomy permitted artists and musicians to break down important barriers, encouraging new aesthetic trends to take root. In 1947, Shûzô Takiguchi and Jirô Yoshihara founded the Japan Avant-Garde Artists Club ("Nihon avangyarudo bijutsuka kurabu"). Critical of market-driven artistic forms of production and formulaic "-isms," Takiguchi envisioned his avant-garde strategy as an exploration of the process or act of creation; for him, "the space of the experimental" connoted the state before artistic languages became conventionalized.[9] The Gutai group (*gutai* meaning concreteness), founded by Yoshihara in the Osaka-Kobe region in 1954, shared a similar ideological basis. The group declared conventional art forms meaningless and aimed instead to "unite the human and material spirits in a cathartic act that simultaneously releases the energy of both."[10] Although averse to political activism, Gutai engaged in its own forms of action events and paintings inspired by Jackson Pollock; as Munroe comments, they pursued art as "an explosive rite to stomp out the dark orthodoxies of pre-war Imperial Japanese culture and usher in the liberal American style democracy which history had unexpectedly granted."[11] The political counterpart of Gutai was to be found in a group of artists with strong Communist Party affiliation who organized Reportage Painting ("Ruporutâju Kaiga") in response to the horrors of war, nuclear holocaust, and social injustices; partly instigated by the JCP, this group sent artists to rural villages and industrial zones to depict instances of imperialism and class struggle.[12] Whether explicitly political or not, such organizations explored art as a form of release and as a means of building new cultural identities that overcame Japan's wartime past.

The aesthetics of the surrealist critic Takiguchi had a profound impact in shaping the first phase of the musical avant-garde. In 1951, he founded the Experimental Workshop (Jikken Kôbo), which brought together figures from a range of fields to collaborate on multimedia projects. The initial members included composers Tôru Takemitsu and Hiroyoshi Suzuki, engineer Hideo Yamazaki, painter Hideko Fukushima, and critic/poet Kuniharu Akiyama. Jôji Yuasa, who joined in 1952, summed up the group's anti-establishment stance as follows: "[I]n liberating music from its own world, we were reacting against the academic conventions, systems, and the establishment."[13] Their artistic visions were unquestioningly modernist in scope and orientation, yet the group sought to incorporate distinctive characteristics of traditional Japanese art forms such as Noh drama and calligraphic paintings.[14] Focusing on the use of new technology, the musical avant-garde sought after new and emerging European trends, such as serialism, dodecaphonic music, and musique concrète, as a way of breaking free from the institutionalized schools of composition based on German or French lineage.[15] Representative works include Takemitsu's *Uninterrupted Rest I* (1952) for solo piano, *Son Calligraphie* (1953); Suzuki's *Metamorphose* (1955) for clarinet and four strings; and Yuasa's *Cosmos Haptic* (1957).

On the political front, the Utagoe ("Singing Voice") movement brought together workers and students in a wide variety of choral activities with leftist and proto-feminist awareness. This movement grew out of the Japanese Association for the Proletarian Arts, founded in 1925, and their meetings included the singing of revolutionary songs to promote the political and social education of the working classes.[16] Although by no means avant-garde with respect to their aesthetic orientation, the mission of the Utagoe movement resonated in the minds of many postwar composers. Hikaru Hayashi, for instance, was a strong advocate of the Utagoe movement, and explored the intersection between and inclusion of folksongs in his original compositions.[17]

In spite of the differences in orientation, many musicians and artists were catapulted into taking concrete political action by the Police Bill controversy of October 1958. The Diet led by Kishi introduced an amendment to the bill that would strengthen police powers to interrogate, search, and arrest people in all public venues. Fearing that this bill was part of Kishi's master plan toward restoring the militarism of the 1930s, the socialists boycotted the Diet and barricaded rooms to prevent deliberations.[18] The earliest written declaration opposing the bill was signed by twenty-seven members of the Seinen Ongakuka ("The Youth Musicians") society of musicians and composers—including Takemitsu, Hayashi, and Toshirô Mayuzumi in November 7, 1958 (a translation of this declaration is provided in figure 9.1). Apparently the public protests against the passing of this bill paid off. After several weeks of uproar and political negotiations, the ruling LDP—which proved to be neither liberal nor democratic—shelved the bill for an indefinite period.[19]

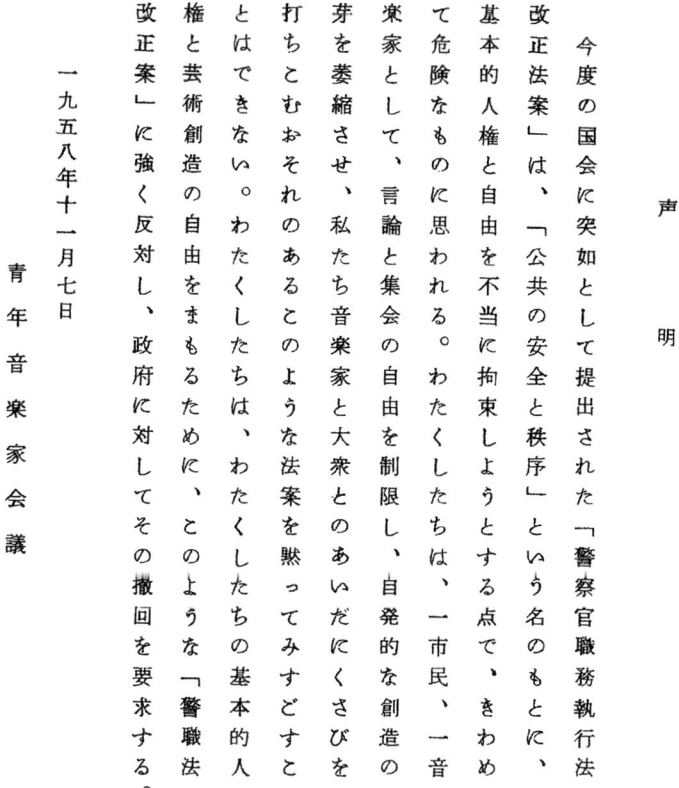

Figure 9.1   Declaration by the Seinen Ongakuka (November 7, 1958).

Declaration

The recent amendment to the bill introduced by the Congress proposes to strengthen police's right to take preventative actions in public venues in promoting public safety and order. We find this to be a great threat to our civil rights and freedom by placing unfair restrictions on our activities. As citizens and musicians, we will not tolerate the passing of this bill, which will severely restrict our freedom to engage in debates, organize meetings, and will place an unnecessary barrier between the musicians and the audience. We strongly oppose the amendment of this bill in order to protect our civil liberties and artistic freedom and ask the government to withdraw the amendment.

November 7, 1958
Seinen Ongakuka Conference

Figure 9.1   Continued.

Despite the ongoing public outcry, the Security Treaty was ratified in January 1960, with additional provisions. This prompted the first Anpo demonstrations, prominent at which were a number of neo-Dadaists, masked and bandaged like mummies. The Neo-Dada Organizers group had been founded the same year, and staged anarchic exhibitions and Happenings. Although they tended to dismiss political ideology altogether, they triggered bloody riots by throwing bricks at police in April 1960.[20] On May 20, prior to Eisenhower's visit, Kishi's party took forceful measures to monopolize the votes on the treaty renewal—bypassing discussion with opposing parties. The public viewed this conduct as antidemocratic and this led the way to the most violent demonstration before the Diet building on June 15 (see figure 9.2).[21] In preparation, numerous musical societies gathered together on June 9 at the Sôgetsu Center for the Arts to plan pro-democratic actions against the renewal of the Treaty. This organization quickly grew to 580 members, and its primary objective was the resignation of Kishi and the dismissal of the Diet. In the event, the demonstration turned into a riot, resulting in hundreds of injured students and police and the death of a twenty-year-old female student.[22] Although forty-seven newspapers published their oppositions to the renewal, the House of Representatives nevertheless passed the bill on June 19.[23]

Participating in a demonstration of this scale was an unprecedented action on the part of Western-trained Japanese composers and musicians, who had mostly occupied a politically neutral position up until this time. While the anarchistic protests ultimately failed to prevent the renewal of the Security Treaty, the artists nonetheless gained a foothold in society by establishing authority and independence against the government. Munroe aptly describes this era in terms of "absolute loss and absolute freedom"; the chaos emanating from the loss or collapse of long-held national

Figure 9.2 Demonstrations before the Diet Building (June 1960). Used by permission of the *Yomiuri* newspaper.

myths (such as the imperialistic configurations of nationhood) ushered in long-awaited freedom for artistic expression without censorship.[24]

Sôgetsu Center for the Arts

Amid the political turmoil and chaos of the early sixties, the Sôgetsu Center for the Arts provided an indispensable venue for artists and musicians to meet, collaborate, and hold performances and exhibitions. Under the directorship of Hiroshi Teshigahara, whose father headed the renowned Sôgetsu Ikebana school, the basement hall of the Center was made available to host a wide range of avant-garde events during its approximately twelve years (October 1958 to April 1971) in existence. In looking back, Teshigahara situates the uniqueness of this period in the unmediated freedom with which artists came together to produce events that included film, dance, music, and Happenings:

> It was a powerful time when artists from different walks of life came together, collided with one another, in pursuit of the unknown. We never had an opportunity like this before and we won't again. Artists could produce what

they want, bring it to the stage and present it. This sort of situation does not happen anymore, now that people count how much it would cost to put together a performance first.[25]

In the initial two years (1958–59), Teshigahara organized viewings of art film and sponsored educational gatherings to promote interest in the traditional arts of Japan.[26] Having established a steady audience base, Teshigahara then launched a series of concerts to promote democratic ideals, which included contemporary music, Happenings, jazz, modern dance, avant-garde film, and underground theater. Within this rich environment of artistic exchange, the musical avant-garde flourished. The different phases of this development can be summarized as follows: concerts by the Sakkyokuka Shûdan (Composers' Group) between 1960 and 1962; *Cage shokku*—a shockwave created by the presence of Cage and David Tudor in 1962; and the emergence of the ensemble New Direction between 1963 and 1964, which contributed further to the era's internationalized outlook. The first of these phases fostered a continuation of the modernist avant-garde idioms established in the fifties, while the second and third phases ushered in the radical branch of the musical avant-garde.

In the first phase, a contemporary music series featured a monthly solo concert of music by nine recognized composers, gathered under the name of Sakkyokuka Shûdan; this included Hayashi, Takemitsu, Mayuzumi, Yasushi Akutagawa, Makoto Moroi, Yoriaki Matsudaira, Akira Miyoshi, and Yoshio Mamiya. Although the pieces typically featured in these concerts were neither political nor unified thematically, they fulfilled the group's mission to promote new works by Japanese composers, which often combined modernist musical idioms with theatrical elements such as pantomime, Noh dance, or projected images. The program notes often conveyed the composer's political or ideological aim. For instance, Hayashi's notes for his solo concert (March 1960) spoke passionately of the importance of foregrounding the human voice—not just by embedding familiar melodies or folk songs in his music, but rather by incorporating the broader mission of the Utagoe movement.[27] Takemitsu's solo concert included an interactive musique concrète piece called *Water Music*, produced with the aid of the engineer Jûnosuke Okuyama. To create the piece, Takemitsu went around Tokyo, recording the sound of dripping water, then cut and spliced the tape for over a month, apparently getting little sleep.[28] The technical skills Takemitsu acquired during these formative years laid the foundation for the musique concrète sounds of urban Tokyo and the electronic manipulation of acoustic instruments in film scores such as *Woman in the Dunes* (1964) and *Double Suicide* (1969).

While the concerts by these "card-carrying" composers received much publicity, the Sôgetsu Center also provided space for less established groups to participate in events. The most significant was the improvisation-based Group Ongaku, headed by Shûkô Mizuno, Yasunao Tone, Takehisa Kosugi, and their colleagues at the Tokyo University of Fine Arts (Geidai). Prompted by Tone, they used forms of intermedia, Happenings, and conceptualism to offer an institutional critique of the arts. Mizuno claims that their performances, which involved engaging in free jam sessions and improvisational activities, echoed much of what Cage was doing around the same time.[29] At the same time, their Fluxus-style events featured gradual processes and disciplined, task-oriented performance to explore the sonic materials of music; for example, Kosugi's *Micro I* (1961) involves wrapping up a microphone in paper and amplifying the crumpled sounds as the paper is gradually removed. After hearing the group's concert at the Sôgetsu Center in 1961, Toshi Ichiyanagi was so impressed by the inventive spirit of the group that he asked them to participate in his first solo concert, which was titled *Happening and Musique Concrète.*[30]

As a further effort to bring international visibility to the Center, Teshigahara invited Edgard Varèse to give a concert in 1961; however, due to illness, the visit had to be canceled. In lieu of Varèse, Ichiyanagi urged Teshigahara to invite John Cage and pianist David Tudor as the first foreign composers to participate in the Contemporary Music Series. In October 1962, the two gave six concerts in Tokyo, Kyoto, and Osaka. In these concerts, Cage and Tudor performed different combinations of music by Cage (*Aria* with *Fontana Mix; Music Walk; Atlas Eclipticalis* with *Winter Music; 0'00"; 26'55.988"*), Christian Wolff (*For six or seven players; For pianist*), Morton Feldman (*Atlantis*), Karlheinz Stockhausen (*Klavierstück X*), Sylvano Bussotti (*Five Piano Pieces for David Tudor*), and graphic scores by Ichiyanagi (*Music for Piano #4*) and Takemitsu (*Corona*). Akiyama recalls how Cage and Tudor's concerts in 1962 shattered every preconceived notion about music, sound, and silence held by Japanese artists and musicians.[31] Utterly fascinated by his experiences in Japan, Cage described his admiration for Tone's work—in particular, the latter's use of maps of the earth's surface to yield directions for the performance of his music. He noted that this technique anticipated a composition he himself had in mind but had not yet written, a sequel to *Atlas Eclipticalis* (1961), which would use maps of the earth rather than of the stars.[32]

The performance of Cage's *Music Walk* (1958) at the Tokyo Bunka Kaikan Hall, with Yoko Ono lying flat across the piano, produced one of the most frequently reproduced images from the Cage/Tudor concerts in 1962.[33] *Music Walk* is an indeterminate piece, consisting of nine sheets of paper with scattered points; a smaller transparent plastic rectangle with parallel lines is placed over the paper, bringing some of the points "out of potentiality into activities." The performers move from one point to another from several playing positions—either at the keyboard, at the back of the piano, or at a radio—and choose one of the lines that refer to five different categories of sounds. Additional small plastic squares with nonparallel lines may or may not be used to make further determinations about the sounds to be produced. By lying across the keyboard, Ono transformed the "music walk" into her own "conceptual walk," and she saw this as her own contribution to the piece; however, the critics dismissed her act as merely eccentric.[34] Her efforts to further "radicalize" the musical avant-garde by pushing the boundaries of performance will be discussed more fully in the following section.

The third phase of development came about through the formation in 1963 of the ensemble New Direction by Ichiyanagi, Takahashi, and Kuniharu Akiyama. The group's statutes emphasized internationalization through the inclusion of composers from abroad, and placed importance upon events that demand the participation of the audience. Although relatively short-lived (1963–64), the group put together six concerts that featured graphic scores by Bussotti, Stockhausen, Feldman, Ichiyanagi, Takahashi, and Kosugi in combination with conventionally notated works by Berg (*Lyric Suite*), Berio (*Sequenza*), Penderecki (String Quartet No. 4), Yuasa (*Interpretation* for Two Flutes I and II), and Boulez (*Improvisations sur Mallarmé* I and II). Most critics welcomed the balancing of repertoire to include a wide range of the contemporary music then in vogue. Akiyama recalls how such events attracted not only composers but also artists, filmmakers, and novelists, who returned week after week to attend the concerts. After Takahashi left Japan to work in Europe, Ichiyanagi organized the concerts by himself until April 1964. The most scandalous event took place when Nam June Paik destroyed the inside of an upright piano with hammer and saw during his solo recital. However, as alternative venues for performances of new music began to open up, composers ceased to gather together at the Sôgetsu Center to work on collaborative projects.[35] After 1965 the Center's focus shifted entirely from music to the promotion of underground theater, film, and animation.

On the Radical Avant-garde

An important breakthrough in the aesthetic orientation of the musical avant-garde took place when the idea of "performance" was opened up, in an effort to break down the traditional barriers that separated audiences from performers, professionals from amateurs, as well as what constitutes music from the noise of daily life. In particular, Happenings played a crucial role in establishing what Michael Kirby has termed a "non-matrixed" model of performance, characterized by the deliberate absence of an information structure containing plot and dialogue.[36] Moreover, "Events," introduced by the Fluxus artist George Brecht, extracted the informational structure of everyday ritual or routine and threw it into high relief for the performer. For example, the performance of Brecht's *Drip Music* required Takahashi to pour water as slowly as possible from a bucket into a fish bowl at the front of the stage, and the audience was completely free to construct whatever meaning they wished.[37] In 1962, the first of Cage and Tudor's visits led many Japanese composers to take radical steps in exploring the emancipatory potential of music making; "Cage's lectures and performances liberated Japanese composers from the rigidities of serialism and notation on a five-line staff."[38] As amateur and professional musicians gathered together at the Sôgetsu Center, their performances often reveled in themes of social alienation and individual autonomy in an attempt to transcend the norms and hierarchies of traditional Japanese society.

Undoubtedly, the difference in aesthetic orientation between the modernist and radical branches of the musical avant-garde pivoted on whether to reject or embrace Cage's experimental views about eliminating the boundary between music and noise. Established composers from the earlier generation (i.e., those associated with Sakkyokuka Shûdan and Jikken Kôbô) were often skeptical: at the time of Cage's first visit in 1962, Mayuzumi openly dismissed Cage's significance as a composer, while Yuasa questioned the premise of abandoning one's will in composing.[39] Even Takemitsu, who shared Cage's interests in Asian philosophy and composed a number of graphic scores, ended up deciding that chance operation was "not structured enough."[40]

Rather than attempting to be comprehensive, I call attention here to the works of three individuals who made distinctive contributions to the Sôgetsu Center in promoting and expanding on Cage's radical aesthetics. In this respect, Ichiyanagi's involvement was critical, along with that of Takahashi and Ono. Having met Cage in New York City in the late 1950s, Ichiyanagi turned his back altogether on traditional conventions of composing (in which he had been trained at the Juilliard School), became involved in Fluxus, and pursued aleatoric and indeterminate procedures in his music throughout the 1960s.[41] In his solo concert at the Sôgetsu Center in November 1961, Ichiyanagi created a sensation by displaying his graphic scores as art in the lobby and offering performances of them on stage. The most striking piece, *IBM: event and music concrète*, called for eight musicians performing different events simultaneously but independently of one another, as the loudspeakers blasted quotidian sounds and noises prepared by Ichiyanagi. The musicians, utterly devoid of expression, performed their individual acts according to the number of repetitions designated by IBM punch cards, and were gradually wrapped up in white paper tape to form a gigantic spider's nest on stage, extending down toward the audience. Although many in the audience questioned the relevance of this work as "music," Kuniharu Akiyama defended its significance in the following manner:

> [T]he disconnected sounds of the electric drill, a falling chair, radio, and piano surrounded us and our eyes simply followed the meaningless

sequence of actions. Yet I was tremendously moved by the experience of utter solitude in the sound and action of each moment that passed by.[42]

In Akiyama's mind, this event clearly stood as a critique of alienation in modern society.

In composing indeterminate scores, Ichiyanagi was very particular about his use of graphic symbols, providing detailed and precise performance instructions. Writing about the significance of graphic notations, he distinguished this form of improvisation from jazz by emphasizing the need to *avoid* preconceived notions for structuring events in time; this was important in order to maximize discontinuity between events and sustain spontaneous interaction between performers.[43] At first glance, his graphic notations do not seem to differ much from those of Morton Feldman, Earle Brown, or Cage from the early fifties. Careful examination of the instructions that accompany Ichiyanagi's graphic scores, however, reveals the extent to which a successful rendering of them depends on the performers' abilities to respond to one another in making decisions on the fly. For Ichiyanagi, liberating sounds through spontaneous musical response signified the liberation of the human spirit. In the program note that accompanied his solo concert at the Sôgetsu Center, he declared that if this new approach to performance represented the extremity of a human cry, "just let out the cry without attaching any kind of meaning to it."[44] Ichiyanagi's emphasis on process and spontaneity curiously echoes Takiguchi's concept of the "space of the experimental" as a state preceding the conventionalization of artistic languages.

As a case in point, the instruction and the first two systems of the score for *Duet for Piano and String Instrument* (1961) are shown in example 9.1. As the instruction states, in addition to interpreting the action corresponding to each symbol, the performer chooses the mode of execution (a or b) based on a choice made by the other performer in the previous event. While the score is read from left to right and there are instructions for how to interpret the different lines that frame the symbols, the time for realizing the events and space in between events is relative and variable. Ichiyanagi's instruction indicates that as a sound comes into being, the performer should follow it with silence or another set of events, without anticipating what comes next. Other notable graphic pieces by Ichiyanagi from this period include *Sapporo* (1962), a piece in which the performers produce sounds associated with different lines in the score while observing other players' signals and the conductor's cues, and *Pratyahara Event* (1963), which calls for the performer to take a specific number of deep breaths in between the execution of successive events.

Even as a student, Yûji Takahashi played an indispensable role in many of the concerts given at the Sôgetsu Center between 1961 and 1963. He quickly became known as a pianist with a niche in contem-

Notations for Piano | Notations for String Instrument

a. Should be used when the pianist hears the string player using the bow
b. Should be used when the pianist hear the string player playing without the bow

a. Should be used when the string player hears the pianist using the keyboard
b. Should be used when the string player hears the pianist playing without using the keyboard

○ a. Play on the keyboard
b. Pizzacato

◇ a. Make harmonics on the keyboard
b. keyboard harmonics produced by piano strings.

–○– a. Armed cluster
b. A noise produced with a tool

□ a. Palm cluster
b. A noise produced without using a tool

↕ a. Glissando upward or downward
b Vertical glissando on strings

↕↕ a. Armed arpeggio
b. Horizontal glissando on the strings

· a. Muted string played on the keyboard
b. Muted pizzicato

⊙ a. Unused way of playing on the keyboard
b. Unused way of producing noise.

a. Oridinary bowing
○ b. Pizzicato

◇ a. Harmonic
b. Pizzicato harmonic

· a. Play between bridge and tailpiece
b. Snapped pizzicato

○‾ a. Sul tasto
b. Make a squeaky sound

○‾ a. Sul poncicello
b. Sweep strings with a cloth

_Ω_ a. Play on tailpiece
b. Strike the fingerboard with the fingertips

○ a. Reverse the playing position of the bow and fingers
b. Strike the body of the instrument

▲ a. Col legno tratto
b. Pizzicato by the bridge

▼ a. Col legno battuto
b. Pizzicato between bridge and tailpiece

↕ a. Glissando
b. Pizzicato glissando

⊙ a. Unused way of playing by using the bow
b. Unused way playing without using the bow

Read the score from left to right with either side up in a horizontal position. Four sheets may be played in any order as long as both the pianist and the string player take the same procedure.

Dotted line frame: play with changes such as accel., rit., crescv., dim., etc.
Thin line frame: play without change in tempo or dynamics
Thick line frame: play with extreme change in tempo or dynamics
Without frame: play freely with regard to range, tempo, and loudness

First two systems of the score:

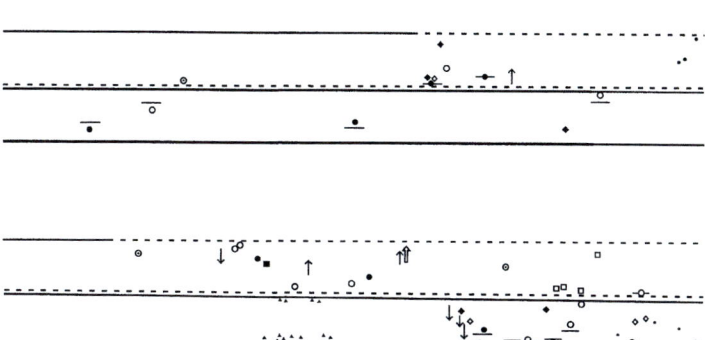

Example 9.1 Ichiyanagi, *Duet for Piano and String Instrument* (1961) (performance instruction, edited by author). Copyright © 1964 by C. F. Peters Corporation. Used by permission.

porary music, acclaimed as a fiercely intelligent virtuoso who could perform Iannis Xenakis's *Eonta* (1963–64)—which was written for him—with complete ease. In the two solo piano recitals he gave at the Sôgetsu Center, he performed Takemitsu's *Piano Distance* (1961), Cage's *Winter Music* (1957), Xenakis's *Herma* (1960–61), as well as

indeterminate works by La Monte Young and Keijirô Satoh. When
Takahashi organized New Direction with Ichiyanagi, the successful realization of many of the aleatoric and indeterminate scores
depended on his unusual versatility and imagination as pianist and
composer—Akiyama described his performances as elegant, relentless,
and metaphysical.[45] Fellow composer Ikebe Shinichirô praised the
ingenuity in Takahashi's simultaneous performances of *L'Ombilic des
Limbes* for tape and *Antonin Artaud's Window* for bassoons, contrabass
clarinets, and double bass (1963), recalling how the bass was played on
its side.[46]

Yet in an essay called "Face the Music" that accompanied the
program to his solo recital, Takahashi expressed a viewpoint opposite
to Ichiyanagi, insisting that freedom in musical expression is fundamentally unattainable. He was fascinated by Cage's indeterminate scores,
which contain multiple possibilities for realization and challenge the
audience to contemplate the resulting "vagueness" of sound. Like Cage,
he insisted that in order to find new avenues of musical expression, it
was necessary to cut oneself off from familiar musical structures and
taste. However, he stressed the importance of formulating one's own
musical "problem" without following Cage's methods.[47] Takahashi's
meandering remarks amounted to a kind of self-declaration, which
ultimately led him to pursue formalized mathematical principles as a
basis for further compositional studies. Encouraged by Xenakis, Takahashi left Japan to perform and study in Europe and the United States
between 1963 and 1972. Most of his compositions, written during this
time, derive from stochastic operations and game theory, such as *Chro-*

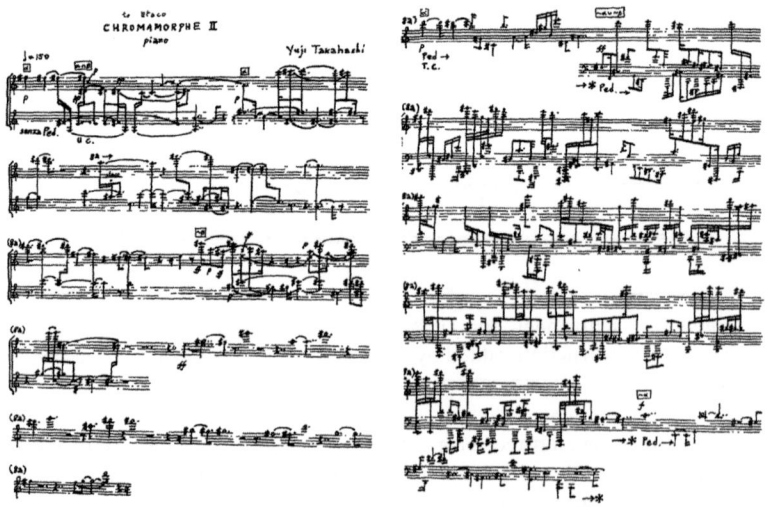

Example 9.2 Takahashi, *Chromamorphe II* (1964). Copyright © 1969 by C. F.
Peters Corporation. Used by permission.

mamorphe II (1964) for solo piano, *Six Stoicheia* (1969) for string quartet, and *Operation Euler* (1969) for three players. *Chromamorphe II* was composed with the aid of Xenakis's program for the IBM7090 computer; two basic motives undergo continual transformation, as the texture alternates between monophonic entries punctuated by silence, and a cacophonic outburst of sounds spread across the registers (see example 9.2).[48]

Finally, Yoko Ono's contribution to the musical avant-garde during the two and a half years she spent in Japan (1962–64) should not be underestimated. For one thing, she is credited for introducing Happenings and Conceptual Art to the Japanese audience. In her conceptual piece *Voice Piece for Soprano* (1961), which ends with a simple instruction to "scream against the sky," she captured the state of angst felt by this generation of artists. In spite of the critics' anticipation of Ono as a promising composer from New York City, her debut performance at the Sōgetsu Center on May 24, 1962 was unfavorably received. Consisting of four multimedia events involving music, poems, and paintings, Ono attempted to break away from the traditional relationship between the audience and performers in the most extreme manner. In an event called *ASO-To David Tudor*, she delivered a nonsensical juxtaposition of declarations taken from Hitler, the Japanese emperor, and French lessons.[49] Her five-hour performance ended at 1:30 a.m. with all the performers standing silently on the stage together with two remaining audience members—the intent behind the *Audience Piece* being that it does not end until the hall is completely vacated. The filmmaker and critic Donald Richie denounced her work as "lacking in originality" and largely "imitative of Cage," and found her passivity on stage and the excruciating length of the events insulting to the audience.[50] Ichiyanagi came to her rescue by explaining the fundamental difference between her aim and Cage's chance operations, emphasizing the point that her artwork invites the audience to actively search for a meaning, and that the piece requires the audience's participation to be complete.[51]

Arguably, the most sensational work Ono produced was *Cut Piece* (1964), in which she invites audience members to get up on stage and cut her clothes with scissors while she maintains a seated pose. This work elicited a wide range of response; when performed as part of her Sayonara concert at the Sōgestu Center, the reception was lukewarm, while in Kyoto a man threatened to stab her with scissors.[52] A video excerpt from the Carnegie Hall performance in 1965 is telling; those who were respectful toward the artist by cutting a small piece of clothing are contrasted by a mocking male subject who "violated" her through aggressive actions that simulated rape.[53] Yoshimoto comments that "[Ono] functioned as a mirror reflecting the feelings of audience members; through watching the performance, the audience discovered voyeurism or violence within itself."[54] This particular work has taken on new politicized meanings in new contexts; as a case in point, Ono performed *Cut Piece* in Paris in 2003 as a form of protest against the Iraq War and in an attempt to promote world peace.[55]

It is deeply ironic that Ono, whose avant-garde art was shunned by the Japanese critics during the early sixties for being too metaphysical, garnered international recognition and flourished as a conceptual artist in New York City. Her mixed reception in Japan reflects the Eurocentric perspective that dominated the reception of the Japanese avant-garde at the time: relying exclusively on Western art-historical discourse to judge Japanese artists, critics were unable to explore critical contexts that departed from this paradigm.[56] Additionally, it seems that the Japanese audience, whose appreciation for art was governed by a high standard of aesthetic refinement and technical mastery, failed to understand the essence of Ono's bold and esoteric approach to art.

In summary, many of the Happenings or Events, be it Ono's *Cut Piece* or Ichiyanagi's *IBM*, may be seen as exterior projections of the collective guilt and fear shared by artists and public at large about Japan's political past and present. Spurred by a common pursuit of liberating one's self from oppressive social conditions, performers engaged in provocative, frivolous, and at times destructive acts as a form of constructive criticism. Regardless of whether such activities would lead to concrete social or political changes, these performances took audiences out of their comfort zone, challenging them to assess the meaning of a work in its social context, rather than simply to marvel at musical or technical refinement as an end in itself. It is precisely in this sense that radical avant-garde musicians ruptured the social norms of artistic performance and laid the aesthetic foundation for creative ventures in theater, dance, and film, filling the void left by the pre-war avant-garde.[57]

Conclusion: The Paradox of the Protest Years

In *Radicals and Realists in the Japanese Nonverbal Arts*, Thomas Havens advances the notion that Japanese avant-garde artists from the sixties later turned into realists by articulating a "post-Western" critique of European modernism through global awareness and local engagement.[58] With respect to developments in postwar theater, David Goodman likewise explores the paradox of embracing European traditions as a means for recapturing and rearticulating the "premodern imagination" that was suppressed by the modernizing agenda of the Meiji reform.[59] In the musical domain, however, Havens's position of "post-Western" critique seems difficult to espouse, since European modernism provided the essential aesthetic foundation of the postwar musical avant-garde. Long before the political conditions that spurred the controversy over the treaty renewal, the first generation of avant-garde composers was driven by a common desire to particularize the language of European modernism in order to explore their subjective positions.

Yet there is little evidence to suggest that these or later composers openly resisted or contested European influences, even in the face of the plurality of aesthetic orientations (e.g., minimalism, collage and quotation, cultural fusion) that they have embraced since the 1970s.

Overall, the praxis of the Japanese avant-garde differed from its Western counterparts in several important ways. First, avant-garde art was absorbed into the mainstream during the 1960s; one can go so far as to say that it was a unique movement in postwar Japanese history, when the avant-garde *became* the mainstream. Housewives, students, professionals, and amateurs flocked to see and participate in events hosted at the Sôgetsu Center.[60] Second, the Japanese avant-garde did not emerge as a reaction against bourgeois ideals, but rather as a radical means to free people from decades of political repression dating back to the Taishô era. Last, the Japanese avant-garde differed from social-democratic countries like Germany and the Netherlands in its reliance on privatized sources of funding. Due to Teshigahara's internal connections, the Sôgetsu Center events were principally financed by the Ikebana institution.[61] Ichiyanagi also confided that his concerts would not have taken place without the generous funding from private donors over the years.[62]

This brings us to the key factor that quashed the protest movement: economic prosperity. In revisiting the relationship between the United States and Japan during the period of occupation, it is important to recognize that Japan profited enormously from this partnership. Protests against the renewal of the treaty reflected a desire to escape from the overwhelming political and materialistic influences exerted by the United States. And for this reason, Packard calls the decade of protests a form of "reactionary nationalism"—Japan's way of asserting and protecting its own identity.[63] Paradoxically though, the enactment of the United States' cold war policies abetted Japanese economic growth at home and abroad in unanticipated ways; both the Korean War and the Vietnam War brought great profits and market breakthroughs in Japan.[64] The capacity for long-time economic planning was also made possible by the domination of the conservative Liberal Democratic Party during the formative years of the rebuilding of the Japanese economy. In simple terms, the political infrastructure that had generated resistance in the 1960s contributed to Japan's emergence as a mature bourgeois society by the early 1970s. As the country gained material wealth, the struggle over the subordinacy of Japan's relationship with the United States diminished in intensity.[65] When the treaty's third renewal was issued in 1970, it triggered another wave of anarchistic movements involving free jazz, underground theater, and Woodstock-inspired rock and folk music, but the level of resistance was considerably tamer.

With economic revival in the 1970s, the production and dissemination of art became increasingly commodified—absorbed into what Frederic Jameson calls the "cultural logic of late capitalism," in which

aesthetic production becomes integrated with commodity production.[66] With materialistic wealth and increased opportunities, the
sense of community that united artists and musicians during the sixties
dissolved. And with it came the near extinction of left-wing political
parties. By then, however, the term "avant-garde" ceased to be a
catchword for contemporary music, as any notions of resistance or
rebellion faded away. This is not to say that the Japanese avant-garde
became institutionalized or superseded by postmodern eclecticism—as
Stuart Hobbs argues was the case in North America and Europe.[67]
While the "political thrust" of the musical avant-garde dissolved by
the mid-sixties, its aesthetic principles and techniques continued to
evolve and became amalgamated into newer trends. The next phase
of development in the 1970s and 1980s was marked by pluralism and
the composers' collective desire to embrace a pan-Asian consciousness
by reclaiming Japan's artistic and historical connections with neighboring Asian countries. Following his involvement with Fluxus artists
in New York City, Kosugi returned to Tokyo to form his improvisational band Taj Mahal in 1969, combining elements of North Indian
music with free jazz and live electronic techniques.[68] After his return to
Japan in 1972, Takahashi surprised everyone by abandoning high
modernism in favor of his own brand of "socialist" music, based on folk
songs collected from all over the world. Reacting against institutionalized
forms of performance, Takahashi sought to establish an ensemble where
musicians can participate in creating, rather than simply recreating
music.[69] His travels to Thailand and the Philippines in 1976, and exposure
there to the indigenous protest songs of workers, led him to form his own
ensemble called Suigyû-gakudan ("Water buffalo ensemble"), which
specialized in the singing of folk songs with simple accompaniments of
Taiko drums, harmonium, and toy piano.[70]

Other opportunities were afforded by the National Theatre of
Japan, which commissioned composers to write for traditional ensembles such as gagaku and reigaku.[71] Takemitsu's *November Steps* (1967)
for biwa, shakuhachi, and orchestra ushered in a new trend of composing music for traditional instruments that were imported originally
from China, Korea, Vietnam, and India. Many Western-trained composers (including other members of the Experimental Workshop)
turned to composing for traditional Japanese and historically extinct
Asian instruments with unprecedented fervor. It is in these contexts
that many of the former avant-gardists gravitated once again toward
the use of aleatoric procedures and graphic notations, as exemplified by
the cadenza in Takemitsu's *November Steps*, Ichiyanagi's *Cloud Shore,
Wind Roots* (1984) for reigaku and gagaku, and Takahashi's *Dream of
Heaven* (1989) for reconstructed qin. And it was in the act of embracing
the premodern Japan through the lens of the avant-garde that the
composers came full circle in claiming their multicultural voice in the
"post" postwar years.

In Japan today, the significance of the postwar avant-garde has not entirely faded, as there is renewed interest in reviving music, film, and art through retrospective concerts and exhibitions.[72] Looking back, it would not be far-fetched to claim that radical avant-garde musicians provided the essential steps toward overcoming societal alienation in the postwar era, through their engagement with "the body as the site of sensation and knowledge," an engagement that echoed the Mavo artists' emphasis on direct experience.[73] The concept of corporeality, previously linked to the idea of nationhood (*kokutai*), was transformed by the Happenings and Events into a site of individual and collective exploration of selfhood. It is no wonder that the idea of a primal scream, literally found in Ono's conceptual piece, became the slogan for the Guggenheim's retrospective art exhibition in 1994. "Scream against the Sky"—its cultural resonances sum up the zeitgeist of the postwar Japanese avant-garde.

Notes

1. Because of the military alignment with the United States, to which Japan agreed in order to regain its sovereignty, the Soviet Union refused to sign the Peace Treaty with Japan in 1951.

2. George Packard, *Protest in Tokyo: The Security Treaty Crisis of 1960* (Princeton, N.J.: Princeton University Press, 1966), 23–25.

3. Ibid., 96.

4. Ibid., 153.

5. Ankoku Butoh literally means "Dance of Darkness." Tatsumi Hijikata introduced the dance form in 1959; it evokes images of decay, fear, eroticism, ecstasy, or stillness through combining elements of traditional Japanese dance, improvisation, mime, and German Ausdrucktanz.

6. David G. Goodman, *Angura: Posters of the Japanese Avant-Garde* (New York: Princeton Architectural Press, 1999), 3–4.

7. While there are different views on the origin of the term "Mavo," Gennifer Weisenfeld speculates that the naming has to do with key concepts underlying the movement, for instance, Marxism, anarchism, and the autonomous role of the individual in society. See Gennifer Weisenfeld, *MAVO Japanese Artists and the Avant-garde 1905–31* (Berkeley and Los Angeles: University of California Press, 2002), 4.

8. Ibid., 251.

9. Miwako Tezuka, *Jikken Kôbô: Avant-Garde Experiments in Japanese Art of the 1950s* (PhD diss., Columbia University, 2005), 28.

10. Alexandra Munroe, *Japanese Art after 1945: Scream against the Sky* (New York: Abrams, 2004), 84.

11. Ibid., 84. Munroe explains further that the formation of Gutai was also influenced by the anti-establishment stance established by the Democratic Artists Association, founded in Osaka in 1951 (86).

12. Ibid., 151.

13. Jôji Yuasa, "Jikken Kôbô Concert," liner notes in *Jikken Kôbô no Ongaku* FOCD 3417 (Tokyo: Fontec, 1996), 11.

14. Kôji Sano, *"Jikken Kôbô,"* in *Nihon no Sakkoku-ka: Nijûseiki* [Japanese Composers: Twentieth Century] (Tokyo: Ongakuno Tomo, 2000), 52; Kôji Sano et al., *Nihon Sengo Ongakushi* [History of Postwar Japanese Music] (Tokyo: Heibon-sha, 2007), 307. Sano argues that works composed by elite, Western-trained composers such as Yoritsune Matsudaira's Theme and Variations on *Etenraku* for piano and orchestra (1951) and Toshirô Mayuzumi's *Ectoplasm* (1954) for tape exemplify the first generation of the musical avant-garde, although neither belonged to the Jikken-Kôbô group. Makoto Moroi and Mayuzumi later founded Ars Nova in 1956, which offered avant-garde concerts featuring works by Pierre Schaeffer, Luciano Berio, and Bruno Maderna, alongside those by Moroi, Mayuzumi, Takemitsu, and others.

15. For a comprehensive study of the pre-war schools of composition, see Luciana Galliano, *Yôgaku: Japanese Music in the Twentieth Century* (Lanham, Md.: Scarecrow, 2002).

16. Ibid., 119. The female leader, Akiko Seki, won the Stalin prize in 1955 for her work.

17. According to Takahashi, the JCP led the Utagoe movement up until 1964. Personal communication with Yûji Takahashi, October 6, 2007.

18. Packard, *Protest in Tokyo*, 102.

19. Ibid., 102–3.

20. Munroe, *Japanese Art after 1945*, 151–52.

21. Sano et al., *Nihon Sengo Ongakushi*, 300. Democracy here refers to liberal, American-style democracy, which was rejected by Kishi's LDP.

22. Munroe, *Japanese Art after 1945*, 151.

23. Sano et al., *Nihon Sengo Ongakushi*, 301.

24. Munroe, *Japanese Art after 1945*, 159.

25. Yoshitomo Nara, ed., *Kagayake Rokujûnendai* [Let the 1960s Shine] (Tokyo: Film Art Publisher, 2002), 93.

26. Ibid., 8–9.

27. In the program note for his solo recital at the Sôgetsu Contemporary Series (March 31, 1961), Hayashi states: "Contemporary music should strive to reincorporate the human voice through song. "

28. Kuniharu Akiyama, "Sokowa Rokujûnendai Zeneigeijutsuno Jûdenchi data" [Sôgetsu was the Battery of 1960s Avant-garde], in *Kagayake Rokujûnendai*, 34–66; 38–39.

29. Shûkô Mizuno, "John Cage ga yatteru kotowa mezurashikumo nantomonai" [What John Cage Does Is Nothing New], in *Kagayake Rokujûnendai*, 162–63.

30. Sano et al., *Nihon Sengo Ongakushi*, 332.

31. While Akiyama, among others, thought of Cage as having radically changed the face of the avant-garde in Japan, other composers such as Mayuzumi and Mizuno remained skeptical toward Cage's role as composer (Nara, *Kagayake Rokujûnendai*, 309).

32. Frederic Lieberman, ed., "A Lecture by John Cage," in *Locating East Asia in Western Art Music*, ed. Yayoi U. Everett and Frederick Lau (Middletown, Conn.: Wesleyan University Press, 2004), 196.

33. The photo is widely distributed on the Internet; see for instance http://www.new-york-art.com/YOko-Works-2.htm (accessed November 1, 2007).

34. Midori Yoshimoto, *Into Performance: Japanese Women Artists in New York* (New Brunswick, N.J.: Rutgers University Press, 2005), 95.

35. Sano et al., *Nihon Sengo Ongakushi*, 342.

36. Michael Kirby, "The New Theatre," in *Happenings and Other Acts*, ed. Mariellen R. Sanford (London and New York: Routledge, 1995), 36.

37. Nara, *Kagayake Rokujûnendai*, 57.

38. Thomas R. H. Havens, *Radicals and Realists in the Japanese Nonverbal Arts: The Avant-Garde Rejection of Modernism* (Honolulu: University of Hawaii Press, 2006), 110.

39. In Sôgetsu Art Center's journal (SAC No. 27, 1962), Mayuzumi stated that he thought of Cage as a brilliant philosopher, but not a great composer—arguing that he stopped composing after 4'33." In an essay from 1961, Yuasa expressed his fascination with Cage and chance operation, but questioned whether the act of liberating sound from predetermined structure resulted in the liberation of selfhood (SAC No. 19, 1961).

40. Havens, *Radicals and Realists*, 113.

41. For Ichiyanagi's involvement in Fluxus, see Luciana Galliano, "Toshi Ichiyanagi, Japanese Composer and 'Fluxus,'" *Perspectives of New Music* 44, no. 2 (Summer 2006): 250–61.

42. Kuniharu Akiyama, "Gendai Ongaku no Jiyû to Bôken" [Freedom and Adventure in New Music], *Yomiuri*, December 8, 1961.

43. Toshi Ichiyanagi, *Ongaku o kiku: Ongaku no ashita o kangaeru* [Listening to Music: Thinking about the Future of Music] (Tokyo: Ishikawashoten, 1984), 69–75.

44. Toshi Ichiyanagi, Program notes from Sôgetsu Contemporary Series No. 10. November 30, 1961.

45. Kuniharu Akiyama, "Atarashii Ongaku no hitopaji" [New Music's Page One], *Yomiuri*, March 2, 1962.

46. Shinichirô Ikebe, "New Direction no koro no omoide" [Recalling the New Direction Years], in *Kagayake Rokujûnendai*, 167.

47. Yûji Takahashi, "Facing Music," SAC No. 19, October 1961.

48. For a recording of *Chromamorphe II*, see *Orchestral Space 1966* (Japan Victor Series VX–69), vol.1.

49. Based on a correspondence with Yoshimoto on July 4, 2007.

50. Donald Richie, "Tsumazuita Saizensen: Ono Yoko no zen'ei shou" [Stumbling Front Line: Yoko Ono's Avant-Garde Show], *Geijutsu Shinchô* (July 1962): 60–61.

51. Toshi Ichiyanagi, "Saizenei no koe" [Voice of the Extreme Avant-garde], *Geijutsu Shinchô* (August 1962): 138–39.

52. Kristine Stiles, "*Cut Piece*, 1964," in *Yes Yoko Ono*, ed. Alexandra Munroe and Jon Hendricks (New York: Abrams, 2000), 158.

53. See http://www.youtube.com/watch?v=qqXSjFB08C8 for a video excerpt from the Carnegie Hall recital in 1965.

54. Yoshimoto, *Into Performance*, 100.

55. Ibid., 101.

56. Midori Yoshimoto, "Off Museum! Performance Art that Turned the Street into 'Theatre,' Circa 1964 Tokyo," *Performance Paradigm* 2 (March 2006): 102.

57. See ibid. for an account of the development of performance art in theater and film circa 1964.

58. Havens, *Radicals and Realists*, 220.

59. David G. Goodman, "Japan's Nostalgic Avant-Garde," in *Not the Other Avant-Garde: The Transnational Foundation of Avant-Garde Performance*, ed.

James M. Harding and John Rouse (Ann Arbor: University of Michigan Press, 2006), 250.

60. Conversations with Ichiyanagi, Hayashi, Takahashi, and Yuasa suggest that the affordable price of admission and multimedia aspects of avant-garde performances attracted a host of professional artists, musicians, filmmakers, as well as lay audience.

61. Havens, *Radicals and Realists*, 115.

62. Based on an interview with Ichiyanagi on May 18, 2006.

63. Packard, *Protest in Tokyo*, 341.

64. John Dower, "Peace and Democracy in Two Systems," in *Post-war Japan as History*, ed. Andrew Gordon (Berkeley and Los Angeles: University of California Press, 1993), 12–13.

65. Gordon, ibid., 450.

66. Frederic Jameson, *Postmodernism or the Cultural Logic of Late Capitalism* (Durham, N.C.: Duke University Press, 1991).

67. Stuart D. Hobbs, *The End of the American Avant Garde* (New York and London: New York University Press, 1997).

68. Sano et al., *Nihon Sengo Ongakushi*, 483–84.

69. Yûji Takahashi, *Tatakau Ongaku* [Fighting Music] (Tokyo: Shôbunsha, 1978), 14–15.

70. Some critics were baffled by the radical change in his musical orientation and could not reconcile the stylistic gap between his "highbrow" modernist compositions and the relatively simple arrangements of folk songs. Takahashi's ensemble disbanded after ten years, but to this day, he still adheres to the ideology of using music to bring about social change.

71. Yayoi U. Everett, "Mirrors of West and Mirrors of East: Elements of Gagaku in Post-war Art Music," in *Diasporas and Interculturalism in Asian Performing Arts: Translating Traditions*, ed. Hae-kyung Um (New York: Routledge, 2005), 182. "Reigaku" is a new term assigned to a genre of newly composed works commissioned by the National Theatre of Japan for the purpose of reviving musical practices of historically extinct instruments from the Imperial Court Repository.

72. According to Ichiyanagi, younger musicians engaged in reviving avant-garde music of the sixties include Tomomi Otachi, Osamu Ikebe, and Akiko Samukawa. In July 2007, Ichiyanagi offered a retrospective concert and lecture of music titled "John Cage and Fluxus" at the Asahi Hall in Tokyo.

73. Peter Eckersall, "From Liminality to Ideology: The Politics of Embodiment in Pre-war Avant-garde Theater in Japan," in *Not the Other Avant-Garde*, 227.

[4]

Central American Revolutionary Music

FRED JUDSON

Music as Social Discourse

Latin America's many musical vocabularies are as evident to consumers and aficionados of World Music as they are to musicians and musicologists.[1] Their variety, beauty, and appeal have engaged and influenced popular and classical music cultures and production far beyond their geographical and social contexts, particularly in Europe and North America. And that influence gathered force during the closing decades of the twentieth century; one need only see or hear the terms *samba, forro, tango, ranchera, salsa, merengue, son, corrido, huayna,* or *mariachi,* for example, to acknowledge it. Though perhaps a cliché, each Latin American musical vocabulary is more than an art form or a cultural expression; it is a social discourse. "Music does not create or realize itself, but is always the result of people doing things together in particular places and times. To understand music is to understand the men and women who make it, and vice versa" (Mellers and Martin 1989: x).

To be Marxist in the understanding of specific Central American revolutionary musics is necessarily to be eclectic and conceptually pluralist. Hence, the analytical point of departure regarding the *subjects* or *social actors* of this music is that of "the people" (*el pueblo*) more than it is of its structural *class* definition. Reflective of the respective Central American *pueblos* the music attributes to the social actors a variety of identities, including those of class (peasantry, proletariat, bourgeoisie), ethnicity (indigenous, black, mestizo and mulatto), gender (the female guerrilla combatant, the mother of the martyred hero, the enduring peasant woman), place (rural, urban, forest, mountain, tropics, province, region, certain towns, etc.), and culture (indigenous, ethnic minority, religious, peasantry, artisans, students, intellectuals, educated, illiterate). It expresses and contributes to a larger, more inclusive and more legitimate societal and national identity than that which prevails and is dominated by national oppressor and imperial social actors. As such, the music is considered as a whole people's cultural expression and thus as *popular* (such usage of the term also refers to the music's production within and alongside the many forms of commercially and socially popular music in Central America) while also political in its role as revolutionary social discourse.

What lends the Central American music examined in this chapter its revolutionary profile is not solely its dramatic social content or its conscious effort to articulate revolutionary social energies and objectives. It is that as concrete cultural production it has been human artifact created and performed in lived social contexts. Those contexts are the respective recent national political, economic, and social histories. The music, its thematic tropes and its forms, are embedded in those histories and in the human and social dynamics that make those histories and shape the respective national presents and futures. In this respect, to understand the music is to situate it in both the larger lived social histories of Central America and in the lived experiences of the music's producers and its "consumers." This chapter examines the themes present in the music with continued reference to those social histories and lived experiences. My own encounters with this music and with selected moments of those histories and lived experiences are central to the "socially constructed understanding" presented in the chapter. From the 1970s through the 1990s, I had the opportunity to act as interpreter/MC at numerous concerts, press conferences, and media interviews given in Canada by Central American musical groups whose work is discussed here. Those experiences provided me with invaluable personal contact with the music and its creators/performers. That cultural exposure was lent context and depth when I served as an interpreter at public meetings and media encounters for activists from various Central American countries who represented social movements and revolutionary political organizations. Research and residential sojourns in Managua, Nicaragua, throughout the 1980s and into the early 1990s put me in a variety of situations in which music was a social actor. To be present at political rallies where some of the groups played the music examined here for the people they intended to hear it deeply influenced my thinking about the music as a repertoire of revolutionary social discourse.

Two examples will suffice to convey the importance of such lived experience for the Marxist-inflected examination of Central American revolutionary music. Attending the 19 July 1985 mass rally on the sixth anniversary of the Sandinista revolution, I joined some half a million Nicaraguans and a scattering of internationalist supporters who sang along with such groups and artists as Mancotal, Carlos Enrique Mejía Godoy y los de Palacagüina, Norma Elena Gadea and Pancasán, whose work is examined in this chapter. To see the faces in the crowd, at times streaming with tears, and to hear the voices rise in songs that had been part of their own revolutionary morale, had been broadcast by clandestine rebel radio or played as part of popular mass in Catholic parishes affiliated with liberation theology during the guerrilla struggle and mass insurrection against the Somoza dictatorship, was an indelible experience. When Salvadorean revolutionary music groups living in exile in Managua took the stage that day, the crowd erupted with repeated slogans (*Si Nicaragua venció, El Salvador vencerá*—If Nicaragua won, El Salvador is next!) and sang the refrains to their well-known and militant tunes. The second occasion was in Managua some months after the Sandinistas lost the 1990 election, at a café where many artists associated with the revolution had performed during the Sandinistas' decade in power. Luis Enrique Mejía Godoy and Norma Elena Gadea sang "Nicagaragua, Nicagaragüita," an affectionate, tender expression of love for the small country, as though for a beloved child. It had been performed at virtually all political meetings, as almost a second national anthem, during the revolutionary government, and was closely associated with the sense that the revolution had been a popular victory, an achievement of the whole nation. Needless to say, the café that night was in emotional overflow; it was the first time since the electoral defeat that the two artists most associated with the song had performed together.

Latin American musics as social discourses[2] vary widely. There is music expressing identities, such as the Peruvian black experience on the CD "Música Negra del Perú" (Various Authors 1999) or the contemporary Afro-Brazilian religious expression on the Virginia Rodrigues CD "Nós" (2000). The popularity and commercial success of the Cuban artists gathered under the loose rubric of the "Buena Vista Social Club" (1997) exemplifies, as one of the CDs' titles announces, what is "distinct and different" about Cuban music, and by extension, about Cubans' social experience of the twentieth century. The universe of Latin American music as radical social discourse in the twentieth century, represented, for example, in the LP *1er Festival Nuevo Canto Latinoamericano. Versión Urgente para Nicaragua* (Various Groups 1982), draws on roots of critical expression regarding slavery, colonialism, and foreign intervention in prior centuries. But its central discourses target the exploitation, repression, and immiseration of Latin America's experiences of modern capitalist development/underdevelopment. As well, the Cuban Nueva Trova (or New Song Movement) following the Cuban Revolution and the Chilean Nueva Canción irruption of the 1960s and 1970s, like others throughout the region, melded critical social protest, musical innovation, contemporary poetry and musical forms of oppressed and dominated groups (e.g., prostitutes, the rural poor, Andean indigenous peoples, sugar workers). They sought consciously both to recuperate and represent a "people's music," to legitimate it as popular and to wield music as a weapon in what they understood to be political class struggles, echoing Woody Guthrie's 1930s maxim: "This guitar kills fascists."

At the same time, such musical social discourses were reflective of global/international popular music genres, as they were of the social specifics of their respective national locales. As Simon Frith (1989: 2) writes, "no country in the world is unaffected by the way in which the twentieth-century mass media . . . have created a universal pop aesthetic." There are numerous contemporary Latin American musicians whose work is clearly a social discourse addressing local as well as larger Latin American situations and at the same time containing a "universal pop aesthetic," the Panamanian artist Rubén Blades (1999) being but one, albeit well-known, example. Central American revolutionary music of the 1970s and 1980s is also character-ized by a discursive and artistic content that is equally disparate and transcendent. Central American artists spoke to specific social interclass dynamics while recovering and popularizing musical forms of whole peoples and their histories. They adapted and improvised on those forms and drew upon musical and social discourses from elsewhere in Latin America and beyond, and from the universal pop aesthetic, producing distinctive work with appeal beyond their immediate circumstances. As Nicaraguan artist Luis Enrique Mejía Godoy remarked in liner notes for the Salvadorean group Banda Tepehuani, "They broke the barrier between 'serious' and 'popu-lar' . . . undertaking the deepening of the folkloric roots and popular music of their [Salvadorean] people, integrating elements from universal music" (Banda Tepehuani 1982).[3]

The social discourse of particular musical vocabularies can be intrinsi-cally and explicitly revolutionary, as, for example, the music of some Sal-vadorean groups affiliated with the Farabundo Martí National Liberation Front (FMLN) written for and broadcast to guerrilla combatants from clan-destine and mobile radio stations (Almeida and Urbizagástegui 1999: 20; Shaull 1990). It can also be revolutionary in specific contexts, where a rev-olution is in power (Cuba, Nicaragua 1979–1990), where an armed revolu-tionary movement is contending for state power (El Salvador, Guatemala, Peru, Colombia at various times in the late twentieth century), where artists identify themselves with revolutionary projects (e.g., in Chile, Argentina, Brazil, Uruguay, Bolivia, Venezuela during periods of repres-sion, dictatorship, and resistance), or where certain musical vocabularies are associated with radical social forces and projects, considered subver-sive and repressed by state authorities. There is also revolutionary music as such due to its internationalism and solidarity with struggles elsewhere. Central American revolutionary music (of Nicaragua, El Salvador, and Guatemala) considered in this chapter meets all these criteria. But just as Frith (1989: 3) declares that "popular music study rests on the assumption that there is no such thing as a culturally 'pure' music," the assumption here is that there is no such thing as purely revolutionary music. It follows that artistic and discursive hybridity, flexibility, dynamism, and variety in Central American revolutionary musical expression are among its crucial characteristics.

A Framework of Understanding

The framework of understanding deployed here contains three general dimensions. One derives from the broad literatures that study revolutions as comparative sociopolitical phenomena, and contains two key assumptions. On the one hand, as Vilas (1995: 9) argues about revolutions in general and the Central American experiences specifically, "[They] are not inevitable, although neither are they accidents. The conditions that fuel and finally ignite a revolutionary process are always particular to each situation, but analysis at the proper level of abstraction brings out recurring elements in the specifics of each case." The "proper level of abstraction" is taken here to be the global character and uneven development of capitalism as the central organizing principle of modern human societies and their governance.[4] Hence, this dimension of analysis falls under the social science category of *political economy*. Following the tenets of that general approach to the study of revolution, represented among others by Moore (1966), Bulmer-Thomas (1987) and Dunkerley (1988), means understanding the social transformations and disruptions of macroeconomic changes, in Central America in the thirty years after World War II, as the crucible for revolutionary upsurges.[5] In effect, the wrenching and rapid modernization of Central America's "traditional" agrarian capitalist societies was the genesis of revolutionary situations.

On the other hand, as Marxist political doctrine and common sense would remind us, objective macroconditions are necessary but not sufficient for revolutionary situations, movements and outcomes to occur. The realm of the subjective, of the consciousness of social forces which may become engaged as revolutionary actors, is just as crucial. This second assumption regarding the causal foundation of revolutionary experiences is embedded in the well-known statement of Karl Marx (1972: 437) that "men make their own history, but they do not make it just as they please; they do not make it under circumstances chosen by themselves, but under circumstances directly found, given and transmitted from the past." It is in the *making*—the collective social action that constitutes history from a Marxist perspective—that consciousness and the realms of the subjective are manifested. Generally, Marxists hold that material life, in particular the human social activity that produces the means to life, determines the content and dynamics of consciousness, hence of culture. Consciousness and culture reflect and represent the ideational, discursive, and symbolic dynamics of those "concrete social relations" and their contradictions, according to Marxist cultural studies.[6] Thus, for example, if social relations are hierarchical, authoritarian, and enforced by violence, it is likely that the dominant cultural values and expressions will be so as well. But it is also within consciousness and culture that "spaces" reside in which ideas and values that contradict a given social order may develop. It is in the relationship between the fundamental social relations of a given society and its culture that revolutionary theorists locate the terrain of subjective conditions.

In the social sciences' inquiries pertaining to revolution and social change, this second general dimension of a framework of understanding derives from the intersection of *political culture* (the study of political values and discourses), *political sociology* (the study of social and class structures' significance for politics), and *political psychology* (the study of political behaviors and their underlying psychological bases). Such inquiries focus on the political syntax of the values and symbolic discourses that maintain or challenge a given socioeconomic and political order, and on those societal and individual processes by which those values and discourses are transformed and become forces themselves in the mass, sustained collective action we call revolutions. A diverse array of scholars and political actors have considered this dimension. Lenin (1975), of course, directly assumed and theorized the historical necessity for the vanguard communist party to mobilize revolutionary ideas, analysis and consciousness in the masses of Russian workers and peasants. Georges Sorel (1925), more representative of the anarchist tradition, focused on the nonrational, symbolic, and mythic structures and discourses of meaning as subjective forces in revolutionary situations. Whereas Marx theorized social contradictions and political struggle as deriving from opposed class interests, and "if . . . both Marx and Lenin stressed the importance of ideas in that struggle, Sorel argued that, in addition to interests and ideas, images and visions propelled human struggles" (Judson 1987b: 20).[7]

This dimension of consciousness, subjective forces and symbolic discourses was famously examined by Antonio Gramsci (1973) in the 1930s, principally through the concept of "hegemony." Gramsci sought to understand the ideological, cultural, and discursive fabrics of class domination under modern capitalism and how practices in those realms interacted with the relations of production and property, arenas of more classical Marxist attention. He also sought to empower subaltern classes and intellectuals through enabling "counterhegemonic" cultures and discourses. And both Marxist and non-Marxist scholarship have shown "in recent years . . . a marked shift from structural explanations of revolutionary processes to explanations integrating more cultural concerns" (Almeida and Urbizagástegui 1999: 14). Charles Tilly (1978), Theda Skocpol (1979), Eric Hobsbawm (1986) and Carlos Vilas (1995) are representative of those who seek to incorporate those concerns.

In combining, then, a political economy or structural dimension of understanding with this broadly cultural dimension, a deceptively elegant argument results: Whatever the structural realities of rapid and wrenching socioeconomic changes (in this case Central America's agrarian capitalist modernizations) people's perceptions and symbolic interpretations of those realities go quite some way in determining their responses to those changes. Those perceptions and symbolic discourses are understood by some, particularly in studies of social movements, as *collective action frames* (Snow and Benford 1988: 14): as dispositions to act. As Vilas (1995: 21) explains, the symbolic elements of a particular culture or society undergoing change do not necessarily orient people to collective action as resistance or revolution:

> Symbolic elements have long offered explanation and justification for the existing social order. Whether the order that is retreating under the assault of the market was objectively better or worse than the new one, therefore, is not the issue; people perceive it as better because the symbolic elements they possess enable them to evaluate it in this way, not merely because the old way of life was objectively less unsatisfactory. Under the old regime, people knew what to expect . . . the arguments that legitimize a social order tend to take on a certain autonomy from their substantive foundations. This is true of any social order and helps to explain the apparently inexplicable "tolerance" or adaptation that people can display under an oppressive or evil order.

Just as the political economy or structural dimension in the framework of understanding elides with that of political culture/sociology/psychology, the latter has a segue with the dimension of *cultural studies*. Almeida and Urbizagástegui (1999) explicitly merge them, drawing on Foran's (1997) concept of "political cultures of resistance and opposition" to focus on the role and content of popular protest music in creating and sustaining a revolutionary mobilization in El Salvador. In their view, popular protest music is a mobilizational resource for a revolutionary movement and is at least an important, even a crucial part of what Gramsci would see as a counterhegemonic culture: "revolutionary movements proffer ideas that emphasize shared injustices and underscore experiences of oppression in a fashion consistent with widespread cultural beliefs" (Almeida and Urbizagástegui 1999: 15). Such music and its conscious political deployment, they argue, achieved a "collective action frame of the insurgent movement in El Salvador between 1975 and 1992, in effect contributing to the movement's mobilization potential" (15) and disseminating a "repertoire of contention . . . the inclusion of contentious repertoires in protest music complements the abstract framing process of general problems, solutions and motivational appeals with precise tactical advice when the moment arises for participants and supporters to engage in collective protest and insurgency" (17).

In a similar elision of political culture approaches and cultural studies that treats Latin American protest and revolutionary music, Rodolfo Pino-Robles (1999: 1) remarks that "to speak of music and social change in the same breath is to speak of a commitment of people exercising this form of art to the service of a social cause." His examples, Atahualpa Yupanqui of Argentina and Violeta Parra of Chile, precede the Central American revolutionary musical discourses but share with them crucial aspects. Their music, in its use of popular forms, "becomes a form of popular memory . . . in which a sense of the past is reconstructed in society questioning and calling attention to the misfortune of those at the bottom of the social ladder" (6). Cuban writer Alejandro Carpentier, says Pino-Robles, captures how such music is "not just a testimony of the past, but a living force which informs the present."

> That music, coming sometimes from remote villages and brought into the city, installed in the suburbs, injected into dances, a lively and inventive music, reinvented daily, it was taking shape, integrating and sketching its own profiles. It was ascending, rising, invading, taking the public taste, to the dismay of those who considered themselves above what they saw as trivial and vulgar. (Carpentier 1977: 13)

Violeta Parra, the Chilean singer who preceded such socially and politically committed compatriot artists as Victor Jara and the world-renowned groups Inti-Illimani and Quilapayun, spoke simply of her connection as a people's artist to her performance materials: "I didn't realize, when I set out to acquire my first song . . . [that] I would learn that Chile is the best folklore reference book written" (1985: 10). Without employing the same conceptual vocabulary, Pino-Robles traces the same sequencing of Chilean and Argentine popular protest/revolutionary music's relationship to macrosocial phenomena of movement, mobilization, and revolutionary commitment as Almeida and Urbizagástegui (1999) find in the Central American experiences.

Themes in Central American Revolutionary Music

This discussion of the three elastic dimensions of a framework of understanding suggests an important enjoinder for contemporary social science: multifaceted social phenomena like Central America's revolutionary experiences and the music that accompanied them may best be understood with combined approaches. The particular framework of understanding presented here, in a certain sense a dynamic synthesis, provides a backdrop of interpretation and meaning for the examination of the music itself. Based in the understanding, a simple content analysis of a score of representative Central American revolutionary music products (LPs and cassettes by Nicaraguan, Salvadorean, and Guatemalan musicians) yields a set of themes. As would be the case with Salvadorean and Guatemalan revolutionary ideologies, a study of *Sandinismo* as Nicaragua's revolutionary ideology/morale (Judson 1987b) had identified several core themes one might expect would be present in the associated music: patriotism and national historical experiential continuity, particularly the linkage of epochs of struggle and figures symbolizing those struggles; anti-imperialism, specifically resistance to United States interventions and control of the region; internationalism and solidarity with similar anti-imperialist and revolutionary struggles, especially in Latin America, but also throughout the world; martyrology, that is, a focus on the sacrifices and losses of those fallen in the struggle, an expressed determination to make the works of the revolution their concrete legacy, and a probing consideration of death's presence for those continuing the struggle; the realm of the future, with its visions, dreams and, in Sorel's terms, *mythes* of the revolutionary society to come. These themes appear throughout Central American revolutionary music's social discourses. In addition to those themes, which together comprise what Central American revolutionaries would call *la mística* or *moral revolucionaria*, several others are evident in the music. Together with the ideological themes, they constitute, as it were, the vocabulary of the social discourses of Central American revolutionary music.

In looking at their respective national societies, Central America's revolutionary musical artists assert the identity of a people as *popular,* as the majority. And they turn that popular identity this way and that, considering class structures, ethnicity, customs, and geographic place. As it is fair to presume, given that the music, by and large, is consciously revolutionary, references to class are prevalent in musical social discourses about who constitutes "the people," *el pueblo,* as the collective social actor. Somewhat in tandem with the theme of solidarity appearing in the revolutionary ideologies, the ideal and practice of unity—of the people, of the revolutionary social forces, and of the different revolutionary organizations—appear frequently. This is especially the case with music that has moved from the raising of consciousness through mobilization to sustaining the political and armed struggle.

In giving discursive contours to the people as protagonist, Central American revolutionary artists, muralists, poets, and painters sharpen the definitions of the enemy. Giving the enemy a collective class name, often "the oligarchy," also serves to show the people as the great majority and the enemy as the powerful and undemocratic few. The instruments of oppression and class rule, the military, police, state security and intelligence operatives, also fall under the category of enemies of the people, though often it is made clear that they are tools and could be morally and patriotically redeemed, especially at the levels of conscript and lower rank. That is not the case with the "enemy behind the enemy," imperialism, the United States government. And in some instances, capital or capitalism is the enemy, though usually the people who control it or serve it are the discursive targets.

With the sharper definition of the enemy, the themes of armed struggle, revolutionary violence and combativity also become more pointed. Metaphors from popular language, intended to inspire courage and diminish the enemy, proliferate, while actual battles add triumphant or angry elements to place names which national and popular audiences are likely to know. And as combat to defeat or repel the enemy increases in ferocity and duration, there

are more appeals for unity, discipline and trust in the revolutionary vanguard
and leadership. There is direct reference to the life, loves, celebrations, priva-
tions and even the diet of the guerrilla combatants or the Sandinista soldiers.
In the case of Nicaragua, there is a call to defend the social, political, and
material achievements of the revolution. There is also an insistent content
given to peace. There are certainly musical expressions of longing for peace
and what it will afford for social development, for the flourishing of democracy, for rebeautifying devastated land and communities, for individual and
family reunions, for love and life. But peace is not seen as arbitrary or given;
it is to be won in confronting the enemy, in maintaining principles at the
negotiating table and being forever mindful of the sacrifices of fallen comrades, in being vigilant in the defense of perceived social gains of the revolution in power (Nicaragua, but also FMLN "zones of control" during the
Salvadorean conflict) or of the revolutionary struggle's organizational and
military gains (El Salvador and Guatemala).

A final element in these revolutionary musical and social discourses,
though also primary, recalls the third dimension of the framework of understanding, the cultural studies perspective, and that is the centrality of the popular. It is the language of the streets and markets, fields and jails, of those who
have limited opportunity for formal education but who are artisans of language
and who love its wordplay, its vibrant metaphors and its humor. And it is the
rhythms, musical forms and instrumentations, the social juxtapositions of the
music with family and fiesta, with dancing and significant life moments, with
campesino/peasant,[8] worker and market life and with regional and local identity
which lends this music perhaps its deepest and most grounded soul. It might be
termed "folk popular," to distinguish it from, but also to acknowledge that popular majorities also listen to and like, domestic and international "pop music."

Revolutionary poetry and liberation theology in Central America found
eloquence in the popular and vernacular: "Poetry by Rubén Darío,[9] Roque
Dalton[10] or Father Ernesto Cardenal[11] frequently proved more inspirational
than obscure Marxist tracts that had little to do with local conditions. Sermons by radical priests and homilies by the martyred Archbishop of El Salvador were often much more influential than quotes from Lenin or supposed
directives from Moscow" (Vanden 1986: 1). The same was true for revolutionary music and its creators/performers. As Luis Enrique Mejía Godoy
declared in liner notes (1992), "Everyday song is not a fad; it is something
always living in the soul of the people."

Nationalism and the Historical Continuity of Struggle

Central American revolutionary thought and practice, which has generally
but not exclusively been Marxist, has more often than not been strongly
nationalist (Castañeda 1993: 267–325; Liss 1991). This is not surprising,

given the national histories of resistance and rebellion, both to colonial rule and imperialism. Such a legacy is a rich resource for the construction of revolutionary discourse, and this theme is one of the most commonly found in the music. The very title of the Nicaraguan group Pancasán's (1983) album *Por La Patria* (For the fatherland) is a portent of the patriotic and nationalist flavor of several of its songs. In "¿Quienes Son?" (Who are they?) Pancasán traces oligarchic complicity with external aggressors to the Spanish "robbery of our Indians," their land and labor power. Pancasán, with perhaps the most militant sound of the Nicaraguan groups, attributes the various invasions and occupations by U.S. troops to "those who made a pact with the Yankees to murder Sandino" (Augusto César Sandino, the nationalist figure who waged guerrilla war against the U.S. Marines from 1927 to 34). They link the FSLN (Sandinistas) to Sandino and prior nationalists who confronted the United States. Time is continuous and mobile in this discourse: "Sandino was here among us, and he is always present," they sing in "El Cuje" (a rural locale). It is an appeal to memory as mobilizer and to a patriotic duty to those who struggled in the past, as Mejía Godoy puts it in his album *Yo soy de un pueblo sencillo* (I'm from a simple people) (1982): "to remember . . . you have to wake up . . . our children will sing what our grandfathers couldn't."

The echo of pre-conquest civilization marks a more distant historical continuity, as well as an alternate indigenous national identity, especially for Maya Guatemala. Kin-Lalat, in their album *Florecerás Guatemala* (1983), sing in the title song ("Guatemala, you will flower") that "we have lived a thousand years of death . . . in the country of eternal spring." The Nicaraguan group Mancotal looks to the precolonial roots for moral, practical and agrarian resources for the struggle to resist aggression and consolidate the revolution. In "Somos hijos del maíz" (We are children of corn) on the LP *Un Son para mi pueblo* (A *Son* for my people) (1981) they draw directly on Mesoamerican indigenous cosmologies. "We will survive," sings Mancotal, "as did our grandfathers, with corn fermented in the blood of heroes . . . corn cultivated here before the cross, the sword, the pirates and capital bloodied our land . . . we've done it for over a thousand sowing seasons." The song counsels Nicaraguans to recuperate the corn-based diet of indigenous peoples, the musicians' voices obviously delighting in listing and pronouncing the many dishes and drinks made from corn, "the irreversible nutrition of the people." With corn, "we will be renewed, we will be fresh corn!" Similarly, Carlos Mejía Godoy and the group Los de Palacagüina (1980) refer to the "millennial presence" of the indigenous community of Monimbó, a district of the Nicaraguan city Masaya. The song features the marimba, an indigenous instrument ("the marimba which plays sounds of liberation"), and links indigenous resistance against "the blond conquistadors" to the role of Monimbó in the popular insurrection against Somoza. Monimbó and its indigenous inhabitants are called "the pure soul of the Nicaraguan people."

The Salvadorean group Yolocamba Ita, in the title song for the album *Canto a la Patria Revolucionaria* (Song for the revolutionary homeland) (1981), pointedly links indigenous resistance to colonialism's commercialization of agriculture and control of labor power to the 1932 rebellion of coffee workers and the armed struggle of the FMLN (Farabundo Martí National Liberation Front) in the 1980s. There have been, their lyrics say, "centuries of lost lives, centuries of overdue revenge for our Pipil [an indigenous people whose remnants were massacred in 1932] land . . . the Indian Aquino [leader of an 1832 rebellion] and Farabundo Martí [leader of the 1932 rebellion] showed us the road we will follow." Both groups consciously took indigenous names, as did the Salvadorean groups Cutumay Camones (Almeida and Urbizagástegui 1999: 20) and Tepehuani.[12] Cutumay Camones also linked the FMLN combatants to Aquino, Feliciano Ama (another indigenous rebel leader in the 1932 events) and Martí: "If you'll glance over there at the mountain, you'll see they've been growing Aquinos in the canefields, Amas in the cornfields, Martís in the coffee groves," went the lyrics of their album *Por eso luchamos* (This is why we fight) (Almeida and Urbizagástegui 1999: 23, 26).

The continuity of suffering, injustice, and truncated sovereignty underlined in the music treating nationalist and patriotic themes finds its response in the appeal to contemporary generations to make good the sacrifices of precursors. An appreciation of national history is validated only by making that selfsame history, continuing and completing its national tasks: liberty, development, sovereignty, as Pancasán's song "Se Está forjando la patria nueva" (The new homeland is being forged) (1979) makes clear even before the 19 July 1979 victory over the Somoza dictatorship. Pancasán's LP *Vamos haciendo la historia* (1981) (Here we're making history) states in the title song: "We go making the history of what will come . . . it costs blows and takes the gun . . . to build the future." Nicaraguan history, plagued consistently by U.S. interventions, is recounted with dates, places, and names in their "Apuntes sobre el tío Sam" (Notes on Uncle Sam). Nicaraguans' pride at Augusto Sandino, known all over Latin America for his resistance struggle against the U.S. Marines, comes to full flower in the song "Adelante Nicaragua" only in the context of the popular insurrection that overthrew the Somoza dictatorship in 1979: "All Latin America is exclaiming: the homeland of Augusto Sandino is battling for its liberty!"

Pueblo, Patria, and Place: Popular Identity

There are several aspects of popular identity that Central American revolutionary music addresses. One of those clearly is social class, while another is nationality and citizenship—a patriotic and nationalist identity. What emerges from listening to this music and its combinations of lyrics, popular language, rhythms, instrumentation, and social discourses is the centrality of the *popular*. It is the music's embrace of the popular that gives its efforts to articulate and reinforce an identity among social forces either engaged or potentially engaged in revolutionary collective action its living discursive content. Collective action frames, as considered by Almeida and Urbizagástegui (1999: 15), "reinforce . . . collective identity, and solidarity among already committed movement members, evoke sympathy from potential supporters, and call the attention of a broader population to a situation that is unjust and in need of change." Particularly in those socioeconomic structures that are *not* what classical Marxism supposed were necessary conditions for socialist revolutions (advanced, industrial capitalist societies characterized by the stark class bifurcation of bourgeoisie and proletariat), a collective action frame has to provide a broader collective identity. Central America's revolutionary music often did that more successfully than did the ideologues and leaderships of the various revolutionary organizations, who tended to replicate vanguardist or Leninist orthodoxies of class (proletariat) and class consciousness.

The key term or trope in the identity discourse of Central American revolutionary music is *el pueblo*. Inclusive, positive, respectful, empowering and democratic are all inferential in the music's articulation of "the people." And it takes poets or musicians who are masters of popular idioms, of the colloquial, of regional and local expressions, to give pueblo its discursive content and form, just as it takes a radicalized and politicized consciousness in those poets and musicians to raise the term to its organic role in revolutionary cultural mobilization. Central America has not lacked for poets and musicians with those attributes. Ernesto Cardenal, Gioconda Belli, Claribel Alegría, Leonel Rugama, and Roque Dalton are among the many names that could come to mind.[13] One of the best-known exemplars among musicians is Carlos Mejía Godoy; Nicaraguan poet Julio Valle-Castillo paid tribute to his gifts in liner notes for the album *Monimbó* (Carlos Mejía Godoy 1980):

> Carlos Mejía Godoy doesn't sing to the people. The people sing in him, through him and with him. A popular voice. Voice and song of the people. Carlos is an eroticist of Nicaraguan speech . . . you can hear the delight of his pronunciation. His lyrics are true poems. Magnificent amorous, social, and political poems. His may be the best libertine poetry—creatively orgiastic—written by the younger generation. These lyrics or poems are in minor meter, octosyllabic even, full of bickering, lines, nicknames, proper names and diminutives: they're a real verbal coitus. (translation by author).

Among the strikingly creative, but genuinely rooted and popular works of Carlos Mejía Godoy is the *Misa Campesina Nicaragüense* (Nicaraguan folk mass) (1977). To sounds of marimba, guitar, accordion and drums, the lyrics identify the pueblo through its faith relationship with God and Jesus Christ: "You're the God of the poor, the human and humble God, who sweats in the street, the God of sunburned and leathery face; that's why I speak to You as my people speak, because you're the worker God, the worker Christ" ("Song of entry"). Such a God, such a Christ are the mirror of the pueblo: "You are there in the pay-line at the harvest . . . I've seen you selling lottery tickets . . . checking truck tires at the gas station . . . Christ, identify with us, not with the oppressor class, but with the oppressed, with my pueblo thirsty for peace" ("Entry" and "Kyrie"). From such a perspective on the pueblo and on faith, the religious credo is: "I believe in You, architect, engineer, artisan, carpenter . . . in You, comrade . . . You shall be resurrected in every arm raised to defend the pueblo against the exploiter's dominion, because You live in the rancho, in the factory, in the school" ("Credo"). The pueblo, in this music, is Christ's pueblo, the "popular classes": "the working class, which from before dawn is on its way to work, which sings to You, Lord, from the plow, from every building site, from the tractor seat, construction workers, tailors, day laborers, everybody equal, stevedores and ironwrights, shoeshine boys in the park" ("Ofertorio"). With the unique ecclesiastical and poetic authority he possesses, Father Ernesto Cardenal, later to be Minister of Culture in the Sandinista government of Nicaragua, paid Carlos Mejía Godoy this homage in the liner notes to *Misa*: "With authentic peasant voices and with the speech of the pueblo which he knows like nobody else, Carlos Mejía Godoy and the Workshop of Popular Sound have composed this Nicaraguan Mass."

The discursive construction of the pueblo as a collective identity has pre-existing materials to appropriate, again particularly in societies with defining features many would term "traditional," or even "folk."[14] When rapid change sweeps through such a society, states Carlos Vilas (1995: 21, 23), like many theorists of revolution, popular social movements and change, people are convinced "that their customs, and the normal order of things, are being violated . . . the speed of change makes custom more difficult to reproduce and to update, and intensifies the feeling of rupture and loss. The development of new modalities of production and access to land, the mercantilization of the labor force, the dislocation of the family, all in the space of a couple of decades, creates an intergenerational break and blocks the transmission of values, attitudes and beliefs." What is crucial for the construction of a revolutionary discourse in these circumstances is that the violated customs, identities, and sense of order take on, potentially, a greater symbolic reality and value than in "normal" or "traditional" circumstances. Vilas (1995: 23) writes: "the fact that the erosion of the traditional way of life arises mainly from an invasion of external factors encourages a certain idealization of the former: the symbolic reality of the traditional order is reinforced at the very moment that its objective reality is vanishing." That "symbolic reality of the traditional" becomes both a discursive space and a resource appropriable for revolutionary symbolic reconstruction. The pueblo's existing sense of itself as people and as *a people* is that cultural resource. As Carlos Nuñez, one of the FSLN *comandantes,*[15] stated in liner notes for the album *Grupo Pancasán* (1979):

> Revolutionary song in our *patria* . . . penetrated our *pueblo*, lighting the flame of insurrection . . . awakening revolutionary fervor in all sectors of the population. It arose from popular throats to sustain us in the hour of defeats . . . opened the doors of our history to show the people the content of their own gestures and actions, their role as protagonists of history. . . . Song has been one of the means for our people to speak of their misery and suffering, of the exploitation. In clandestinity, in underground activity, in combat we have heard those voices singing to life and communicating hopes for the future, demanding bread, freedom, a new regime, a more just society.

Ubiquitous on billboards in revolutionary Nicaragua, and still emblazoned on the pedestal of the monument to the worker-combatant near the old cathedral in Managua's earthquake-ruined (1972) city center, Sandino's declaration that "only the workers and peasants will go to the very end" links the pueblo to genuine citizenship. Classical Marxism (Marx, Lenin, Gramsci, Trotsky) argued that bourgeois democracy was a form of class domination and thus incomplete until the proletariat achieved supremacy and completed the respective national historical projects of democracy with socialism transcending class domination. Similarly, Central American revolutionary discourses, in concert with the precepts of Latin American dependency theory, held that "dependent bourgeoisies" and U.S. imperialism were a historical obstacle to national sovereignty, popular democracy, and concomitant development. Thus the historic responsibility of the *pueblo* as conscious "maker of its own history" was to fulfill those national agendas, as Sandino declared. It would take a *revolutionary pueblo*, conscious and organized, but "when the people have the will, there is no tyrant who can resist them," Tepehuani sings in the progressive salsa tune "Organizete" (Organize yourself) (1982).

The full and historically deserved citizenship which would identify the pueblo with the patria was to result, with the pueblo achieving "an eternal joy when worker/peasant power *is* the power" ("Cuando venga la paz" [When peace comes],) (Norma Elena Gadea 1985). And unlike the selfish, self-absorbed, and oppressive oligarchy, which was incapable of achieving or sharing a true patria and an inclusive national citizenship, the pueblo would know how: "It was the pueblo that most hated you [the torturer for the oligarchy's dictatorship] when the song was in the language of violence . . . but it is the pueblo, now, beneath its red-black [Sandinista and universal revolutionary colors] skin, which has a generous heart . . . [capable] of saying hello to you in the streets without beggars, of ensuring your children have schools and flowers" ("Mi venganza personal" [My personal revenge],) (Mejía Godoy 1982).[16]

The identity of the pueblo, then, is ultimately with the patria, when that patria is liberated, when that patria is fully *popular*. Such an identity is pointedly political, in that it is only realized with access to state power, as well as being nationalist and patriotic. It is also a popular identity of *place*, a theme appearing throughout Central American revolutionary music. There is national, and also natural place, in references to Central America as a region of Latin America and of the world's South/Third World, as a "brother of so many peoples" (from the title song on *Yo soy de un pueblo sencillo*, Mejía Godoy 1982) characterized by being an isthmus of volcanoes, lakes, and earthquakes. *Pueblo* becomes "*mi tierra*" (my/our land), as in Tepehuani's songs "Cumbia de mi tierra" and "El volcán" (Tepehuani 1988), where "earth tremors are human tremors . . . ready to explode . . . boiling up with humanity's love . . . blow, volcano! Get angry, blow now! Be that lava of light, stopping the darkness." One of Luis Enrique Mejía Godoy's songs is "Juan Terremoto" (Earthquake Juan), who has to live in ruins after the 1972 Managua earthquake, when the dictator Somoza appropriated the reconstruction materials arriving from other nations for his own construction companies and the "new mansions were for the rich man" (*Del 70 al 80; Diez Años*). Yolocamba Ita also sings of volcanoes and the combative *pueblo*, literally in the same breath, naming the San Vicente/Chinchontepec volcano where the FMLN maintained control for years: "Above the ravine of Cayetana village, where the male volcano flirts with the female, when the sun has just risen, early in the morning you can see the fighters of the popular movement" ("Canción al FMLN," Yolocamba Ita 1981). The whole country of El Salvador becomes a place defined by its anti-imperialism: "If the Yankees intervene here like they did in Vietnam, if the Marines invade, here they'll find their graves, like Cayetano [FMLN commander Salvador Cayetano Carpio] said."[17]

Place is addressed in two more ways in Central American musical discourses about the pueblo. In the popularization and celebration of the local, this music makes people's, especially rural people's, attachment to place a central feature. It is replete with place names, both in song titles and in lyrics. It tells people that where they are from, and hence they themselves, are important, that the music belongs to them. And place names situate the heroic actions and martyrs of past and contemporary popular struggles in the symbolic firmament of the pueblo. The album *Marimba Revolucionaria* (Hermanos Palazio 1980), for example, has instrumentals with place-name titles of revolutionary significance to Nicaraguans: "Vivirás Monimbó," for the combative indigenous neighborhood of the city of Masaya; "Pancasán," for the site of a failed 1967 FSLN rural guerrilla front in the north-central mountains (the group Pancasán, of course, took its name from that front); "El Niquinomeño," for the "man from Niquinohomo," Augusto César Sandino. Tepehuani (1982) dedicates a song to the Morazán region of El Salvador, where the FMLN established a liberated zone during the war and enjoyed almost complete popular support, effectively establishing governance. The all-peasant Salvadorean group Los Torogaces de Morazán and many of the fifty or more protest/revolutionary musical groups aligned with the revolutionary organizations from 1975 to 1992 all made locales an integral part of their lyrics, in celebrating popular identity and events of the armed struggle (Almeida and Urbizagástegui 1999). And Carlos Mejía Godoy, master of Nicaraguan vernacular and folklore, could have specific locations be nationally known with songs like "Terencio Acahualinca" and "Ticuantepe sin vós" (1980).

Place in Central American folk culture, in tradition and in modernity, is physical and emotional. It is filial and familial, associated closely with life, death and agricultural cycles, and with national, local and personal history. Its very physicality comes from the exuberance and drama of nature and Central American revolutionary music emphasizes the natural aspects of place. Tepehuani's near-avante-garde composition "Madre Tierra" (1982), for example, combines the patriotic and popular sentiment for mi tierra with an ecological sensibility ("Mother Earth") and echoes of indigenous cosmology. Tepehuani uses plants and animals, both to highlight nature in the pueblo's social and symbolic world and as metaphor: "Butterfly, your flight is our flight . . . dreaming of the spring of equality . . . [and] its multiple colors on the horizon" ("Mariposa"); in "Pájaro Guazapa" (Bird of the Guazapa volcano), a song that opens with helicopter gunship sounds, presumably over the slopes of Guazapa, an almost continuous combat zone just outside San Salvador during the 1980s, they sing of "the green bird of my hope . . . the bird of the poor . . . the guerrilla bird" (El Zamaquión 1988).

In a somewhat different idiom, Norma Elena Gadea (1985) uses the images and metaphors of birds, trees, and flowers both for highlighting popular identity ("El almendro" [The Almond Tree], in which she sketches the peasant, rural setting of a young girl's life) and to pay homage to the fallen and martyred combatants ("El zenzontle pregunta por Arlen Siu" [The Zenzontle bird asks for Arlen Siu]). Nature becomes the patria and the very earth, its creatures and its foliage, embrace the pueblo's heroes and martyrs. And nature will celebrate the people's triumph, "when peace comes" (the album title): "the necessary bird, the revolutionary bird freed from its cage, flies to the future . . . with the Guatemalan bird, the Salvadorean bird"; in that future "the fiesta will be of children and birds."

The Class Identity of *El Pueblo*

In the social discourse of Central American revolutionary music, it has been argued, the *popular* elements of the pueblo's identity are central, and those popular elements can be understood as transcending stricter class characterizations. They can be considered as cultural, as "placed," and as reflections of nationality. Nonetheless, as seen in the references to the Campesino Mass and the discussion of respective national societies' capacities to achieve the historical goals of a nationalist agenda, class is durably embedded in the discourses. Using class categories when singing of the pueblo sharpens the understanding and consciousness of those social forces held responsible for making the revolution and undertaking the nationalist agenda: "Rise up, working class, the time has come to take this thing seriously and liberate El Salvador. The *patria* needs you, with your fist and your voice. Let's fire our guns and shout revolution" (Cutumay Camones, cited in Almeida and Urbizagástegui 1999: 30).

And it is a classically Marxist delineation of social contradictions as outlined, for example, in "The German Ideology" (Marx 1972b), which is articulated in this music, speaking to relations of production and property, to exploitation and the class character of the state responsible for maintaining those relations and suppressing resistance or challenge. It is also classically Marxist in identifying the desired outcome of popular revolution as socialist, even when the music is not so explicit. This is not surprising, as a social discourse which gives a class name to domestic and international enemies, which attributes underdevelopment, dictatorship, and state terror to capitalism, and which assigns to "the popular classes" national historic agendas that the national bourgeoisie is deemed incapable of carrying out, is likely to identify the overarching goal of those popular classes as socialism.

The music locates suffering in the popular classes and connects that suffering to class domination, that is to the unequal structure of property ownership and access to means of production; to the lack of worker's rights and protections; repression of labor organization; to outright forceful appropriation of peasant property for large capitalist farming, and so on. To be "poor and humble" is to be "exploited, peasant, worker" ("Pajarito de la paz" [The little bird of peace], Norma Elena Gadea 1985). It is the Guatemalan highlands Maya peoples "in [peasant] rubber boots," who are the pueblo and the guerrilla fighters in Kin-Lalat's song "Amante Alzado" (My insurgent lover) (*Florecerás Guatemala*). Luis Enrique Mejía Godoy, in "Venancia," recounts how the campesina woman Venancia became a guerrilla fighter after the Nicaraguan National Guard killed her companion "because he was in the union." In "Jacinto," he sings of "María, who shapes tortillas of hope . . . her hands protested the misery of the *rancho* [working for a cruel landlord]," and in "Abajo," returns to the nineteenth century and sings of "the suffering Indian . . . mistreated by the landlord . . . without letters and speech, barefoot and hungry for liberty"(*Del 70 al 80*). For Banda Tepehuani, two main classes, equally exploited by capital and repressed by the oligarchy's state (and by imperialism, by extension) are the protagonists of revolutionary struggle: the peasantry and the workers. Tepehuani points to land reform and worker control of enterprises as their goals in "Llegaremos" (We will get there) (*El Zamaquión* 1988).[18] And when government conscript soldiers become aware of their class identity and allegiance, it shall be "soldiers on our side, with workers, peasants and students," musically and politically aligned with the revolutionary *cumbia* music of "El Zamaquión" (*El Zamaquión*).

Most Central American revolutionary music groups, of course, went beyond class characterizations of the suffering pueblo to laud the worker and peasant origins of specific guerrilla fighters and give a class character to the goals of the struggle, that is a revolutionary socialist society controlled by workers and peasants. In the FMLN's zones of control, such as Morazán or Chalatenango, revolutionary production not only to support the fighters, but also to manifest a revolutionary culture of work, was an objective of the musicians, their concerts in those zones and the clandestine radio broadcasts of their music. In "Producción de Guerra" (War production), Yolocamba Ita plays in a *típica* musical idiom, like a campesino musical group, about producing food for the popular revolutionary army: "Let's ready the plows and machetes, let's prepare the ground for planting, for our liberation . . . here everybody is learning to be organized . . . isn't it great to feel this and be able to work [army sweeps and bombing disrupted much of Salvador's agriculture during the war] . . . we're sowing a delicious revolution" (*Canto a la patria revolucionaria*).

And there was high praise for those who aligned themselves with the two main protagonist classes. The young Nicaraguan student and guerrilla fighter Luisa Amanda Espinoza, killed by government troops early in the 1970s and for whom the Sandinista women's organization was named, had "your girl's heart made grand by the patria . . . the hope of campesinos in your hands" (Norma Elena Gadea, 1985). In the lush, slow tune "Despertar" (Awakening), Banda Tepehuani pays tribute to a guerrilla fighter who "saw injustices before my very eyes . . . strikes and curfews . . . I felt one with my brothers" (*El Zamaquión*). Yolocamba Ita sings of Sister Silvia, a nun who worked as a nurse with wounded FMLN fighters, eventually taking up arms and dying in combat: "You gave your fresh and vigorous blood to your beaten and hungry people . . . your soft nurse's hands grew with the Gospel and you grasped the liberating arms in this holy war of the poor" (*Canto a la patria revolucionaria*). Taking listeners to the loneliness and terror of a political prisoner in the Somoza dictatorship's filthy cells, Pancasán's "Canción para un reo político" (Song for a political prisoner) reassures: "in the small hours of your moaning, torture embracing you, workers and peasants sustain you" (*Haciendo la historia*).

Unity of the Pueblo, Support for the Vanguard

While the main class protagonists of the pueblo, in virtually all of Central American revolutionary music, are the workers and peasants, the category of pueblo is inclusive. The urban poor, those employed in petty commerce and

services, the small rural producer, and the rural landless who are not technically proletarian clearly belong to the pueblo. The Sandinista government
spoke of a proportion of the larger capitalist farmers and industrialists as
"patriotic producers."[19] The crucial role of faith communities, especially the
liberation theology current within the Catholic Church, helped make the mul-
ticlass and multi-identity coalitions that gave Central American revolutionary
movements and organizations some unique characteristics. Yolocamba Ita's
"Homenaje a Monsignor [Oscar] Romero" (*Canto a la patria revolucionaria*) is but one recognition of that role, which helped bring literally millions of Central Americans to radical social consciousness. Guatemala's
ethnocultural and linguistic realities[20] made Maya identity a problem for
stricter Marxist doctrines of class issues above all others, but increasingly
focused the attention of revolutionary organizations under the umbrella of
the URNG (Guatemalan National Revolutionary Union) in the 1980s.

Revolutionary music spoke to the reality of disparate social and organizational forces in promoting unity and support of the vanguard, in both a
sociocultural and an ideological sense. In other words, commitment to and
consciousness of the pueblo, including the idea that campesinos and workers
were the two central classes, would qualify anyone for inclusion, no matter
what their class background or position. Students, professionals, clergy,
intellectuals, artists, artisans, small merchants, the "middle class," and here
and there genuinely bourgeois individuals were all present in the popular
mass organizations, in revolutionary organizations and in guerrilla forces.
Rarely, revolutionary music's social discourses articulated a specifically feminist inclusion of women in the pueblo, though individual women martyred in
the struggle received considerable attention.

Musical groups affiliated with specific organizations, and many of the
best-known groups were so affiliated, certainly conveyed symbolic messages
to militants and factions on the need for unity. But they also produced messages cast more broadly to the pueblo on the generic necessity for unity
among revolutionary organizations and for popular unity against the enemy:
"town and country, *barrio* and factory . . . everybody get ready to fight"
(Pancasán 1981); "this thing has gotten really serious . . . enough already,
let's put an end to this shit . . . it's insurrection time" (Tepehuani 1988). Yolocamba Ita, in "El Casor'o de los Compas" ("The multiple wedding of the
Compañeros"), conveys the image of campesinos from different organizations coming together in marriage and in revolutionary unity. And in its fable
"El Baile de los animales" (The animals' ball), the animals, representing different organizations, get together to rid themselves of the oppressor gorillas
(the military), the mean pigs (the oligarchy) and the brutal donkey (U.S.
imperialism): "and so ends this song, which has taught us quite a lesson: if
the animal kingdom can organize, why can't we do the same?"(*Canto a la
patria revolucionaria*). Banda Tepehuani's very album title, *Por la paz, El*

Salvador vencerá (With peace, El Salvador will win) captures the same spirit: it is the pueblo and the patria for whom the struggle is waged.

Spirit is not sufficient; organization, unity, and discipline are required. That is the social discourse of revolutionary music at critical points in the struggle.[21] Kin Lalat's "Canción de la unidad" equates pueblo, organization, and unity, and their hymn to fallen 1960s guerrilla commander and ex-military officer Turcios Lima pointedly notes that he "carried the unitary and liberatory flag" (*Florecerás Guatemala*). Deep into the war against the U.S.-backed Contras, Nicaraguan musicians at the seventh anniversary of the 1979 Sandinista triumph sang "Seguimos de frente con el Frente," a wordplay in Spanish: "We keep up front with the [FSLN] Front." And in "Vamos a la plaza" (Let's all go to the plaza), they urge the pueblo to "celebrate the victory's anniversary; it's a fiesta *and* a responsibility . . . if you're with Sandino, yesterday, tomorrow and forever, you're with the Frente." Responsibility means defense of the revolution: "all arms to the people!" (Various Nicaraguan Groups 1986). In the same vein, Pancasán (1983) links the broad anti-Somoza coalition of the pueblo to the patria and both to the vanguard party, the FSLN: "For the *Patria*, it is our victory, our hope, our dawn. In order to fight, to win, to build, to live . . . to the battle . . . we are millions with the vanguard . . . we demand it for the *patria*." Pancasán's song "Pueblo, ejército, unidad: garantia de la Victoria" (Pueblo, army, unity: The guarantee of the victory) (1981), which spoke to the immediate period after the 1979 victory, was echoed in the FSLN poster slogan of the mid-1980s "One single army in defense and production."

Morale, Mística, and Martyrology

This music's homage to those fallen in the struggle, particularly to the martyrs of the contemporary revolutionary generation, is a natural lament and mourning for the dead which any people, family, or individual would feel and express. As a social discourse, the remembrance, naming, and exaltation of those whose died in the struggle moves into the realm of sacrifice and martyrdom. The music seeks to honor and socialize those sacrifices, to make those martyred a crucial part of the mística and revolutionary morale of both vanguard and pueblo. It links their actions and sacrifices to the goals of the struggle, not just in terms of military victory over the oppressor or the aggressor, but to the expected works and achievements of the revolution in power: democracy, freedom, justice, equality, development, education, health, housing, employment, culture, social services. The mística of those who continue the struggle and the achievements of the struggle are considered the legacy of the fallen heroes and martyrs. At the deepest levels of symbolic discourse, the deaths of martyrs are transcended. They live in the morale and works of the revolution and the revolutionaries. They incarnate *pueblo* and *patria*, symbolically endowing them with popular identity.

It could be argued, and certainly can be the impression for a visitor to Central America, that death is culturally more present than in some of the world's wealthier societies. A socioeconomic and cultural environment that social science quite recently would have termed "underdeveloped" objectively experiences more deaths per population, at earlier ages, as a result of poverty, disease, and marginalization. There is, then, likely to be a popular death trope, as it were, a certain familiarity and informality with death in cultural expression: language, music, literature, art, religion. That trope is imported easily into the social discourses of revolutionary music and gives some surrounding cultural shape and substance to the music's treatment of fallen heroes and martyrs. The music validates and enhances the meaning and symbolic significance of their deaths and of death itself.

Historical continuity and temporal cyclicity are evident in Central American revolutionary music's treatment of martyrdom. The sacrifices of the contemporary revolutionary generation of militants and combatants are linked to those of previous generations and of outstanding national heroic figures, just as they are held up as examples for their surviving comrades and those generations to come. Sandino is told, in Pancasán's "Requiem a la muerte" (Requiem for death) that he lives "forever in your awakened people and the revolution" (*Vamos haciendo la historia*). Carlos Fonseca, martyred leader of the FSLN during the hard years of guerrilla struggle, is exalted in the anthem by Carlos Mejía Godoy and Tomás Borge "Comandante Carlos Fonseca," which every Sandinista militant and much of the country could sing by heart in the 1980s: "you defeated death . . . a bullet found your stubborn saint's heart and spilled your blood into our lives . . . and when the traitors and cowards are but a footnote of an old history, coming generations of the free and luminous Nicaragua will eternally remember you, firing auroras from your carbine" (Frente Sandinista de Liberación Nacional 1979). The "Hymn of Sandinista Unity," also almost universally known in Nicaragua in the 1980s, declares that "the children of Sandino neither sell out nor surrender . . . a new sun will illuminate the whole land which our martyrs and heroes gave us, a land of strong rivers of milk and honey" (Frente Sandinista de Liberación Nacional).

Fallen comrades in current struggles are equally exalted, whether they are specifically named in the music or not. Kin Lalat sings of Guatemala's flowering from "every drop of blood, every tear shed . . . every piece of torn skin, every bullet . . . it's blood that nourishes the cry of freedom" (*Florecerás Guatemala*). The history of the patria, both before and currently, the Salvadorean group Cutumay Camones sings, "is made with the blood of thousands of massacred brothers and sisters" (cited in Almeida and Urbizagástegui 1999: 22). Scores of songs seal the martyrdom of individuals and of the nameless: "from north to south, from sea to sea . . . they sowed the sun . . . life is the harvest of the revolution" ("Canto Final" [Final Song], Various

Nicaraguan Groups, 1986). Some, like assassinated Salvadorean Archbishop Oscar Romero or the Jesuit priests killed by army troops in their dwellings at the University of Central America campus in San Salvador, are very well-known symbols, people who took the side of the pueblo (Romero said: "I am at the service of the organizations of the people") and were killed for it. Father Gaspar García, a Spanish priest who joined the armed struggle in Nicaragua, is celebrated for his internationalism, solidarity, and commitment to the pueblo: "He changed his parish robes and the confessional for the mountains and the gospel of a revolutionary rifle" (Frente Sandinista de Liberación Nacional). His sacrifice is seen as a victory over death: "He knew that death arrives unannounced, but death is a seed when there is a pueblo behind it."

Others, like the 16-year old Salvadorean fighter María Elena Salinas, a "daughter of the people . . . a responsible proletarian," are made examples and are remembered in songs meant for her combatant comrades. To love and honor her, sings Yolocamba Ita (*Canto a la patria revolucionaria*), is to wage "the prolonged war . . . that red love of autumn, your love, announced the springtime of liberation's hopes." And popular musical idioms symbolically identify the popular origins of such martyrs; típica Nicaraguan country music is the idiom in "María Soledad," a working peasant woman who died fighting the Contras (Luis Enrique Mejía Godoy 1986). The music acknowledges the close humanity of martyred combatants, that they have loved ones and that they are loved. The tender love duet "Si me quitan tu flor" (If they take your flower from me) by Norma Elena Gadea and Luis Enrique Mejía Godoy (Norma Elena Gadea 1985) captures the sacrifice of guerrilla lovers who know the risks combatants take. In Norma Elena Gadea's "Te quiero más" (I love you more), from the same album, the lover says "I know I'm not the only love in your life . . . but in pain, in love . . . I love you/share you with my pueblo."

Musically expressed martyrdom arises as mourning and celebration for the life and significance of the fallen and symbolically embraces the martyred in the bosom of the pueblo. As revolutionary social discourse, such a theme is directed to the reinforcement of morale and mística. It encourages militants, combatants, and the pueblo not to weaken, to be more determined, to be inspired. Guerrilla life and underground struggle are not easy, and developing morale and mística is a crucial element.[22] Just as "Sandino fell . . . in order to grow" ("Cantame Nicaragua" [Sing to me, Nicaragua], Banda Tepehuani 1982), the martyrdom of contemporary heroes, as well at the pueblo's suffering and hopes, should make one "happy to be a *guerrillero*, fighting for the pueblo, running off the tyranny" ("Cumbia de mi tierra" [Cumbia of my land], *El Zamaquión*). The pueblo should honor the martyrs by waging "the people's war" (Kin Lalat), "laying ambushes against the army, explosives for their trucks, taking care of business . . . ," just as musicians should wield their guitars "like a machine gun" and the Maya, the "enslaved Indian, illiterate and screwed over . . . [should] rise up to free-dom," while guerrilla fighter-lovers know that "our love will be present in the pueblo; if we die, we shall be together in a thought and a song."

Such morale in music is "food, light and encouragement in the difficult hours, remembering fallen brothers . . . it's a stone to smash the enemy" (FSLN Comandante Carlos Nuñez, liner notes, Pancasán 1981). It prepares people to follow the example of the martyred, like Arlen Siu- "*la chinita*[23] fought to the very end" (Norma Elena Gadea, 1985). The pueblo has to emu-late their grit: "Like a lioness I will defend this land and my cubs . . . they [the Contra] shall not pass . . . we'll defeat these criminal hordes" ("No pasarán"[24] [They Shall Not Pass], Norma Elena Gadea, 1985). For the fallen comrades, revolutionary musicians deploy "this song as a shot . . . guitar, ready, aim, fire and sing . . . a song of love for my brothers and hatred for the enemy . . . firing at the heart of imperialism."

Such music and its martyrology readies people for revolutionary vio-lence, as Luis Enrique Mejía Godoy tenderly acknowledges in "Para amar en tiempo de Guerra" (To love in wartime): "We'll have to kill, but our motive is love" (Luis Enrique Mejía Godoy 1992). The music of mística does not have to be sober or solemn, either, in respecting the example of martyrs and stim-ulating the morale of the pueblo and combatants. It can be humorous and popular, ironic, sarcastic, and full of slang. It uses dance music and lively campesino rhythms. "This lovely little *chavela* [girl] is four years old," sings Luis Enrique Mejía Godoy in "Todas las armas al pueblo" (All the arms to the people) for the fourth anniversary of the Nicaraguan revolution (Various Nicaraguan Groups, 1986). The Contras "came for salad and we gave them yams [slang for "turds"] . . . come get your song, baby!" And to the strains of jumping Atlantic Coast music we hear that "this pueblo is no idiot . . . you [Contras and imperialists] ain't gettin' your *zumba, macumba!* [won't find your jollies here, dudes!]." Just as much bite is in Banda Tepehuani's "La Pelota" ("The soccer ball," a euphemism for the U.S.-made anti-personnel bombs the Salvadorean military used during the war, and also a slang refer-ence to testicles). To jazzy tempos and a pretty melody, Tepehuani sings that "we *guanacos* [colloquial term for Salvadoreans used all over Central Amer-ica] don't give up . . . you gringos will never know where our blows are com-ing from . . . you want to fight on Guazapa [the volcano], we'll make you dance, we'll send you to the cemetery, we'll break your teeth, we'll take your 'pelota' . . . so take off" (*El Zamaquion*).

Myths, Dreams, the Future, and Revolutionary Works

In "Salsa Nicaragüense" (Various Nicaraguan Groups, *Bienvenidos a Nicaragua Libre* 1982) the singer joyfully proclaims it salsa *pinolero* [*pinolero* is a colloquial term for "Nicaraguan" used throughout Central

America, taken from the popular corn-based Nicaraguan drink *pinole*]. In the next song, the musician is "singing to you [Nicaragua] because I love you." This direct and simple sentiment as revolutionary social discourse is one of triumph, of being able to equate pueblo with patria and patriotism with revolution. The album's music has a generally light-hearted pop feeling (its title is "Welcome to free Nicaragua"), inflected with some popular and folkloric motifs, but the titles bear the sentiment of cherishing and protecting the revolutionary people and homeland: "I sing to you because I love you," "This great love," "My pueblo," and "They shall not pass." Though there is Guatemalan and Salvadorean revolutionary music which expresses such deep love for pueblo and patria, it was only in Nicaragua that the fundamental *mythe* (Sorel) and dream of revolution, that is, of taking state power, was realized. Notwithstanding that revolutionary shortfall, themes based in that dream appear in all three Central American revolutionary musics.[25]

During the struggle, the future is musically expressed, as has been seen, in the metaphors of birds and flowers, in the imagery of happy children and reunited lovers. The metaphors of maternity and birthing lend the revolutionary future some of the strongest lyrical imagery. In "Mujer, mujer" (Woman, woman, Pancasán 1983), the band combines the combative, violent present with the portent of the future: "Made of fire and gunpowder, woman of time and history, you gained your place in history, leading in combat . . . the future is in your womb." Armed struggle and revolutionary violence can be a national and popular birthing: El Salvador, "in your armed struggle you advance to the future" ("El Salvador vencerá," Pancasán 1983). To "love in wartime" (Luis Enrique Mejía Godoy, *Del 70 al 80; Diez Años*) is "to allow our cause to grow in the womb of history."

The reality of revolutionary power is that some things desired during the struggle have been achieved, but also that they must be defended. The Cutumay Camones song "Las Milicias Populares" (The popular militias) names the people's gains from the armed struggle of the FMLN in the "zones of control" in the Chalatenango region of El Salvador: they are defended against the attacks of government forces, they can organize and participate in popular production, education, health care, and culture. The popular militias, "that's us, thousands of men and women in the countryside and the city, we've come from every part of the popular masses to defend the victories of the revolution" (Cutumay Camones, *Por eso luchamos*, 1984, cited in Almeida and Urbizagástegui 1999: 27). Peace has to be won, in such circumstances, by force of arms. In El Salvador, the FMLN in effect fought the government forces, and behind them the United States government, to a stalemate. The FMLN controlled significant portions of national territory, established effective "dual power" in several regions and achieved some international diplomatic status, eventually engaging in UN-sponsored peace negotiations with the reluctant government of El Salvador. To get to that point cost many lives and continuing militancy, as Cutumay Camones high-lighted in the "Peace Cumbia" (*Patria Chiquita mía*, "My little homeland," 1987, cited in Almeida and Urbizagástegui 1999: 28): "Thousands of fists are raised . . . chants are raised because if the issue is peace, the people become gigantic . . . what we want is social justice, all the people await peace with dignity. Dialogue is necessary when there is much to discuss, for we have a war that we want to end. But, one thing, my brother: don't forget that this war is the product of social inequality."

In Nicaragua's case, musicians declared in the cassette *Seguimos de frente en lucha por la paz* (We continue in the struggle for peace, Various Nicaraguan Groups 1986) that "you see, we've grown somewhat . . . now our house is open in this liberated Nicaragua"; at the same time, defense of the state is necessary, but it is a revolutionary and popular defense— "here you see our youth armed with rifles and smiles, smiles we were able to sow among the ashes" (Luis Enrique Mejía Godoy, "Canción de aniversario"). The Cuarteto Segoviano, in "Hay que hacerle güevo" (You gotta make an effort), celebrates the revolution's gains, while reminding listeners that counter revolutionary and external hostile forces require vigilance. With típica campesino music from north-central Nicaragua, the area bordering Honduras and experiencing the bulk of Contra attacks from their bases inside Honduran territory, the Cuarteto urges campesinos to "raise produc-tion . . . while our *cachorros* ["cubs," the affectionate name given young mil-itary conscripts defending the country] defend the revolution" and secure peace.

Some of the most moving expressions of that desired state of affairs are both personal and social; Norma Elena Gadea's ballad "Cuando venga la paz" (When peace comes) articulates the deep-felt desire to have the violence cease, however justified it may be from a revolutionary standpoint. It asks and answers, "What will it be like? What will *we* be like then?" Separated lovers will be reunited; revolutionaries and the pueblo "will sing the old rev-olutionary songs . . . and recall the fallen comrades . . . with the [state] power of workers and peasants" (Norma Elena Gadea 1985). And lovers will have what they wanted for the future, for themselves and for the pueblo: "to live fully . . . in a space of sunlight where death does not fit" ("Para luchar y quer-erte" [To fight and to love you], Luis Enrique Mejía Godoy, *Del 70 al 80: Diez Años*).

With peace, those in exile will come home, enforced separations will be ended in the "dreams of a springtime of equality . . . [and] I will not rest until I find you, along with those who dream of the return home, feeling the deli-cious fever-chill of peace" ("Mariposa" [Butterfly] and "No descansaré" [I won't rest], Banda Tepehuani, *El Zamaquión*). It will be a new society, where "we have cut the distance between human beings" ("Que no se escucha hoy la madrugada" [Today we won't hear the early morning], Luis Enrique Mejía

Godoy, *A pesar de Usted* 1986), because though "implacable in combat [this pueblo] is generous in victory" and former enemies will have a place; there can be reconciliation within popular power. The pueblo has the opportunity to realize its historic capacities: "As my grandfathers dreamed, we'll have a proud and free patria" ("La Herencia" [The heritage], Luis Enrique Mejía Godoy, *Del 70 al 80; Diez Años*); "as you and I dreamed . . . we are going to make a country and . . . our bird of peace will fly" ("Vamos hacer un país" [Let's make a country], *A pesar de Usted*).

The first few years of Sandinista revolutionary power showed what positive popular social energies might be released. Notable and rapid improvements in social conditions, in access to popular health, education, production and culture and in spaces for popular organization to flourish characterized the 1979–1983 period. It was a time of "a new day advancing" ("A pesar de Usted," Luis Enrique Mejía Godoy 1986), when families "had a son [or daughter] on the border [in defense] or picking coffee" and a time when hopes for rapid improvements in life for the peasantry and the urban poor were being met. The social works of the revolution were felt in every part of the country, as the song "Pobrecito mi cipote" (My poor little boy) (Luis Enrique Mejía Godoy 1982) reflected. It recounts the poverty, hunger, ill health, and scarcity of paid work for campesinos, but "the *compañero* [local Sandinista organizer] says all that will change; the revolution is bringing health workers, vaccination teams, the literacy campaign and food." In a mass popular literacy campaign surpassed only by Cuba's of the early 1960s, Nicaragua saw one hundred thousand mostly young people fan out across the whole of the national territory and rapidly reduce illiteracy. Very lively music, created especially for and about the National Literacy Crusade, captures the excitement, the challenges, and the achievements of that remarkable year of 1980 (Various Nicaraguan Groups, *Convirtiendo la oscurana en claridad* 1980). The album's title ("Converting the darkness into clarity" and its song titles tell the story: "Hymn to literacy," "The ABCs," "You got to learn to read," "The *son* of ABC," "The *Corrido* of the literacy brigade," "Let's together leave ignorance behind," "It's never too late to learn, *Compañero*" and "Josefana's going (to alphabetize)."

The motives of revolutionaries in Central America, on the reactive existential level, are not difficult to understand: outrage at suffering and injustice, resistance to oppression and brutality. Within the symbolic realms of patria and pueblo, a deeply emotional identification with the people and homeland collides with the structural and political barriers to patria and pueblo realizing their potential for freedom, sovereignty, dignity, development, and citizenship. Those strongly nationalist and popular objectives of revolutionary commitment and activity coexist relatively easily in Central American experience with the classically Marxist goals of socialism and the "new man." Central American revolutionary music brought imagery and language articulating all those discursive and symbolic elements together in its notes on and to the future.

Concluding Remarks

In assuming Central American revolutionary music to be a mobilizing and sustaining set of social discourses articulated in the specific historical circumstances of the 1970s and 1980s, this chapter has sought to address both context and content. The framework of understanding presented was intended to give context some outlines, but without falling into analytical or theoretical rigidities. Its three dimensions—political economy, political culture, and cultural studies—were considered as elastic, incomplete and hence still useful, themselves hybrids that borrow and receive from each other and from elsewhere in the social sciences. If not so specified in much of the chapter devoted to the music's thematic content, they were nonetheless present in delineating the tropes of that content and exploring their meanings. Those meanings suggest that an expanded and undogmatic, culturally infused Marxist worldview is appropriate for appreciating Central American revolutionary music as social discourse.

Such a worldview situates the music in the structural political economies of uneven and dependent capitalist (mal)development, with their attendant social stresses, their undemocratic, authoritarian, and repressive political regimes of accumulation, and with their fragmenting of (however unequal or unjust) cultures of consent, consensus, and legitimation. It is a worldview that emphasizes the realm of the subjective in seeking the roots of consciousness moving individuals, groups, and masses to a disposition for revolutionary thought and action. In the cultural, political, and social contexts of Central American societies, such a worldview perforce includes categories aside from class, relations of production and property, and social contradictions arising from those relations. Hence, it considers the key tropes of pueblo and patria from a broader perspective. It gains from a cultural studies perspective an appreciation of Central American revolutionary music's origins in and command of the *popular*, in its language and musical forms. From the strand of social science that studies nationalist political cultures, such a worldview can perceive the organic link of patriotism to Central America's revolutionary organizations and ideologies. And from an encounter with Sorel it can assume an existential outlook with respect to this music's martyrology, mística and the death trope. Perhaps most of all, such a worldview can hear the myriad of life, which is the music.

Notes

1. Brazilian guitarist Paulo Bellinati remarked at a concert in Chico, California, in February 1997 that he was researching twenty-two regional music traditions in Brazil, only one of which was represented at that particular concert.
2. See Foran 1997 for a theoretical discussion.

3. Author's translation. Unless otherwise indicated, all translations from the Spanish are the author's.
4. For a discussion of the concept of "regime" as "organized governance experience," see Judson 1999.
5. For an illustration of the political economy approach as it pertains to Central America, see Judson 1987a.
6. A prime Nicaraguan example is found in the work of Orlando Nuñez (1988).
7. Judson 1984 applies Sorel's approach to the Cuban revolution.
8. The term *campesino* includes almost all rural dwellers and is thus more expansive a category than the English word "peasant." Generally, it does not mean "capitalist farmer," in the sense that the English term suggests sizable holdings and regular employment of wage labor, though many *campesinos* with land produce commodities for the market. Throughout Latin America, *campesino* includes the rural landless, seasonal workers, and wage employees.
9. Nicaragua's poet laureate of the decades around the turn of the century.
10. Salvadorean poet of the 1960s and 1970s.
11. Minister of Culture in the Sandinista government, 1979–1990, who founded the peasant artists' and contemplative community of Solentiname and developed the "folk mass" in the 1960s and 1970s.
12. Personal communication to author by Eugenio Andrade, Tepehuani arranger/composer/keyboardist, Managua, 1993.
13. See the personal and poetic *testimonio* for Leonel Rugama and Roque Dalton by Canadian poet Jim Smith (1998).
14. See Burns 1991 for an elaboration of the concept of "folk society" as applied to Nicaragua.
15. There were nine, all of whom occupied high government posts in the 1979–1990 period of Sandinista government.
16. The lines are from the poem "My personal vengeance" by Tomás Borge, one of the FSLN *comandantes*, written to and about the man who tortured him in Somoza's dungeons.
17. In responding to a journalist's question about a possible U.S. invasion force, Cayetano is purported to have answered: "Our country would become a 21,000 km² tomb for the Marines" (Yolocamba Ita 1981).
18. *El Zamaquión* appears to be a rural locale in El Salvador.
19. See the thorough discussion of the Nicaraguan bourgeoisie and Sandinista policies in Ryan 1995, especially pp. 80–90.
20. For merely four informed sources of the hundreds that exist, see Lovell (1995), Noval (1992), Perera (1993) and Bastos and Camus (1993).
21. There are various mappings of these "critical points." See Almeida and Urbizagástegui 1999 for a formulation.
22. See Shaull 1990 and especially Cabezas 1983 and Payeras 1985 for vivid *testimonios* of guerrilla existence. See Diaz 1992 for a *testimonio* about prison and torture.
23. *La chinita*—"the Chinese girl"—visible minority and physical characteristics appear in popular language with much less stigma or social discomfort attached than in "the North."

24. The cry of the legendary Spanish revolutionary "La Pasionaria" during an onslaught of the fascist forces during the 1936–1939 civil war.

25. Such themes could doubtless be found in revolutionary and protest music in the rest of Central America: Panama, Costa Rica, Honduras, and Belize.

References

Almeida, Paul, and Rubén Urbizagástegui. 1999. "Cutumay Camones. Popular Music in El Salvador's National Liberation Movement." *Latin American Perspectives* 26(2): 13–42.

Banda Tepehuani. 1982. LP *Por la paz. El Salvador vencerá* (For peace. El Salvador will win). Managua: ENIGRAC.

———. 1988. Cassette *El Zamaquion*. Managua: ENIGRAC.

Bastos, Santiago, and Manuela Camus. 1993. *Quebrando el silencio. Organizaciones del Pueblo Maya y sus Demandas*. Guatemala: FLACSO.

Bellinati, Paulo. 1993. CD *Serenata. Choros and Waltzes of Brazil*. San Francisco: GSP Recordings.

Berryman, Phillip. 1984. *The Religious Roots of Rebellion. Christians in Central American Revolutions*. Maryknoll, N.Y.: Orbis Books.

Blades, Rubén. 1999. CD *Tiempos*. New York: Sony Music International.

Buena Vista Social Club. 1997. CD *Buena Vista Social Club*. Red Bank, N.J.: World Circuit.

Bulmer-Thomas, Victor. 1987. *The Political Economy of Central America since 1920*. Cambridge: Cambridge University Press.

Burns, E. Bradford. 1991. *Patriarch and Folk. The Emergence of Nicaragua 1798–1858*. Cambridge: Harvard University Press.

Cabezas, Omar. 1982. *La Montaña es algo más que una inmensa estepa verde*. Managua: Editorial Nueva Nicaragua.

Carpentier, Alejandro. 1977. "América Latina en la confluencia de coordenadas históricas y su Repercusión en la musica." In *América Latina en su Música*, edited by Isabel Arets. Mexico: Siglo XXI/UNESCO.

Castañeda, Jorge. 1993. *Utopia Unarmed. The Latin American Left after the Cold War*. New York: Alfred A. Knopf.

Diaz, Nidia. 1988. *Nunca Estuve Sola*. San Salvador: UCA Editores.

Dunkerley, James. 1988. *Power in the Isthmus. A Contemporary History of Central America*. London: Verso.

Foran, John. 1997. "Discourses and Social Forces: The Role of Culture and Cultural Studies in Understanding Revolutions." In *Theorizing Revolutions*, edited by John Foran, 203–26. London: Routledge.

Frente Sandinista de Liberación Nacional. 1979. LP *Guitarra Armada* (Armed guitar). San José: INDICA.

Frith, Simon, ed. 1989. *World Music, Politics, and Social Change*. Manchester: Manchester University Press.

Gadea, Norma Elena. 1985. Cassette *Cuando venga la paz* (When peace comes). Managua: ENIGRAC.

Gramsci, Antonio. 1973. *Selections from the Prison Notebooks of Antonio Gramsci*.

Edited and translated by Quentin Hoare and Geoffrey Nowell Smith. New York: International Publishers.

Hobsbawm, Eric. 1986. "Revolution." In *Revolution in History*, edited by Roy Porter and M. Teich, 5–46. Cambridge: Cambridge University Press.

Judson, Fred. 1984. *Cuba and the Revolutionary Myth. The Political Education of the Cuban Rebel Army 1953–1963*. Boulder, Colo.: Westview Press.

———. 1987a. "Capitalist Crisis, Imperialist Crisis and the Nicaraguan Revolutionary Response." In *Frontyard/Backyard: The Americas in the Global Crisis*, edited by John Holmes and Colin Leys. Toronto: Between the Lines.

———. 1987b. "Sandinista Revolutionary Morale." *Latin American Perspectives* 14(1): 19–42.

———. 1999. "Political Regimes." In *Critical Concepts: An Introduction to Politics*, edited by Janine Brodie, 57–74. Scarborough, Ontario: Prentice-Hall.

Kin Lalat. 1983. Cassette *Florecerás Guatemala* (You will blossom, Guatemala). Amsterdam: KKLA.

Kirk, John. 1984. "Revolutionary Music Salvadorean Style: Yolocamba Ita." *Literature and Contemporary Revolutionary Culture* 1: 338–52.

Liss, Sheldon. 1991. *Radical Thought in Central America*. Boulder, Colo.: Westview Press.

Lovell, W. George. 1995. *A Beauty that Hurts. Life and Death in Guatemala*. Toronto: Between the Lines.

Mancotal. 1981. LP *Un Son para mi pueblo* (A *Son* for my people) Managua: ENIGRAC.

Marx, Karl. 1972a. "The 18th Brumaire of Louis Napoleon." In *The Marx-Engels Reader*, edited by Robert Tucker. New York: Norton.

———. 1972b. "The German Ideology." In *The Marx-Engels Reader*, edited by Robert Tucker. NewYork: Norton.

Mejía Godoy, Carlos. 1977. LP *Misa Campesina Nicaragüense* (Nicaraguan peasant mass). San José: INDICA.

Mejía Godoy, Carlos, and Los de Palacagüina. 1980. LP *Monimbó*. San José: INDICA.

Mejía Godoy, Luis Enrique. 1982. Cassette *Yo soy de un pueblo sencillo* (I am from a simple people). Managua: ENIGRAC.

———. 1986. Cassette *A pesar de Usted* (In spite of you). Managua: ENIGRAC.

———. 1992. Cassette *Del 70 al 80; Diez Años*. San José: Sony Music.

Mellers, Wilfrid, and Pete Martin. 1989. Preface. In *World Music, Politics, and Social Change*, edited by Simon Frith, vii–x. Manchester: Manchester University Press.

Moore, Barrington, Jr. 1966. *The Social Origins of Democracy and Dictatorship: Lord and Peasant in the Making of the Modern World*. Boston: Beacon Press.

Noval, Joaquín. 1992. *Resumen Etnográfico de Guatemala*. Guatemala: Editorial Piedra Santa.

Nuñez, Orlando S. 1988. *La Insurrección de la conciencia*. Managua: Editorial de la Escuela de Sociología de la Universidad Centroamericana.

Pancasán. 1979. LP *Grupo Pancasán*. San José: INDICA.

———. 1981. LP *Vamos haciendo la historia* (We are making history). Managua: ENIGRAC.

———. 1983. Cassette *Por la Patria* (For the homeland). Managua: ENIGRAC.

Parra, Isabel. 1985. *El Libro mayor de Violeta Parra*. Madrid: Ediciones Michay.

Payeras, Mario. 1985. *Days of the Jungle*. New York: Monthly Review Press.

Perera, Victor. 1993. *Unfinished Conquest. The Guatemalan Tragedy*. Berkeley: University of California Press.

Pino-Robles, Rodolfo. 1999. "Music and Social Change in Argentina and Chile: 1950–1980 and Beyond." Unpublished conference paper, Canadian Association of Latin American and Caribbean Studies Conference, Ottawa, Canada, October, 15 ms. pp.

Randall, Margaret. 1984. *Christians in the Nicaraguan Revolution*. Translated by Mariana Valverde. Vancouver: New Star Books.

Rodrigues, Virginia. 2000. CD *Nós*. New York: Natasha Records.

Ryan, Phil. 1995. *The Fall and Rise of the Market in Sandinista Nicaragua*. Montreal: McGill-Queen's University Press.

Skocpol, Theda. 1979. *States and Social Revolutions*. Chicago: University of Chicago Press.

Shaull, Wendy. 1990. *Tortillas, Beans, and M-16s. A Year with the Guerrillas in El Salvador*. London: Pluto Press.

Smith, Jim. 1998. *Leonel/Roque*. Toronto: Coteau Books.

Snow, David, and Robert Benford. 1988. "Ideology, frame resonance, and participant Mobilization." *International Social Movement Research* 1: 197–217.

Tilly, Charles. 1978. *From Mobilization to Revolution*. Reading, Mass.: Addison-Wesley.

Vanden, Harry. 1986. *National Marxism in Latin America. José Carlos Mariátegui's Thought and Politics*. Boulder, Colo.: Lynne Rienner.

Various Authors. 1999. CD *Música Negra del Perú*. Lima: Producciones IEMPSA.

Various Groups. 1982. LP *1er Festival Nuevo Canto Latinoamericano. Version Urgente para Nicaragua*. Managua: ENIGRAC.

Various Nicaraguan Groups. 1980. LP *Convirtiendo la oscurana en claridad* (Converting the darkness into clarity) Managua: ENIGRAC.

Various Nicaraguan Groups. 1982. Cassette *Bienvenido a Nicaragua Libre* (Welcome to free Nicaragua). Managua: ENIGRAC.

Various Nicaraguan Groups. 1986. Cassette *Seguimos de frente en lucha por la paz* (Let's continue forward in the struggle for peace). Managua: ENIGRAC.

Vilas, Carlos. 1995. *Between Earthquakes and Volcanoes. Market, State, and Revolutions in Central America*. Translated by Ted Kuster. New York: Monthly Review Press.

Yolocamba Ita. 1981. LP *Canto a la patria revolucionaria* (Song to the revolutionary homeland). Vancouver: Goldrush Studios.

[5]

Ska and the Roots of
Rastafarian Musical Protest

Stephen A. King

To the casual listener, "ska" may appear to be nothing more than some form of speedy and spirited reggae. This is not entirely inaccurate. Ska is actually the pop-based precursor to reggae.

—Dale Turner

By the late 1950s, a newfound optimism permeated Jamaica's warm tropical breezes. In a country with a history of slavery, institutionalized racism, class disparity, and economic dependence, this optimism appeared justified, at least at first glance. Despite its troubled past, Jamaica over the next few years would gain its national independence and experience an economic boom lasting until the late 1960s. The leaders of one of Jamaica's leading political parties, the Jamaica Labour Party (JLP), were excited by the prospect of independence. Yet they also realized the island was experiencing a host of sociopolitical problems, from overcrowding to crime. While the government launched a vigorous national campaign to stress Jamaica's transition to independence as a positive, uplifting event, "[n]epotism, vio-

Roots of Rastafarian Musical Protest

lence and political victimisation came to characterise the transition from colonialism to neo-colonialism" (Campbell, "Rastafari" 10).

These political tensions coincided with the emergence of a new musical form known as ska. Ska was a mixture of mento, a Jamaican indigenous musical form, American jazz, and rhythm and blues.[1] On the surface, ska was a happy, content—even cheery—music. But if one listened closely between the polyrhythmic pulses of the music, ska was as deceptive as the government's attempt to paint the country with a color-blind palette of national unity. Ska may have sounded happy, but it also expressed a musical angst rooted in the tenement houses and yards of West Kingston, a dilapidated area of open sewers, rampant unemployment, and rival political gangs.

Despite the fact some ska songs were routinely banned from Jamaican radio stations, popular critics and music scholars generally have failed to appreciate their protest message. Erna Brodber, an observer of Jamaican music, has contended that Jamaican ska was not a medium of protest, claiming that most of the songs spoke of "morals and with love" and were little more than "re-issues of folk songs" ("Black Consciousness" 59). Writing in *The Black Scholar*, Patrick Hylton agreed that early ska songs were primarily love songs (27). In the same vein, other scholars have claimed that the music's lyrics "tended to be light, [and] were generally about love and lovemaking" (Alleyne 118), concluding that ska closely resembled a Caribbean music known as calypso (Winders 68). Jamaican native and longtime observer of Jamaican music, Pamela O'Gorman, has dismissed ska as little more than a "regional variant of a broad U.S. style, namely rhythm and blues" (86).

As Jamaica's leading popular music historian, Garth White, has observed, however, "critical social commentary and protest were in ska almost from its inception" ("Mento" 39). Although few observers have acknowledged ska's protest themes, ska actually represented the first form of a popular protest music, albeit a "mild" protest against social and political conditions in Jamaica. Ska songs suggested more a politics of passive suffering rather than active resistance. Yet, ska played a significant role in creating a musical "community" of both Rastafarians and those sympathetic to the movement, and it gave early expression to the Rastafarian's social and

Roots of Rastafarian Musical Protest

political ideology. Lyrically, ska promoted Rastafarian ideology through faint themes of repatriation and the introduction of the term "Mount Zion," the Rastafarian's heaven in Africa. Instrumentally, the ska song "Oh Carolina" featured Rastafarian drumming, and even the instrumental songs bore titles such as "Another Moses" and "Babylon Gone," highlighting the movement's belief in the divinity of Ethiopian emperor Haile Selassie and the hope for deliverance from oppression, or "Babylon." With the advent of ska, Rastafarians thus began to explore a new mode of political expression, popular music, with far more reach than their traditional outlets: street preaching, church sermons, pamphlets, and word of mouth within Rastafarian communes.[2] In the end, ska portended the development of popular music as the chief communicative medium of the Rastafarian movement.

JAMAICA: FROM COLONIALISM TO INDEPENDENCE

Following the arrival of Columbus in 1494, Jamaica became one of many Caribbean countries to be colonialized by European powers. From 1494 to 1655, the Spanish nearly extinguished Jamaica's indigenous population, the Arawak Indians, while plundering the island for silver and gold. When the English became Jamaica's new colonial rulers in 1655, they brought another source of forced labor, the West African slave. By the end of the seventeenth century, African slaves were being brought to Jamaica in increasing numbers to cultivate the vast fields of sugar cane. Even after the end of slavery in 1834, Jamaica continued to be under the thumb of British colonial rule, supporting a small white planter class and a large peasantry consisting mostly of former slaves. The white planter class denied the peasants' independence by restricting the sale of land. Since most of the peasants could not obtain land, they were forced to work for the white planter class, subject to deplorable working conditions and cheap wages, as low as a penny a day (Beckford and Witter 40–1).

In 1938, a national workers' strike set in motion a series of events that led ultimately to Jamaica's independence in 1962. Rural sugar and banana

Roots of Rastafarian Musical Protest

workers and urban dockworkers rebelled against low wages and demanded improved working conditions. During the national strike, several were killed, hundreds were injured, and many others were jailed for their participation in the rebellion (Post 276–84).

To pacify the enraged workers, the British Crown established a Royal Commission, led by Lord Moyne, to investigate the workers' demands (Beckford and Witter 62). The Moyne Commission established several new policies, including steps to establish representative self-government in Jamaica. Meanwhile, Jamaica's colonial office conceded to the leaders who voiced the workers' grievances against the colonial state, Alexander Bustamante and Norman Washington Manley (Beckford and Witter 61). In 1938, Manley became the leader of Jamaica's first mass political party, the People's National Party (PNP), and Bustamante assumed the leadership of one of Jamaica's first organized labor unions, the Bustamante Industrial Trade Union (BITU).

In 1942, Manley and Bustamante disagreed over the PNP's political role in Jamaica. Manley envisioned the PNP's mission as seeking Jamaica's constitutional independence, while Bustamante's interests were to "secure the new relationship of direct bargaining of the laboring class with the ruling class" (A. Brown, *Color, Class, and Politics* 103). Tension between the two leaders became so great that Bustamante left the PNP and used his BITU to launch Jamaica's second political party, the Jamaica Labour Party in 1943.

Following the split, the relationship between the two parties remained tense; the conflict often moved from simmering hostility to open warfare. The PNP was considered "left wing," sponsoring economic and social reform, a high profile in international affairs and, at times, a socialist government. The JLP, in contrast, was described as a "right-wing" party maintaining a conservative ideology that favored capitalism, free enterprise, and a close link with western countries.[3] A number of rival political parties, including the People's Political Party (PPP), never achieved much success in Jamaica. Led by Barrister Millard Johnson, the PPP was a socialist party that ran political advertisements in Jamaica's national newspaper, the *Daily Gleaner*, advocating the redistribution of wealth, eradication of racial discrimination, and developing economic and social ties to Africa (B. Johnson 25).

Roots of Rastafarian Musical Protest

From 1944 to 1962, Jamaica's political leaders and the British Crown worked on a plan for Jamaica's full independence. In 1944, the British Crown signed into law a new Constitution, granting Jamaica Universal Adult Suffrage (Beckford and Witter 62). Ultimate authority for Jamaica's internal and external affairs still rested with the governor-general who represented the British monarchy in Jamaica. By 1957, however, Britain began to undertake serious steps to relinquish control of Jamaica because of the financial burden the Caribbean colony placed on British taxpayers (Panton 26). In 1957, the PNP implemented a Cabinet government that enabled the Jamaican government to play a more influential role in determining the nation's economic policies (Panton 26). Two years later, the PNP established Jamaica's first fully autonomous government (Panton 26). This new arrangement allowed the prime minister to assume full responsibility for all internal affairs and reduced England's authority in Jamaica to issues of foreign policy. On August 6, 1962, Jamaica finally secured full constitutional independence and became an independent parliamentary state within the British commonwealth. While the governor-general still remained officially head of the state, his role was now reduced to appearing at ceremonial events. The prime minister and his Cabinet government now had full executive power to make policy decisions in domestic and international affairs.

Less than four months before Jamaica became a sovereign nation, Manley and the PNP were voted out of office, and the JLP's Alexander Bustamante became prime minister. Bustamante presided over a remarkable economic resurgence which occurred prior to and following independence. From 1950 to 1968, Jamaica's gross domestic product (GDP), adjusted for inflation, increased 6.7 percent (Kuper 17). In 1960, the unemployment figure dipped to 13.5 percent, one of the lowest unemployment rates on record (Boyd 8–9). In addition, between 1956 and 1967, Jamaica's manufacturing sector expanded as Jamaican entrepreneurs profited from an assortment of exports, including furniture, garments, and footwear (Stone, "Power, Policy and Politics" 27). Jamaica also continued to be one of the world's leading exporters of bauxite. The Jamaican government encouraged American and Canadian companies to invest in Jamaican bauxite; bauxite continued to be

Roots of Rastafarian Musical Protest

Jamaica's chief export for the next decade. As economist Derick Boyd has summarized: "The decades of the fifties and sixties were, in the main, good years for the Jamaican economy" (5).

While workers mined the "unlimited" deposits of bauxite in the hills of Jamaica, the Jamaican government also began to develop an equally appealing, less physically demanding "gold mine." In order to catch the eye of the wealthy foreign traveler, the Jamaican government actively encouraged foreign investors to expand the tourist industry on Jamaica's north coast. The sunny attractions, including Negril, Montego Bay, and Ocho Rios, sprouted new resort hotels, airport runways, and private beaches.

As foreign visitors celebrated their new tropical escape, the JLP continued to face both old and new social and political problems. There are at least four factors that plagued Jamaica as it made the transition from a British colony to an independent nation. First, Jamaica became even more economically dependent on foreign powers. The JLP and the PNP strived to emulate the "Puerto Rican Model" to create a "new" Jamaica. The effort to emulate this model, nicknamed "Operation Bootstrap," encouraged foreign investors to establish manufacturing activities in Jamaica. By 1962, Jamaica's economy was heavily tied to foreign investors, with dramatic increases in exports to Britain, the United States, Canada, and Japan. Jamaica's dependence on foreign countries turned the island into a "peripheral attachment to the international capitalist system" (Beckford and Witter 79). In the case of bauxite, for example, Jamaica possessed the raw materials but did not possess the management and technological resources. In effect, Jamaica lacked the means of processing raw materials, such as bauxite and sugar. Because Jamaica depended on foreign powers for production, the island suffered from trade deficits, high interest rates, and high fees charged for technological and management services (Beckford and Witter 79).

Second, multinational corporations continued the process of purchasing Jamaica's rural land. American and Canadian companies had taken over control of the bulk of the bauxite industry, and these multinational companies often drove small farmers from the rural areas of Jamaica's parishes,

Roots of Rastafarian Musical Protest

including St. Ann and St. Elizabeth (Campbell, *Rasta* 93). Between 1943 and 1970, according to Campbell, 560,000 rural inhabitants were displaced from Jamaica's countryside (*Rasta* 86). As these multinational corporations purchased the farms to mine for bauxite, Jamaica's agricultural output dropped steadily, and Jamaicans began to rely more and more on imported food products.

Third, because of the land seizures and Britain's 1962 immigration law that severely restricted Jamaicans from migrating to England, thousands migrated to Kingston, Jamaica's capital city. There they suffered from unemployment, food shortages, and a high infant mortality rate. Many who could not find work turned to hustling, prostitution, and crime. In the slums, food shortages and disease played a significant role in a high death rate for children under four years of age. The *Life Tables for British Caribbean Countries* indicated that, from 1959 to 1961, 5,980 out of 100,000 infant males died during their first year of life (32). This was the highest death rate of all age groups in Jamaica.

Fourth, with the increasing migration of the populous to the city, Jamaica experienced a severe housing shortage. Although Jamaica's *Town Planning Department Report* in 1961 stressed a need to redevelop some of Kingston's poorer suburbs, including Trench Town and Kingston Pen, the commission was unable to make any substantial changes in these areas, building very few domiciles (3). For the very poor who could not rent a single-story tenement or a small apartment in a government housing project, squatting on government land became a matter of survival (Clarke 234). As the need for housing increased and the available housing slowly turned into crumbling tenements, middle-class Jamaicans built new houses in the Kingston Heights. Soon, Kingston visibly displayed the contrast between the rich and poor, as "mansions climbed up the hillsides while ghettoes spawned along Spanish Town Road" (Beckford and Witter 74). The increasing economic disparity between the middle and upper classes and those crowded in the urban ghettos made Jamaica's national motto, "Out of Many, One People," seem more and more an empty slogan.

9

Roots of Rastafarian Musical Protest

THE RASTAFARIAN MOVEMENT: "CULT OF OUTCASTS"

During the 1950s, the Rastafarians were viewed by many in Jamaica as bearded drug addicts, a national eyesore, or a "cult of outcasts" (Patterson, "Ras Tafari" 15). The *Daily Gleaner* reported frequent clashes between Rastafarians and police, and the work of sociologist George E. Simpson confirmed the stereotype of the Rastafarians as black racists who wanted to rule over the white man (134–5). While the Rastafarian movement did indeed promote racial pride, the movement in reality posed little threat to Jamaica's ruling class. Largely lower class, politically passive, and nonviolent, most Rastafarians were committed only to repatriating members to Africa and to worshiping the divinity of Haile Selassie.[4] For the most part, Rastafarians avoided the political world, preferring meditation and prayer.

At the same time, however, the Rastafarian movement had developed a language of protest that later became prominent in Jamaica's popular music. The first of three terms important to understanding this emerging political consciousness was "Babylon," a term borrowed from the Bible but given unique meanings by the Rastafarian movement. In studying the Old Testament, the Rastafarians had "identified the Black Jamaicans as the chosen people of which the Bible spoke. In the bondage and oppression of the Hebrews in Egypt, they saw their own bondage and oppression in this latter day Babylon [Jamaica]" (Beckford and Witter 76). Since this biblical interpretation became common among Rastafarians, the term Babylon has been applied to a variety of entities that Rastafarians consider oppressive. Rastafarians have used the term Babylon to refer to the Jamaican government, the police, the Christian church, and western culture in general (Davis and Simon, "A Rasta Glossary" 69). Babylon has come to be associated with any symbol of oppression, as well as with any person who intentionally hurts others out of personal greed or prejudice (Gibson 25).

A second term that developed unique and special meanings within the Rastafarian movement was "Jah." In Rastafarian culture, "Jah" referred to former Ethiopian emperor Haile Selassie. In 1929, Jamaican black nation-

Roots of Rastafarian Musical Protest

alist Marcus Garvey's fictional play, *The Coronation of the King and Queen of Africa,* spotlighted the crowning of an African king. In 1930, when Ras Tafari Makonnen, the great grandson of King Sahela Selassie of Shoa, was crowned emperor of Ethiopia (and renamed Haile Selassie I), many Jamaicans were convinced that he was literally the "King of Kings," the living black messiah. Many Rastafarians believed Selassie's status as a deity was a rejection of the white Christian church. The living black messiah reject-ed both the Bible's portrait of Jesus Christ as white and the story of his death. For the Rastafarians, "Jah" was a "symbol of resistance" to the white church (Beckford and Witter 76).

The third protest term with unique significance in the Rastafarian movement was "Mount Zion." Lamenting their own captivity in Jamaica, Rastafarians consulted their Bibles and identified their suffering with the plight of the Jews in the Bible. Consequently, Zion was torn from its biblical context and came to express the Rastafarians' hope for repatriation to Africa. Through the Rastafarian lens, Mount Zion moved from Israel to Africa. Rastafarians rejected the traditional Christian interpretation that heaven was a spiritual place "in the sky" and promoted the belief that Mount Zion was, literally, a "heaven on earth."

In the late 1950s and early 1960s, the Rastafarian movement actively began to seek repatriation to Mount Zion in Africa. In 1959, a self-declared Rastafarian "prophet," Claudius Henry, sold fifteen thousand tickets to Rastafarians and other poor Jamaicans promising repatriation back to Ethiopia on October 5 (Smith, Augier, and Nettleford 16). Many abandoned their homes, sold their belongings, and traveled long distances to the port in Kingston where Henry promised that a ship would be waiting. The tickets even included a written promise that "[n]o passport will be necessary for those returning home to Africa" (Smith, Augier, and Nettleford 16). After Henry could not deliver on his promise of repatriation, he was jailed and fined for disturbing the peace.

The arrest of Claudius Henry only served to confirm what many had already thought about the Rastafarian movement—that they were a bunch of crackpots, deluded by visions of returning to Africa. After his release

Roots of Rastafarian Musical Protest

from jail in December 1959, Henry became increasingly hostile toward Jamaican authorities. Preaching to the members of his Rastafarian group, the African Reformed Church, Henry's sermons often condemned the oppressive British government. During one sermon, Henry allegedly threatened the life of Prime Minister Norman Manley (Gray 50–1). On April 6, 1960, the *Daily Gleaner* announced that police, suspicious that Henry was planning to overthrow the government, had raided Henry's headquarters and found twenty-five hundred electrical detonators, plus a cache of shotguns, machetes, and dynamite ("Weapons Seized" 1). In October of that same year, Henry went to trial on a variety of charges, including treason. During his trial, Henry announced he was a "prophet" and encouraged Jamaicans to "reform themselves" and seek repatriation to Africa ("Drilled Men" 4).

In the same year, Henry's son, Ronald Henry, was training a guerrilla band of Rastafarians and sympathetic African Americans in Red Hills, a suburb overlooking Kingston. Ronald Henry and his followers had returned to Kingston from New York with the intent of overthrowing the Jamaican government (Stone, *Class, Race, and Political Behavior* 154–5). The government sent in a police force and soldiers from the Royal Hampshire Regiment, a military unit of the British command in Jamaica, and quickly suppressed the "Red Hills" incident (Barrett 98–9). The younger Henry and four of his followers were captured and sentenced to death for conspiring to overthrow the government.

In 1963, a Rastafarian "uprising" once again struck fear in the hearts of many Jamaicans. The altercation began near Montego Bay when a group of Rastafarians protested against restrictions that prohibited them from walking across the Rose Hall estate to their small plot of land. Rose Hall was quickly being transformed into a tourist attraction called Coral Gardens, and authorities feared the Rastafarian presence would frighten tourists (Campbell, *Rasta* 106). The conflict turned ugly, as a group of Rastafarians allegedly burned down a gas station, attacked a police officer with a spear, and killed eight people. The *Daily Gleaner* speculated that the Rastafarians

Roots of Rastafarian Musical Protest

were under the influence of drugs when they launched their "Holy Thurs-day rampage" ("8 Killed" 1). Within twenty-four hours, more than 150 Rastafarians were arrested on assorted charges, including vagrancy and unlawful possession of drugs and weapons ("8 Killed" 1).

Because the Rastafarian movement continuously evolved, it is difficult to describe its doctrines at any given stage of its development. At the request of some members of the Rastafarian movement, three University of the West Indies (UWI) researchers conducted two weeks of intensive research on the movement in July 1960 and summarized the movement's core beliefs in a brief pamphlet entitled the *Report on the Rastafari Movement in Kingston, Jamaica*. Their report found that the Rastafarian movement unanimously believed in the divinity of Haile Selassie and favored the repa-triation of all its members to Africa. After discussions with Rastafarian members, the authors also summarized the movement's goals: to end police persecution, to improve economic conditions and access to adult education, and to strengthen human rights, including freedom of movement and speech (33–4).

Despite occasional incidents like the "Coral Gardens" uprisings, most Rastafarians preached love and peace. In a 1964 article in the daily news-paper, *Public Opinion*, one Rastafarian said: "A Rastaman can't bruk shop, a Rastaman can't chop up no one with machete,—Rastaman him no business with gun" (Heymans 8). In the *Star*, a Jamaican afternoon newspaper tabloid, Brother Aubrey Brown, a Rastafarian spokesperson, argued that the Rastafarian movement did not condone preaching "race hatred . . . against the pink nor the yellow" (qtd. in "Watch Word" 7). The *Report* of the UWI research team confirmed this nonviolent attitude when it reported that a "great majority of Ras Tafari brethren are peaceful citizens who do not believe in violence." The *Report* did suggest, however, that the movement was heterogeneous, and that a small minority of Rastafarians were criminals, revolutionaries, or "mentally deranged" (27). However, most Rastafarians did not seem to fit the Jamaican government's portrait of their cause as a violent, revolutionary social movement.

Roots of Rastafarian Musical Protest

SKA AND THE ROOTS OF RASTAFARIAN PROTEST MUSIC

In the late 1950s, many Jamaicans loved American music. Jamaica's affection for U.S. musical forms reflected the worldwide dominance of the U.S. music industry and the fact that until the late 1950s Jamaica lacked its own recording industry. In a 1994 interview, Dermot Hussey, a former employee of the Jamaica Broadcasting Corporation (JBC) and Radio Jamaica Rediffusion Limited (RJR), noted that American music—big band, swing music, and jazz—had long been popular in Jamaica, and many Jamaicans believed foreign music was more "sophisticated" than their own indigenous forms. By the late 1950s, a new American music, rhythm and blues (R&B), had begun to captivate Jamaicans. While some R&B and rock-and-roll artists (such as Bill Haley and the Comets) played to cheering Jamaican audiences, most of the music was either brought back from the United States or heard on transistor radio from U.S. radio stations, such as WINZ in Miami, Florida (Witmer 15).

Early American R&B stars became role models for struggling young Jamaican musicians. Fats Domino was extremely popular in Jamaica because he "dealt with black life" (G. White, "Mento" 38). Early ska bands, such as the Wailers, even imitated the appearance of the R&B artists. Peter Tosh, one of the Wailers' founding members, recalled in the documentary *Caribbean Nights: The Bob Marley Story* that the "slick style" of short Afros, silk clothes, and sunglasses was adopted by ska bands hoping to "look like the ting." Recording under the direction of Clement "Sir Coxsone" Dodd in the two-track Studio One in Kingston, ska groups such as the Charmers and the Gaylands modeled themselves after the Impressions and the Platters, singing about sexual temptation, longing, and lost love. Some Jamaican groups, such as the Three Tops, even named themselves after American R&B stars in their efforts to emulate black American musical forms.

Even before the rise of ska, Jamaica had produced a generation of legendary jazz and big band musicians. According to Dermot Hussey:

Roots of Rastafarian Musical Protest

> We had turned out a generation of musicians that were able to not only
> win acclaim here, but migrate to Britain primarily. People like Bertie King . . .
> established themselves also in the United States, and recorded for Blue Note
> records. So, there was this kind of level of musical excellence, particularly
> from the instrumental point of view. And that carried over into the ska period
> for a bit.

The popularity of this music was often credited to the influence of the Europeanized school missions in Jamaica. The Alpha Boys' School, a kind of reform school located in West Kingston, was the best example of how European schools of music were established in Jamaica to train Jamaican musicians to emulate the "European wind band tradition" (Witmer 12). The Alpha Boys' School sported an extraordinary music school and graduated some of Jamaica's finest big band, swing, and jazz instrumentalists. The Alpha Boys' School also trained musicians to fulfill national duties, such as playing for the Jamaica Military Band (Witmer 12).

The popularity of both R&B and ska was linked directly to a technology known in Jamaica as the "sound system." Sound systems were portable music systems on wheels; vans would carry high-fidelity playback equipment to neighborhood dances in Kingston (Winders 68). These gatherings usually took place in outdoor venues, such as neighborhood yards (Witmer 16). In order to provide this service, all that was needed was access to a power line. With an available power source, a sound system could envelope the community in music with two to eight speaker systems (Davis, "Talking Drums" 33).

The sound system promoted R&B, music typically unavailable to many Jamaicans. Legendary ska producer and promoter Clement Dodd often traveled to the United States and reentered Jamaica with copies of American recordings. The sound systems were instrumental in exposing Jamaicans to American music, because the "majority of Jamaicans then could not afford the radios that could pick up foreign stations, and so were not exposed to the kinds of music coming out of America. It was left to the sound-systems to educate and entertain the average Jamaican to the musical happenings" (Jingles 1).

Roots of Rastafarian Musical Protest

More important, the sound system became the focal point for the development of a community of dissent. As one of the few affordable social activities for the poor, the sound system brought music to places where the voice of the poor could be heard without interference by local authorities. As cultural critic Dick Hebdige has written, the "sound-system came to represent, particularly for the young, a precious inner sanctum, uncontaminated by alien influences, a black heart beating back to Africa" (*Subculture* 38). At a sound-system gathering, a deejay encouraged dancing and made toasts to the audience.[5] Yet the deejay also would engage in a running commentary on political events in Jamaica.

By 1962, Jamaican ska was a hot musical item. A 1962 issue of *Spotlight Newsmagazine*, a Jamaican music magazine, reported that "whether or not it catches on in the States, there is no doubt that Ska is a big business in Jamaica" ("Ska—The Up Beat" 31–2). The ska sound (called "blue beat" in England) even created a national tremor in England. In "blue beat," the music's "monotonous, pulsating and compulsive" rhythms inspired a frenzied dance underscored by "the guttural grunts and groans of the dancers, who act like an exhausted person gasping for breath" (Patterson, "The Dance" 401). Edward Seaga, future JLP prime minister and a pioneer in recording Jamaican Revivalist music, managed to book a ska band at the 1964 World's Fair in New York. Despite ska's popularity, however, Jamaica's upper classes often ridiculed the music as an inferior art of the lower classes.

Protest Lyrics

Many ska songs were either searing, jazzy instrumentals or romantic love songs. Borrowing from the American black music tradition of jazz and blues, the theme of personal angst was materialized in ska lyrics that highlighted male-female relationships. Within these genres, especially the blues, women were portrayed as embodying love and loneliness, devotion and infidelity (Spencer 126). One might read some ska songs, such as the Checkmates' "Turn Me On" and Lee Perry's "Sugar Bag," as strictly "trivial" love songs (*Ska Bonanza*). In most of the songs, however, ska musicians expressed deep personal pain, brought about by the "corrupting" female influence. The

Roots of Rastafarian Musical Protest

temptation of female flesh and sexual pleasures ultimately led to "lonesome feelings," "teardrops," "broken hearts," and "lost love." The Wailers' "I Need You" found the dejected male "ashamed" of his "lost love." In order to fight from being a "small man" the victim declared: "I don't need you" (*One Love*). The woman thus became a symbol of only temporary pleasure, followed by hard luck, separation, and alienation.

However, many of the music's references—the social conditions of the ghetto, God as a redeemer, and repatriation to the "promised land"—clearly demonstrated ska's budding political concerns.

For example, ska musicians hinted at the brewing discontent of Jamaica's poor. In the shantytown, where an insult could quickly turn into a fatality, Bob Marley warned "Mr. Talkative" that too much gossip would lead to an early demise (*One Love*). Eric "Monty" Morris, an early ska musician, sang about a single mother raising children in poverty: "Old lady who live in a shoe / She had so many children / She didn't know what to do." Other artists, such as Theophilus Beckford, discussed the problem of youth in jail: "Georgie and the Old Shoes has gone to jail / Well if you're looking for poor Georgie / He's behind de [the] wall" (qtd. in G. White, "Mento" 41). Jamaican musician and record producer Prince Buster explored the issue of racial tension in the ghetto with the hit "Blackhead Chinee Man." The song was not just a direct attack against Derrick Morgan, a successful ska musician, but a warning about the potentially explosive conflict between "native" blacks and the foreign merchant class in Jamaica (Clarke 79). While calling attention to such social and political problems, however, ska stopped short of calling for rebellion. In 1963, the Wailers' first hit single, "Simmer Down," actually called upon Jamaicans to "cool" their tempers:

> *Simmer down, control your temper*
> *Simmer down and you'll get stronger*
> *Simmer down. Can't you hear what I say?*
> *Simmer down. Why don't you, why don't you*
> *Simmer down?* (One Love)

17

Roots of Rastafarian Musical Protest

Ska musicians frequently looked to God for solace. Spirituals and gospel music had historical roots in a country populated with Christian churches. American gospel music has a direct link to the slave experience in the cotton fields. Gospel music draws on African tribal music, black spirituals, slave work songs, and Protestant church hymns (Carpenter 405). Gospel music has since influenced folk, blues, and R&B. In particular, the Wailers' string of gospel singles, including the songs "Amen" and "Habits," reflected the importance of the Christian church in the lives of many of these musicians (*One Love*).

As in most spirituals, God's role was that of a silent redeemer. As a "shining light" or "spirit," the faithful experienced God's presence and patiently waited for God to fulfill biblical prophecy. In "Over the River," the Jiving Juniors invoked the imagery of the Second Coming: "I'll be here when he come / My savior, my savior / I'll be here when he come" (*Ska Bonanza*). In the Wailers' song, "I Am Going Home," Bob Marley cried for God to "carry me home" (*One Love*). With God's will at work, the oppressed passively waited for liberation and deliverance.

The theme of repatriation to the "promised land" also can be located in a variety of ska songs. Despite the fact that ska musicians did not focus attention on the Rastafarian goal of returning to Africa, the repatriation motif was important in developing subsequent Rastafarian themes. Ska musicians associated biblical references to the River Jordan with the theme of returning home. In the Bible, the River Jordan stretched from the Sea of Galilee to the Dead Sea and symbolically represented the watery impasse between the wandering "lost" Jewish tribe and the promised land. Over the opening chords of the Wailers' "I Am Going Home," Bob Marley sang of the River Jordan while the background vocals cried, "I am going home." In another ska song, "River Jordan," Clancy Eccles's backup vocalists repeated the chorus "roll River Jordan roll," while Eccles described Noah's Ark, thunderous rain, and God's return to rescue the faithful from oppression (*Tougher Than Tough*). Although the Maytals' "Six and Seven Books of Moses" simply recited the books of the Old Testament, the song hinted at the Israelites' return to the promised land (*Tougher Than Tough*).

Roots of Rastafarian Musical Protest

In one of the few ska songs to employ Rastafarian images explicitly, "Carry Go Bring Come," Justin Hines and the Dominoes invoked the image of Mount Zion, an image that would echo through reggae songs during the 1970s. In the song, Hines alerted followers to "seek in Mount Zion high / Instead of keeping oppression upon an innocent man" (*Tougher Than Tough*).

While some ska songs hinted at repatriation "back home," "Carry Go Bring Come" discussed the oppressive experience in Jamaica and specifical ly acknowledged Mount Zion in Africa as the promised land. Although the ska sound was mostly a blend of several genres of popular music, Rastafarian themes were clearly expressed in song titles and instrumentation.

Musical Instrumentation

Ska music blended a variety of musical styles. Kenneth M. Bilby, a scholar of Jamaican music, has referred to the blending of musical styles as the process of creolization. Creolization refers to a "meeting and blending of two or more older traditions on new soil, and a subsequent elaboration of form" ("The Caribbean" 2). American musical forms such as jazz and big band music inspired ska's horn sound, and R&B influenced the music's guitar style, the types of chords used, and the length of the song (usually under four minutes). Jamaican music expert Garth White has also suggested that ska was influenced by its predecessor, mento: ska's "shuffle-rhythm [is] close to mento but even closer to the backbeat of the r&b" ("Mento" 38).[6] Ska also contained a mix of blues and African elements such as call and response (Turner 148).

Ska's top music producers, Clement Dodd, Leslie Kong, and Duke Reid, would invite young, upstart ska musicians like Jimmy Cliff to record songs with a studio "house band," consisting of some of the best musicians on the island. Because of the limitations of two-track recording, a producer would be forced to record the band "live" (i.e., all the musicians would play in the same room at the same time). One of Jamaica's most influential bass guitarists, Jackie Jackson, recalled the limitations of the two-track studio:

> It was all of the instruments on one track and the vocals on the
> other. Thank the Lord 4-track came along. You used to play out your

Roots of Rastafarian Musical Protest

soul on 2-track because every time you take a cut, all of the instruments pop up on one track. Sometimes you go back and listen and you can't hear something. So you take another cut, you go back in and listen, and now something too *loud*. It went on like that for ever and ever because there was no separation. (qtd. in Gorney 41)

Although the limitations of the recording technology played a significant role in the often uneven and "raw" production, ska songs clearly reflected the joyful celebration of independence and the bustling urban life of West Kingston. And the music's relatively fast tempo accounted in large measure for ska's joyful sound. Compared to reggae music of the 1970s (averaging approximately 72 beats per minute [bpm]), ska songs achieved a faster tempo of approximately 110 to 130 beats per minute. Songs such as the Wailers' "Simmer Down" (124 bpm), Justin Hines and the Dominoes' "Carry Go Bring Come" (126 bpm), the Skatalites' "Nimble Foot Ska" (128 bpm), and Don Drummond and Roland Alphonso's "Roll On Sweet Don (Heaven and Hell)" (131 bpm) exemplified ska's quick, often festive, beat.[7]

Like most western music, ska music was played in 4/4 or common time (four quarter notes per bar).[8] The ska ensemble included a rhythm guitar and, occasionally, a lead guitar, an upright bass, drums, lead and harmony vocals, and often an extensive horn section that included a trombone, trumpet, and a tenor or alto saxophone (or both). Unlike later rocksteady and reggae bands, a ten-piece ska band took on the appearance of a large jazz ensemble or a big band.

Although ska borrowed heavily from other musical genres, the musicians created a unique rhythmic sound and style. In the early 1960s, ska singer and producer Prince Buster asked his guitarist Jah Jerry to emphasize the offbeat in an attempt to move ska beyond simply copying the R&B sound (Barrow 11). In most American popular music, the rhythm guitar accented the downbeat or played on the underlined numbers: (1 & 2 & 3 & 4 &). In contrast, ska guitarists played on the offbeat or the "and" (1 & 2 & 3 & 4 &). The guitarist's emphasis on the offbeat, rather than the downbeat, created the distinctive sound that has since characterized all of Jamaica's popular music.

Roots of Rastafarian Musical Protest

In the typical ska arrangement, the piano and horns would help the guitarist emphasize ska's offbeat sound. For example, Don Drummond's instrumental, "Man in the Street," featured a guitar, piano, and horns playing the same rhythm, each instrument emphasizing the offbeat. However, in songs such as Derrick Morgan's "Forward March," when a guitarist was not available, the horns and piano provided the offbeat pattern (*Tougher Than Tough*).

As a musical experience, the rhythm guitar created a positive, almost optimistic sound. The ability of the guitarist to create this "happy" and "uplifting" sound was a result of the usage of major, as opposed to minor, chords and keys. For centuries, western musicians have used major chords and keys to convey "happy" and "optimistic" feelings to listeners. Although some ska songs did utilize minor keys, most songs were written in major keys, relying on the three major or primary chords (I, IV, V). Playing a short, choppy rhythm, the ska guitarist enhanced this "happy" sound by playing mid-register voicings on the top three or four smallest strings near the middle of the guitar neck. Some guitarists further emphasized this sound by employing more frequent chord changes. In "Simmer Down," the guitarist used two chords, changing every two beats (1 & 2 & 3 & 4 &) within the 4/4 framework.

While the rhythm guitar, piano, and horn section anchored ska's offbeat sound, the drummer typically emphasized downbeats 2 and 4. The drummer typically played a timekeeping role, utilizing only a minimal number of percussive instruments: snare drum, hi-hat, ride cymbal and, occasionally, the bass drum. In most ska songs, the drummer would hit the snare drum on beats 2 and 4, while playing a steady eighth-note pattern on the hi-hat or a ride cymbal. Yet, in songs such as "Man in the Street" and "Nimble Foot Ska" (*Ska Bonanza*) the drummer played a more adventurous role, using bass drum accents, snare fills, and busier improvisational work on the hi-hat to add color to the sound. Despite these occasional rhythmic flourishes, the drummer played a subordinate role in the ska arrangement. It was not until the birth of international reggae that the drums became an extremely important, if not dominant, musical instrument.

21

Roots of Rastafarian Musical Protest

The bass, along with the rhythm guitar and drums, served as an important part of ska's percussive sound. Employing a stand-up bass (electric bass
guitars were not widely used in Jamaica until the mid-1960s), the ska bassist
would frequently play a "walking" bass line, a bass figure often heard on jazz
and blues records. To achieve this sound, the bassist would play four quarter
notes per bar illustrating the "one-note-per-beat" style. For example, in
Jimmy Cliff's 1962 song "Miss Jamaica" (*Tougher Than Tough*), the bass
player played this ska bass line (figure 1.1):

A simplified version of this bass rhythm would look like this (figure 1.2):

X	X	X	X
Beat 1	Beat 2	Beat 3	Beat 4

While the electric guitar, piano, upright bass, and drums functioned as
ska's unwavering rhythmic "heartbeat," the horn section would have far
more latitude and freedom to explore the boundaries and scope of its collective function and sound. The horn section performed multiple roles,
including sustaining chord tones, doubling the guitar's offbeat staccato
chords, playing a song's main riff or theme, and—at times—even improvis-
ing solo passages. For example, in "Carry Go Bring Come" the trombone
provided the opening statement, while additional horns acted in a supportive manner by blowing unison lines in the background. After a four-bar
theme, the trombone joined the other horns, and for the remainder of the
song, the tenor sax, trumpet, and trombone played in unison, while additional horns doubled the guitar's offbeat figure. In this song, one horn sec-

Roots of Rastafarian Musical Protest

tion functioned harmonically and rhythmically by doubling the offbeat guitar chords, while the other horns played a unison melody.

Frequently, ska songs such as "Nimble Foot Ska" featured complicated horn arrangements. In this song, after the drummer provided a brief introductory snare fill, the tenor sax introduced the song's eight-bar theme before the rest of the horn section (trombone, alto sax, and trumpet) entered with a well-structured background theme. Early in the song, the horn section played a harmonized theme, while the tenor sax improvised a brief solo. As the song progressed, a horn trio consisting of trumpet, trombone, and sax alternated between playing harmony and unison lines. Similar to many early ska songs, "Nimble Foot Ska" demonstrated the genre's reliance on horns and the complexity of these arrangements.

Ska songs would also include another important "instrument," the human voice. Typically, ska songs featured a lead vocal and two or three backup singers. While most vocal arrangements were fairly rudimentary, some songs previewed the more complex vocal arrangements that would be heard in future rocksteady and reggae songs. In the Jiving Juniors' song "Over the River," for example, the lead singer and three backup singers harmonized during the song's introduction. As the song shifted into the chorus, the backup singers vocalized the phrase "I'll be here when he come," while the lead singer repeated the words "over the river." Later in the song, the two vocal parts switched roles: the backup singers repeated "over the river" while the lead singer enthusiastically proclaimed: "I'll be here when he come." Despite vocal workouts like "Over the River," which reflected a type of call-and-response approach, most ska songs employed more basic vocal arrangements such as a lead vocal and backup harmony parts.

In sum, even though the ska sound was heavily dominated by the accented offbeat, it also exploited the tension between the offbeat and the downbeat. While the electric guitar, piano, and occasionally one or more horns emphasized the offbeat, the drums and the bass anchored the downbeat. Another important characteristic of the ska sound was the combination of structured repetition and improvisation. The electric guitar, bass, piano, and drums played with very little variation; in comparison, one or

Roots of Rastafarian Musical Protest

more horns and, occasionally, the vocals would improvise "around" the rest of the ensemble to help create ska's "happy," "joyous," and "uplifting" sound. Some of these vocal arrangements harkened back to traditional American black music, especially gospel music, which is often marked by vocal improvisations. Perhaps ska can best be characterized as a product of creolization, borrowing heavily from black American music (jazz, gospel, and R&B), while also incorporating indigenous (mento) and African elements into its sound. In addition, ska music began to reflect the influence of the Rastafarian movement.

The connection between Rastafari and ska music was most evident in the work of two pioneering musicians: Oswald Williams, popularly known as "Count Ossie," and Don Drummond. In the 1940s, Count Ossie was inspired by Burru drumming, an African drumming pattern, and he established several Rastafarian camps and invited many sympathetic to the Rastafarian movement to be part of his musical experiments (G. White, "Mento" 39). His earliest recordings have not survived, but Ossie highlighted Rastafarian drumming in the haunting song "Oh Carolina" (*Tougher Than Tough*). The song was sung by the Folkes Brothers with Count Ossie and other Rastafarian musicians adding traditional Rastafarian drumming and backup vocals.

Rastafarian influences were also evident in the titles of his instrumental songs such as "Another Moses" and "Babylon Gone." "Another Moses" referred cryptically to the divinity of Haile Selassie, and "Babylon Gone" expressed the Rastafarian hope in being delivered from Jamaica's oppressive social structure to their home in Africa (G. White, "The Development" 64). In the mid-1960s, Ossie formed a group called the Mystic Revelation of Rastafari. Cedric Brooks, a noted Jamaican musician, said that "Count Ossie was the pioneer in bringing the Rasta Music into the open" (Brooks 14).

Don Drummond has been credited with introducing Rastafarian influences into the musical nucleus of ska. As the leading trombonist for the Skatalites, Drummond's songs—"Tribute to Marcus Garvey," "Reincarnation," and "The Return of Paul Bogle"—reflected his Rastafarian faith (Jerry 1). Dermot Hussey explained in an interview the connection

Roots of Rastafarian Musical Protest

between Drummond and Rastafarian themes: "If you noticed all the themes that had an African orientation in ska music, "Don de Lion," "Father East," . . . all those things, he was the one that I think that had a great association with the kind of Rastafarian sensibility."

In 1965, Drummond, who had a history of mental illness, murdered his girlfriend, and in 1969 he committed suicide in a Jamaican asylum. The black nationalist newspaper, *Abeng*, mourned Drummond's death and praised his contribution to ska. One Rastafarian writer, Bongo Jerry, characterized Drummond as the "melody of Freedom Sounds." Recognizing Drummond's incredible musical skill and tragic life, Jerry confessed: "[W]e hurt inside when we remember that he was pushed around, pushed about and then finally shoved out by Babylon" (1).

The influence of Count Ossie and Don Drummond created the opportunity for ska musicians to enter Rastafarian camps, to engage in musical experiments, and to become sensitive to the Rastafarian ethos. Because of their association with the movement, these musicians were "always kept under surveillance by the police" (Clarke 67). In effect, the fusion of ska and Rastafari initiated the process of creating a musical community unified against an oppressive social system.

By the mid-1960s, however, Jamaica's popular music would evolve into rocksteady, a more aggressive, more politically minded protest music. Although not politically explicit protest music, ska initiated this evolution of Jamaican popular music toward a message of dissent against repression, intolerance, and discrimination.

Notes

1. Mento emerged in the 1930s and is generally characterized by its experimentation with European (trumpet) and African (drums) instruments. While mento was heard throughout Jamaica, it is largely a rural-based music. See, for example, Garth White,

Notes

Traditional Musical Practice in Jamaica and Its Influence on the Birth of Modern Jamaican Popular Music (Kingston, JA: African-Caribbean Institute of Jamaica, 1982).

2. Rastafarians also use "reasoning," an informal dialectic, to debate issues and seek wisdom.

3. From 1940 to 1952, the PNP espoused socialism until the more conservative members of the PNP convinced Norman Manley that the party's extreme left wing, a group of self-proclaimed Marxists, were a threat to his authority. In 1952, Manley expelled the four Marxists, popularly known as the four H's—Ken and Frank Hill, Richard Hart, and Arthur Henry—from the party. For the next twenty years, the PNP would remain dedicated to a liberal, democratic policy until Norman Manley's son, Michael Manley, reintroduced the political philosophy of democratic socialism in 1974. See, for example, Carl Stone, "Power, Policy and Politics in Independent Jamaica," *Jamaica in Independence: Essays on the Early Years,* ed. Rex Nettleford (Kingston, JA: Heinemann Caribbean, 1989), 21.

4. In 1961, Norman Manley decided to send delegates (from the Rastafarian movement and a governmental council) to search for land in Africa. The committee traveled to five African states to experiment with the idea of emigration and eventual citizenship. Unfortunately, for the Rastafarian movement, the "first official mission to Africa" (1961) and a nongovernment-sponsored "second mission to Africa" (1963–1965) did not result in achieving the movement's goal of repatriation. See *Majority Report of Mission to Africa* (Kingston, JA: Government Printer, 1961) and Douglas R. A. Mack, *From Babylon to Rastafari: Origin and History of the Rastafarian Movement* (Chicago: Research Associates School Times Publications and Frontline Distribution International, 1999).

5. For the Jamaican DJ, the term "toasting" often refers to sexual bragging.

6. According to Caribbean music expert Kenneth M. Bilby, the "influence of mento, in particular, has been underrated. Not only would some argue that the characteristic ska afterbeat actually stems in part from the strumming patterns of the banjo or guitar in mento, but ska versions of traditional mento tunes were common during the early 1960s" ("Jamaica" 29). Bilby also suggests that the mento influence actually "increased during the reggae era" and that "[f]ew listeners outside of Jamaica know that there was a whole substyle or genre of mento-reggae (sometimes called 'country music') that enjoyed tremendous popularity in the island during the 1970s" (30).

7. The beat, according to the *New Grove Dictionary of Jazz*, is "[t]he basic pulse underlying measured music and thus the unit by which musical time is reckoned; the beat, though not always sounded, is always perceived as underpinning the temporal progress of the music, and it is only the presence of the beat that allows rhythm to be established" (Kernfeld 85).

8. The following is a nontechnical description of quarter notes, eighth notes, and sixteenth notes: Using a heartbeat as an example of a steady rhythm, four consecutive beats represent a typical bar or measure of music. Count and repeat the numerical sequence: (1 2 3 4 1 2 3 4 1 2, etc.). Each beat is called a quarter note. The upbeats

Notes

or offbeats exist "half-way" between each beat, yielding eight notes to a bar, thus the term "eighth note." This beat is identified by an "&," and can be represented by the following illustration (1 & 2 & 3 & 4 & 1 & 2, etc.). Dividing each of these eight notes in half produces sixteenth notes. This is illustrated in the following way (1 e & a 2 e & a 3 e & a 4 e & a 1 e & a, etc.). Of course, musicians can further subdivide the beat and are free to combine these rhythms with rests or silence to create infinite forms of expression.

WORKS CITED

Books and Pamphlets

Alleyne, Mervyn C. *Roots of Jamaican Culture*. London: Pluto, 1988.

Barrett, Leonard E. *The Rastafarians: Sounds of Cultural Dissonance*. Rev. ed. Boston: Beacon, 1988.

Beckford, George, and Michael Witter. *Small Garden . . . Bitter Weed: The Political Economy of Struggle and Change in Jamaica*. Morant Bay, JA: Maroon, 1982.

Bilby, Kenneth. "Jamaica." *Reggae, Rasta, Revolution: Jamaican Music from Ska to Dub*. Edited by Chris Potash. New York: Schirmer, 1997. 29–36.

———. "The Caribbean as a Musical Region." *Caribbean Contours*. Edited by Sidney Mintz and Sally Price. Baltimore: Johns Hopkins UP, 1985. 1–38.

Boyd, Derick A. C. *Economic Management, Income Distribution, and Poverty in Jamaica*. New York: Praeger, 1988.

Brown, Aggrey. *Color, Class, and Politics in Jamaica*. New Brunswick, N.J.: Transaction, 1979.

Campbell, Horace. *Rasta and Resistance: From Marcus Garvey to Walter Rodney*. Trenton: Africa World, 1987.

Carpenter, Bill. "Gospel." *All Music Guide: The Best CDs, Albums, and Tapes*. Edited by Michael Erlewine and Scott Bultman. San Francisco: Miller Freeman, 1992. 405.

Clarke, Sebastian. *Jah Music: The Evolution of the Popular Jamaican Song*. London: Heinemann, 1980.

Davis, Stephen. "Talking Drums, Sound Systems and Reggae." *Reggae International*. Edited by Stephen Davis and Peter Simon. New York: Rogner and Bernhard, 1982. 33–4.

Davis, Stephen, and Peter Simon. "A Rasta Glossary." *Reggae International*. Edited by Stephen Davis and Peter Simon. New York: Rogner and Bernhard, 1982. 69.

Works Cited

Gray, Obika. *Radicalism and Social Change in Jamaica, 1960–1972*. Knoxville: U of Tennessee P, 1991.

Hebdige, Dick. *Subculture: The Meaning of Style*. London: Routledge, 1988.

Kernfeld, Barry. "Beat." *The New Grove Dictionary of Jazz*. Edited by Barry Kernfeld. New York: St. Martin's, 1995. 85–8.

Kuper, Adam: *Changing Jamaica*. London: Routledge & Kegan Paul, 1976.

Mack, Douglas R. A. *From Babylon to Rastafari: Origin and History of the Rastafarian Movement*. Chicago: Research Associates School Times Publications and Frontline Distribution International, 1999.

Majority Report of Mission to Africa. Kingston, JA: Government Printer, 1961.

Panton, David. *Jamaica's Michael Manley: The Great Transformation (1972–92)*. Kingston, JA: Kingston Publishers, 1993.

Post, Ken. *Arise Ye Starvelings: The Jamaican Labour Rebellion of 1938 and Its Aftermath*. Hague: Martinus Nijhoff, 1978.

Smith, M. G., Roy Augier, and Rex Nettleford. *Report on the Rastafari Movement in Kingston, Jamaica*. U of the West Indies, JA: Department of Extra-Mural Studies, 1978.

Spencer, Jon M. *Protest and Praise: Sacred Music of Black Religion*. Minneapolis, Minn.: Fortress, 1990.

Stone, Carl. *Class, Race, and Political Behaviour in Urban Jamaica*. U of the West Indies, JA: Institute of Social and Economic Research, 1973.

———. "Power, Policy and Politics in Independent Jamaica." *Jamaica in Independence: Essays on the Early Years*. Edited by Rex Nettleford. Kingston, JA: Heinemann Caribbean, 1989. 19–53.

White, Garth. "Mento to Ska: The Sound of the City." *Reggae International*. Edited by Stephen Davis and Peter Simon. New York: Rogner and Bernhard, 1982. 37–42.

———. *Traditional Musical Practice in Jamaica and Its Influence on the Birth of Modern Jamaican Popular Music*. Kingston, JA: African-Caribbean Institute of Jamaica, 1982.

———. *The Development of Jamaican Popular Music—Part II*. Kingston, JA: African-Caribbean Institute of Jamaica, 1984.

Journal Articles

Brodber, Erna. "Black Consciousness and Popular Music in Jamaica in the 1960s and 1970s." *Caribbean Quarterly* 31.2 (1985): 53–66.

Brooks, Cedric. Interview. "Interview with Cedric Brooks." By Shirley M. Burke. *Jamaica Journal* 11.1–2 (1977): 14–17.

Campbell, Horace. "Rastafari: Culture of Resistance." *Race and Class* 22.1 (1980): 1–22.

Clarke, Colin G. "Dependency and Marginality in Kingston, Jamaica." *Journal of Geography* 82 (1983): 227–35.

Hylton, Patrick. "The Politics of Caribbean Music." *Black Scholar* 7 (1975): 23–9.

O'Gorman, Pamela. "On Reggae and Rastafarianism—and a Garvey Prophecy." *Jamaica Journal* 20.3 (1987): 85–7.

Works Cited

Simpson, George E. "Political Cultism in West Kingston, Jamaica." *Social and Economic Studies* 4 (1955): 133–49.

Winders, James A. "Reggae, Rastafarians and Revolution: Rock Music in the Third World." *Journal of Popular Culture* 17.1 (1983): 61–73.

Witmer, Robert. "A History of Kingston's Popular Music Culture: Neo-Colonialism to Nationalism." *Jamaica Journal* 22.1 (1989): 11–18.

Magazine Articles

Gorney, Mark. "Jackie Jackson and the Roots of Reggae." *Bass Player* May 1999: 37–41.

Hussey, Dermot. "Bob Marley, The Man of Music for 1975." *Pepperpot* Dec. 1975: 41, 43–5.

Patterson, Orlando. "The Dance Invasion." *New Society* 15 Sept. 1966: 401–3.

———. "Ras Tafari: The Cult of Outcasts." *New Society* 12 Nov. 1964: 15–17.

"Ska—The Up Beat." *Spotlight Newsmagazine* Apr./May 1964: 31–2.

Turner, Dale. "The Skinny on Ska." *Guitar One* Dec. 1997: 147–53.

Newspaper Articles

"Drilled Men Not for Earthly Purposes." *Daily Gleaner* 25 Oct. 1960: 1, 4.

"8 Killed after Attack on Gas Station." *Daily Gleaner* 13 Apr. 1963: 1.

Heymans, Peter. "What the Rastaman Sey." *Public Opinion* 12 June 1964: 8.

Jerry, Bongo. "Roll on Sweet Don." *Abeng* 17 May 1969: 1.

Johnson, Barrister Millard. "The Peoples Political Party." Advertisement. *Daily Gleaner* 14 Apr. 1961: 25.

"Watch Word Should Be Love." *Star* 25 May 1961: 6–7.

"Weapons Seized in Raid on Church Headquarters." *Daily Gleaner* 7 Apr. 1960: 1, 14.

Government Documents

Jamaica. Census Research Programme. *Life Tables for British Caribbean Countries, 1959–61*. Kingston, JA: U of the West Indies, 1966.

Jamaica. Jamaica Town Planning Department Report 1961/62. *Town Planning Department Report for Financial Year April 1st 1961–31st March 1962*. Kingston, JA: Government Printer.

Convention Paper

Gibson, Dirk. "I and I Downpressor Man: Reggae as an Instrument of Social Change." Intercultural/International Communication Conference. Florida. Jan. 1990.

Works Cited

Music, Television and Film

Barrow, Steve. Liner notes. *Tougher Than Tough: The Story of Jamaican Music*. Island,
    1993.

The Bob Marley Story: Caribbean Nights. Dir. T. Wall and Anthony Finch. Island, 1985.

Jingles, Julian. Liner notes. *Ska Bonanza: The Studio One Ska Years*. Heartbeat, 1991.

Marley, Bob, and the Wailers. *One Love at Studio One*. Heartbeat, 1991.

Ska Bonanza: The Studio One Ska Years. Heartbeat, 1991.

Tougher Than Tough: The Story of Jamaican Music. Island, 1993.

[6]

Playing at Poverty:
The Music Hall and The Staging
of the Working Class

Ian Peddie

"It's Nice to Be Common Sometimes"
—Daisy Hill

In 1935, the year in which Daisy Hill's yearning to be free of middle-class constrictions first appeared, the music hall was in its final death throes. The rise of cinema and later television had done for the music hall just as the halls had sounded the death knell for free-and-easies and song-and-supper rooms whence they emerged. Nevertheless Hill's song, written and composed by George Ellis, registers more than an evolution in live entertainment; as it implies an ideological impulse beyond a nostalgic longing for "the good old days," the song implicitly gestures towards the transformation of the image of the working class that had occurred on the music hall stage. At its core this reconfiguration, the origins of which may have begun as early as the 1860s, was crucial in damping down any vestigial antithetical political agitation remaining in the wake of the Chartist movement. At the same time, in their role as a stage for redefining existing social structures, the music halls effectively became a platform for propaganda. The dynamics that informed the correlation between these two issues were essential to the universalizing process to which the working class was subject and in which the role of music hall was central. But the influencing of social and political visions was far more subtle and profound than it may at first appear. The patronizing noblesse oblige of popular Victorian novels, to take one example, may have been suitable for the parlor but it simply acknowledged the presence of despair and misery. Instead, and with no little irony, because the reassertion of hierarchy necessitated the complicity of the working class, any rationale for inequality in the social landscape had to take into consideration the vast numbers hierarchy would inevitably emasculate. In ways both insidious and shrewd, those condescendingly referred to as the "salt-of-the-earth" were invited to participate in the refashioning of their own image, or, to paraphrase E.P. Thompson, the working-class audience in the music hall was "present at its own making."[1] What all this meant was that

---

[1]   E.P. Thompson, *The Making of the English Working Class* (New York: Vintage, 1966), 9.

by 1935 Daisy Hill could safely assume that implications arising from the notion of what being "common" actually entailed were understood and shared for reasons other than the uniformity of the audience's social rank. At stake here, of course, were issues beyond questions of gentility: the staged manipulation of the image of the working class functioned to ensure that the meanings disseminated actually became part of the social identities of the working classes.

Hill's assertion unwittingly makes sense because it points to the internalization of distinctions similar to those which the working classes would have to accept were they to accede to the reconfiguring of their images. From this perspective, populist images of the music hall as an escapist and ideologically neutral form of leisure marked by communal entertainment "of the People, for the People, by the People" were important means of concealing agendas that sought to eradicate the politics of class antagonism in favor of the maintenance of deference and hierarchy.[2] So often and in so many ways was the alleged innocuous essence of the music hall articulated that Max Beerbohm, one of its most famous critics, came to think of the music hall as "Demos's Mirror."[3] Beerbohm, as Barry J. Faulk points out, considered music hall entertainment synonymous with English character, and he also viewed it as an exemplar of public organic expression and populist taste.[4] According to Beerbohm, music hall entertainments "have grown, feature for feature, from the public's taste," a belief that invites the conclusion that "they are things which the public itself has created from its own pleasure," and consequently "they know no laws of being but those which the public gives them."[5] The notion that the music hall offered authentic working-class expression was widespread and ensured that as a form of entertainment it was an important site of struggle. After all, as many critics have pointed out, Britain was a nation built upon "cohesive inequality," and there were many willing to invest time and effort in ensuring it remained that way.[6] Behind such sentiments, however, lay the

---

[2]   W. Macqeen-Pope, *The Melodies Linger On: The Story of the Music Hall* (London: W.H. Allen, Nd), 3.

[3]   Beerbohm saw the music hall as a mirror on life: "There is no nonsense about the Halls, no pretence. The mirror is held up, and in it the face of Demos is reflected, whole and unblurred. Thus for those who, like myself, have the misfortune to hate humbug, a Hall is preferable to a theatre. It has an air of honest and freshness not to be found in a theatre. It is nearer to life. The average song, maybe, does not distort life less than the ordinary play; but, at least, it distorts life exactly as the public likes to see life distorted. It shows us, in fact, what are the tastes and sentiments of the public. It is an always trustworthy document. And, in this sense, it is near to life." *More Theatres, 1898–1903* (London: Rupert Hart-Davis, 1969), 274.

[4]   *Music Hall & Modernity: The Late-Victorian Discovery of Popular Culture* (Athens: Ohio University Press), 30.

[5]   Beerbohm, *More Theatres*, 273.

[6]   Philip Williamson, "The Doctrinal Politics of Stanley Baldwin" in *Public and Private Doctrine: Essays in British History Presented to Maurice Cowling*, ed. Michael Bentley (Cambridge: Cambridge University Press, 2002), 198.

dilemma of the experience of class and, crucially, how it would be represented. Ensuring that the "common" was interpreted as a shared and palatable affirmation of Hill's song was the result of a process of social shaping and reinforcement through which the meaning and image of what constituted appropriate notions of working class were contested. Consequently, songs such as "It's Nice to Be Common Sometimes" owed their very existence to the fact that by the time they appeared so much of the entertainment the music halls identified as threatening to the social order, especially anything approximating to class conflict, had either been purged or appropriated and reconfigured to the point where it had been emptied of much of its original potency.

From this perspective, there is no more important figure than that of the cockney, or more specifically that of the costermonger, who by the opening of the twentieth century had been repeatedly staged and completely reinvented.[7] The costermonger as a figure of some independence, with his own barrow from which he sold vegetables, and his historic antipathy towards figures of authority, no doubt elicited much consternation in a Victorian world extremely concerned with exercising paternalistic social control. While these reasons alone made costermongers a target for propaganda, their presence and visibility, with their own distinctive uniforms which later gave rise to the exaggerated attire of Pearly Kings and Queens, ensured that theirs was an image whose effacement and subsequent replacement with a sanitized, staged mockney would prove especially useful. Again, at the risk of laboring a point, this process required the mobilization of narratives that sought to redefine the image of the working class in terms of the political and social aspirations of an establishment cadre; and, any such narratives would also have to function as a template the working class could be invited to adopt. For those who conceived of Britain as a layered social hierarchy contingent upon the maintenance of established categories for its very survival, here was a moment that granted a useful opportunity to reinforce social divisions while simultaneously offering the working classes the illusion that they too had a participatory role in society.

Fundamental to this process were the critics and commentators who saw the music hall and its entertainers as the essence of Englishness. To envisage things in this way necessitated an ideological commitment that banished Henry Mayhew's charges, made in *London Labour and the London Poor* (1851), that the halls were vulgar and coarse; instead, the largely post-1900 cultural shift that imbued "a decidedly low-brow practice" with more significant meaning is invariably explained as a response to the growing commercialism—and implicit connotations of associated artistic banality—that affected the music hall as the twentieth century approached.[8] In this hypothesis, the middle class emerges as a

---

[7]   The term is derived from "costard," which is an apple, and "monger," one who sells.

[8]   Barry J. Faulk, *Music Hall and Modernity* (Athens: University of Ohio Press, 2004), 24.

kind of philistine buffer between the working class, producers of art synonymous with organic "national" expression, and intellectuals, who are beleaguered by middle-class conformism. Appealing though this reading is, it runs the risks of partially removing intellectuals from the political aspects involved in attributing to the working classes ownership of a form of entertainment some intellectuals argued was indistinguishable from the national character. But intellectual privileging of working-class music-hall entertainment was not only a transparently self-serving strategy, it was a form of appeasement, a way of diluting the reality of inequality and reasserting the primacy of hierarchy.

Crucial to this enterprise was the poet and critic T. S. Eliot, whose homage to the music-hall singer Marie Lloyd (1870–1922) elevated her to a synechdocal, representative role of near-angelic status, where "'Marie Lloyd,' as the poet imagined her, comes to stand in *for* the working class."[9] In so doing, Eliot took his place among a long line of critics for whom music-hall entertainers were the true purveyors of an essential and immutable working-class essence. In ways both ingenious and incredulous, critics as diverse as George Orwell, G.H. Mair, and Max Beerbohm have been quick to assert that, as the latter put it, "there is not one peculiarity of our race, good or bad, that is not well illustrated in the Music Halls."[10] At stake here were not merely issues of authenticity: instead an idealized image of the working class realized through its allegedly representative entertainers suggested a sense of anxiety that fostered a desire to co-opt an idealized image of the working class as an ally against the deadening effect of mass consumer society. Hence cultural custodians like Eliot, whose interest in the working-class at times bordered on salacious, revealed an investment in reproducing and sanctioning a working-class that typifies their concept of not what the working-classes might be but what they wanted it to be. The threat posed by the rise of a new commercial lower-middle class, of which the carbuncular clerk of "The Waste Land" is Eliot's archetypal example, suggests that the championing of music hall as the touchstone of working-class experience effectively hid an agenda desirous of what it implicitly purported to oppose: a still more stratified society.[11]

---

[9]   Ibid., 44. See also Eliot's "Marie Lloyd," in *Selected Prose of T.S. Eliot*, ed. Frank Kermode (New York: Farrar, Strauss and Giroux, 1975), 172–174, where the poet asserts his belief in Lloyd's "moral superiority" over other performers. "It was her understanding of the people and sympathy with them, and the people's recognition of the fact that she embodied the virtues which they genuinely most respected in private life, that raised her to the position she occupied at her death. And her death is itself a significant moment in English history. I have called her the expressive figure of the lower classes. There is no such expressive figure for any other class. The middle classes have no such idol: the middle classes are morally corrupt" (173).

[10]   *More Theatres*, 276.

[11]   Useful discussions of the Victorian and Edwardian lower middle class include G.L. Anderson, "The Social Economy of Late-Victorian Clerks," in *The Lower Middle Class in Britain 1870–1914*, ed. Geoffrey Crossick (New York: St. Martin's Press, 1977), 113–133, and Rae Harris Stoll, "The Unthinkable Poor in Edwardian Writing," *Mosaic* (December, 1982), 23–45.

Such significant attempts to exercise influence over the social landscape were contingent upon the assumption that the importance of the music hall as a site of class struggle owed much to its socially diverse audience. The fact that audiences were, as one critic points out, "never homogenous" underlines the relevance of the staging of class just as it amplifies how significant it was that the audience received and interpreted the appropriate social messages.[12] For those invested in promoting a social agenda, the opportunity to transmit selected class values and attitudes in front of a hierarchically diverse audience must have been of inestimable importance. That an elemental contrast between working-class and middle-class attitudes towards the music hall existed is not in doubt. According to Dagmar Kift, the values propagated in the mid-Victorian music hall, those of "hedonism, ribaldry, sensuality, the enjoyment of alcohol, the portrayal of marriage as a tragic-comic disaster, and the equality of sexes at work and leisure" were all "diametrically at odds with those propagated by and attributed to the Victorian middle class."[13] While these were the broad frames of reference that governed social approaches to the music hall, they also encouraged the kind of consistent intervention in music hall programmes that can only be read in terms of class interest. A useful example in this respect is the case of the popular entertainer Charles Godfrey, whose song sketches of Crimean War veterans moved patrons to "volcanic excitement and thunders of applause."[14] Yet towards the end of the nineteenth century, Godfrey was censored in the West End when another of his songs from his Crimean War set, "On Guard," a song about poverty, met with "complaints from the better seats."[15] This suggested that while it was acceptable to invoke patriotism illuminating the neglect of former soldiers was another thing altogether. Considered in the aggregate, these examples intimate a pattern of intent that dovetails with the evolution of the music hall as a medium through which hierarchy and social standing could be defended. Viewed from the standpoint of the working classes, the dilution of class antagonism in the music halls was deepened as the halls became an increasingly commercial venture and their potential as a pulpit for propaganda became evident.[16]

The core assumptions that informed these ideas, the reassertion and maintenance of hierarchy, a social vision consistent with traditions of rank and station, and fear of social conflict between capital and labor, were invariably interpreted

---

[12]   Dave Russell, *Popular Music in England, 1840–1914* (Montreal: McGill-Queen's University Press, 1987), 91.

[13]   Dagmar Kift, *The Victorian Music Hall: Culture, Class and Conflict* (Cambridge: Cambridge University Press, 1991), 176.

[14]   Quoted in Kift, 4.

[15]   Quoted in Russell, 90.

[16]   Useful on the commercial aspects of music hall ownership is Penelope Summerfield, "The Effingham Arms and the Empire: Deliberate Selection in the Evolution of Music Hall in London" in *Popular Culture and Class Conflict, 1590–1914: Explorations in the History of Labour and Leisure*, eds Eileen Yeo and Stephen Yeo (Brighton: Harvester Press, 1981), 209–240.

through the dominant metropolitan culture. Hence while few critics disagree that the music hall possesses impeccably working-class roots, fewer still oppose the truism that London was the fulcrum of the music hall. The fact that the music hall largely began in London and was subsequently disseminated in the provinces has important implications not least because so much of music hall entertainment defined itself with this proviso in mind. Not surprisingly in this light, many of the provincial artists hoping to "make it" on the London music-hall circuit relied for effect upon provincial stereotypes popular in "the smoke." Typical in this respect was George Formby senior (1875–1921), who was wont to introduce himself to London audiences as "George Formby fra' Wigan" to which he added the rejoinder, "I've not been in England long ..." Born James Booth in Ashton-under-Lyne, Lancashire, the illegitimate son of an illiterate mother, after a dreadful childhood Formby became a comedian known for his dry wit. Ironically, however, perhaps he is best known for a distinctive cough, which he would excuse with "it's not the cough that carries you off, it's the coffin they carries you off in," which was always guaranteed to raise a laugh. But the cough was no act: Formby died of tuberculosis. His London appearances centered around his adoption of the persona of a gormless northerner, John Willie, a provincial notable for his failed attempts at "Playing the Game in the West" (End) as one of his song titles has it. The game that had to be played was, in effect, a form of reassertion of identity consistent with the attitudes of social acquiescence that became an increasing feature of the halls as the twentieth century approached. Read in this way, Formby's naïve provincial invites the kind of paternalism that critics such as Laurence Senelick has suggested is the defining feature of the music hall.[17] No doubt similar conclusions might be applied to the legions of provincial entertainers who trod the boards in London. The authenticity of many of the portrayals they offered might best be judged in the light of a couple of representative acts. First, the Scots singer and comedian Harry Lauder (1870–1950), who was one of the most famous of all music hall performers. Allegedly described by Winston Churchill as "Scotland's greatest ever ambassador," Lauder actually first appeared as an Irish comic singing "Calligan-Call Again." Just as quickly as he dropped his Irish persona, however, Lauder became the stereotypical Scot; replete with kilt, tam and walking stick, he is perhaps most famous for "Roamin in the Gloamin" and "I Love a Lassie." But for all his considerable success the identity Lauder created has always been contentious, not least during his heyday. One of the most striking comments on his act came during his 1917 tour to Australia, where an anonymous correspondent challenged not only the image Lauder was projecting but also the extent to which that image influenced Lauder's imitators. As "a typical Lowlander of the towns, corresponding to the London Cockney," the reviewer asserted, "there is no good reason why it [a kilt] should be worn by Lauder."[18] But while the persistence of

---

[17]   Laurence Senelick, "Politics as Entertainment: Victorian Music-Hall Songs," *Victorian Studies*, Vol. 19, No. 2 (1975), 149–180.

[18]   Quoted in Paul Maloney, *Scotland and the Music Hall, 1850–1914* (Manchester: Manchester University Press, 2003), 179.

the stereotypical vision of the Scot Lauder created particularly rankled, it is the interpretation of the staged Scot in terms of a metropolitan comparison that proves most revealing. Dismissing the presence of "kilt jokes or songs" as "cockney rubbish," the reviewer concluded that "comic songs from London" which made reference to Scots were invariably written by "the slum-brained type of Cockney song-writer."[19] Compelling correlations of this ilk exist in myriad forms, not least in the person of Chas W. Whittle, who "gained his major success not with the proud "My Girl's a Yorkshire Girl," but "Let's All Go Down the Strand.""[20]

While such examples indicate the dominance London exerted over music-hall entertainers, it would be wrong to conclude that the situation was uniform. Away from the capital, many provincial music-hall entertainers built their reputations upon the fact that they were part of the local community. Edward "Ned" Corvan (1829–1865) was "a favourite everywhere" on Tyneside, not least because his "localized pieces spoke to the experience of workers."[21] Corvan, who did odd jobs and played the violin at the Victoria Theater before his singing career blossomed, actively resisted the collaborationist pressures at work from the mid-nineteenth century onwards. The "quiescence" of working-class music after the Chartist decades of the 1840s, marked by "a transition from protest, street music and spontaneous sing-song to formalised performance in choirs and brass bands," and where "the outlines of a qualitatively distinct workers' music culture become even mistier" in hindsight makes Corvan's resistance seem all the more admirable.[22] Yet because "music-hall was a participatory form of activity," then Corvan's success must be read in terms of the class homology he engendered with his audience.[23] Establishing himself as vox populi for the class identity he shared with onlookers, Corvan articulated a sense of solidarity his audience understood well, as the following verse from "The Funny Time Comin'" indicates:

> There's a funny time comin' lads,
> A funny time comin'
> We'll hae ne shippin maisters then,
> I' the funny time comin';
> We'll hae nae cutlashes on the Quay,
> The bairns and wives to anger;
> We'll hae a better North Shields M---r,
> Ony wait a little langer. [24]

---

[19] Ibid., 180.

[20] Russell, 98.

[21] Dave Harker, "The Making of the Tyneside Concert Hall," *Popular Music*, Vol. 1 (1981), 49.

[22] Richard Middleton, "Articulating Musical Meaning/Re-constructing Musical History/Locating the 'Popular,'" *Popular Music*, Vol. 5 (1985), 19.

[23] Gareth Stedman Jones, *Languages of Class: Studies in Working Class History, 1832–1982* (Cambridge: Cambridge University Press, 1983), 224.

[24] Quoted in Harker (1981), 51.

Opposition to the "maisters," who, as the singer in "Astrilly [Australia] or The Pitmen's Farewell" points out "keeps us striking,'" would have found the same kind of favorable reception as that of "The Rise in Coals," a song decrying an increase in the price of winter fuel:

> The snaw fell doon fast, an' poor folks seem'd shy,
> Clos'd up I' thor hyems as the storm pelted by;
> An they wished roond their nooks such times soon wad pass,
> For provisions had risen an' they'd saved little brass,
> And as money an' firin' was meltin' away,
> Thor seemed nowt but caud dops for us poor sons of clay,
> The women folks flew ti' fill thor coal holes,
> To the depoe but hand them they've raised wor small coals.
> O What a price for sma' coals, how they've raised wor sma' coals.[25]

The almost Dickensian opening of this song quickly gives way to the kind of serious social critique that marks so much of Corvan's best work. In the final verse, the dishonest tactics of the unscrupulous coal-merchants are implicitly contrasted with honest "toil" of the pitmen who dig the coal:

> They ken hoo ti swindle poor folks wi' thor loads,
> Pretendin' thor raised, and that snaw stopped the roads,
> But a pitman tell'd me ti stop up sic jaw,
> For it niver rained hailstones nor snawed doon belaw.
> An' he says if thou'll teeyke advice fra a feul,
> When thors a greet vast o' weather, get thaw holes a chock full
> An while thou's warmin' thaw shins by the fire, as the snaw
> Drops doon through the loom, think o' the pitmen belaw.
> For they toil hard and sair for sma' coals, how they toil for sma' coals.[26]

As an organic intellectual of some importance, Ned Corvan understood the value of recording events from the perspective of those not usually quoted. "When 'eer owt happens in the toon," he pledged in the song "£4 10s Or, the Sailor's Strike," "aw'll take maw pen and write it doon."[27] And so he did, as the following verse, taken from "The Queen Has Sent a Letter, or The Hartley Calamity" (1862) indicates:

> The collier's welfare, as he toils, more interest might command
> Among the wealthy owners and rulers of the land.
> Are they like beasts of burthen, as Roebuck once did rave,
> Will government in future strive the collier's life to save?
> Why should the worn-out collier amid his abject gloom
> Eke out the life his Maker spared to share the pauper's doom?[28]

---

[25]　Quoted in Middleton, 28.

[26]　Ibid., 28–29.

[27]　Quoted in Harker, 51.

[28]　Ibid., 53.

This was written to commemorate the mining disaster at New Hartley in 1862, where a shafthead collapse entombed and subsequently killed many miners; one cannot help wondering if there is a sense of irony in a song that begins with "Bless the Queen of England" and ends with the above-quoted verse. Corvan's defense of collective, communal, working-class interests was reinforced by local circumstances that were difficult to understand by those from outside the area. Given that the shared identities upon which so much of his work depends were coming under increasing pressure as the influence of the London music hall burgeoned, the appearance in his repertoire of parodies of cockney songs, many of which he wrote as a consequence of seeing London entertainers performing in Newcastle, indicates that he too had begun to look over his shoulder.

Ned Corvan had good reason to be worried. After a spell as a publican in the late 1850s, he returned to the music hall, though by now many of the small halls had gone under in the face of pressure from commercial chains just as local artists were losing out to London stars. "What had happened," Dave Harker asserts, "was that big capital had seen a promising investment, and had bought up most of the 'machine tools." Thus when Corvan appeared at the Tyne Theater, *"even in spite of his sustained popularity*, he was continuously made to play second fiddle . . . to the imported, London-based stars, to the foreign attractions like the Christy Minstrels and, most decisively of all, to the culture and ideology of the proprietors."[29]

Although examples of genuine working-class expression continued during this period, so much of the evidence suggests that as the nineteenth century progressed the music hall became a tool to endorse the prevailing social order as well as the desires of those at the apex of the social hierarchy. Joe Wilson, Ned Corvan's contemporary and fellow Geordie, is a useful example of how ideologically subtle some of the significant changes that affected the music hall actually were. While Wilson was often regarded as a working-class radical, Dave Harker has shown that he was "really useful in helping to popularize the values, attitudes and ideas espoused by the bourgeoisie, and by those who aspired to that status."[30] In fact, while Wilson's style panders to prevailing notions of respectability and his belief in temperance, his work offers little or no concession to those too desperate to worry about the state of their boots nor those driven to drink by circumstance. In "Bad Beuts" the social ostracism Wilson suggests awaits those afflicted with worn footwear is as certain as the social order is immutable. After all, as the song has it, "it's the way o' the world if a chep's hard up."[31]

Such attitudes nurtured a social vision far removed from the collective identities so important to Ned Corvan. For Joe Wilson, who ironically once played

---

[29]   Ibid., 54.

[30]   Dave Harker, "Joe Wilson: 'Comic Dialectical Singer' or Class Traitor?" in *Music Hall: Performance and Style*, ed. J.S. Bratton (Milton Keynes: Open University Press, 1986), 127.

[31]   "What That Man Might Heh Been," <http://www.geocities.com/matalzi/priests18. html#songs>. Accessed December 9, 2006.

244   *The Working-Class Intellectual in Eighteenth- and Nineteenth-Century Britain*

at a benefit concert for his fellow Geordie, the self-help culture, which he seems
to have been completely captivated by, leads to his condemnation of alcohol and
those who use it:

> Thor once wes a time-when i' bizniss his-sel,
> He held a fine place I' the toon,
> An' bore a gud nyem as a nice sort o' man
> That few, varry few wad run doon;
> But the hyem that he had wassint peaceful aw've heard,
> He'd trubbles that cuddint be seen,
> So he flew te the drink-an' it myeks a chep sad,
> When he thinks what that man might heh been.
> He had wealth-as a scholar he gain'd greet renoon,
> An' respect frae the foaks that he knew;
> But noo, man, he's poor, for the money he had
> Like chaff on a windy day flew;
> He drinks day an' neet- but he's not biv his-sel,
> For thor's cases like this daily seen,
> An' hoo often ye'll hear iv a cumpny the words
> Wiv a sigh, "What that man might hev been![32]

Inasmuch as it records a standard fall from grace, "What That Man Might Heh
Been," is a fairly typical example of Wilson's many temperance pieces. Typically, in
this song and in others too, Wilson admits no other explanation for alcoholism save
that vaguely intimated kind of moral failure which Victorians attributed to those
they routinely condemned as inadequate. On the other hand, while articulations
of the social order emphasizing respectability became ten-a-penny in Victorian
Britain, the claims to authenticity implicit in the vernacular idiom Wilson uses
make his songs a particularly useful barometer of prescient embourgeoisment.

One might, then, interpret the likes of Joe Wilson as a kind of bridging figure
spanning the distance between the antithetical radicalism of Ned Corvan and the
more overtly pro-establishment "coster" entertainers that emerged in the latter
decades of the century. This particular vision of the music hall, which Martha
Vicinus characterized as a movement from a "class to a mass entertainment," was
a gradual process that entailed the appropriation and manipulation of working-
class images and minds.[33] Once under way, this progressive rearticulation of the
politics of music hall songs could be deployed to buttress dominant ideologies in
limitless ways. Particularly towards the end of the nineteenth century, music hall
narratives, for instance, played an important role in legitimizing the British empire
to a Glasgow audience many of whom no doubt saw their own country as a victim
of English imperialism. Hence expressions of loyalty to the British Empire in
this respect reveal how widespread invitations to identify with British imperialist

---

[32]   Ibid.

[33]   Martha Vicinus, *The Industrial Muse: A Study of Nineteenth Century British
Working Class Literature* (New York: Barnes and Noble, 1974), 238.

goals masked the reassertion of class hierarchy at home. If those Scots "ready tae fecht [fight] for auld England" as one song put it, bear testimony to the powerful internal and cultural hegemony England was asserting north of Hadrian's Wall, they also suggest allegories of class of a strength similar to those that encouraged the suppression of antithetical opinion in the music halls of England.[34] Piecemeal and at times arbitrary though these processes of change were, it is worth pausing to remind ourselves that they required a remarkable ideological journey from the militant opposition of songs such as "The Funny Time Comin,'" where hierarchy is abolished as "the lads" vow to make the "shipping maisters ... work like other men," to songs such as the Scot William C. McPhie's imperial triumphalism wherein "Britain's flag has risen over Afric's sunny plains," and Scots "with their bayonets fixed soon put Britannia's foes to rout".[35]

Behind these questions, which not surprisingly have inspired considerable debate, lay the extension of capitalism, for while it may be that "in the 1860s many of the songs sung in the working-class halls were still anti-aristocratic and populist in tone" it is also the case that capitalist entrepreneurs and institutions provided the means through which the working-class could be manipulated and shaped.[36] In fact, music halls were vulnerable to profit-seeking capitalists as well as those authorities attempting to encourage and control the kind of behavior they believed should be promoted. Even though "opportunities for relatively autonomous working-class experience were still created and used . . . these were under mounting pressure from other social groups with a stake in shaping working-class culture."[37] Equally, no doubt in a further attempt to control song content, it was not unknown for hall owners to employ songwriters. But these were far from the only reasons why the music hall was one of the key ideological battlegrounds of the nineteenth and early twentieth centuries.

Criticism of the music halls also came from a combination of the pressure applied by reformers, often in the guise of temperance groups, who associated the halls with drinking, prostitution, and other examples of debauchery and vice. At the same time, the withholding of entertainment licenses could be and was used as a disciplinary measure against halls associated with behavior to which licensing boards objected. In conjunction with the erosion of political comment of an anti-establishment stripe from the halls, these changes became key elements in the reconfiguration of what was deemed acceptable in the music hall. Among a number of influential directives, "House Rules," which demanded that performers eschew derogatory remarks towards the royal family as well as members of parliament, closed off another avenue of expression. Not surprisingly in this light, as the social composition of the audience became more varied in the later decades of the nineteenth century—though established hierarchy was still visible in the

34 Quoted in Maloney, 165.
35 Quoted in Harker, "The Making," 51; Quoted in Maloney, 166.
36 Stedman Jones, 231.
37 Summerfield, 209.

form of seat price segregation—the content of entertainment in the halls began to reflect social ideologies and visions consistent with establishment values. Little by little, in the aggressive, interventionist attempts to preserve and reassert what many saw as an organic hierarchy crucial to Britain's very existence, the impact of the politics to which the audience was exposed "continued over the course of decades to grow into a creed."[38] But advocating a sense of national identity around the promotion of Empire and one's duty to it fostered more than the advancement of patriotism as a civic responsibility; because it conceals class distinctions under the umbrella of imperial obligation, this conception of "duty" implies unquestioning acceptance of one's "lot" or station in life. Ideas that repeatedly presented hierarchy as sacrosanct and class position as immutable fostered the ingredients with which entertainers could manipulate the visions and images of the working class to the point where the working class was presented with an idealized image of itself. As we have seen, granting the working class an essentialist authenticity of experience, as intellectuals and others did, offered an added layer of legitimacy. However important though all these issues were perhaps the most crucial figure in the rearticulation of the working-class image was that of the staged cockney, especially the persona of the costermonger.

As I noted earlier, the relative autonomy and cohesion of the costermonger community, with its own working hours, meant that costers appeared to be under the command of no one, an issue that, given the Victorian propensity towards vigorous attempts at social control, must have made them an especially appealing target for music hall appropriation. The nature of their profession, especially their visibility and mobility, also made them ideal for the dissemination of political opposition through the sales of broadsides. According to Penelope Summerfield, costermongers "composed many of their own broadsides" wherein they "asserted their political identity in songs opposing restrictive legislation.[39] But there was another reason, no less political, why the coster image was so dramatically altered. Certainly from the 1860s onward, the influence of theatrically trained performers meant that the regional artists, many of whom represented local class interests, were eased out of the halls. If there was a hint of Victorian Darwinism to this theatrical evolution, it could be explained away as a contest between authenticity and acting. After all, the changing composition of the hall audiences, which included an increasing number of patrons whose viewing experiences were defined by the theatre, invited such a conclusion. Accordingly, the audience "decided that class relationships were of less importance than dramatic expertise" and, as "primarily men [sic] of the theater" they "didn't expect to admire performers for the 'authenticity' of their origins as much as for their acting power."[40] It was this kind of subtle shift in emphasis, with pathos replacing authenticity as the benchmark of quality, that opened the way for

---

[38]   Senelick, 155.

[39]   Summerfield, 232.

[40]   John Stokes, *In the Nineties* (Chicago: University of Chicago Press, 1989), 90.

the appropriation of the costermonger image and subsequent rearticlation of the working class.

Alfred Peck Stevens (1839–1888), better known as Alfred Vance or "The Great Vance," was one of the earliest artists to exploit the coster image. Theatrically trained, Vance established his cockney credentials in the 1860s with such "rorty sketches of real life" as "The Ticket of Leave Man," "Costermonger Joe," and "The Chickaleary Cove."[41] The latter, in which the performer affected a curious Jewish articulation, now seems more mockney than Cockney:

> I'm a Chickaleary bloke, with my one—two—three—
> Vitechapel was the willage I was born in;
> To catch me on the hop,
> Or on my tibby drop,
> You must vake up wery early in the mornin'.
> I've got a rorty gal, also a knowing pal,
> And merrily together we jog on.
> And I doesn't car a flatch
> So long as I've a tach,
> Some pannum in my chest—and a tog on!"[42]

In the parlance of the time, one is inclined to cry "well fancy that!" And this, after all, may well be the intended response because this song, with its later references to back-slang ("yenom" = money) and other Cockney fixtures such as "dipping blokes" (pickpockets), is fairly typical of the genre. For all these reasons, it appears difficult to agree that the song's "cockney dialect" is "an assertion of local solidarity and pride."[43] Nonetheless, "The Chickaleary Bloke" and songs of a similar sentiment began to resonate powerfully as they contributed to the changing image of the costermonger. And as there were no shortage of performers willing to impersonate what was becoming a standard version of the stage costermonger, the evolving image became "a desired image created by the music hall and perpetuated by the music hall's feeding upon itself" rather than being a representation founded in the reality of costermonger London.[44] No one contributed more to this process than "the Coster's Laureate," Albert Chevalier (1861–1923).

Chevalier was a character actor who initially thought the halls beneath him. But a period of unemployment quickly removed any inhibitions he may have held about "playing down" in the halls. He made his debut at the Tivoli Theatre in 1891 singing among other songs, "The Future Mrs. 'Awkins" and "Knocked 'Em in the

---

[41] Chance H. Newton, *Idols of the Halls* (Wakefield: E.P. Publishing, 1975 [1928]), 23.

[42] Quoted in Newton, 25.

[43] J.S. Bratton, *The Victorian Popular Ballad* (Totowa: Rowan and Littlefield, 1975), 99.

[44] Derek B. Scott, "The Music-Hall Cockney: Flesh and Blood, or Replicant?" *Music and Letters*, Vol. 83, No. 2 (May, 2002), 256.

Old Kent Road (Wotcher!)." Both of these songs assume only a tenuous pretence towards realism; in the former the singer attempts to woo "sweet Lizer" on the romantic basis that if she dies "an old maid" then she will "only 'ave erself to blame." "Knocked 'Em in the Old Kent Road," which purports to describe typical coster behavior, continues in a similar lexicon:

Last week down our alley came a toff
Nice old geezer with a nasty cough
Sees my missus, takes 'is topper off
In a very gentlemanly way
Wot cher! all the neighbors cried
Who yer gonna meet, Bill
Have yer bought the street, Bill?
Laugh! I thought I should've died
Knocked 'em in the Old Kent Road
Ev'ry evenin' at the stroke of five
Me and the missus takes a little drive
You'd say, Wonderful they're still alive
If you saw that little donkey go
When we starts the blessed donkey stops
He won't move, so out I quickly lops
Pals start whackin' him, when down he drops
Someone says he wasn't made to go
Wot cher! all the neighbors cried
Who yer gonna meet, Bill
Have yer bought the street, Bill?
Laugh! I thought I should've died
Knocked 'em in the Old Kent Road. [45]

"I was there," H. Chance Newton wrote of "Chivvy's" debut, "and well remember the deep impression Chevalier's quaint and semi-pathetic manner and his finished acting made upon the usually rollicking Tivolians."[46] Clearly, as Derek B. Scott points out, Chevalier "was important to the growing respectability of the halls."[47]

Chevalier, in fact, was important in so many ways because his songs underscored and naturalized the established hierarchy in significant ways. At a time when a growing number of lower-middle class clerks were aspiring to rise in the class system—and Leonard Bast in E.M. Forster's *Howards End* became the archetypal example—lines of class demarcation, which were an important means of establishing benchmarks of gentility, were underscored at every opportunity. So thoroughly had the ground in fact been prepared that as the twentieth century opened it mattered little to critics such as Max Beerbohm that Chevalier's costermonger

---

[45]   <http://lyricsplayground.com/alpha/songs/k/knockedemintheoldkentroad.shtml>. Accessed May 15, 2007.

[46]   Quoted in Newton, 121.

[47]   Scott, 250.

was "unfaithful to the Old Kent Road."[48] What was of concern to the same critic was Chevalier's over-acting, or more correctly his didactic delivery. After commending Chevalier's for his lyrics, Beerbohm then castigates his manner and delivery, concluding that "his points do not need such an unconscionable amount of hammering, to drive them home for us."[49] In other words, Beerbohm's anxiety centers on a fear that Chevalier's act runs the risk of undermining the ideological goals it is designed to serve. But given the rapturous reception some of Chevalier's more famous sketches received, it appears that Beerbohm failed to grasp the extent to which the audience had already been taught how to perceive such acts. Such perceptual frameworks were reinforced through sketches such as "The Coster's Serenade" (1890), a song constructed around a staged glimpse at courtship. Here Chevalier first establishes his undying love for "'Arriet" and then proceeds to take her on a mawkishly sentimental trip enlightened by what must have been the customary Cockney attractions:

> You ain't forgotten yet that night in May,
> Down at the Welsh 'Arp, which is 'Endon way;
> You fancied winkles and a pot of tea.
> 'Four-'alf', I murmured, 'is good enough for me'.
> 'Give me a word of 'ope that I may win.'
> You prods me gently with the winkle pin.
> We was as 'appy as could be that day
> Down at the Welsh 'Arp, which is 'Endon way.
> Oh! 'Arriet, I'm waiting, waiting for you my dear.
> Oh! 'Arriet, I'm waiting, waiting alone out here.
> When that moon shall cease to shine,
> False will be this 'eart of mine;
> I'm bound to go on lovin' yer, my dear,
> (spoken) D'ye 'ear? [50]

Ensuring the survival of hierarchical privilege and the social codes and attitudes that gave rise to them, to which this verse makes a strong contribution, necessitates the repeated demonstration of exactly what separates the classes and why those distinctions should be preserved. And what could be more natural in this respect than language, the incorrect usage of which marked the offender out as vulgar? An important denominator in ascertaining degrees of gentility was the "dropped aitch," which at times even functioned as an indicator of social origin. In fact, as P.N. Furbank points out, "the privileging of an artificial and ideal metropolitan accent ... put Cockney, the dialect of the humbler inhabitants of the metropolis, in a special position. If regional dialects were to be 'corrected,'" he goes on,

---

[48]   *More Theatres*, 436.

[49]   Ibid., 437.

[50]   Quoted in *Best Music Hall and Variety Songs*, ed. Peter Gammond (London: Wolfe Publishing, 1972), 27.

"this one was nearest to hand ... and accordingly the one most likely to figure as the archetype of 'incorrectness.'" From this premise it was but a short step "to selecting some feature of Cockney as a shibboleth distinguishing the gentleman from the non-gentleman."[51]

At the time Chevalier was performing commentators saw the development of his stage coster in terms of "a fully-rounded theatrical type or 'mask.'" But the act that accompanied the song was also an important feature of the mask: "The verse finishes, the coster turns, toys with his hat, in one quick movement the billycock has struck ten attitudes, and then the shoulders are squared, the elbows stick out, and the foot leaps forward before the straightened leg into that inimitable coster stride."[52] These exaggerated affectations, which formed an important part of the image of the costermonger Chevalier was projecting, reached their apotheosis in "My Old Dutch," his most popular song. This was the song around which Chevalier created an act of unbelievable sentimentality. Martha Vicinus describes the staging of the song thus:

> 'My Old Dutch' began with a pantomime act: the curtain would open showing the front of a workhouse with its entrances marked 'Men' and 'Women'. Chevalier would enter arm in arm with 'my old Dutch', and the guardian would separate the two, gesturing to the appropriate doors. With a look of horror, Chevalier would say 'You can't do this to us – we've been together for forty years', and break into song.[53]

While Vicinus is correct to argue that "Chevalier's emotional scene pandered to his audience's expectations in a way that made rigid, and ultimately false, the emotions he expressed," that he could expect spectators to take this kind of thing seriously is indicative of his skill in manipulating the audience and the image of coster.[54] Nonetheless, as I have tried to argue, the song's success depends upon the fact that the ground upon which it could be accepted had already been prepared. A couple of representative verses and the chorus run as follows:

> I've got a pal,
> A reg'lar out an' outer,
> She's a dear good old gal,
> I'll tel yer all about 'er.
> It's many years since fust we met,
> 'Er 'air was then as black as jet,
> It's whiter now, but she don't fret,

---

[51]   P.N. Furbank, *Unholy Pleasure or The Idea of Social Class* (Oxford: Oxford University Press, 1985), 102.

[52]   D.F. Cheshire, *Music Hall in Britain* (Rutherford: Fairleigh Dickinson University Press, 1974), 66.

[53]   *The Industrial Muse*, 275.

[54]   Ibid, 275. J.S. Bratton provides a compelling argument that "My Old Dutch" was meant to be taken seriously. See *The Victorian Popular Ballad*, 100.

Not my old gal!
We've been together now for forty years,
An' it don't seem a day too much;
There ain't a lady livin' in the land
As I'd 'swop' for my dear Old Dutch!
There ain't a lady livin' in the land
As I'd 'swop' for my dear Old Dutch!
I calls 'er Sal,
'Er proper name is Sairer,
An' yer may find a gal
As you'd consider fairer.
She ain't a angel - she can start
A jawin' till it make yer smart;
She's just a woman bless 'er 'eart,
Is my old gal![55]

Described by Chance Newton as a "famous domestic monologue," it is difficult to see this song as anything other than jejune. Nevertheless, at the time it was written and performed arguments as to its didactic purpose were seriously entertained.[56] For instance the reformer Laura Ormiston Chant, felt that "My Old Dutch" expressed "the finest sentiments of the human heart ... in a language understood by the people," while Lewis Carroll was moved to record that Chevalier's influence on public taste "is towards refinement and purity."[57] To what extent these opinions are in any way representative is virtually impossible to tell. What such comments do alert us to, however, is the presence of emotionally paternalistic attitudes towards the working class; by the same token, the implication that the working class could understand only a limited register provides its own rationale for the manipulation of the costermonger: it is done for working class's own good. Hidden behind these various forms of noblesse oblige is a congruity of thought and attitude much of which to one extent or another turns upon the preservation of hierarchy, station, and authority; the affinity between allegorized visions of life and the social order reinforced this compact. At issue, of course, is the duplicitous yet paradoxically impressive extent to which those in a position to exert influence understood that "the social order was not simply 'out there' in social and economic structures, but 'in here,' being actively constructed in the imaginative life of audiences ..."[58] This was the kernel of knowledge that set in motion the staged sublimation of working class interests and their replacement by "compensatory" claims that theirs was the only true authentic British experience.

Throughout the critical canon that comprises music hall historiography, representations that affirm the logic of working-class experience as organically

---

[55] Quoted in *Best Music Hall and Variety Songs*, 86.

[56] Newton, 122.

[57] Quoted in Vicinus, 275; Quoted in Cheshire, 67.

[58] Patrick Joyce, *Visions of the People: Industrial England and the Question of Class 1848–1914* (Cambridge: Cambridge University Press, 1991), 225.

authentic invariably work at one level or another to camouflage and deny vestigial class agitation. By the very same process, hierarchy was reinforced and station and rank re-asserted. Hence it comes as no surprise to find that "political music-hall songs never really attacked the system as such."[59] Instead, they were used to buttress a system wherein Conservative values dominated. As one critic put it, the music hall was a place in which "Toryism must be seen as a theatrical convention as traditional and as unquestioned as the comedian's red nose."[60] The extent to which social aspiration was viewed as a subject fit only for scorn corroborates such apposite conclusions. Yet the fact that many members of the working class saw class as immutable belies how much ideological reinforcement was required for such a position to be reached. In this ideological aim the music hall had few peers; as a means of reinforcing social distinctions it fostered a myth of British community contingent upon the acceptance of one's "lot" or "place." These were lessons that in one way or another were repeated so frequently that they became second nature.

Aspirations towards working-class social advancement were universalized as a topic suitable solely for scorn long before the arrival of *Me and My Girl*, that 1930s lesson in adherence to one's social station. Written by Douglas Furber, Arthur Rose, and Neol Gay, this musical enshrined as fit only for parody working-class pretensions to what Lewis Carroll referred to as "refinement." The plot is familiar: the death of Lord Hareford precipitates the news that he had fathered an illegitimate child, who becomes the heir to his fortune and his title. To the horror of Hareford's friends and relatives, the heir is Lambeth costermonger Bill Snibson. Worse still, Snibson's girlfriend, Sally, is a cockney. Predictably, the plot centers upon attempts to make Snibson into a gentleman and Sally a lady, a desire the servants at Hareford Hall condemn as impossible. Eventually, after much confusion, assorted cockney characters, complete with Pearly King and Queen (an exaggerated version of the distinctive buttoned costumes worn by costers), teach the upper-class characters a song and dance, "The Lambeth Walk." But in the context of the staged image of the working class, one cannot help but wonder whether the immensely popular "Lambeth Walk" is the corollary of decades of social manipulation. Is this song really anything other than the working class reverting to its "rightful place," a position to which legions of music hall entertainers had invited it to assume? In much the same way that Daisy Hill's contention "it's nice to be common sometimes" lauded the alleged simplicity of working class life, "The Lambeth Walk," where everything was "free and easy" and you could "do as you darn well pleasy," made much of the notion that cheerful cockneys could sometimes teach the toffs a thing or two.[61]

But, as we have seen, this was a concession contingent upon the working class accepting the place assigned to it by those who sought to purge the music halls of

---

[59]   Kift, 41.

[60]   Senelick, 165.

[61]   "TheLambethWalk,"<http://www.lyricsfreak.com/m/me+and+my+girl/the+lambeth+walk_10177677.html>. Accessed May 12, 2007.

class antagonism and political agitation. Those who presented the staged image of the working class, those who played at poverty, were a crucial element in a process that arguably at some level involved a shift in working-class attitudes from the social agitation found in the early music hall to the collaborationist acquiescence of its final years. And this was a process that is inscribed in the lyrics of the periods in question; it entailed a move from the antagonism of Ned Corvan's "Sum people's born wi' silver spoons i' thor gobs, but it strikes me mine's been a basin o' soop" ("The Soop Kitchin"), to the acceptance of one's lot in *Me and My Girl*, where Sally Smith, Bill Snibson's sweetheart, is encouraged to "take it on the chin, cultivate a little grin and smile!" ("Take it on the Chin").[62]

Works Cited

"Knocked 'Em in the Old Kent Road." <http://lyricsplayground.com/alpha/songs/k/knockedemintheoldkentroad.shtml>. Accessed 15 May 15, 2007.

"Take it on the Chin." <http://www.lyricsfreak.com/m/me+and+my+girl/take+it+on+the+chin_10177679.html>. Accessed April 1, 2007.

"The Lambeth Walk." <http://www.lyricsfreak.com/m/me+and+my+girl/the+lambeth+walk_10177677.html>. Accessed May 12, 2007.

"The Soop Kitchin." <http://www.geocities.com/matalzi/priests16.html#The%20Tyneside%20Chorus>. Accessed April 1, 2007.

"What That Man Might Heh Been." <http://www.geocities.com/matalzi/priests18.html#songs>. Accessed December 9, 2006.

Anderson, G.L. "The Social Economy of Late-Victorian Clerks," *The Lower Middle Class in Britain 1870–1914*, ed. Geoffrey Crossick. New York: St. Martin's Press, 1977.

Beerbohm, Max. *More Theatres, 1898–1903*. London: Rupert Hart-Davis, 1969.

Bratton, J.S. *The Victorian Popular Ballad*. Totowa: Rowan and Littlefield, 1975.

Cheshire, D.F. *Music Hall in Britain*. Rutherford: Fairleigh Dickinson University Press, 1974.

Eliot, T.S. "Marie Lloyd," in *Selected Prose of T.S. Eliot*, ed. Frank Kermode. New York: Farrar, Strauss and Giroux, 1975.

Faulk, Barry J. *Music Hall & Modernity: The Late-Victorian Discovery of Popular Culture*. Athens: Ohio University Press, 2004.

Furbank, P.N. *Unholy Pleasure or The Idea of Social Class*. Oxford: Oxford University Press, 1985.

Gammond, Peter, ed. *Best Music Hall and Variety Songs*. London: Wolfe Publishing, 1972.

Harker, Dave. "Joe Wilson: 'Comic Dialectical Singer' or Class Traitor?" in *Music Hall: Performance and Style*, ed. J.S. Bratton. Milton Keynes: Open University Press, 1986.

---

[62]   <http://www.geocities.com/matalzi/priests16.html#The%20Tyneside%20Chorus>. Accessed April 1, 2007; <http://www.lyricsfreak.com/m/me+and+my+girl/take+it+on+the+chin_10177679.html>. Accessed April 1, 2007.

254   *The Working-Class Intellectual in Eighteenth- and Nineteenth-Century Britain*

———. "The Making of the Tyneside Concert Hall," *Popular Music*, Vol. 1 (1981).

Jones, Gareth Stedman. *Languages of Class: Studies in Working Class History, 1832–1982*. Cambridge: Cambridge University Press, 1983.

Joyce, Patrick. *Visions of the People: Industrial England and the Question of Class 1848–1914*. Cambridge: Cambridge University Press, 1991.

Kift, Dagmar. *The Victorian Music Hall: Culture, Class and Conflict*. Cambridge: Cambridge University Press, 1991.

Macqeen-Pope, W. *The Melodies Linger On: The Story of the Music Hall*. London: W.H. Allen, n.d.

Maloney, Paul. *Scotland and the Music Hall, 1850–1914*. Manchester: Manchester University Press, 2003.

Middleton, Richard. "Articulating Musical Meaning/Re-constructing Musical History/Locating the 'Popular,'" *Popular Music*, Vol. 5, 1985.

Newton, Chance H. *Idols of the Halls*. Wakefield: E.P. Publishing, 1975.

Russell, Dave. *Popular Music in England, 1840–1914*. Montreal: McGill-Queen's University Press, 1987.

Scott, Derek B. "The Music-Hall Cockney: Flesh and Blood, or Replicant?" *Music and Letters*, Vol. 83, No. 2, May, 2002.

Senelick, Laurence. "Politics as Entertainment: Victorian Music-Hall Songs," *Victorian Studies*, Vol. 19, No. 2, 1975.

Stokes, John. *In the Nineties*. Chicago: University of Chicago Press, 1989.

Stoll, Rae Harris. "The Unthinkable Poor in Edwardian Writing," *Mosaic*, December, 1982.

Summerfield, Penelope. "The Effingham Arms and the Empire: Deliberate Selection in the Evolution of Music Hall in London," in *Popular Culture and Class Conflict, 1590–1914: Explorations in the History of Labour and Leisure*, eds Eileen Yeo and Stephen Yeo. Brighton: Harvester Press, 1981.

Thompson, E.P. *The Making of the English Working Class*. New York: Vintage, 1966.

Vicinus, Martha. *The Industrial Muse: A Study of Nineteenth Century British Working Class Literature*. New York: Barnes and Noble, 1974.

Williamson, Philip. "The Doctrinal Politics of Stanley Baldwin," in *Public and Private Doctrine: Essays in British History Presented to Maurice Cowling*, ed. Michael Bentley. Cambridge: Cambridge University Press, 2002.

Part II
Resistance, Struggle and Conflict

[7]

Irony, Deception, and Political Culture in the Works of Dmitri Shostakovich

JENNIFER GERSTEL

The existence of irony in music is a topic that has recently attracted the attention of both musicologists and literary theorists. Focusing on the "double-voicedness" employed by Shostakovich under the Soviet regime, this essay explores the ways that the production and reception of musical irony are influenced by cultural and political context.

The fact that the arts in the Soviet Union survived the 1930s and 40s is amazing, for Joseph Stalin had no more taste for art than he had for insubordination. Yet somehow, despite the constant threat of silencing, Soviet artists managed to produce masterpieces which revolutionized the art world and were globally acclaimed, especially in the field of music. Richard Taruskin, in *Defining Russia Musically* (1997), writes that "no one alive today can imagine the sort of extreme mortal duress to which artists in the Soviet Union were then subjected, and Shostakovich more than any other" (516). If there is something ironic about the achievements of artists like Shostakovich, however, the question that arises in turn is where does the irony lie and to what extent was it a deliberate strategy adopted by musicians under the Stalinist regime?

Although irony as an artistic strategy has traditionally been associated primarily with literary works, such "double-voicing" has a long history that spans the spectrum of artistic endeavor, as Linda Hutcheon has recently argued in a far-ranging study provocatively titled *Irony's Edge* (64). Highlighting the differences and similarities between irony in literature and in other modes of art, Hutcheon taps into the difficulty of delineating exactly where irony is located and how ironic meaning is generated. She titles one section

36 *Mosaic* 32/4 (December 1999)

of her study "The unbearable slipperiness of irony," and musicologists have noted the same frustrating inability to pin down ironic effect in music, perhaps more so in the case of Shostakovich than with any other composer. Indeed, in an analysis of Shostakovich's *Tenth Symphony*, David Fanning concludes: "it is still no more possible to prove the existence of irony in music than to define the parameters of an ironic 'oh yes' in literature." As he also observes, however, listeners do seem to recognize the existence of irony and respond to it, a situation he sees as owing partly to extra-musical factors: "Timing, context, and cultural conventions, some would say ideology, too, all contribute to the instinct which may lead us to impute such meaning; and performance...plays a crucial role in its communication" (73).

In this essay, I want to pursue both a musical and an extra-musical reading of Shostakovich's use of irony, showing how the extreme cultural and political circumstances surrounding his activity as a composer entwine content and context and how a perception of the ironies built into his works are largely dependent on what Hutcheon calls "discursive communities" (18). As Taruskin puts it, "[w]hat made Shostakovich's music the secret diary of a nation was not only what he put into it but what it allowed listeners to draw out" (474). I will begin my analysis with a brief history of Shostakovich's unique position in the Stalinist regime, and move forward to investigate how Hutcheon's theory of irony operates when applied to several musical texts by Shostakovich, taking into account the external problems of authorial intention, a shifting historical context, and what Taruskin describes as the "social value" of Shostakovich's music (476). Finally, I will draw attention to the continuing critical debates and lack of consensus surrounding the interpretation of Shostakovich's music, with a view to suggesting how such controversy provides perhaps the best indication of all that the essence of ironic expression continues to elude its pursuers.

In *The Irony Tower*, Andrew Solomon writes that "one seldom needs to search for ironies in Moscow; more often than not, they are given like gifts" (7). Indeed, the collection of strategies used by 20th-century Soviet artists reads like a recipe for the range of methods possible in the production of irony. It is hardly surprising that these artists turned to ironic expression so heavily during the most critical period in their struggle for survival, for, as Hayden White notes, the history of irony everywhere reflects its usage as a powerful "transideological" tool (38). Similarly, as Hutcheon observes, irony "can and does function tactically in the service of a wide range of political positions, legitimating or undercutting a wide variety of interests" (10). The majority of Soviet artists creating works with covert meanings used irony to highlight the difference between the true and the false, deliberately engaging in deception in order to question the tenets of the political system which governed both their lives and their work.

To varying degrees, the system of threats and rewards was applied to all artists, collectively and individually, according to what the government identified as their talent, power, and potential to be useful or subversive. In *Art Under Stalin*, Matthew Cullerne Bown observes that artists developed different methods of resistance for coping with the stringent and constantly shifting requirements that "had nothing in common with reality," and he goes on to note that some, especially those in the visual arts, reacted by "depicting a fictitious land 'flowing with milk and honey' in the most banal and bombastic manner," knowing that "the more ingratiating [the] falsity, the more trustworthy [an artist's] work was deemed" (154, 156). Some composers created works privately according to their own tastes, performed them only for friends, and hid them from public performance until more critically favorable—or physically safer—times. Russians called this strategy composing "for the desk," a phrase which by its very existence suggests that the practice was prevalent. Some broke down and "reformed" their habits, composing pieces in "ideologically unassailable" genres; thus Prokoviev's and Myaskovsky's "work lists[are] studded with cantatas to the glory of Stalin and Kirov" (Schwarz 244, 174). Some became Party functionaries responsible for punishing their former colleagues or colluded in the censuring of their fellow artists after Zhdanov's decree in 1948 which "decisively condemned all attempts to separate art from politics" (Cullerne Bown 206).

Other artists, however, those of the younger generation such as the cellist Mstislav Rostropovich and the writer Alexander Solzhenitsyn, spoke out defiantly against the post-Stalinist regimes, whereby they found themselves exiled and stripped of their citizenship. In the late 1960s and early 70s, dissidents in many areas of the arts and sciences commonly made their escapes to Israel, western Europe, or the United States. But perhaps the most creative approach to dealing with early mid-century intellectual repression, and certainly the most difficult to effect successfully in art, was the phenomenon of double-voicedness, that is, the ability to communicate two or more opposed meanings at once. To lie and tell the truth at the same time was the supreme act of subversion during Stalin's tyranny. And no one did it better, or with more wit, humor, sarcasm, and irony, than Shostakovich.

38 *Mosaic* 32/4 (December 1999)

The Soviet government early recognized that Shostakovich, once he had come to its attention by his first public successes, might be groomed as the showpiece of modern Soviet music, both at home and abroad. Born in 1906 in St. Petersburg, he came of age in the highly politicized culture of the early 1920s. With the best training in Moscow, Shostakovich began to turn out acutely original and topical works, despite the political instability associated with the death of Lenin and Stalin's rise to power around 1928. It was in the Party's best interest to see that the young composer's rare talent was molded to conform to the Stalinist public-relations machine of nationalist self-congratulation. This meant portraying Russian history and culture as the sole inspiration for all artistic endeavors, glamorizing peasant life, displaying foreign influence, if at all, as degenerate, and paying extravagant homage to the rapidly developing cult of Stalin. Shostakovich, however, made several serious errors early in his career. He objected to being the trick pony of the Communist party; he was attracted to a humanism which could not be reconciled with the ideology of Stalin and his "culture minister" Andrei Zhdanov; and, as an artist, he demanded the luxury of being allowed to think for himself and determine the direction of his own music. As a creative intellectual and a popular national figure, the young Shostakovich posed a threat to Stalin's control. In the words of an old Russian proverb, Shostakovich was learning to "kiss but spit" (Roseberry, *Shostakovich* 121).

A study of Shostakovich's musical career, which spanned the fifty years between 1925-75, is necessarily a study in survival tactics, which began with his adoption of the role of *yurodivy* (or "holy fool"), and grew increasingly complex, layered, and desperate with the composer's gain in stature and with Stalin's tightening of ideological control. This tacit "relationship" between Shostakovich and Stalin, of course, was hardly voluntary. Yet the strategy was shockingly successful; Shostakovich's swift, exaggerated apologies and *mea culpas* served to keep him from being imprisoned, exiled, or killed. Shostakovich's most recent biographer, Elizabeth Wilson, argues that the classic figure of the *yurodivy* in Russian culture works by "us[ing] arcane symbols or simplistic parables to express the truth...[so that] every statement could have more than one message," thus stopping just short of outright offending the Czar (428). Also, as Solomon Volkov makes clear, traditionally, the "holy fool...protests in the name of humanity, and not in the name of political changes" (xxxiii), thus claiming what Wilson calls "the historical right to expose evil" (428). Eric Roseberry similarly supports the theory of Shostakovich's attraction to the concept of the *yurodivy* when he remarks that the Fool in

Shakespeare's *King Lear* was one of Shostakovich's favorite characters (*Shostakovich* 13).

On the strength of his peculiar "relationship" with Stalin, Shostakovich was likely to be protected from the worst types of harm that came to some of his colleagues, but this did not mean that he could openly criticize Stalin or the Soviet political system. Thus, in two great waves of governmental intervention in the arts, in 1936 and 1948, Shostakovich was stripped of his teaching job at the Leningrad Conservatory, his works were forbidden to be performed, he was publicly insulted and criticized, shunned on the street, notified of his "errors," and instructed by "Party musicologists" what type of music he should create: songs reflecting the glory of Stalin, the Soviet land, and the Soviet people. So while others were jailed or "disappeared," Shostakovich was left to squirm and confess; Stalin reserved for him the special mental torture of fear without end. Thus it was that his *Fourth Symphony* was put away for years and left unperformed while he struggled to compose music fit for public consumption according to the dictates of the authorities.

Wilson argues that Shostakovich adapted the "holy fool" of traditional Czarist culture "to the conditions of Soviet Russia"—i.e., where "the modern *yurodivy* revealed the truth at the level of the 'sub-text', making this apparent by deliberately communicating banalities on the surface level" (428). Such a method of truth-telling in secret requires a purposeful and exaggerated mediocrity with which the composer must blanket his deeper, meaningful statements. It requires two distinct audiences and levels of competency: one to understand nothing more than the "surface level" which appears as mere melody and harmony, and one to distinguish the composer's intended real message—variously described as existing behind, underneath, through, or inside the shell of "meaningless beautification"(MacDonald 260)—and available only to the discerning and privileged listeners who share a certain "cultural or philosophical competency" with the composer (Hatten 47).

In such a binary model, the hermeneutics become difficult to untangle: musical deception and the presentation of truth are placed in opposition with both levels of reception and interpretation being enabled and defined by each other, yet all listeners hear the same combinations of sounds at the same time. The challenge for Soviet composers was to be both inclusive and protective. What set Shostakovich apart, however, was his disinterest in mere "banalities" as a surface gloss. Mediocrity made him impatient; he demanded that his compositions provide an immediate richness and engagement for even the most casual listener, whose

40 *Mosaic* 32/4 (December 1999)

burden in turn was to hear and take away from a piece more than just music. This, of course, makes interpretation of Shostakovich as the transmitter of only two qualitatively different messages much more difficult.

Shostakovich was once asked near the end of his life why he agreed to sign his name to articles and statements which Soviet ideologues composed for him, and which did not reflect his true opinions. Many younger artists who were fighting openly in the 1960s and early 70s had a difficult time condoning his submissive behavior and wondered which side he was on. Instead of responding directly, Shostakovich referred skeptics to his music: "Look," he replied, "words are not my genre. I never lie in music. That's enough" (qtd. in MacDonald 252). Shostakovich's unease with words and preference for music reveal his divergence from the traditional *yurodivy* who juggled vocabulary and rhetoric both to please the czar and criticize him. To Shostakovich, music was the true language of multiplicity, which always expressed the truth, never lied, yet was always subject to interpretation. With music he felt that he was able to say everything but admit nothing. In the last public statement before his death, Shostakovich described music as "an art that is especially communicative, an art that travels all over the world without a visa and requires no translation into other languages" (qtd. in Schwarz 573).

As I see it, while Shostakovich's use of irony can sometimes be approached through the concept of the *yurodivy*, he also goes beyond the traditional oppositional stance of the "holy fool" to encompass a more nuanced range of meanings and suggestions. Alternatives to a superficial reading of the music may be expressed in language suggesting geographical proximity, such as "behind" or "underneath," but the possibilities do not necessarily have to be limited to the juxtaposition of opposites. With strictly political ironies, those produced specifically as "oppositional rhetoric," there may well be an intending ironist who aims a politically charged message at a self-selecting community, with the instructions to elicit a reaction of dissent disguised or coded within the seemingly innocuous. Or the message(s) may be more general, but still fully intended and opposed to that expressed.

Hutcheon contends that irony by definition "comes into being in the relations between meanings...so that both the said and the unsaid together make up th[e] third meaning," the ironic and critically evaluative one (12, 60). Thus double-voicedness—a traditional cornerstone of irony—may actually be triple-voicedness, or even polyphonic expression. In fact, Hutcheon quotes the musicological phrase used by T. McCracken in

"Triple-voicing: the multicultural canon" in order to explain the phenomenon: "two notes played together produce a third note which is at once both notes and neither," perhaps indicating the affinity of irony for a medium structured to generate multiple layers of meaning simultaneously (60). Yet if irony need not be definitively separated into the true and the untrue, as Hutcheon argues, then how do we categorize the many specific and meaningful counter-statements in Soviet art, which are aimed at a particular audience, but which could not be openly expressed? Hutcheon argues that "it is because of its very foregrounding of the politics of human agency...that irony has become an important strategy of oppositional rhetoric" (11-12). Soviet artists knew this implicitly.

Indeed, Hutcheon departs from what she refers to as "the party line [which] says that there is an intending 'ironist' and her/his intended audiences—the one that 'gets' and the one that doesn't 'get' the irony" (10), an approach exemplified most prominently by Wayne Booth in *The Rhetoric of Irony* (1974). The "party line," as she describes it, is precisely what we have in the simplified example of the *yurodivy*: "neat theories of irony that see the task of the interpreter simply as one of decoding or reconstructing some 'real' meaning (usually named as the 'ironic' one)," a meaning "that is hidden, but deemed accessible, behind the stated one" (11). Hutcheon's suggestion is that real-life ironies—rather than those devolved from theory—are much more complex and difficult to grasp, for they do not stabilize as separable binaries: "The ironic meaning is not...simply the unsaid meaning, and the unsaid is not always a simple inversion or opposite of the said"; rather, irony functions as a set of "dynamic and plural relations among the text or utterance (and its context)," where meanings are slippery, multiple, and find their locations "in the space *between* (and including) the said and the unsaid" (12-13, 11, 12). Taruskin also negatively cites Wayne Booth in an effort to show what Shostakovich does not do; he argues that the question of "intent" here is "naive, unanswerable, and irrelevant," and that the social power of the music is derived from its "uncontrollable play of subtexts" (472).

Fanning's concluding chapter in his monograph on the *Tenth Symphony* is titled "The Language of Doublespeak," and his comment that "more often than not the surface of the music is not to be trusted" seems to imply that he subscribes to a theory of irony as inversion. In the second movement of this symphony he finds an "[e]motional numbness behind trivial physical activity" and sees this as "one of the most characteristic Shostakovich utterances" (74). How, then, is Shostakovich's irony to be characterized? Is irony here simply a clear case of duplicity featuring the

Music and Protest

said versus the unsaid, the true contrasted yet blended with the untrue, as
Wilson believes, and possibly Fanning? If so, what precisely is the unsaid
message, and are we, as late 20th-century Western listeners, qualified to
understand it as the "ironist" intended? Or does Shostakovich as a composer go beyond the programme of the double message to embrace an
untranslatable, polymorphous, polyphonic, yet universal vision? The
answer, quite predictably, is both.

What further complicates the untangling of the intended, the equivocal and dialogic, and the polyphonic here, however, is that in the mid-century Soviet Union, *everything* was politicized and subject to state control,
including the personal. Therefore any personal or individual preference
publicly stated needed to be deceptively designed in order to be disclosed.
It is no coincidence that the works of Mikhail Bakhtin, a contemporary of
Shostakovich, became publishable only toward the end of his life for reasons similar to those which explain why Shostakovich's compositions
were often withheld from public performance. Bakhtin's unpublished
essays, which later became *The Dialogic Imagination*, were not collected
until 1975, the year which saw the death of both men. Bakhtin's major
writings from the 1930s share many of the tensions and concerns apparent in Shostakovich's work of the period, and his theoretical vocabulary is
well-suited to an analysis of Shostakovich's musical philosophy, as
Taruskin suggests.

Furthermore, in a striking argument made about Russian visual artists
in the 1980s—a quite different group from Shostakovich's generation of
composers—Solomon suggests that after decades of repression, concepts
like deception and subterfuge are now firmly embedded in Russian arts,
despite the end of the Cold War: "to tell the truth by way of a lie is as basic
to Soviet artists as the telling of a lie in the vocabulary of truth has historically been to Soviet bureaucrats" (14). For Russians in the 20th century,
according to Solomon, the practice of deception evolved as a Darwinian
trait: those who could do it best had the greatest chance of survival in an
unstable environment. Commenting on the conditions which shaped
modern Soviet artists and their work, he observes:

> [I]t was necessary for serious artists working in the Soviet Union to com-
> municate their truths in fragments, because whole and simple acts of
> communication—given the subversive inclinations behind those acts—
> would have won their authors governmental disapprobation, with all its
> attendant punishments....truth itself took on the status of a forbidden
> indulgence.   (11)

By the beginning of the post-Stalinist era, most Russians had become sus-picious of "whole and simple acts of communication"; several genera-tions of fear instilled in them that an honest approach to personal expression was a danger to be avoided. The status of fiction itself was in jeopardy, for the distinctions between "fictional" and "real" became solely a matter of propaganda. As Solomon puts it, these artists were "[b]red to believe that what is worth saying cannot be said" (39). Therefore the transmission of disguised or elusive messages among Soviet citizens would likely be understood by others within the same cultural milieu.

Deceptive art, or deception *as* art, however, is a concept entirely alien to the West, so that it is not surprising that Western art historians and musicologists have only recently begun to appreciate the formation of the Soviet aesthetic. Historically, Western expectations of openness on the part of Soviet artists have been met with disbelief and even disgust. Tactics such as evasiveness, outright denial of the truth, or representing with eagerness the exact opposite of their true opinions in both public life and public work confused those Westerners accustomed to being able to speak and act in a straightforward manner. For Shostakovich's fellow Soviets, it is precisely the "eagerness" of his pro-Communist public state-ments which would have raised suspicions as to the real state of the case—obsequious exaggeration or understatement being one of the common structural markers for irony. Yet to non-Soviets, the public image of Shostakovich the man often appeared merely as that of an aloof Soviet patriot, confounding those who heard the dissident strains present in his music.

Many Westerners did hear this dissonance, but felt that it was not only at odds with the public statements emanating from the Soviet media but also with statements by the composer himself in interviews with the press. Which to believe? As early as 1943, the American critic of Russian music Gerald Abraham wrote of the *Third Symphony* (1929): "one cannot help feeling that the composer is playing a part....He tries to be Marxian, but fantastic Gogolian humour keeps breaking in" (qtd. in Schwarz 81). Different "discursive communities"—groups who share a similar social-cultural context and thus a similar interpretative framework—responded to Shostakovich's music in different ways, which illustrates the capacity for irony to act as a cultural marker (Hutcheon 82). But Shostakovich's gift to music was his ability, beyond those of all others, to "give voice to truths in terms that were incomprehensible to the bodies responsible for alienating truth itself," in the process transforming irony into art (Solomon 11).

44 *Mosaic* 32/4 (December 1999)

Several examples from Shostakovich's repertoire suggest the ways he ironized music to "give voice to truths" which could not be overtly expressed. The symphonies he wrote in his middle period, culminating with the *Tenth Symphony* (1953), are full of hidden messages, in-jokes, and allusions through which Shostakovich could phrase his frustrations, alienation, doubt, hope, and yearning, for an informed group of listeners. Certainly Shostakovich elicits special meanings from specific combinations of musical notes in a piece such as the *Tenth*, where his musical characterization of Stalin in the short and brutal second movement (see Fig. 1) signals his disgust, blending emotions of furious anger with a technical refusal of melody. Noting the "dual process of intensification...and constraint," Fanning suggests that the "frenetic surface activity and underlying tonal paralysis ...have the music spinning like a rat in a trap" (44).

Fig. 1. Dmitri Shostakovich, *Tenth Symphony*, second movement, fragment. From David Fanning, *The Breath of the Symphonist: Shostakovich's "Tenth."* Reproduced by permission of the Royal Musical Association

The fact that this movement, at its slowest, takes only four minutes, that it begins *fortissimo*, "continues with some 50 *crescendos*" with "no relaxation from the fast opening tempo" emphasizes its extremity and what Fanning calls its "naked violence" (39, 76). As for how Shostakovich was able to get away with such a seemingly obvious "structural metaphor," as Fanning puts it (44), we should note first that the music conveys not two opposite and reversible messages, but rather potential for infinite interpretation, with the listener being asked to determine the music's emotional context and what it might signify. Secondly, we should bear in mind that this was not an attempt to capture Stalin musically while the dictator was still alive; the *Tenth Symphony* is the first orchestral work by Shostakovich to have been written after Stalin's death, in fact, shortly thereafter, and as a result, Shostakovich may have felt that he could assume a higher level of risk than when Stalin was alive.

Moreover, to symbolize his personal freedom from Stalin's tyranny, in this symphony Shostakovich took his Russian initials, "D" for Dmitri, "SCH" for Shostakovich, and transposed them into musical notes (the equivalent in our alphabet of the pitches D, E flat, C, and B), used as a musical signature here in the third and fourth movements of the piece. (see Fig. 2). The controlled racing and clashing of the second movement

'DSCH'

Fig. 2. Dimitri Shostakovich, *Tenth Symphony,* second movement, DSCH motif.
Reproduced by permission of the Royal Musical Association

gives way in the third movement to a first hesitant recital of the DSCH melody, which then gathers strength to override and "shout down" the few last Stalinist interruptions by the fourth movement. Toward the end of the third movement, as Fanning notes, "DSCH has now been heard over modal G, F, and E. From this point through to the coda the phrase-structure is very clearly in four-bar units, with DSCH asserting itself at the end of each phrase" (56; see Fig. 3). While nothing in the piece is apparent to the casual listener, and while nothing in the score or the instructions to the performers overtly links the piece with depictions of Stalin or the composer himself, the repeated musical monogram, as it were, allows the composer to assert his individuality, to maintain his principles and a measure of artistic integrity through a private symbolic system. Yet in an environment potentially hostile to his work Shostakovich was still able to present to the unenlightened listening public—and Party

46 *Mosaic* 32/4 (December 1999)

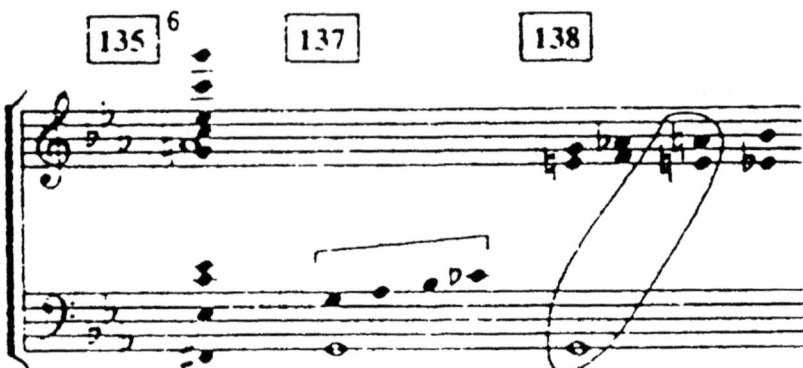

Fig. 3. Dmitri Shostakovich, *Tenth Symphony*, third movement,
fragment with DSCH melody.
Reproduced by permission of the Royal Musical Association

officials—what appeared as ideologically unthreatening, but still very
powerful music. Such a division between the knowing audience and the
ignorant audience, however, becomes increasingly difficult as
Shostakovich's musical language becomes more and more diffuse; a piece
like the *Tenth Symphony* tells an audience *how* to feel, but not necessarily
why. Nevertheless, Shostakovich counted on the fact that contemporary
Soviet audiences who had also suffered under Stalin would tacitly understand him, since they belonged to a similar discursive community—what
was happening to him was also central in the lives of every Soviet citizen.

Several other examples of this type of extended, intended deception-
allusion exist in Shostakovich's corpus as strategies against Stalinist
repression. In general, Shostakovich turned to the string quartet form for
themes of a more "intimate, confessional nature," whereby it became "a
diary into which the composer confided secret, private thoughts"
(Roseberry, *Shostakovich* 13). In contrast to the large public statements
and official stature required of the symphonic genre, the quartet was an
outlet for thoughts which could be shared with a smaller and more sympathetic audience. The later *Eighth Quartet* (1960) is especially famous for
portraying private emotions and politically sensitive material alongside a
veneer of relative normalcy. Yet again, there are no precise oppositional
messages. The intimacy is available and interpretable for those who know
where to look; in some cases, no doubt, Shostakovich structured into his
music personal associations known only to himself. MacDonald refers to
the *Eighth Quartet*, not unkindly, as "the densest mass of self-quotation
Shostakovich ever committed to paper," despite the fact that, most likely
for protection, he inscribed the work impersonally "To the Memory of the

Victims of Fascism" (222). Some evidence suggests that Shostakovich originally intended this quartet as a final work, a kind of musical suicide note, composed immediately after he was forced to join the Communist Party. In a letter to Isaak Glikman of 19 July 1960, he writes: "I have been considering that when I die, scarcely anyone will write a work in my memory. Therefore I have decided to write one myself" (qtd. in Redepenning 210).

The *Eighth Quartet* is saturated with the DSCH motto, combined with several melancholic, wandering themes from his previous works. Roseberry shows how the piece calls upon an "association of ideas" in which the initial DSCH motif, through transposition, addition, and expansion, evolves into a recollection of the "opening gesture" of his *First Symphony (Ideology* 271; see Fig. 4). In the *Eighth Quartet,* in addition to direct musical quotations from his *Eighth Symphony* and the *Second Piano*

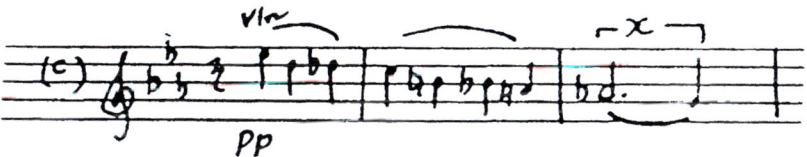

Fig. 4. DSCH theme from Dimitri Shostakovich, *Eighth Quartet.*
As transposed by Roseberry.
Reproduced by permission of Garland Publishing

Trio, other melodies and snatches from his own previous work include his opera *Lady Macbeth of Mtensk.* Among quotations from other works, particularly important are a Russian revolutionary song "Tormented by the hardships of prison," and a Jewish folk song from World War II, whereby he positions himself with the victims of the Holocaust and suggests that he is forced to dig his own grave. Again, this is deeply subversive material because of the institutionalized anti-Semitism of 20th-century Russia. In fact, Joachim Braun argues that Shostakovich frequently adopted "a Jewish idiom as a language of dissent," a highly risky but profoundly resonant maneuver, since at the time he wrote the *Song Cycle From Jewish Folk Poetry* in 1948, "the entire Jewish intellectual elite was either under suspicion or under arrest, including the compilers of *Jewish Folk Songs,* Dobrushin and Yuditsky" (262, 263). It is also worth noting that amid the political controversy and charges of "cosmopolitanism" (a euphemism for anti-Semitism) in the late 1940s, Shostakovich held back the public performance of his most Jewish work until 1955, two years after Stalin's death.

48 *Mosaic* 32/4 (December 1999)

The *Eighth Quartet* also includes an allusion to Shostakovich's most famous work, the *Fifth Symphony* (1937), which according to MacDonald "sp[ins] out its optimism to ridiculous lengths" in the finale in order to mock Stalin. He calls this "satire by overstatement," with Shostakovich being "terrorized into artificial enthusiasm" (110). As he explains it, "the commonest reaction the *Fifth* seems to have called from contemporary Russian listeners was simple relief at hearing tragic emotion expressed during a time when genuine feeling was being systematically destroyed" (125). The ovation for the *Fifth Symphony* at its Leningrad premiere in November 1937 continued for forty minutes, and was first performed during a time when the country was gripped by "mass arrests, disappearances, and executions" (Taruskin 516). As MacDonald suggests, "tragic" and "satirical" are terms frequently used together to describe Shostakovich's music. Similarly, Fanning's commentary on the finale of the *Tenth Symphony* calls the piece a "pessimistic comedy" (72). Indeed, most critics find it difficult to resist juxtaposing opposites in an effort to access Shostakovich's musical vocabulary. If Shostakovich highlights the difference between truth and fiction in the *Fifth*, however, he does so, ironically, by blending them together; it is that subtle critical edge to his blending of the two which alert listeners would recognize.

The Soviet authorities constantly complained and warned Shostakovich that his compositions were too elitist and that he did not write for "the people." As Schwarz notes, he was frequently found guilty of "formalist distortions and anti-democratic tendencies which are alien to the Soviet people and its artistic taste," charges for which he either had to apologize or risk "disappearance" (219). The image of Shostakovich as anti-populist was a label he vehemently rejected and a topic which caused him much consternation. Schwarz, together with other modern critics, argues aggressively on his behalf that Shostakovich "never posed as an 'ivory tower' artist...he had a need for communication...He wanted to be 'understood' by the people. But, like all genuine artists, he wanted to be understood through his *best* efforts, not by 'writing down' to the people." Schwarz, who himself escaped with his family from Russia during World War II, identifies the errors of the Stalinist "populist aesthetic" as "not so much that 'art must be understandable by the people', but that *all* art must be understood by *all* the people" (245). Interestingly, the Stalinist position here reflects the same basic criticism often mustered against irony itself—that its very nature is not universally accessible and therefore that its use is suspect.

Having lived his entire adult life under the Soviet system, Shostakovich somehow still retained an unshakable belief in the power of the individual, in human agency and integrity. Thus he quietly refused to supply the demand for Soviet musical propaganda. Yet as he grew older, and while he was still composing, he signed ridiculously pro-Soviet articles and made speeches written for him without protest. As Taruskin observes, Shostakovich "was the one and only Soviet artist to be claimed equally by the official culture and the dissident culture" (482). The balancing act drove him close to suicide several times and nearly catapulted him into insanity on many occasions. His seeming inconsistency, however, has left a legacy of wildly divergent opinions among critics and musicologists as to his true opinions and attitudes. He continues to be seen, depending on interpretation and ideology, as either a hero or heretic, or somewhere inexplicably between.

The field of Shostakovich interpretation was also vastly complicated in 1977 with the publication of Solomon Volkov's *Testimony: The Memoirs of Dmitri Shostakovich*, which purported to be the texts of interviews between Volkov and Shostakovich over a period of months late in the composer's life. The memoirs portray Shostakovich as a zealous and bitter anti-Communist victim who admits freely to Volkov many things not corroborated elsewhere. Soviet attempts at recovering the official image of Shostakovich as a Communist patriot led to repudiation of *Testimony* as a piece of anti-Soviet propaganda invented by Volkov. The Volkov text, moreover, has equally come to be regarded as highly suspicious by many Shostakovich biographers, to the point where they refer to the image of Shostakovich propagated there as "Volkov's Shostakovich." Indeed, in a fascinating investigative article titled "Shostakovich versus Volkov: whose *Testimony*?" Laurel E. Fay has traced discrepancies between Volkov's claims about Shostakovich and those from other sources. At the same time, serious scholars of the composer, including Taruskin, do find useful and irreplaceable the insights into Soviet cultural conditions and Shostakovich's milieu that Volkov's own voice provides. Despite their discomfort with the idea of Shostakovich's "memoirs" as told to Volkov, many scholars continue to quote him.

Since Shostakovich's public verbal statements and writings were known to have been tainted by coercion, and the interpretation of his music seemed to be mired in as much controversy as his beliefs, in the 1980s a reassessment of the music took place in the West. Not surprisingly, the conclusion reached by many critics was that his music "eludes

50 *Mosaic* 32/4 (December 1999)

any superimposed single order of meaning, whether of the orthodox or the Western-revisionist cast" (Norris 9). By the mid 1990s, in turn, a second wave of Shostakovich studies appeared, one which had recovered from the confusions of the newly post-Communist era, and is exemplified by the 1995 collection entitled *Shostakovich Studies*, edited by Fanning. Until very recently, however, there has been difficulty in treating Soviet music solely in its historical context, as Taruskin relates concerning his participation in a 1991 conference with the theme "Soviet Music toward the 21st Century," when "Between the planning and the convening, the history of Soviet music came dramatically to an end" (511).

Of the theories of irony available to account for the exigencies of Shostakovich's art, Hutcheon's model, which posits a third meaning generated by the friction of the two others, therefore seems closest in application to the way his music actually works. In particular, Fanning's efforts to capture in words Shostakovich's unique brand of ironic expression in the *Tenth Symphony* are particularly evocative precisely because they demonstrate the inability to do so. He compares Shostakovich's irony to "a smile held beyond its natural duration" or "a tragic speech delivered with merry inflections" (71, 72), drawing on verbal analogies to enlarge our understanding just as Hutcheon borrows a musical vocabulary. More cross-disciplinary theory on the nature of irony in music is needed, but for the moment we should note that Shostakovich often goes beyond what Hutcheon calls the "semantic third note" (61) to elicit a whole range of ideas and associations, a multiplicity of voices to which the mode of music is particularly well-suited. Of course, most of these voices would have been unacceptable to the Soviet authorities—if they could hear them.

Shostakovich's secret form of protest was not characterized simply by two single ideas attacking each other, and it is this greater complexity that enabled him to say convincingly "I never lie in music." If irony is "simultaneously disguise and communication," as Hutcheon argues (95), then such communication for Shostakovich is always equivocal, framed, refracted, and projects multiple truths. It is in fact the very opacity of his true thought which made him subversive in a society demanding unity, collectivity, and congruity in every movement of life and art. Thus critics of Shostakovich are both frustrated and inspired by music which "somehow defeats the methods of even the closest and most sensitive formal analysis" (Norris 166). Even the most complex theory of irony or music cannot fully anatomize the phenomenological suspension in which Shostakovich's multiple meanings are held, that friction of interpretations in which all truths are finally held to be inseparable.

WORKS CITED

Braun, Joachim. "The Double Meaning of Jewish Elements in Dmitri Shostakovich's Music." *The Musical Quarterly* 71 (1985): 68-80.

Cullerne Bown, Matthew. *Art Under Stalin.* Oxford: Phaidon, 1991.

Fanning, David. *The Breath of the Symphonist: Shostakovich's "Tenth."* London: Royal Musical Association, 1988.

——————, ed. *Shostakovich Studies.* Cambridge: Cambridge UP, 1995.

Fay, Laurel E. "Shostakovich vs Volkov: whose *Testimony*?" *The Russian Review* 39 (1980): 484-93.

Hatten, Robert. "Interpreting Deception in Music." *In Theory Only* 12 (1992): 31-50.

Hutcheon, Linda. *Irony's Edge: The Theory and Politics of Irony.* London: Routledge, 1994.

MacDonald, Ian. *The New Shostakovich.* London: Fourth Estate, 1990.

Norris, Christopher, ed. *Shostakovich: The Man and his Music.* London: Lawrence and Wishart, 1982.

Redepenning, Dorothea. "'And art made tongue-tied by authority': Shostakovich's Song-cycles." *Shostakovich Studies.* Ed. David Fanning. Cambridge: Cambridge UP, 1995. 205-28.

Roseberry, Eric. *Ideology, Style, Content, and Thematic Process in the Symphonies, Cello Concertos, and String Quartets of Shostakovich.* New York: Garland, 1989.

——————. *Shostakovich, His Life and Times.* Kent, UK: Midas, 1982.

Schwarz, Boris. *Music and Musical Life in Soviet Russia, 1917-1981.* Bloomington: Indiana UP, 1983.

Shostakovich, Dmitri. *Symphony No. 5* in D Minor, Opus 47, 1937.

——————. *Symphony No. 10* in E Minor, Opus 93, 1953.

——————. *String Quartet No. 8* in C Minor, Opus 110, 1960.

Solomon, Andrew. *The Irony Tower: Soviet Artists in a Time of Glasnost.* New York: Knopf, 1991.

Taruskin, Richard. *Defining Russia Musically: Historical and Hermeneutical Essays.* Princeton: Princeton UP, 1997.

Volkov, Solomon, ed. *Testimony: The Memoirs of Dmitri Shostakovich.* New York: Harper & Row, 1979.

White, Hayden. *Metahistory: The Historical Imagination in Nineteenth-Century Europe.* Baltimore: Johns Hopkins UP, 1973.

Wilson, Elizabeth. *Shostakovich: A Life Remembered.* London: Faber, 1994.

JENNIFER GERSTEL is a Ph.D. candidate in English literature at the University of Toronto, focusing on science and the Victorian novel. Her doctoral dissertation is entitled "Sexual Selection in Darwin, Gaskell, Eliot, and Hardy."

[8]

IRAN

"Like a Flower Growing in the Middle of the Desert"

Mark LeVine

To travel from Beirut to Tehran is to move between two poles of the "Shi'ite Crescent" that couldn't be more different from each other. Beirut is a seaside city where even walking in the poor, Shi'i southern suburbs you can't escape the Mediterranean culture. Its legendary nightlife a few kilometers uptown doesn't stop even for suicide bombings and civil war. Tehran is roughly eight times the size of Beirut. With twelve million people, it is at least three times as large as all of Lebanon, yet the city seems devoid of character, and has no nightlife to speak of. At least aboveground.

My arrival at the recently opened Imam Khomeini Airport was quite a shock. The airport's hypermodern glass-and-steel design puts Milan's Malpensa or Paris's Charles de Gaulle airports to shame. It seemed a world apart from the stern-looking photos of Khomeini that stare down at you from

various angles in the arrival terminal. I was nervous about getting into Iran—and even more so about getting out—given
the tense state of relations between Iran and the United States
and the United Kingdom. But the passport officer waved me
through when he saw my American passport. No questioning, no heavy-handed security people following me. Just "Welcome to Iran," and off I went.

⁂

"Let's see . . . you've got the British hostages, the crackdown
on insufficiently headscarved women, and the escalating nuclear showdown. There always seem to be at least three crises
involving Iran these days, don't there?" Behnam Marandi
asked as we walked down Jomuri-ye Eslami street in downtown Tehran, about a block and a half from the British Embassy. A computer programmer and Web designer by
profession, Behnam is also one of the main forces behind
Tehran Avenue, a semi-underground online magazine cover-
ing the arts, especially music in and around the city. Not only
does Behnam know every important musician in Tehran, he
knows what they have to do to survive in the era of President
Mahmoud Ahmadinejad.

Behnam was actually off by at least one crisis. There was
also an American "tourist"—who some people claimed was
a CIA operative (it turned out that he was a former FBI
agent)—who had disappeared on one of the small Iranian islands in the Persian Gulf. But where were all the protesters I
had seen in front of the British Embassy while watching the
BBC a few minutes earlier in my hotel room? This was only
day five of the "British hostage crisis" that began when Iranian Revolutionary Guards detained a small British naval

vessel patrolling the waters close to (Iran claimed inside) the country's territorial waters. Surely I should have heard them chanting their amusingly histrionic 1970s-era chants, this close to the embassy.

But, as with almost everything in Iran, reality rarely corresponds to the images of the country we see on television. Aside from the 150 or so protesters, many of them either "professionals" brought in for the cameras (and indeed, many milled around until given the cue to chant and march for the cameras) or die-hard regime supporters, Tehran's twelve million or so residents apparently had better things to do that afternoon. Even a block away from the protest site life went on as usual.

Officially, Iran is a country still obsessed with past humiliations. Newly printed posters of martyrs from the Iran-Iraq war, now a generation removed from public consciousness, cover buildings and utility poles. If you drive by Palestine Square, it's hard to miss the giant bronze sculpture of a map of Palestine, with life-size figures of women and children on one side, and fighters taking on the Zionist Goliath on the other. "But who thinks or cares about Palestinians?" a friend asked, with derision in her voice. As we walked by the former American Embassy, now home to a museum and offices of the dreaded Revolutionary Guards, we passed a huge, freshly painted mural on a building that read, ISRAEL SHOULD BE WIPED OUT, while the walls of the embassy featured numerous insults in Persian and English against the United States. No one pays much attention to them; and indeed the government allows Iranian Jews to visit the country's mortal enemy, Israel.

Most Iranians don't want revolution; they just want to manage their lives with as little interference as possible from the government. It's not easy to stay out of the government's way, however, when the Ahmadinejad regime constantly shifts the parameters of what's "Islamically acceptable" behavior, clothing, or music. Yet Iranians also seek to raise their standard of living by pressuring the government to maintain or increase public services and provide a better social infrastructure. It's the tension between these two desires that gives the ayatollahs and Ahmadinejad breathing room to enforce a social and political system that few Iranians care for.

Officially, I had been invited to Iran to give some academic lectures and meet with members of the religious establishment. But my real reason for coming to Iran was to meet with musicians. "The first thing you need to understand about music in Iran today," Behnam explained, "is that you can't show instruments on TV because that's considered against religion. You can have people playing them on TV, and you can hear instruments and the music, but you can't see the musicians playing the instruments, except for the daf [a type of drum] or flute—unless, of course, you've got an illegal satellite dish."

We were looking for a quick bite to eat, but that's not easy to find in downtown Tehran. In most cities of the Middle East, you can't walk a block without passing several restaurants or food stands. There are restaurants and fast-food-type storefronts in Tehran, to be sure, but compared with most of the region, there's never been much of a café and restaurant culture in Iran, so most meals are eaten at home.

Indeed, in a society where there's not much to do outside the home, dinner has become one of Iran's most important social lubricants. A member of Iran's top metal band, Ahoora, told me, "Our whole life is inside." Inside you don't need to wear your veil, you can blast your music, dance, watch pirated copies of the latest Hollywood—or Bollywood—movies, kiss your girlfriend, and otherwise feel free.

Of course, most Arab/Muslim countries try to control the use of public space by citizens—both where and how they can come together and what they can do and say when they do so. But in Iran the level of control is greater than in any other country aside from Saudi Arabia and parts of Afghanistan; it's surely the envy of the Egyptian or Pakistani Interior Ministries. As in the old Soviet Union, there simply is no public sphere in the traditional meaning of the term, as a space where citizens meet publicly and freely discuss issues of social or political concern.

There is one big difference between the Iranian regime and its predecessors behind the Iron Curtain: East Germany and the Soviet Union had elaborate internal intelligence networks that reached deep into the private lives of average citizens; in Iran, private space has become increasingly free of government interference in seemingly inverse proportion to crackdowns on the public sphere. Successive governments have come to understand that the majority of Iranians will not tolerate policing of their private lives anywhere near the extent that they'll accept control of their public identities and actions. And so, for the most part, the state leaves Iranians alone behind closed doors.

And even outside the home, Tehranians have long been adept at finding spaces to gather outside the official gaze— publicly, if not politically. They often take to the mountains north of the city in order, literally, to "get away from it all," particularly the control of the various arms of the state and its guardians of public morality, the *basij* (Persian for "mobilized"). This feared volunteer force is made up largely of young members of the Revolutionary Guards. For three decades now, when not engaged in war, the *basij* have roamed the country's main cities, harassing anyone who violates their interpretation of proper Islamic conduct or dress.

The *basij*, and the interests they serve, have made it nearly impossible to find a good place to play or hear heavy metal in Tehran. For the most part, nontraditional music, and rock in particular, is heard not just indoors, but quite literally underground, in basements, the storage rooms of apartment buildings, and parking garages. Performances are occasionally allowed, but only under tightly controlled conditions, and even then they can be canceled with little notice, sometimes in mid-performance. Few countries in the world have repressed non-official public culture, and particularly music, as thoroughly as has Iran.

࿇

What most defines Iran for me is a particular musical interval, one traditionally unique to Persian and Indian music. Called the *koron* in Persian, and a "neutral third" by Western musicologists, the first time I heard the *koron* it literally stunned me, since it's almost completely unknown in Western classical or popular music. It is a microtone, an interval less than the semitone (for example, C to C#), which is the smallest interval traditionally used in Western music. The *koron* is formed by taking the major third of a key and lowering it by somewhere between a quarter-tone and a third-tone, which produces a very strange and unsettling yet somehow "neutral" sounding interval, so it's difficult for a westerner to tell whether the piece is being played in a major or minor key.

The *koron* is not used very often in Iranian metal because it's difficult for fretted instruments (and impossible for the piano) to play microtonal intervals. But it helps us understand the complexity of Iranian culture more broadly—that is, the ability to hold two seemingly contradictory positions and achieve a kind of reconciliation, or harmony.

The Roots of Iranian Rock

Rock 'n' roll has long been popular in Iran. It came of age in the mid-1970s during the reign of the secularizing Shah, who placed far fewer restrictions on foreign cultural practices and products than did his successors in the Islamic Republic (one metal musician explained that his mother "was a big fan of Pink Floyd, Hendrix, and the Stones"). Heavy metal joined the sonic environment around the end of Iran's brutal eight-year war with Iraq. Perhaps the first band to achieve something of a breakthrough in the metal scene was O-Hum (Illusions), founded in 1999. The band plays a well-orchestrated blend of Western hard rock and Persian traditional music and instrumentation, with many of the lyrics taken from the fourteenth-century poet Hafez. After its first album was rejected by the Ershad, or Culture Ministry, band members created their own website and offered free downloads of the album—one of the first Iranian examples of using the Internet to get around state restrictions on cultural production. By 2000, there were roughly fifty bands just in Tehran, but the scene had a hard time growing because it's so difficult to make it as a musician in Iran and the government routinely cracks down on alternative cultural expression.

O-Hum also began playing publicly—or rather, privately—at venues such as the Russian Orthodox church in

Tehran and at a few charity concerts. This was a period when the Khatemi government mainly policed public "Islamic" spaces. So churches, foreign embassies, and private homes became quasi-public spaces where musicians could perform for sometimes hundreds of people without fear of harassment or arrest. This would change in 2007, when the Ahmadinejad government began to invade private homes and arrest metal fans.

Paradoxically, during the last five years more underground bands have approached mainstream popularity, even when officially banned. For some this has been a sign of success: "Unlike in other countries, we're aggressive, we keep fighting to keep metal alive," one artist told me. Others would prefer never to see the light of day: "Maybe it's good that the best music is all underground. It keeps us on the edge. It keeps us fresh," another musician said with a sigh. But everyone believes that the music must go on. "The death of metal would be the death of Iran," explained a guitar player, "so we keep fighting to keep it alive."

Despite the crackdowns, as recently as 2007, 3,000 fans could be expected to show up for shows such as the one performed by the band SDS at the University of Tehran, even though it wasn't allowed to perform with vocals. "We were not allowed to headbang or even stand up," one fan present explained to me. "It was 'metal theater,' not a metal concert," continued Pooya, one of the founders of the scene who did the first, and to this day one of the only, public metal concerts with vocals. "Everyone had to sit politely. At one gig, at Elm-o-San'at (Science and Industry) University, we managed to play for forty minutes before the *basij* tried to force us to stop. They weren't supposed to enter the university. So they drove up to the front and started roaring their motorcycles, and the manager of the place begged us to stop. We were the last metal concert with vocals."

Even without vocals, explained another musician, when bands played classic death-metal anthems, like the songs from Slayer's classic 1986 album *Reign in Blood,* "the whole crowd would fucking explode with headbanging, nobody could control them. They'd go so wild, you know? Needless to say, the next gig was canceled, because the whole thing was about control, and we were out of their control. We were arrested and charged with satanism."

A professor who works closely with the Miras Maktoob Institute (Institute for the Written Heritage) explained the larger phenomenon reflected by Iranian metal this way: "On the one hand, in the current political situation you can't come to the surface here; the 'real underground' is in Iran these days, and one would imagine that because of this we are isolated from the rest of the world. Yet Iran has been at the crossroads of culture since Cyrus the Great. We've always been open, that's why the Iranian government has tried, and failed, to suppress our instinctual drive to reach out and absorb other cultures."

Censoring the Uncensorable, Foregrounding the Underground

The restrictions the regime has imposed on the performance of music are many. As Behnam explained, "The most important thing is that you can't see women singing on TV, and they aren't allowed to sing solo in public, so musicians have to do special arrangements of their music in order to have at least two women singing, or singing in the chorus of a performance featuring a male singer." Women are clearly the most heavily censored and filtered "item" on the Internet in Iran as well. Tens of millions of websites are blocked, as part of what one scholar terms the "gender apartheid of Iran," just because they contain the word "women" in them. The government automatically assumes that any website with women as a subject is "immoral."

Politicians, prophets, and even philosophers have been warning societies about the threat posed by music, and especially the female voice, to the social order since Homer introduced the Sirens to literature and Socrates urged the banning of eight types of music in the *Republic* on the belief that they encouraged drunkenness and idleness. Early Muslim leaders—although not the Qur'an—held similar views. After the Iranian Revolution, one newspaper explained, "We must eliminate music because it means betraying our country and our youth . . . Music is like a drug, whoever acquires the habit can no longer devote himself to important activities."

The mullahs weren't that far off the mark in comparing music-listening to drug use: more than one musician explained to me, in the words of one of the country's leading metal guitarists, that "buying music was like buying drugs" when metal first arrived in Iran in the late 1980s. Even getting a black-market cassette was comparable to scoring; you had to take two taxis and meet at a neutral location and make the hand-off as quickly as possible before hiding the tape in your pants for the ride home.

On the other hand, the late Ayatollah Khomeini wavered on his opinion of music. He argued that "music dulls the mind because it involves pleasure and ecstasy, similar to drugs," but he became more lenient after hearing a musician playing something he thought sounded beautiful outside the window of his home one day. Ultimately, the near-total ban on rock music during the Revolution's first fifteen years was loosened a bit under the presidency of Mohammad Khatemi, who was more responsive to the demands of the younger generation than had been his predecessors Khamenei and Rafsanjani. Metal bands even managed to get permission to hold a few concerts during this period, but President Ahmadinejad's election in 2005 led to the banning of all Western music from state-run TV and radio stations, making it harder—but not impossible—for fans to hear live metal in Iran.

To make a government-approved CD, without which you aren't allowed to perform legally, you have to take your music to the Ershad, or Culture Ministry, where several committees determine whether the music, lyrics, and presentation are technically professional and Islamically acceptable. The absurdity of the categories that must be approved in order to receive permission to release an album reflects the larger absurdities of Iran's political and social orders today. Bad grammar, shaved heads, an "improper sense of style," and even "too many riffs on electrical guitar and excessive stage movements" can all get your music banned. "It's like this," Behnam said. "When you submit a request, they have a department to check the music, especially vocal content. The Ershad will often order a singer or band to change the lyrics, melody, or rhythm in a song. Lyrics are especially important for them. They need to check whether it's against the system, which is forbidden."

By "system," Behnam meant the entire ideological, political, and economic apparatus of the Iranian state. So if a censor listening to a song decides that the guitar distortion is too intense, and therefore threatens state security by exciting emotions that the state can't control or that could be turned against it, the band will have to lighten up on the guitar. Or perhaps the melody is too Western, or just not Iranian enough, or the lyrics are a bit too risqué. You can imagine how death-metal bands might fare against an Iranian censor, which is why most don't bother trying to obtain government approval. But this tactic can be dangerous during periodic crackdowns by the government, which can use the "illegal" circulation of an artist's or band's music as a convenient excuse to arrest or otherwise harass them.

Schools have been on the frontline in the struggle for the soul of young Iranians since the Revolution. High schools were both where most metalheads were introduced to the music and where the government tried to clamp down on it from the start. Guitarist Ali Azhari, one of the most important artists in the Iranian scene, recalled with a smile, "The principal of my school had a shelf in his office filled just with my T-shirts and bracelets. He was trying to demetalize me," Ali said, coining a new word to explain exactly what was being done to him. "But it didn't work." Later on, when metalheads started to become a more public, if strange-looking, presence on the streets, the government began to accuse—and soon after, indict—them for being satanists, spreading Western culture, and simply for being in a metal band (which didn't seem to be part of the criminal code when I checked). Convictions of musicians were almost always overturned, but the government's point was made.

❦

Almost every Arab/Muslim country has some sort of official censor of music, but Iran's has proved more proactive and aggressive than others'. Iran's mullahs have legitimate reasons to fear metal: it reflects the mood of a young generation (65 percent of the country's population) roiled by drug use, prostitution, increasing AIDS, and, most important, a nearly complete rejection of the values of the Revolution.

Perhaps the best indication of how strongly the country's metal community—and, by extension, a large share of the rest of Iran's younger generation—oppose the ethos of the Revolution comes from the popularity of the pioneering British metal band Iron Maiden. "For sure, Iron Maiden would have to be the most important band for us," explained Armin Ghaouf, a twenty-eight-year-old mechanical engineer and guitar player who's been on the metal scene since its inception. Tall, with shoulder-length hair (it was much longer until the police cut it after arresting him) and a pleasant face, Armin plays a role similar to Slacker's in Egypt: he knows everyone and everything about the scene and connects all its dots, even though he doesn't play much these days. Sitting next to him, Ali Azhari agreed: "Maiden gives me a vision at a time when the chief symbol of Iranian culture is that of the martyr. Maiden is so visual—just think of the album covers with their tanks and other images of war and death—it's like a dream combined with music. The band allows you to imagine being somewhere else you can't physically be."

Just a few weeks earlier, Ali, Armin, and I had stood about twenty feet from the stage watching Maiden's first-ever performance in the Arab world, at the Dubai Desert Rock Festival. The images of war's violence and futility—particularly as embodied by the band's mascot, the skeleton-monster war robot Freddy, blundering across the stage pretending to shoot the crowd—served as the perfect rebuttal to Khomeini's valorization of war and martyrdom as the holiest acts within Islam. As Ali pointed out afterward, "There are so many images of war and guns on the streets and buildings of Tehran, it's the same symbolism really." Except that the Revolution's martyrs died "in the path of God," while Iron Maiden's die for nothing.

The mullahs celebrate violence; the metalheads critique it. Being a metal fan offers—however paradoxical it might seem—a "community of life" (as one musician described it to me) against the community of death and martyrdom propagated by the Iranian government. But the risks are both real and substantial. As Pooya explained, "Even my family thought I was dangerous." Pooya was arrested so many times he stopped counting. "I just wanted to dress like a metalhead, and I was arrested and beaten, first in the cars of the *basij,* then in jail." It wasn't just long hair that could get one in trouble. Ramin Sadighi, the founder of the innovative and respected Iranian world-music label Hermes Records, said that during the long period when Western instruments were effectively banned in Iran, he had to rent delivery vans and travel well before and after rehearsal times to get his upright bass to rehearsal and performances. "We sacrificed so much," he informed me, "more than the current generation of musicians can understand."

Other musicians were accused of being Jewish or of looking like "savages" because of their long hair and metal attire.

In response, one metalhead offered the most pejorative insult in the Iranian repertory: "The government is Arab! It's like we're occupied. That's why the music is so strong." (Many Iranians are intensely nationalist, and harbor a millennium-old grudge against Arabs for supposedly overshadowing them in the larger Muslim world.) Armin recounted one such incident: "I was walking down the street and a passing police patrol car stopped and the cops asked, 'Where are you going with long hair?!' I said, 'What's the matter? None of your business,' and they took me in and said, 'We'll call your father, we'll take his documents, and if you let us cut your hair he'll get them back.' What could I do? After that I started to put my hair in a ponytail, tuck it in my collar, and tie it up, and walking around on the street it didn't look like I had long hair. When we were playing or jamming, I took it out, that was it."

Of course, musicians aren't the only group targeted by the Ershad. Mojtaba Mirtahmasb, a well-known documentary filmmaker in Tehran, has also had his run-ins with the government, for two documentaries (*Back Vocal* and *Off Beat*) he made about the difficulties faced by Iranian musicians today. We watched the films in his apartment, since naturally they are banned from public view. Mojtaba explained that one Iranian jazz band had two concerts approved by the government, only to have the second show canceled hours before it was to start.

The government can prevent public performances, but in other ways music censorship is increasingly irrelevant in Iran. After three decades of a revolutionary regime, Iranian artists have gotten very good at making the best of a bad performance environment. Among the most interesting examples comes from Farzad Golpayegani, one of the top two or three metal guitarists in Iran, and one of the country's most talented graphic artists as well. Although he loves to play outside Iran, "where at least kids can headbang," Farzad remains committed to building the rock scene in his country, and has become expert at putting on shows that defy the restrictions placed on him, often at the last minute, by authorities. "The last concert was half unplugged because we were not allowed to bring drums, so I tuned my acoustic guitar like a setar," he laughed. (The setar is a three-stringed country cousin of the sitar.) "Another time I played with percussionists and a video of my paintings projected on a screen behind me; we had about 500 people for that show."

It's also relatively easy to buy foreign music in stores, while the Internet and music downloading have made it impossible to control the spread of "illegal" music. Yet if the central government has reached a seeming truce with young Iranians concerning what goes on between their headphones, local governments are closing music schools and jailing and even lashing people caught listening to "thumping tunes in their cars."

Is This Music or Magic?
How Metal Invaded Iran

The practice of tightly policing music goes back to the start of the Revolution, but it is one of the ironies of Iranian political culture that the very technology and clandestine means of communication that made the Iranian Revolution possible (in particular, the circulation of contraband cassette tapes of the Ayatollah Khomeini's speeches) were also used by the early metalheads to spread the word about, and the music of, heavy metal. Khomeini realized the possibility for cassettes to be used against him in the same way he used them against the Shah, so he banned them after taking power. Nevertheless, by the time Khomeini died, cassette tapes of the world's best metal were circulating to a small but fanatical community of metalheads in Tehran and other major cities like Isfahan, Shiraz, and Mashad.

Indeed, metal "fever" had spread among young Iranians at the very moment that the fever of the Revolution began to dim. As Pooya put it during yet another four-course meal at the home of a musician, "Out of the death of Khomeini the flowers of metal grew." Another musician picked up on the paradoxical image of metal as beauteous and life-affirming, explaining that when it first hit Iran, metal was "like a flower growing in the middle of the desert" of Iranian politics and culture.

❧

I never thought it was possible to find a musician as devoted to death metal as Marz until I met Ali Azhari. "I remember when I was thirteen years old," Ali said during our first meeting in his apartment, "I was looking for serious music, not just party music or music to get drunk to. I was into reading books and wanted to be, I dunno, an important guy. And I remember I listened to—can you believe it—Def Leppard, and I said, 'Whoa! What is this? Is this music or is this magic? Is it a kind of spell?'"

I got lost trying to find Ali's house in northern Tehran, the upscale part of the city whose numerous high-rise condo developments, many of them with apartments costing well over $1 million, begin to look the same after a while (in one neighborhood the high-rises are all painted white, blending into the snow-covered mountains above them). Ali's apartment is in a nondescript building in a neighborhood where dozens of satellite dishes are illegally set up away from the street. "It doesn't matter, though," he explained. "They [meaning the *basij*] know it's here. They'll come by and rip them out eventually, and then everyone will wait a while and put them back in."

Ali is one of the best guitarists in Iran. He plays incredibly fast and cleanly, and he has a taste for the theatrical that gives his music an added sense of importance. His round face yet sharp features, long jet-black hair, and black metal T-shirt give him the look of a young Iranian Alice Cooper, although his videos might make even Alice Cooper a bit queasy.

The first thing you notice about Ali's apartment (after realizing that he seems to be one of the few metalheads in the Middle East who doesn't live with his parents) is that it's quite dark, even in the middle of the day. The second thing you notice is how neat it is. This is not the abode of the typical metaler; there are no beer cans or crumpled fast-food wrappers or potato chip crumbs lying around. Ali is much too artistic and professional for that.

As I inhaled the scent of Persian incense burned to keep out the malevolent spirits of the Revolution, my ears were assaulted by an extreme metal video by the group Hate Eternal, blasting from his television. Slowly the apartment came into focus. It was laden with 1970s goth-futuristic furniture and stuffed animals—real ones, including a fox with a squirrel in its mouth and a couple of birds of prey as well.

At the other end of the apartment is Ali's control room, a two-by-three-meter padded room with just enough space for his computer, a mixing board, and a window to connect to the even tinier "live" room. The walls are covered with posters and stickers of metal and rock bands, including Hendrix and Bob Marley. Ali's Marshall TLS 100 amp and a couple of microphones took up the entire room. "I used to have the dual-lead Marshall," he explained, but even though he had almost no chance of ever playing in a space big enough to use it, "I moved up to the triple," an even more powerful amplifier.

On Ali's computer desktop is a huge photo of Twisted Sister frontman Dee Snyder. "Metal owes him because he stood alone against the PMRC [Parents Music Resource Center], and others trying to demetalize the world," Ali said proudly. "When you're a kid in the middle of a war, it stays in your mind for a long, long time. Heavy metal was considered totally Western and unacceptable, but we heard it and said, 'We like it and we're gonna get it.' We started trading tapes and starting bands with old instruments not destroyed during the Revolution, and when people would travel we'd ask them to buy tapes."

Armin, a long-time friend of Ali, remembered, "Everyone was greedy and hungry to get albums, and they would be copied literally a million times, which meant you wanted to make sure to get one of the first copies, because cassettes lost quality with each copy. And we were also tricky. We'd always keep a song for ourselves, and people would have to beg to get it. Of course with the Web, you can't play those games anymore," he said with a laugh.

Ali laughed too, at the thought of all the changes that have occurred in the last decade. "I remember a female friend asking, like this sixty-year-old guy, 'Would you please bring me this CD?' and it was, like, a Cannibal Corpse CD. Naturally the guy hears the name and says, 'Lady, this kind of music is not for you!' And she lies and says, 'Oh no! I don't want it for myself, it's not for me, it's for someone else.' "

The clandestine "microshows" that characterized the early Iranian metal scene (and are still one of the few ways to hear metal performed live today) were ad hoc and improvised. To many of the attendees, the shows could be truly disorienting, almost like religious experiences—the perfect antidote to the hyper-ritualized, formulaic, and in-your-face Islam propagated by the Islamic state. For Armin, "The first show I played at left me so dizzy. It was in someone's home because there were no discos to play in, and there were maybe thirty kids. The host asked my band to play 'Altars of the Abyss' by Morbid Angel, and everyone just freaked out, they couldn't bear the level of extremity, they couldn't take it after five minutes. You know, the timing was perfect, because metal hit Iran at the same time DM [death metal] became big. It was the perfect time because it was just after the war ended and death was everywhere, and then, boom, it [metal] exploded."

Strolling Down Tehran Avenue

As the sun set, I headed with Behnam to the apartment of Sohrab Mahdavi, on a pretty, tree-lined street in the well-heeled Fereshteh neighborhood in the hills of northern Tehran. Sohrab is one of the gentlest and purest souls I ever met. He and his wife, Mahsa Shekarloo, a UNICEF official in Tehran working on women's issues, are keen observers of Iranian culture and politics.

Sohrab and Mahsa's apartment is a bit sparse, but tastefully decorated, with a nice sound system. As soon as we

arrived, Sohrab laid out a delicious meal of *kuku,* an omelet
with minced vegetable, rice, and yogurt, and some fresh *sabzi,*
a plate of local herbs that normally includes mint, basil, dill,
parsley, coriander, cilantro, tarragon, and watercress.

After dinner, we had tea and snacked on salted marijuana
seeds. Not surprisingly, these are popular with college students because they help them to stay awake during long
nights of studying for exams (before going to bed, students
will chew poppy seed to come down). As we drank and ate, we
listened to some traditional setar music.

Like the sitar, the setar has movable frets that make it
possible to play various modes of Persian music and the combination of semitones, quarter-tones, and *korons* that characterize it. I was aware of how versatile the instrument was, but
I'd never listened to the kind of traditional Persian music
Sohrab was playing for me, particularly the songs based on
the *segah* mode, which combines a *koron* with a semi-flat *re,*
or second, for a truly haunting sound.

Sohrab is the founder of *Tehran Avenue,* where Behnam
works. The online zine was created in 2001 to explore cultural
life in Tehran. "Basically, *Tehran Avenue* is a bunch of people
trying to find out what's going on in their society," said
Behnam. While it was started with only a small group of writers, in the last six years it has grown into a sizable community
to "push the limits of understanding" of Iranian culture.
Sohrab and his team see the site as a means of bringing the vibrant underground scene of Tehran aboveground. Aided by the
"back alleys of the website," they employ both English and Farsi
to bring expatriate and local Iranians into one community.

The activity that put *Tehran Avenue* on the global cultural
map was Sohrab's idea to hold a virtual battle of the bands in

2004. Called Tehran Avenue Music Open, the competition prompted interest from hundreds of bands—itself an indication of how big the underground music scene is just in Tehran—with dozens sending in their music to be judged. A couple of years earlier, *Tehran Avenue* ran an "Underground Music Competition," the existence of which was spread entirely by word of mouth and, in a non-publicized manner, via the Internet. But sympathetic officials from the cultural establishment let them know that calling the competition "underground" could actually put the bands who participated in harm's way, so they decided to make it an open, albeit virtual, forum. Both competitions helped to solidify the identities of the country's emerging rock and metal bands.

The submissions showed how many great young musicians were coming of age in Tehran, and also pointed to the desperate need for an accessible space for them to get together and share their music. As of 2007, there were three Web-based competitions. Sadly, it's not yet possible to arrange live competitions to determine the winners, but the competitions have helped Iranian rock artists learn more about their own scene, and have opened their music to the world at large.

Like Walking Without Legs

Very soon after the Revolution, Tehran was transformed into what the anthropologist Roxanne Varzi aptly describes as an "Islamic revolutionary space." Old monuments were replaced by new ones celebrating the Revolution, billboards featured photos of clerics and Islamic symbols instead of ads for the latest Western goods, and women could no longer walk the city's wide boulevards in anything but the full-length outer

garment known as a chador. "An all-encompassing Islamic reality" was created, according to Varzi, and it didn't include
rock 'n' roll.

The Islamic public sphere became even more narrowly
focused once Saddam Hussein attacked Iran in late December 1980. The war intensified the already powerful cult of
martyrdom in post-Revolution Iran. The massive casualties
produced by the war, and particularly by the Iranian tactic of
using human waves to counter Iraq's superior firepower, required that Iranians—not just the young men fighting, but
the families sacrificing them—have a thirst for martyrdom.

After Khomeini's death in 1989, Iranian society gradually opened up during the Rafsanjani and particularly the
Khatemi governments of the next decade and a half. Increasing numbers of young people became disaffected with the
cult of martyrdom and complete self-sacrifice. Instead of the
religious idea of *bi-khodi,* or self-annihilation, being the dominant mode of religious expression, the more liberal idea
of *khod-sazi,* or individualistic self-help, began to take hold
among young Iranians disillusioned by the waste of war.
Some of them were led to metal as an alternative value system
rather than just as a form of musical escapism. As Armin
Ghaouf explains, "What makes heavy metal so important are
the eight years of brutal war—twice the length of America's
involvement in World War II. I remember the missiles coming to Tehran, so wearing a metal or Maiden T-shirt with a
tank on it is very relevant to me. We didn't know if we'd live
through the war. And even today, at twelve years old we are
still forced to learn how to use AK-47s and to defend against
chemical weapons."

With such experiences, it's no wonder that death metal

became popular among young people. But how do they make it part of their everyday lives on the streets of Tehran? They do it by blasting music in their cars until the *basij* pulls them over, or by wearing skimpy headscarves until the *basij* force them to pull them completely over their scalps; and by wearing their iPods or Walkmans, which, especially for women with their mandatory headscarves, has become a favorite way to tune out the existing regime and into one's own world while walking down the street. Some even tag the logos of their favorite metal bands on walls across Tehran—whether in their bedrooms or on the street—claiming their bit of territory from a society in which they feel they have little stake.

Finally, Iranians connect with their music through the Internet, not just in English but in Farsi as well (while only one in sixty people in the world speak Persian, the language ranks fourth in frequency of use in Internet blogs). As Behnam explained about *Tehran Avenue*'s focus on creating a Web-based community of artists and fans: "Increasingly we've chosen to go through the cyberworld because of the ban on live shows." But, I wondered, how do you do music without live shows? Behnam thought for a second and agreed, "Yes, it's like walking without legs. Music is supposed to bring people together and create communities—real, not virtual. If you can't do that, then something is missing."

But even without the chance to perform in truly public settings (and therefore in front of large crowds), metal musicians argue that playing metal gives them confidence for life, and a safe place to work out feelings of aggression and hopelessness that otherwise would lead to more-unhealthy activities (from violence to drug use), which are commonplace in Iran today despite the regime's self-image as a paragon of

Islamic virtue. As Armin puts it, "Metal is like an asylum. A mental asylum that rejuvenates you and gives you hope."

New Gods and Old Martyrs

"When you breathe in our country, it's political," admitted Ali Azhari. "But even so, we're not doing stuff to harm the system, we're just trying to survive." Ali was trying to convince me of his innocent intentions. But it was hard to take his protestations of innocence very seriously when he was wearing a T-shirt that read, YOUR GOD IS DEAD. Ali's T-shirt, but not his argument, made more sense when he introduced his new project, Arthimoth. "Arthimoth is a newborn god I created myself, a combination of an ancient Persian name with the Greek goddess Artemis [the goddess of the wilderness and fertility]. I thought that this is the time to re-create ancient gods as a legacy of our fathers. Musically, we try to remix very old, traditional Iranian village music with contemporary music and especially extreme metal. In other words, we root the metal in our culture."

Creating other gods, however metaphorically, is certainly a good way to get into trouble in Iran—even more so when it's obvious. As Ali and Armin admitted, "We chose this metal in order to communicate. We write on behalf of the kids." Yet if you watch Ali in the recording studio, Baphomet shirt drenched with sweat as he records a brutal vocal that sounds—and looks, if the grimace on his face is any indication—like it's coming from his bowels, it's hard not to take his theology seriously. Certainly the government does—to a certain degree.

As we were talking, Ali loaded the video for "Baptize"

onto his computer. Ali is rightfully proud of the video because it demonstrates his skills as a metal songwriter, guitarist, and filmmaker. It's among the most disturbingly powerful music videos I've ever seen, riffing on the futility of violence first brought to metal cinema with Metallica's groundbreaking video "One" (which depicts a horrifically wounded soldier—without arms or legs, blind, deaf, and mute—using morse code to tap out a message to his doctors to kill him). But "Baptize" takes the message of "One" to a far higher degree of intensity than Metallica's innovative video—both musically, as the chromatic minor riffs of the song have enough of a hint of the unsettledness produced by the *koron* to keep the listener constantly off balance, while the drums never settle down into a beat you can groove to, and visually (something I wouldn't have imagined possible before seeing his video).

Ali uses the word "baptize" to indicate how Iranians are forcibly submerged, body and soul, in a system in which there is no room for independent thought. The video's lead actor is a man, mostly naked, who is led, seemingly willingly, to a chair. Immediately upon sitting down, he has the top of his head sawed off; his brain is shocked with electrodes and then nibbled on by a rat while another man screams into his ear from an occult-looking book (Ali actually used a Hebrew book because using the Qur'an would have really gotten him into trouble). The images move back and forth between shots of the band headbanging in unison and Ali singing as the rat eats the man's brain. Finally, as the song ends, the "doctor" sews the man's scalp back on and he stumbles away, like a zombie, into the world.

Ali's studio was raided while he was completing production for the video. The original masters of the video were confiscated, and he was questioned by the secret police. But he managed to hide another master copy and upload the video onto YouTube, where he's received comments from both Israel and Lebanon with the same message: "Don't let religion ruin your art; 'keep it brutal.' " It's a sentiment that's shared by many Iranian metalheads. A member of Iran's hottest young metal band, Tarantist, put it this way: "Metal is in our blood. It's not entertainment, it's our pain, and also an antidote to the hypocrisy of religion that is injected into all of us from the moment we're born."

From Boom Boxes to Mobile Phones: Tehran's Streetcorner Public Sphere

Bahman, rhythm guitarist for Tarantist, explained that in Iran the idea of a unique Iranian identity is so strong that "anything that looks like a foreign culture is frowned upon. Especially if it comes from the U.S." Yet hip-hop, which even more than heavy metal is identifiable as a product of the "Great Satan," has had an easier time of it in Iran than its hard-rock counterpart (the baggy clothing preferred by rappers does have the advantage of being more Islamically acceptable than the tight leather pants, T-shirts, and menacing-looking jewelry that define metal style). Indeed, rap has played a central role in creating a broad sense of community against the grain of the regime's wished-for Shi'i utopia, very often without arousing the suspicion that it's doing just that.

The Iranian rap scene is still small compared to the much better established hard-rock scene, but its rapid growth is described by many metalheads with envy. That doesn't mean that rappers are off the government's radar screen; several

were arrested around the time I was in Iran, including one of
the country's leading rappers, Hich-Kas, for being too overtly
political. But in general, hip-hop in Iran is more tolerated
than heavy metal, as long as it doesn't deal directly with sexual issues or take on the government.

While it has strong working-class and lower-class roots,
many rappers and fans are from the wealthier segments of society. No matter their origin, most Iranian rappers have chosen the genre both because of its connection to worldwide
musical trends and because of rap's history of political and social criticism. One of Iran's rising female rappers, Salome, explained: "The true meaning of hip-hop culture [is] a lot deeper
than it looks on the surface. It's become much more eclectic
than it was previously, and much more out in the open. As
important, it's become Persianized instead of just copying the
West. For example, I only use natural instruments, without
samples [the digitally recorded bits of instruments or other
songs that have long been the foundation of hip-hop produc-
tion] in my songs."

Salome is half Iranian and half Turkish, and makes her
living as a designer since doing so as a rapper is out of the
question. (That she can make a living as a fashion designer in
the Islamic Republic says something about the complex politics of cultural production in Iran today.) When we met in the
office of *Tehran Avenue,* she was dressed, fashionably, in black,
including her headscarf, which she kept adjusting as we
spoke. A connoisseur of alternative hip-hop in the States, Salome is a fan of Dead Prez, Immortal Technique, and Paris.
She raps in Persian and Turkish on top of beats influenced by
these artists, yet unlike her heroes, she goes out of her way to
define herself as apolitical: "I'm not political, just social, so I'll

do songs about our rage at all the Iranian rappers who say meaningless stuff imitating commercial American rap, stuff that has no connection to our culture."

When rappers in the Arab/Muslim world say they're "social, not political," it means they're not critical of their own government; foreign governments are another matter entirely. After the United States invaded Iraq, Salome wrote a rapid-fire, nationalistic America-basher called "Petrolika." But while she doesn't mind performing abroad (as she did at the Intergalactic Music festival in Amsterdam in 2006), in Iran "I want to stay underground. I don't want to do interviews, to make that sacrifice, particularly being a woman." Rapping is not high on the Ahmadinejad list of approved feminine vocations.

Iran's male rappers are equally aware of what lines they can publicly cross without getting arrested or otherwise harassed. This was clear from a visit to one of Tehran's best—but still underground—hip-hop recording studios. The studio, which has no official name, is located in a wealthy neighborhood, but—as usual—it's in the basement so that neighbors, at least those outside the building, won't know it's there (although the steady coming and going of young men in hip-hop clothing, or with instruments slung over their shoulders, must surely indicate that something un-Islamic— from the regime's point of view—is going on there). As soon as I entered, I had a case of déjà vu; its smell and look reminded me of almost every other studio I've been in. Cigarette smoke filled the air, mixed with the odor of fried fast food, while chips and empty soda cans were scattered on tables and the floor.

It was here that I met two of the leading rappers on the

Iranian scene, Reveal and Hich-Kas. Reveal grew up largely in the UK and is currently completing a degree in Persian language at the School of Oriental and African Studies in London. Hich-Kas, whose name means "nobody" in Persian, is a home-grown rapper who chose his name specifically as a play on rappers who try to blow themselves up with pompous-sounding names. "I just wanted to show that somebody that calls himself 'nobody' can say big things." Both rappers are critical of the current situation in Iran and the problems their fans face, but neither was very comfortable talking explicitly about politics.

Reveal is one of the most educated rappers I've ever met, but for sheer grandeur of vision the prize has to go to the eighteen-year-old Tehran rapper Peyman-Chet. "The 'chet' means 'stoned,' " Peyman explained to me as we sat in a tiny rehearsal/recording studio on the third floor of a working-class neighborhood of central Tehran. This was not the Tehran I had grown used to. The streets were narrower, the buildings older. Peyman chose his stage name not because he likes drugs, but rather as a play on the way rap and drug culture are mixed in the States—"It's quite the opposite in Iran, where it's more techno and rock and dance music that attract the drugs. I chose the dope imagery to focus on addicted people." Drugs are in fact a huge problem among Iran's youth. According to a 2005 UN report, the country has the highest addiction rate in the world, especially for heroin and related drugs. "Natural and synthetic heroin, even synthetic crack; we got it all in Iran," a member of the metal band Ahoora admitted. "Yeah, we have an abundance of everything here—drugs, oil, money—everything except freedom," another band member chimed in.

Ahoora and Peyman are seemingly from opposite sides of the tracks. Peyman practices in a dingy studio with old equipment, Ahoora has a state-of-the-art Pro Tools recording system in the villa of the guitar player's father, a wealthy pistachio merchant whose faux-1920s Hollywood-style home boasts an intricately carved wood-paneled barroom that must have seen its share of fabulous parties in the Shah's day. Peyman has a new Yankees cap, Ahoora's lead guitarist has five electric guitars (two Jacksons, one Ibanez, one BC Rich, and one I'd never seen before), three Marshall amps (a JCM 2000, a Valvestate 2000, and a G30R), sixteen effects pedals, and an eighteen-button effects board hooked up to a rack-mounted digital effects system.

Of course, being a rapper, Peyman doesn't need any of that stuff. All he needs is a pen, a notebook, and a few hundred dollars to record a song that will be downloaded by thousands, if not tens of thousands, of people all over the world soon after he uploads it to his site. And while his name parodies hip-hop's fascination with dope, his clothing is as authentic as it can get when you're living 8,000 miles east of New York: baggy pants, sports jersey, baseball cap, and a big gold chain. "I wear baggy clothes because when people see me it makes them think. It shows that I want change," he explained.

The small studio, which was normally used by rock bands, was filled with posters of Pantera, Megadeth, and Cowboys from Hell, a cheap drum set, and a small amp, on which rested, of all things, a menorah with *Shalom* written in Hebrew and English in the middle of it. "What's that doing there?" I asked incredulously. "I think it's cool. It's beautiful, and it pisses off the state," said the owner of the studio, who prefers that I do not use his name because, while Iran's

25,000-strong Jewish community faces little persecution in the Islamic Republic, thinking menorahs are cool is not something you want to advertise publicly.

Although he's very young, Peyman enjoys a certain notoriety as a result of his music's distribution over the Internet and a video of his being broadcast on Dubai or European channels. He doesn't just see himself as a rapper. "I became interested in Persian poetry and Irfan—mysticism—and try to mix all of that into my raps and send it to the streets with a bit of Tupac thrown in. We're like modern Firdusui or Rumi [the two most famous Persian poets]," he argued. He played me the rhythm of a new song he's working on while he rhymed in a strange mixture of classical and postmodern Persian. "Eminem inspired by Rumi," he said.

As I chatted with Peyman, I understood why rap was spreading so quickly and deeply in Iran: rappers have succeeded in reclaiming public space for themselves in a way that metalheads can only dream of. "There's around 1,000 rappers just in Tehran," Peyman explained, "and we constantly meet and have battles in the parks. One of the most important is [the appropriately named] 'Joint Park,' or 'Cigari Park' in Persian. Basically, when we want to meet and have a battle, the word goes out through SMS messages or announcements on Persian-language rap sites. At least two times a month we have these gatherings, and up to 200 rappers and fans show up. Once we have a critical mass of people"—and he took out his mobile phone to play me a video of one of these battles while he was talking—"someone takes out a mobile phone and plays a beat that's stored on it, and we start rhyming. But it's not just the park, we get together and rap on streets, sidewalks, corners, even though it's illegal. Usually the *basij* check us out and leave us alone, and so do the cops, but we can disperse and regroup very quickly if the cops hassle us."

Peyman is very focused on "doing something that will be loved on the streets." But in Iran, street cred doesn't come from the gangsta or thug life. Instead, it comes from writing a song that is an innovative combination of Persian and Western music and raps, and deals with real social issues without focusing the regime's attention on you. "The problem is, nothing is underground in Iran. You can do a political song in a third-class studio in Tehran and you'll be caught in a week. They have spies everywhere. My friend did a song called 'Objection' against everything that's going on, and he was caught and put in jail for a week. He had to sign something saying he'd never do a political song again. I just drop some of Tupac's more political lyrics into my songs. Those who know, get it."

Despite the government's overwhelming power, Peyman feels that "the only way to push the government is to grow the movement beyond the point it can easily be destroyed. That's why I focus not on gangsta rap but on our problems here. Yet those rappers who rap about drugs and sex, or are hard-core nationalist, get more famous than those who rap about social problems. Kids today are much more interested in drugs and sex than in fighting to change society," he said with disgust. "But if someone could give them the energy and inspiration to do something, things would change."

Needing Each Other, or Needing to Defeat the Other?

I thought about how the Iranian government must view the growing popularity of rappers like Peyman-Chet and their metal counterparts as I sat in the Tehran office of Massoud Abid, a professor of philosophy and human rights at Mufid University in Qom (the center of Shi'i scholarship in Iran). Although he is a Hojatul Islam, the rank just below ayatollah, if anyone from the establishment would be sympathetic to—or at least tolerant of—the dreams of young music fans, it would be Abid, who is well known to Iranian scholars and activists as one of the more progressive religious scholars and officials in Iran.

Neither my spoken Persian nor his English was fluent enough to carry on a complicated conversation solely in either language, so we spoke in Arabic mixed with the other two. The trilingual texture of the conversation symbolized one of Abid's key points, which is that Iran is becoming ever more globalized today, even as the United States seeks to isolate it politically and economically. And along with being globalized, Iranian young people are becoming more politicized, he felt, contrary to what Peyman-Chet had said. "Viewed from the outside, it might seem that young people are increasingly depoliticized and alienated from the state today," Abid argued. Yet, from his position on the inside, things looked very different. The public sphere was neither absent nor deep underground: "It's just developing in less noticeable ways, outside of mainstream popular culture. Just look at the large increase in the number of NGOs in Iran in the last last four to five years."

But at an even more basic level, the universities are where much of the most interesting developments are taking place, according to Abid. He sees this especially in how students in seminaries and "secular" universities are combining religious and nonreligious courses of study. "Seminary students are taking courses in human rights or sociological theory, more women than ever are enrolled in universities; you can see the change in the personality of students, as the focus on politics of the post-Revolution generation has also given way to more of a focus on personal issues," he explained.

Abid believes that most Iranians want better relations with the West. "We have to do two things: first, get rid of this conflict between Islam and the West; and, second, learn how to understand the West for both good and bad. The changing position of the religious establishment toward music is a good indication of the possibilities for such a rapprochement. Today most senior ulema [Muslim legal scholars] are opposed to rock not because of religious reasons as much as because it's not part of Iran's cultural heritage."

The hope is that as Iran's overwhelmingly young population expands the horizons of what is a legitimate part of Iranian culture, that too will change. Indeed, Abid expressed confidence that a rapprochement with the United States, and with the West more broadly, would ultimately occur. In the end, he told me as I got up to leave, "the two sides need each other a lot more than they need to defeat the other."

Abid's philosophy is certainly far from the politically dominant conservative philosophy of Khamenei and Ahmadinejad. But there is a well-developed strand of relatively progressive theology and social and political thought in Iranian Shi'ism today, especially around the issue of women. As Ziba Mir Hosseini describes it in her book *Islam and Gender,* "If clerics want to stay in power they cannot ignore popular demands for freedom, tolerance, and social justice." Whether it's women working through sympathetic ayatollahs to reinterpret Islamic law in less oppressive ways, or metalheads using online zines to pry open their society's public sphere, most Iranians refuse to yield to the repressive dreams of their leaders. This has produced a cultural tug-of-war that will continue for the foreseeable future, and metal and hip-hop will be an important part of its soundtrack.

Iran's Unplugged Heavy Metal Heroes

During my last few days in Iran, I was lucky to meet up with two of the bravest and heaviest musicians in the country. The first was Mahsa Vahdat, one of the best young singers of traditional Persian music in Iran, who gained international notice with her beautiful duet with British singer Sarah Jane Morris on the celebrated 2004 album *Lullabies from the Axis of Evil*. Mahsa's soft face, long dark hair, and captivating eyes draw people toward her the moment they see her, and her almost-whisper when she speaks brings you even closer. But when she starts to sing, her rich, sad, trembling voice is commanding.

"It's not easy to perform in Iran today," Mahsa explained, given the restrictions on women singing solo, and on live performances by women more broadly. "We are forced to perform outside the country if we want to perform our material as it's supposed to be played." But Mahsa has been lucky; at least she can write new music and record it in Tehran despite the cultural clampdown by the Ahmadinejad government. "The problem isn't religion. Everything in Iran is in the end about politics; religion is just the excuse."

It's also about power—wielded by men over women—which frustrates her more than most any other dynamic. "On the face of it, it's hilarious, their policy of restricting people and telling them that you can only sing for women. But it's also humiliating." Ironically, the very thing that limits her opportunities to perform in Iran—being a woman with an exceptional voice—makes it easy for her to get invited to international festivals and collaborations with artists from Europe and the United States. It's far harder for most rock bands, the success of Tarantist and Hypernova notwithstanding.

One artist who should be getting lots of offers in and outside Iran is Mohsen Namjoo, one of the country's most respected younger musicians. Mohsen plays the light and airy setar, though he looks like a weathered rock star of at least forty-five—a kind of Iranian Keith Richards with better teeth and skin. In fact, Mohsen is in his early thirties, but he's been through enough pain, drugs, and suffering in the last few years to last a lifetime.

When we finally managed to arrange a joint performance, at the apartment of one of Tehran's leading gallery owners, I understood just how heavy Persian rock could be, even unplugged. Most of the artists I've met in Iran believe, as one metal musician put it, that "you can't make a career out of music in Iran unless you are willing to compromise." Mohsen clearly hasn't heard about that philosophy. He lives purely and only to play music, and couldn't care less about the latest trends in pop music or the most recent three political crises. His years studying in some of Iran's most prestigious conservatories have produced an improbably wild yet somehow controlled style of setar playing, with a voice that can change from growled whispers to howls to tearful falsettos in the space of a measure.

With his talent has come quite a bit of ego (as more than one musician who's worked with him warned me); the best

strategy I could think of halfway through our first song together was to play a simple rhythm on the guitar, or setar
when we switched instruments for a couple of songs, and let
him do his thing. This was certainly what everyone at this
party had come to hear (several brought camcorders or mp3
players to record the "show," which quickly made its way onto
YouTube). As I quickly learned, Mohsen's thing includes
blues progressions seemingly shorn from Robert Johnson
and heavy-metal riffs drawn directly from Deep Purple and
Black Sabbath, interlaced with the intricate melodies of the
segah mode, which he has transformed into an Iranian all-
around blues-rock mode that left me, and most of the small
audience, trying to figure out whether he was playing an
Iranicized version of Western rock or blues, or a Westernized
version of traditional Iranian music.

Mohsen might be an ex-junkie whose prodigious talent is
matched only by his outsized ego. But he seems to have
figured out the best strategy to defeat the mullahs and the repressive Iranian state that keep going after other musicians:
ignore them. Rather than take them on with political lyrics,
just get everyone high on your infectious music. Tear at the
legitimacy of the regime with each *koron* and each three-
stringed power chord strummed—when necessary, with a
paper clip bent over a broken nail—with violent intensity on
your setar. Get the metalheads and the traditional artists to
give you props and support you, move from party to party and,
when possible, from concert to concert, with a ferociously joyful music that links together almost every style heard in Iran,
from the Zoroastrian era to the arrival of hip-hop.

As Mohsen explained in his very broken English, he just
"lets the music do the talking, and the music will set you

free." It's a sentiment that more and more members of Iran's metal, rock, and hip-hop scenes are taking to heart. It's not an easy task—at almost the same moment I was flying out of Tehran, an Iranian American colleague of mine at UC Irvine, Ali Shakeri, was arrested at the airport, and languished for months in jail or under house arrest with several other Iranian Americans on charges of being CIA agents and "velvet revolutionaries." Yet only a few months later I was able to meet up with Farzad Golpayegani and his band in Istanbul, where we—three Iranians, a Brit, and an American—performed before 30,000 fans at the biggest (and perhaps the only) peace festival in the Muslim world. That's the way life goes in Iran today, and however disheartening it can be, no one I know would risk the status quo for the risky and dangerous business of another revolution ("Look what happened last time we had one!" was the universal response I received every time I broached the subject).

Everyone agrees that the struggle for Iran's soul will be long and hard, but if the activists, intellectuals, and artists I've met, religious and secular alike, can muster enough patience and strategic foresight, there's a good chance that they'll succeed in cracking open the public sphere a bit more each year. And soon enough, it will grow so wide that no one—be it Ahmadinejad, the *basij,* or the ayatollahs—can force it closed again.

Bibliography

Arash BT. "An interview with one of the organizers of 'Tehran Avenue Music Open.' " *Zir Zaman,* October 2003.

"Arthimoth: Death Metal Band from Iran." Danish TV documentary, on YouTube in three parts.

Basmenji, Kaveh. *Tehran Blues: Youth Culture in Iran.* London: Saqi Books, 2005.

Mir-Hosseini, Ziba. *Islam and Gender: The Religious Debate in Contemporary Iran.* Princeton: Princeton University Press, 1999.

Peterson, Scott. "You Say You Want a Revolution? Iran Bands Rock On." *Christian Science Monitor,* October 1, 2003.

Tala'i, Darius. *Radif Mirza Abdallah: Natnavisi Amuzishi va tahlili (The Traditional Persian Art of Music: The Radif of Mirza Abdallah).* Tehran: Nashreney Publishing, 2007.

Varzi, Roxanne. *Warring Souls: Youth, Media, and Martyrdom in Post-Revolution Iran.* Durham, NC: Duke University Press, 2006.

Websites:

ahoora-band.com

arthimoth.com

farzadonline.com

mahsavahdat.com

mohsennamju.com

myspace.com/hichkas21

peyman-chet.com/

revealed

Tarantists.com

tehranavenue.com

[9]

Yugoslav and Post-Yugoslav Encounters with Popular Music and Human Rights

Rajko Muršič

In October, 2009, the Croatian Minister of Foreign Affairs, Gordan Jandroković, sent a note to the Swiss embassy in Zagreb to protest against the decision of the Swiss authorities to ban a performance in Switzerland by the well-known Croatian rock singer Thompson (Marko Perković) (Ivanović, 2009). Marko Perković/ Thompson, who started singing while a member of the Croatian defense forces in 1991/92, took his stage name from the Thompson machine-gun used in the war in Croatia. A couple of days after Jandroković had sent his note, the Croatian Prime Minister, Jadranka Kosor, supposedly seriously considered dismissing the minister. Although she refrained from doing so, the incident is proof enough that music can become an important political issue, and that such incidents may question or change our points of view. Although I have occasionally been active in defending freedom of expression in music (see Muršič, 1999, 2000), I sympathized with the Swiss government's decision. This was a situation that effectively demonstrated that we cannot advocate unchangeable universal principles of freedoms and rights. Why?

Only two months before the incident, while giving a presentation on popular music and its political implications in the former Yugoslavia, I played one of Thompson's patriotic songs ("Duh ratnika" [The Spirit of the Warrior]) to an audience of non-Croatian-speaking students and asked for their opinion. It was perceived by the students, who sincerely enjoyed it, as a very nice rock ballad. Some of them considered it just another love song. To some extent, I agreed. Then, after presenting them with some other examples of music from the 1990s period, when war ravaged the region, I played the song again, this time accompanied with video footage. After a few seconds it became clear to everybody that the song was not just about love, but about a very specific kind of love: love of a country. In glorifying the *Ustaše*, Croatian war heroes who in World War II collaborated with the Nazis, Thompson's "love song" acquires a fascist patina. For someone who is not a Croatian nationalist to have enjoyed the song, only to discover its meaning is not what they thought, this could present quite a dilemma.

Thompson is a product of the violent breakdown of the Yugoslav socialist federation. Taking his music as the mark of a structural shift from nationalism, or postnationalism, to "pop-nationalism," his example may not be as threatening as it at first seems. Using nationalist symbolism in a pop milieu, pop-nationalism substitutes hard chauvinist-nationalist sentiments for just another pop charade. With its aestheticized ritual it can transform nationalist emotions, power, and "truth" into a pop event, providing the stage for the catharsis of accumulated postwar public sentiments and concerns in facing structural uncertainty about future "nationhood." However, there is no guarantee that such pop music will not be used for real nationalist and chauvinist mobilization. After all, the same music could be used in immensely different ways.

New musical styles that articulate widespread needs and aspirations with the minimal level of artistic expression are a common response to war and postwar trauma. Just such a style—dubbed "turbo-folk" in 1988 by Montenegrin singer and author Antonije Pušić (known as Rambo Amadeus)—appeared during Yugoslavia's dissolution. The "cathartic" function of this turbo-folk had the potential to lead to two radically opposed outcomes: on the one hand, this pop-nationalism expressed in patriotic popular music and in an unrestricted mélange of sex, hedonism, splendor, and "supermodern traditionalism" could provide symbolic attachment without any profound "real-political" consequences; on the other it could not only stimulate nationalist sentiments but provoke acts of intolerance, ethnic hatred, and violence.

Is this a situation that was specific to the former Yugoslavia? Considering Bulgarian *chalga*, Turkish *arabesk*, and other similar genres, it is more likely a rule than an exception. After all, "pop's 'offence' can bring to light problems that might otherwise not gain attention" (Cloonan, 1996, p. 34). Since Walter Benjamin warned about aestheticized political rituals and their sublime power, it is well known that partying, having fun, and the expression of mutual sentiments through song can play a crucial role in the success of populist, (neo)nationalist, and fascist movements. Indeed, by the power of ecstatic interpellation, anger and aversion to "others" are often expressed by those who feel socially excluded from their own society (by social rank, age, and territorial distance from the centers of power) through ongoing symbolic and ideological struggles in support of their own people.

Thompson's example reveals important points to be considered when analyzing music and its relationship to human rights. First, music alone—that is, as humanly organized sound (Blacking, 1973), or as a nonverbal sound game (Muršič, 1993)—never carries its inherent meaning; it is its social context, use, intentions, and additional carriers of meaning that make a piece of music a meaningful means of communication (or at least a shared experience). Second, when music is being used to mobilize the masses, there is always the possibility of it being used in opposite or alternative ways. Third, when music is being used as a means of political mobilization, defense, identity-making, or even torture, social situations need also to be considered as crucial in its understanding, not just the musical material itself. More simply put: it is not music but people who harm other people. The question though is, are harmful acts any different if people use music as a means of violence?

Music as an Act of Violence

Despite the fact that music, especially military and court music, has been used to mobilize masses since time immemorial—and many examples of the power of music are found in ancient myths—music scholars have only very recently started to examine the use of popular music as a means of violence (Johnson and Cloonan, 2008). With its nonverbal appeal and sound structure, music is very powerful. It can even reach the existential core of individuals as social beings, affecting them profoundly with subtle cumulative effect at physiological, psychological, and aesthetic levels.

Making music is, in essence, making sense of a cacophonic experience by turning manifold social experiences into symbolic commonalities with other "insiders." This role is often ascribed to "the stranger within," who can manage to cultivate fields of identification and a "more complete experience of Self" (Port, 1999, p. 292). Such strangers within, members of marginal and often suppressed minorities, are often important as the carriers of musical traditions (Merriam, 1964, pp. 123-44). In the case of Yugoslavia such minorities were the Roma and, especially after the turbulent 1960s, the youth.

The Roma played wedding music on instruments popular in particular places and at particular times. They would use string instruments in the north and brass instruments in the south. Among the brass orchestras worth mentioning are the Feat Sejdić Orchestra, the Boban Marković Orchestra, and the Kočani Orchestra, and among musicians the king of Roma saxophone from Skopje, Ferus Mustafov. One of the first big stars of Romani ethno-pop was Esma Redžepova, with her magnificent voice, later joined by Šaban Bajramović and other Romani singers. Esma Redžepova is an active member of the Lions Club, sponsor of the Romani Women's Association "Esma," and was named an ambassador of the United Nations for refugees. In 2002 she was nominated for the Nobel Peace Prize. With its appeal, music could make a significant contribution to the struggle for Roma emancipation. Nevertheless, the Roma are still waiting for true recognition as equal citizens in European countries.

In the former Yugoslavia (as in other countries) Roma musicians are seen as people who play their music with great pleasure. While urbanized and industrialized people who moved from the countryside were seen as unable to enjoy their lost "traditional" music in the same way that their forebears had, Roma musicians, by continuing to play their music, were able to continue enjoying it. An oppressed and stigmatized minority, who didn't choose to be marginalized, Roma are considered to play music "with heart." However, it is their suppressed social position that is believed to be what makes them seemingly more "musical" than the dominant population. The same could be said of African Americans in the United States. Recent appropriations of hip-hop and rap, and more distant appropriations of reggae, among worldwide "colored" populations, including, for example, Bulgarian gypsies (cf. Rice, 1996, p. 196; Silverman, 1996, p. 243), prove that music can be used as a means of gaining or promoting self-confidence.

Very similar observations can be made regarding youth as a permanently marginalized group in industrialized societies. For example, Slovene youth turned to Yugoslav or Balkan popular music at a time when their own no longer gave them what they were looking for: for them, "Yugo rock" or "Balkan rock," as it was called, preserved what Slovenian popular music did not: identification with passionate and authentic music.

As a collective symbolic activity, playing or listening to music has manifold social implications, but it cannot be taken as a magic wand with which to change society's ills. Though music is essentially a social phenomenon, it is not possible to master its social impact. Only exceptionally are its social effects predictably encoded into the music, but even in these cases (anthems, jingles or other advertising music are possible examples), universal social consensus about its meaning is hardly to be established. Consequently, when considering music's social effects, the contextual dimensions in which the meaning of music is socially achieved need also to be taken into account. If, for example, certain music intervals are officially forbidden, as indeed some were at the time of Shostakovich's well known struggles with the Soviet authorities, and a composer chooses to employ them, it is not the intervals or other music materials themselves that are subversive, or even the imposition by others of meaning upon the composer; it is the decision of the composer who opposes the regulations that gives rise to the charges of subversion.

Music in the Time of War

The dissolution of Yugoslavia was violent. During more than a decade, war and conflict dictated daily life, having dramatic effects on the popular music of the region. With the first armed conflicts, the popular music market was effectively destroyed. Nonetheless, exchange of music between the republics was never completely halted. And although audiences were changed along with dramatic changes in the popular music infrastructure, especially within the public and commercial media in the region, the idea of common popular music survived.

Throughout the 1990s it was almost impossible for Serbian bands and performers to perform in Croatia, as much as it was for Croatian groups and singers to play in Serbia. After the fall of Slobodan Milošević in 2000, however, the situation changed, though not as fast as expected. In 2002, for example, a Belgrade magazine, *Ilustrovana Politika*, wrote that an unofficial ban on playing Serbian artists was still in force at national radio and television stations in Croatia. Meanwhile, big Serbian (or former Bosnian) stars like Ceca, Zdravko Čolić, or Goca Tržan were privately very popular. Similarly, while the Croatian singer Severina was frequently played by the Serbian media (Gajić, 2002), Dalmatian superstar Oliver Dragojević still claims he will never again perform in Serbia no matter how much he's offered—not even for 200,000 EUR, which was possibly the largest amount paid to any singer from the area to perform in Belgrade (Gajić, 2002). Leaving aside noncommercial acts, one of the first singers to perform in Croatia after the war was Serbian Bajaga (Momčilo Bajagić) with his band Instruktori, promoting his album *Zmaj od Noćaja*. It has been claimed that Bajaga and Instruktori sold more albums in Croatia than in Serbia (Gajić, 2002). Đorđe Balašević was another of the first mainstream Serbian acts to perform in Croatia after the fall of Milošević. In Slovenia too, Serbian musicians were the first to be invited to play after the country gained international recognition. Back in 1992, however, only those who did not support Milošević were booked. Interestingly, among the concert audiences of singers like Đorđe Balašević or Bajaga, who regularly performed in Slovenia, there were perhaps more Croatian attendees than Slovene.

War and armed conflict affect society more dramatically than perhaps any other kind of exceptional circumstance. When grenades fall and arms are fired around one's home it is impossible simply to dismiss the fact. After the initial shock, everything changes. For a musician, too, it is almost impossible simply to stand by and pretend that nothing is happening. When armed conflict begins, how an individual becomes involved in the conflict is essential: as a victim, as a helpless observer, as an aggressor, and so on. But whatever happens, it is impossible to remain silent. Consequently, musicians from the former Yugoslavia reacted to the conflicts in many different ways. The majority of Slovene and Croatian musicians reacted to the atrocities as the victims of aggression, or in solidarity with their co-citizens, while their fellow Serbian musicians, especially the younger ones, found themselves in a much more difficult position: some rejected the violence and organized antiwar events, others responded individually to the atrocities, some remained silent and waited, others supported their country's regime, some emigrated before or during the conflicts, others defended "Yugoslavism." Whatever choice they made, it was impossible to pretend that nothing had happened. And even if popular musicians tried not to get involved, they could not avoid the facts of everyday life in their surroundings, which were in many cases marked with unprecedented violence, first in Croatia and then in Bosnia and Herzegovina. While it is impossible to make a general assessment of musicians' responses to the war, after almost two decades since the beginning of the conflict, and almost a decade since its end, it is more or less clear that popular music became actively involved in the processes. The following sections present some examples "from the field."

Bosnia and Herzegovina

Bosnia and Herzegovina was one of the cradles of Yugoslav rock music, starting with the first famous Yugoslav rock band Indeksi, followed by the most successful Yugoslav rock group ever, Bijelo Dugme, and the famous "new primitivism" of the 1980s in the form of bands such as Zabranjeno Pušenje and Elvis J. Kurtović. Among alternative acts were SCH and the art group Zvono. Bosnia and Herzegovina was also an important center of Yugoslav pop and ethno-pop. The singer Zdravko Čolić attracted an audience in the 1970s and made his comeback (from Belgrade) in the 2000s when he sang in all parts of the former Yugoslavia. In the 1980s, the extraordinarily popular Lepa Brena paved the way for turbo-folk.

At the beginning of the war in Bosnia and Herzegovina in 1992, newly-composed folk music was for a while "expelled" from all electronic media in Sarajevo. Nevertheless, cassettes were smuggled across the front lines in both directions (Šavija, 1998). During the siege, for younger Sarajevans the creation of alternative culture was the only means to keep urban culture alive (Šavija, 1998). Thus in the 1990s, during and soon after the war, the most vivid alternative cultural scene to emerge in all the former Yugoslav cities, with several dozen rock bands, art groups, culture magazines, and fanzines, did so in Sarajevo (see Janjatović, 1997; Šavija, 1998; Jeffs, 2005). This music scene was documented on the compilations *Rock Under the Siege* A and B, released by the independent radio station Radio Zid. Furthermore, rock concerts, many of which had been organized during the siege of Sarajevo, were in many instances the first events that proved life was returning to normality after the war. The concert performed by Croatian and Bosnian acts in Skenderija, Sarajevo, on December 28, 1996, entitled *Pjevajmo do zore* (Let's Sing until Dawn) was one such positive sign (Sinclair and Janjatović, 1997).

Further positive signs can be read in other developments and achievements in the music world. At the end of the 1990s, commercial domestic ethno-pop, influenced by Serbian turbo-folk, merged with pop (Andree Zaimović, 2004, p. 163). The pop-music-oriented *Glorija*, published simultaneously in Zagreb and Belgrade, became one of the most widely distributed magazines in Bosnia and Herzegovina (Andree Zaimović, 2004, p. 164). On May 7, 2001, five years after the Dayton Peace Agreement, national public radio service BH Radio 1 was among the first national institutions established in postwar Bosnia and Herzegovina, which had been divided into two entities, the Republic of Srpska and the Federation of Bosnia and Herzegovina, and further divided into cantons (Andree Zaimović, 2002, p. 125). Much later, in late 2009, public support was mobilized for the defense of the radio station Radio 202 which was about to lose its frequency, but which was finally incorporated into the newly-established Sarajevo city radio and television.

One of the most serious problems Bosnia and Herzegovina faced after the war, a problem deeply related to its popular music, was the massive exodus of educated people. It is estimated that around 300,000 university-educated people (Andree Zaimović, 2002, p. 126) left the country in the decade after the dissolution of socialist Yugoslavia. Many musicians found new residence in Croatia, Serbia, Slovenia, other European countries, or in the United States. Hence one of a number of exciting Bosnian rock acts, Culture Shock, comes from Seattle.

In the 2000s many exciting alternative acts also appeared. Among them perhaps Damir Avdić (sometimes under the name Balkan Psycho) from Tuzla produces the most poignant and profound lyrical and artistic reflection of postwar Bosnia. Also of note is Vuneny from Mostar.

Croatia

Croatia was undoubtedly a center of the Yugoslav popular music industry. It had a vivid postwar jazz scene (Boško Petrović is of especial note in this regard; see Vrdoljak, 2008) and produced the majority of domestic pop songs. The Zagreb Song Festival (since 1953) introduced great singers and songwriters such as Ivo Robić, Vice Vukov, Tereza Kesovija, Oliver Dragojević, Severina, and others, and composers and directors Miljenko Prohaska and Nikica Kalodjera (Luković, 1989; Vrdoljak, 2008). Zagreb was home to the first Yugoslav rock singer Karlo Metikoš (Mat Collins), the first domestic rock album (Grupa 220's *Naši dani*), and many successful bands, such as Time, Parni Valjak, Prljavo Kazalište, etc. (see Janjatović, 1999; Mirković, 2004).

During the war in Croatia, the vast majority of Croatian musicians responded to the atrocities with projects and songs directed at the war. The most well-known song was the late Tomislav Ivčić's "Stop the War in Croatia." It had international appeal and reached the Top 10 in Australia. On the compilation CD *The Best of "Rock za Hrvatsku,"* which accompanied an edited volume on music during the war in Croatia (Pettan, 1998), we find peace songs, militant songs, and others. Among these, perhaps the most interesting is "E, moj druže beogradski" (Hey, My Belgrade Comrade), in which the singer, Jura Stublić of the famous new wave group Film, directly addressed his former Belgrade friends for not openly opposing the war in Croatia.

Although the Croatian media attempted to promote the preferred urban forms of popular music as Croatian, in opposition to the "rural" forms of ethno-pop as Serbian, this divide was not proven in the field. Many Croats preferred ethno-pop, while many Krajina Serbs preferred rock. Some militant Croatian musicians, such as Marko Perković/Thompson, intending to mobilize audiences for war (see Pettan, 1998, pp. 24-5), used Balkan rock (or Yu-rock) as a background to the image of self-confident fighters, although they were actually at the same time fighting against something they conceived as "Balkanism."

During and immediately after the war very few bands from Croatia were willing to perform with Serbian artists. When in late 1992 the alternative band Vještice performed for peace in Prague with their Serbian antiwar friends, they faced public discontent. Among the bands that tried to avoid disputes with their Serbian friends, or were critical of Croatian nationalism, were punk and post-punk bands Kud Idijoti, Fuck off Bolan, Let 3, Dark Busters, and others (Sinclair and Janjatović, 1997). After the war, Croatian musicians did not perform in Serbia until the fall of Milošević in the year 2000. Among the first were Alka Vuica (Janjatović, 2000) and the superstar singer Mišo Kovač. The first artist from Serbia to perform in Croatia after the war was well-known anti-Milošević alternative singer and songwriter Rambo Amadeus (Janjatović, 2000).

Macedonia

Due to the difference in language and Macedonia's geographical distance from other centers, the country's popular music scene produced only a few famous bands and singers, including the jazz-rock group Leb i Sol, Roma singer Esma Redžepova, and pop singer Ljupka Dimitrovska. After the dissolution of Yugoslavia, new talents, acceptable to all regions in the former Yugoslavia, appeared. Two examples, DD Synthesis and Anastasia, both used folk elements in their new musical synthesis. Another, who rose to superstardom, was Toše (Todor) Proeski. His untimely death in 2007 prompted perhaps the first display of unanimous sentiment in audiences from all over the former Yugoslavia who united to show respect for this artist's work and efforts, among which were charity and activism for peace.

The alternative music scene in Macedonia began to grow only in the last decade. When the national radio and television network RTV Macedonia wanted to cancel Kanal 103, a semi-autonomous station that played primarily alternative and noncommercial music, the response of its listeners and civil society in general was very strong. It is possible this event further stimulated development of the local alternative music scene with excellent bands such as Foltin, PMG Collective, Bernays Propaganda, and others coming to the fore.

Serbia (and Montenegro)

Despite being the capital of Yugoslavia, Belgrade was not the country's most important popular music center. However, the first famous Serbian rock group, Siluete, hailed from there and was followed by supergroups Yu Grupa and Smak. Then, in the early 1980s Belgrade exploded with new wave groups including Šarlo Akrobata, Idoli, Električni Orgazam, and Ekaterina Velika (see Janjatović, 1999).

Together with domestic pop, a new hybrid style had developed in the late 1950s, combining a couple of decades of older local adaptations of popular music in towns—the so-called *starogradska pesma* (old-town song)—with pop, jazz, and rural traditional music, producing a local ethno-pop genre called *novokomponovana narodna muzika* (newly-composed folk music). Based on the specific use of accordion and melismatic (Oriental) vocals, it further developed with the introduction of modern pop, until it became a dominant music genre in the early 1990s when it developed into what is now known as "turbo-folk."

In the late 1980s, a sharp division was established between the audiences attached to ethno-pop music, the so-called "narodnjaci," who would mostly follow nationalist ideals, and domestic rock, which took another direction, more openly cosmopolitan and antinationalist. Some would claim that the dividing line was between rural and urban cultures, although the division was not so clear. For example, some musicians, such as Boris Kovač, who took their inspiration from traditional music, did not follow this nationalist path at all, while some Serbian rockers, most notably Bora Đorđević from Riblja Čorba, "dived head-first into the nationalist waters" (Janjatović, 1999, p. 33). Turbo-folk, or neo-folk (Dragičević-Šešić, 1994), fused "love songs and older folk tunes" with contemporary dance music in an explicitly or implicitly ethnic Serbian manner (Monroe, 2000).

If the development of turbo-folk was directly related to Serbian nationalist politics in the 1990s, and nonnationalist rock was vehemently marginalized with the destruction of alternatives (Gordy, 1999), two events, both related to rising international interest in music festivals, exemplify these strands in post-Milošević Serbia. The first is the annual festival of brass bands in Guča (near Dragačevo) in central Serbia. The festival offers a very strange mix of ecstatic music performances, dance, heavy drinking, and the gathering of fans of Romani brass bands. At the same time it is an exhibition of Serbian nationalist relics. The second is a more cosmopolitan event that brings the most exciting popular music acts to Serbia: the Exit Festival. This festival is the result of urban youth opposition to the Milošević regime throughout the 1990s. In the summer of 2000, students and youth activists from Otpor (Resistance) organized a festival in Novi Sad which lasted 100 days. Since 2001 the festival has been organized annually in the Petrovaradin fortress across the river Sava. It very quickly developed into one of the most exciting summer festivals in Europe with strong urban and multicultural characteristics (see Žolt et al., 2004; Bizjak et al., 2005). The festival boasts a very broad range of modern popular music. It is a gathering, it is fun, but it is also the main symbol of modern, nonnationalist, urban Serbia. Furthermore, the Exit Festival also gives space to presentations from civil society projects and nongovernmental organizations.

It is well known that the student movement Otpor was closely related to cosmopolitan rock promoted by the independent media. For more than a decade, Radio B92, the student station Radio Index, and the network of independent radio stations had an important role in the continuing struggle against Milošević's regime. Many musicians, at least for a while, especially if they wanted to speak out, left the country. However, during protests against Milošević in 1996, protesters who had shifted their social engagement from the political field to carnivalesque "spheres of culture, personal identity, individual style, spare time and everyday life" (Milić and Ćičkarić, quoted in Grlja, 2002. p. 41) sang an adaptation of the Beach Boys' "Surfin' U.S.A." by pop band Eva Braun, entitled "Serbia Whistling" (Sinclair and Janjatović, 1997). That year, unfortunately, the street noise—including whistles, shouts, and the beating of pans—that protesters employed did not help. Nevertheless, independent releases, such as the compilation albums *Nas slušaju svi, mi ne slušamo nikoga!* (Everybody Listens to Us, We Don't Listen to Anybody) and *Ovo je zemlja za nas?!? Radio Boom 93 (1992-1997)* (Is This Country for Us?) (Sinclair and Janjatović, 1997), did have a profound effect on people who did not accept the predominantly nationalist call and resisted further. The compilation *Korak napred 2 koraka nazad* (Step Further, Two Steps Beyond), with adaptations of old Yugoslav hits, even helped pave the way to a warming of relations between Croatia and Serbia (Janjatović, 2000). Prior to this, while the Serbian media had not banned Croatian music, it was not being played as frequently as before the war. However, at the beginning of the NATO bombing of Serbia in March, 1999, the majority of radio stations stopped playing music in English (Pančić, 1999).

Slovenia

Despite being a small republic, Slovenia played an important role in the development of Yugoslav popular music. In Ljubljana the first Yugoslav jazz ensembles (Jazz Negode in 1922) were formed and the first jazz festival was organized in Bled in 1960. Rock band Kameleoni achieved Yugoslav recognition in the 1960s while in the 1970s the lyrics of the underground band Buldožer faced censorship. In the late 1970s, a very strong and politically conscious alternative scene developed, not only with punk rock, but with many post-1960s movements in culture and arts, as well as with new social movements. As a consequence, during the 1980s it was possible to follow step by step the processes of liberalization and the ongoing questioning of the limits of expression. Early punk and alternative new social movements helped pave the path toward democratization. The leading ideas of the growing new civil society were the abolition of the death penalty and the abolition of so-called "verbal crime," Article 133 of the Civil Penalty Code, that could see someone jailed merely on the basis of his or her public expression of thoughts that might disturb the public.

Many other human rights and basic freedoms were promoted through processes that were closely related to music activism, such as environmentalist activism and new spiritual movements, and, perhaps the most important and symbolically powerful, gay and lesbian movements. These movements are the main reason why at the end of the 1980s Slovenian politics was not overwhelmingly nationalist. Popular music, especially alternative rock and other kinds of underground music, played a major role in these processes. Having said that, examples of new patriotism and nationalism were to be found in popular music as well (Agropop), though even these might have been interpreted ironically (Barber-Keršovan, 1999).

Soon after June, 1991, in particular, a certain amount of music censorship existed in the media, and it was very difficult to hear songs in the Croatian and Serbian languages on Slovene radio stations. However, the media blockade in Slovenia did not last for long. Some media, like independent Radio Študent, played music from Serbia and other parts of the former Yugoslavia all the time. On September 16, 1991, Radio Študent launched a legendary show in the Croatian/Serbian language: *Nisam ja odavde* (I Am Not from Here), initially titled *Balkan urnebes* (The Balkan Pandemonium), was partly nostalgic, partly activist, and partly devoted to refugees.

After the war in Slovenia, and during the wars in Croatia and Bosnia and Herzegovina, it did not seem opportune to invite Serbian acts to play in Slovenia. At the beginning of 1994, Bajaga and his band Instruktori were refused visas, and only after the intervention of the then Slovenian president Milan Kučan were the visas acquired. It was not until February, 1996, that Slovenian bands (four of them) visited Serbia, and in May of the same year four Serbian bands (Love Hunters, Nothing but Logopedes, Svarog, and Goblins) responded in kind (Janjatović, 1996). The interruption in the exchange of music had somehow been unexpected, because many Slovenian citizens originated from other Yugoslav republics. Before the dissolution of Yugoslavia, these citizens were stigmatized and named "južnjaki" (the southerners), "bosanci" (bosnianers), or "čefurji" (a derogatory term for migrants from other former Yugoslav republics). One pop singer, Robert Pešut, also known as Magnifico, turned this stigma around with his album *Kdo je čefur* (Who is *čefur*). In the past few years it has become fashionable for Slovenian youth to act as stigmatized "čefur," and in 2009, the writer Goran Vojnović was awarded the national prize for the novel *Čefurji raus!* (*Southerners Go Home!*). Music and popular culture proved to be powerful tools in turning stigma around and empowering minorities.

National and Cosmopolitan Popular Music in the Light of Human Rights and Freedoms

That Serbian turbo-folk was popular in Croatia and Bosnia and Herzegovina even in the most tragic times of war is extremely interesting. Not only did civilians listen to it, but also mobilized soldiers who would appropriate music from behind the enemies' lines and use it for their own purposes. This popularity was coterminous with the unprecedented burst of creativity among the people in areas of conflict. The Croatian rock singer Thompson and the Serbian neo-folk singer from Croatia Baja mali Knindža (Mirko Pajčin) are typical examples of the spontaneous wave of militant popular music that flourished at the time. They sang songs entitled "Serbs Aren't Afraid of Anyone," "Tears Aren't for Serbs," "Kosovo Is Our Soul" (Baja), and "Because We Are Croats," "The Spirit of the Warrior," and "Shut the Gun" (Thompson), among others.

With imagery in the music videos of "nouveaux riches, gangsters, beautiful girls, femmes fatales, luxurious interiors, and fancy cars" (Kronja, 2004, p. 8), turbo-folk not only became the dominant popular culture in Serbia, but spread to other countries in the region, including Bulgaria, Albania, Macedonia, Bosnia and Herzegovina, Croatia, and Slovenia. The most popular acts would play for audiences of thousands. In 2002, the most popular Serbian singer in Croatia was Ražnatović Ceca and "even soldiers in Croatian barracks listened to her" (Gajić, 2002). Belgrade based TV Pink, established in 1994, became the most important center for the promotion of turbo-folk. In 2009, much remained the same: in Croatia, Svetlana Ceca Ražnatović was still by far the most sought after Serbian performer. However, although she was announced the No.1 "folk music" star in

Croatia (according to the website of her Croatian fan club[1]), she continued to claim that she would never perform there.

Despite proclamations of freedom of expression in the former Yugoslavia and the world over, some bands still face censorship. The primary motives for suspension of freedom of expression are public moral and religious issues. The Croatian band Let 3, for example, is well known for provoking outrage, including by sometimes performing nude on stage. Indeed, their performance on the program "Tistega lepega popoldneva," on Slovenian national television on November 11, 2006, was censored, and their performance in Travnik (Bosnia and Herzegovina) was banned (Jaušovec, 2007).

When using a human rights framework to understand cultural movements, it is important to remember that universal human rights were introduced into the international language of law only after World War II was concluded and the human atrocities that were perpetrated therein were revealed. These declared human rights are the lowest possible denominator from which it is possible to deduct something we can comprehend as the universal human existence underlying the dignity of each individual human being. Thus the provisional notion of "human rights" relates to manifold dimensions of human existence. The Universal Declaration, however, was a political compromise, and hence it supports only basic freedoms without explicitly rejecting censorship and other "softer" ways of regulating freedom of expression.

Music, as well as other kinds of art, transcends and rises above the particular "and reaches for the universal" (Ostertag, 2009, p. 8). Ostertag's *Yugoslavia Suite*,[2] performed by American artists Bob Ostertag and Richard Board in Slovenia and Serbia immediately after the NATO bombing of Serbia in October, 1999, as well as concerts in Sarajevo in 1995 by U2 and (the internationally renowned and somewhat controversial Slovenian avant-garde group) Laibach, efficiently transcended dead-end situations in the region without having any immediate impact. This is how music affects social life. It is an essential part of new social movements, especially the carnivalesque rebellion of youth against the constraints of nationalist politics or against global capitalism. The organization of protest concerts (see Grujičić, 1999), the adaptation of pop songs, chanting on the streets, the release of antiwar compilation albums, and carefully chosen music played in the media all proved to be relatively effective ways of mobilizing the youth in the former Yugoslavia, especially in Serbia. The famous line of the antiwar song "Slušaj 'vamo!" (Attention!) by Rimtutituki, comprising members of Električni Orgazam, Partibrejkers, and Ekaterina Velika, declares "we don't want folk music to win." This was not merely a statement about aesthetic preferences (Žolt et al., 2004, pp. 373-4), but a clear declaration of resistance to the homogenization of cultural space in a modern European country. Given the limited appeal of this

---

[1]   http://ceca-fans.bloger.hr/, accessed July 30, 2009.

[2]   See http://bobostertag.com/music-liveprojects-yugoslaviasuite.htm, accessed May 27, 2010.

song, and of rock music in general, music journalist Petar Janjatović would claim that "rock was absolutely never a real force here," though many people in Serbia believe that "Milošević was brought down by rock and roll" (Janjatović and Rogošić, quoted in Mijatović, 2008).

Some rock musicians are still involved in breaking the barriers between countries. In August, 2008 a monument to Bob Marley was erected in the Serbian village of Banatski Sokolac. The statue was unveiled by the famous Croatian rock musician Dado Topić (Time) and Serbian reggae rocker Jovan Matić (Del Arno Band), and the event was accompanied by a concert by Croatian and Serbian bands. However, the common belief that "rock is engaged in the music of rebellion" is clearly unfounded (Grujičić, 1999). No music in its essence is rebellious or supportive of a regime. The Serbian movement Otpor adopted rock music as its common music expression with groups like Eyesburn, Love Hunters, Atheist Rap, Kanda Kodža i Nebojša, and Darkwood Dub. And when the ethno-pop (*narodnjak*) star Dragan Kojić Keba expressed his desire to participate in an Otpor protest, he was rebuffed (Grujičić, 1999). In contrast, some rock and pop singers openly joined the nationalists, for instance Serbian and Croatian rock singers Bora Đorđević and Marko Perković (Thompson). In 1992, ethno-pop singer Zoran Kalezić, pop singer Vladimir Savčić Čobi, and rock singer Bora Đorđević came together to sing "U boj, ustani, Srbine moj!" (To Fight, Arise, Oh My Serb!).[3] Montenegrin singer Zoran Kalezić explained: "We can't expect Sloba [Milošević], [Vojislav] Šešelj, or Arkan to Sing! They'll do some other things, and we'll sing" (Tarlač, 2003).

Together with the escalation of war in Yugoslav republics, traditional music forms were revived and were either considered as markers of national or regional exclusiveness or as a means of military mobilization (*gusle* singing in the Dinaric region,[4] for example). It is well known that the political leader of the Bosnian Serbs, Radovan Karadžić, performed as a *gusle* singer (Tarlač, 2003). However, it is less widely known that all parties in the conflict revived *gusle* singing. In 1998 the international authorities in Bosnia and Herzegovina were supposedly preparing an Act banning *gusle* singing events in the Republic of Srpska, because they would promote ethnic hatred and celebrate war criminals (Milojević, 2007).

Music has always been used, in some form or another, not only as a mobilizing force, but also as a weapon aimed at the "enemy." Serbian patriotic neo-folk singers, though not so different from the Croatian and Bosnian variants, with their megalomaniac and mythomaniac expressions of kitsch, sang about "Kosovo, Serbia, God, tradition, territory, faith, blood, land, pride, children, spite, love, language, hearth, graves, traitors, fights, and borders" (Tarlač, 2003).

---

[3] A version of the song can be viewed on YouTube: http://www.youtube.com/watch?v=2yOlp91IMQY, accessed April 9, 2011.

[4] *Gusle* singing is a musical form comprising the singing of epic songs accompanied by the single-stringed instrument after which the form is named.

Yet surprisingly the production of offensive music in the former Yugoslavia has not been limited to the locals. In 2005, under the name Shiptare Boys, Norwegian KFO soldiers recorded the song, "Kosovo," a kind of a bad joke with an anti-Serbian message which scandalized the Serbian public.[5]

Conclusions

Freedom of expression and freedom to associate in public, together with freedom of the press and of other forms of public communication and expression, shall be guaranteed. Each person may freely collect, receive, and circulate information and opinions. Except in such circumstances as are laid down by statute, each person shall have the right to obtain information of a public nature, provided he or she can show sufficient legal interest as determined by the statute. These are basic principles declared in the Universal Declaration of Human Rights. Why should popular music be excluded from these principles? Popular culture is, after all, as Noam Chomsky and others have repeatedly argued, "Integral to the construction of consent for the dominant ideologies of the West ..." (Monroe, 2000). In his writings on freedom, John Stuart Mill claimed that there is no interest in banning words or the gestures of people unless they can cause harm to others (Cloonan, 1996, p. 12).

Freedom of expression and unrestrained creativity in popular music are essential constituents of modern democratic society. Together with other forms of freedom, freedom of artistic expression is the essential basis for a democratic and tolerant society. Wittgenstein's frontiers of one's language, which become frontiers of one's world, are constantly changing. The question is whether the actors are approaching an open or closed universe.

---

[5]   See http://www.youtube.com/watch?v=cpu8IQH4B9U, accessed April 12, 2011.

Bibliography

Andree Zaimović, Vesna, "Muzička politika na javnom radijskom servisu Bosne i Hercegovine—muzikološki izazov u specifičnoj poslijeratnoj stvarnosti" [Music Policy in the Public Radio Service of Bosnia and Herzegovina— Musicolocigal Challenge in Specific PostWar Reality], in Ivan Čavlović (ed.), *Zbornik radova 3. međunarodnog simpozija "Muzika u društvu"* [Proceedings from the 3rd International Symposium "Music in Society"] (Sarajevo: Muzikološko društvo, 2002): 125-31.

Andree Zaimović, Vesna, "O medijskom pristupu popularnoj muzici zemalja bivše SFRJ" [On the Media Approach to Popular Music in the Countries of the Former Socialist Federative Republic of Yugoslavia], in Tamara Karača and Senad Kanić (eds.), *Zbornik radova 4. međunarodnog simpozija "Muzika u društvu"* [Proceedings from the 4th International Symposium "Music in Society"] (Sarajevo: Muzikološko društvo, 2004): 161-5.

Barber-Keršovan, Alenka, "Na sledi kulturni identiteti. Kaj je 'slovenskega' v slovenski rock glasbi?," *Glasnik Slovenskega etnološkega društva*, 39, 1 (1999): 4-9.

Bizjak, Anja, et al. (eds.), *Petrovardinsko pleme: Raziskovanje fenomena Festivala EXIT/Petrovaradinsko pleme: Istraživanje fenomena Festivala EXIT /Petrovaradin Tribe: Reflections of the Phenomenon of Music Festival EXIT* (Ljubljana: KUD Pozitiv, 2005) <http://www.pozitiv.si/petrovaradintribe/>, accessed July 25, 2009.

Blacking, John, *How Musical is Man?* (Seattle: University of Washington Press, 1973).

Cloonan, Martin, *Banned! Censorship of Popular Music in Britain, 1967-92* (Aldershot: Arena, 1996).

Cohen, Ronald D., *Rainbow Quest: The Folk Music Revival and American Society, 1940-1970* (Amherst: University of Massachusetts Press, 2002).

Dragičević-Šešić, Milena, *Neofolk kultura: Publika i njene zvezde* [Neofolk Culture: Audience and Its Stars] (Sremski Karlovci and Novi Sad: Izdavačka knjižarnica Zorana Stojadinovića, 1994).

Gajić, Branka, "Neće Oliver, neće ni Ceca" [Oliver Does Not Want, and Ceca Does Not Want], *Ilustrovana politika*, 2279 (September 21, 2002), <http://ilustrovana.com/2002/2279/7.htm>, accessed July 5, 2009.

Gordy, Eric D., *The Culture of Power in Serbia: Nationalism and the Destruction of Alternatives* (University Park, Pa.: Penn State University Press, 1999).

Grlja, Dušan, "(De)generation in 'Protest' or the Defense and the Last Days of 'Other Serbia'," *Break*, 2, 2-3 (2002): 34-44.

Grujičić, Nebojša, "R'n'r i protesti: Kamenje na system" [R'n'r and Protests: Stones to the System], *Vreme*, 464 (November 27, 1999).

Ivanović, Goran, "Mesić oštel hrvaško diplomacijo zaradi Thompsona" [Mesić Blamed Croatian Diplomacy for Thompson], *Dnevnik* (October 6, 2009): 6.

Janjatović, Petar, "Global Music Pulse: Slovenia/Serbia," *Billboard*, 108, 25 (1996): 61.

Janjatović, Petar, "Global Music Pulse: Bosnia," *Billboard*, 109, 5 (1997): 49.

Janjatović, Petar, "A Retrospect: Yugoslav Pop and Rock," *Novi zvuk*, 13 (1999): 30-35.

Janjatović, Petar, "Global Music Pulse: The Latest Music News from around the Planet. Belgrade," *Billboard*, 112, 9 (2000): 53.

Jaušovec, Matjaž, "CD-teka: Let 3—Bombardiranje Srbije i Čačka" [Review of Let 3's Bombing of Serbia and Čačak], *RockOnNet* (August 23, 2007) <http://www.rockonnet.com/>, accessed December 9, 2008.

Jeffs, Nikolai, "Some People in This Town Don't Want to Die Like a Hero: Multiculturalism and the Alternative Music Scene in Sarajevo, 1992-1996," in Mark Yoffe and Andrea Collins (eds.), *Rock 'n' Roll and Nationalism: A Multinational Perspective* (Newcastle: Cambridge Scholars Press, 2005): 1-19.

Johnson, Bruce, and Martin Cloonan, *Dark Side of the Tune: Popular Music and Violence* (Aldershot: Ashgate, 2008).

Kronja, Ivana, "Politics, Nationalism, Music, and Popular Culture in 1990s Serbia," *Slovo*, 16, 1 (2004): 5-15.

Luković, Petar, *Bolja prošlost: Prizori iz muzičkog života Jugoslavije 1940-1989* [Better Past: Scenes from the Musical Life in Yugoslavia, 1940-1989] (Beograd: Mladost, 1989).

Merriam, Alan P., *The Anthropology of Music* (Chicago: Northwestern University Press, 1964).

Mijatović, Brana, "'Throwing Stones at the System': Rock Music in Serbia during the 1990s," *Music and Politics*, 2, 2 (2008) <http://www.music.ucsb.edu/projects/musicandpolitics/archive/2008-2/mijatovic.html>, accessed July 19, 2009.

Milojević, Jasmina, "Novo guslarstvo: Ogled o tradicionalnom muzičkom obliku u popularnoj kulturi" [New Gusle Music: A Study of Traditional Musical Form in Popular Culture], *Kultura*, 116-17 (2007): 123-40.

Mirković, Igor, *Sretno dijete* [The Lucky Kid] (Zaprešić: Fraktura, 2004).

Monroe, Alexei, "Balkan Hardcore: Pop Culture and Paramilitarism," *Central Europe Review*, 2, 24 (July 19, 2000), <http://www.ce-review.org/00/24/monroe 24.html>, accessed April 15, 2005.

Muršič, Rajko, *Neubesedljive zvočne igre: Od filozofije k antropologiji glasbe* [Non-verbal Sound Games: From Philosophy to the Anthropology of Music] (Maribor: Akademska založba Katedra, 1993).

Muršič, Rajko, "Popularna glasba v krempljih represije in cenzure" [Popular Music in the Clutches of Repression and Censorship], *Časopis za kritiko znanosti, domišljijo in novo antropologijo (ČKZ)*, 27, 195-6 (1999): 179-99.

Muršič, Rajko, "Provocation and Repression after Socialism: The Strelnikoff Case," in Tony Mitchell, Peter Doyle, and Bruce Johnson (eds.), *Changing Sounds: New Directions and Configurations in Popular Music. IASPM 1999 International Conference Proceedings* (Sydney: University of Technology, 2000): 309-18.

Ostertag, Bob, *Creative Life: Music, Politics, People, and Machines* (Urbana: University of Illinois Press, 2009).

Pančić, Teofil, "Muzika i rat: imate li srca?" [Music and War: Are You Human?], *Vreme*, 9 (May 8, 1999) <http://www.vreme.com/arhiva_html/vb9/8.html# Muzika>, accessed July 5, 2009.

Pettan, Svanibor (ed.), *Music, Politics, and War: Views from Croatia* (Zagreb: Institute of Ethnology and Folklore Research, 1998).

Port, Mattijs van de, "The Articulation of Soul: Gypsy Musicians and the Serbian Other," *Popular Music*, 18, 3 (1999): 291-308.

Rice, Timothy, "The Dialectic of Economics and Aesthetics in Bulgarian Music," in Mark Slobin (ed.), *Returning Culture: Musical Changes in Central and Eastern Europe* (Durham, NC: Duke University Press, 1996): 176-99.

Rodionov, I., "Vecher v diskoklube," *Dneprovskaia pravda* (January 14, 1979): 4.

Šavija, Nebojša, "Ambrosia Souvenir: Department for Text Pathology," Performance/presentation in the event *On Divided Society*, IUC Dubrovnik, April 1-11, 1998 (unpublished manuscript, 1998).

Silverman, Carol, "Music and Marginality: Roma (Gypsies) of Bulgaria and Macedonia," in Mark Slobin (cd.), *Returning Culture: Musical Changes in Central and Eastern Europe* (Durham, NC: Duke University Press, 1996): 231-53.

Sinclair, David, and Petar Janjatović, "Music Acts as Healing Force in the Balkans: A Special Report on the Music and Musicians of the Balkans since the Breakup of Yugoslavia and the War of 1991-95," *Billboard*, 109, 23 (1997): 1-4.

Tarlač, Goran, "Turbo Folk Politics," *Transitions Online* (April 14, 2003) <http://www.tol.cz/>, accessed July 19, 2009.

Vrdoljak, Dražen, *Moje brazde: Bilješke o hrvatskoj zabavnoj, pop i jazz glazbi* [My Grooves: Notes on Croatian Entertainment, Pop and Jazz Music] (Zagreb: V.B.Z, 2008).

Žolt, Lazar, Aleksandra Višnjevac, and Anđelija Vučurević, "Aktuelno stanje omladinskih potkultura i publika Exit-a" [Current State of Youth Subcultures and Audience of the Exit Festival], *Teme*, 28, 4 (2004): 361-80.

Discography

Baja Mali Knindža, "Srbi se nikog ne boje" ["Serbs Aren't Afraid of Anyone"], *Još se ništa ne zna* [It is Not Yet Known] (Serbia Music, 1994).

Baja Mali Knindža, "Nisu suze za Srbina" ["Tears Aren't for Serbs"], *Još se ništa ne zna* [It is Not Yet Known] (Serbia Music, 1994).

Baja Mali Knindža, "Kosovo je naša duša" ["Kosovo is Our Soul"], *Biti il ne biti* [To Be or Not To Be] (Renome, 1999).

The Beach Boys, "Surfin' USA" b/w "Shut Down" (Capitol, 1963).

The Best of "Rock za Hrvatsku" (Croatia Records, 1992).

Grupa 220, *Naši dani* (Jugoton, 1968).

Ivčić, Tomislav, *Stop the War in Croatia* (Croatia Records, 1991).

Korak napred 2 koraka nazad [Step Further, Two Steps Beyond] (B92, 1999).

Nas slušaju svi, mi ne slušamo nikoga! [Everybody Listens to Us, We Don't Listen to Anybody] (Radio Index, 1997).

Ovo je zemlja za nas?!? Radio Boom 93 (1992-1997) [Is This Country for Us?] (B92 and Radio BOOM 93, 1997).

Rock under the Siege A (Radio Zid, 1995).

Rock under the Siege B (Radio Zid, 1996).

Stublić, Jura, "E, moj druže beogradski" ["Hey, My Belgrade Comrade"], Stublić, Jura and Film, *Hrana za golubove* [Food for Pigeons] (Croatia Records, 1992).

Thompson, "Jer, Hrvati smo" ["Because We Are Croats"], *Moli mala* [Prey, My Baby] (Croatia Records, 1992).

Thompson (Marko Perković), "Pukni, puško" ["Shut the Gun"], *Vjetar s Dinare* [Winds from Dinara] (Croatia Recorts, 1998).

Thompson, "Duh ratnika" ["The Spirit of the Warrior"], *Bilo jednom u Hrvatskoj* [It Was Once in Croatia] (Croatia Records, 2006).

[10]

Shooting and Crying: The Emergence of Protest in Israeli Popular Music[1]

~ Scott Streiner ~

INTRODUCTION

Dissent has long been woven into popular music. Indeed, for at least two generations, it has almost been taken for granted that popular music is a site for protest: from "Blowin' in the Wind" through "Sunday Bloody Sunday" to "The Ghost of Tom Joad," expressions of opposition to prevailing policies have been a part of the masses' music.

That does not mean, however, that political protest has been the norm for popular music, nor that the challenges to the status quo by popular musical artists have known no bounds. Indeed, what is striking upon close examination is how rare dissent is in practice, impressions to the contrary notwithstanding.[2]

At least one obvious explanation for this is rooted in the very fact that the music is *popular*. To retain commercial appeal among a wide cross-section of the populace can be tricky at the best of times; to do so while espousing views which run counter to conventional wisdom can be next to impossible. Thus, the creator or purveyor of music who aspires to sales and adoration faces a built-in disincentive against open dissent. This disincentive will presumably be especially pronounced in situations where the conventional wisdom is preoccupied with matters fundamental to a society—such as its self-definition or survival—and where social consensus is broad and deep.[3]

What is fascinating from an analytical perspective, then, are instances where political protest emerges in popular music despite these seeming obstacles to it. This article will focus on one such case: the gradual appearance and normalization of protest in Israeli popular music. The specific type of dissent of interest here is protest from the left about the Israeli government's security/peace policies, rather than, say, protest over social inequities or political corruption. The rationale for this focus is straightforward: because Israel has lived in a state of real or potential war since its establishment in 1948, security/peace issues have consistently dominated the national agenda, to the near exclusion of matters that are of central concern elsewhere. The perpetual shadow of conflict has meant that, despite deep internal cleavages, Israeli society has encouraged and subtly enforced a significant degree of consensus on core security issues. Like many collectivities that feel vulnerable (and regardless of whether others think this feeling sensible), Israelis have tended to view a degree of cohesion around certain fundamental matters as a *sine qua non* of survival. Thus, protest from the left—that is, demands for security/peace policies which involve greater compromise and increased short-term

Scott Streiner is currently employed with Canada's federal government as a senior public servant and would like to point out that this essay was prepared exclusively in his academic capacity and does not reflect official policy.

772   SCOTT STREINER

risks—has never been simple. The limits of legitimate protest from the left have, inevitably, been much debated and have only shifted substantially in the wake of major events.

With respect to the arena for protest, the article's focus will be music which is broadly recognized as "mainstream" and played most frequently on the country's radio stations. "Popular music" is a good framework in which to explore the appearance and development of protest for at least two reasons. The first relates to the dynamics of structure; that is, the shaping of individual action by social forces. Because artists and companies producing popular music are worried about staying fashionable and making a profit—and so, are inherently predisposed to tread cautiously around any subject likely to provoke excessive controversy—we learn something important about transformations in the socio-cultural milieu when previously proscribed protest emerges in popular music. The second reason relates to the impact of agency; that is, how individual choices alter social structures. Because popular artists have a privileged status and because of the ongoing exposure of the population to their music, the opinions conveyed by the lyrics they sing can potentially have a significant effect on public attitudes.[4]

One caveat is in order: in the Israeli context, popular music as I am using the term (it essentially means a variant of Western pop-rock) needs to be distinguished from the more Middle Eastern music enjoyed by a substantial proportion of the populace but rarely treated seriously by music critics and broadcasters. The latter, which is sometimes called "central bus station music" because of the plethora of shops around Tel Aviv's old central bus station that sell it, traditionally tended to be disparaged by those in a position to arbitrate on what constitutes "quality" creativity. Although this has started to change in recent years as more "crossover" music has been recorded and as critics have responded to charges of paternalism, "central bus station music" is still a distinct and less recognized genre. This state of affairs probably has much to do with Israel's continued conflict with the Arab world and desire to see itself as Western, as well an internal hierarchy in which Ashkenazi (European-origin) Jews do better in socio-economic terms than Mizrachi Jews (those with roots in Arab countries). The exclusion of Middle Eastern music from my own analysis is not intended to justify the treatment that such music has received; it simply recognizes its relative marginalization as a fact relevant to the establishment of analytical boundaries. In addition, it reflects the reality that Middle Eastern music has not been a sphere for protest from the left, perhaps because Mizrachi Jews, for a variety of reasons too complex to enter into here, have tended to be hawkish on security/peace issues.[5]

The remainder of the article will be divided into three general sections: the history of protest in Israeli popular music; case-specific explanatory factors; and a conclusion which briefly considers theoretical implications of the case.

HISTORY OF PROTEST IN ISRAELI POPULAR MUSIC[6]

1948 TO THE EARLY 1970s

For years after Israel's establishment, there was little serious protest of its security and peace policies from the left. While a few thinkers and groups had advocated far-reaching compromise with the Palestinian–Arab population prior to the Second World War, the Holocaust and the feeling of being besieged from all sides during the 1948 war generated a deep sense of moral justification and little sympathy for anyone calling for significant concessions.[7] Moreover, Zionism's success in setting up a state led, perhaps invariably, to the ascendance of the ideology's nationalistic features over its universalistic, humanistic ones.[8] True, criticism related to specific incidents or issues erupted from time to time but, by and large, there was consensus that the state's security and peace policies were dictated by forces beyond its control. Feeling threatened by a hostile and much larger Arab world, Israeli society concluded that it had no choice but to defend itself vigorously, lest another Holocaust take place right in the Land of Israel.

On the rare occasions that protest on security/peace matters from the left did materialize, it was usually expressed by poets and intellectuals with impeccable credentials. This reflected the relative status of different types of "art" in the society at the time. Poets and scholars were the most highly respected creative communities in the Yishuv—the pre-1948 Jewish community in Palestine—and in the young state of Israel. Thus, Natan Alterman, Israel's leading poet, could publish a piece attacking violent acts perpetrated by Jewish soldiers against Palestinian–Arab civilians (acts officially denied by Israeli officialdom until recently) during the newly independent state's military struggle with the Arabs. And the well-known philosopher, Martin Buber, could safely raise moral concerns about the state's policies towards Arabs inside and outside its borders.[9] Such expressions of protest, however, were infrequent and peripheral, and therefore were easily dismissed by those in power.

Given its embryonic and lower-status condition, popular music was not a site even for limited protest during this period. Indeed, the opposite was true: for some 25 years, popular music reinforced rather than challenged the Zionist ethos and government policy. The voices on the radio sang about attachment to the Land of Israel, celebrated daily life in the new state, recalled victories over adversaries, mourned those killed in battle, quoted national poets and biblical verse, and (increasingly over time but still much less regularly than in Europe and North America) pined for love. Typical titles from the popular repertoire of Israel's first two-and-a-half decades include "Song of the Valley" (*Shir ha'Emek*),[10] "Song of the Tide" (*Shir ha'Reut*), "Someone Who Has Dreamed" (*Mi sh'Chalam*), "Just Another Weekday" (*Stam Yom Shel Chol*), "A House Facing the Golan" (*Ba'it el Mul ha'Golan*), "There Are Flowers" (*Yesh Prachim*), "At Night on the Grass" (*Ba'Laila al ha'Deshe*), and "Lesson About the Homeland" (*Shi'ur Moledet*).

The epitome of this style of popular music was Naomi Shemer's "Jerusalem of Gold" (*Yerushalayim Shel Zahav*), which was released just before the 1967 war and which remains a staple in Jewish musical curricula around the world. Shemer was among the best known of popular musicians, and her timing was, in hindsight, perfect, if inadvertent. In "Jerusalem of Gold," Shemer sang longingly for Jerusalem's Old City, from which Israelis had been cut off since 1948, and bemoaned its empty alleyways. Needless to say, the alleyways were not exactly empty at the time: they were full of Palestinians, though empty of Jews. But the song did capture Israelis' genuine attachment to the Old City along with their sense that it had been placed beyond their reach because of Arab animosity. Thus, it is not surprising that when Israel captured the Old City in the 1967 war—along with the West Bank, Golan Heights, Gaza Strip, and

Sinai—"Jerusalem of Gold" became something of a national anthem. Euphoric after their unexpected military victory, Israelis embraced the paeon to their reunited capital.

The 1967 triumph, however, planted the seeds for an eventual erosion of the consensus around security/peace issues or, to put the matter slightly differently, for an expansion of the limits of legitimate protest. As the excitement subsided, some Israelis began to gradually realize that they were facing a new reality: the reality of being a strong occupying power rather than a weak, threatened, infant state. This reality did not hit all at once, did not become obvious to many, and never displaced the parallel sense of vulnerability that persists in the Israeli psyche. But it did mean that, at least for some Israelis, the possibility of choice in security/peace policy became much more palpable. And by extension, the potential for open dissatisfaction with government policy increased.[11]

EARLY 1970S TO EARLY 1980S

Fascinatingly, the first real protest song to appear in Israeli popular music was released by an Israeli Defence Forces' (IDF) musical group. These groups had long been maintained by the IDF as a morale-boosting option for draftees with exceptional talent and as a breeding ground for popular artists. But in the early 1970s, one of the groups released "Song of Peace" (*Shir l'Shalom*), a composition that, despite the use of metaphorical language, left no doubt about its unprecedented call for less obsession with the casualties of past battles and greater effort to prevent future ones:

> Let the sun rise
> And light up the morning
> Even the purest prayer
> Can't bring us back
>
> He whose candle has been snuffed out
> Who is buried in dust
> Won't be returned
> Or awoken by bitter tears
>
> No one can bring back those of us
> At the bottom of a dark pit
> Here, the joy of victory
> And songs of praise are of no use
>
> So, sing only a song of peace
> Don't whisper a prayer
> Just sing a song of peace—with a great shout
>
> Let the sun rise
> Between the flowers
> Don't look back
> Let those who have departed be
>
> Look up in hope
> Not through gun sights
> Sing a song for love
> Not war

Don't say "the day will come"
Bring the day
Because it isn't just a dream
In every square, cheer for peace.

For some, the song was a welcome expression of discontent with the government's passivity on the question of peace. For many, however, it was nothing less than scandalous. There was a period during which it was shunned by radio stations and for many years it was tainted in the public eye by its disregard for consensual limits and the controversy it had provoked. Still, a precedent had been established, and the song itself would enjoy a remarkable revival more than two decades later.

There was a scattering of other songs through the 1970s that captured Israeli society's yearning for peace, including Naomi Shemer's bittersweet "The Last War" (*Ha'Milchama ha'Achrona*), released in the wake of the devastating 1973 war, which spoke sadly of how each of Israel's battles was expected to be the final one, but never turned out to be. Shemer, however, was certainly not on the left, and songs such as "The Last War" wished for peace without suggesting that the country's leaders bore significant responsibility for its absence. It was only in the late 1970s that another popular song candidly criticized government security and peace policies: "Things Will Be OK" (*Yihiyeh Tov*), by David Broza. The song was written in the wake of Menachem Begin's election as Prime Minister (the first time the so-called National Camp had taken the reigns of power from the Labour Party) and Anwar Sadat's historic visit to Jerusalem. This was also the period that witnessed the emergence of "Peace Now," a left wing, soldier-led movement that publicly challenged the government's security and peace policies.[12] "Things Will Be OK" registered a sardonic protest against the petty bickering of political leaders charged with peace-making, and expressed a mixture of hope and doubt about the potential for living a normal life in Israel. Again, the protest was somewhat metaphorical, yet unmistakable. Broza sang:

I look out of the window
And it makes me feel pretty sad
The spring has passed, it's gone
Who knows if it will ever return
The clown has become king, and the prophet, a clown
And I've lost my way, yet I'm still here ...

Children spread their wings
And fly off to the army
But two years later
They come back without any answers

Governments of generals
Divide up the landscape
Into "ours" and "theirs"
When will we see the end of it?

Ironically, the song's tone and its metaphorical quality allowed those on the other end of the spectrum to use Broza's lyrics for their own purposes—right-wing protests against Menachem Begin's decision to trade the Sinai for a peace treaty with Egypt. Condemning the government for its concessions to Sadat and arguing that "peace in exchange for peace" should be sufficient, the right quoted the following lines from "Things Will Be OK":

> Here comes Egypt's President
> I was so happy as he arrived
> Pyramids in his eyes
> And peace in his pipe
> So we said, "Let's bury our differences
> and live like brothers"
> Then he shouted, "Yes, forward!
> Just so long as you get out of the territories"

Like "Song of Peace," "Things Will Be OK" was a rather isolated event in Israeli popular music: other artists did not release protest songs in the late 1970s and, within a few years, Broza himself had left Israel for an extended period of residence and recording in North America.

LEBANON WAR

By 1982–83, the mood among many in Israel was souring. Begin had been re-elected and had allowed his hawkish Defence Minister, Ariel Sharon, to launch a war in Lebanon that was widely seen as the first war Israel had chosen, rather than been forced, to fight. Moreover, the fighting was carried much further into the territory of Israel's Northern neighbour than the government had led Israelis to believe it would be; casualties among Israeli soldiers, Lebanese civilians, and Palestinian refugees were high; and increasingly, Israel seemed enmeshed in an *ad hoc*, semi-permanent occupation. The result was an unprecedented wave of protest: Peace Now organized the largest demonstration in Israeli history (a reported 400,000 people—about one-tenth of the population if accurate) after the massacres at the Sabra and Shatilla refugee camps, and a new movement, "There's a Limit" (*Yesh Gvul*), appeared to the left of Peace Now to promote conscientious objection to military service in Lebanon.[13] The Lebanon War, in short, spurred previously unseen levels of public denunciation of official security/peace policies.[14]

Popular music reflected this development. Shlomo Grunich, a musician highly regarded by music critics and "avant-garde" Israelis, protested the initial apathy of some of his compatriots and the commercial pressure to produce de-politicized lyrics in "Simple Songs" (*Shirim P'shutim*):

> They go out to dance
> They want to be happy
> Not think too much—to sing in harmony
> That the People of Israel is still alive ...
>
> Everyone wants to have a good time
> And clap their hands
> But the times are pretty bad
> See how I look.

I want to cry
I want to scream
But that's not something anyone will broadcast
It's to my advantage to be nice
For the People of Israel is still alive.

Even stronger lyrics were recorded by Shalom Chanoch, a leading popular musician whose past career risks had mainly involved experimenting in rock genres "harder" than those to which Israelis were accustomed. In "He Doesn't Stop at Red Lights" (*Lo Otzer b'Adom*), Chanoch took a pointed, personal swipe at Defence Minister Sharon and encouraged Israelis to oppose his actions in Lebanon:

Going quickly, he shortens the trip
Leaving behind an avalanche of destruction
For him, time is wasting and there's not enough space
Careful—he doesn't stop at red lights

Clear the way, here comes the murderer
A raging bull, he doesn't even bother to slow down
Watch out for your life
He doesn't stop at red lights

You shut up—he'll set the agenda
You sleep—he'll lead the flock
And if suddenly you wake up in an abyss
Too late—he doesn't stop at red lights

Tellingly, during this period, the military itself got back into the business of tacit protest, permitting an army production team to film a rather despondent, cynical movie on the Lebanon War called "Two Fingers from Sidon" (*Shtei Etzbaot m'Tzidon*). The film, which enjoyed an extended run in Israeli cinemas, had a title track which contained undeniable strains of dissatisfaction:

Two fingers from Sidon
I'm sitting here depressed
All day long, patrols, guard duty
Looking for someone to shoot at ...

It was just as telling—in some respects, more so—when the two-man duo, the Duda'im, slipped a line into their version of "By the Rivers of Babylon" that asked: "When will we get out of Lebanon?" What was interesting about this single line was less what was being said than who was saying it. The Duda'im were an archetypal group of the "early period" in Israeli popular music, specializing in upbeat songs about the Land of Israel and the Jewish People. For them to insert even a short note of open protest into a recording revealed how far the limits of legitimate protest had moved as a result of Israel's bloody entanglement North of its border.

INTIFADA

More than three years after the start of Sharon's war, Israel was breathing a sigh of relief as a joint Labour–Likud coalition pulled most military units out of Lebanon.

Predictably, this contributed to a lull in protest music. However, the interregnum was rather brief: in late 1987, the Intifada broke out in the Gaza Strip and West Bank. Soon, the evening news was showing pictures of soldiers firing on stone-throwing youngsters, and Israeli society began to slip into its most intense debate yet over security/peace policy. The breaking point for many on the left came when Defence Minister Yitzchak Rabin was reported to have told troops, in reference to Palestinian rioters, to "break their bones," and when clips of soldiers beating and burying Palestinians were broadcast. For the first time, Peace Now called unequivocally for talks with the Palestine Liberation Organization (PLO) and for the establishment of a Palestinian state alongside Israel. And the segment of the political spectrum to the left of Peace Now began to get crowded; in addition to "There's a Limit," there appeared militant groups such as "The 21st year" and "Women in Black."[15] The social convention that had long discouraged far-reaching critiques of the government's security/peace policies—a convention which had already been challenged during the Lebanon War—was placed under intense pressure. Israelis were at something of a loss, and were deeply divided. Confronted by a new form of civil combat, the government tried brute force, and a substantial proportion of the population unabashedly declared its disapproval.[16]

In the midst of the tumult, protest stopped being the exception to the rule in Israeli popular music. One after the other—with the women leading the way—many mainstream artists released strongly worded songs expressing pain over innocence lost, denouncing government policies in the West Bank and Gaza Strip, and calling for decent treatment of the Palestinian population. Si Heeman, daughter of Nahum Heiman (a quintessentially apolitical composer of the 1950s and 1960s), prompted reactions comparable to those provoked a decade-and-a-half earlier by "Song of Peace" (including calls for a broadcast and performing ban) when she sang these lyrics in "Shooting and Crying" (*Yorim u'Bochim*):

> Boys play with lead
> Girls with dolls made of iron
> Life looks different
> In the shadow of the filth.
> And I couldn't care less
> Who's going to win this time around
> The world I had is gone
> The great light has been turned off.
>
> Shooting and crying
> Burning and laughing
> When did we ever learn how to bury people alive ...
> When did we forget
> That once, our children were also killed ...
>
> On both sides, people just want to live
> In the midst of all this fear, it's becoming impossible to see
> People want some shelter from the whole conflict
> I really don't give a damn who—is strong.

Chava Alberstein, a hitherto apolitical songstress known for her melodic voice, pushed heresy a step further when she embedded powerful protest in the traditional

Passover song, "Chad Gadya." In Alberstein's version, the words adored by generations of Jewish children were followed by:

> What are you doing singing "Chad Gadya"?
> It isn't spring, Passover hasn't arrived
> What's changed for you? What's changed?
> I've changed this year
>
> Every night, every night
> I asked myself just four questions
> But tonight, I have one more question:
> How long will the cycle of terror continue?
> Those who attack, those who are attacked
> Those who beat, those who are beaten
> When will this insanity be over?
>
> What's changed for you? What's changed?
> I've changed this year
> Once, I was a sheep and a gentle goat
> Today I'm a leopard, an aggressive wolf
> I've already been a dove and a deer
> Today I have no idea who I am.

Yehudit Ravitz and Nurit Galron, who with Alberstein were probably the best-known female pop artists, also voiced blunt protest.[17] Speaking, as it were, to Palestinians (but of course, actually making an ethical statement to Israelis), Ravitz sang, "We're both children of [Noah's son] Shem/I breath, you breath …/Mother earth is tired, fed up with burning." And, with caustic sarcasm, Galron assailed the readiness of some Israelis to ignore the harsh effects of the country's policies in the occupied territories when she sang, "Don't tell me about a little girl who has lost her eye/It just makes me feel bad."

Even Shlomo Artzi, a musician sometimes criticized for supposedly writing lyrics thin on substance, released a protest song during this period. In "We Haven't Learned A Thing" (*Lo Lamadnu Klum*), Artzi lamented the blinkers that seemed to keep Israel from understanding the human dimension of the Palestinian experience and moving towards reconciliation:

> By the intersection there's a traffic jam from the heat waves and the humidity
> Abed on his donkey, we inside our car
> "Take two soft drinks, sunflower seeds, very cheap, man"
> Says Abed in Hebrew filled with gravel and rocks
>
> Grossman calls these bad times "The Yellow Wind"…
> There's no love here, just donkey shit …
> In Tel Aviv and Qalqilia, people are out of strength
> "It's all just politics"
> Says Abed as he rushes …
>
> It has to be said, to be sung with sadness
> We haven't learned a thing—so it turns out

780   SCOTT STREINER

"With time, you'll learn something about us yet—it's essential"
Says Abed as he rushes, exhausted, but without regrets
"How your sky is the same as our sky ...
And how I am of my field as fruit is of the tree"

With his donkey, he passes next to the well
A bullet or stone falls, hitting Abed as he rushes
It's all because of people, not Fate
We still haven't learned anything—so it turns out

AFTER OSLO

The Intifada ended with the surprise 1993 deal (the Oslo accords) between the Labour Party government led by Yitzchak Rabin and PLO Chairman Yasser Arafat. The abatement of the conflict in the West Bank and Gaza Strip meant that much of what the left had been protesting was history—with Oslo, the government had, in broad terms, adopted the left's policy prescriptions. As a result, Peace Now temporarily withdrew from the scene, giving the government quiet support as it pursued peace with the Palestinians. On the right, however, there was fury, which seemed to build from one angry demonstration to the next. Soon, support for Rabin's government began to soften, and with elections on the horizon, Peace Now decided it was time to organize a counter-rally. Government leaders agreed to attend and, on the evening of 4 November 1995, Rabin joined some 100,000 demonstrators in singing "Song of Peace" (a remarkable rehabilitation for a work once viewed as bordering on the blasphemous). Moments later, he was assassinated by a radical right-wing university student—the first Israeli government leader ever to be murdered for political reasons.[18] Within less than a year, the right had regained power, as Benjamin Netanyahu won a razor-thin victory in the race for the Premiership against Shimon Peres, Rabin's Labour Party successor. After three years of dithering and dodging, Netanyahu lost power to Labour's Eud Barak who, in turn, was unseated by Ariel Sharon after his dramatic bid for a peace deal collapsed and a new, more violent Intifada erupted.

The post-Oslo reality led to a interesting development in popular music. On the one hand, a degree of leftist political expression continued among more respected artists—especially after Rabin's assassination—but was characterized by a tone less directly critical of the government than that which had been typical during the first Palestinian uprising. On the other hand, varieties of protest that had been unheard of not long before made their appearance—and yet, did not seem to be taken particularly seriously. It was as if protest had been normalized to the point where it could be seen as a fad in popular music and consequently, its sincerity could be viewed with some scepticism. Most notable in this "radical but dubious" protest category was Aviv Geffen, son of a well-known Israeli poet and something of a Michael Jackson wanna-be. Geffen was widely (though incorrectly) thought to have dodged the draft—a rumour that once would have been a quick ticket to social ostracization—and got away with recording songs that mocked key social values, particularly around military service. However, perhaps because he was perceived to be a bit of a youthful charlatan, Geffen's lyrics never seemed to have quite the shock value to which he aspired. Indeed, Geffen was even invited to sing at Peace Now's November 1995 demonstration—and was standing on the stage near Rabin singing "Song of Peace" just moments before the Prime Minister was gunned down.

One example of the slightly muted protest that has continued to appear in some songs is "Winter '73" (*Choref '73*), a bittersweet composition released by the IDF's Educational Corps Choir (which may have been seeking to repeat the success of "Song of Peace" and in so doing, revive the flagging fortunes of the military's musical units). In the song, soldiers born in the wake of the 1973 war suggest that their parents might have done more to make the dream of peace a reality:

When we were born, the country was wounded and desolate
You looked upon us, embraced us, tried to find some consolation
When we were born the old folks blessed us with tears in their eyes
Saying—God willing, these children won't have to go off to the army
And your faces in faded photos show that you meant what you said
When you promised to do everything for us—to turn enemy into friend.

You promised a dove
An olive branch
You promised peace in our home
You promised spring
And blossoms
You promised to keep promises
You promised a dove

We're the children of winter '73
We've grown up and now we're in the army with weapons and with helmets on our
heads ...
We won't pressure you, make demands, or threaten
When we were little you said promises should be kept
We just wanted to whisper—we're the children of that winter
The year 1973.

Another example of post-Oslo protest was David Broza's "Howling Dove" (*Homa
Yona*), released shortly after the singer's return to Israel, which contained these lyrics:

Little children
Learn to pick out the enemy
To be suspicious of the whisper of grass in an open field ...

Above the canyon the moon is climbing
Beneath the window a dove howls
And I think of you
And listen to her
Sing an ancient song about beaches and dangers

About the roots of the olive tree
About watersheds
About an eye for an eye
About those who rely upon their swords
How Cain still weeps
Among the gravestones.

A third manifestation of the persistence of quiet discontent was a song on the
Rabin assassination entitled "Goodbye Friend" (*Shalom Chaver*)[19] by Arik Einstein, the
much-loved granddaddy of Israeli popular music, who is better known for his interest
in sports than politics. Recalling the night Rabin was killed, Einstein sang:

Even as you were immersed in joy
Bursting with a song of peace
Out there in the dark, the murderer
Was waiting for the right moment

782   Scott Streiner

The square was packed and ...
Hearts opened to one another like flowers
His pistol was loaded for death
His eyes, cold as ice.

All three of these songs were characterized by melancholy as much as anger. At the
other end of the spectrum, the rebellious Aviv Geffen, in "Now It's Cloudy Out"
(*Achshav Me'unan*), opined: "We're a generation that's been fucked/Now it's cloudy
out/We want to leave this place." And in "97 Profile" (*Profil 97*), a reference to the
highest fitness rating that a new draftee in the IDF can receive, he sang:

Now the blossom's blossoming, and screaming
Kids wilt there, in the territories
A plant has grown now, and he's parachuting
Kids, mostly, become vegetables

A 97 Profile—but much less inside
The commander says, "shoot"
In uniform, he salutes, fighting for his sanity
The Death Defence Forces.

Geffen, like Broza and Einstein, has sold hundreds of thousands of records. Clearly,
whatever its sources, protest against official security/peace policies has ceased to be
taboo in Israeli popular music. Twenty-five years ago, most popular artists celebrated
Israel's valleys and victories; today, some sing of the stupidity of military service and of
abandoning the country. Reasons for this transition will be explored in the section that
follows.

Case-specific Explanatory Factors

The history discussed above may be broadly mapped as follows: from 1948 to the
early 1970s, there was no leftist protest on peace/security issues in Israeli popular music;
from the early 1970s to the early 1980s, limited protest surfaced on a few rare occasions;
during the Lebanon War, a greater degree of open protest appeared; with the outbreak
of the Intifada, blunt protest went from being exceptional to being quasi-normal; and
since the Oslo agreements protest has been present in both muted and extreme forms.

This is a history marked by sharp twists and turns, which suggests that we are
speaking less of a gradual, endogenous process of evolution than of a phenomenon
profoundly shaped by powerful events and trends in the political, social, and cultural
environment. Proceeding from this premise, I would argue that there are five key,
interrelated explanatory factors relevant to this case: (1) the sense that there were
realistic alternatives to government policy; (2) exposure, through media coverage, to the
dehumanizing effects of existing policy; (3) the erosion of social solidarity; (4) the
legitimization of protest; and (5) the impact of globalization. I will now examine each
in turn.

BELIEF IN REALISTIC ALTERNATIVES

Until the election of the first Begin government, the majority of Israelis believed that their leaders were deeply and genuinely committed to peace with the Arabs, and that the only real barrier to peace was the hostile refusal of the Arab world to accept the reality of the state of Israel and to allow the Jewish people to live with security. To the extent that there was any doubt on this front, it attached mainly to the sudden shift to the role of conqueror in 1967, and to the policies of Golda Meir's government in the early 1970s, which had a reputation for arrogance. For the most part, however, the foci of protest during the Meir era were social issues, the Prime Minister's seeming callousness, and the government's failure to anticipate the Arab attack on Yom Kippur, 1973. Examples of such protest included the civil disobedience of the Israeli Black Panthers, a movement of militant Mizrachi Jews, and the stage play, "Queen of the Bath" (*Malkat ha'Ambatia*). It is not particularly surprising, then, that the early 1970s saw one, but only one, significant protest song ("Song of Peace").[20]

In contrast to his predecessors, Begin was not seen by many Israelis as a supporter of reconciliation with the Arab world. Known for his hawkish attitudes and belief in the Jews' God-given right to the entire "Land of Israel"—and having won power because of an unexpected alliance with a new centrist bloc backed mainly by elite sectors that would never have supported a Likud government—Begin was expected by many to be a strident foe of compromise. Hence, the appearance of "Things Will be OK" shortly after his ascension to the Prime Minister's Office. The surprise timing of Sadat's peace initiative, however, and Begin's unanticipated willingness to give up the whole of the Sinai, temporarily won the Prime Minister the grudging tolerance (if not exactly the sympathy) of Israelis who might otherwise have been quick to protest his government's security and peace policies. But that tolerance—which reflected the possibility that Begin would actually go the distance to avoid violent confrontation with the Arabs—crumbled when it became clear that the Lebanon War was going to be a major and prolonged conflict. In this connection, it is important to remember that even the 1973 war was viewed by Israeli public opinion as a disaster not because (as Sadat later argued) the Meir government's rather hard-nosed policies had contributed to its outbreak, but because the government had been lulled into thinking that there was little serious danger of war.[21] The Lebanon War was generally viewed as the first time an Israeli government had departed from the principle of fighting only "no-choice wars" (*milchemot ain breira*). As such, it was a natural spark for unprecedented protest.

The feeling that government policies were significantly more aggressive and obdurate than necessary emerged with even greater force during the Intifada. Here, again, the sense among many Israelis on the left was that other options existed but were not being considered by a regime incapable of insight and vision.[22] This feeling was especially pronounced because of the lopsided nature of fighting during the Intifada— for the first time, Israeli soldiers were battling not enemy troops with guns and tanks, but young civilians with crude, homemade projectiles. And no matter how many times government leaders insisted that slingshots, stones, and Molotov cocktails were danger- ous weapons requiring a firm military response, a substantial portion of the Israeli populace was not convinced. Moreover, many Israelis could not help but feel a certain respect and sympathy for the struggle of a people seeking self-determination—a people whose past passivity had sometimes been treated with disdain. Even Defence Minister Rabin was eventually reported to have seen some of his youthful self—when he was a member of the Yishuv's Haganah fighting British rule—in the crowds of rock-wielding Palestinians. It follows, then, that a large number of Israelis would be uncomfortable with the government's iron-fisted response. With their ingrained sense of vulnerability, Israelis have always been ready to countenance virtually any action required for the sake of survival, but many were not prepared to acquiesce to brutality aimed at suppressing a popular and relatively unthreatening uprising in occupied lands. Instead, they loudly insisted that sound alternatives were available.

Once government policy had embraced those alternatives, with Oslo, most of the left returned to the view that the Israeli government was, generally speaking, doing all that it reasonably could to advance peace. This helps explain the relatively restrained tone among many artists in the post-Oslo period particularly since the breakdown of the peace process in autumn 2000, which is generally attributed by Israelis, rightly or wrongly, to the intransigence of the Palestinian leadership.

MEDIA COVERAGE

Media censorship for security reasons has always existed in Israel. Since the early 1980s, however, such censorship has been increasingly difficult to enforce—and thus, has been in steady decline. A central cause of this trend is the availability of news from abroad. If Israelis watching the BBC or reading *Time* can learn of the massacre at Sabra and Shatilla or the burying of Palestinian protesters (in both cases, the government initially tried to suppress press coverage), then it becomes hard to justify the prohibition of Hebrew-language reports by the domestic media.

In part, the nature of events themselves conspired to rob the censor of much of his work. The wars before Lebanon had been fierce and relatively brief, leaving reporters little opportunity to get to the field, dig for stories, and sharpen critical perspectives. The Lebanon War, however, dragged on. Moreover, foreign reporters were often headquartered outside Israeli zones of control—and thus, free to tell the world of things that the Begin government would have preferred to leave unreported. The Intifada, too, was an extended conflict, and one that journalists from abroad were determined to cover in-depth—leading to repeated quarrels with Israeli authorities seeking to restrict access to the occupied territories and to vet dispatches. While the Israeli media initially followed rather than led the foreign press corps—reflecting the continued social legitimacy of restrictions related to security/peace issues—follow they did, and with growing assertiveness. As the universe of matters deemed "beyond the pale" of media coverage shrank, the exposure of the Israeli public to the effects of official policy ballooned.

This development was not unlike that which occurred in the United States during the Vietnam War. Then, too, assertive journalists gained access to the field of a drawn-out conflict and relayed home images of the destruction wrought by government-ordered actions. And then, too, the result was a hitherto unthinkable wave of public dissent (Washington's cognizance of this dynamic was plainly evident in its tight control of the media during the Gulf War).

Exposure to the violence of the Lebanon War (particularly Sabra and Shatilla) and the Intifada had a significant effect on the willingness of many Israelis to accede to government calls for an unquestioning consensus around issues of security and peace. In the past, it had been possible to minimize or deny unsettling rumours—since little concrete evidence was accessible to the Israeli public—and thus, easier to maintain comparatively strict, narrow limits on protest against official security and peace policies. Overall, Israelis were persuaded (not always incorrectly, it should be emphasized) that their military was relatively restrained and that the much-trumpeted notion of the "purity of arms" (*tohar ha'neshek*)—which was supposed to ensure that the Israeli soldier never used more violent force than necessary—was uniformly respected. This helps to explain why events such as the sometimes ruthless expulsion of Palestinians during the 1948 war did not "take hold" in Israelis' historical consciousness. However, once proof of outrages started to appear in the daily papers and on the evening news, Israelis inclined towards humanitarian attitudes and compromise with the Arabs could no longer be convinced to swallow their doubts or muffle their dissent. The images and information conveyed though media coverage of the war in Lebanon and the uprising in the West Bank and Gaza Strip prompted those already inclined to question government policy to push the boundaries of legitimate protest, while reducing the likelihood that the broader public would repudiate this protest as utterly illegitimate.

EROSION OF SOLIDARITY

Israeli society was, for many years, characterized by a much greater degree of collective solidarity than is typical in liberal democracies. This solidarity did not express itself in docile obsequiousness towards authority, but rather in an atmosphere of familiarity that made chance encounters between strangers seem like meetings between long-lost companions and that ensured a degree of unity, after all the internal debating was done, in the face of a sometimes unfriendly world.

The sources of this solidarity were complex. Chief among them was the archetypal Jewish experience of being an imperiled minority—a Diaspora experience that reached its terrifying climax in the Holocaust and that was "imported" into Israel not only through the demographics of immigration, but also through the geopolitical reality of being a small country surrounded by seemingly implacable adversaries. In addition, the collectivist ideology of many of Israel's founders—who emerged from Eastern European Marxist–Zionist movements and saw the communitarian kibbutz as the embodiment of a just society for a revitalized nation—meant that a greater premium was placed on the collective's needs than the individual's desires. Finally, the deliberate efforts of David Ben-Gurion and his Labour Party to foster a culture of "statehood-ness" (*mamlachtiut*) as an antidote to fractious political divisions had a solidarity-inducing effect on the behaviour of opinion-shapers, the nature of public debates, and the content of educational curricula.

Over the past two decades, however, Israel has seen a substantial decline in internal solidarity, though it remains a more "family-like" society than, say, Britain or Canada.[23] This decline has had much to do with the developments discussed above (for example, the increasing sense that government policy is unnecessarily rigid) but, arguably, it has also been a function of sheer exhaustion with the demands of the group. Like the once-committed members of African communes or the long-suffering fans of mediocre sports teams, Israelis simply got tired of the various individual hardships that went with support for the collective. The perpetual tension, the annual stint of reserve duty in the military, the inability to visit many parts of the world with an Israeli passport, the need to accept lower standards of living than appeared to be typical in Europe and America—these sorts of deprivations could be embraced for a decade or two, and accepted even longer, but at some point, they began to eat into the collectivist solidarity of many Israelis, particularly those members of the elite most influenced by individualist philosophy and most exposed to morés in the West.[24]

The drop in solidarity has found expression in growing interpersonal competitiveness, reflected in the ubiquitousness of phrases such as "I deserve it" (*magia li*) and "I'm nobody's fool" (*ani lo friar shel af echad*), which are used to justify requests for preferable treatment or attempts to circumvent rules of fair play. Increased individualism has been manifested in, and stimulated by, a boom of materialism and consumerism—a boom initially sparked, somewhat ironically, by the Begin government's policy of "treating the people well" (*l'hativ im ha'am*) through consumption-promoting measures that eventually produced hyper-inflation. Reduced identification with the nation has been evident in declining enthusiasm for Independence Day—once a focus of intense collective celebration. And growing fragmentation has been reflected in the demands of socially disadvantaged groups for attention to past wrongs; for example, the insistence of Yemenite Jews that there be a full investigation into the possible abduction of Yemenite babies in the early 1950s, an outrage long the subject of rumours that (because of the imperatives of social cohesion) few dared to mention out-loud.

While it is true that Israel still retains an unusual degree of collective spirit—spirit which may often be latent, but which quickly emerges during crises such as the Gulf War scud missile barrages—since the early 1980s, it has clearly gone through a process of escalating dis-integration and individualization. And as social solidarity has declined, the constraints on self-expression dictated by the "greater good" have loosened, producing an environment in which artists are far more likely to ponder strong expressions of protest against official policies in areas once deemed sacrosanct.

LEGITIMIZATION OF PROTEST

Whatever the urge to oppose, mainstream singers concerned about popularity and sales are unlikely to risk protest if they expect that it will be seen by the overwhelming majority of the public as illegitimate. One need only recall the rapidity with which John Lennon retracted his "Beatles are bigger than Jesus" comment in the face of wide condemnation to realize how large public opinion looms in the minds of popular musicians and the companies that underwrite them.

For this reason, artists interested in voicing disapproval of government policy can be expected to consider, consciously or otherwise, how close their lyrics are to the boundaries of legitimacy before stepping into the recording studio. In the Israeli case, the fact that the social trends noted above expanded those boundaries from *circa* 1980 onwards was, therefore, critical. Equally important was the fact that protest was initially undertaken by those with particularly high credibility; in other words, the first to test and stretch the limits of legitimate dissent were those who could most afford the gamble. Within popular music, the premier example of this phenomenon was IDF-sponsored compositions—first, "Song of Peace" (a composition so controversial for its time that, arguably, it could only have been released by a military musical group) and later, "Two Fingers from Sidon." Once the armed forces had appeared to sanction certain types of dissent, it became much more difficult to sustain social norms that excluded those types. It is also significant that many of the musicians involved in protest were themselves products of the IDF musical groups or, in the cases of Si Heeman and Aviv Geffen, the offspring of well-known composers/poets (with all the attendant status and protection).

Outside of popular music, it is notable that the pathbreakers were the soldiers who organized Peace Now and respected authors such as Amos Oz, A.B. Yehoshua, and David Grossman.[25] Both soldiers and authors arguably enjoyed a more "assured" status within Israeli society than the creators of popular music—and thus, could go further in testing the boundaries of what that society would tolerate in terms of protest. Finally, it is worth recalling that protest erupted in popular music after the rise of the Likud to power, a political watershed known by a word for "transformation" (*ma'hapach*) that is grammatically rooted in and reminiscent of the word for "revolution." After three decades of interrupted Labour Party rule, the elites connected to Labour—elites who tended to be better-educated, more Westernized, and wealthier than most of the population—found the new political reality hard to digest. And because this is the section of society that tends to arbitrate with respect to what constitutes "quality" art, it makes sense that its loss of power would be accompanied by a corresponding rise in tolerance for criticism of official policies.

This combination of factors lent enhanced legitimacy to forms of dissent previously inhibited by social norms—sufficiently so that popular musicians could engage in protest of their own without imperilling their careers. This does not negate the genuine courage shown by the artists in question, but it does suggest that those artists' decision to protest was more a considered step than a reckless leap; as "mainstream" creators, they expressed their views in a way that did not risk moving them too far beyond boundaries others had already probed.

GLOBALIZATION

That globalization has become one of the dominant forces of our age is less and less a matter of debate, and more and more a truism.[26] Certainly, in the Israeli context, one can easily identify the penetration of global (read: Western) cultural influences. These influences arrive *via* European and American television stations such as CNN and MTV, movies, increased travel, and, of course, popular music. They include individualism, materialism, increased cultural and intellectual relativism, suspicion of explicit political ideologies, and decreased commitment to particularistic visions.[27] Needless to say, such influences are not evenly felt across the population: while the effects of the first two are widespread, the impact of the last three is concentrated among the more highly educated sectors and among youth. Indeed, an opposite reaction—one of closure, heightened nationalism, and antipathy to democratic notions—is materializing among groups resistant to the dilution of culture and unlikely to benefit from an opening to the world.

Popular musicians, however, are situated squarely within the circles whose response to globalization is enthused rather than antagonistic, and sell most of their albums to those circles. Thus, as globalization has accelerated, the likelihood of popular artists feeling motivated to protest and feeling safe in doing so has increased. Furthermore, the fact that protest is a well-ingrained tradition in Western popular music provides an extra "incentive" for protest by popular artists in any region heavily affected by globalization. In effect, protest can become a badge of honour, giving musicians a stronger sense of personal legitimacy when they reflect on their actions in a global perspective, even as they take some risks with their domestic reputations. If "the world" (meaning, essentially, Western mores) becomes a psychological point of reference for defining valid self-expression, then the power of local taboos to curb that expression will inevitably decline. In light of this, it is not altogether surprising that Israeli musicians who have engaged in protest from the left have also attempted English-language musical careers (David Broza, Shalom Chanoch), made deliberate efforts to import Western music styles (Shlomo Grunich), or sung the praises of life abroad (Chava Alberstein).

CONCLUSION: SOME THEORETICAL REFLECTIONS

Despite the risks inherent in any attempt to generalize from specific instances, this article will conclude with some brief speculation on what the case discussed above can teach us about processes which contribute to the emergence of authentic political protest in art.[28]

Let us begin by asking why, in so many instances, art is bereft of real protest. In light of the Israeli case, I would propose that where protest is absent, it is because *artists do not feel that there is any policy that can and should be protested within the boundaries of "safety."* This may be the case because: (i) the artist is basically satisfied with things as they are; or (ii) although dissatisfied, the artist would have to step past the boundaries of safety in order to voice what is on his or her mind. Where boundaries are at issue, their precise breadth and (in)flexibility will depend on case-contingent conditions, and the definition of safety will depend not only on prevailing social norms, but also on the artist's aspirations and tolerance for risk. Among mainstream artists, the general pattern is likely to be one of caution, since there is a concern not only with opprobrium or arrest, but also with sales; yet, ironically perhaps, mainstream artists actually have more of the credibility required to successfully protest and thereby expand the limits for everyone.

When protest does appear, it is presumably because the artist is motivated to denounce something, and can do so within the boundaries of safety. It follows that where a change in the level of protest has occurred, it is either because there is a new reason to oppose (or to stop opposing), or because the boundaries permitting opposition have shifted. Either of these changes could be linked to the personal development of the artist; for example, someone may have direct experience with a social problem that inspires indignation, or enter a relationship with a partner who encourages greater outspokenness, or return from a life-threatening experience determined to speak his or her mind. However, in cases where protest erupts as a broad phenomenon rather than an isolated incident, the likely cause is changes in the socio-cultural–political milieu— changes that involve shifts in official policy, movement in the limits of permissible expression, or, as in the Israeli case, both.

The factors that produce a rise in protest, then, are *increased frustration with the status quo* and/or *increased safety in dissent*, and the factors that prompt a reduction in protest are *increased satisfaction with the status quo* and/or *increased risk in dissent*. The development of these factors is a complex process involving the ongoing shaping of the individual by society, and of society by the individual. And the specific conditions that ignite and fuel such changes will vary from instance to instance though, extrapolating again from the Israeli case, we could surmise that they might involve the adoption of new policies by the authorities, increased information on the effects of these policies, a decline in the influence of the powers-that-be over social norms, legitimization of protest by highly credible individuals or groups, and a growth in external influences.

Embedded in society and anxious to cultivate rather than squander influence, yet accustomed to the cathartic gratifications of self-expression and possibly burdened by a sense of social responsibility, the artist has a great many questions to ponder before any foray into the precarious territory of politics. We cannot predict with any certainty when the mantle of protest will be taken up (by and large, social theory is belatedly distancing itself from such insipid pretensions to precision), but we can engage in informed conjecture on the conditions under which political protest by artists is more probable. I hope that this article, with its in-depth account of a particular case and its preliminary theoretical reflections, makes a small contribution towards that discussion.

NOTES

1. The author is a senior manager in the Canadian Public Service and a Doctoral Candidate in Political Science at Carleton University, Ottawa, Canada. The views expressed in this article are solely those of the author. The author wishes to acknowledge helpful insights provided during preparation of this article by Noam Kochavi, Eli Achdut, Dana Arieli-Horowitz, and Zohar BenDavid-Streiner.
2. For an article which highlights the timidity of seemingly politicized popular music and the manner in which it is manipulated and regulated by political parties and the state, see Martin Cloonan and John Street, "Politics and Popular Music: From Policing to Packaging," *Parliamentary Affairs* 50 (April 1997): 223–34.
3. Numerous studies have been conducted on how music can be used not to challenge the existing order, but to reinforce it. For two very different examples, see Stephen H. Lewiston Barnes, *Muzak: The Hidden Messages in Music* (NY: Mellen, 1988), and Felicia Hughes-Freeland, "Art and Politics: from Javanese Court Dance to Indonesian Art," *Journal of the Royal Anthropological Institute* 3 (September 1997): 473–95.
4. The conception of interrelated, mutually constructive structure and agency implicit in this paragraph draws upon Anthony Giddens' notion of structuration, and informs my analysis throughout the article. For one of Giddens' more parsimonious accounts of structuration, see Anthony Giddens, *The Nation-State and Violence* (Oxford: Polity Press, 1985). For a discussion of the theoretical underpinnings of emerging Canadian International Relations scholarship—including an increasing tendency to probe the links between geopolitics and domestic developments—see Teresa Healy and Mark Neufeld, "Critical Reflections on a

790   SCOTT STREINER

Discipline: A Canadian Perspective," in *AntePodium*, an electronic journal published by the Victoria University of Wellington, 1997 (http://www.vuw.ac.nz/atp/).

5. Those interested in analyses of this phenomenon might wish to consult David Hall-Cathala, *The Peace Movement in Israel, 1967–87* (London: MacMillan, 1990); Oren Yiftachel, "Israeli Society and Jewish–Palestinian Reconciliation: 'Ethnocracy' and its Territorial Contradictions," *The Middle East Journal* 51 (Autumn 1997): 505–19; and Yael Yishai, "Hawkish Proletariat: The Case of Israel," *Journal of Political and Military Sociology* 12 (1985): 53–73.

6. A major source on the history of Israeli popular music (it does not deal with protest *per se*) is the excellent doctoral dissertation of Mordechai Regev, which includes an English-language abstract: *Bo'o Shel ha'Rock (The Coming of Rock)*, an unpublished Ph.D. thesis, Tel Aviv University, 1990.

7. On the atmosphere in the country in the late 1940s—and the tendency to dampen criticism in order to bolster the fledgling state's ability to confront multiple crises—see Tom Segev, (Arlen Neal Weinstein, English language ed.), *1949: The First Israelis* (New York: The Free Press, 1986).

8. On the complex interrelationships between ideology, culture, and politics during Israel's history, see the cogent analysis in Yaron Ezrachi, "Democratic Politics and Culture in Modern Israel: Recent Trends," in *Israeli Democracy Under Stress*, ed. Ehud Sprinzak and Larry Diamond (Bolder and London: Lynne Rienner Publishers, 1993), 255–71.

9. For a collection of Buber's remarkably farsighted writings on the subject, see Martin Buber (Paul R. Mendes-Flor, ed.), *A Land of Two Peoples: Martin Buber on Jews and Arabs* (NY: Oxford University Press, 1983).

10. All translations in this article are my own. Where lyrics are quoted, they are sometimes relevant extracts rather than entire songs. And where a link is made between a song and an artist, the artist is the musician who recorded and became associated with the song, even if the words were actually written by someone else.

11. To get a sense of the dramatic political and psychological transformations that took place in Israel from 1967 onwards, one of the best sources is Amos Elon, *A Blood-Dimmed Tide: Dispatches from the Middle East* (NY: Columbia University Press, 1997).

12. For an excellent insider's account of the growth of Peace Now and the Israeli peace movement more generally, see Mordechai Bar-On, *In Pursuit of Peace: a History of the Israeli Peace Movement* (Washington, DC: United States Institute of Peace Press, 1996).

13. The key Hebrew-language text summarizing the arguments for conscientious objection—and a premier expression of leftist distress and protest during the Lebanon War—is Yesh Gvul's text *Gvul ha'Tziut (the Limits of Obedience)* (Tel Aviv: Siman Kri'a Books, 1985).

14. For an exploration of some of the reasons why the Lebanon War sparked unprecedented protest, see Lilly Weissbrod, "Protest and Dissidence in Israel," in *Cross-Currents in Israeli Culture and Politics*, ed. Myron Joel Aronoff (New Brunswick, NJ: Transaction Books, 1984), 51–68.

15. An account of the methods and achievements of the last group may be found in Sara Helman and Tamar Rapoport, "Women in Black: Challenging Israel's Gender and Socio-Political Orders," *The British Journal of Sociology* 48 (December 1998): 681–700.

16. Meron Benvenisti provides a characteristically insightful analysis of the psychology of Israeli attitudes towards Palestinians and the impact of the Intifada in *Intimate Enemies: Jews and Arabs in a Shared Land* (Berkeley: University of California Press, 1995).

17. At first glance, the central role played by female artists during this period seems striking, and it is tempting to infer that Israeli women have generally been more dovish than Israeli men. However, even an Israeli academic and activist who has striven specifically to engage women in the peace movement has had to acknowledge that in the aggregate, the female half of Israel's population is no more supportive of peace policies than the male half. See Galia Golan, "Militarization and Gender: the Israeli Experience," *Women's Studies International Forum* 20 (September/December 1997): 581–86.

18. This being said, political assassinations more generally have not been altogether unknown

in Jewish history. See Nachman Ben-Yehuda, *Political Assassinations by Jews: a Rhetorical Device for Justice* (Albany, NY: SUNY Press, 1993).

19. It is interesting and a little strange that this phrase, used by President Bill Clinton on the night of the assassination, came to symbolize Israelis' emotions around the traumatic event. One can only speculate on the reasons why the words of the US President, rather than an Israeli leader, attained such cachet.

20. A description of some of the marginal but fascinating (and in some instances, prescient) voices of dissent in the 1970s can be found in David J. Schnall, *Radical Dissent in Contemporary Israeli Politics* (NY: Praeger, 1979).

21. It has been argued that Sadat's overtures had a profound effect on the thinking of those who were in their formative years at the time of his visit to Jerusalem, as they demonstrated that peace was a concrete option—and that the longer-term impact of this realization was seen in the growth of the Israeli peace movement in the mid-1980s. See Miriam Spielmann, "If Peace Comes ... Future Expectations of Israeli Children and Youth," *Journal of Peace Research* 23 (1986): 51–67.

22. Two well-documented overviews of protest in Israeli politics argue that increasing political protest in Israel can be directly linked to the frustration of Israelis (who have a very high rate of political awareness) with situations where their ability to influence policy is minimal. See Sam Lehman-Wilzig, *Stiff-Necked People, Bottle-Necked System: The Evolution and Roots of Israeli Public Protest, 1949–1986* (Bloomington: Indiana University Press, 1990); and Gadi Wolfsfeld, *The Politics of Provocation: Participation and Protest in Israel* (Albany, NY: SUNY Press, 1988).

23. As early as the mid-1970s, scholars began to identify symptoms of an erosion of social solidarity in Israel: see Eva Etzioi-Halevy, *Political Culture in Israel* (NY: Praeger, 1977).

24. Researchers now confidently speak of a incremental but continuous "winding-down" of the Arab–Israeli conflict, and of a gradually decreasing tendency in Israeli school texts to emphasize unquestioning patriotism and ethnocentrism: see Hemda Ben-Yehuda and Shmuel Sandler, "Crisis Magnitude and Interstate Conflict: Changes in the Arab–Israeli Dispute," *Journal of Peace Research* 35 (January 1998): 83–109; and Daniel Bar-Tal, "The Rocky Road Toward Peace: Beliefs on Conflict in Israeli Textbooks," *Journal of Peace Research* 35 (November 1998), 723–42.

25. *The Yellow Wind* (NY: Farrar, 1988), Grossman's seminal account of the bitter reality of daily life for Palestinians in the occupied territories, is actually cited in the second verse of "We Haven't Leaned a Thing," Shlomo Artzi's Intifada-era protest song, quoted above.

26. A cogent (if sometime overstated) examination of the multiple cultural axes of globalization can be found in Roland Robertson, *Globalization: Social Theory and Global Culture* (London: Sage, 1992). Some scholars, particularly neo-Marxists, have contended that globalization is more an ideology used to perpetuate exploitation than a novel or inexorable trend: see, for example, Samir Amin, "The Challenge of Globalization," *Review of International Political Economy* 3 (Summer 1996): 216–59; and Philip McMichael, "Globalization: Myths and Realities," *Rural Sociology* 61 (1996): 25–55. However, globalization arguably remains "real" as a socio-political phenomenon regardless of whether it is constructed ideology, an inevitable metamorphosis, or a little of both.

27. Hall-Cathala, *The Peace Movement in Israel, 1967–87*, contends that the rise of Israeli peace activism has had much to do with a desire to counter increasingly assertive particularism (manifested, for instance, in the West Bank settlers' movement) with universalistic values.

28. I should note here that much excellent work has been done on the relationship between art, including popular music, and leftist/protest politics in a wide range of historical contexts. See, for example, Sanjib Baruah, " 'Ethnic' Conflict as State–Society Struggle: The Poetics and Politics of Assamese Micro-Nationalism," *Modern Asian Studies* 28 (July 1994): 649–71; Ron Eyerman and Andrew Jamison, "Social Movements and Cultural Transform-ation: Popular Music in the 1960s," *Media, Culture, and Society* 17 (July 1995): 449–68; Chang-tai Hung, "The Politics of Songs: Myths and Symbols in the Chinese Communist War Music," *Modern Asian Studies* 30 (October 1996): 901–29; Kimani Gecau, "Popular

792   Scott Streiner

Song and Social Change in Kenya," *Media, Culture, and Society* 17 (October 1995): 557–75; Stephen King and Richard J. Jensen, "Bob Marley's 'Redemption Song': The Rhetoric of Reggae and Rastafari," *Journal of Popular Culture* 29 (Winter 1995): 17–36; Robbie Lieberman, *"My Song is My Weapon": People's Songs, American Communism, and the Politics of Culture, 1930–1950* (Urbana, IL: University of Illinois Press, 1989); Eliana Moya-Raggio, "Arpilleras: Chilean Culture of Resistance," *Feminist Studies* 10 (Summer 1984): 277–90; and Siew-Chye Phua and Lily Kong, "Ideology, Social Commentary, and Resistance in Popular Music: A Case Study of Singapore," *Journal of Popular Culture* 30 (Summer 1996): 215–31.

[11]

MOVING IN DECENCY: THE MUSIC AND RADICAL POLITICS OF CORNELIUS CARDEW

By Timothy D. Taylor

ONE OF THE most memorable graffiti I have seen was a rubber-stamp message on a wall in the Music Library at Yale University:

> NOT ART

Judgements about what is and what is not art are not easily made, of course, and they are seldom as clear-cut as this rubber stamp suggests. But the claim is made seriously from time to time that political art—art that overtly promotes a political message—is not art, or that it negates art.[1] Cornelius Cardew (1936–81) was a maker of radical political art, and the ways he negotiated the often obscure terrain of aesthetics and society are worth examining.[2]

Cardew wasn't always a composer on the Left. Born in Gloucestershire in 1936, he attended the Royal Academy of Music, where he studied composition with Howard Ferguson. He gravitated to Stockhausen and Cologne, and his study there eventually led to his realization of the score to Stockhausen's *Carré* (1959–60). 'Realization' is indeed the right word: as Stockhausen himself said, 'I left the independent working-out of composition plans to [Cardew]'.[3] Cardew eventually became the central figure of the musical avant-garde in England, a position recognized by other members of it.

In time, Cardew reacted against serialism, the most prestigious European method of composition in the 1950s and '60s. In a lecture delivered in 1967, he said:

> Since the war Folk music has become dissipated and internationalized (at least in Europe and America) to the point that one can hardly call it folk music. The fate can be compared to the heroic pseudo-scientific universalism of serial music in the early 50s; at that time you were quite likely to hear serial compositions by a Bulgarian, a Japanese, or a South African on the same programme and be virtually unable to tell the difference between them. At that time serial music was not available on disc, so we may attribute the effect to the pervasiveness

Many friends and colleagues have helped with this article. I would like to thank, first and most important, Sherry B. Ortner for support and encouragement of all kinds; Judith Becker, John Canaday, Richard Crawford, Jonathan Freedman and Glenn Watkins also contributed insights and useful comments. Finally, Matthew Greenall, the director of the British Music Information Centre, was extremely hospitable during my visit there in 1992, providing access to many recordings and materials unavailable in the USA. That visit was funded by a Rackham Dissertation grant from the University of Michigan.

[1] See, for example, Bernard Holland, 'Music and Virtue: Is Making Art Good Making Good Art?', *The New York Times*, 20 July 1993, B2.

[2] Like most contemporary composers, Cardew has received scant scholarly attention. The two major sources on his music are Richard Barrett, 'Cornelius Cardew', *New Music '87*, Oxford, 1987; and John Tilbury's extensive liner notes to *Cornelius Cardew Memorial Concert* (London: Impetus IMP 28204, 1985), a recording difficult to obtain. Cardew is also a significant presence in Michael Nyman's excellent *Experimental Music: Cage and Beyond*, London, 1974. See also Paul Griffiths, *Modern Music and After: Directions since 1945*, Oxford, 1995.

[3] Quoted in Karl H. Wörner, *Stockhausen: Life and Work*, ed. & trans. Bill Hopkins, London, 1973, p. 43.

of the idea. However, death in a vacuum is not a happy thought and around 1960 many of the reputable composers were beating a hasty retreat, taking with them just as much of the original idea as they were able to carry. Nono went into political music. Stockhausen into the grand operatic tradition. Boulez into impressionism and a glorious career as a conductor.[4]

On 12 September 1967 Cardew wrote in his diary:

From America Columbus brought us back syphillis [*sic*], or Death through sex; there is no reason why the compliment should not be returned with myself as the humble vehicle, in the form of total serialism—or Death through music. In the case of serialism the damage has already been done; Schoenberg is the bearer of that intolerable guilt.[5]

Retreating from serialism, Cardew pursued an interest in improvisation, which resulted, as it had for his former mentor Stockhausen, in the composition of prose pieces. A typical work is *Sextet—The Tiger's Mind* (1967),[6] which is as much a Confucian or Zen parable as a musical score. And his 'Interpretation' (notes towards the interpretation of the score, included with it) provides a discussion of the four characters as much as directions to performers.

Cardew's alienation from European avant-garde music can be traced back to the mid to late 1960s, when, in 1966, he joined the former jazz musicians Keith Rowe, Lou Gare and Eddie Prévost in the improvisation group AMM (the meaning of these initials, if any, still isn't publicly known)[7] and, more important, in 1969 co-founded the Scratch Orchestra. Much of the impulse behind the birth of the Scratch Orchestra came from Cardew's growing concern to liberate the performer and encourage amateur musicians to make music. He spoke of the importance of the Scratch Orchestra not just for his own work but because it allowed those who wished to express themselves musically to do so. This encouragement of musical expression formed the gist of much of his career to make 'a musical life' for himself and to facilitate others in doing so. In an interview for the BBC first heard in 1972 and re-broadcast in 1991, Cardew discussed the genesis and philosophy of the Scratch Orchestra:

The Scratch Orchestra came about in response to the demand of a lot of young people who weren't trained musicians to get together to make what we called experimental music on a large scale. It has nothing in common with a conventional orchestra.
Nonetheless it is people capable of playing music in the ordinary way.
Well, not at all. These people may be visual artists, they may be people interested in theatre, they may be perfectly ordinary office workers or students or what have you. They're not necessarily trained in playing any instrument at all. Some of them would perform activities of one kind or another, not necessarily producing sound, because scratch music was really a composite of people making their own activities, so that some of these activities would involve people playing conventional instruments like saxophones or flutes or this, that and the other. And other things would simply involve making motions with a hand or arranging a scarf, or all kinds of activities which would not necessarily make sound. The only limitation was that it should be fairly low-key, so as to allow somebody who wanted to express a solo to be able to do it on top of several people playing scratch music.
So, allowing for the fact that we can't see what's going on, can we hear what goes on?
Well, yes. Let's listen to a bit of this tape. (Plays) [Speaking over tape:] Yes, we don't actually mean it as though it was a fully-composed piece of music, because the essence of

---

[4] Notes for a lecture delivered at the State University of New York at Buffalo, 1967, quoted in Tilbury, liner notes to *Cornelius Cardew Memorial Concert*.

[5] Quoted ibid.

[6] Cardew, *Sextet—The Tiger's Mind*, [London], 1967.

[7] For a history of AMM, see Edwin [Eddie] Prévost, *No Sound Is Innocent: AMM and the Practice of Self-Invention; Meta-Musical Narratives; Essays*, Matching Tye, Essex, 1995.

scratch music is that people are asked to write accompaniments, so each person writes accompaniments and plays these accompaniments and everybody else plays their accompaniments together. So in fact this whole body of sound that makes up a lot of people playing scratch music could be used as a background for somebody playing a solo, and in fact we can go on talking.[8]

'THE GREAT LEARNING' (1968–72)

During his time with the Scratch Orchestra, Cardew produced one of his most important scores, *The Great Learning*, based on a text by Confucius. This remains a noteworthy work of experimental music, combining verbal and musically-notated directions for performers with a prominent ritual element. The original text is divided into large paragraphs, a structural division that Cardew adopts in his score. The score calls, generally, for chorus, although other instruments and objects occasionally make appearances. For example, paragraph 1 calls for 'chorus (speaking and playing whistles and stones) and organ'.

The Great Learning is virtually a catalogue of the experimental musical techniques of the 1960s, combining unconventional instruments and noises with conventional ones, and prose notation with standard. Cardew's quip about paragraph 5 is applicable to the whole work: 'I simply included everything which cropped up at the time'.[9] Despite his move away from serial procedures and his espousal of a freer model of composition because of his work with AMM and the Scratch Orchestra, *The Great Learning* provides evidence of a highly orderly musical sensibility. For example, paragraph 2 consists of 25 collections of pitches for singing and 26 rhythms for drumming. Cardew's performance notes indicate that the pitches and rhythms are to be used freely but within certain boundaries: the pitches sung for the duration of one 'very long breath', the rhythms repeated for the length of one bar of the vocal part. On the surface, paragraph 2 is freely composed and performed (see Ex. 1[10]).

Despite the seeming intuitiveness of the pitch material, a close analysis shows that it is tightly organized. The pitch materials of paragraph 2 are all pentachords or tetrachords, and the interval contents of all the pentachords are identical, as are those of the hexachords. Additionally, the pitch collections are meticulously, if not serially, arranged: six pitch collections (pentachords with a repeated pitch) or hexachords occur every five bars (in bars 1, 6, 11, 16 and 21—the first bar of each staff). As is clear in Table I, the six-note collections of pitches occur only in the first column. Also, Cardew's fastidiousness with pitch material is revealed since each pitch-class set raises one pitch class in the previous set by a semitone; Cardew is systematically working through the twelve different permutations that comprise a particular pitch-class set. The letters I have assigned to recurring pitch-class sets reveal the pattern: once Cardew runs out of pitch-class sets, he starts again, at bar 13. Cardew has applied his expertise in organizing pitch material, learnt from his study of serial procedures, to this work, which, on the surface, is completely intuitive.

The rhythmic material shows a similar ingenious organization. Despite an initial

---

[8] Peter Paul Nash, interview with Howard Skempton and John Tilbury, 'Music Weekly', BBC Radio 3, 26 November 1991. A recording of this broadcast is held at the British Music Information Centre, London, and I thank them for making it available to me when I visited there in May 1992.

[9] Brian Dennis, 'Cardew's *The Great Learning*', *The Musical Times*, cxii (1971), 1066–8, at p. 1067.

[10] Despite persistent efforts, I have been unable to locate a copyright holder for the quotations reproduced in Exx. 1 and 2; the Performing Rights Society Ltd., London, have no record of a 'publisher assigned to [Cardew]' (private communication).

Ex. 1 Cardew, *The Great Learning*, paragraph 2, 'Singing'

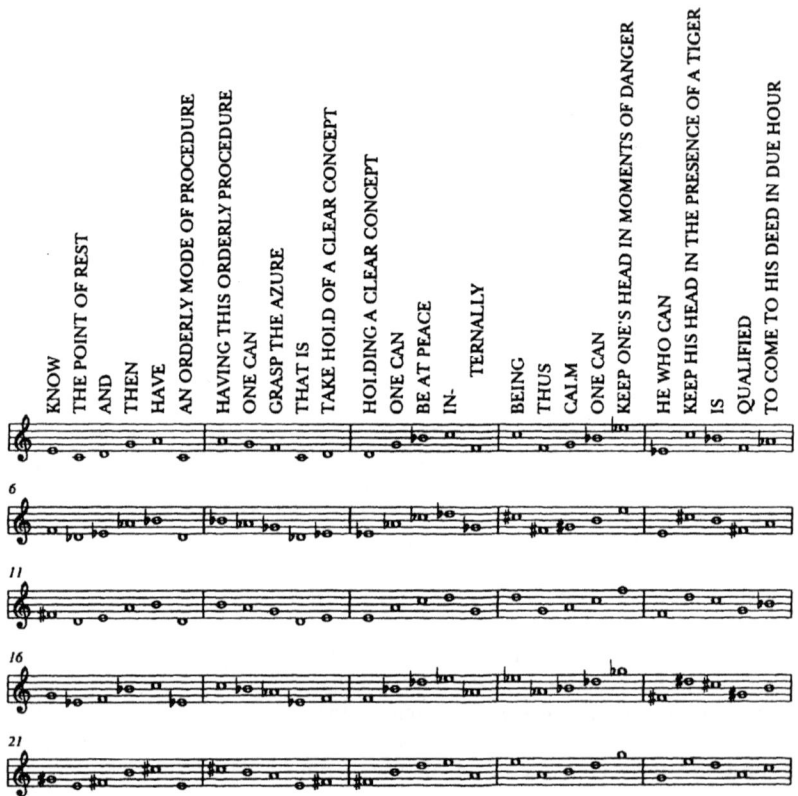

impression of discrete, independent patterns, even a cursory analysis reveals the similarities between the various groups of rhythms. In Ex. 2, the pairs Castor/Pollux and Romulus/Remus, for example, are the only patterns with fermatas. All the patterns in the playing-cards tetrad begin with two simultaneous notes; the Romulus/Remus pair begin with two grace notes; and so on.

Each of Cardew's drumming patterns comes with a label, apparently randomly chosen and organized, but turning out to fall into regular patterns: the Great Lakes, the five senses, the suits of cards, mythological characters. Arranged on a grid in Table II, they, like the pitch material, make patterns: the pairs are arranged vertically in columns 1 and 2; the Great Lakes and the senses are arranged vertically in columns 3 and 4; the suits of cards are arranged in column 5; and the uniques fill in the blanks. Within columns, the elements are always reversed alphabetically, except in the case of the Great Lakes, which are instead arranged geographically, from north to south; there is no alphabetical organization in the pairs and uniques, although the uniques always come in the conventional order (except White/Black).

Cardew's fascination with Chinese calligraphy—which may reflect his earlier work

TABLE I

Cardew, *The Great Learning*, paragraph 2: Grid of Pitch Class Sets

1* [0,2,4,7,9] {6–0} A′ †	2 {0,2,5,7,9} B	3 [0,2,5,7,10] C	4 [0,3,5,8.10] *unique 1*	5 [0,3,5,8,10] D
6 [1,2,3,5,8,10] hexachord 1	7 [1,3,6,8,10] E	8 [1,3,6,8,11] F	9 [1,4,6,8,11] G	10 [1,4,6,9,11] *unique 2*
11 [2,4,6,9,11] {6–2} H′	12 [2,4,7,9,11] I	13 [0,2,4,7,9] A	14 [0,2,5,7,9] B	15 [0,2,5,7,10] C
16 [0,3,4,5,7,10] hexchord 2	17 [0,3,5,8,10] D	18 [1,3,5,8,10] *unique 3*	19 [1,3,6,8,10] E	20 [1,3,6,8,11] F
21 [1,4,6,8,11] {6–4} G′	22 [1,4,6,8,11] G	23 [2,4,6,9,11] H	24 [2,4,7,9,11] I	25 [0,2,4,7,9] A

* Bold numbers indicate bar numbers.

† Bold letters indicate labels given to non-unique pitch-class sets. A letter with a prime symbol (′) indicates that that particular set has a repeated pitch; this is indicated immediately above with a 6 (to indicate the number of pitches) followed by the pitch class that is repeated.

as a graphic artist—informs other portions of *The Great Learning*, in paragraph 7 for example. It is as if he were following the 'orderly mode of procedure' and 'careful deliberation' of the original Confucian paragraph in the making of the portion of the piece I have highlighted. No other paragraph in *The Great Learning* reveals such tight organization. Perhaps no other work is so rigorously organized while simultaneously allowing the performers so much freedom. In this longest and probably most respected of his works, Cardew has not completely abandoned form-orientated 'academic' music, however.[11] His control of pitch and rhythmic material in paragraph 2, for example, is total. The other paragraphs of *The Great Learning* show many other kinds of compositional process at work, including improvisation, graphic notation and prose directions.

The late Brian Dennis wrote that Cardew derived the rhythmic patterns in paragraph 2 from the original Chinese characters, the short strokes interpreted as quavers, the long strokes as crotchets.[12] Like the drum rhythms of paragraph 2, Chinese calligraphy plays a role in paragraph 7. On the other hand, in paragraph 7, the

[11] For a characterization of 'academic music', see my 'The Gendered Construction of the Musical Self: the Music of Pauline Oliveros', *The Musical Quarterly*, lxxvii (1993), 385–96

[12] Dennis, 'Cardew's *The Great Learning*', loc. cit.

Ex. 2 Cardew, *The Great Learning*, paragraph 2, 'Drumming'

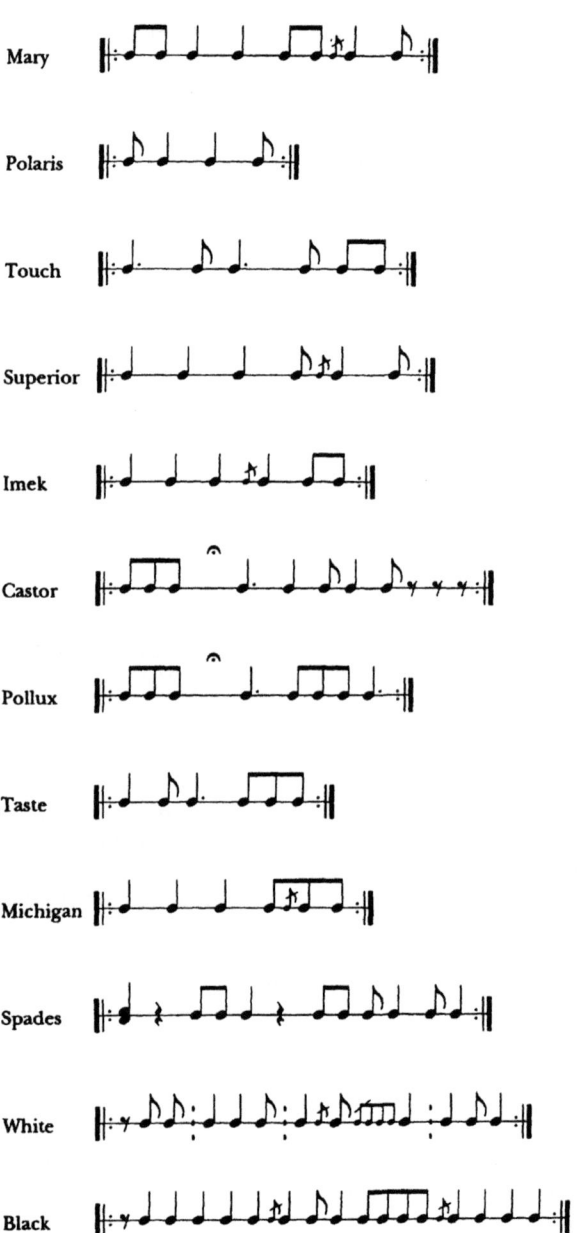

TABLE II

Cardew, *The Great Learning*, paragraph 2: Grid of Drumming Patterns

1* Mary unique 1	2 Polaris unique 2	3 Touch pentad 1.1	4 Superior pentad 2.1	5 Imek unique 3
6 Castor pair 1/a	7 Pollux pair 1/b	8 Taste pentad 1.2	9 Michigan pentad 2.2	10 Spades tetrad/1
11 White pair 2/a	12 Black pair 2/b	13 Smell pentad 1.3	14 Huron pentad 2.3	15 Hearts tetrad /2
16 Romulus pair 3/a	17 Remus pair 3/b	18 Sight pentad 1.4	19 Erie pentad 2.4	20 Diamonds tetrad /3
21 Right pair 4/a	22 Left pair 4/b	23 Hearing pentad 1.5	24 Ontario pentad 2.5	25 Clubs tetrad /4
		26 Brabazon unique 4		

* Bold numbers indicate pattern numbers.

numbers 8, 5 and 13 from the following passage are derived from the number of strokes in a particular character:

$$= = = = = >\quad \text{sing } 8\qquad \text{IF}$$
$$\text{sing } 5\qquad\qquad \text{THE ROOT}$$
$$\text{sing } 13 \text{ (f3)}\qquad \text{BE IN CONFUSION}$$

The meaning of the characters sometimes affects Cardew's choice of borrowed characters; at other times it does not, as with the example just quoted. Linda Dusman has also considered the role of Chinese calligraphy in this particular paragraph, concluding that Cardew achieved a perfect balance between the individual and the whole, the compositional process and the philosophical message.[13]

THE SHIFT TO THE LEFT

Following the composition of *The Great Learning*, Cardew and the Scratch Orchestra increasingly took a Marxist–Leninist–Maoist turn. This was precipitated in part, according to Cardew's friend and fellow Scratch Orchestra member John Tilbury, by a quotation from *The Concept of Freedom*, by the Marxist writer Christopher Caudwell in which he criticizes the distance of an art work from its creator and its audience, the fetishization of the work by both artist and audience, the reification of the individual

[13] Linda J. Dusman, 'The Individual as Structure in Cornelius Cardew's *The Great Learning*: Paragraph 7', *Interface*, xvi (1987), 201–17.

artistic creator and the individual interpreter.[14] Keith Potter writes of a more gradual shift away from positions associated with Stockhausen towards those of John Cage.[15]

Cardew's study of Marx and his long-standing interest in Chinese culture eventually led him to Mao Tse-Tung's 'Talks at the Yenan Forum on Literature and Art' from 1942. His *Stockhausen Serves Imperialism* is filled with quotations from Mao.[16] Much of his earliest music protesting against contemporary 'academic' compositional values consisted of attempts to infuse music with use-values in the Marxian sense, such as the functional values of ritual and ceremony. He was similarly concerned with convincing his public that the point was not the final 'object' but the process of making music, or, in his own words, of 'making a musical life'. Such ideas appear in Mao's writings; a passage from the Yenan talks that speaks to Cardew's new attitude reads: 'There is in fact no such thing as art for art's sake, art that stands above classes or art that is detached from or independent of politics. Proletarian literature and art are part of the whole proletarian revolutionary cause; they are, as Lenin said, cogs and wheels in the whole revolutionary machine.'[17]

Cardew's study of Marx, Lenin and Mao brought a dramatic repudiation of his mentors and a revaluation, if not outright denial, of his own earlier work. He shocked an international gathering of musicians in Rome in 1972 when, in a paper on the problems of notation, he disavowed his earlier compositions. 'As Marx said of philosophy', he told his audience, ' "It is not enough to understand the world, the point is to change it", so we should say to artists, "It is not enough to decorate the world, the point is to influence it".'[18]

Cardew's programme notes to the score of *Piano Album 1973* contain the most forthright and succinct statement of his change in ideology and composition:

> I have discontinued composing music in an avantgarde idiom for a number of reasons: the exclusiveness of the avantgarde, its fragmentation, its indifference to the real situation of the world today, its individualistic outlook and not least its class character (the other characteristics are virtually products of this). I have rejected the bourgeois idealistic conception which sees art as the production of unique, divinely inspired geniuses, and developed a dialectical materialist conception which sees art as the reflection of society and at the same time promoting [*sic*][19] the ideas of the ruling class in a class society. At a time when the ruling class has become blatantly vicious and corrupt, as it must in its final decay, it becomes urgent for conscious artists to develop ways of opposing the ideas of the ruling class and reflecting in their art the vital struggles of the oppressed classes and peoples in their upsurge to seize political power.[20]

Cardew goes on to wonder what kind of musical material can fulfil these goals, and proposes the ten movements in *Piano Album 1973* as examples: his arrangements of music from China, 'the most advanced socialist country in the world'; Ireland, because of the Irish people's 'heroic efforts to achieve liberation from the British colonial yoke';[21] and other movements drawing on or praising Mao Tse-Tung.

Cardew's earliest anti-bourgeois music addresses the dilemmas involved in making

---

[14] Quoted in Tilbury, liner notes to *Cornelius Cardew Memorial Concert*.

[15] Keith Potter, 'Cornelius Cardew: Some (Postmodern?) Reflections on Experimental Music and Political Music', *New Music, Aesthetics and Ideology*, ed. Mark Delaere, Helga de la Motte & Herman Sabbe, Wilhelmshaven, 1995, pp. 152–69.

[16] Cornelius Cardew, *Stockhausen Serves Imperialism and Other Essays*, London, 1974.

[17] Mao Tse-Tung, *On Literature and Art*, Peking, 1967, p. 28.

[18] Cardew, *Stockhausen Serves Imperialism*, 81.

[19] This is a strange choice of word: rather than 'promoting' the ideas of the ruling class, Cardew was interested in 'opposing' them, as the next sentence makes clear.

[20] Cornelius Cardew, programme notes to *Piano Album*, London, 1973.　　　　[21] Ibid.

political art works, and marks a turn to writing music that would not only serve the revolution but would also be accessible to those disenfranchised in his own society: the workers. An early example is 'Soon' (1971), for voice and piano; Cardew's note to the score says that the text is based on Mao's injunction that 'A single spark can start a prairie fire'. (This is a well-known example that is reprinted in its entirety in Michael Nyman's *Experimental Music: Cage and Beyond*.[22])

While the song's text carries the political meanings, the music illustrates clearly Cardew's reliance upon many of the formal aesthetic values of contemporary 'academic' music that Cardew was committed to leaving, especially complexity and virtuosity. What untrained (i.e., proletarian) or even amateur musician could make sense of this song? The metre changes almost every bar. Fermatas break up the flow. The key (D flat major) would be difficult for amateurs to read. And the second phrase is a contrapuntal inversion of the first. The complexity of this piece forces a consideration of its intended performers and audience. The difficulty of the music plus the recurring first person would seem to indicate a trained musician.[23] What, then, about community music? Cardew suggests that his piece may be used as such, at least in part: his note at the bottom of the score says 'Bars 6, 12–18, 35 may be omitted in community singing'. Is this supposed to be a neo-folksong? Perhaps, rather than being for someone else to perform, this is Cardew writing down his own singing, his own thought.

Cardew's mixture of Eastern and Western musical idioms in *Piano Album 1973* and in works such as *The East Is Red* (1972)[24]—elaborations and arrangements of Chinese pieces—is paralleled by a troubling confusion of philosophical assumptions. Cardew conflates the Chinese individual as representative of a collective self with the capitalist conception of an autonomous individual, a product of the composer's marriage of convenience between Chinese traditional thought and the Western avant-garde in general. This confusion helps highlight a problem in Western revolutionary thought: criticizing bourgeois culture from within the system requires the critic to adopt some aspects of that system. So while Cardew may well have understood that his conception of self was bourgeois, he nonetheless kept it, for he remains the singular presence behind this work—and indeed all his works. There is no similar transformation of the figure of the bourgeois composer-individual, or, as Foucault might have it, the composer-function.[25] Unlike the Chinese arranger of 'The East in Red Glow'[26] (the source music for Cardew's *The East Is Red*), who goes uncredited save for his/her collective identity as a member of the Union of Chinese Musicians, Cardew never relinquished his compositional identity in *The East Is Red*.

Cardew was dissatisfied with this and other music from this period, believing that it did not go far enough in critiquing bourgeois culture and providing alternative visions of society. This dissatisfaction eventually turned to criticism of the avant-garde in general. In a 1976 essay entitled 'Wiggly Lines and Wobbly Music' Cardew identified graphic notation—which he had explored exhaustively in his *Treatise* (1963–7)—as a trend representing the increasing *embourgeoisement* of 'art' music. Graphic notation in his view had become an aesthetic object in its own right.[27] Cardew argues generally

    [22] Nyman, *Experimental Music*, p. 148.
    [23] And it is a trained soprano (uncredited), with an operatic voice, who sings 'Soon' on *Thälmann Variations* (London: Matchless Recordings MR10, 1986).
    [24] Cardew, *The East Is Red*, London, 1988.
    [25] Michel Foucault, 'What Is an Author?', *The Foucault Reader*, ed. Paul Rabinow, New York, 1984, pp. 79–85.
    [26] 'The East in Red Glow', in *Historical Revolutionary Songs*, 1971.
    [27] The most prominent example is Cardew's own *Treatise*, which Paul Griffiths has called the *Ring* of graphically

that the artistic avant-garde is part of the imperialist superstructure. The values implicit in avant-garde art, he contends, help 'to protect that [imperialist] society against radical social change':[28]

> Composers who adopt such approximate graphic indications of what their music is to sound like have lapsed ideologically into the fallacy that music can consist solely of a series of doodles, textures, outbursts, stops, and starts. Never mind how artfully arranged, this amounts to adopting the attitude that your score can be used by anyone, to express any ideas, in any context.[29]

Later Cardew writes: 'a number of people with relatively progressive ideas were swept into the avant-garde and dallied for a shorter or longer time with the manipulative techniques and pseudointellectual ideologies that were currently on show [in the 1950s and '60s]. But where could they go? Their subjective rebellion against the establishment left them in limbo.'[30]

One of Cardew's musical activities after his ideological conversion was to refashion *The Great Learning*. Cardew explains that this change was brought about by Mao's 'Talks at the Yenan Forum on Literature and Art', in which he said that art works that did not serve the masses can be altered to do so. In Mao's words: 'We must take over all the fine things in our literary and artistic heritage, critically assimilate whatever is beneficial, and use them as examples when we create works out of the literary and artistic raw materials of the life of the people of our own time and place'.[31]

Cardew left the music in *The Great Learning* unchanged, but he altered the translations of the original text by Confucius. The original version used a translation which began: 'The great learning takes root in clarifying the way wherein the intelligence increases through the process of looking straight into one's own heart and acting on the results; it is rooted in watching with affection the way people grow; it is rooted in coming to rest, being at ease in perfect equity'.[32] The new version reads: 'The Great Learning means raising your level of consciousness by getting right to the heart of a matter and acting on your conclusions. The Great Learning is rooted in love for the broad masses of the people. The target of the Great Learning is justice and equality, the highest good for all.'[33] The revolutionary content of the new version is clear.

Eventually, Cardew criticized even his need to 'reform' *The Great Learning*, as he came to believe that intentions to reform are bourgeois and thus unacceptable: 'Bourgeois ideology cannot be reformed, it must be smashed'.[34] Cardew now thought that *The Great Learning*, from the worker's standpoint, was 'inflated rubbish' (he himself put this phrase in quotation marks), and only continued to perform and discuss the work because it was 'a carrier for its criticism'.[35] His view of the work became highly ironic; in a footnote to *Stockhausen Serves Imperialism* he described the

notated works: see *The Thames and Hudson Encyclopaedia of 20th-Century Music*, London, 1986, p. 84. Also see Brian Dennis, 'Cardew's "Treatise": Mainly the Visual Aspects', *Tempo* (1991), No. 177, pp. 10–16. Composers who employed the kind of notation that Cardew decried include Robert Ashley, Earle Brown, John Cage and La Monte Young.
28 Cornelius Cardew, 'Wiggly Lines and Wobbly Music', *Breaking the Sound Barrier: a Critical Anthology of the New Music*, ed. Gregory Battcock, New York, 1981, p. 236.
29 Ibid., p. 241.
30 Ibid., p. 247.
31 Mao Tse-Tung, *On Literature and Art*, p. 18.
32 Cornelius Cardew, *The Great Learning*, London, 1971.
33 Cardew, *Stockhausen Serves Imperialism*, p. 99.
34 Loc. cit.
35 Ibid., p. 92.

effect of the first paragraph as 'extremely solemn and ritualistic, provided, that is, that it is not disrupted by justifiably irreverent laughter'.[36]

Just as *The Great Learning* represents Cardew's mature experimental-music phase, his final repudiation of it marks the beginning of his mature radical political phase. His associates, the composer Howard Skempton and the pianist John Tilbury, summed up his radical musical aesthetic in the above-mentioned BBC interview. They thought that, for Cardew, music must be essential to one's everyday life; it should never be merely an embellishment but, rather, a menace, a challenge.[37] Music, as Cardew himself said, 'must make waves in our environment'.[38] The problem he still faced was how to turn sound waves into political ones without simply reverting to soapbox oration. And the problem with repudiating any dominant ideology is that you have to replace it with something else. Ideology is, as assumed here, more than beliefs, it is a world view, something that, in the Althusserian sense, constructs us to a large degree.[39] Once you become conscious of your ideological predispositions you cannot simply get rid of them; you cannot avoid ideology in some form or another. Particular structures of bourgeois ideology are tenacious, as we saw in the residual avant-garde musical ideas appearing in Cardew's 'Soon'. Yet ideology is susceptible to alteration by individual subjects: one can, within limits, choose to adopt an alternative ideology. But even if an individual succeeds in this, any new ideology will prove to be as binding as the jettisoned one, and still permeated by it.

The analogous situation in the realms of 'art' or 'government' is similarly difficult. Marshall Berman, in a discussion of Michel Foucault, writes of trading in one ideological structure for another. He points out the virtual impossibility of criticizing ideology, since the critic must approach one ideology from the position of another.[40] This point also surfaced in a discussion between Foucault and a couple of 'Maoist militants' in June 1971, in which Foucault spoke at length of the necessity of not reinstating bourgeois structures of power after the citizenry had been proletarianized. One of the students asked him where the new bureaucracy will come from, and Foucault admitted that he didn't know.[41]

THE PROBLEM OF RADICAL AESTHETICS

Cardew's attempts to write political music raise powerful questions about the roles of art and artists in society and about meanings in art. A few avant-garde (or ex-avant-garde) composers preceded Cardew in their turn towards revolutionary or anti-bourgeois music, notably Hanns Eisler and Hans Werner Henze.[42] But, as Paul Griffiths has noted, approaches to Leftist musics vary as much as in the wider

---

[36] Loc. cit. n. 63.

[37] Nash, interview (see n. 8).

[38] Quoted in Dennis, 'Cardew's *The Great Learning*', p. 1066.

[39] The term 'ideology' is used here as it is in Marxian theory: 'the system of ideas and representations which dominate the mind of a man or a social group'. This is the summary that Louis Althusser offers: see 'Ideology and the State', *Lenin and Philosophy and Other Essays*, trans. Ben Brewster, New York, 1971, p. 158. In addition to Marx's writings, other useful sources on this concept of ideology include Terry Eagleton, *Ideology: an Introduction*, London, 1991; David McLellan, *Ideology*, Minneapolis, 1986; and Raymond Williams, *Marxism and Literature*, Oxford, 1977. For a particularly cogent recent discussion of music and ideology (among many other issues), see Rose Rosengard Subotnik, *Developing Variations: Style and Ideology in Western Music*, Minneapolis, 1991.

[40] Marshall Berman, *All that Is Solid Melts into Air: the Experience of Modernity*, New York, 1988, pp. 34–5.

[41] Michel Foucault, 'On Popular Justice: a Discussion of Justice', *Power/Knowledge: Selected Interviews and Other Writings, 1972–77*, ed. Colin Gordon, trans. idem, Leo Marshall, John Mephan & Kate Soper, New York, 1980, pp. 27–8.

[42] Alan Bush is another British composer whose music expresses his radical Left political beliefs.

'bourgeois' musical field.[43] Stylistically, Cardew is closest to Eisler.[44] Both repudiated what they considered to be bourgeois music and adopted accessible musical styles, writing straightforward songs that would, they hoped, further the revolution. Given the similarity of their polemics[45] and music, it is odd that Cardew rarely mentioned Eisler in any of his writings or interviews;[46] perhaps, like so many composers, he was simply asserting his originality as a reflex conditioned by his involvement in a Western tradition that valued it.[47]

Cardew's aesthetics

Cardew said and wrote very little about aesthetics, although it is clear that he recognized its existence. In 1971 he participated in a composers' discussion in London entitled 'The Composer, Performer and Audience', and seemed to provoke the other panellists (Sven-Erik Bäck, Alexander Goehr and Witold Lutosławski) with his comment, reported by *Music and Musicians*, that the Darmstadt audience was fed 'on an exclusive diet of "aesthetic" music and [was] unable to kick the habit in favour of anything more human'.[48]

Several years later Cardew's comment, in an interview with Adrian Jack, that he did not think there could be a unified, standard aesthetic, led to an interesting exchange. Jack espoused the viewpoint common among some contemporary composers that if you expose audiences to enough of a new style of music they will appreciate it and learn to discriminate between good and bad. He then proposed an analogy: 'It's not until you have lived in a country for some time that you can discriminate between buildings with similar architecture'. Cardew replied: 'What you say is quite right from the aesthetic point of view, but I maintain that the main thing will be whether the building is a palace or a wash house'.[49] In other words, what the building was for and who used it were more important than its form or appearance. Much of Cardew's energy was directed, as this quotation indicates, to wresting art away from conceptions

[43] Griffiths, *The Thames and Hudson Encyclopaedia of 20th-Century Music*, p. 140.

[44] Henze, for example, while committed to the Left, consciously decided to write music in the bourgeois style: 'I have taken the decision that in my work I will embody all the difficulties and all the problems of contemporary bourgeois music, and that I will, however, try to transform these into something usable, into something that the masses can understand': Hans Werner Henze, *Music and Politics: Collected Writings, 1953–81*, trans. Peter Labanyi, London, 1981, p. 180.

[45] Compare, for example, Eisler's writings collected in *Hanns Eisler: a Rebel in Music. Selected Writings*, ed. Manfred Grabs, trans. Marjorie Meyer, New York, 1978. See also Lydia Goehr's discussion of Eisler and political music generally in 'Political Music and the Politics of Music', *The Journal of Aesthetics and Art Criticism*, lii (1994), 99–112; and Stephen Hinton, 'Hanns Eisler and the Ideology of Modern Music', *New Music, Aesthetics and Ideology*, ed. Mark Delaere et al., pp. 101–20.

[46] One rare exception is Keith Potter's interview, 'Some Aspects of a Political Attitude: Cornelius Cardew Interviewed by Keith Potter', *Contact*, x (1974–5), 23–6.

[47] In addition to precedents, there have been followers, such as Frederic Rzewski and Christian Wolff; of these two, Rzewski has been the more assiduous in pursuing the kind of explicitly political agenda and deliberately simplified music associated with Cardew, in works such as *The People United Will Never Be Defeated!* (1973), virtuoso piano variations on the Chilean—now pan-Latin—protest song '¡El pueblo unido jamás será vencido!' (recorded by Ursula Oppens on Vanguard VSD 71248, 1978). For a discussion of Rzewski's music and politics, see Christian Asplund, 'Frederic Rzewski and Spontaneous Political Music', *Perspectives of New Music*, xxxiii (1995), 418–41; this article, however, curiously omits all reference to Cardew, whom Rzewski himself has frequently credited as a significant influence.

There have also been fellow travellers, such as Louis Andriessen, who has taken a somewhat different route in his espousal of a wide variety of musical styles, including those from the popular realm, nonetheless rooted in avant-garde musical idioms that refuse to pander to audiences, in works such as *De Staat* (1972–6) (recorded by Reinbert de Leeuw and the Schoenberg Enzemble on Elektra Nonesuch 9 79251–2, 1991). See David Wright, 'Louis Andriessen: Polity, Time, Speed, Substance', *Tempo* (1993), No. 187, pp. 7–14.

[48] Meredith Oakes, 'Composers Talk and Talk', *Music and Musicians*, xix (1971), 4.

[49] Adrian Jack, 'Cornelius Cardew', *Music and Musicians*, xxiii (1975), 31.

that ignored its social effects. As he said elsewhere, 'If music was a purely aesthetic experience it would not occupy the central place it does in our affairs'.[50]

Cardew summarized his new views on the role of music in *Stockhausen Serves Imperialism*, where he asks: 'How can a composer truly reflect society if he ignores the lessons of that society? If a composer cannot or refuses to come to terms with such problems then the matter should be thrown open to public criticism. The artist serves the community, not vice versa.'[51]

In the Rome talk in which he repudiated his earlier music, Cardew spoke of the requisite overtness of political art. He ended his talk with these words:

> The ideology of a ruling class is present in its art implicitly; the ideology of a revolutionary class must be expressed in its art explicitly. Progressive ideas must shine like a bright light into the dusty cobwebs of bourgeois ideology in the avantgarde, so that any genuinely progressive spirits working in the avantgarde find their way out, take a stand on the side of the people and set about making a positive contribution to the revolutionary movement.[52]

Some of Cardew's earliest political music was for the Scratch Orchestra, which he was attempting to lead in a political direction. Believing that the 'end-product' of an artist's work was 'ideological influence',[53] he began to think that the role of the artist was to promulgate this influence. Such a stance produced some forgettable music. One work, entitled *Ten Thousand Nails in the Coffin of Imperialism* (1972), is an example of the most off-putting kind of radical, proselytizing music. This piece has not been commercially recorded, and no score appears to be extant, but the British Music Information Centre, London, has a tape of a live performance by the Scratch Orchestra. The work begins with roughly 30 seconds of hammering sounds, then a call and response begin between a solo voice which is probably Cardew's, and a group which repeats what the soloist says, with a piano playing dissonant chords in the background. The spoken parts go something like this:

> One thousand nails in the coffin of [inaudible]!
> Two thousand nails in the coffin of property!
> Three thousand nails in the coffin of oppression!
> Four thousand nails in the coffin of sterling [?]!
> Five thousand nails in the coffin of Minister Heath![54]
> Six thousand nails in the coffin of [inaudible]!
> Seven thousand nails in the coffin of [inaudible]!
> Eight thousand nails in the coffin of capitalism!
> Nine thousand nails in the coffin of war!
> Ten thousand nails in the coffin of imperialism!

More hammering sounds follow, the piano continues, and then the work stops.

In addition to offending some listeners because of its overt message, this piece fails because a clear aesthetic function is nowhere to be found. This, given the general elevation of form over content in modern musical aesthetics, is another in a string of ironies surrounding Cardew and his output. *Ten Thousand Nails in the Coffin of Imperialism* shows an interest in a message but little in composition. If the range of meanings of art contains, at one end, form and, at the other, ideology, this work is

---

[50] From an introduction he gave to a performance of *The Great Learning*, quoted in Dennis, 'Cardew's *The Great Learning*', p. 1066.

[51] Cardew, *Stockhausen Serves Imperialism*, p. 39.

[52] Ibid., p. 86.

[53] Ibid., p. 7.

[54] Edward Heath, Conservative MP, and British Prime Minister from 1970 to 1974.

probably too close to one pole to be effective. Rather than uniting aesthetics and ideology as Mao would have artists do, it ignores one end of the spectrum. Of course, 'aesthetic function' does not refer to the aesthetics critiqued here but, rather, to an attention to compositional craft, to sonic beauty as well as to 'ideological influence'.[55] If an unthinkable and exclusive devotion to compositional form is open to criticism, Cardew's single-minded interest in ideology seems equally problematic. As Adorno said about Brecht, 'Whatever is educational in Brecht's plays can be taught more convincingly by theory—if it needs teaching at all'.[56]

Offering an 'aesthetic' criticism of *Ten Thousand Nails in the Coffin of Imperialism* does not necessarily mean that it would be a 'better' work if it somehow achieved a 'balance' between form and content, composition and ideology, or whatever sort of binary opposition describes this polarization, if 'binary' describes it at all. Adorno points out that these poles, usually labelled 'formalism' and 'socialist realism', are not useful, for they make it appear as though there were a clear-cut distinction. He says that the real way to deal with formalism and socialist realism is not to find 'some spurious middle ground' between them but to point out the distance between them.[57]

The main problem with *Ten Thousand Nails in the Coffin of Imperialism* is not that it lacks a 'balance' between socialist realism and formalism, or that the distance between these poles is not highlighted, but simply that there is little attention to the form. The work proselytizes, appears to preach only to the converted, the music comes wrapped so blatantly in political language that the message probably will not get through. This, of course, is the problem faced by all political artists: how to convey a message without preaching. But most overtly political musicians have been popular musicians, and the most enduring of such messages have been packaged in memorable melodies and compelling lyrics by the likes of Woody Guthrie, Bob Dylan and, more recently, the English rock musician Billy Bragg and the American band Rage Against the Machine. All these musicians have other attributes that help promulgate their message: they are witty and self-reflexive, and their brand of politics, while leftist in some sense, is more populist than identifiably Marxist or Maoist.

Cardew may well have realized the foregoing limitations. In abstract or experimental music, the problem is that listeners have nothing to hang on to but the words, since the music is not appealing in the way that much pop or folk music is. Perhaps this was one of the reasons why Cardew wrote for Peoples' Liberation Music, a rock band consisting

---

[55] 'Aesthetic function' is a term used by Jan Mukarovsky in *Aesthetic Function: Norm and Value as Social Facts*, Ann Arbor, 1970. Mukarovsky, a Czech sociologist whose brand of literary theory owes much to the Russian formalist critics, thought that all cultural forms contain aesthetic properties, but only those in which the 'aesthetic function' is primary should be considered as art.

In many ways this is an important argument, for it is premissed on the pervasiveness of an aesthetic sensibility: anything people make has an aesthetic value as well as a functional one—we look for beautiful stones on the beach, we make our living spaces more than merely liveable in. But problems with Mukarovsky's ideas enter when abstract qualities such as 'aesthetics' or 'beauty' become even more abstracted (into 'aesthetic function') and are subject to quantification. (It is here that his debt to the Russian formalists becomes clear, since they were less interested in what is literature than in what is *literary*. So he removes his critical lens from the cultural form and asks not what is aesthetics, but what is the aesthetic function.)

An example of how wrong-headed quantifications of art works can be is provided by Guy Sircello, who puts forward a theory of PQDs ('properties of qualitative degree') in his *A New Theory of Beauty*: '*A PQD of an "object" is beautiful if and only if (1) it is not a property of deficiency, lack, or defect, (2) it is not a property of the "appearance" of deficiency, lack, or defect, and (3) it is present in that "object" in a very high degree; and any "object" that is not a PQD is beautiful only if it possesses . . . at least one PQD present in that "object" to a very high degree*'. Quoted in Peter Kivy, *The Corded Shell: Reflections on Emotions and Music*, Princeton, 1980, p. 123 (italics in the original).

[56] Theodor W. Adorno, *Aesthetic Theory*, trans. C. Lenhardt, ed. Gretel Adorno & Rolf Tiedemann, London, 1984, p. 349.

[57] He singles out Schoenberg, Klee and Picasso, who, he believes, have best accomplished this: ibid., pp. 362–3.

of John Marcangelo, Laurie Baker and John Tilbury, whose existence must have been short and obscure, since, except for an introductory article when the band was first formed, it is virtually unmentioned in the leading British music press.[58] The other reason could be that Cardew wanted to reach listeners other than 'the same old audience'. Herein lies yet another dilemma for political art. If it departs from the dominant aesthetic, it will appeal to no one but the converted. But if it tries to mix this aesthetic with a radical political content, it risks being co-opted by the ideology underlying that aesthetic and hence becoming another commodity of the bourgeois culture industry. In the terms of Walter Benjamin in his famous essay 'The Work of Art in the Age of Mechanical Reproduction', the impact of the art work shifts from 'cult value' to 'exhibition value'.[59]

From a strict revolutionary standpoint, seemingly the *only* alternative to bourgeois art is to give up capitalist conceptions of the individual self and of 'art' and to turn the production of music from a professional to a community activity. Cardew, however, talks frequently of 'working musicians'—those who are paid for their services—so it is clear that he does not think that all music-making should be amateur. Yet the thrust of the Scratch Orchestra was community music-making, by both 'professional' and 'amateur' musicians. After repudiating avant-garde music, Cardew devoted much of his compositional energy to finding ways of bringing music-making to everyone. He retained notions of music as 'art'. Music remained something special, with its own distinct place in the world. Cardew never advocated getting rid of art; rather, he only questioned and sought to redefine its role in society. Marx himself, in fact, strongly believed in 'art'.[60] In practical terms, even the most radical positions leave some room for art, despite its bourgeois history.

Like Marx, Mao Tse-Tung had a use for art, as well as the art of the past, ideas that for a time were extremely influential on Cardew, as is shown by the quotation applied to his revision of *The Great Learning*. In his 'Talks at the Yenan Forum on Literature and Art', Mao spends a great deal of time discussing the role of art in a socialist society, and the importance of making art for the masses—art that serves the cause of the proletariat. Here he poses the question 'literature and art for whom?' as his first, and evidently most fundamental, problem.[61] He then notes the two criteria for judging art, the political and the artistic, and argues that all classes in all class societies invariably put the political criterion first and the artistic criterion second.[62] However, he stresses again and again the compatibility of aesthetic and political values: 'What we demand is the unity of politics and art, the unity of content and form, the unity of revolutionary political content and the highest possible perfection of artistic form'.[63] For him, art is inherently neutral; its reception and interpretation determine its political meanings.

In addition to viewing aesthetics as a bourgeois construct, we could also see it as inherently conservative, helping to maintain the *status quo*. Not only does art encode the values of the dominant culture, in the Western tradition it does so while at the same time appearing to have no overt values other than formal ones. This function of art

[58] The one article I have found is Richard Williams, 'Up against the Wall', *Melody Maker*, xlviii (25 August 1973), 27, which does not mention Cardew as a composer for the group. Williams praises their music, calling it a cross between Stevie Wonder's 'Superstition' and Terry Riley's *A Rainbow in Curved Air*.

[59] Walter Benjamin, 'The Work of Art in the Age of Mechanical Reproduction', *Illuminations: Essays and Reflections*, ed. Hannah Arendt, trans. Harry Zohn, New York, 1969.

[60] As did Trotsky, who is better than many early Marxians on art and the use of art in society: see *Leon Trotsky on Literature and Art*, ed. Paul N. Siegel, New York, 1970.

[61] Mao Tse-Tung, *On Literature and Art*, p. 10.

[62] Ibid., p. 30.

[63] Loc. cit.

tends to turn anything overtly political in it into a self-marginalizing mechanism. But this is not to say that art itself must reflect a conservative view. Although 'official' discourses about art—the various academic disciplines, mainstream criticism, aesthetics—tend to reinforce dominant cultural norms, art remains more than a product of the dominant culture's ideology. It is too complex to be reduced only to this means of signifying, no matter how broad. Ironically, the common effort of political art to impose a unitary interpretation on its audience ultimately undermines its effectiveness. Put another way, one of the qualities present in overtly political art is its lack of ambiguity. This is one of the reasons why political art often seems not to act like art: historically, modern artistic forms have never made any attempt to develop the techniques of maintaining stable and hegemonic interpretations.

The earliest formulation of modern aesthetics was an attempt to wash ideology out of art, thereby making it susceptible to many interpretations, as long as they were non-political.[64] Ambiguity has become one of the most valued of all aesthetic criteria with the onset of modernity. Umberto Eco, for example, seconds Roman Jakobson's notion that one of the functions of language, the 'poetic' function, comes into play when the message is ambiguous and self-focusing. For Eco, ambiguity appears to be the first prerequisite of art: 'ambiguity is a very important device because it functions as a sort of introduction to the aesthetic experience; when, instead of producing pure disorder, it focuses my attention and urges me to an interpretive effort'.[65]

Related to ambiguity is Pierre Bourdieu's term 'facile'. He argues that aesthetics has a disgust for the 'facile', the cheap, the easy. If the meaning is too near the surface, then the work is, in effect, 'Not Art'. In Bourdieu's words, 'it could be shown that the whole language of aesthetics is contained in a fundamental refusal of the *facile*'.[66]

Adorno identified the lack of ambiguity in what he called 'tendentious' works, and he used the phrase 'preaching to the converted' when discussing some of Brecht's work. He recognized that 'Brecht's didactic posture reflects intolerance of ambiguity, the sort of ambiguity that touches off thought and reflection'.[67] But Adorno's real interest is in the work itself—he celebrates art's autonomy, and views people's reactions to it as unimportant: '. . . the subjective experience of art in itself is meaningless, and . . . in order to grasp the importance of art one has to zero in on the artistic object rather than on the fun of the art lover'.[68] So while he identified this problem of political art, he did not see the fundamental reason why political art appears to fail, and fail ineluctably.[69]

[64] This is a complex concept, relevant to all cultural products. See *Music and Society: the Politics of Composition, Performance and Reception*, ed. Richard Leppert & Susan McClary, Cambridge, 1987; Susan McClary, 'Historical Deconstructions and Reconstructions', *Minnesota Composers Forum Newsletter* (April 1982), 1, 'Historical Deconstructions and Reconstructions II: the Roots of Alienation', ibid. (June 1982), 2–5, 'Historical Deconstructions and Reconstructions III: Autonomy and Selling Out', ibid. (June 1983), 4–5, (March 1983), 2–5, 'Historical Deconstructions and Reconstructions IV: the Living Composition in Social Context', ibid. (February 1984), 3–5; Timothy D. Taylor, 'Aesthetic and Cultural Issues in Schumann's *Kinderszenen*', *International Review of the Aesthetics and Sociology of Music*, xxi (1990), 161–78; and idem, 'When We Think about Music and Politics: the Case of Kevin Volans', *Perspectives of New Music*, xxiii (1995), 504–36.

[65] Umberto Eco, *A Theory of Semiotics*, Bloomington, 1976, pp. 262–3. Eco pursues the concept of ambiguity in his later books, most importantly in *The Open Work*, trans. Anna Concogni, Cambridge, Mass., 1989.

[66] Pierre Bourdieu, *Distinction: a Social Critique of the Judgement of Taste*, trans. Richard Nice, Cambridge, Mass., 1984, p. 486.

[67] Adorno, *Aesthetic Theory*, p. 344.

[68] Ibid., p. 20.

[69] Elsewhere Adorno discussed the ambiguity of music. 'Music points to true language in the sense that content is apparent in it, but it does so at the cost of unambiguous meaning': *Quasi una fantasia: Essays on Modern Music*, trans. Rodney Livingstone, London, 1992, p. 3.

Cardew's attempt to imbue his music with political values is contrary to bourgeois aesthetics, whose main purpose is to remove politics, hence defending art from claims that it must demonstrate functionality. The question faced by Cardew and other radicals, then, is: Can there *be* such a thing as radical aesthetics, since aesthetics was invented by the bourgeoisie and propagates its values under the guise of 'art for art's sake'?

It could be, too, that Cardew's notion of the power of art is untenable, for it assumes that art and society are separate, and that the one can thus influence the other. Yet this cannot be so, since they are not separate to begin with; any society and its forms are inseparable.[70] The assumed separateness of art and society could be another way in which the dominant culture attempts to circumvent any concept of subversive content in art. Terry Eagleton writes that teaching English literature became a way for the waning aristocracy to inculcate its values in the burgeoning middle class.[71] As the rising bourgeoisie began reading, it would have been useful for the aristocracy to teach them that literature and the real, social, lived world are unrelated, and that literature is formal, not social or political. This certainly happened in music. So dominant cultural values can be promulgated covertly, and universalized, and overtly political cultural forms become self-marginalizing, as are people who insist on reading art in overtly political ways.

Alongside this argument one must ask whether popular culture is unambiguous, since its assumed lack of ambiguity is the reason why it is subjected to criticism by people who have invested in art: straightforwardness makes it banal. But there are ways of looking at popular arts other than those once validated and practised by the academy, ways in which the underlying meanings can be uncovered. There is no reason why Fredric Jameson's concept of the political unconscious cannot apply to popular works as much as to literature.[72]

In political art, however, the political *is* conscious. There is no need for a critic to argue for the primacy of a political response, since the works themselves request, even demand, such a response. This means that they simultaneously force aesthetic considerations and the whole structure of Western interpretative conventions into second place. In a way, therefore, political art cannot work, because it tries to pre-empt interpretation, which helps to explain why much political art is unpopular with audiences: it allows them no room for interpretative manoeuvring. They are being told what to think, or do, and there is hardly any, or indeed no other, way to interpret the material, as in Cardew's *Ten Thousand Nails in the Coffin of Imperialism*.

But interpretation is arguably the primary way in which we define ourselves as individuals, staking out a semiotic territory of 'our own'. Put another way, interpretation of art works allows us to reinforce the Western bourgeois ideology that encourages us to believe that we are all autonomous individuals with specific, unique, complex reactions to every cultural form we encounter. In the last chapter of *Musical Elaborations*, 'Melody, Solitude, and Affirmation', Edward Said implies a similar

---

[70] This point is made most forcefully by Raymond Williams in *Marxism and Literature*, where he insists repeatedly that cultural forms are caught up in dynamic processes, never fixed or apart from the culture in which they are made and consumed.

[71] Terry Eagleton, *Literary Theory: an Introduction*, 2nd edn., Minneapolis, 1996. Adorno talks at length about the 'neutralization' of art that can occur if it is not understood properly. He invokes Sartre at one point, writing that Sartre thought that the principle of *l'art pour l'art* 'was perfectly acceptable to the bourgeois because it served as a means to neutralize art', and goes on to say that, in Germany, the 'bourgeois appropriated art by assigning to it the role of an ally in its attempt to institute social control': *Aesthetic Theory*, p. 336.

[72] Fredric Jameson, *The Political Unconscious: Narrative as a Socially Symbolic Act*, 1981.

argument concerning the ambiguity of music and its ability to individuate listeners.[73] For Said, listening to Brahms evokes a set of meanings and associations so complex and individualizing that no one but Said himself could have experienced them. This outcome accords with the tenets of Western culture. When one does not make music oneself but instead pays others to do so, one gives up group identity and participation for a heightened sense of one's own individualism and that of the great artists whose commodities one consumes. But interpretation, like ambiguity, is something we all exercise regardless of our political inclinations. While reinforcing bourgeois notions of individuality occur, many other interpretations are possible: some might even be anti-bourgeois.[74]

Cardew thus found himself in an ironic situation. Much of his compositional career was invested in freeing the performer from the shackles of conventional notation as he saw it and encouraging everyone to make music. But his political music, in its proselytizing, actually denies his audience the chance to participate unless they are already converted to his message; and in that case no new belief or activity is produced—he is merely reinforcing what his listeners already believe.[75] Thus, while his music provides a systematic critique of bourgeois culture from a socialist/communist position, it fails to offer a vision other than a familiar notion of a socialist Utopia. Nothing wrong with that, but 'socialism' as a concept has become so debunked by the powers-that-be that most people will not be convinced.

The marginal revolutionary

> If you go carryin' pictures of Chairman Mao
> You ain't gonna make it with anyone anyhow.

The Beatles

As would be expected, Cardew's ideological shift marginalized him almost out of sight. He is never mentioned in *Composer*, the journal of the Composers' Guild of Great Britain and the British Music Information Centre; Peter J. Pirie devotes one paragraph to him in *The English Musical Renaissance* and calls his music 'simple-minded'.[76] Cardew is not mentioned in *British Composers in Interview*.[77] And his appearances in the *Musical Times*, to which he had been a regular contributor early in his career, drop noticeably after his turn to writing political music.

Before his embracing of Maoism, many of Cardew's works had been published by leading European music publishers such as Peters and Universal Edition. Thereafter, his works were published by small, unknown firms. One of these, Experimental Music Catalogue, seems to have been run by Cardew himself, for they published only his music, all in his own manuscript. Like all of Cardew's political music, this is extremely

---

[73] Edward Said, *Musical Elaborations*, New York, 1991.

[74] Popular culture is no less active in the construction of our individual identities. Unlike much political art, it simultaneously provides us with material that is attractive according to traditional norms. *Melody Maker*, interviewing fans at a Billy Bragg concert in England, discovered many who did not share Bragg's democratic socialist politics: they go to his concerts just to hear the tunes. For a discussion of this and other issues relating to Billy Bragg's music, see my 'Re-Signing Mass Culture: Billy Bragg's "There is Power in a Union"', *Popular Music and Society*, xv (1991), 33–48. For an excellent discussion of the popular culture and left politics, see Tony Bennett, 'The Politics of "the popular" and Popular Culture', *Popular Culture and Social Relations*, ed. idem, Colin Mercer & Janet Woollacott, Milton Keynes, 1986.

[75] The denial of individuality is a criticism that Cardew himself made of John Cage's *HPSCHD* (1967–9), saying that, among other things, it reduces the listener as individual 'to the position of a mere spectator': *Stockhausen Serves Imperialism*, p. 84.

[76] Peter J. Pirie, *The English Musical Renaissance*, London, 1979, p. 241.

[77] R. Murray Schafer, *British Composers in Interview*, London, 1963.

difficult to find, although the small English publisher Forward Music is currently issuing some of his political works. Some of his friends and colleagues reacted to his conversion with the sort of scepticism and discomfort with which the non-religious treat the openly devout. Howard Skempton, for example, said that he 'lost touch with Cornelius for political reasons in the early seventies', although he continued to acknowledge Cardew's influence, especially through the tonal works, on his own music.[78] Part of the problem is that bourgeois culture offers no viable 'middlebrow' cultural space, cultural space; cultural forms are categorized as 'high' or 'low', political or not political, aesthetic or not aesthetic; little space exists between any of these binary oppositions. So while Cardew was no longer accepted by most 'highbrow' composers, the nature of his music did not allow his acceptance in 'lowbrow' musical circles. Neither, it seems, did Peoples' Liberation Music.

The marginalization of overtly political art also estranges composer and audience.[79] Cardew believed that a composer's access to a mass audience was controlled by the State and was thus severely limited. The BBC is a 'national' organization, and musicians are 'in the employ of capitalists (publishers, record companies)' who attempt to profit from the musicians' work.[80] Furthermore, Cardew probably realized that he continued to be a part of the State's hegemonic structures himself: his shift in ideology did not remove him from the bourgeoisie. Even in his overtly critical works he could not escape what he condemned, for, as Roland Barthes writes, criticisms of the bourgeoisie are bourgeois themselves:

> True, there are revolts against bourgeois ideology. This is what one generally calls the avant-garde. But these revolts are socially limited, they remain open to salvage. First, because they come from a small section of the bourgeoisie itself, from a minority group of artists and intellectuals, without public other than the class which they contest, and who remain dependent on its money in order to express themselves.[81]

Barthes's observation resonates with Adrian Jack's criticism of some of Cardew's music. Cardew admitted: 'We simply don't have access to a working-class audience'.[82] He said later in the interview that his music should be simpler, that he is not interested in breaking new ground as he once was:

> I would be much happier if music were much simpler, more straightforward and communicated about something in the real world.
> *Whom do you communicate with?*
> The same old audience.[83]

Cardew's music was thus susceptible of becoming re-aestheticized: judged, that is, purely by standards of form, complexity, originality. And in these terms it was 'bad' music and therefore unimportant; or, as Peter J. Pirie said, 'simple-minded'.[84]

Many critics who wrote about Cardew's music mentioned his audience. Steve Lake,

---

[78] Kevin Volans, *Summer Gardeners: Conversations with Composers*, Durban, 1985, pp. 39–40.

[79] Although I am arguing, in essence, that political art is self-marginalizing, out of the mainstream, there are others who view 'proletarian' art as part of the mainstream of high art. Here William Empson is useful. In his pathbreaking book *Some Versions of Pastoral*, he identified the techniques used in 'proletarian literature' as the same as those used in other kinds of literature: the worker could represent something more complex, in the same way that the shepherd (in the pastoral tradition, which was what Empson was considering) could. But Empson is concerned with the ways things mean, not what they mean, which is my concern here. (I used the New York, 1974, edition of his book.)

[80] Cardew, *Stockhausen Serves Imperialism*, p. 7.

[81] Roland Barthes, *Mythologies*, trans. Annette Lavers, New York, 1975, p. 139.

[82] Jack, 'Cornelius Cardew', p. 31.

[83] Ibid., p. 32.

[84] See n. 76, above.

writing for *Melody Maker*, noted that Cardew seemed like a 'cartoon revolutionary' and that if he really wanted a working-class venue (instead of the 'highbrow' St Pancras Assembly Rooms in London) he should 'play the Reading Pop Festival'.[85] In a feature on contemporary music in *Melody Maker*—usually a chronicle of popular music—the unnamed author makes a similar observation: 'The irony of Cardew's situation is that for all his theories about the artist functioning as a member of society, he continues to present his music in "bourgeois" (to use his terminology) concert halls, and his audience remains as of old, willing, apparently, to be outraged both politically and musically'.[86]

These tensions began to tell on the musicians themselves. Rod Eley, in his history of the Scratch Orchestra included in *Stockhausen Serves Imperialism*, describes the growing tension within the orchestra as its members delved further and further into Marxist and Maoist thought. He quotes John Tilbury's summary of the problem: 'After two years of activity, during which the whole gamut of contemporary bourgeois art has been explored, the Scratch Orchestra has reached an impasse. Either you sell your product on the market, or you drop out; this constitutes the dilemma of the bourgeois artist.' Tilbury went on to echo Mao's question of art—whom does it serve?—answering: 'clearly the ruling class of the bourgeoisie'.[87]

The binary choice Tilbury poses here is of course over-simplified. As Jacques Attali has written, one way of regaining control over one's own music is, in the classic Marxian way, to seize the means of production.[88] Attali cites the free jazz musicians of the 1960s who founded their own recording and publishing company. This is also an option that the English socialist rock musician Billy Bragg has considered. With the advent of cassette recording, producing and marketing one's own music is easier than ever before and is something that the Scratch Orchestra could have considered. But their decision to play music that was attempting to be 'art' severely limited the venues at which they could appear. They couldn't 'play the Reading Pop Festival', as the anonymous *Melody Maker* critic suggested, since few at that festival would have wanted to hear them.

Rod Eley notes the point at which the Scratch Orchestra realized its ineffectiveness. In June 1971 they gave a concert in a club for young immigrants where there had been a riot and several arrests the previous week. They played the 'Toy Symphony'.[89] 'We experienced at last the true nature of our almost total incompetence, and the total irrelevance of the Scratch Orchestra in its present form in the modern world.'[90] But Cardew refused to be silent. He went on composing, never moving from his political stance, although there are a few works with odd titles, such as *Three Bourgeois Songs* of 1973. These songs are settings of Confucian odes that Cardew also employed in *The Great Learning*, but they are written in a fairly complex, barely tonal idiom. It is as if Cardew were longing for his old avant-garde values, just as Schoenberg longed to write, and occasionally did write, tonal music after beginning to compose methodically with twelve notes in the 1920s.

And it may be that he was on his way back to these earlier, more recognizably avant-garde musical values, which, as we have seen, left traces in 'Soon'. He enrolled on a Master's Theory and Analysis course at King's College London in the autumn of 1981,

[85] Steve Lake, 'Rzewski/Cardew' (concert review), *Melody Maker*, li (7 February 1976), 47.
[86] Anon., 'Sages, Seers and Prophets', *Melody Maker*, li (24 April 1976), 27.
[87] Cardew, *Stockhausen Serves Imperialism*, p. 28.
[88] Jacques Attali, *Noise: the Political Economy of Music*, trans. Brian Massumi, Minneapolis, 1985.
[89] Presumably Leopold Mozart's. The Scratch Orchestra did occasionally play popular classics.
[90] Cardew, *Stockhausen Serves Imperialism*, p. 22.

just before he died; and Susan Bradshaw, in an obituary, wrote: 'What a tragic pity that he should have been torn away just as he appeared to be on the verge of returning to the world of a more self-demanding kind of music-making . . .'[91] At the bottom of a recording of some of Cardew's piano music, a message appears: 'The Cornelius Cardew Foundation would like to make it clear that later in his life Cardew rejected Maoism'.[92] But there is no evidence for this turning back in Cardew's own writings, of which there are few from the last few years of his life.

CONCLUSIONS

Cardew occupies an extreme position—one not currently represented so visibly by anyone else. What is more, despite the marginalization brought on by his shift in ideology, Cardew's presence on the English contemporary music scene over a decade after his death remained surprisingly strong. In the span of less than a week in May 1992, he appeared twice in the British press. In a weekly feature called 'Notes & Queries' in the *Guardian* newspaper, a reader asked: 'Can a person like Wagner's music and still be a socialist?' There were a variety of answers, including this one from a Liverpool reader: 'Try listening to the works of the right-on composer of revolutionary people's "music", Cornelius Cardew. You'll be desperate for the politically dubious pleasure of *Parsifal* in no time.'[93] Also, a full-scale article about his mysterious death appeared in the *Independent* newspaper.[94] Many of Cardew's friends believe that the hit-and-run accident that killed him was not an accident but that he was murdered by the government for his political views and activism. This is doubtful, for he had so successfully marginalized himself that he was not a real threat to the *status quo*. But his was a restless spirit, and he continues to define, if only by his absence, a crucial role of music in society today.

[91] Susan Bradshaw, 'Cornelius Cardew (1936–1981)', *Tempo* (1982), No. 140, p. 22 (ellipsis in the original).
[92] Cornelius Cardew, *Thälmann Variations* (1974).
[93] 'Notes & Queries', *The Guardian*, 11 May 1992.
[94] Edward Fox, 'Death of a Dissident', *The Independent Magazine*, 9 May 1992, pp. 24–30.

Part III
The Politics Within

[12]

The Language of the Young People

Rap, Urban Culture and Protest in Tanzania

José Arturo Saavedra Casco

El Colegio de México, Mexico

Abstract

The main aim of this article is to show through a brief recount of the history of rap in Tanzania the social and political contents of Tanzanian hip-hop songs, mentioning the characteristics of the messages and their impact on Tanzanian youth. This article also remarks on the local elements, beside the use of Swahili language, contained in Tanzanian rap that are inherited from Swahili precolonial poetry. Finally, it gives several examples of the social and protest contents in songs of remarkable Tanzanian hip-hop artists, such as Mr. II, Professor Jay and Wagosi wa Kaya.

Keywords hip-hop • poetry • Swahili • Tanzania • youth

Introduction – Tanzanian Hip-hop: A Global Phenomenon

Tanzania is an East African country still considered one of the poorest in the world; it is highly dependent on foreign aid and many of its people live below the World Bank poverty line (the GNI per capita is under US$300).[1] We nevertheless find here an amazing cultural phenomenon, a movement that combines both foreign and local elements. This movement originates in the creativity and willingness of young Tanzanians who have chosen hip-hop as a way to express themselves, by writing their own music and lyrics which depict the problems, worries and dreams of their generation. In a relatively short period of time, hip-hop has changed dress codes and also created new spaces in Tanzanian society. Furthermore, it represents a new industry that gives opportunity for young rappers to prosper in ways that previous musicians never imagined. The rise of rap has been simultaneous with the spread of the mass-media networks in Tanzania. Hip-hop performers not only use radio and television channels, but also produce audio CDs and video clips that are currently available on VHS tape and DVD, thereby pushing beyond the typical musical market that is based only on audio-cassettes. Rappers also have shown extraordinary skill in organizing

230   Journal of Asian and African Studies 41(3)

companies and creating new forums where they share the stage with newcomers in order to give the opportunity to these beginners to display their talents.
Some Tanzanian rappers or *maemesi* (MCs) have succeeded in establishing
careers that have given them self-reliance and wealth. Tanzanian hip-hop domi-
nates the East African music scene, selling its songs in Kenya, Uganda and even
overseas in Europe and North America where there are Swahili-speaking expatriate communities. In record time, it has spanned the generational gap between
older generations, who initially considered rap *musiki ya kihuni* – music for
vagrants, thieves and criminals – which 'could spoil the behavior of youngsters',
and younger generations who were not convinced by the values inherited from
the government of *Ujamaa* which were professed until the middle of the 1980s.
Finally, Tanzanian hip-hop, although highly influenced by American rap philosophy and values, integrated the old tradition of Swahili poets who, since pre-
colonial times, composed verses to express the people's grievances, joys and
feelings toward events that affected their everyday lives. The social function of
rap is the same as that which these Swahili poets practised for centuries along
the East African coast. Later educational policies also stressed this same
function by placing emphasis on narrative poetry that depicted the remarkable
historical events of the country.

The aim of this article is to examine how a genuine African element is present
in many hip-hop songs and also to trace how social and political concerns are
still addressed in Tanzanian rap, in spite of more romantic and banal subject
matters that are welcomed by those who want to turn Tanzanian rap into a very
profitable business. In order to reach this goal I will make a brief review of
Tanzanian hip-hop history based on current available scholarship, together with
other materials that show the African elements of hip-hop in order to stress the
continuity of the Swahili poetic tradition and its influence on young rappers.
Then I will discuss the social function of poetry present in rap, mentioning as a
representative sample the works of famous rap performers such as Mr. II,
Professor (or 'Profesa') Jay and Wagosi wa Kaya.

The Origins and Development of Hip-hop in Tanzania

According to available data, we can trace the first signs of American rap in
Tanzania to the mid 1980s, when the first examples of American rap began to
circulate among youth in Dar es Salaam. Even though researchers believe this
music was first listened to by children from well-off families (Gesthuizen and
Haas, 1998; Englert, 2003; Mwisheshe, 2004; Perullo, forthcoming), the location
and character of the city, a port which receives ships and goods from all over the
world, surely contributed to the introduction of this music in several social
sectors in a short period of time. One should also remember that until the beginning of the government of Benjamin Mkapa the process of privatization and
liberalization of the economy increased the number of high-class families with

links abroad. Since these beginnings, the images of American rappers dominated the scene and for young Tanzanians the glamour, dress and luxurious way of living associated with American rappers created a series of images and symbols that new Tanzanian rappers admired and tried to recreate in their own environment. In the years to come, hip-hop fashion was very visible in areas like Coco Beach, near Masaki, and Swahili comics such as *Bongo, Tabasamu* and *Sanifu* took from American hip-hop movies the image of youth gathering on the beach in the latest gear, equipped with sound systems (Gesthuizen and Haas, 1998: 7).

One undeniable fact is that even if the arrival of hip-hop impacted consumers from a wide range of social classes, only a limited group of individuals could afford to initiate their own local hip-hop production. By the end of the 1980s there were only a few radio stations in the country. There were no television stations until 1994, and the most common way to listen to Tanzanian bands was to buy audio-cassettes of very poor sound quality or to attend live performances (Gesthuizen and Haas, 1998: 2).[2]

In the early 1990s rap competitions began in several venues in Dar es Salaam, such as the New Africa Hotel and the Kilimanjaro Poolside, where youth gathered to listen to American hip-hophits. The most notorious competition of these early times was the 'Yo! Rap Bonanza' organized by DJ Kim & the Boyz promotion. This event, where the first *emecis* (masters of ceremonies) performed American rap songs, took place on the seventh floor of the New Africa Hotel (Perullo, 2005: 12–13). One of these young men, Saleh Jabir, would become the pioneer of Swahili rap when he dared to put into Swahili the lyrics of 'Ice Ice Baby', a hit that had recently come from America. People were shocked when they listened to Swahili lyrics inserted in the original version 'without losing the concept' (Gesthuizen, 2002b). According to Saleh, his friends, without telling him, sold a copy of the single to an Indian businessman and after a short time several copies were distributed among Indian shops in Uhuru Street. Saleh was from a rich coastal family and he was actually not directly interested in making a big profit with his songs. Nevertheless, he released the first Tanzanian hip-hop album. Unfortunately, Saleh's career did not last for long. By that time hip-hop began to be considered by older generations as *uhuni* (gangsterism) associated with crime and drugs. The first generation of rappers had to cope with this situation, and Saleh, as the first public figure, suffered most from the hostile attitude toward rap (Gesthuizen and Haas, 1998: 3).[3] Instead of producing a second album, Saleh decided to leave Tanzania and settle in the United Arab Emirates, where he is still living today (Gesthuizen and Haas, 1998: 4; Buyanza, 2002; Gesthuizen, 2002b).

In spite of the negative attitude toward hip-hop in many sectors, the number of groups increased significantly in the following years. Kwanza Unit, K.B.C, Rhymson, Gangsters & matatizo G.W.M, E-Attack, Deplow Matz, Afro Reign, Bantu Pound and Hard Blasters, among others, stormed the scene and captured

232 Journal of Asian and African Studies 41(3)

the attention of many new fans. By this time, these artists were writing their own songs in Swahili and did not limit themselves to translating American rap songs as Saleh Jabir did. One of them, Joseph Mbilinyi – who initially called himself 'Mr. II', or 'Two Proud', and then changed his name to 'Sugu' – is the hip-hop artist whose career has been sustained most successfully. He not only composed his songs in Swahili, but also addressed politics, social inequalities and other problems that affected Tanzanians. He became so popular that his music reached audiences even in rural areas where rap had not been heard before. Unlike Saleh Jabir, Mr. II enjoyed greater acceptance by older people; the quality of his music contributed to making him the first Tanzanian rapper who could make a living from his music. He was also the first Tanzanian hip-hop musician who toured abroad, going to Holland in early 1998. He currently lives in London and is preparing his first internationally released album (Buyanza, 2002; Gesthuizen, 2002c).

In the second half of the 1990s rap music experienced an incredible expansion due to the growth of Tanzanian mass media – there appeared five television stations, numerous new radio stations and more than 350 newspaper and magazine publications – the result of liberalization that generated financial resources for investment in Tanzanian urban sectors. This environment encouraged the arrival of modern technology that in turn facilitated access to Internet services and modern equipment for the music industry (Gesthuizen and Haas, 1998: 2).[4] In only a few years many new record studios appeared, and local and international hip-hop was daily broadcasted on radio and television.

Since 2000, many new hip-hop bands and solo artists have emerged and many new companies – most of them created by the rappers themselves – have produced albums and videos and appeared in television programmes, films and soap operas – like the famous *Siri* (The Secret) featuring the successful Banana Zorro. The current situation is clearly the opposite of those initial years when rappers had to deal with the intolerance of the older generation and a limited budget to distribute their production.

Based on this, I propose dividing the history of Tanzanian hip-hop into two periods, in order to distinguish the different contexts that existed during these stages. The first ranges from the emergence of hip-hop in Tanzania in the mid-1980s and up to 1999, when rap had developed into a well-established industry. The second, from 2000 onwards, represents a period of a boom of artists and the consolidation of business related to rap. I derive the first period from an article written by Thomas Gesthuizen (2000c) published by the website *africanhiphop.com,* which listed the names and profiles of the 41 most prominent Tanzanian rappers who emerged between 1991 and 1999. In most cases the artists on this list, called 'the old school', share the characteristics that define this first stage of the history of Tanzanian hip-hop. They encountered several of the same problems, such as hostility toward their music, lack of opportunities, poor quality audio production and a very limited market. The beginning of the second period is marked by the inclusion of Tanzanian rap as a musical category accepted by the Tanzanian Arts Councils, *Baraza ya Sanii ya Tanzania* (BASATA). The implementation of yearly awards for the best albums and artists since 1999 by BASATA has also contributed to the consolidation of local hip-hop. From 2001, BASATA recognized rap as an official genre within Tanzanian music and has also engaged young rappers in campaigns addressing social problems, such as drugs, AIDS, sexual abuse and lack of education (Gesthuizen, 2002a; Englert, 2003: 78; Edward, 2004). Thus, this official support meant a radical change for Tanzanian rap industry. From 2000 local hip-hop has constantly grown. A few survivors of the first stage, such as Sugu (the former Mr. II) and Mr. Ebbo still shock audiences with new productions, while at the same time new prominent stars have invaded the scene using radio, television and also the emerging Internet space. Professor Jay, with his hit 'Ndiyo Mzee' (Yes Sir!), showed blatantly that sharp critique of local politicians was not inconsistent with commercial success. Wagosi wa Kaya, a group from the coastal city of Tanga, demonstrated on their part that high standard hip-hop is no longer exclusive to Dar es Salaam. Numerous rap contests have been held in Arusha, Morogoro, Dodoma and other regional capitals. These are the main recruitment sites for new talents (Englert, 2003: 80; Edward, 2004).

This hip-hop boom helped to create the style known as *Bongo Flava*[5] (the flavor of Dar es Salaam), which includes young artists based in Dar and all those in the country who follow its musical tendencies. This genre mixes hip-hop with pop rhythms – locally known as R&B – and also with *rumba, taarab* and *lingala* styles. Ferooz, Banana Zorro, Dully Sykes, Dudubaya and Mwanfalsafa are very popular nowadays, as are young female artists who compete to consolidate women's presence in local hip-hop, such as Zay-B and Sista P. Also, other pop female artists like Rehema Chalamila (Ray C), Judith Wambura (Lady Jaydee) and the Zanzibari V-2 are clearly succeeding not only in Tanzania but in the whole East African region. Some artists share several musical fields. Luca Mkenda, 'Mr. Nice', has successfully combined his *takeu* style with hip-hop concepts; the late James Cool, 'Mtoto wa Dandu', re-released old East African dance classics such as Les Wanyika's 'Sina Makosa' and Maquis Original's 'Kalubandika', introducing hip-hop elements in his versions on the album, *Sukuma Land* (2000) (Gesthuizen, 2002c). If collaboration among rappers was a common feature in the past, now this tendency has been extended to musicians of all the genres. Bw. Misosi collaborates with Wagosi wa Kaya and also with Muumin Mwinjuma, one of the most popular musicians of the *Musiki ya Dansi* (dance music) genre. Even the famous Mr. II has Remmy Ongala – a real icon of East Africa rumba – as a guest on his album, *Itikadi* (2002).

Nevertheless, not all young rappers are happy with the results of this tendency toward mixing genres. In the first stage of rap, most of the lyrics showed a very great social concern, with critiques of the establishment and the country's economical situation. Now many rappers like Dully Sykes, Ray C and Mwanafalsafa sing about the 'sunny side of life', which is considered by some as contrary to the original concept of 'keeping it real' (talking of real problems) found in the first Swahili hip-hop lyrics (Englert, 2003: 76).

The tendency to 'lighten' the social protest content in many hip-hop songs is evident in a context where more big business sponsors are supporting hip-hop rallies and competitions, where there are more recording studios and production companies, and where more rappers are closer to TV show-biz with productions such as *Girlfriend* and *Siri*, stories absolutely involved in a hip-hop environment (Englert, 2003: 79).

There is also evidence of a growing concern among rappers with having the support of local firms and participating in their advertising campaigns (Toroka, 2002). Rap has also become a very attractive and profitable career that breaks with the old tradition of the 'hopeless poor musician'. An article in an East African newspaper asserts that Tanzanian rappers have extended their market to the whole of East Africa and that artists, such as Mr Nice, TID or Wagosi wa Kaya, earned in around US$30,000 (Tsh30 million) in royalties from their hit CDs – serious money in Tanzanian terms (Suleyman, 2004). The promotion of young rappers is now for some a successful enterprise. Eric Shigogo, head of Ericom Limited, is launching an aggressive campaign to promote young Tanzanian artists in the USA. The goal is to show western countries that 'in Africa not everything is negative, and music is a product that currently the Afro American population is getting more interested in knowing and acquiring' (Lengua, 2004). Recently, for example, Albert Mangwair, Banana Zorro, Mwanafalsafa Ruta Bushoke and Ray C travelled to the UK where they performed a very successful concert in the city of Reading. Furthermore, Ray C continued her own tour to Maryland to give her first performance on the American continent (*Bongoxplosion*, 2004).

In the face of this growing commercialization some artists have fallen to some of the common problems of show-biz, and, inevitably, several scandals have erupted which threaten to taint again the reputation of hip-hop in Tanzania. Recently, Dudubaya badly beat Mr Nice on stage in front of hundreds of fans. Also, it has not been long since rapper Steven Gerald (Steve 2K) was stabbed to death by his own promoter, Castro Ponela Fusi, after a bitter argument between them. Finally, another artist, Khaleed Mohamed, was detained by police, accused of rape (Mkangara, 2004).

Thus, a group of producers, promoters and artists joined to organize the 'hip-hop Summit 2004' in order to discuss these and other problems that worry many rappers: the increasing lack of social consciousness in lyrics, poor earnings for many artists and the illegal production of CDs, audio tapes and video materials. This event took place in Dar es Salaam in early December 2004. As we can see, then, the rap music industry is growing to an unanticipated extent. Gone are the days when rap was marginal and its activity was reduced to a very few spaces.

It is still too early to judge whether this process will completely change the original characteristics of this movement.

The African Influence: Swahili Poetry and Social Themes in Tanzanian Hip-hop Songs

Scholarship on Tanzanian hip-hop, though still very scarce, has already pointed out several essential aspects of this cultural phenomenon. On the one hand, Gesthuizen and Haas (1998: 7), using research conducted in Tanzania during 1997, have convincingly shown the strong borrowing of cultural symbols and images from American rap and from the cults surrounding some American rappers, such as 2Pac, whose violent murder, depicted in the comic *Bongo*, shocked Tanzanian rap's audience. On the other hand, Perullo (2005: 15–19) shows in his history of the early years of Tanzanian hip-hop how the creation of rap songs in Swahili contributed to the rapid acceptance of this music by a wide young audience who appreciated social messages set in a Tanzanian context. These researchers reached a common conclusion on the importance that the rap audience gave to Swahili lyrics, which this audience judged by the hip-hop concept of 'keeping it real'" introduced by American hip-hop. That meant that these lyrics had to be identified with real life and the real problems that youth suffered. Additionally, Tanzanian rappers, unlike their American counterparts, tried to avoid violent messages and the use of vulgarities (Perullo, forthcoming: 26–7), in this regard following the criteria that ancient Swahili poets followed. These poets believed that their works should contribute positive messages to the community through sophisticated prosodic rules and an elegant use of the language (Lienhardt, 1968; Massamba, 1983; Pouwels, 1987; Shariff, 1988; Middleton, 1992: 189–91). Furthermore, Gesthuizen (2002a) has recognized the strong importance of Swahili poetry in the composition of hip-hop lyrics. He mentions that since many young people are unable to speak and understand English fluently, they have found inspiration in the Swahili pop music of the past, even in Swahili poetry. He adds: 'An example is rapper Cool Para from Zanzibar who uses the metre of taarab lyrics, and whose lyrics are – quite unusual for a rapper – composed by an older poet who is also active in politics'.

Englert (2003: 81–2) tells us that the *darhotwire* website opened an online poll where people could vote about which elements they considered the most important in the elaboration of a hip-hop song. Astonishingly, 41 per cent voted that the most important thing is the content and quality of the lyrics and *mashairi* (verses). Only 25 per cent said that the singer's voice was more important, and, finally, 18 per cent considered that the beat and rhythm was the most important aspect.

Since pre-colonial times Swahili poetry has represented an important way to express social concerns and to mark Swahili identity in relation to hinterland

236   Journal of Asian and African Studies 41(3)

and non-Muslim peoples (Lienhardt, 1968: 2–3; Pouwels, 1987: 73–4). Around the 16th century Muslim scholars produced the first manuscripts of Swahili poetry written in Arabic script. They saw this literary form as a useful tool for teaching the Islamic faith to younger generations (Knappert, 1979). In the centuries to come this poetry incorporated local themes originally preserved by oral means and became an important way of expressing social concerns. It was also used in contests of composition ability during public festivities. The most remarkable poets participated in competitions (*mashindano*) that took place during public festivities. Contenders had to compose verses replying to what their opponents previously said (Biersteker and Shariff, 1995; Biersteker, 1996). Often the subjects of Swahili poetry were social matters and complaints against oppression of local or foreign rulers, rivalries between cities or regions, or the depiction of memorable events for the community. Political poetry existed since the 19th century in Lamu and Mombasa, and in the previous years to European colonization there was sophisticated historical narrative poetry written under the *utenzi* genre (Harries, 1962; Abdulaziz, 1979). During German and British colonial rule European scholars studied ancient Swahili poetry and preserved very old materials (Saavedra, 2002). Also during European rule, colonial policies promoted the use of Swahili language by inland peoples, expanding the language's area of influence to the whole of East Africa. Logically, they encouraged poetry written with reference to western standards. Brilliant poets, such as Shabaan bin Robert, were successful in developing Swahili poetry using both traditional and western models (Mulokozi and Sengo, 1995). Later, by the time of Nyerere's *Ujamaa* government, the status of Swahili as the main official language made Swahili literature – especially poetry – a subject that students had to study at elementary and secondary levels.

Instead of 'free verse' lyric poetry, intellectuals of the *Ujamaa* regime chose the narrative genre of *utenzi*, which follows the complex prosodic rules of traditional poetry, to honour the ruling party *Chama cha Mapinduzi* (Party of the Revolution) (Mahimbi, 1981), the Tanzanian Army (Mdundo, 1987) and the government of Zanzibar (Khatib, 1975). This genre was also used to narrate the war of Kagera between Tanzania and Uganda, the outcome of which was the end of the dictatorial regime of Idi Amin Dada (Muhanika, 1981). After the *Ujamaa* system collapsed, the function of poetry as a tool of communication was gradually undermined by the expansion of the radio network and also by the establishment of television stations in the country. However, a residue of this tradition is found in the newspapers that have a section where people can send poems about public worries, complaints, or topics of general interest. There is still very much present a custom of reciting improvised verses at weddings and other family celebrations together with public festivities. In the coastal areas and also on the Islands of Zanzibar and Pemba, where the Muslim tradition of the *Maulidi* (the commemoration of the birth of the prophet Mohammed) is widely celebrated, the recitation of ancient verses that involve all the participants is the central part of the event. Thus, it is not strange that with this background composition of poetry is a familiar skill for old and new generations.

Certainly, the first and second waves of Tanzanian rappers may not have been directly influenced by traditional poetry, since, according to experts, today's students do not feel attracted to ancient poems whose vocabulary, with many loans from Arabic, needs glossaries and specialized dictionaries to be understood (Mazrui and Shariff, 1992; Mulokozi, 1999, 2000). Nevertheless, the young generation of Tanzania may have also been influenced by poetry through the local dance music that their parents enjoyed during the first decades after independence. The musical genre known as *Musiki ya dansi* became very popular in the *Ujamaa* era and many of the bands that played this music participated in competitions decided by the preference of the audience. Each band developed a style (*mtindo*) that in many cases had influence from traditional local dances (*ngoma*). Many *ngoma* were connected to Swahili poetry in various ways. Competitions among bands and the link with the poetic genre *nyimbo* (song), which gave its name to lyrics used for telling stories inside dancing compositions, are two of the most remarkable points. According to Graebner (2000: 302–8), musicians also followed some genres of dialogue poetry such as *malumbano*, 'a tradition in Kiswahili poetry [which] refers to a kind of cross-questioning between poets, either in written verse or in oral discourse'. The author also mentions that the lyrics, 'part of the larger universe of Kiswahili poetry', are familiar to fans who are very well-versed in the art of decoding songs and reading between the lines. The lyrics must also give positive messages and omit insults or vulgar expressions. Rivalry between *Musiki ya dansi* bands was a common feature by the time of hip-hop's arrival in Tanzania.

Tanzanian hip-hop inherited various elements from this musical context that also had influence from the Swahili tradition of poetry performance: competitions among composers, (*mashindano*); the mutual consensus between them and their audience of norms for the adequate use of poetry and language; the use of poetry as a way to express social and political concerns; and, finally, the ability to improvise verses with a suitable rhyme. Precisely, the role of Tanzanian rap as a vehicle for social and political expression is still very present in spite of a growing process of commercialization that is currently taken place. This is quite evident when we listen to the lyrics of several artists who in recent years have stormed the hip-hop scene and have continued the concept of 'keeping it real', which inspired the first Tanzanian rappers at the beginning of this cultural phenomenon.

Urban Protest and Social Complaints: Mr. II, Professor Jay and Wagosi wa Kaya

Among hip-hop performers who have produced successful albums in the last three years we find three good examples of those who address social topics expressed in songs and reflect the current problems that many young Tanzanians face. The first, Mr. II, is one of the few survivors of the first stage of evolution of Tanzanian hip-hop and, as mentioned previously, he is also the first internationally successful artist in this musical category. The other two, Professor Jay and Wagosi wa Kaya, have succeeded in attracting the respect and preference of young audiences due to the quality of their music and the strong and thought-provoking content of their lyrics, which continue the old tradition of using poetry as a means of expression and as a tool of protest.

Mr. II, throughout his prolific career, has composed many songs that express the typical concerns and worries of many Tanzanian people: poverty, lack of opportunities, difficult access to education and jobs, and the essential rights of citizens. Even though Mr. II has not limited his production to political or social topics, these are the subjects that have mainly attracted the attention of Tanzanian audiences and also particularly captivated researchers interested in Tanzanian hip-hop. Gesthuizen and Haas (1998) do not hide the influence of this artist in their research named after his successful album *Ndani ya Bongo* (Inside of Dar es Salaam). They include translated fragments of his song 'Moja kwa Moja' (Straight On) to show the strong personality of Mr. II as he plays with egocentric posturing in front of his fellow artists (p. 1). They also include the whole translation of 'Sema nao' (Talk to Them), a song that addresses Mr. II's own role as a leader of the hip-hop movement while calling for unity among rappers (pp. 12–16). And Perullo (forthcoming: 26–7), analyzes the song 'Nimesimama' (I've Just Stood Up), also from the album *Ndani ya Bongo*; he considers it 'the final push' to call attention to the localization of rap music in Dar es Salaam and a clear example of how important the 'social message' in lyrics has become for the young audience. 'Nimesimama' tells the story of a young man being questioned by a police officer and touches on sensitive matters such as abuse of authority, unemployment and the despair of Tanzanian youth who envisage leaving the country as the only option in the case of boys, or becoming prostitutes in the case of girls. Mr. II has not abandoned this tendency in composition. A good example is the song 'Haki' (Right), which is included in his 2002 album produced in Dar es Salaam: *Itikadi* (Faith). In this song, Mr. II, now using the nickname 'Sugu', affirms that everyone, with no distinction of gender, race, age or social class, must enjoy the same rights. In his main chorus, Sugu asserts:

Wabongo mnataka nini?	What do people of Dar es Salaam want?
Watoto wa mitaani mnataka nini?	What do street children want?
Wagenja wa viwanja mnataka nini?	What do those who live in wasteland want?
Majenzi mnataka nini?	What do the builders want?
Waskaji yumo jelani unataka nini?	What do people in prison want?
Madenti wantaka nini?	What do students want?
Mapromota munataka nini?	What do promoters want?

Saavedra Casco: Rap, Urban Culture and Protest in Tanzania 239

Na sisi wasanii tunataka nini?	And what do we artists want?
Haki, herufi zake chache sana neno haki,	Rights! Very few letters for the word
Haikuiazimu kushika bunduki, haki!	It must not be necessary to hold a rifle to get it.

(Excerpt of 'Haki', from Sugu's album *Itikadi*, G.M.C Records 2002.
Transcript and translation by JASC)

In the final line, he argues that rights are a necessity for everyone and that obtaining them by violent means is the final and most extreme action that must be taken. He argues that people must claim their rights; Mr. II himself claims that as a Tanzanian and human being he will continue expressing the idea that the rights of everyone must be acknowledged, whether they are rich or poor, young or old, learned or uneducated, and so forth.

Joseph Haule, also known as Professor Jay (or Profesa Jay), began his career as rapper as a member of Hardblasters in 2000, using at that time the name of Nigga Jay. He contributed some of the best tracks to the successful album *Funga Kazi* (Fasten the Work), including the hit 'Chemsha Bongo' (Use Your Brain), which impressed the audience with its new and fresh style (Gesthuizen, 2002c). In 2001 Professor Jay initiated his solo career with a remarkable album *Machozi, Jasho na Damu* (Tears, Sweat and Blood). In this album Professor Jay deals with several topics. In the introduction to the title song of the album, he enacts an imaginary conversation between himself and an old man who questions the validity of rap music, arguing about its reputation as *musiki ya kihuni* (music for vagrants and thieves). Professor Jay replies brilliantly with what is probably the best synthesis of the significance and objectives of Tanzanian hip-hop. He asserts that rap not only is not a bad influence for youth but, on the contrary, is the best instrument to expose injustice, inequality and all the other problems that affect Tanzanian society; it is also a medium to create consciousness about these problems in order to solve them.

Several of the songs on this album are good samples of Professor Jay's commitment. 'Machozi, Jasho na Damu', for instance, is an excellent summary of the difficult times that many Tanzanians encounter with poverty, insecurity and lack of opportunities. Another track, 'Ndio Mzee' (Yes Sir!) portrays an imaginary encounter between a politician – by his voice we deduce that he is an old, experienced man – with a crowd who listens to his speech. The politician promises a lot of things, many impossible to achieve in the current situation of the country, only to gain support in the elections. In the middle of the song the politician asks the audience for questions, then a young man questions all these useless promises and asks why politicians take into account the people only while campaigning. This song is a clear reference to the growing lack of credibility that the ruling political class has for many Tanzanians. It was a hit in Dar es Salaam, and the main radio stations, such as Radio One, frequently played the track and contributed to its popularity. In spite of the fact that the song is an acerbic criticism of the Tanzanian political class, it seems that authorities respected the public freedom of expression (probably helped by the fact that the song does not mention specific allusions to, or names of, any real politicians).

Another standout song is 'Bongo Dar es Salaam', an ingenious, incisive depiction of Dar es Salaam. In recent years a sense of uncertainty about personal safety in this city has grown among residents and visitors. Many who are familiar with Dar es Salaam feel that the city has very unsafe areas not only for the most obvious victims – *Wazungu* (white people) and other foreign visitors – but for many local residents as well. By looking at local newspapers we see that these fears are not unfounded. Pickpocketing, theft and abuse by the authorities against local inhabitants, rural newcomers and those unfamiliar with the city are facts that occur in a context of legal impunity and pose a continuous threat for personal safety. Professor Jay criticizes this situation, arguing that in Dar es Salaam many inhabitants have lost respect for the values taught by elders, that they only want to have fun without working, and that they rob people who are themselves in need. This song also decries the way lack of manners are degrading the behavior of younger generations in the city. In the chorus listeners are given a blunt warning about all the dangers of the city:

Kiitikio	*Chorus*
Bongo eeee bongo Daressalaam	Bongo eeee bongo Daressalaam
Utalialialialia bongo Daressalaam	You will cry in bongo Daressalaam
Kaa chonjo ee Ndani ya Daressalaam	Watch out inside Dar es Salaam
Utalialialialia ndani ya Daressalaam	You will cry inside Daressalaam
Bongo ya sasa si ya mwaka arobaini na saba	'Bongo' nowdays is not that of the year 47, even gradmothers become prostitutes
Mpaka bibivizee sasa wanafanya ukahaba	I don't know what to say that you can understand me
Sijui niseme nini ili mniweze kunielewa Na sijui nifanye nini nisaidie wanaoonewa	And I don't know what to do to help all those who are ill-treated
Hakuna heshima ni vurugu mechi katika jamii	There is no respect, there is complete confusion in the society
Hakuna utii wala mafunzo ya manabii na wezi wa mfukoni wanachomwa moto kinyama	There is no obedience nor teachings from the prophets
Mwingine hajaiba kapewa kesi kwa uhasama	And pick pockets are sent to the fire like animals while someone who has not stolen is sent to the court

Ni nani atayejua na sheria iko mkononi	Who shall know that law is at hand?
Watu wa bongo mbona hamna utu moyoni	Why do people of 'Bongo' lack humanity in their hearts?
Vijana wamejibana ili wapate mtaji wa biashara	Youth squeeze each other to get money to make business
Mnawaita Machinga ingawa wote si kutoka Mtwara	You call them 'Machinga' although None of them are from Mtwara
Mbaya kuliko zote mnapovunja vibanda vyao	The worst thing is when they destroy their huts
Wengine walikuwa wezi je warudie zama zao?	And others who were thieves, when shall they have their turn?
Ni mshike mshike sometimes vita na polisi	They are arrested sometimes when there are clashes with the police
Wao na sisi rungu na pingu kama ibilisi	For them and us only clubs and handcuffs as if we were the Devil
Kwetu uswahilini ni mambo ya kila siku	These matters happen every day in our homeland
Na ni kama kuibiwa cheni kweye ngoma ya mchiriku	It is like when they steal your gold chain when you are in a Mchiriku's dance
Wabongo wanapenda sana starehe kuliko kazi	'Bongo' dwellers much prefer fun than work
Wanatamani wangezaliwa Brunei ili wamwage radhi	They'd have liked to be born in Brunei In order to be full of satisfaction

(Excerpt of 'Bongo Dar es Salaam', from Professor Jay's album *Machozi, Jasho na Damu*, FKW Records, 2001. Transcript by Africanhiphop.com/Madunia foundation, translation by JASC)

This fragment of the song shows us the straightforwardness of Professor Jay's message, a consistent characteristic of many of his songs that, together with superb music, has given him well-deserved popularity in Tanzania.

Finally, we mention the work of the Wagosi wa Kaya duo, which has been storming the Tanzanian hip-hop scene since the beginning of the new century. The members are Mkoloni (Fredy Mariki) and Dr. John (John Simba Evans). They formed the group in Tanga, a port city north of Dar es Salaam, which has an old and strong tradition of Swahili poetry (Knappert, 1979: 209–32). The name of this duo is taken from Kisambaa, a local language of the Tanga region and means 'The men of the village'. Contrary to the case of Mr. II and several other artists that appear on Internet websites, the two members who form this group have only a limited space on specialized websites and there is little information about them. However, nowadays Wagosi wa Kaya are very popular in

Tanzania among both young and old people and their songs have reached remote areas where radios and audio tape sets are only run on batteries. Their two albums – *Ukweli Mtupu* (The Naked Truth) and *Ripoti Kamili* (The Complete Report) – broke all sales records, and with the support of the company GMC productions this dynamic duo have succeeded in making two music videos with most of the songs that appear in their albums. They also contributed one track to the album *Bongo Flava*, the first compilation of Tanzanian hip-hop launched internationally at the end of 2004, a fact that will surely help to make them known abroad (Gesthuizen, 2004: 4–5).

Many reasons can explain the fast success of Wagosi wa Kaya. One is a musical style that combines several influences, making their work sound more like accessible pop than hardcore rap. They also collaborate with some of the most famous local rappers, such as Dully Sykes, Bw. Misosi, Johnny Walker, Comorien and Professor Jay. Their lyrics – which combine the sophisticated vocabulary of coastal Swahilis with slang and local language – almost always display a social commitment or depict of the common problems that affect the Tanzanian society. One song alerts youth to the danger of HIV: 'Titamtambuaje?' (How Will You Recognize It?). Another song, 'Traffic', narrates a common story about the corruption of police officers that control traffic in the main avenues of the city. We also find a song that portrays a habit that has become common among urban Tanzanians, the use of mobile phones: 'Simu za Mkononi' (Mobile Phone). However, the most remarkable lyrics are those that express political protest. 'Tanga kunani?' (What Is There in Tanga?) is a brilliant description of the current state of Tanga. The city was an important economic centre during the last years of the colonial period and the first two decades of the *Ujamaa* regime. Nevertheless, its prosperity has gradually been fading away up to the present day. That has meant that many youth have had to migrate to Dar es Salaam and many local businesses have collapsed. In this context, Wagosi wa Kaya talk about a city that still preserves many of its Swahili customs. They complain about the current state of many inhabitants of the city and evoke the wealth of the city's past to contrast with the current economic depression. As in Professor Jay's 'Bongo Dar es Salaam', the chorus of the song is quite indicative:

Kiitikio	*Chorus*
Tanga, kunani paleee, mbona kila kitu pale kimekufa, Tanga, kunani paleee, mbona maisha pale yanasikitisha.	What is there in Tanga? Why has everything faded away there? What is there in Tanga? Why is life there so disappointing?
Halafu hali ya sasa sii kama ile ya zamani, ukaenda ovyo tu utauza kila kitu chako cha thamani.	Now things are not like in the past, If you are not careful you will Sell all your valuables.

Matajiri wa enzi zile ukiwaona
leo hii tena hawana thamani Enzi
zile bwana mkoa wa Tanga kila
kitu mambo yalikuwa swafi.
Mijikazi ilikuwa tele, na
kulikuwa hakuna mambo ya
ukorofi, lakini sasa hivi thubutu,
twandelea kuchakaa mpaka tutoke
ukurutu, hakuna ndimaa, kilo mtu
ambiwa ajifanya mvuvi ati, na
ukamshauri mtu akushushia
varangati, astaghafirullai laadhim!

If you see the rich men of the past
Nowadays, they are ruined.
For the gentleman of the old Tanga
Region, everything was ok.
There was plenty of jobs everywhere
And there were not wicked deeds, but now
certainly we are so worn out we get rashes.
There are no jobs but people are told not to
be lazy, and you advise a man to leave
vagrancy,
For God's sake!

Ndege pia kwa mwezi twaona
mara moja, basi balaa hili watu
tumekuwa twaishi maisha ya
tumbiri, sijui tusomeane alubadili,
ili tumkamate alotu filisi utajiri.
Bandari nayo sasa yachungulia
shimo, zamani waweza ona miji meli
palee

We see a plane once a month
Thus, this misfortune
We have been living the life of a monkey
I don't know what we must learn in order
to catch those who left us in bankruptcy
If you take a glance at the harbour
You will see only a vacant hole, and in the
past there were many ships!

wala haina kipimo, lakini!
sasa hivi si meli tena, wala hazina
uwezo wa kubeba hata kontena.
Ukiondoa Wahindi na Waarabu,
Waswahili wenye pesa ni wa
kuhesabu, halafu wikiendi angalia
nyendo zao, kuchukua wake za;
watu na kutaka mambo nje ya
uwezo wao.

No calculations are made, but!
There are no ships now, neither is there
possibility of carrying even a container.
Except for the Indians and the Arabs
You can count the Swahili with money
With the fingers of your hand, but then, look
at their behaviour! They get women of other
people and want things beyond their
possibilities.

(Excerpt from 'Tanga kunani?', from Wagosi wa Kaya's album *Ukweli Mtupu*, GMC Records, 2001, Dar es Salaam. Transcript by Bongoxplosion/darhotwire.com/, translation by JASC)

Another striking song is 'Tumeshtuka!' (We Are Shocked!), which narrates in an acidic and eloquent way the attitude of Tanzanian authorities who currently privilege foreign companies – mainly from Britain – in order to get the best investment opportunities. The song starts with a strong assertion: privileged treatment for foreign companies has not significantly changed since the beginning of the independent era. The chorus once again stresses the artists' opinion on this topic:

Kiitikio	*Chorus*
Kwenye ubia kitu gani tunapata? Tunaibiwa! Kwenye ubia kitu gani tunapata watu? Ehh! Tumeshtuka!	What do we get with foreign corporations? We are getting robbed! What do we get with foreign corporations people? Ehh! We are really shocked!
Nimepata uhuru tokea mwaka wa sitini na moja, lakini mpaka leo maendeleo utanikungoja Sasa watanzania hivi ninakwenda wapi? Inaelekea mpaka sasa na mimi nijue niko wapi!	I got freedom in the year 61 But up to now development is still waiting for me Tanzanians! Where am I going right now? It has led me to the point where now I do not know where I am!
Wa maingereza mengi sana juu ya ubia, ukweli kwamba hakuna kinachotuingia Elimu ya nandoa juu ya huu binamshaji haendelewi bwana, mimi naona ni wa ubabaishaji	Many English (companies) are in this partnership, and certainly there is nothing that reaches us, wisdom is not evident in this privatization, it is not going anywhere Sir, and I see it only makes confusion.
Mambo ya kiongozi jamani yanakwenda Na tupaji na najua kiongozi wengine hawana daimu ya kupata kinachohitaji Wanachuma hapa kwetu Ulaya na wanakwenda kuifasi Kama uliko humjui unakosa si naweza wasiwasi Unakuta ni wewe na mwandiko kwa heri, Indas Indas,	The leaders' concerns go on, my God, As usual, and I know other leaders do not have enough time to get all they need They pick everything from here for Europe And go there to refresh themselves Don't feel bad if you don't know what your mistake is You find what your fault is when the agreements have been made [...]
Wananchi imekataa hata hakuna wasiwasi Ni mtindo asubuhi siku hio ni shela Ya kiongozi, wazazi wetu imempaswa Wasije wa vimeskosi wakafikia uamuzi wa kutaka kuminamshia jeshi.	Citizens are refused without any doubt That is the style in the morning when everything is covered up for leaders, but in the case of our parents they must not arrive with rolls sweet, if they do they shall confront the army officers!

(Excerpt from 'Tumeshtuka', from Wagosi wa Kaya's album *Ripoti Kamili*, GMC Records, 2003, Dar es Salaam. Transcript and translation by JASC)

The song continues with a blatant critique of the government's policy of giving many advantages for investment to foreign companies, while Tanzanians face many disadvantages if they try to start their own businesses. According to Wagosi wa Kaya this situation makes them feel in an state of complete helplessness. '*Wananchi tunaishi kama watoto yatima inchi haina Baba hii wala haina Mama*' (we citizens live as if we were orphans, without neither father nor mother!). They refer to how *wazungu* can invest in any field, while at the end of the song they compare this benevolent attitude towards foreigners with all the obstacles that Tanzanian entrepreneurs have to face, making an allusion to the case of the hip-hop music companies. This composition has been included among Wagosi wa Kaya's songs in the video named after their second album, *Ripoti Kamili*. Although the video is not particularly attractive, the freedom to perform it publicly shows again an apparent absence of censure for hip-hop songs with blunt critiques of the government policy to privilege foreign investors. As in the case of Professor Jay's political songs, there is no mention of any specific politician.

From all these examples it is possible to see how messages in hip-hop songs demonstrate a tremendous commitment to express popular non-conformity with the current political, social and economic situation of Tanzania. They share a clearly defined style in which the lyrics denounce the negative actions of politicians, police and ordinary citizens; they also advise people not to imitate those attitudes.

Conclusion: Will Social Protest Remain in Tanzanian Hip-hop?

In this article I have described how Tanzanian hip-hop has developed since its first appearance and how it was transformed from an underground and marginal musical genre to a successful, expanding industry. The article also refers to the links between Tanzanian hip-hop and Swahili poetry, stressing that competition, social protest and collective attention to appropriate behaviour are common features establishing cultural continuity over time and across generations. Certainly, the rapid change that Tanzanian rap has experienced does not help us to deduce the extent to which the genre will maintain these qualities. Of special interest is the issue of the commercialization and internationalization of rap music, together with opportunities for rap artists to acquire wealth. Up to the present time successful rappers and promoters have continued with their original communal vision of the industry, organizing contests and congresses and joining forces to promote new hip-hop performers. One also sees a collective acceptance of the principle of maintaining a critical attitude in lyrics consistent with the concept of 'keeping it real', as conceived since the first years of Tanzanian hip-hop. It is difficult to guess if the growing earnings of this industry might spoil this communal spirit in the short term. It is also difficult to predict whether there might be a gradual change of lyric contents, from the social and political

246   Journal of Asian and African Studies 41(3)

to banal and naïve matters. If Tanzanian hip-hop artists wish to keep on using their music as a way of expression and a vehicle of communication, Swahili language will still be used, and this fact will surely help to maintain many of the characteristics mentioned in this article.

A systematic study of Tanzanian hip-hop is needed from the perspective of social and cultural history. A careful study of lyrics through analysis of the difficult, but amazingly meaningful *Kiswahili cha mtaani* (literally 'Swahili of the street' – Swahili slang) will also contribute to understanding the mentality of rappers and their arguments, and the relationship between them and their audience. Such a study, complemented with an analysis of the current Tanzanian socio-political context, would surely provide a framework for the changing environment of young Tanzanians in an era of globalization. The growing interest in this subject by scholars of diverse social disciplines around the world is a clear testimony of its importance. It shows that in Africa not everything is sadness and despair, but that on the contrary, as Tanzanian rappers have shown us, there is also vitality and hope.

Acknowledgement

I would like to thank James Brennan and Prakash Shah who read the manuscript of this article and gave me helpful comments regarding its contents. I am also very grateful to John Marston who reviewed the text and helped me to correct the writing of this article, and finally I give my gratitude to Katherine Hunt for her valuable assistance in editing this research.

Notes

1. Information from: http://news.bbc.co.uk/1/hi/world/africa/country_profiles/1072330.stm
2. Information from: http://news.bbc.co.uk/1/hi/world/africa/country_profiles/1072330.stm#leaders
3. It is worth mentioning that associating musicians with vagrancy, alcoholism and drugs was common in Tanzania society before arrival of rap, a feeling depicted by the famous Remmy Ongala in his song 'Musiki Asili yake Wapi?' (Where is the origin of music?) from the album, *Songs for the Poor Man* (1989).
4. Information from: http://news.bbc.co.uk/1/hi/world/africa/country_profiles/1072330.stm#leaders.
5. The term comes from the nickname '*bongo*' (brain), given to the city many years ago and is very common today.

References

Abdulaziz, Mohamed H. (1979) *Muyaka: Nineteenth-century Swahili Popular Poetry*. Nairobi: Kenya Literature Bureau.

Biersteker, Ann (1996) *Kujibizana. Questions of Language and Power in Nineteenth- and Twentieth-century Poetry in Kiswahili*. East Lansing, MI: Michigan State University Press (African Series, 4).

Biersteker, Ann and Ibrahim Noor Shariff (eds) (1995) *Mashairi ya Vita vya Kuduhu* (Poem of the Kuduhu War). East Lansing, MI: Michigan State University Press (African Historical Sources, 7).

Bongoxplosion (2004) *Wasanii wa bongo wakamua* (Bongo's Artists Squeeze out UK). Available at: http://www.darhotwire.com/Bongoxplosion/2004/11/04/546.htlm

Buyanza, Eric 'DoT' (2002) *Historia ya Bongo Hip-hop* (History of Bongo Hip-hop). Available at: http://www.darhotwire.com/

Edward, Willy (2004) 'Tuzo za Kilimanjaro. Mkombozi wa wasanii Tanzania' (Kilimanjaro's Awards. The Redeemer of Tanzanian Artists), *Majira*, 17 July. Available at: http://www.bcstimes.com/majira/viewnews

Englert, Birgit (2003) 'Bongo Flava (Still) Hidden "Underground" Rap from Morogoro, Tanzania', *Vienna Journal of African Studies* 5(3): 72–93.

Gesthuizen, Thomas (2002a) *Hiphop in Tanzania*. Available at: http://www.niza.nl/

Gesthuizen, Thomas (2002b) *Saleh J: Tanzanian Pioneer*. Available at: http://www.africanhiphop.com/

Gesthuizen, Thomas (2002c) *Tanzanian Hip Hop: The Old School (1991–1999)*. Available at: http://www.africanhiphop.com/

Gesthuizen, Thomas (2004) *X Plastaz & Bongo Flava: Tanzanian Hip Hop Released Internationally*. Available at: http://www.africanhiphop.com/

Gesthuizen, Thomas and Peter-Jan Haas (1998) *Ndani ya Bongo. Kiswahili Rap Keeping It Real*. Available at: http://www.africanhiphop.com/

Graebner, Werner (2000) 'Ngoma ya Ukae: Competition Social Structure in Tanzanian Dance Music Songs', in Frank Gunderson and Gregory Barz (eds) *Mashindano! Competitive Music Performance in East Africa*, pp. 295–318. Dar es Salaam: Mkuki na Nyota Publishers.

Harries, Lyndon (1962) *Swahili Poetry*. Oxford: Clarendon Press.

Khatib, Muhammed Seif (1975) *Utenzi wa Ukombozi wa Zanzibar* (Poem of the Liberation of Zanzibar). Dar es Salaam: Oxford University Press (Vito vya Kiswahili, 3).

Knappert, Jan (1979) *Four Centuries of Swahili Verse: A Literary History and Anthology*. London: Heinemann Educational Books.

Lengua, Emmanuel (2004) 'Wamarekani Kuinua Wasanii Tanzania' (Americans Raise Tanzanian Artists), *Majira*, 11 August. Available at: http://www.bcstimes.com/majira/viewnews;

Lienhardt, Peter (1968) 'Introduction', in Hasani bin Ismail (ed.) *Utenzi wa Swifa ya Nguvumali* (Poem to Praise Nguvmali), pp. 1–80. Oxford: Clarendon Press.

Mahimbi, E.M. (1981) *Utenzi wa Chama cha Mapinduzi* (Poem of the Revolutionary Party). Dar es Salaam: Tanzania Publishing House.

Massamba, David P.B. (1983) 'Utunzi wa Ushairi wa Kiswahili' (Composition of Swahili Poetry), in *Fasihi* (Literature), Makala za Semina ya Kimataifa ya Waandishi wa Kiswahili, Taasisi ya Uchunguzi wa Kiswahili (Procedures of the International Seminar of Swahili's Writers, Institute of Kiswahili Research), pp. 55–95. Dar es Salaam.

Mazrui, Alamin M. and Ibrahim Noor Shariff (1992) *The Swahili, Idiom and Identity of an African People*. New York: Africa World Press.

Mdundo, Minaeli O. (1987) *Utenzi wa Jeshi la Wananchi Tanzania* (Poem of the Popular Army of Tanzania). Dar es Salaam: Tanzania Publishing House.

248   Journal of Asian and African Studies 41(3)

Middleton, John (1992) *The World of the Swahili: An African Mercantile Civilization.* New Haven, CT: Yale University Press.

Mkangara, Seleman (2004) 'Kongamano la hip hop ni dira ya muziki' (Hip Hop Congress is the Vision of Music), *Majira*, 30 October. Available at: http://www.bcstimes.com/majira/viewnews

Muhanika, Henry R. (1981) *Utenzi wa Vita vya Kagera* (Poem of the Kagera's War). Dar es Salaam: Dar es Salaam University Press.

Mulokozi, M.M. (1999) Interview with author, Dar es Salaam, October and November.

Mulokozi, M.M. (2000) Interview with author, Dar es Salaam, April.

Mulokozi, M.M. and T.S.Y. Sengo (1995) *History of Kiswahili Poetry.* Dar es Salaam: Institute of Kiswahili Research.

Mwisheshe, Said (2004) 'K-Bazil: Musiki Unataka Watu Wenye Elimu' (K-Bazil: Music Wants People with Education), *Majira*, 24 October. Available at: http://www.bcstimes.com/majira/viewnews

Perullo, Alex (forthcoming) '"Here's a Little Something Local": An Early History of Hip Hop in Dar es Salaam, Tanzania, 1984–1997', in James Brennan, Andrew Burton and Yusuf Lawi (eds) *Dar es Salaam: The History of an Emerging East African Metropolis.*

Pouwels, Randall. L. (1987) *Horn and Crescent.* New York: Cambridge University Press.

Saavedra, José Arturo (2002) 'Swahili Poetry as a Historical Source: Utenzi, War Poems and the German Conquest of East Africa, 1888–1910', PhD dissertation, SOAS, University of London.

Shariff, Ibrahim Noor (1988) *Tungo Zetu* (Our Compositions). Trenton, NJ: The Red Sea Press.

Suleyman, Miguel (2004) 'Seventies Music Is All the Rage Again', *The East African*, 10 May.

Toroka, Erick (2002) *Why Local Firms Ignore Tanzanian Artists?* Available at: http://www.africanhiphop.com/

José Arturo Saavedra Casco was born in Mexico City, Mexico. He holds a PhD in African History and Swahili Literature from the School of Oriental and African Studies (SOAS), University of London. He has published several articles in Germany, Mexico, USA and Tanzania on historiography, African history and Swahili poetry as a historical source. He has given lectures on Swahili language and culture, African history and historiography in several prestigious Mexican universities since 1993. He has also given seminars at SOAS, at the Institute of Kiswahili Research, University of Dar es Salaam and in several other academic institutions in Mexico. He is currently a member of the academic staff of the Centre of Asian and African Studies at El Colegio de México, Mexico City. He is also a member of the African Studies Association (ASA).
Address: Camino al Ajusco no.20, Pedregal de Santa Teresa, C.P. 10740 Mexico D.F. MEXICO. (jsaave@colmex.mx)

[13]

"ROCKING THE BOAT" IN SOUTH AFRICA? VOËLVRY MUSIC AND AFRIKAANS ANTI-APARTHEID SOCIAL PROTEST IN THE 1980S

By Albert Grundlingh

The British social and cultural historian, Arthur Marwick, concluded his magisterial book on the cultural revolution of the 1960s in the West with a very brief final sentence on the transformation: "there has been nothing quite like it; nothing will be quite the same again."[1] This deceptively simple and deliberately vague assertion masks an array of nuanced historical judgments in which Marwick teased out the complexities and contradictions of the sixties.

In trying to characterize the decade, American author Hunter Thompson has succinctly formulated the analytical problem inherent in the dynamics of the period:

> History is hard to know—but even without being sure of "history" it seems entirely reasonable to think that every now and then the energy of a whole generation comes to a head in a long fine flash, for reasons that nobody really understands at the time—and which never explain, in retrospect, what actually happened.... You could strike sparks anywhere.[2]

While there seems to be a firm understanding that the 1960s represent the confluence of meaningful social forces, there are some explanatory doubts as to how and why it happened. The conundrum invites historical analysis; the outlines of the phenomenon may appear clear, but the reasons for that are not immediately apparent nor is its historical significance self-evident.[3]

In a similar vein Afrikaans anti-apartheid social protest music during the 1980s was reminiscent, albeit in a much more muted form, of the cultural and social challenges to the status quo in the West two decades earlier. Perceptive

---

[1] Arthur Marwick, *The Sixties: Cultural Revolution in Britain, France, Italy, and the United States of America* (Oxford, 1998), 806.

[2] Hunter S. Thompson, *Fear and Loathing in Las Vegas: A Savage Journey to the Heart of the American Dream* (New York, 1971), 67–68.

[3] For conflicting views in the American context see for example Domick Cavallo, *A Fiction of the Past: The Sixties in American History* (New York, 1999) and Roger Kimball, *The Long March: How the Cultural Revolution of the 1960's Changed America* (San Francisco, 2000).

observers picked up on this. Thus American journalist Tom Masland, who was based in South Africa, reported in mid-1989 on the similarities in dress, lyrics, and general political outlook between the followers of Afrikaans counterculture and what he considered to be their earlier American counterparts.[4] The analogy, suggestive as it is, should not however be overdrawn. The South African variant had its own local character and emphases that impacted in a particular manner and generated its own complicated processes and codes of understanding. These need to be untangled and assessed primarily in the context they were moulded.

This article has several related aims. It seeks to understand the conditions under which anti-apartheid Afrikaans protest music emerged in the '80s and why it took about twenty years after oppositional youth movements in the West for roughly comparable developments among Afrikaner youth to gain some traction. Central to the protest was an attempt to question, and even to reformulate through the medium of music, what it meant to be an Afrikaner during the latter phases of apartheid. The analysis disaggregates the dynamics and nuances of this process. Moreover, the actual impact of the phenomenon at the time is evaluated through a critical assessment of the claims made by band members and journalists. Finally the way in which the memory of this movement continued to have an influence among young Afrikaner people well into the post-apartheid era is explored.

Emergence and Social Background

One of the salient features of the tumultuous 1980s in South Africa was the cycle of on-going black protest orchestrated by the United Democratic Front and other extra-parliamentary anti-apartheid organizations and the declaration of successive states of emergencies by the predominantly Afrikaner National Party government. Overtly anti-apartheid Afrikaner voices were relatively mute during this period. However, initiatives such as the meeting between mainly Afrikaner intelligentsia and some of the leaders of the banned African National Congress in Dakar in Senegal in 1987 as well as the appearance of an uncompromisingly critical Afrikaans newspaper, the *Vrye Weekblad* (Free Weekly) stand out as distinct markers. To this must be added a sprinkling of Afrikaans literary works and some tentative soul searching in some Afrikaner churches about the morality of apartheid. [5]

---

[4] Cited in "Kerkorrel en die nuwe ANC," *Die Burger*, 23 June 1989. The report appeared in the *Chicago Tribune* of 8 June 1989, under the heading "Afrikaans Rock Tweaks Noses of Conservative Elders."

[5] Herman Kitshoff, "Andersdenkende verset: Afrikaanse kulturele verset teen apartheid en Afrikaner kontak met die African National Congress in die tagtigerjare" (M.A. thesis, University of Stellenbosch, 2002), passim; C. Faure, "*Vrye Weekblad* (1988–1993): Profiel van 'n

Afrikaans anti-apartheid musicians saw themselves as quite distinct from ₀these developments. As aprominent band member explained cryptically: "Our protest was not as subtle as those of the novelists; ours was an in your face, f—k you movement."[6] In rock and roll style, with an overlay of punk, hard-hitting lyrics satirized the state, Afrikaans political leaders, the South African Defence Force, the apartheid system, and white middle-class values. [7] Known as the "Voëlvry" musicians with a band called the "Gereformeerde [Reformed] Blues Band" as the main act, they toured the country in 1989. "Voëlvry" could be interpreted as free as a bird or outlawed—the double meaning was probably intended—and the band's name was a satirical word play on the Dutch Reformed Churches. These young(ish) musicians with their explicit anti-apartheid message unleashed an enthusiasm that was succinctly described as "Boer Beatlemania." [8]

It was seen as a unique phenomenon by the media; for the first time full-blown rock and roll with biting social commentary was seen to challenge the generally perceived staid and shackled Afrikaans cultural and political world. The Afrikaans establishment media, though it may have had reservations about the way the musicians expressed themselves, nevertheless gave them ample coverage. One of the possible reason for the media investment in Voëlvry was that it was involved in its own repositioning at the time. During the late '80s the mainline Afrikaans press, which used to enjoy cordial relations with the government, became increasingly uneasy with the way in which an aging president P.W. Botha seemed to blunder from crisis to crisis. Apart from the newsworthiness of Voelvry, giving them exposure was also a way of asserting a modicum of independence from the government.[9]

---

alternatiewe Afrikaanse koerant," *Communicatio* 19, 2 (1993), 22–31: Max du Preez, *Pale Native: Memories of a Renegade Reporter* (Cape Town, 2003), 16–167, 171–211; Gary Baines, "'South Africa's Vietnam'? Literary History and Cultural Memory of the Border War," *South African Historical Journal* 49 (2003), 172–92.

[6] M-Net TV Documentary, 12 August 2003 (Koos Kombuis).

[7] The lyrics of some of the key songs appear in the Appendix to this article.

[8] "Nuwe lied vir jong Suid-Afrika," *Die Suid-Afrikaan*, June 1989.

[9] For the Afrikaans media see George Claassen, "Breaking the Mold of Political Subservience: 'Vrye Weekblad' and the Afrikaans Alternative Press," in Les Switzer and Mohamed Adhikari, eds., *South Africa's Resistance Press: Alternative Voices in the Last Generation Under Apartheid* (Athens, Ohio, 2000), 403–57; Jon-Adriaan Stemmet and Leo Barnard, "The Relationship Between P.W. Botha and the Pro-establishment Press during the 1980's," *Historia* 49, 1 (May 2004), 154–65.

Voelvry could claim diverse places of birth, but central in its making was the small "Black Sun" theater in Yeoville in Johannesburg, where various irreverent Afrikaans cabaret artists under a variety of stage names plied their trade. As the acts attracted a growing and increasingly enthusiastic audience, some of them moved on to bigger venues. With a small sponsorship of the *Vrye Weekblad* and an enterprising record company, Shifty Records, the musicians decided to take a collection of the shows on a nationwide tour in 1989.[10]

The driving force behind Voëlvry was a number of young men in their twenties or early thirties: Ralph Rabie, known as Johannes Kerkorrel—a stage name taken from a trademark Dutch organ (the adoption of such a name carried strong mocking tones of the somber music of the Dutch Reformed Church), played a major role in dealing with the media. James Phillips who had something of a bilingual background and assumed the stage name, Bernoldus Niemand (Mr. Nobody as he liked to style himself) was a talented musician with a degree in music from the University of the Witwatersrand. André du Toit, known successively as André Letoit and Koos Kombuis, had a fine turn of phrase and a dry wit. They were managed by "Dagga" (Marijuana) Dirk Uys who shared the general quirkiness of the musicians, but was blessed with certain entrepreneurial and organizational skills. Other musicians were

> Willem Moller (known as Mr. Volume), Gary Herselman with the *pseudonym* of Piet Pers and Jannie (Hanepoot) van Tonder. The lone female was Tonia Selley, who went under the name of Karla Krimpelien.[11]

Although these musicians received considerable media attention as a remarkable anti-apartheid strand, seen in a broader African context they slotted into a time-honored tradition. Oppositional music and decolonization have a long and complex interwoven history in Africa.[12] In South Africa black protest music has been a well-established feature of the cultural landscape. In the 1930s and 1940s jazz and blues music as well as distinctive forms of township music such as *marabi* carried with them their own implicit and sometimes explicit political messages. During the repressive 1960s with the banning of the African National Congress and strenuous government attempts to implement a divide-and-rule

---

[10] "Voëlvry," *Die Burger*, 29 April 2002; Du Preez, *Pale Native*, 207; "Rustelose gees," *Insig*, 28 February 2003, 34.

[11] "Voëlvry," *Die Burger*, 29 April 2002; M-Net TV Documentary, 12 August 2003; "Rustelose gees," *Insig*, 28 February 2003.

[12] For example Thomas Turino, *Nationalists, Cosmopolitans and Popular Music in Zimbabwe* (Chicago, 2000); Christopher Waterman, *Juju: A Social History and Ethnography of an African Popular Music* (Chicago, 1990).

policy based on ethnic divisions, earlier popular music had to contend with officially sanctioned traditional, neo-traditional, and religious music. Many jazz and
other musicians shunned by the South African Broadcasting Corporation which
followed government policy by promoting narrow ethnic music, and left in the
lurch by recording companies that followed suit, had emigrated, disillusioned with
political developments in South Africa. During the 1980s, however, a vibrant and
virile popular culture reappeared in tandem with the resurgence of opposition to
apartheid. Increasingly, township bands and choirs shared the stage with politicians at huge United Democratic Front and trade union meetings.[13]

Voëlvry musicians were aware of these developments and some moved in
the same social circles as certain black artists. One member used to play in a
multiracial band, "Winston's Jive Mix." This does not imply, however, that their
music incorporated elements of township music or that their lyrics reflected the
specific concerns of black people. Their music spoke to a young(ish) white
audience and the nature of the issues differed accordingly.[14] The use of the term
"blues band" is perhaps significant. Blues music is of course originally an
African-American genre and the use of this term, like their stage names, may have
been a deliberate attempt to jar existing Afrikaner sensibilities.

Despite their on-stage appearance as down-at-heel dissolute punk rock
artists, the musicians came from respectable middle class homes. A good sprinkling had had tertiary education. What is striking, is that at least three members
were the sons of ministers of religion and some of the others had a strict religious
upbringing.[15] Given the nature of the clerical profession, the parents were probably quite articulate and exposure to such a home environment might go some way
in understanding the verbal acuity of the musicians and their facility for assem-
bling novel lyrics. Moreover, their intimate knowledge of the inner workings of
the Afrikaner social world in which "dominees" played a prominent part, might
have honed their senses for selecting suitable cultural elements for subversion. On
another level, while bearing in mind that psychoanalytical interpretations of the

---

[13] On the history of South African black music, see, for example, David Coplan, *In
Township Tonight! South Africa's Black City Music and Theatre* (Johannesburg, 1985); Louise
Meintjes, *Sound of Africa! Making Music Zulu in a South African Studio* (Durham, 2003); Ingrid
Byerly, "Mirror, Mediator, and Prophet: The Music Indaba of Late-apartheid South Africa,"
Ethnomusicology 42, 1 (1998), 1–44; Chris Ballentine, "A Brief History of South African Popular
Music," *Popular Music* 8, 3, (1989), 305–310.

[14] M-Net TV Documentary, 12 August 2003; E-mail interview with Koos Kombuis, 5 July
2004.

[15] M-Net TV Documentary, 12 August 2003.

488   ALBERT GRUNDLINGH

wellsprings of behavior can be overdetermined, the dynamics of defiance against parental authority may indeed have featured in the make-up of some Voëlvry musicians.[16]

The texture of this social composition shows some similarities with what had happened over two decades before in the much-vaunted cultural revolution of the sixties in the West. Irwin and Debi Unger have pointed out that in the United States, counterculture

> was the child of prosperity. Hippies renounced the bourgeois rat race of nine-to-five jobs, manicured suburban lawns, and prudent lives. Some professed to despise private property and possessions generally, but most of them came from that very milieu. Almost all of them were suburban dropouts who lived off the surplus and cast-offs of an affluent society. Some were straight remittance men and women who survived on checks sent by Dad or Mom.[17]

In the case of Afrikaans anti-establishment elements, the degree of financial dependency might have varied, but in general their outlook accorded with that of their counterparts of an earlier epoch in the West.

A Delayed "Sixties"

The time lag between developments in the West in the sixties and their late arrival for Afrikaner youth in the eighties calls for an understanding of the social and cultural dynamics at work at different historical junctures. In Afrikaner circles the 1960s were the high point of apartheid and the system was touted as the solution to potential racial conflict.[18] Illusionary as it was, the ideology nevertheless held out the promise of a secure future as far as Afrikaners were concerned, Consequently there was little need to question the system or the underlying issues and values. In conjunction with this, a conformist youth culture flourished.

Although a so-called "ducktail" subculture—recognizable by distinctive hairstyles and clothing and marked by what was considered antisocial behavior—had made its appearance in the larger cities during the late 1950s, it lacked

---

[16] Koos A. Kombuis, *Seks en drugs en boeremusiek: die memoires van 'n volksverraaier* (Cape Town, 1998), 231 (Kombuis explaining the problematical relationship with his parents); M-Net TV Documentary, 12 August, 2003.

[17] Irwin Unger and Debbie Unger, eds., *The Times Were a Changin': The Sixties Reader* (New York, 1998), 158.

[18] The most informed recent analysis of Afrikaners' belief in apartheid in the sixties is that of Hermann Giliomee, *The Afrikaners: Biography of a People* (Cape Town, 2003), esp. 534–36.

an overt political dimension and was restricted to predominantly white English speakers, failing to make significant inroads in Afrikaner ranks.[19] Rock and roll music was closely associated with "ducktails." Afrikaner culturalists were quick to regard the rock hysteria in the West during the sixties and its emergence in South Africa as an "alien and dangerous culture" representing—in contradistinction to sober and idealized Afrikaner values—a moral collapse in decadent Britain and America.[20] Elements of Afrikaner youth in the sixties nevertheless did listen to the music of the time, often transmitted from radio stations in neighboring Mozambique as it was seldom given official local airtime on the South African Broadcasting Corporation, but to them it was merely enjoyable music and they remained largely oblivious to the possibility of linking it to subversive political agendas or even thinking of it as undermining Afrikaner culture.

A further deterrent to cultural fragmentation was the introduction of compulsory military service for all white males in 1967. Cultural conformity and a firm set of assumptions about Afrikaners as a beleaguered nation in a hostile world became further entrenched as the military assembly line churned out a series of like-minded young males. Initially conscription was for nine months, but in the mid-seventies it was extended to two years as the so-called "border war" on the South West African/Namibian and Angolan borders against the South West African People's Organization and Cuban surrogates intensified. Internal and cyclical black unrest in South Africa from 1976 onwards also saw the deployment of white troops in black townships, which further added to the increased militarization of South African society. Gradually, however, the efficacy of the state's strategy and the imposition of compulsory military service were being questioned in well-coordinated and innovative initiatives such as the End Conscription Campaign (ECC) during the eighties.[21]

Although the ECC was led mainly by white\ English speakers, the emergence of the organization opened up more space for Afrikaans speakers to challenge the status quo through creative cultural expression. One such medium was music, which captured the personal disillusionment and angst generated by conscription for a war that was increasingly perceived as morally questionable and

---

[19] Kate Mooney, "Ducktails, Flick-knives and Pugnacity: Subcultural and Hegemonic Masculinity in South Africa, 1948–1960," *Journal of Southern African Studies* 24, 4 (1998), 5.

[20] Charles Hamm, "Rock and Roll in a Very Strange Society," in Richard Middleton and David Horn, eds., *Popular Music 5: Continuity and Change* (Cambridge, 1985), 160.

[21] Merran W. Phillips, "The End Conscription Campaign, 1983–1988: A Study of White Extra-Parliamentary Opposition to Apartheid" (M.A. thesis, University of South Africa, 2002).

destined to drag on in a futile manner.[22] For the first time, songs also started to appear in Afrikaans, prompting young men not to march to war but to challenge a system that forced conscription on them. Songs such as "Hou My Vas, Korporaal" (Hold Me Tight, Corporal) by James Phillips sung in a rock and roll mode, as well as offerings by Koos Kombuis in ballad form, suggested the appearance of a new Afrikaans cultural dimension. The choice of music as a vehicle of Afrikaans disenchantment took place in the absence of other overt forms of specifically Afrikaans anti-apartheid political protests. In turn the lack of other contenders helped ensure that the frustrations of the youth expressed through music were highly profiled in the press. The pressures on white middle-class young people and the exposure of their predicament added a more overtly political edge to the music than otherwise might have been the case. What had happened in the U.S. in the late sixties (with anti-war songs and protests against the American presence in Vietnam) resonated in South Africa two decades later, albeit in a muffled way.

An additional dimension in understanding the late emergence of Afrikaans protest music is the evolving dynamics of class and ethnic subjectivities. Although the Afrikaner middle-class expanded rapidly in the sixties when South Africa had one of the highest economic growth rates in the world, the identification of this class with the state and its support of apartheid had the effect of creating an inward-looking bourgeoisie, suspicious of cultural influences from the West that might contaminate what was regarded as "pure" Afrikaner values. However, as the belief in apartheid slowly eroded, the possibilities of exploring other forms of identification outside the earlier subjectivities shaped by the ethnic fold, presented themselves. Increasingly, Afrikaners regarded themselves in a less insular way. Aided by outside influences such as the introduction of television in 1975, they came to view themselves in more overtly cosmopolitan terms and thus participated more self-consciously in styles of consumption prevalent among the middle classes elsewhere in the West.[23]

This was a significant development, as Afrikaner children born in the sixties were socialized in a world where globalizing cultural impulses held more

---

[22] Michael Drewett, "Satirical Opposition in Popular Music Within Apartheid and Post-apartheid South Africa," *Society in Transition* 33, 1 (2002), 80–90; Michael Drewett, "It's My Duty Not My Choice': Narratives of Resistance to the South African Border War in Popular Music," in Chris van der Merwe and Rolf Wolfswinkel, eds., *Telling Wounds: Narrative, Trauma and Memory; Working Through the South African Armed Conflicts of the 20th Century*, Proceedings of the Conference held at the University of Cape Town, 3–5 July 2002, 127–33.

[23] Compare Jonathan Hyslop, "Why Did Apartheid's Supporters Capitulate? Whiteness, Class and Consumption in Urban South Africa, 1985–1995," *Society in Transition* 31, 1 (2000), 38–40.

sway than before and this carried a greater potential of subjectivities being rear-ranged and narratives of self being renegotiated. Elements from this generation led the quest for a new way of asserting themselves as being white and Afrikaans. They found it in rock and roll. It was a fusion of cultural ingredients not thought possible before—Afrikaans as a language had been considered too guttural and formal to be turned into credible rock and roll lyrics. Johannes Kerkorrel made the modernizing and globalizing notion of their work explicit when he stated in an interview in 1989: "Rock and roll is a universal language. It works in Europe, it works in Australia, America—and it works here."[24]

Performance

The Voëlvry countrywide tour in 1989 represented the high point of Afrikaans protest rock. Operating on a shoestring budget and under surveillance and threats from the security police, it was not a trouble-free logistical exercise. Ironically though, Dirk Uys, the manager, claimed that organizational experience he had picked up as an officer in the Defence Force during his period of conscription came into good use running an operation of this nature.[25]

They managed to draw a full house for most of the concerts but had some problems acquiring suitable venues. Some Afrikaans universities banned perfor-mances on campus and they had to find alternative venues. Their banishment from the University of Stellenbosch campus gave rise to a particular furore as Stellenbosch was supposed to be the heartland of "liberal Afrikaners." The university authorities claimed that the use of offensive language by the bands ran counter to the refined art of academic debate and they were therefore unwelcome on campus. What is more likely is that the political content of their songs, which included a particular sardonic mockery of State President P.W. Botha ("Sit Dit Af"; "Switch it Off"), was of decisive importance. Botha also happened to be chancellor of the university and the authorities could hardly condone the brazen upbraiding of its highest symbolic functionary. While petitions, counter-petitions, and letters appeared in the newspapers, protesting students (both for and against) also made their voices heard on a campus more known for its political docility than activism. The concert was held at another venue and attracted close to 4,000 raucous students. To demonstrate what they considered the infantile behavior of the Stellenbosch rector, Mike de Vries, they started the concert off by chanting the adapted lyrics of an Afrikaans nursery rhyme: "Siembamba, Mike bewaar die

---

[24] "Kerkorrel and Kie," *The Star*, 25 May 1989. "Softer" forms of Afrikaans rock music have appeared in the mid-eighties by artists such as Anton Goosen.

[25] "'Dagga' Dirk is stryder vir Afrikaanse rock," *Die Burger*, 30 March 2002.

sedes, x2, Voëlvry gaan die kampus ontsier, toffie vir Mike ons is hier!"
("Siembamba, Mike protects the values, x2, Voëlvry is a disgrace for the campus,
but we have outsmarted Mike, we are here!")[26]

Elements of the Afrikaner establishment were equally perturbed by the
messages conveyed by the Voëlvry musicians, but this did not deter the intrepid
pioneers of Afrikaans rock and roll. One journalist described their visit to
Welkom, a mining town in the Free State countryside, in racy prose:

> There was a full moon shining over the mealiefields of Welkom on the
> night the Boere punks came to town. They checked in at the Heavenly
> Bodies Gym, an Olympian fortress of brick and corrugated iron—. But
> they hadn't come to pump iron. They had come to party. Banned in Bethle-
> hem, pilloried in Potch, told to "voertsek" [to leave] in Vanderbijlpark, the
> Voëlvry Alternatiewe Boeremusiek bandwagon has been rock and rolling
> around the platteland [countryside] with all the momentum of an oxwagon
> stuck in a donga [ditch]. You can't blame people for feeling a little
> nervous. Hiding behind subversive pseudonyms, yelling inciteful slogans
> ... the Voëlvry brigade mocks the total onslaught with a rock and roll
> beat.... They are sowing a germ of cultural and spiritual liberation ... of
> politics beyond Parliament and life beyond Welkom.[27]

Proselytizing in towns such as Welkom could be a thankless mission, however, as
a section of the audience pelted them with eggs. [28]

But not all responses in the countryside were hostile. At Kroonstad, close
to Welkom, Antjie Krog, destined to become a celebrated author and whose
family had a farm in the Kroonstad district, waxed lyrically about their performance. "The familiar outlines of one's town," she wrote, assumed a new
dimension as the Voëlvry musicians "launched an attack on the alliance between

---

[26] "J. Kerkorrel en sy Blues Band maak vriende," *Die Burger*, 15 May 1989. For a sample of
the reporting and correspondence see "Voëlvry-groep ontstoke oor Matie verbod," *Die Burger*, 5
May 1989; "Maties hou by verbod op 'Voëlvry,'" *Die Burger*, 10 May 1989; "US-dosent praat oor
Voëlvry," *Die Burger*, 9 May 1989; "Foto's van betoging uit blad na versoek," *Die Burger*, 8 Nov.
1989; "Laat kritiek deur musiek toe," *Die Burger*, 5 June 1989; "Verbod op Voëlvry- konsert
geregverdig, kritiek nie," *Die Burger*, 12 June 1989; "Alle bewakers is nie paronoïes nie," *Die
Burger*, 25 May 1989; "Maties gee een van hulle menseregte prys," *Die Burger*, 30 May 1989.

[27] "When the Boere Punks Came to Town," *Sunday Times*, 30 April 1989.

[28] Kombuis, *Seks, drugs en boeremusiek*, 214–15.

politics and religion which allowed you to clap your hands and stamp your feet." It was "possible for everyone to participate in protest." [29]

In Johannesburg and Pretoria Voëlvry attracted not only students, but also other young urbanites. The audience in Johannesburg was described as

> youngsters with earrings, acne infested girls with purple hair and bright eyes, barefooted pseudo-ethnics, nature lovers with beads and kikois, sulking no-goods with bovver boots and other remnants of Britain *circa* 1978, Teds, Mods, Lefties—all with reddish eyes. But with the important difference that they all spoke Afrikaans.[30]

Apart from attracting a particular set of young people, Voëlvry extended its generational reach to thirty- and forty-year-old professionals who formed a noticeable part of the audience at some concerts.[31]

On tour, underlying personal animosities, coupled with a degree of drug and alcohol abuse, gave rise to occasional frayed tempers.[32] It was a rollercoaster experience, as the musicians appeared to take the Afrikaner youth by storm. Kerkorrel reflected on this in 1992:

> The adaptation was not easy, but it was exhilarating. I got high on many of the experiences. All of a sudden we met many interesting people. We saw places and did things which otherwise would not have been the case. It was very pleasant, but it also had its downside— You had to cope—you had to be the big star, number one. Things were hunky dory and bright and beautiful and then they started to ban us in certain places, public controversy followed and Afrikaans ministers of religion started playing records backwards to find satanic messages—. But if I had to add up the pros and cons, it was more than a worthwhile experience.[33]

Voëlvry concerts were intense affairs. Kerkorrel was known to "whip his audience into ecstasy with his whooping bopalong brand of boogie and brazen energy."[34] While the rapport between the musicians and their audiences appeared

---

[29] "Protes weerklink luid, vinnig en toeganklik," *Vrye Weekblad*, 12 May 1989 (my translation).

[30] "Oranje, Blanje—Blues," *Vrye Weekblad*, 14 April 1989 (my translation).

[31]" Boereblues oor apartheid," *Rapport*, 4 June 1989; "Nuwe lied van jong Suid-Afrika," *Die Suid-Afrikaan*, June 1989.

[32] M-Net TV Documentary, 12 August 2003; Kombuis, *Seks, drugs en rock*, 14.

[33] "Johannes Kerkorrel word groot," *De Kat*, 30 April 1992 (my translation).

[34] "Afrikaans Pride and Passion Mix with Fun and Laughter," *Sunday Times*, 9 July 1989.

to be one of mutual synergy, there was also an element of power play involved. Johannes Kerkorrel, the band's front man, was well aware of the way an adroit performer could influence his audience. With a certain measure of arrogance he commented:

> I have found that audiences here love to be told what to do. They have been brought up in a country where they are virtually told from the minute that they walk into school—Do this, do that. Audiences don't know what to do. They like to be told and then they feel reassured—.[35]

It is certainly not without irony that Kerkorrel used the very same conformity that he had claimed to despise, to further his dialogue with some audiences.

As part of their political agenda, the Voëlvry musicians also sought to ridicule other forms of Afrikaans music. They took issue with those popular Afrikaans singers who sang about beaches, seagulls, puppy love, and rugby and argued that these songs lulled Afrikaners into a false consciousness. Typifying this brand of music was a balladeer, Bles Bridges. Bridges had a huge appeal among predominantly working-class and rural Afrikaners eager to escape into a fantasy make-believe world. He wore gold lamé, waiter-type jackets and sequenced sequinned pants with cowboy boots to complete a Las Vegas–like kitsch glitter package. Bridges sang his songs in safe, easy, antiseptic Afrikaans and showered adoring women with red roses as a grand conclusion to his shows. He made it clear that "love is the only thing worth singing about. To sing about politics has never done anybody any good."[36] It was the exact antithesis of what the Voëlvry musicians stood for and they responded by openly denigrating his music and distributed T-shirts with the logo: "Ek Verpes Bles" ("I Detest Bles").

Ethnic Dynamics and Social Characteristics

It is easy to read into the Voëlvry critique of Afrikaner culture, as some analysts have done, a call for radical social change that proceeded from a decentered base intent on an outright rejection of a particular identity.[37] This can be misleading. While Voëlvry rejected a certain form of Afrikaner identity, at the core of what

---

[35] "Kerkorrel en kie," *The Star*, 27 May 1989.

[36] Cited in Brendan Jury, "Boys to Men: Afrikaans Alternative Popular Music, 1986–1990" *African Languages and Cultures* 9, 2 (1996), 101. See also "There Is Life After Bles," *Sunday Times*, 11 December 1988; "Bless My Soul, Mr Kerkorrel," *Sunday Times*, 12 February 1989; "Bles en Kerkorrel bly maar haaks," *Die Burger*, 10 February 1989.

[37] Compare Jury, "Boys to Men," 102; Dan O'Meara, *Forty Lost Years: The Apartheid State and the Politics of the National Party* (Johannesburg, 1996), 371.

they represented was a broader formulation of Afrikaansness in line with the pressures of the time. Although they sought to recast Afrikaner identity in a different mould, they were well aware that the very success of their enterprise depended on their being Afrikaans. Without that distinctive hallmark, they would have disappeared into the amorphous grey of the wider anti-apartheid movement. Besides the strategic advantage of Afrikaans, Kerkorrel also had a strong belief in the political potential of Afrikaans speakers:

> I am mad about Afrikaans people and therefore I do what I do in Afrikaans, because I think that is where it can happen. These are the people who can make a difference. If I look at these people, our fans, then I scheme; these are the people necessary to get a new South Africa started—for sure. Then I am glad that I am part of this thing—.[38]

Kerkorrel was impatient with establishment critics who regarded their lyrics as unsophisticated and who failed to realize that they sought to add an essential new dimension to Afrikaans and wished to uncouple the language from the apartheid state:

> We get a lot of flak from most of the Afrikaans press. They say we are unpractised and "dik gerook" [stoned] and that our lyrics are naïve. They obviously don't realise that our whole idea is to write naïve lyrics. We are liberating the language. If you can make a language into rock and roll, it can't be an oppressive language anymore. It's got to be free. It is just an African language like any other and it is certainly not the exclusive property of the "volk."[39]

Underlying their position was also an attempt to make Afrikaans part of a wider world through rock and roll. As Bernoldus Niemand explained, "The Afrikaner was the polecat of the world, part of nothing, rejected. I tried to bring him in, make him feel part of something."[40] Similar concerns also fed into their rejection of the term "alternative Afrikaners" which the media bestowed upon them. To them the term implied that they were being "othered," and it carried negative associations they regarded as inappropriate and superfluous.[41]

In addition, they found the overtures of some "liberal" English speakers patronizing and overbearing. They felt insulted to be called "thinking" Afrikaners

---

[38] "Eet Kreef," *De Kat*, 30 June 1989 (my translation).

[39] "It Is Not Just What the Okes Say, Man," *Weekly Mail*, 5 December 1988.

[40] "Oupa Phillips se klong mik kop toe," *Die Burger*, 4 January 1994.

[41] "'Alternatief?' Nee, ons rock en roll!" *Die Burger*, 20 May 1989.

496   ALBERT GRUNDLINGH

by the English media and were of the opinion that such a formulation could only stem from a mindset that believed that all Afrikaners "secretly had pictures of Hitler behind their toilet doors."[42] Charles Leonard, a music journalist of the *Vrye Weekblad,* recalled in 2002 that at the time foreign journalists regarded "alternative Afrikaners" as peculiar anthropological species. He caustically commented on these journalists' perception of "alternative Afrikaners." "Check that cute one with the ear-ring, chuck him another piece of boerewors [traditional sausage]," was their attitude according to Leonard.[43] On the same score Koos Kombuis was also irritated by their record company, Shifty Records. Although he found some of the individuals companionable, he summarized their superior attitude towards the musicians in the phrase: "Jolly good show, old chap, let us help these Afrikaner boykies."[44] Kombuis, moreover, viewed the deferential attitude of some "liberal" English speakers towards black people as insincere and condescending. There was no point in trying to curry favor with black people, he argued; all South Africans, regardless of color, had to learn to share the same space.[45] Their basic point of departure, as Kerkorrel articulated it, was not to pontificate about other groups, but to help Afrikaners "find a new meaning in the country and a new place for us in the country."[46]

While Voëlvry proclaimed a new role for Afrikaners, their performances were marked by an unexamined gender assumption. Tonia Selly (Karla Krimpelien), a fine vocalist, was cast in the role of a mini-skirted "doo wop" girl and not given much prominence in the overall projection of a "new" identity. Moreover, the lyrics were written from a predominantly male perspective and although sensitive to the way in which Afrikaner women were implicated in the militarization of South African society, they failed to give women an active voice in their protest lyrics.[47] Jennifer Ferguson, a fellow white anti-apartheid activist, welcomed their appearance on the musical scene but viewed them, in perhaps somewhat exaggerated terms, as swaggering males who play "big cock rock" on stage and who imagined that they could ride "John Wayne style through South

---

[42] "Oranje, Blanje—Blues," *Vrye Weekblad,* 14 April 1989 (my translation).

[43] "Onskuld-era het gesterf," *Beeld,* 16 November 2002.

[44] http://www.litnet.co.za/koosbrief.asp, copy of a letter from Koos Kombuis to Dirk Uys, c July 1990.

[45] "New Afrikaners Sing Different Tune," *The Sunday Star,* 5 March 1989.

[46] "Kerkorrel sing steeds die blues," *Insig* (December 1988) (my translation).

[47] Lydia Hagen, "Kulturele identiteit die 'alternatiewe Afrikaanse beweging' van die tagtigerjare" (M.A. thesis, Rand Afrikaans University, 1999), 50, 88.

Africa to save the country."[48] It was a charge that Kombuis found a bit worrying, but not sufficiently so to ponder upon it with any anguish. "Obviously we were sexist," he responded later. "We were the 'Voëlvry' tour. So what?"[49] This does not imply, however, that they were oblivious to the function of a specific form of white masculinity in shaping the military environment Underlying the lyrics of some of Bernoldus Niemand's songs in particular, there was a clear rejection of the social construction of male gender that forced him to assume the role of a soldier.[50]

In dealing with the complicated relationship between music, culture, and politics in the sixties, the work of R. Eyerman and A. Jamison is conceptually suggestive in probing the dynamics of the Voëlvry movement. They see social movements as involving more than pure political activities inasmuch as they open up accessible public space for cultural experimentation and allow for various forms of critiques of the existing order. Social movements then, they argue, can alter "structures of feeling and underlying sensibilities," while "harder" politics are being played out elsewhere.[51] A hallmark of social movements is their nebulous nature. Nevertheless, while social movements do not emerge fully formed with an explicit programme and can take shape in amorphous ways, they are fundamentally affected by the political cultures of the societies of which they are part. Social movements coalesce over time and display a certain hybridity of ideas as part of the convoluted process of producing reworked identities and political visions.[52] It is in this context that music as one element becomes "both knowledge and action, part of the frameworks of interpretation and representation produced within social movements and through which they influence the broader societal culture." [53]

The Voëlvry tour and the well-attended shows, combined with a strident political message, soon earned the appellation of a "movement." It was perhaps more than just convenient journalistic shorthand. "Voëlvry," like other similar movements, was the product of particular historical circumstances and evolved in

---

[48] "Nuwe lied van jong Suid-Afrika," *Die Suid-Afrikaan*, June 1989.

[49] Kombuis, *Seks, drugs en boeremusiek*, 231 (my translation).

[50] Drewett, "It's My Duty, Not My Choice," 130–31.

[51] Ron Eyerman and Andrew Jamison, *Music and Social Movement: Mobilizing Traditions in the Twentieth Century* (Cambridge, 1998), 42–43.

[52] Ron Eyerman, "Social Movements: Between History and Sociology," *Theory and Society* 18, 3 (1989), 543.

[53] Eyerman and Jamison, *Music and Social Movement*, 23–24.

498   ALBERT GRUNDLINGH

an inchoate way. Koos Kombuis recalled in 2000 what he regarded as the founding moment:

> The last thing that I, Ralph, and Dirk were aware of at the time was that we
> were busy with an important cultural movement. We would only realize
> that later, when the tour began and then only vaguely at the back of our
> heads—we were simply too busy most of the time and too freaked out to
> reflect logically about everything.[54]

He stated their non-programmatic political involvement pithily: "We knew there
was sh*t in the land and we felt that our music might just make a difference."[55] It
later dawned on him that "Something was busy happening. And we were at the
centre of it. And the power of the regime was suddenly not all that absolute."[56]
Antjie Krog in her description of the show at Kroonstad also picked up on the
birth of a new set of perceptions and emotions: "The somber pessimism and
burdens of impotent guilt dissolved. Here is the start of something."[57]

The embryonic but palpable sense of imminent change and the appeal to
new Afrikaner cultural and political sensibilities as well as the enthusiastic
following it attracted certainly gave Voëlvry the appearance of a social movement. But the case should not be overstated. It failed to evolve beyond protest
music, lacked wider connections, and did not inspire their followers to express
themselves in unambiguous and meaningful political terms. At best it can be
described as a moderate to weak social movement.

A pertinent characteristic of Voëlvry was the way it dealt with tradition.
"Traditions," as Eyerman and Jamison have argued, "are inherited ways of interpreting reality and giving meaning to experience; and thus provide the underlying
logical structure upon which all social activity is construed."[58] During times of
stress, these authors claim, a selective reworking occurs in which traditions are
infused with new kinds of meaning. As a result "traditions are made and remade
in a process of mobilization."[59] Despite the apparent rejection then of what has
gone before, cultural redefinitions are informed as much by the past as the

---

[54] Kombuis, *Seks, drugs en boeremusiek*, 204.

[55].Article by Sam Woulidge, 5 August 2003, http://www.kooskombuis.co.za/english.htm.

[56] Kombuis, *Seks, Drugs en boeremusiek*, 211 (my translation).

[57] "Protes weerklink luid, viriel en toeganklik," *Vrye Weekblad*, 12 May 1989 (my
translation).

[58] Eyerman and Jamison, *Music and Social Movement*, 20.

[59] Ibid., 39.

present; their efficacy depends on an adroit use of an intelligible and known past and adapting it in such a way that it speaks anew in a changed context. Through a process of connecting a selected or usable past with ongoing contemporary life, the potential critical impact is heightened as the familiar is recognizable but in a defamiliarized shape.

Some Voëlvry musicians had an appreciation of South African history in which the association of Afrikaners with apartheid since 1948 was regarded as an aberration when viewed against the background of a more varied past that goes back much further than 1948. As Kerkorrel explained, in response to a journalist's question in 1989 whether he sought to unshackle Afrikaners from their past:

> I mean, what is the past? The past 40 years? This country has a past that goes back a long, long way. Must we take the past 40 years as the past? Definitely not. I think it is a little perverse twist, you know, and it's done an incredible amount of damage to us as Afrikaans people. But at the moment there is a whole "new future" type of feeling.[60]

Kombuis also gave considerable thought to South African history. In 1989 he published a novel in which he took the reader on a tour through his version of South Africa's convoluted past.[61] For Kombuis, like Kerkorrel, there was much more to South Africa's history than forty years of apartheid. Apartheid was seen as a present curse and he preferred to reach back further into the past. "Each generation rebels against its fathers and makes friends with its grandfathers," as he concisely summarized his position.[62]

The keen understanding of history and the way it could be redeployed in the present found creative expression in some of their lyrics. Traditional Afrikaans songs and symbols were reworked and presented in rock and roll style. A particular popular song in this respect was "Ossewa" (Oxwagon). In Afrikaner representations of history the oxwagon has become the symbol of God-fearing 19th-century Voortrekkers (Boer pioneers) who "tamed" the "wild" interior of South Africa. At night the Voortrekkers were occasionally known to arrange the oxwagons in a *laager,* a defensive circle, as precaution to possible attacks from the indigenous population. In the late 20th century Voëlvry interpretation of this history, the oxwagon is transformed into a modified modern car with a V6 engine and a tape deck blaring Elvis Presley music. The passengers in this new oxwagon are on their way to the beach for a carefree holiday. Symbolically the oxwagon is

---

[60] "Kerkorrel and Kie," *The Star*, 25 May 1989.

[61] André Letoit, *Suidpunt Jazz* (Pretoria, 1989).

[62] "Letoit, Punk en plesierig," *Die Burger*, 20 August 1988.

500   ALBERT GRUNDLINGH

now being put to a different use. Where the oxwagon was usually associated with closed, inward-looking worldviews (often referred to as the *laager* mentality), the new revamped oxwagon was to lead Afrikaners out of their political and cultural impasse into a brighter future. But even though it was now billed as a "funky" oxwagon, the refrain of the song—"sweet, sweet *ossewa*"—was a constant reminder of the enduring familiarity and almost endearing reliance of the symbol. "We did not discard or write off the oxwagon," they explained, "we gave it a facelift, repainted it, and filled it with a V6 engine. It was the kind of attack the Botha apartheid government did not expect."[63] Kerkorrel took the analogy further: "It is as if we are Voortrekkers again, breaking away and looking for a new future, finding new boundaries, building bridges and experimenting."[64]

Another song that drew upon the past is that of "Boer in Beton" (A Boer in Concrete) by Koos Kombuis, known as André Letoit at the time. The lyrics deal with the process of Afrikaner urbanization and adaptation to city life. The artist's on-stage rendition of this was well described by a journalist:

> Then the music faded, the lights dimmed and André Letoit mooched on stage. Cocooned in a sunflower yellow pullover, he hunched over his scratchy guitar and sang a song about the pain of being a misplaced urban Boer, mummified in concrete like Oom Paul [President Paul Kruger] in old Church Square. Lost in his freedom in the city, Letoit resented his heritage and history as much as he felt it calling him somewhere in the bitter watershed of his soul.[65]

The occurrence that prompted this song is instructive, as it carried within itself a certain tension between the past and what was then the present. Letoit explains that he was sitting in a café in Pretoria:

> Some CP [Conservative Party] "toppies" [elderly men] were talking at the table next to me and I resented everything they stood for. Then I started feeling empathy when I realized that in their way they were completely honest and their fears were completely justified. Believing that democracy can work is a very high-risk thing. I got this nostalgic feeling. When they left I wrote *Boer in Beton*.[66]

---

63 "Uit die perd se bek," *Beeld* 29 April 2002 (my translation).

64 "Ruk en rol saam met Kerkorrel," *Die Husigenoot*, 20 April 1989 (my translation).

65 "When the Boere Punks Came to Town," *Sunday Times*, 30 April 1989.

66 "Afrikaans Pride and Passion Mix with Fun and Laughter," *Sunday Times*, 9 July 1989.

Voëlvry music, as Ingrid Byerly has pointed out, "served prominently as a site of contemplation concerning the image of the Afrikaner—whether the old stereotype or the new incarnation of Afrikaner." [67]

Although in form and presentation Afrikaans rock was a radical new departure, it should be clear that Voëlvry did not emerge out of a vacuum. Particularly in the search for lyrics, they seemed to have scoured earlier sources for possible subversive lyrics. Some of the songs that appeared in the time-honored and revered songbook of the "Federasie van Afrikaanse Kultuurkringe" (FAK) found their way in a revised form into the repertoire of the Voëlvry musicians.[68] In addition, they searched for earlier Afrikaans music that reflected realities other than those that appeared in the ethnically inclined lyrics of the FAK songbook. They discovered these in the music of the Briel family singers. The Briel family's first long-playing record appeared in 1956 and their songs were heartfelt renditions of Afrikaner poverty and working-class life on the Rand during the 1930s and 1940s. The Briel music was considered authentic and committed social commentary of an earlier era that could complement that of Voëlvry some decades later. These linkages were demonstrated by playing Briel music as fillers between events, and later some surviving Briel members were also invited to perform live.[69]

Certain elements of the way Voëlvry presented itself as a movement resonated with those of the punk movement in Britain during the late 1970s and early 1980s. In an analysis of the punk movement abroad, P Lamy and J Levin have outlined its characteristics:

> The punks have taken to expressing their disillusionment with society by mocking it in exaggerated style. Punk breaks all codes of accepted behaviour and lifestyle and reproduces entire philosophical and sartorial history of subcultures in "cut-up" form, combining elements that had originally belonged to different epochs.[70]

The use of offensive language on stage and the proclamation of an apocalyptic prophecy completed the repertoire.

---

[67] Byerly, "Mirror, Mediator, and Prophet," 19.

[68] Hagen, "Kulturele identiteit," 45.

[69] "Die Briels was toeka al betrokke," *Die Burger*, 31 May 1990; "Briels helde van Houtstok," *Beeld*, 2 June 1990; "Kerkorrel se doodsbrief," *Rapport*, 17 November 2002.

[70] P. Lamy and J. Levin, "Punk and Middle-Class Values: A Content Analysis," *Youth and Society* 17, 2 (1985), 160. See also Craig O'Hara, *The Philosophy of Punk* (San Francisco, 1982), 4–5.

502   ALBERT GRUNDLINGH

Kerkorrel was wary of accepting the punk label. Part of this reluctance might have been due to an artistic desire to be seen as original and independent, but he also felt that overseas artists made no sense in South Africa because they did not address South African issues.[71] This did not deter him from dressing local content up in a distinctly punk fashion, however. The parodies of Afrikaner society, the uses of history and the disaffection with middle-class establishment values, often expressed in swear words on stage, all carried punk overtones. Kerkorrel though, when criticized for swearing, sought to provide an indigenous rationale:

> I learned to swear during my compulsory military service and I do swear on stage and some people find it a bit much. But if you think about it carefully, Afrikaans has the most wonderful swear words. Nobody swears better than the boers. What is Afrikaans without its swear words?[72]

Voëlvry musicians did not gravitate towards hard punk activities such as the physically destructive behavior on stage that was a hallmark of some punk bands overseas. Theirs was a somewhat softer expression. But as the British punks who advocated anarchy as an antidote to society's perceived ills, Voëlvry had similar problems dealing with the intricacies of the South African situation. Hence the escapist message with which they sought to end their shows and round off their commentary on the South African condition:

> "Almal moet gerook raak, so hoog soos 'n spook raak—die gemors hier skoonmaak—ja—almal!" (Everybody must get stoned—become as high as a ghost—clean up the mess here—yes—everybody.)[73]

Impact

Although Voëlvry was widely heralded in the media as a unique and significant movement, its importance beyond that bestowed by the media is harder to fathom. As far as the musicians themselves and their sympathizers were concerned, the movement certainly had a major effect on Afrikaner consciousness. In 2000 Koos Kombuis considered the impact to have been "moerse" (extremely) big. He explained that "under normal circumstances, what we did might not have been that important, but it was the right thing, in the right place, at the right time."[74] In

---

[71] "Alternatief? Nee, ons rock en roll"! *Die Burger*, 20 May 1989.

[72] "Ruk en rol saam met Johannes Kerkorrel," *Die Huisgenoot*, 20 April 1989 (my translation).

[73] "When the Boere Punks Came to Town," *The Suday Times*, 30 April 1989.

[74] Article by Sam Woulidge, 5 August 2003, http://www.kooskombuis.co.za/english.htm.

his autobiography Kombuis duly acknowledges the wider political forces at work during the eighties, but still believes that their contribution was the *doodskoot* (the killer blow).[75] The journalist, Max du Preez, was of the opinion that Voëlvry is "entitled to more recognition for the fundamental change in the minds of Afrikaners which made 1994 possible than the politicians such as F.W. de Klerk who, like to receive all the accolades."[76] Bernoldus Niemand was equally outspoken about their perceived influence: "It was the type of encouragement the reformers required, the knowledge that the *laaities* (the youth) were with them."[77] These assumptions, appealing as they might appear, are difficult to prove analytically. Hence, to try and determine the movement's reach and powers of persuasion it is necessary to probe wider and deeper.

Political surveys undertaken at Afrikaans universities such as Rand Afrikaans University in Johannesburg and the University of Stellenbosch in 1989 and earlier reflected that students were wedded to the status quo and not given to entertain fundamentally changes.[78] One of the researchers, Susan Booysen of Rand Afrikaans University, expressed grave doubts about the impact of Voelvry and in an interview with a newspaper dismissed the response of the students on campus as a mere "flirtation."[79] While making allowance for possible methodological shortcomings in questionnaire-type surveys that fail to register qualitative subterranean disaffection, the evidence of the surveys nevertheless serves as a salutary reminder that beyond the Voëlvry movement there was a vast number of white young people set in their ways and untouched by the Voëlvry message. By the same token though, the fact that Voëlvry did manage to attract some apparent dissidents is significant.

In evaluating the impact of "Voëlvry," the nature of the concerts and the reception of their songs should also be taken into account. At face value the concerts certainly signaled change, but the level of commitment and the degree of

---

[75] Kombuis, *Seks, drugs en boeremusiek*, 218.

[76] Max du Preez, "Die kunste of die politiek: wie doen die meeste om iets nuuts in Afrikaans aan te vang?" 2002, http://www.afrikaans.be/artikels/htm.

[77] "Oupa Phillips se klong mik kop toe," *Die Burger*, 4 January 1994.

[78] Susan Booysen, "Politieke verandering en die sosialisering van Afrikaanse studente: 'n gevallestudie 'n gevallestudie," *South African Journal of Sociology* 21, 4 (1990), 181–92; Hennie Kotze, "Political Education and Socialization: A Comparative Perspective at Two Afrikaans Universities," *South African Journal of Sociology* 21, 3 (1990), 133–43; Jannie Gagiano, "Ruling Group Cohesion," in Hermann Giliomee and Jamie Gagiano, eds., *The Elusive Search for Peace: South Africa, Israel, Northern Ireland* (Cape Town, 1990), 191–208.

[79] "Boereblues oor apartheid," *Rapport*, 4 June 1989 (my translation).

504   ALBERT GRUNDLINGH

change (and even whether there was a clear understanding of what the Voëlvry lyrics implied) need to be examined. There is no doubt that the concerts were popular and that Voëlvry music, being banned from the state-run South African Broadcasting Service, sold very well.[80] Youthful enthusiasm can, however, be deceptive. Dirk Uys the manager on tour, conceded that many attended the concerts primarily as a "jol" and according to him only about 40 percent of the audience understood and agreed with the lyrics. But he regarded it as "socialising process and even the aggressive ones could learn something from the concerts."[81] It remains doubtful though what they learnt. At some concerts the ironies in the lyrics were completely misunderstood. The song "BMW" was a biting satire on white middle class values. ("I drive a BMW; I give black people f—k—l"; do not talk politics or I'll shout blue murder" – translation). In Potchefstroom, however, the lyrics were met with a roar of approval from a section of the audience who interpreted it very literally that no concessions should be made to black people and politics should not be discussed. There was very little indication that the Voëlvry performance was creating a sense of uneasiness.[82]

Apart from those who were evidently tone-deaf in picking up a different ideological beat, for another section of the audience it was a matter of preaching to the converted. Although it was not his intention, Kerkorrel implied as much when he revealed: "We all thought the Afrikaans youth supported the National Party, but when we went on stage and told them, the 'king has no clothes,' they responded with, 'Yes, we know.'"[83] These youths were thus predisposed to receive the message favorably. Writing in a wider context about the role of music in social movements, R Rosenthal has pointed out that the test is to "find proof from *the audience* that the power of music goes beyond raising the spirits of those already committed—."[84]

The reach of Voëlvry was mainly restricted to white Afrikaans audiences. At the predominantly brown campus of the University of the Western Cape, known for its activism in the eighties, the Voëlvry concert had some novelty value but a low turnout and a lukewarm response. Nor did the musicians have any

---

80 "Kerkorrel Out of Tune on SABC," *Pretoria News*, 18 May 1989; "Eet Kreef uitverkoop," *Die Burger*, 11 May 1989.

81 "Nuwe lied van jong Suid-Afrika," *Die Suid-Afrikaan*, June 1989 (my translation).

82 Ibid.; "Die swart gevaar in Potch," *New Nation*, 27 April to 4 May 1989.

83 "Gryser en wyser," *Rapport*, 9 June 2002.

84 Ron Rosenthal, "Serving the Movement: The Role(s) of Music," *Popular Music and Society* 25, 3/4 (Fall/Winter 2001), 15 (emphasis in original).

contact with major black political organizations.[85] One also searches in vain in the African National Congress mouthpieces of the time for evidence that the movement registered with the exiled organization. Koos Kombuis, though, relates that he met former Robben Island political prisoners after 1990 who claimed that they had "cheered" the movement on.[86]

While it is clear that the movement's impact is more problematic than often projected, its influence in a less formalistic sense cannot be ignored. Analyzing the influence of social movements in Latin America, Alvarez, Dagnino, and Escobar have made the point that social movements, even if they are politically relatively weak, often involve dense webs of different forms of understanding. They argue that "discourses and practices circulate in weblike, capillary fashion (e.g., are deployed, adopted, appropriated, co-opted, or reconstructed, as the case may be) in larger institutional and cultural arenas."[87] These processes can happen almost imperceptibly. In a similar vein it can be argued that Voëlvry carved out a new space for cultural contestation where the vague discomforts of Afrikaner youths could be addressed and perhaps assume a different form. As a student at Stellenbosch in 1989 recalled:

> At that time our air waves were filled with government-filtered, imported pop music and our local artists, English and Afrikaans, were churning out sterile songs about abstract concepts like love, loss, and clowns who drink too much—. The first time I played my *Eet Kreef* cassette—I realized that I was listening to real songs about real problems that at that moment transcended the petty issues of love and alcoholism—. This was something I have never encountered before and it struck a ready chord.[88]

While surveys among university students in Britain have shown them to be more attentive to lyrics than other comparable youth groups,[89] there is no ready evidence to claim that it was broadly the same with Voëlvry music. Nevertheless Voëlvry did introduce Afrikaner youth to a new and vibrant discourse at a particular important historical juncture—*before* the watershed announcement of

---

[85] "Kerkorrel on kie," *The Star*, 27 May 1989; "Protes hier om te bly?" *Vrye Weekblad*, 19 May 1989.

[86] Kombuis, *Seks, drugs en boeremusiek*, 218.

[87] Sonia Alvarez, Evalina Dagnino, and Arturo Escobar, eds., *Culture of Politics/Politics of Culture: Re-visioning Latin American Social Movements* (Boulder, Colo., 2000), 16.

[88] "Kerkorrel," 13 November 2002, http://www.andrew.co.za/article.

[89] Peter G. Christenson and Donald F. Roberts, *It Is Not Only Rock and Roll: Popular Music in the Lives of Adolescents* (Hampton Press, N.J., 1998), 63.

506   ALBERT GRUNDLINGH

F.W. de Klerk on 2 February 1990, unbanning the formerly proscribed and exiled
political organizations. This meant that on the eve of the post-apartheid South
Africa of the 1990s, an element of Afrikaner culture has already been publicly
moulded to accept change. However, it remains conjectural whether this actually
facilitated the political transition in the mid-nineties in a meaningful way.

Legacy

Predictably Voëlvry musicians welcomed the changes in the country. In 1990
Kerkorrel declared: "I have great faith in the political abilities of both Nelson
Mandela and F.W. de Klerk. At least one gets the feeling these days that maybe
we are not going to kill everybody."[90]

Slowly, however, a sense of caution set in as to what the political future
held in store and there was a certain wariness in accepting the credentials of the
ANC. In 1994, just before South Africa's epochal election, Koos Kombuis who
five years earlier had rejected the National Party in no uncertain terms, stated that
he would be voting, ironically, for none other than the National Party.[91] In the
post-1994 period and particularly after the advent of Thabo Mbeki, Kombuis
became increasingly critical of what he regarded as authoritarian tendencies in the
ANC and a romanticized representation of the African past in ANC circles.[92] Dirk
Uys, again, was concerned about the white "brain drain" from South Africa and
he claimed that a fair number of those who had left the country were Voëlvry
supporters in the eighties.[93] Kerkorrel, the only white Afrikaans artist asked to
perform at the inauguration of Nelson Mandela in 1994, shared the rising tide of
white disillusionment with the direction of the ANC after 1999. Mbeki in
particular was accused of re-racializing South Africa. Kerkorrel could not,
however, bring himself to sing in public about what he considered the ills of
contemporary politics:

> It was just so disappointing that somebody [Mbeki] came to breathe life
> into the racial ghosts of "there are whites, and there are blacks," and so on.
> It was nauseating. I did write songs about it, but I decided not to bring it

---

[90] " 'Gatvol' of Being Branded," *The Daily Mail*, 17 July 1990.

[91] "Daar is 'n boemelaar in die kombuis," *Die Burger*, 25 March 1994.

[92] K. Kombuis, *Afrikaans, My Darling* (Cape Town, 2003), 33–38.

[93] "Vroumense en ou karre rock," *Beeld*, 6 April 2002.

out. I felt, just give these guys a break. Don't break them down, it is a new broom finding its feet.[94]

On a personal level Voëlvry musicians also had to adapt to a new reality. Their rationale as protest musicians fell away in 1990 and the group broke up. The switch from minor cult heroes in the eighties to ordinary musicians in the nineties was not always easy. For individuals like Koos Kombuis, the aftermath of the Voëlvry period was marked by an increase in the use of drugs.[95] Over the course of time though, Kombuis succeeded in reinventing himself as an entertainer and noted author.[96] Kerkorrel experimented with more sedate cabaret music and also established links with Flemish singers in Belgium. In the process he lost some of his earlier appeal. Known to be a complex and temperamental person, Kerkorrel was also given to fits of depression; during one of his dark and despondent moods he committed suicide on 12 November 2002.[97] Another Voëlvry member, James Phillips (Bernoldus Niemand), passed away seven years earlier after a car crash.[98]

Kerkorrel's death in particular sparked a renewed interest in the Voëlvry movement. The tragic circumstances of his suicide received considerable media attention and he was widely hailed as a fine musician and anti-apartheid activist. Remembrance services were held in Johannesburg and Cape Town; in Parliament speeches were made in his honor and during the annual Klein Karoo Arts Festival in Oudtshoorn in April 2003, a special exhibition of his work was showcased.[99]

Death bestowed on Kerkorrel an exalted position. While due allowance must be made for the fulsome nature of obituaries, some commentaries amounted to unrestrained exaggerations. In one tribute Kerkorrel was unashamedly linked to international figures who had died tragically:

---

[94] "Die mond is nie geheim nie," 2002. (Interview with Kerkorrel), http://www.litnet.co.za/mond/kerkorrel.

[95] Kombuis, *Seks, drugs en boeremusiek*, 219.

[96] "Boesembroers," *Insig*, November 2003; http:// www.boekwurm.co.za/blad/koos/html "Koos Kombuis Voëlvry Puppie", Ons rebelle nou die nuwe establishment," *Rapport*, 12 October 2003.

[97] "Gefolterde mens," *Beeld*, 14 November 2002.

[98] "East Rand Cowboy: A Son of Springs," *Sunday Times*, 21 September 2003.

[99] "Hulde in parlement," *Die Burger*, 14 November 2002; "Remembering Kerkorrel," *Mail and Guardian*, 14 November 2002; "Troebadoer leef voort," *Die Burger*, 3 April 2003; "Moving Tribute to Kerkorrel," *Cape Times*, 2 April 2003; "Rock Icon Recognized," *Star*, 2 April 2003; "Nog geen vrede oor Kerkorrel," *Beeld*, 20 December 2002; "Andersheid lê nie in kleur nie," *Die Burger*, 19 July 2003.

508   ALBERT GRUNDLINGH

> Many creative people ... burn too brightly to survive the night. Not all of
> them actively commit suicide but there is often a distinct tendency towards
> self-destruction that shortens their lives. One only needs to think singers
> and musicians like Billie Holliday, Janis Joplin, Jimi Hendrix, Jim Morri-
> son, and Kurt Cobain.....[100]

For a journalist of an Afrikaans newspaper in the Free State there was no doubt
that "his death ensured his iconic status."[101] In numerous tributes he assumed a
central role in converting Afrikaners from apartheid ways.[102]

The beatification of Kerkorrel was based on a generalized understanding,
with a certain degree of romanticism, of what the movement had achieved in the
eighties. The complexities of defining the political reach of Voëlvry as well as
Kerkorrel's increasing disillusionment with the ANC in the late nineties were
elements that ran counter to sanctification and thus remained outside the orbit of
appraisal. The movement was now assigned a pure and powerful past.

Such dynamics are not unique; certain interpretations of the significance
of the sixties in the West suffer from the same overload. In reviewing the associations engendered by "Voëlvry," it is instructive to note the work of Eleanor
Townsley who has explained the general phenomenon of "the sixties" in America
in terms of semiotic tropes:

> The answer is that "the Sixties" is an important political trope of the last
> quarter of the 20th century; that is, a figurative use of words, which orga-
> nizes our understanding of contemporary U.S. politics and society. The
> trope's specific function is to compress and inscribe historically developed
> collective understandings in a very short space; it reduces complexity and
> represses contentious detail in favor of "what everyone knows."[103]

In a similar way Voëlvry in Afrikaner circles came to represent "common
knowledge." The outcome of developments after 1989 placed Voëlvry on the
winning side of history, which imparted an element of prescience to the move-

---

[100]"Visionary Outsiders," *Natal Witness*, 22 November 2002.

[101]"Kerkorrel," *Die Volksblad*, 16 November 2002.

[102] For example, "Kerkorrel het nasiebou gehelp," *Beeld*, 14 November 2002; "Hy het
geweet sy tyd is verby," *Rapport*, 17 November 2002; "Sanger was ook aktivis, komponis," *Die
Burger*, 13 November 2002; http://www.litnet.co.za/sênet/asp "Ralph het ons geleer," http://www.
pretoria.co.za/survey "Gaan julle Kerkorrel mis," November 2002; "Johannes Kerkorrel was reg
oor die onreg," *Beeld*, 27 November 2002. For a more skeptical view, see "Diè mense laat hom
wriemel," *Die Burger*, 23 November 2002.

[103] Eleanor Townsley, "The Sixties' Trope," *Theory, Culture, and Society* 18, 6 (2001),99

ment. For a new generation of Afrikaners, eager to be redeemed from what they consider to be apartheid guilt, particularly after the unsettling revelations before the Truth and Reconciliation Commission, Voëlvry *represented a dimension of* Afrikaner culture untainted by apartheid. In contrast to much else relating to the Afrikaner past, it was argued, Voëlvry could be construed as compatible with post-apartheid South African society. Hence in the quest for a new identity, the movement readily presented itself as a useful trope. One Afrikaner of this generation made it clear:

> The Voëlvry tour indirectly paved the way for us—the generation that still played marbles in the eighties while the country was burning—to tackle the future without the chains, the stresses, and the angst of the past.[104]

Afrikaans music went through various permutations during the nineties, some of it drawing musically on "Voëlvry," but overtly political elements remained absent from the lyrics. Certain Afrikaans artists involved with the music scene, did wish, however, to demonstrate their attitude towards the new dispensation by invoking personalized domestic images of the Afrikaans cultural past and juxtaposing these with scenes of black people rioting. These images were reflected on huge screens that serve as backdrops to rave and trance music concerts. In essence it was an attempt to balance "good" memories (homely poems, stories, popular objects, sport) with "bad" memories (violence, troops in the street, and protesting black youths under apartheid). The visuals were soft and the two sets of images were seen to cancel each other out, deliberately making light of politics. As one of the organizers of the rave explained: "Whatever needed to be said, has already been said. It is time for people to enjoy their freedom."[105]

An analyst of this development has recently criticized this position and claimed that it stood in contradistinction to the Voëlvry movement of the eighties, which was about resistance and political engagement and not about fun and freedom.[106] Such an interpretation is something of an oversimplification; at least part of the appeal of the Voëlvry movement was precisely its ability to bring a light and mocking touch to the heavy hand of politics. Perhaps the irreverent and creative probing of politics can even be seen as potentially the movement's most enduring legacy to a country where a new round of politicians are not necessary immune to illusions of grandeur.

---

[104] "Al lê die berge nog so blues" (E. Grundling), http://www.litnet.co.za/klank/ernsjk.asp.

[105] Stephanie Marlin-Curiel, "Rave New World: Trance-mission, Trance-Nationalism and Trance-scendence in the 'New' South Africa," *The Drama Review* 45, 3 (Fall 2001), 4.

[106] Ibid., 4.

510   ALBERT GRUNDLINGH

Conclusion

Voëlvry did rock the boat, but more gently than has often been assumed. It was mainly a white middle-class movement that sought to redefine elements of Afrikaner ethnicity in the eighties without fully rejecting it. Although the movement was largely restricted to the white community and its proselytizing effects were uneven, it was a brave stand to take at the time. As a social movement it was overtaken by events from 1990 onwards and predictably it lost its impetus; the boat did not sink. The Voëlvry stance taken in the eighties still resonated sixteen years later to help manufacture an anti-apartheid past for a younger generation of Afrikaners grappling with a sense of identity in quite a different context.

Writing on the potentially explosive mix between social movements and music and their longer-term effects, Eyerman and Jamison comment perceptively:

> For brief, intensive moments, the habitual behaviour and underlying values of society are thrown open for debate and reflection, and, as the movements fade from the political center stage, their cultural effects seep into the social lifeblood in often unintended and circuitous ways.[107]

This accords well with the creative turmoil unleashed by Voëlvry and the subsequent unscripted trajectory of their abiding influence.

---

[107] Eyerman and Jameson, *Music and Social Movement*, 6.

Appendix

SIT DIT AF!	SWITCH IT OFF!
Die ander dag toe voel ek lam	I was somewhat tired the other day
Ek wou 'n klein bietjie ontspan	I wanted to relax
En 'n boer maak 'n plan	A boer devises a plan
Ek sit my TV set toe aan	I switch on my TV set
Jy sal nie glo wat ek sien	You won't believe what I saw
Op my TV screen	On my TV screen
Dit was 'n nare gesig	It was an unpleasant sight
Dit het my heeltemal ontwrig	It completely unhinged me
Dit was 'n moerse klug	It was a huge joke
Dit was PW se gesig	It was PW's face
En langs hom staan oom Pik	And next to him stands uncle Pik
O, ek dog ek gaan verstik	Oh, I thought I'll choke
Sit dit af x4	Switch it off x4
Want dit was 'n helse straf	Because it is heavy punishment
Ek stap kombuis toe, kry 'n bier	I then walked to the kitchen for a beer
En skakel oor na TV 4	And switched to channel four
O my God wat het ons hier	Oh my God, what have we here
Wat my TV screen ontsier	That is spoiling my screen
Is daar nêrens om te vlug	Is there nowhere to hide
Van daai man se mooi gesig ?	From that man's pretty face?
Met sy vinger in die lug	With his finger in the air
Gaan hy my lewe net ontstig	He is an annoyance in my life
In die programme op die lug	In the programmes in the air
Sien jy net PW se gesig	You only see PW's face
Ek vat jou nog 'n wed	I'll take you another bet
Al die bure het M-net	All the neighbours have M-net
Sit dit af x 4	Switch it off x 4

512   ALBERT GRUNDLINGH

HOU MY VAS, KORPORAAL	HOLD ME TIGHT, CORPORAL
Hou my vas korporaal, ek is 'n kind skoon verdwaal	Hold me tight corporal, I am a child completely lost
Gaan ek weer my cherry sien,	Will I see my cherry again
as ek van die trein afklim?	when I get off the train?
Ja sowaar korporaal	Yes, indeed, corporal
Dis maar swaar korporaal	It is difficult, corporal
Ek speel oorlog met my beste dae	I am playing war with my best days
Ja, ja, ja	Yes, yes, yes
Ek en al my maatjies bymekaar	Me an all my mates
Sal so doen kolonel	Will do that, colonel
Sal nie weier alhoewel	Will not refuse, though
Elke dag deurgekruis	Every day is a cross
Al hoe nader aan my huis	One day closer to home
Hot en haar korporaal	Here and there, corporal,
Ek word naar korporaal	I am getting nauseous, corporal
My ou man se eerste kamp is klaar	My old man's [father's] first camp is finished
Ja, ja, ja	Yes, yes, yes
Amper al sy maatjies bymekaar, bymekaar	Almost all his mates, together, together
Oogklappe sorg vir 'n skoon gewete	Blinders make for a clean conscience
Dis my plig nie my keuse	It is my duty, not my choice
Hier sit ek, ek sit en vrek	Here I sit , I sit and die
Dis nie my skuld maar ek hou my bek	I am not guilty, but I have to shut up
Hou jou bek boet	Shut up, young man!
Sy is my nooi en haar naam is min dae	She is my girl and her name is "min dae"
Ja ja ja	Yes yes yes
Ek en al my maatjies bymekaar	Me and all my mates together, together, together
Ja x7	Yes x7
Korporaal	Corporal
Yo yo	Yo yo
Troep kom hier	Troop come here
Sien jy daai boom	Do you see that tree
Niemand sien die boom nie	Nobody sees the tree
Bring hom hier ek wil hom rook	Bring it here, I would like to smoke it
Hou my vas, korporaal	Hold me tight, corporal

"ROCKING THE BOAT" IN SOUTH AFRICA? **513**

BMW

Ons ry 'n BMW x3
Ons gaan elke jaar oorsee
Miskien gaan ons volgende jaar twee keer
Ons ry 'n BMW x 2
Ons sal jou nie 'n lift gee [Ons sal jou fo-k-l gee]
Ons ry 'n BMW x 3
Vir 'n ryloper sê ons nee
Ons ry 'n BMW x 3
Moet ons dan alles verniet weggee
Ons ry 'n BMW x 3
Polina gaan maak vir die miesies tee
Ja ja toe Polina
Ons drink net suurlemoentee
Ons ry'n BMW x 3
Wel jy weet, ons stem vir die PFP
Ons stem vir die NP
Ons stem vir dieKP
Ons stem vir alles met 'n P
Net nie die ANC, nee
Ons ry 'n BMW x 2
Moenie politiek praat hier nie
Ons sal blou moord skree
En dan sal ons vir Mevrou moet Valiums gee
My kop is so seer
Kan iemand asseblief vir 'n sonbril aangee
Die lig, die son is so helder
En het enige iemand nog 'n idée
Geen rus, niks meer rus
Ek weet nie meer nie x2
Waarom ry ons nie weer 'n keer nie ?

BMW

We drive a BMW x 3
We go overseas annually
Perhaps we'll be going twice next year
We drive a BMW x 2
We won't give you a lift[We will give you fo- k-l]
We drive a BMW x 3
For a hitch hiker we say no
Do we have to part with everything, and get nothing in return
We drive BMW x 3
Polina, go and make tea for the madam
Yes, yes, Polina
We only drink lemon tea
We drive a BMW x 3
Well, you know, we vote for the PFP
We vote NP
We vote KP
We vote for anything with a P
But not the ANC, no
We drive a BMW x 2
Do not talk politics here
We'll shout blue murder
And then we'll have to give the Mrs Valium
My head is so painful
Can somebody please pass me dark glasses
The light, the sun is strong
Does anyone have an idea
No more rest, no more rest
I don't know any longer x 2
Why don't we go for another drive?

514   ALBERT GRUNDLINGH

BOER IN BETON	BOER IN CONCRETE
Ek is 'n Afrikaner in die stad	I am an Afrikaner in the city
Ek dra my masker soos 'n kat	I wear my mask like a cat
Deur donker stegies en geboue	Through dark alleys and buildings
Vat vyf, my broer vat vat	Take five, my brother, take five, take take
En iewers in my onderbewussyn	And somewhere in my subconsicious
Sien ek nog die Karooson skyn	I still see the Karoo sun shining
Hoor ek die grensdrade se gesing	I hear the boundary fences sing
Voer ek die kabouters in my tuin	I feed the gnomes in my garden
Ek rook ingevoerde fags	I smoke imported fags
Ek lees Engelsprekende mags	I read English mags
Ek gaan nooit kerk toe	I never go to church
Want dis 'n drag	Because it is a drag
Want ek's boer in beton	Because I am a boer in concrete
Soos Oom Paul op ou Kerkplein	Like "oom" Paul on my old Church Square
Niemand weet van my pyn	Nobody knows about my pain
Want ek is goed vermom	Because I am well camouflaged
Ek is 'n boer in beton	I am a boer in concrete
Iewers in my klink die stem	Somewhere in me is the voice of Strydom,
Van Strydom, Verwoerd en die knipmeslem	Verwoerd and the blade of a pocketknife
Van die patriotisme wat nog flits	Of a flash of patriotism
Al maak ek Sondae nog vuur met Blits	Although I use Blits to make a fire on Sundays
Elke voorvader 'n pionier	Every ancestor a pioneer
En ek weet ek hoort nie hier	And I know I don't belong here
Ek sit in laatnag kroeë rond	I sit in bars late at night
Maar ek ken nie meer die reuk van grond	But I no longer know the smell of the land
Daar is iewers nog velde wat roep	There is still somewhere fields that are calling
Daar is iewers nog 'n Boerestoep	There is still somewhere a Boer veranda
Die Groot Trek oor die savanna	The Great Trek over the savanna
Die blink loop van 'n sanna	The glittering rifle-barrel
Daar is 'n ketel wat nog kook	There is a kettle boiling
Daar is 'n kampvuur wat nog rook	There is a campfire still smoking
Daar is vroue wat nog ween	There are women still crying
En uitlanders wat brande stook	And 'uitlanders' still stoking fires
En ek net so vreemd soos jy	And I am just as estranged as you are
In hierdie stad van fuifery	In this city of carousing
Hier tussen die wolkekrabbers	Here between the sky scrapers
Waar speedcops spied en karre ry	Where speed cops speed and cars ride
My handpalms is wit soos jy	The palms of my hands are as white as you are
Ek bedel troos waar ek kan	I beg to be consoled where I can
In hierdie land van blik en glas	In this land of tin and glass
Is ek in sak en as.	I am in sackcloth and ash.

[14]

Mühsam, Brecht, Eisler, and the Twentieth-Century Revolutionary Heritage

David Robb

IN MARCH 1873, *two* years after German unification, Georg Herwegh wrote the poem "Achtzehnter März" for the twenty-fifth anniversary of the 1848 revolution in Vienna. The poem laments the revolution's failure while simultaneously prophesizing that its legacy would live on in future revolutions:

> Achtzehnhundert vierzig und acht,
> Als im Lenze das Eis gekracht,
> Tage des Februars, Tage des Märzen,
> Waren es nicht Proletarierherzen,
> Die voll Hoffnung zuerst erwacht,
> Achtzehnhundert vierzig und acht?
>
> Achtzehnhundert vierzig und acht,
> Als du dich lange genug bedacht,
> Mutter Germania, glücklich verpreußte,
> Waren es nicht Proletarierfäuste,
> Die sich ans Werk der Befreiung gemacht?
> Achtzehnhundert vierzig und acht?
>
> Achtzehnhundert vierzig und acht,
> Als du geruht von der nächtlichen Schlacht,
> Waren es nicht Proletarierleichen,
> Die du, Berlin vor den Zitternden, bleichen,
> Barhaupt grüßenden Cäsar gebraucht,
> Achtzehnhundert vierzig und acht?
>
> Achtzehnhundertsiebzig und drei,
> Reich der Reichen, da stehst du, juchhei!
> Aber wir Armen, verkauft und verraten,
> Denken der Proletariertaten —
> Noch sind nicht alle Märzen vorbei,
> Achtzehnhundert siebzig und drei.[1]

Yet again we see here the utopian sentiment alongside the disappointment of the *deutsche Misere*, the recurring failure of Germany to alter the political status quo from within. This double-edged condition would mark the German political song throughout the twentieth century, from the Spartakus movement in 1919 to the anti-fascist campaigns of the 1930s and from the 1968 student movement in West Germany to the 1989 *Wende* in the GDR.

Thematically the continuance of this tradition is apparent in recurring poetic motifs of the *Liedermacher* from the 1960s up to the 1990s. On another level, however, the early twentieth century represented a time of groundbreaking innovation in terms of literary form and performance techniques. These innovations had a lasting influence on the genre of political song. The appropriations by East and West German *Liedermacher* of the political song *Erbe* of the early twentieth century and the Weimar Republic will form the focus of this chapter.

Utopia and Defeat 1: The Legacy of Erich Mühsam

The history of the early twentieth-century German cabaret has been well documented in books such as Peter Jelavich's *Berlin Cabaret*[2] and Alan Lareau's *The Wild Stage: Literary Cabaret of the Weimar Republic*.[3] German cabaret was based on the original "Chat Noir" model of Paris in the 1880s and 1890s. Embodied by the figure of Aristide Bruant, creator of the "Chanson realiste," the French blueprint was a combination of song, satire, and entertainment. Many political lyricists in Germany saw the cabaret as a medium with which to earn money as well as to disseminate political thought. In the German political cabaret of the early twentieth century, Erich Mühsam (1878–1934), alongside Frank Wedekind (1864–1918), played a substantial part in the renewal of balladesque satire in the tradition of Heinrich Heine.[4] In his early bohemian years in Berlin, Mühsam performed in Germany's legendary first cabaret *Überbrettl* (1901–2) and later in Die elf Scharfrichter in Munich. Along with Wedekind, Christian Morgenstern, Otto J. Bierbaum, and Arno Holz, he was one of the most influential cabaret writers of his day. Mühsam's songs were more radically satirical than those of his colleagues, as were his pieces in the magazines *Simplicissimus* and *Der wahre Jakob*. In "Lumpenlied" from 1912 he identifies with the dispossessed, who are set in opposition to the *Bürger* and the *Philister*:

> Kein Schlips am Hals, kein Geld im Sack.
> Wir sind ein schäbiges Lumpenpack,
> auf das der Bürger speit.
> Der Bürger blank von Stiebellack,
> mit Ordenszacken auf dem Frack,
> der Bürger mit dem chapeau claque,
> fromm und voll Redlichkeit.[5]

MÜHSAM, BRECHT, EISLER & 20TH-C. REVOLUTIONARY HERITAGE ◆ 37

Mühsam's most famous cabaret song was "Der Revoluzzer" from 1907. Since the 1860s a unified workers' movement had been organizing itself: workers' associations and clubs had formed, demanding rights that had been promised but not carried through in 1848, such as free elections. This had culminated in the formation of the Social Democratic Party (SPD) in 1869. The gradual institutionalization of this party, however, necessitated a compromise with the system, which left radicals such as Mühsam dissatisfied. His song "Der Revoluzzer" parodies the half-hearted revolutionary approach of the SPD in the figure of the "Lampenputzer" who does not want his street lamps damaged by the building of barricades (see Kauffeldt, 165–67):

> War einmal ein Revoluzzer,
> Im Zivilstand Lampenputzer;
> Ging im Revoluzzerschritt
> Mit den Revoluzzern mit.
>
> Und er schrie: "Ich revolüzze!"
> Und die Revoluzzermütze
> Schob er auf das linke Ohr,
> Kam sich höchst gefährlich vor.
>
> Doch die Revoluzzer schritten
> Mitten in der Straßen Mitten,
> Wo er sonsten unverdrutzt
> Alle Glaslaterne putzt.
>
> Sie vom Boden zu entfernen,
> Rupfte man die Gaslaternen
> Aus dem Straßenpflaster aus,
> Zwecks des Barrikadenbaus
>
> Aber unser Revoluzzer
> Schrie: "Ich bin der Lampenputzer
> Dieses guten Leuchtelichts.
> Bitte, bitte, tut ihm nichts!
>
> Wenn wir ihn' das Licht ausdrehen,
> Kann kein Bürger nichts mehr sehen,
> Laßt die Lampen stehn, ich bitt!
> Denn sonst spiel ich nicht mehr mit!"
>
> Doch die Revoluzzer lachten,
> Und die Gaslaternen krachten,
> Und der Lampenputzer schlich
> Fort und weinte bitterlich.

> Dann ist er zu Haus geblieben
> Und hat dort ein Buch geschrieben:
> Nämlich wie man revoluzzt
> Und dabei doch Lampen putzt.[6]

In its parodic role characterization, "Der Revoluzzer" is — despite its greater balladesque simplicity — a forerunner of the *Rollengedicht* of Franz Josef Degenhardt in the late 1960s. In "Verteidigung eines Sozial-demokraten vor dem Fabriktor," for example, Degenhardt uses the inter-play between third-person narrator and character role-play to parody a Social Democrat politician who is persuading workers not to strike:

> und heute
> guck dir das doch mal an
> wohnzimmer teppich
> couch sessel
> alles was du willst
> auto sogar
> die kinder arbeiten verdienen
> und dann kommt ihr ARBEITER DU BIST AUSGEBEUTET
> [. . .]
> ich sag dir so geht das nicht
> [. . .]
> sagt der alte ewige sozialdemokrat und spricht und spricht
> und spricht und spricht
> bloß ändern das will er nicht[7]

In general, however, Mühsam rated his own cabaret work as trivial (Kauffeldt, 148). Of more importance to him were his non-satirical *Kampflieder* targeted specifically at an audience of revolutionary workers. In their pathos and choice of metaphors, these Mühsam texts show inspiration from the songs of 1848. The hymnic rhetoric — similar to that of Freiligrath and Herwegh — is meant to enthuse the reader and lis-tener (Kauffeldt, 147). Mühsam was inspired by the communicative folk style of the *Kampflieder* of 1848 and their practical use in the context of revolution. He was to bemoan the lack of such songs during the German uprisings of November 1918.[8] A forerunner of Brecht and Hanns Eisler, Mühsam's *Kampflieder* had the express purpose of enlightening the pro-letariat. In 1912 he wrote in the journal *Kain:*

> Das ist nämlich der Sinn alles Werbens und aller Agitation: in stim-
> mungsverwandten Intelligenzen Gedanken zu wecken, Gefühle zu
> Überzeugungen zu erweitern und Sehnsüchte mit dem Drange zur
> Tat zu erfüllen.[9]

In "Generalstreikmarsch," as Diana Köhnen writes, the collective "we," as well as the highly accessible structure of four-line verse, alternating rhymes, and refrain, point to its intended use in the daily political struggle (163–64): "Wir waren lang genug die Knechte, / wir wollen unsre Herrn nicht mehr! / Wir setzen uns für unsre Rechte, / für unsre Freiheit nun zur Wehr" (Mühsam 1906, 1). The song agitates for a general strike as a response to the Russian Revolution of 1905. The relationship to 1848 is evident in the depiction of the master-servant opposition and in the metaphors of a sleeping people who are to be woken up by the revolutionaries: "Schläft denn das Volk? Wir woll'n es wecken. / Heh! Arbeitsmann, Rebell, Wach auf!" (1906, 1). Drastic metaphors such as blood-sucking and the slaughterhouse (later used by Brecht) are similarly borrowed from the style of *Vormärz* poetry: "Sie saugen uns das Blut vom Leibe, / Sie greifen frech nach unserm Glück / Daß man das Volk zur Schlachtbank treibe, / das ist das Ziel. — Was kost' das Stück?" (1906, 1).

A decade later the reverberations in Germany of the Russian Revolution of October 1917 presented a more immediate context for Mühsam's *Gebrauchslieder*. "Räte-Marseillaise," for example, relates to the daily political struggle leading up to the Bavarian revolution in April 1919, and directly appeals to the masses:

> Wie lange Völker, wollt ihr säumen?
> Der Tag steigt auf, es sinkt die Nacht.
>   Wollt ihr von Freiheit träumen,
> das schon die Freiheit selbst erwacht?
>   Vernehmt die Rufe aus dem Osten!
> Vereinigt euch zu Kampf und Tat!
>   die Stunde der Befreiung naht!
> Laßt nicht den Stahl des Willens rosten![10]

As in 1848, after the euphoria of rebellion came the analysis of failure. When the short-lived Soviet Republic of Bavaria was toppled on 13 April, Mühsam, a member of the Revolutionary Workers' Council, was arrested and jailed until he was granted amnesty in December 1924. Texts he wrote during this period take stock of the defeat. In "Ruf aus der Not" of October 1919, a poem reminiscent of Freiligrath's "Die Toten an die Lebenden" (see Köhnen, 170), Mühsam appeals to the dead revolutionaries Marat and Bakunin to inspire renewed revolt. An image of the *deutsche Misere* is presented again in political lyric with respect to a betrayed people:

> Marat! Bakunin! Steigt aus eurer Gruft hervor!
> Wacht auf, schaut um euch, staunt, empört euch,

> lebt und helft!
> Oh, unerhört in aller Menschheit Freiheitskampf,
> seht sterben in Verrat des deutschen Volkes
> Glück!
> Marat! Bakunin! Gebt mir Geist von eurem
> Geist! (1920, 86)

Requiems to Liebknecht and Luxemburg (1928, 206) and Sacco and Vanzetti (1928, 208) continued in this vein. Mühsam believed nothing fundamental had changed since 1848 and saw himself as part of that same literary tradition, as the reference to "Herwegh, Weerth und Freiligrath, / Pfau und Heinrich Heine" in "Der freie Geist"[11] indicates. Köhnen explains the significance of Mühsam's reference to the dead revolutionaries:

> Das Beispiel der toten Revolutionäre soll die Überlebenden mahnen, die Revolution zu vollenden. Die Beschwörung revolutionär-anarchistischer Vorbilder, wie auch den pathetischen, stark mit Metaphern überfrachteten Stil des Gedichts kann man als Versuch verstehen, den revolutionären Elan der Arbeiter erneut zu entfachen. (183)

Mühsam's revolutionary ideals were never realized. In 1934 he was brutally murdered by the Nazis in the Oranienburg concentration camp. Forty years later in the GDR, however, his legacy survived in the work of singers who also saw themselves as part of the same literary protest tradition as Herwegh and Heine, which by now also included Mühsam and Brecht. Wolf Biermann, for example, conjured up an image of bygone revolutionaries in "Der Hugenottenfriedhof" from 1969. Like Mühsam's "Der freie Geist," this song laments the passing away of the revolutionary verve associated with icons of the past. In the song Biermann strolls past socialist dignitaries such as Brecht, Hanns Eisler, and John Heartfield, who lie buried in the Berlin "Hugenotten" cemetery. As the chorus "Wie nah sind uns manche Toten, doch / Wie tot sind uns manche, die leben"[12] suggests, the example of the dead revolutionary artists is a reminder to the living leaders that their so-called revolution in the GDR was a phony one.

As explored in the last chapter, the evoking of such iconic images of revolutionary heritage had the aim of questioning the GDR's self-image as the historical continuity of the revolutionary *Arbeiterbewegung*. As Karen Leeder writes of Steffen Mensching's early poem "Traumhafter Ausflug mit Rosa L.," the subject's erotic but unfulfilled encounter with the dead Spartakus revolutionary Rosa Luxemburg serves to depict "how far the present falls short of revolutionary aspirations of the past" (1996, 127). Idealistic, youthful, and vibrant images of the heroine standing barefoot among the red poppies in a Polish field clash with the theme of funerals ("Marmor, Schleifen und Lilien") and official remembrances

("Kränzen und Märschen des Winters"),[13] which is all that revolutionary heritage had come to amount to in the GDR.

Mühsam himself was the "dead revolutionary" conjured up in Karls Enkel's *Liedertheater* program "Von meiner Hoffnung laß ich nicht — Der Pilger Mühsam"[14] in 1980. As in Mensching's poem mentioned above, the motif of funeral and remembrance features strongly. This was controversial. SED Party functionaries would have preferred that such an official remembrance of Mühsam focused on his utopian *Kampflieder*.[15] But examples of those are interspersed with poems relating to death and defeat, as well as playful cabaret texts that lent themselves to ironical present-day interpretations. An example of the latter is Hans-Eckardt Wenzel's rendition of Mühsam's satirical poem "Das Volk der Denker" from 1925, which forms the highpoint of the program. Wenzel's ironic facial expressions and gestures indicate clearly the significance of this text to the present day. It parodies the complacency and ultimate naivety of comrades who believe in the historical inevitability of the communist utopia:

> [. . .]
> Die Zukunft kommt! Von selbst und ungerufen!
> Nur eine Serie von Entwicklungsstufen
> steht noch bevor. — So lehrt's die Theorie.
> Du liest und lernst. Den Rücken krumm gebogen,
> durchwühlst du Heft um Heft und Band um Band.
> O armes Volk! Von aller Welt betrogen,
> betrügst du selbst dich um dein Sehnsuchtsland.

But it is the funeral motif that provides the aesthetic focal point of the program, which begins and ends with Mühsam's poem "Ehrung der Toten." In the lines "Menschen laßt die Toten ruhn / und erfüllt ihr Hoffen!" yearning for utopian change is relativized by the image of death. The members of the cast, wearing black funeral dress, carry the coffin onto the stage, and Mensching, leader of the funeral procession, announces: "Wir möchten jetzt mit den Trauerfeierlichkeiten beginnen." Here arises an irresolvable contradiction: they celebrate Mühsam's life, but in emphasizing his funeral — the coffin remains on stage for the duration of the show — Karls Enkel mourns the loss in the socialist present of the utopianism that Mühsam stood for.

The contradiction runs throughout. Inherent in the title of the Mühsam poem "Von meiner Hoffnung laß ich nicht" was the belief of the group's leaders Hans-Eckardt Wenzel and Steffen Mensching in the struggle for change. This spirit is, however, constantly relativized by the context of performance, that is, by the reality of the political impotence of the individual in the GDR. In "Gesang des jungen Anarchisten," for example, they sing with a hint of irony: "Von Gesetzen nicht gebunden, /

42   ◆   DAVID ROBB

Ohne Herrn und ohne Staat — / frei nur kann die Welt gesunden, / Künftige, durch eure Tat." Stefan Körbel's interpretation of "Der Ge-fangene" alludes to similar restrictions in the present. In emphasizing the refrain, "Sich fügen, heißt lügen," he mirrors the historical parallel of the dangers of social conformism.

In light of the above, the GDR can be viewed as being at a historical standstill: just as Mühsam had protested that nothing had changed since 1848, Karls Enkel boldly questioned what had changed for the better in the GDR. This is the implied message of Wenzel's rendition of "Kalender 1913": "Im Jahre achtundvierzig schien / die neue Zeit heraufzuziehn / Ihr, meine Zeitgenossen wißt, / daß heut noch nicht mal Vormärz ist."

The funereal motif is never far away. Karls Enkel's reciting of Müh-sam's German translation of "The Internationale" was significant on two levels. Despite severe beatings by Nazi *Sturmabteilung* (SA) guards during his captivity, Mühsam had refused to sing the popular Nazi song "Das Horst-Wessel-Lied" (also known as "Die Fahne hoch," from its first line) and had sung "The Internationale" instead.[16] Here it is sung unaccompa-nied as a lament, Wenzel beating out a slow rhythm on the sound board of his guitar. The lines are separated by long theatrical pauses, creating an alien-ation or defamiliarization effect. This provokes the audience to view the protesting sentiments of the song in terms of their present-day validity: "Vom Staat und vom Gesetz betrogen, / in Steuerfesseln eingeschnürt, / so wird uns Gleichheit vorgelogen / vom Reichen, der kein Elend spürt."

The production climaxes with the juxtaposition of the "Soldatenlied" with the funeral of Mühsam. The song urges soldiers — again with a con-troversial subtext in the GDR context — to turn their weapons against the rulers and to free the world. Such rebelliousness is, however, coun-tered by despondency in Mensching's announcement of the funeral pro-cession: "Die Revolution ist vorüber. Räumen Sie die Straßen auf. Wir wollen mit den Trauerfeierlichkeiten beginnen." The production thus ends in an unresolved contradiction. While the positive perspective on the fu-ture is sustained, it is held in check by the all-pervading image of death.[17]

Despite intermittently coming into conflict with the authorities, such attempts by Karls Enkel to give the proletarian and literary *Erbe* a renewed significance for the present day were welcomed by the critical intelligent-sia of the literary establishment. Influential figures such as Wolfgang Heise from the *Kulturwissenschaft* department at the Humboldt University in Berlin, where group members Wenzel, Mensching, and Stefan Körbel were studying, frequently gave good references to fend off potential bans or censorship.[18] Heise was also a prominent member of the Kulturbund der DDR, which sponsored two of the group's productions: "Deutsch-land meine Trauer. Ein Johannes-R.-Becher-Abend" (1981)[19] and "Die komische Tragödie des 18. Brumaire nach Karl Marx" (1983).[20]

In West Germany such delving into the proletarian past was perceived as having much less cultural significance. In 1986 Dieter Süverkrüp and Walter Andreas Schwarz released a record of Mühsam songs entitled *Ich lade Euch zum Requiem*. It is clear that Mühsam's requiem for his dead revolutionary colleagues had different connotations for a West German audience than for one in the GDR. The final verse proclaims: "Das Heut' erkennt das Gestern nicht, / trotz Ruhmeskranz und Seelenmessen. — / Wer Zukunft schuf, bleibt unvergessen. / Erst die Geschichte hält Gericht." In the GDR, these lines were dripping with irony even as late as the 1980s because of the hollowness of the state's claims to be the continuation of this past — the dead revolutionaries had indeed effectively been forgotten. In the West German version, on the other hand, there is no intended irony, only the invoking of a tradition in a country where radical socialism has ceased to play a major cultural role. By 1986, the heady days of student rebellion were long gone. Süverkrüp and Schwarz's modest motivation is to keep the spirit alive "für die, die auf dem beschwerlichen Weg in die Zukunft Mühsams Idealismus brauchen als Stärkung und Bestätigung," as the CD booklet informs us.

In the course of the 1980s, however, dealing with the concept of utopia became questionable even for a GDR audience. Karls Enkel's approach was dismissed by the young avant-garde "Prenzlauer Berg" poets of the 1980s and accused of being a new form of didacticism for daring to deal *at all* with an utopian discourse that had long lost its relevance (Leeder 1996, 40). We shall later examine this accusation with regard to Karls Enkel's treatment of the Spanish Civil War in its *Liedertheater* production "Spanier aller Länder" in 1985. First let us look at some of the aesthetic categories of the early twentieth-century political song that influenced the genre from the 1960s onwards.

The Aesthetics of Resistance: The Grotesque

The end of censorship that occurred with the fall of the *Kaiserreich* in late 1918 and the continued political turmoil of the 1920s resulted in a creative climate of artistic experimentation that initiated a golden age of political song. Max Reinhardt revived the Schall und Rauch cabaret in Berlin in December 1919. Wedekind and Mühsam's mantel as the leading satirical songwriters of prewar cabaret was now taken over by Kurt Tucholsky, Walter Mehring, and Erich Kästner.

One of the techniques used and developed in the literary cabaret milieu was the grotesque. Horror stories with elements of the macabre had been a historical feature of the sensationalist *Moritat* variety of the street ballad. The shock effect of this ballad type had been exploited by Frank Wedekind in the satires he performed at the turn-of-the-century cabaret Die elf

44   ♦   DAVID ROBB

Scharfrichter in Munich. These included the provocatively anti-bourgeois "Der Tantenmörder," for which he was taken to court:[21]

> Ich hab' meine Tante geschlachtet,
> Meine Tante war alt und schwach;
> Ich hatte bei ihr übernachtet
> Und grub in den Kisten-Kasten nach.
>
> Da fand ich goldene Haufen,
> Fand auch an Papieren gar viel
> Und hörte die alte Tante schnaufen
> Ohn' Mitleid und Zartgefühl.
>
> [...]
>
> Ich hab' meine Tante geschlachtet,
> Meine Tante war alt und schwach;
> Ihr aber, o Richter, ihr trachtet
> Meiner blühenden Jugend-Jugend nach.[22]

In the Weimar Republic Walter Mehring used this shock technique, for example, in "Die kleine Stadt," where he exposes the hypocrisy of social attitudes towards single mothers, the song ending with the ominous hint of a tragic ending for mother and child.[23] Brecht used it in "Von der Kindesmörderin Marie Farrar" from *Hauspostille*. Here the macabre subject matter of infanticide is contrasted starkly by the moral of the refrain: "Doch ihr, ich bitte euch, wollt nicht in Zorn verfallen / Denn alle Kreatur braucht Hilf von allen."[24]

The shock effect could be intensified by the use of directly grotesque imagery as in Brecht's song "Legende des toten Soldaten." He had written this as a satire of the German *Heldenballade* when he was a medical student in a military hospital at the end of the First World War. In this satire of the concept of "Treue über den Tod hinaus" (see Riha, 63–75), the military authorities deem the corpse of a soldier fit to return to battle. Brecht's grotesque comic perspective portrays a dead, stinking, and decaying soldier goose-stepping at the front of a military parade. This is reminiscent of a trait of the grotesque in the history of painting such as the tradition of the *Totentanz*, in which a procession of skeletons are depicted dancing towards the grave. Combined here with a satirical poetic distance the grotesque element exposes the hypocrisy of the rulers and military and the pointlessness of war. With the image of the dead soldier Brecht addresses the concept of the interchangeability of men in war.

Forty years later in the GDR the young Wolf Biermann encountered the literary and theatrical *Erbe* of Brecht while an apprentice at the Berliner Ensemble. Risking the wrath of the SED, which presumed to dictate how Brecht's heritage was to be interpreted, Biermann appropriated several aesthetic aspects of Brecht in his writing as well as in his performance techniques, using these to criticize the GDR. For example, he, too, played on the image of the grotesque body. "Soldat, Soldat," an anti-war song from 1963, is reminiscent of Brecht's "Legende des toten Soldaten" in referring to the facelessness and interchangeability of soldiers: "Soldaten sehn sich alle gleich / lebendig und als Leich" (Biermann, 103). His "Ballade vom Mann, der sich eigenhändig beide Füße abhackt," also from 1963, parodies the self-defeating policies of the SED: a man steps in a pile of feces and finds a solution in chopping off his foot:

> Es war einmal ein Mann
> der trat mit seinem Fuß
> mit seinem nackten Fuß
> in einen Scheißhaufen.
>
> Er ekelte sich sehr
> vor seinem einen Fuß
> er wollt mit diesem Fuß
> kein Stück mehr weitergehn
>
> Und Wasser war nicht da
> zu waschen seinen Fuß
> für seinen einen Fuß
> war auch kein Wasser da
>
> Da nahm der Mann sein Beil
> und hackte ab den Fuß
> den Fuß hackte er ab
> in Eil mit seinem Beil (98–99)[25]

He cuts off the wrong foot and then, in his rage, cuts off the other one too. Biermann, who was expelled from the Party in 1963, makes the parallel clear: "Es hackte die Partei / sich ab so manchen Fuß / so manchen guten Fuß / abhackte die Partei." But at this early stage in his career, Biermann still holds onto the possibility of reform, singing that unlike this man's, the Party's foot can still grow back on: "Jedoch im Unterschied / zu jenem obigen Mann / wächst der Partei manchmal / der Fuß schon wieder an" (99).

It is highly likely that Biermann's grotesque imagery in "Ballade vom Mann" was influenced by the dismemberment of the character Herr Schmitt by two clowns in Brecht's play *Das Badener Lehrstück vom Einverständnis*. This had been intended as an abstract portrayal of the brutality of power relationships in capitalist society — in short: to demonstrate that people do not help one another. The slapstick was an example of Brecht's alienation technique, also known as the estrangement or defamiliarization effect (*Verfremdungseffekt*), which he developed in his theater productions throughout the 1920s and 1930s. The intention was to use artificial (un-naturalistic) performance techniques to prevent the audience's identification with the characters and thereby keep its attention focused on the political message.

This alienation technique is evident in Biermann's "Ballade vom Mann." We see it in the song's function as a parable (here of how the Party cuts its own nose off to spite its face); in the aforementioned grotesque lyrical imagery; but also on the level of performance: in the singer's exaggerated fricative on every repetition of the word "Fuß" and the jarring elongations of certain vowels, for example, the "ei" in "Partei." These guide the audience towards the parodic intent.[26]

A further example of Biermann's use of the grotesque can be found in relation to his identification with the figure of François Villon. This will be dealt with in chapter 3 on "Narrative Role-Play."

In the 1980s Wenzel and Mensching, too, used strong elements of the grotesque. Their clown costumes — Wenzel appeared as a white clown with painted, fat, red lips and Mensching as a dark Mephisto figure — immediately created a grotesque, alienating milieu for their songs and scenes. In traditional folk culture, according to Mikhail Bakhtin, the clown's large, red-painted mouth is a symbol of the carnivalesque grotesque body "that swallows the world and is itself swallowed by the world."[27] In this, it symbolizes transformation; the unfinished; the never completed. When Wenzel and Mensching made use of this fair-ground tradition, this heightened the alienation effect in their — for GDR standards — highly risky portrayals of political leaders. As mentioned, Mensching's 1982 poem "Égalité" from the *Hammer-Rehwü*[28] is a mocking degradation of political leaders sitting on the toilet. In the *Liedertheater* program "Altes aus der Da Da eR"[29] from autumn 1989 (adapted for film by Jörg Foth in 1990[30]) Wenzel and Mensching grotesquely caricature the aging Politbüro. In one scene, the duo, in clown masks and costumes, sprinkle powder on each other's hair, bow their heads and shoulders, and transform into decrepit old men. Wenzel, in a traditional carnivalesque inversion whereby objects are employed in an arbitrary topsy turvy fashion, uses his guitar as a walking stick. With mock pathos they perform the tragicomedy of the soon-to-be deposed leaders, singing: "Eh du dich versiehst mein Freund / Ist die Zeit verronnen/ Und vom Glücke dieser Welt / Hast du nichts gewonnen / Ja, ja, ja, ja / Weißt ja wie gut ich dir bin." The clowns continue to relentlessly lampoon the GDR political hierarchy in the song "Undank ist der Welten Lohn," singing with ironical self-pity of the personal tragedy unfolding:

Ich hab mich nie gebremst für meinen Staat
Regierte viel parteilich Tag und Nacht
Jetzt bin ich alt und ernte den Salat
Das alte Eisen wird nun ausgelacht
Bin selber schuld das hab ich nun davon
Undank ist der Welten Lohn.

Montage Technique

Singers such as Wolf Biermann, Wenzel and Mensching, and Konstantin Wecker were also highly influenced by the montage technique that had been pioneered in the Weimar Republic. The montage aesthetic was a reflection of the ambiguous, hybridic nature of the political song between high and low culture that was particularly evident in the early Weimar cabarets. The concept of *Gebrauchsmusik* and *Gebrauchslyrik* (music and lyrics "for use") was widespread. It encompassed the ideals of practicality, usefulness, relevance, didacticism, and utilization of modern technology (Cook 1988, 21). In a modern, fast-moving, urban world, where communication could not be taken for granted, music and words were now written with a particular target audience in mind and with a specific purpose, for example, for political enlightenment or agitation. Montage was a major communicative technique in this respect.

Montage was pioneered in Berlin dada, cinema, and cabaret. The dada movement had been founded at the Cabaret Voltaire in Zurich in 1916 by artists and writers such as Hugo Ball, Tristan Zara, Hans Arp, and Richard Huelsenbeck. Due to the dadaists' rejection of bourgeois values in general (particularly militarism) figures such as John Heartfield and George Grosz had aspects in common with the communists. But the communists distrusted dada because of its rejection of logical systems of thought. In fact the dadaists were essentially apolitical, as this 1924 poem by Kurt Schwitters indicates:

Was ist Wahnsinn?

Wahnsinn läßt sich teilen.
Wahnsinn ist dividierbar und multiplizierbar.
Man lernt Wahnsinn am besten kennen, wenn man sich von
    ihm entfernt.
Wahnsinn ist Politik.
Dada ist gegen Politik, weil gegen Wahnsinn.
Politik steht im Weichbild unserer Zeit.
Möge selbiges Bild bald weichen und unserer Zeit freien
    Raum lassen.[31]

Dada was intended, according to Ball, to be apolitical, whimsical, spontaneous, foolish, and should represent "a farce of nothingness."[32] In the wider cultural picture this latter aspect was in tune with the nihilism of Brecht and the poets returning from the war. The randomness of the dadaist montage principle in art and poetry reflected — in the wake of the slaughter of the First World War — the fragmentation of modern life devoid of sense or purpose. There emerges a dislocated relationship to time and history. The senseless catastrophe of the war had shattered the illusion of progress and temporal continuity embedded in the ideals of the Enlightenment. The principle of randomness, breaks, and interruptions was a major strategy in the montage-based dada art of John Heartfield and George Grosz and in the poems of their Berlin colleague Walter Mehring.[33] With its reportage style, Mehring's "Achtung Gleisdreieck," for example, refers to the chaos of the famous triangular station junction in Berlin where trains and people converged and departed: "Jeder in / Anderer / Richtung und / Achtung! Das /Gleisdreieck."[34] The poem is a montage consisting of image fragments of different aspects of Berlin city life: forms of entertainment, modes of transportation, and political sloganeering, none of which have much in common with each other apart from their random simultaneity in the big city (Jelavich 1996, 146–47). Mehring's "Berliner Simultan" (1920), sung by Rosa Valetti, was typically dadaesque in its approach, with frivolous, throw-away lines such as: "Her mit dem Scheck! / Schiebung mit Speck / Komm, süsse Puppe! / Is' alles schnuppe." Such references to black marketeering appear amidst a collage of random, fast-flowing images from public life, which among other things point to the rise of the far right and anti-Semitic violence: "Das Volk steht auf! Die Fahnen raus! [. . .] Die Reaktion flaggt schon am DOM/ Mit Hakenkreuz und Blaukreuzgas — / Monokel contra Hakennas' / — Auf zum Pogrom / Beim Hippodrom!" (Mehring, 78–79).

If modernist art after the First World War reflected a crisis; a break with cultural traditions and assumptions, it is interesting to look at GDR lyric and song from the mid-1960s onwards. For example, the significance of the use of montage in GDR *Liedertheater* must be viewed in terms of the general trend in GDR literature of this period to reflect discontinuities and ruptures. After the conviction of the *Aufbau* period of the 1950s and early 1960s, the SED's claim of continuity with the revolutionary tradition was becoming increasingly problematic. For many critical writers, history could no longer be viewed in the traditional Marxist sense "as a rationally transparent, dynamic, and linear process, which would ultimately lead to the communist goal" (Leeder, 108). Rather, from the late-sixties onwards, there was the acute sense of being "out of step," of a "gap in time."[35] This idea of a break with cultural tradition was expressed by an adoption of modernist, anti-realist literary techniques by writers such as Christa Wolf, Heiner Müller, and Volker Braun. But it was younger writers, those "born into"[36] this historical standstill, who experienced its contradictions most keenly. In the poetry of Steffen Mensching, Hans-Eckardt Wenzel, Uwe Kolbe, Jörg Kowalski, and others, this resulted in a "subjective acquisition" of history (Leeder, 115). The montage aesthetic behind this approach is reflected in Steffen Mensching's poem "London, fünfzehnter März dreiundachtzig" (1982) in which the poet adapts a telegram sent by Friedrich Engels announcing the death of Karl Marx:

> Gestern mittag, 2 Uhr 45. Das stärkste Herz
> Das ich gekannt,
> Hat ausgeschlagen. Die Menschheit ist um
> Einen Kopf kürzer. Lokalgrößen
> Und kleine Talente, wo nicht Schwindler,
> Bekommen freie Hand [. . .]

In Mensching's presentation of Engel's call to keep up the utopian struggle there is a subjective slant: the poet's basic optimism is tinged with an ironic sadness bordering on resentment. It reflects the skepticism that was felt at the time regarding postponing a "life in the now" for the sake of a future utopian goal:

> [. . .]   Ja
> Der endliche Sieg bleibt sicher, aber Umwege,
> Lokale und temporäre
> Verirrungen werden anwachsen. Nun — wir
> Müssens durchfressen. Wozu
> Anders sind wir da. Unsere Courage verlieren
> Wir darum noch nicht. Dein Engels. (1984, 24)

This poem was recited by Mensching in Karls Enkel's *Liedertheater* production "Die komische Tragödie des 18. Brumaire" in 1983. Reminiscent of the group's treatment of Erich Mühsam, it was accompanied by music in the style of a funeral lament. The montage effect is clear in the convergence of two time levels: the one reflects Engel's sadness at the death of Marx in 1873; the other reflects contemporary sadness at how, 100 years later in 1983, Marx's ideas had not been realized.

Musical Montage

The montage-based use of music by performers such as Biermann, Wenzel and Mensching, and Konstantin Wecker can also be traced back to the 1920s. Montage was a feature of the trend of *Neue Sachlichkeit* (New Objectivity) in literature, music, photography, and art. This entailed sobriety, detachment, and a non-expressionistic matter-of-factness, and was evident in the lyric of Brecht, Tucholsky, Mehring, and Kästner. In the world of serious music, *Neue Sachlichkeit* was pursued in the *Zeitoper* (Opera for Our Time) composed by Kurt Weill, Paul Hindemith, and Ernst Krenek in the late 1920s. Like *Gebrauchsmusik, Zeitoper* recognized the gulf between composer and the modern musical audience and sought to create music for the members of that wider audience.[37] *Zeitoper* renounced the dramatic, expressionistic model of Wagnerian opera and incorporated features of the genres used in revues, such as popular song (including the sentimental German *Schlager* variety), American jazz, and modern dance-steps such as the Charleston. It also made use of new technology (slide projections, film clips, and elaborate new stage settings) which had been pioneered in the political theater of the communist director Erwin Piscator (Cook 1988, 34–39).

In Weill's collaboration with Brecht on *Die Dreigroschenoper* in 1928 and *Aufstieg und Fall der Stadt Mahagonny* in 1929, the music took on a new political function. Here, the concept of *Zeitoper* was combined with Brecht's emerging theory of alienation effects (*Verfremdungseffekte*). Music, text, and performance now had to shake audiences out of their passive consumption of art, to lead them to a critical awareness of its themes. Weill's compositions supported Brecht's satire on the illusionist consumer paradise represented by the city Mahagonny. A musical montage technique was employed in which elements of opera, popular ballads, jazz, and sea chanty (as well as rhythmic influences from Stravinsky) formed dissonances with one another or created tension with the content of the lyrics to create an alienation effect.[38]

The legacy of Weill and Hanns Eisler (whose theory of the dialectical interplay between text and music will be dealt with below) continued to be a major strategy in the revived political song from the 1960s onwards. This was particularly so in the GDR, where the proletarian musical heritage was most heavily nurtured. While Wolf Biermann did not write Eislerian *Kampflieder* — his ballads, *Moritaten,* and *Spottlieder* reflected an altogether more subjective style[39] — he had learned, as one of Eisler's most famous pupils, "daß die Musik nicht nur ein Transportmittel sein soll."[40] Biermann's songs illustrate the Eislerian practice of using music to promote dialogic interplay between different textual levels. In "Enfant perdu" from 1969, Biermann's lament for Florian Havemann, son of the political dissident Robert Havemann, who had abandoned the GDR for the West, the church tonality of the harmony in the minor key expresses the sadness of loss (Kühn, 89). This mood is abruptly broken up, however, by a change in rhythm to a staccato pulse, as Biermann acknowledges the fact that for many in the GDR emigration is never far from their thoughts: "Abgang ist überall" (217).

The use of music to support parody is evident in Biermann's 1965 song "Acht Argumente für die Beibehaltung des Namens Stalinallee." Here the singer mocks the changing of the name of the street to Karl-Marx-Allee after the revelations of Stalin's crimes at the Soviet Union's Twentieth Communist Party Congress in 1956. For Biermann the name should stay as a monument to the legacy of the Stalinism, which had so corrupted the GDR:

> Es steht in Berlin eine Straße
> Die steht auch in Leningrad
> Die steht genauso in mancher
> Andern großen Stadt
>
> > Und darum heißt sie auch STALINALLEE
> > Mensch, Junge versteh
> > Und die Zeit ist passé
> > [. . .]
>
> Die weißen Kacheln fallen
> Uns auf den Kopf ja nur
> Die Häuser stehen ewig!
> (in Baureparatur!!)
>
> > Auch darum heißt das Ding STALINALLEE
>
> Karl Marx, der große Denker
> Was hat er denn getan
> Daß man sein' guten Namen
> Schreibt an die Kacheln dran?!
>
> > Das Ding heißt doch nicht KARL-MARX-ALLEE
> > Mensch, Junge, versteh:
> > STALINALLEE (160–62)

The air-pumping effect of the harmonium conjures up the sound of a carousel and street party celebrations (Kuhn, 124). Through this use of music Biermann caricatures the abandon with which the Party renames streets and towns in order to manipulate history.

The influence of Weill and Eisler is also evident in the music of Konstantin Wecker in West Germany. Musical montage was a means of expressing contradiction and ambiguity. This can be contrasted with the monotony of the music of some of the more militant Burg Waldeck *Liedermacher* (such as the later Degenhardt), for whom music became subordinated to the political statement. But Wecker's message was also political: in a response to increased police surveillance of alleged political deviants following the activities of the Red Army Faction in the late 1970s Wecker wrote

"Hexeneinmaleins": "Immer noch werden Hexen verbrannt / auf den Scheitern der Ideologien. / Irgendwer ist immer der Böse im Land / und dann kann man als Guter / und die Augen voll Sand / in die heiligen Kriege ziehn!" (1978). This song is a montage of rock and classical musical styles. The Carl Orff-influenced operatic motifs support the idea of a hunt, thereby underscoring the theme of the *Hexenjagd,* or witch-hunt. As Matthias Henke observes:

> Expressive Rhythmik, vielseitiger Einsatz der Stimme (geflüstert, gerufen, gesungen, solistisch, im Chor) und der ikonographische Gebrauch der Instrumente (Orgel und Trommel als Symbol für Kirche und Militär) lassen aus den Texten die Schreie der Gequälten hören.[41]

Wecker's song "Einen braucht der Mensch zum Treten" from 1984 also reflects a modernist aesthetic of disruption. Wecker uses the chorus, in a way reminiscent of an Eisler *Lehrstück-Lied* (Henke 1987, 212), to disrupt the conventional song structure, having it burst in unexpectedly and repeatedly. This defamiliarization, also caused by starkly contrasting musical accompaniments throughout the song, intends to draw attention to the textual content: how feelings of inadequacy are often at the root of social ills such as xenophobia: "Es gibt ein ganz probates Mittel / Um den Alltagsfrust zu überstehen / Dazu braucht man keinen Doktortitel / Man löst mit einem Türken das Problem."[42]

In the post-Biermann generation in the GDR Karls Enkel was another example of a younger generation using montage to express dissent from the dogmas of cultural tradition. Here, too, music could have a supportive or an ironic, undermining function. Forms with certain associations (folk, pop, waltzes, marches, tangos, classical string-quartets) formed a dialectical relationship with lyrical content. An example was Wenzel's performance of the previously quoted poem "Égalité" in the *Hammer-Rehwü* of 1982. The rococo string arrangement with its rather prudish associations supports the mock innocence of the white clown Wenzel's delivery. This is, however, contradicted by the profanity of the text, which, in carnivalesque fashion, brings the lofty world of leading politicians down to the level of what Bakhtin terms "the bodily lower stratum."[43] Similarly in Karls Enkel's Goethe program "Dahin! Dahin!"[44] of 1982, defamiliarizing, festive klezmer and folk accompaniments of Goethe's poetry were juxtaposed with more conventional Schubertian arrangements. In this way they alerted the audience to a plebeian dimension in Goethe's work hitherto unacknowledged in GDR literary reception of the poet (Robb 1998, 39–40).

Agitprop Revue

Montage was also an important aspect of the agitprop revue of the 1920s, elements of which were revived in the political song scenes of both the Federal Republic and the GDR. In the 1920s agitprop revue had been distinct from the bourgeois literary cabaret in that it had overtly revolutionary aspirations. A major player was Erwin Piscator, a war veteran and Communist Party member who had founded the first proletarian theater in Berlin in 1920. He staged the *Roter Rummel* revue in Berlin in support for the KPD election campaign of 1924. It was a multimedia event comprising songs and sketches. The action was augmented by film or slide projections, in keeping with the montage aesthetic of the age. In the scenes the players acted out various social roles, for example, the policeman, the worker, and the capitalist. They directly engaged the audience and agitated with political slogans and arguments that demonstrated the power relationships of the class conflict.[45]

In the late 1960s in West Germany a variation of this agitprop tradition — as opposed to established political cabaret acts like Wolfgang Neuss and Hanns Dieter Hüsch — was practiced by the group Floh de Cologne.[46] Stemming from the radical student movement, their first album in 1968 was a collaboration with Dieter Süverkrüp entitled *Vietnam*. All royalties were transferred to a foundation to benefit the Vietnamese. With their montage of rock music, political lyrics, humor, and lunacy, they became known as the German answer to the American rock groups The Fugs and Mothers Of Invention.[47] The sleeve of their album *Fliessbandbabys Beat Show* shows a nineteen-point step-by-step guide to becoming politically active. Their most acclaimed album was *Profitgeier* (1971), "a highly imaginative rock opera" executed at a furious tempo, in which "the group members acted as different characters or proclaimed political views on the class-divided society."[48]

Floh de Cologne performed several times at the annual Festival des politschen Liedes in East Berlin. But their form of agitprop rock theater was too politically direct to be practiced by GDR groups. From the mid-1970s onwards a new form known as *Liedertheater*, distinct from GDR cabaret,[49] was pioneered by groups such as Schicht, Brigade Feuerstein, and Karls Enkel. Disenchanted with the limitations on the political song form imposed by the censorship in the GDR,[50] they used parodic techniques from 1920s proletarian revue to expose contradictions in their own society. A technique employed by Erwin Piscator in the 1920s was that of dismantling ("Demontage"), whereby well-known quotations are cut up and satirically recast. This is evident in the *Hammer-Rehwü* of 1982, where, for example, Spencer Davis's 1960s rock hit "Keep on Running" becomes "Halt zur Stange," the motto of a social conformist or "Mitläufer" and Zarah Leander's "Es wird einmal ein Wunder geschehen," from the 1942 film *Die große Liebe,* is transformed into a parody of the utopian delusions of the GDR leadership and their love affair with the socialist ideal: "Es wird einmal ein Wunder geschehn, / Und dann werden tausend Märchen wahr. / Ich weiß, so schnell kann keine Liebe vergehn, / Die so groß ist und so wunderbar."

Similarly the opening song, "Du, laß dich nicht bescheißen," constitutes a play on the line "Laßt euch nicht verführen" from Brecht and Weill's *Mahagonny.*" The new version laughs at the utopian belief in a future communist paradise and implies that the government uses people as mere objects in the pursuit of that goal. The parodic hybrid functions by adapting the original *Mahagonny* lines "Laßt euch nicht verführen / Zu Fron und Ausgezehr. / Was kann euch Angst noch rühren / Ihr sterbt mit allen Tieren / Und es kommt nichts nachher"[51] to become: "Du, laß dich nicht einwickeln / Von Liebe, Fron und Ehr / Wir sind Verbrauchsartikel / Und sterben wie Karnickel. / Und es kommt nichts nachher."[52]

Although it appropriated the form and structure of the proletarian revue, the *Hammer-Rehwü* turned the whole concept on its head. Rather than propagating socialism, it made fun of the symbols of GDR authority, namely the general, the dictator, and the worker (see Robb 1998, 55). And in a clear distancing from the didacticism of proletarian revue, the cast declares to the audience in the epilogue that there will be no moral:

> Ihr aber, die ihr nutzlos rumgesessen / Mit euren fiesen Füßen, dicken Bäuchen, / Schiefgegrinsten Fressen, / Was sagt ihr nun? / Was nehmt ihr mit ins Heim? / [. . .] Mein Freund, ich will nicht sagen, du bist bös / Doch etwas dümmlich hockst du hier / Nervös, auf deinem Stuhl, / Weil die Moral, es ist fatal, / Nicht mitgeliefert wurd in diesem Fall.

The Political Song Theory of Hanns Eisler

Despite the satirical provocation of the literary chanson, it seldom proposed a revolutionary solution to society's ills. Furthermore, the fact that it was targeted at a bourgeois taste group (Jelavich, 134–35) undermined its political effectiveness, according to Benjamin, who wrote in 1931 that "linke Melancholie" had merely become a marketable commodity within a bourgeois avant-garde milieu.[53] By 1929 Brecht was departing from the subjective approach of his *Hauspostille* poem collection and was increasingly writing songs for the political use of a mass audience. He began collaborating with Hanns Eisler, a composer who shared Brecht's own increasingly Marxist beliefs. Eisler conceived a theory of the political song that combined current modernist aesthetics with a revolutionary ideological stance. In the mid-1920s he had been influenced by the Soviet avant-garde and was impressed by the agitprop group Blaue Blusen, which made current problems tangible by means of photography, film, and radio.[54] Working with the Berlin group Das rote Sprachrohr, Eisler learned to use music to represent political concerns. He found that "music, if intelligently used, was in a position effectively to indicate the relationship between the various topics and to intimate the emotional level" (Betz 1982, 65). This approach to composition — geared towards agitation and enlightenment of a proletarian audience — contrasted to that of bourgeois music, which Eisler believed was composed for passive consumption, for the purpose of recovery and reproduction.[55] Within this broad category of "bourgeois music," serious music, such as Schönberg, was a means of entertainment for an educated elite, while popular music such as the *Schlager* merely served to dull the minds of the masses (Eisler 1973, 178). Proletarian music therefore had to rid itself of all trappings of bourgeois music. This included the melodic logic and harmony of the *Schlager* and *Volkslieder,* which Eisler believed to be corrupt in their encouragement of passivity and conformity (170).

Eisler's approach mirrored Brecht's theory of Epic Theater in that ac tors had to preserve distance, that is, not lose themselves in their roles. In this respect the affectation of bourgeois music, as reflected in the personality cult of a conductor, had to be replaced in the militant songs by a "kalte Grundhaltung" that helped impart the political message (170). The words should be presented rhythmically and precisely, as if in a lecture. For Brecht and Eisler this particular attribute was to be found in the singing style of Ernst Busch.

In short, workers' music should be challenging, should not promote conformity, but should be as transparent as possible. Its first aim should not be to revel in its own artistry, but to demonstrate a particular *Gebrauchswert.* As Betz states, "beauty, aesthetic charm and enjoyment were no longer the highest aim [of the music], but were pressed into its service" (82). To these ends, the technique of musical montage was used to communicate the Marxist vision of social dialectics and the class struggle, as illustrated in the discussion of songs that follows.

Eisler's composition for Tucholsky's "Lied der Wohltätigkeit" is a montage of cabaret chanson, marching rhythms, and jazz counterpoints. The song, which was sung by Ernst Busch, is laden with sarcasm. It protests at the hypocrisy of the capitalists, who pretend to be working in the interests of the proletariat:

> Sieh, da steht das Erholunggsheim
> Einer Aktiengesellschaftsgruppe;
> morgens gibt es Haferschleim
> und abends Gerstensuppe,
> und die Arbeiter dürfen auch in den Park

> Sie reichen euch manches Almosen hin
> Unter christlichen, frommen Gebeten;
> sie pflegen die leidende Wöchnerin,
> denn sie brauchen ja die Proleten.
> Sie liefern auch einen Armensarg.
>
> Gut, das ist der Pfennig
> und wo ist die Mark?

The lighthearted, almost decadent, cabaret aspect of these verses and chorus underline the parody of Tucholsky's lyrics — exposing the sham of the capitalists' good intentions toward the workers. A dialectic tension, however, is continually created by the accompanying march pulse and the jazz inflections. Changes in tempo are used to highlight certain ideas and insights. In the third and final section, the cabaret music subsides, to be replaced entirely by an agitative march rhythm as Busch shouts the emphatic conclusion:

> Proleten fallt nicht auf den Schwindel, rein!
> Sie schulden euch mehr als sie geben.
> Sie schulden euch alles, die Länderei'n,
> die Bergwerke und die Wollfärberei'n. . .
> sie schulden euch Glück und Leben!
> Nimm, was du kriegst! Aber pfeif auf den Quark.
> Denk an deine Klasse und die mach stark![56]

Similarly, Eisler's composition for Brecht's "Solidaritätslied" from 1931 constitutes a montage of agitative text, march rhythms, modal ecclesiastic music, and popular jazz. The march provided urgency, the jazz inflections were inserted to increase accessibility, and the collective associations of church music were used to promote class consciousness (Betz, 80). "Solidaritätslied" became the theme song for Brecht and Eisler's *Kuhle Wampe* (1932), a film starring Ernst Busch, which clearly illustrates the milieu of the mass workers' gathering for which the *Kampflied* was conceived. The text itself contains distinct echoes of the militant songs of 1848 and those of the early Mühsam in its call to break the chains of tyranny and overturn the master-slave relationship:

> Unsre Herrn, wer sie auch seien
> Sehen unsre Zwietracht gern
> Denn solang sie uns entzweien
> Bleiben sie doch unsre Herrn.
> [. . .]
> Proletarier aller Länder
> Einigt euch und ihr seid frei.

> Eure großen Regimenter
> Brechen jede Tyrannei!

This, however, is combined with a more purposeful, less romantic vision within the structure of an organized world solidarity movement: "Vorwärts und nicht vergessen / Worin unsre Stärke besteht! / Beim Hungern und beim Essen / Vorwärts, nie vergessen/ Die Solidarität."[57]

Utopia and Defeat 2: The Legacy of the Anti-Fascist Movement and the Spanish Civil War

With the coming to power of the Nazis in 1933 Eisler was unable to properly test the intended effects of the *Kampflied* that he had envisaged in his theory. With the exodus from Germany of left-wing artists including Brecht, Eisler, and Busch, it now remained to be seen how songs could contribute to the international anti-fascist movement. The history of the particular relationship between Brecht, Eisler, and Busch in the early years of exile has been well documented in Albrecht Dümling's *Laßt Euch nicht verführen: Brecht und die Musik.*[58] It was in this period — up until he was arrested by the Nazis in Belgium in 1940 — that Busch made an international name for himself on his journeys between Amsterdam, London, Moscow, and Barcelona as the singer of the anti-fascist song.

Busch was originally a metal worker who had joined the Kiel Arbeiterjugend in 1916 at age 16. After taking singing and acting lessons he became an actor in the Kiel Stadttheater, later moving to Berlin in 1927, where he found roles in Erwin Piscator's Theater am Nollendorfplatz. He greatly impressed as a singer and was invited by Edmund Meisel to sing his settings of Walter Mehring lyrics. Brecht invited him to play Constable Smith in *Die Dreigroschenoper* at the Theater am Schiffbauerdamm in 1928. A year later he worked again with Hanns Eisler in Piscator's production of Mehring's play *Der Kaufmann von Berlin.* Mehring was later to say of Eisler: "[sein] bestes Instrument war Ernst Busch."[59] Busch also performed in the cabarets, where he sang workers' songs such as Julien Arendt's "Seifenlied," Erich Weinert's "Roter Wedding," and David Weber's "Stempellied." Eisler wrote the music for these and often accompanied Busch on the piano.

Busch fled from Nazi Germany to the Netherlands in March 1933, where he performed radio broadcasts specifically targeted at an anti-fascist audience within Germany. In the summer of 1933 Brecht and Eisler compiled a new book entitled *Lieder, Gedichte, Chöre.* With songs such as "Ballade vom Baum und den Ästen," "An die Kämpfer in den KZ Lagern," and "Ballade vom SA-Mann" they hoped to invigorate the anti-fascist resistance. As Dümling writes, it was intended, somewhat idealisti-

cally, that the book could be smuggled into Germany to resistance fighters. Three thousand copies were printed, but it is likely that few reached
their intended destination (394).

In 1935 Busch went to Moscow, where he worked with lyricist Erich
Weinert and played for German communist exiles. He performed on the
radio station Komintern, which, with 500 kilowatts of power, was broadcast all over the world. Later, on the eastern front, the Red Army played
Busch's singing over public address systems to spread propaganda among
the German troops. Author Heiner Kipphardt, confirming the quality of
Busch's singing, which had so impressed Brecht and Eisler, recalls as a
young German soldier hearing Busch's voice: "Die Stimme verjagte meine
Apathie [. . .] Diese Stimme wußte, daß [. . .] die Wahrheit triumphieren
würde."[60]

In July 1936 workers and left-wing intellectuals from around the world
joined together in the International Brigades to fight against General
Franco's overthrow of the democratically-elected socialist government in
Spain.[61] In his Moscow exile, Busch began compiling the volume *Canciones
de las Brigadas Internacionales*,[62] which appeared in Spain in 1937. It contained Spanish Republican songs such as "Bandera Roja" (best known for
its Italian version "Bandiera Rossa") and compositions from Eisler and
Paul Dessau, among a host of international worker's songs in several languages. The songs reflected the utopian spirit of the International Brigade
fighters, as exemplified by Dessau's "Spaniens Himmel" (otherwise known
as "Die Thälmann-Kolonne"):

> Spaniens Himmel breitet seine Sterne
> Über unsre Schützengräben aus
> Und der Morgen grüßt schon aus der Ferne,
> Bald geht es zu neuem Kampf hinaus.
> Die Heimat ist weit, doch wir sind bereit
> Wir kämpfen und siegen für dich: Freiheit. (1937)[63]

The self-sacrifice and resolve of the brigade is evident in Busch's
"Lincoln-Bataillon": "In dem Tal dort am Rio Jamara / Schlugen wir unsre
blutigste Schlacht / Doch wir haben auf Tod und Verderben / Die
Faschisten zum Stehen gebracht" (1937). Erich Weinert's song "Jarama-
front" proclaims how the battle of Jamara will serve as a model for the
world revolution to come: "wenn die Stunde kommt, /[. . .] Wird die
ganze Welt zur Jaramaschlacht." And Busch's "Die Herren Generale"
evokes, to the tune of the Spanish folk song "Mamita Mia," a new era in
which the chains of servitude will be broken: "Und alle deinen Tränen /
mamita mia, / die werden wir rächen. / Und alle unsre Knechtschaft /
mamita mia, / die werden wir brechen." Busch journeyed from Moscow
to Spain in February 1937 for the publication of *Canciones*, and he him-

self sang for the brigades. In 1938, under wartime conditions in Barcelona, Busch recorded *Discos de las Brigadas Internacionales,* songs that Jürgen Schebera described as "Höhepunkte kämpfender Kunst unseres Jahrhunderts." In a tribute to Busch, who died in the GDR in 1980, Schebera rated *Canciones* on par with Picasso's *Guernica* in terms of its artistic contribution to the Spanish Civil War.[64]

This musical legacy of the Spanish International Brigade was carried on in the GDR, initially by the workers' choirs and from the mid-1960s onwards by the FDJ-sponsored *Singebewegung.* An altogether more provocative relationship to the Spanish *Kampflieder* was established in 1975 by Wolf Biermann with his recording *Es gibt ein Leben vor dem Tod.* Initially the project had been inspired as a critical response to the GDR's diplomatic recognition of Franco's Spain. But there was a more general cultural criticism: the utopian spirit of the songs of the International Brigade clashed with the stagnation of the socialist ideal in the GDR. Biermann emphasized the irony of this in his performance of Dessau's "Spaniens Himmel." Having long been a compulsory item at FDJ or Party meetings, the song had lost any association with freedom for the average citizen of the GDR. Biermann's response was to parody it, singing it as a slow dirge as opposed to a vibrant, optimistic march. He sang as if he were a cold, frightened young soldier stumbling over words that, according to Biermann, would have been remote to the immediate reality of war in any case. There is a non-commitment: words such as the usually declamatory "Freiheit" tail away at the end of lines or are not sung at all, as in the case of the "nicht" in "Mit uns stehn Kameraden ohnegleichen, / Und ein Rückwärts gibt es für uns nicht." He remembers: "Ich hatte dieses Lied durch meine Interpretation dermaßen gegen den Strich gebürstet, daß es für die Wissenden im Osten eine herzerfrischende Provokation gegen die herrschende Ideologie war, in den Augen der Obrigkeit ein Sakrileg."[65] A comment from Otto F. Riewoldt illustrates the tensions between Biermann and the West German Communist Party (DKP) of the time, whose members mistrusted Biermann's criticism of the GDR. Riewoldt says his approach was in keeping with the defeatist mood among socialist intellectuals of the time: "Biermanns kommunistische Utopie [nährt] sich von Niederlagen, Trauer um die verraten Revolution, Lob der toten, gescheiterten Revolution."[66] This comment foreshadowed the controversy that surrounded Karls Enkel's 1985 program "Spanier aller Länder," with its treatment of the themes of utopia and defeat.

If the 1983 production "Die komische Tragödie des 18. Brumaire" had expressed Karls Enkel's identification with the defeated Parisian proletariat of 1848, 1985's "Spanier aller Länder"[67] explored the group's relationship to the failure of the International Brigade. In this *Liedertheater* production, a collaboration between the group and the well known musician and veteran of the Spanish campaign, Eberhard Schmidt, utopian fighting spirit is again balanced against death and defeat. The heroism of writers who fought on the Republican side is highlighted. This is countered with a mood of melancholy that is conveyed through the medium of montage. As Mensching shouts out "Gestern alles Vergangene [. . .] Doch heute der Kampf" from W. H. Auden's "Spanien 37," the cast, dressed in the uniforms of the International Brigade, sing Schubert and Uhland's "Frühlingsglaube" quietly in the background. The pathos of the fighting spirit is doubly relativized, the optimistic refrain "Nun muß sich alles wenden" from "Frühlingsglaube" contradicted by the sadness of the singing. In this way a moment of revolutionary history is projected onto the contemporary GDR.

Again, mirroring the narratives of the songs of the *Vormärz* and the 1848 revolution, the utopian aspirations of the International Brigade are countered with images of sleep and death. Rilke's "Schlußstück" is adapted as follows: "Groß ist der Tod / Wir sind die seinen / Lachenden Munds / Wenn wir uns mitten im Leben meinen / Wagt er zu weinen / Mitten in uns." A dialogue between Wenzel and Mensching, playing the roles of Don Quixote and Sancho Pansa, relates the dangerous similarity of death and sleep. As they watch the sleeping Republican fighters in the valley below, Quixote observes: "Ein einziges böses Ding hat der Schlaf [. . .] daß er namlich dem Tode so ähnlich sieht, denn zwischen einem Schlafenden und einem Toten ist nur ein geringer Unterschied." Here Walter Benjamin's idea that Western society had not yet awoken from the dream of the nineteenth century[68] is applied to the GDR. With echoes of the Biedermeier period, it relates to the retreat en masse into the inner self that Wenzel and Mensching felt so characterized their own society. Through this technique of association, the GDR appears as a land in slumber.

"Spanier aller Länder" finishes with the internment of the International Brigade fighters in the Gurs concentration camp. Don Quixote acknowledges this defeat in his final speech. As in "Die komische Tragödie," the levels of past and present blend together and the GDR appears as bereft of any utopian perspective. The ghosts of revolutionary ancestors still weigh heavily, but Wenzel and Mensching's sense of responsibility toward them cannot be fulfilled because of the constraints of their time. As the "Jetzt noch nicht" sentiment in Mensching's poem "Für Peter Weiss" provocatively reflects, the GDR in 1985 was simply not yet ready to confront the taboos of the past.[69] As if to underline this fact, the concluding words "Jetzt noch nicht" were omitted from the published version of the poem:

Einmal, später, irgendwann
werden wir die Siegel der Archive brechen.
Beieinander sitzend dann
Das nie Ausgesprochene aussprechen.

[. . . .]

Irgendwann, hoffentlich bald, aber später,
Werden wir die ganze Wahrheit ertragen.
Nennen werden wir Helden Helden
     Verbrechen Verbrechen

Nacheinander werden wir zu Wort uns melden,
das Schweigen brechen,
das taktische dumpfe beredsame Schweigen.
[. . .]
Einmal, später, jetzt noch nicht.[70]

By the same token, the fact that Karls Enkel did not challenge taboo subjects more openly earned them fierce criticism from their audience. Many felt the depiction of the International Brigade's heroism amidst spirited marching music and pathos-laden songs such as "No pasaran" and "Santa Barbara" overshadowed the level of contradiction presented in the clowns' dialogues or in the treatment of the defeat. In retrospect Mensching confessed to having been too much in awe of the sacred socialist heritage that the International Brigade and Eberhard Schmidt represented: "Spanien [war] für uns etwas Hehres [. . . .] Es war sehr schwer für mich, an dieses Heiligtum frech heranzugehen."[71] Wenzel explained they had overestimated their audience's continuing readiness in 1985 to embrace the basic concept of utopia at all:

> Aller bisheriger plebejischer Protest/Karneval bei *Karls Enkel* basierte auf der stillschweigenden Übereinkunft, daß es nicht um konservative Weltmodelle geht, die als unausgesprochene Utopie in den Köpfen existierte. Dieser Zustand war, als wir *"Spanier"* produzierten, vorbei [. . .] Das naive Experiment wurde nicht mehr zugelassen.[72]

No matter how challengingly and creatively Karls Enkel treated the theme of utopia in "Spanier aller Länder," by 1985 it was in essence already too late to present it to a critical GDR audience. This was an indication of how rife disillusionment was in the final few years of the state's existence.

In conclusion, the combination of literary movements and revolutionary flashpoints from 1900 until the late 1930s inspired a wealth of German protest song. This formed both a thematic and stylistic reference point for the revived political song of the 1960s onwards. On an artistic level, avant-garde techniques developed for song, agitprop theater, and cabaret in the 1920s were acquired and exploited by the new *Liedermacher*. As in the Weimar Republic, diverging artistic forms reflected differences in approach to the issue of revolution. Cabaret chanson and *Kampflied* reflected the opposition between literary satire and didactic agitation. This was later mirrored in the diverging approaches of, for example, Wolf Biermann and the *FDJ-Singegruppen,* Konstantin Wecker and the Burg Waldeck activists, as well as in the different approaches to political revue of Floh de Cologne and the GDR *Liedertheater* groups. Finally, on the thematic level, the political song movements of the *Vormärz* and 1848, the Weimar Republic, West Germany, and the GDR — for all their differences — are connected by a common strand in which the gesture of rebellion is juxtaposed with the despair of failure. And here the importance of the relationship between content and form becomes evident: the contradictoriness embodied in the recurring theme of *deutsche Misere* demanded an ambiguity of approach — to music and text — which the artistic techniques developed in the earlier part of the twentieth century facilitated.

Notes

[1] Georg Herwegh, "Achtzehnter März," in *Herweghs Werke. Erster Teil. Gedichte eines Lebendigen* (Berlin: Deutscher Verlagshaus Bong & Co., 1909), 142–43.

[2] Peter Jelavich, *Berlin Cabaret* (Cambridge, MA and London: Harvard UP, 1996).

[3] Alan Lareau, *The Wild Stage: Literary Cabaret of the Weimar Republic* (Columbia, SC: Camden House, 1995).

[4] Rolf Kauffeldt, *Erich Mühsam Literatur und Anarchie* (Munich: Fink Verlag, 1983), 147.

[5] Erich Mühsam, *Der Ruf,* Heft 1, 1912, 1–2. Quoted in Kauffeldt, *Erich Mühsam,* 152–53.

[6] Erich Mühsam, *Der Krater. Gedichte* (Berlin: Morgen Verlag, 1909), 142–43.

[7] Franz Josef Degenhardt, "Verteidigung eines Sozialdemokraten vor dem Fabriktor" in *Im Jahr de Schweine 27 Neue Lieder mit Noten* (Hamburg: Hoffmann und Kampe, 1970), 32–33. Other songs by Degenhardt from the early 1960s such as "Rumpelstilzchen" and "Wölfe mitten im Mai" from *Spiel nicht mit den Schmuddelkindern* (Reinbek bei Hamburg: Rowohlt, 1969, 15–17 and 28–32) show an influence from the grotesque ballad style of Christian Morgenstern, a cabaret contemporary of Mühsam.

[8] Diana Köhnen, *Das literarische Werk Erich Mühsams* (Würzburg: Königshausen & Neumann, 1988), 171.

[9] Mühsam, "Generalstreik!" in *Kain,* II, 5, 1912, 65. Quoted in Köhnen, *Das literarische Werk Erich Mühsams,* 170.

[10] Mühsam, "Räte-Marsellaise" in *Brennende Erde: Verse eines Kämpfers* (Munich: Kurt Wolff Verlag, 1920), 73. See Köhnen, *Das literarische Werk Erich Mühsams,* 176–79).

[11] *Welt am Montag,* 27 July 1925. Quoted in Kauffeldt, 270.

[12] Wolf Biermann, "Der Hugenottenfriedhof" (1969), in *Alle Lieder* (Cologne: Kiepenheuer & Witsch, 1991), 215. All subsequent references to Biermann unless otherwise stated concern this book.

[13] Steffen Mensching, "Traumhafter Ausflug mit Rosa L.," in *Erinnerung un eine Milchglasscheibe. Gedichte* (Halle and Leipzig: Mitteldeutscher Verlag, 1984), 14–15.

[14] Karls Enkel, "Von meiner Hoffnung laß ich nicht — Der Pilger Mühsam," unpublished manuscript and video, collected by Karin Wolf, archive of the Akademie der Künste der DDR, Berlin, Liedertheater-Dokumentation, Forschungsabteilung Musik/Liedzentrum, 1980. All subsequent unreferenced quotations from this program can be found in the above unpaginated manuscript.

[15] See chapter 8 of this book on political song in the GDR for the reactions of the GDR Stasi to this production.

[16] F. C. Weiskopf, quoted in concert program for *Von meiner Hoffnung laß ich nicht.*

[17] The treatment of the "revolutionary dead" by Karls Enkel has been addressed in David Robb, "Reviving the Dead: Montage and Temporal Dislocation in Karls Enkel's Liedertheater," in *Politics and Culture in Twentieth-Century Germany,* ed. William Niven and James Jordan, 143–61 (Rochester, NY: Camden House, 2003). For an account of Wenzel and Mensching's respective tributes to Mühsam in their own poems see Karen Leeder, *Breaking Boundaries: A New Generation of Poets in the GDR* (Oxford: Clarendon, 1996), 87–88.

[18] See chapter 8 of this book on political song in the GDR.

[19] Karls Enkel, "Deutschland meine Trauer — neun Arten einen Becher zu beschreiben. Ein Johannes-R.-Becher-Abend" unpublished manuscripts and tape recording, collected by Karin Wolf, archive of the Akademie der Künste der DDR, Berlin, Liedertheater-Dokumentation, Forschungsabteilung Musik/Liedzentrum, 1981.

[20] Karls Enkel, "Die komische Tragödie des 18. Brumaire. Oder Ohrfeigen sind schlimmer als Dolchstöße. Nach Karl Marx," unpublished manuscript and video, collected by Karin Wolf, archive of the Akademie der Künste der DDR, Berlin, Liedertheater-Dokumentation, Forschungsabteilung Musik/Liedzentrum, 1983.

[21] See Riha, *Moritat, Bänkelsong, Protestballade,* 16.

[22] Frank Wedekind, "Der Tantenmörder," in *Gesammelte Werke,* vol. 1 (Munich: Georg Müller Verlag, 1920), 107.

[23] See chapter 3 of this book, "Narrative Role-Play as Communication Strategy in German Protest Song."

[24] Bertolt Brecht, "Von der Kindesmörderin Marie Farrar," in *Gesammelte Werke,* vol. 8 (Frankfurt am Main: Suhrkamp, 1967), 176.

64   ◆   DAVID ROBB

[25] All quotations from Wolf Biermann's lyrics in this book are copyright © and used by permission of Wolf Biermann.

[26] Biermann, "Ballade vom Mann," on the live CD *Es geht sein' sozialistischen Gang* (CBS, 1977).

[27] Mikhail Bakhtin, *Rabelais and His World* (Bloomington: U of Indiana P, 1984), 317.

[28] Karls Enkel, Wacholder, and Beckert & Schulz, "Hammer-Rehwü," unpublished manuscripts and video, collected by Karin Wolf, archive of the Akademie der Künste der DDR, Berlin, Liedertheater-Dokumentation, Forschungsabteilung Musik/Liedzentrum, 1982. CD *Hammer-Rehwü von 1982* (Nebelhorn, 1994).

[29] Wenzel and Mensching, "Altes aus der Da Da eR," unpublished manuscript and video, collected by Karin Wolf, archive of the Akademie der Künste der DDR, Berlin, Liedertheater-Dokumentation, Forschungsabteilung Musik/Liedzentrum, 1989.

[30] Wenzel and Mensching, *Letztes aus der Da Da eR,* directed by Jörg Foth (DEFA, 1990). The various textual versions of the Altes and Letztes revue series are published in Wenzel and Mensching, *Allerletzes aus der Da Da eR/ Hundekomödie,* edited by Andrea Doberenz (Halle and Leipzig: Mitteldeutscher Verlag, 1991).

[31] Kurt Schwitters, "Was ist Wahnsinn?" in *Eile ist des Witzes Weile: Eine Auswahl aus den Texten* (Stuttgart: Reclam, 1987), 51.

[32] Hugo Ball, *Flight Out of Time: A Dada Diary* (New York: Viking, 1974), 65. Quoted in Roy F. Allen, "Zurich Dada, 1916–1919: The Proto-Phase of the Movement" in Stephen C. Foster, ed., *Dada/Dimensions* (Ann Arbor: UMI Research Press, 1985), 7.

[33] Mehring, Grosz, and Heartfield, together with composer Friedrich Hollaender, produced and performed a puppet show called "Einfach Klassisch" for the opening Schall und Rauch cabaret in December 1919.

[34] Walter Mehring, *Chronik der Lustbarkeiten: Die Lieder, Gedichte und Chansons 1918–1933* (Düsseldorf: Classen Verlag, 1981), 117–18.

[35] Marilyn Sibley Fries, ed., *Responses to Christa Wolf: Critical Essays* (Detroit: Wayne State UP, 1989), 47.

[36] Leeder, 4. Here Leeder is referring to Uwe Kolbe's term "Die Hineingeborenen," also the title of his poetry collection: *Hineingeborenen: Gedichte 1975– 1979* (Berlin and Weimar: Aufbau, 1980).

[37] Susan C. Cook, *The Opera for a New Republic: The Zeitopern of Krenek, Weill, and Hindemith* (Michigan: UNI Research Press, 1988), 30–31.

[38] Ronald Sanders, *The Days Grow Short: The Life and Music of Kurt Weill* (London: Weidenfeld and Nicolson, 1980), 145–53.

[39] Georg-Friedrich Kühn, "Kutsche und Kutscher. Die Musik des Wolf Biermanns," in Heinz Ludwig Arnold, ed., Wolf Biermann (Munich: Edition Text und Kritik, 1980), 111.

[40] Biermann, in *Frankfurter Rundschau* (30 December 1972), 5.

[41] Matthias Henke, *Die großen Chansonniers und Liedermacher: Verflechtungen, Berührungspünkte, Anregungen* (Düsseldorf: ECON, 1987), 212.

[42] All quotations from Konstantin Wecker's lyrics in this book are copyright © and used by permission of Konstantin Wecker/Management Konstantin Wecker.

[43] See Mikhail Bakhtin, *Rabelais and His World,* 23. See references to the carnivalesque in the work of Biermann and Karls Enkel in chapter 3 of this book, "Narrative Role-Play as Communication Strategy in German Protest Song."

[44] Karls Enkel, "Dahin! Dahin!" unpublished manuscript and tape recording, collected by Karin Wolf, archive of the Akademie der Künste der DDR, Berlin, Liedertheater-Dokumentation, Forschungsabteilung Musik/Liedzentrum, 1982.

[45] See Christa Hasche, "Bürgerliche Revue und 'Roter Rummel.' Studien zur Entwicklung massenwirksamen Theaters in den Formen der Revue in Berlin 1903–1925." Diss. (Berlin: Humboldt University, 1980).

[46] For a wider examination of agitprop rock see Annette Blühdorn, *Pop and Poetry — Pleasure and Protest: Udo Lindenberg, Konstantin Wecker and the Tradition of German Cabaret* (Bern: Peter Lang, 2003), 135–37.

[47] http://digilander.libero.it/mguitarweb/KrautRock/F1.htm.

[48] http://digilander.libero.it/mguitarweb/KrautRock/F1.htm.

[49] See Joanne McNally, "Shifting Boundaries: An Eastern Meeting of East and West German 'Kabarett,'" *German Life and Letters* 54: 2 (2001).

[50] See chapter 8 of this book, "Political Song in the GDR."

[51] Bertolt Brecht, *Aufstieg und Fall der Stadt Mahagonny* (1928), in *Die Stücke von Bertolt Brecht in einem Band* (Frankfurt am Main: Suhrkamp, 1987), 214.

[52] The "Du" at the start of the first line is also a blatant reference to the banned Wolf Biermann song "Du, laß dich nicht verhärten, in dieser harten Zeit." From "Ermutigung," *aah-ja!* (CBS, 1974). Because Biermann's songs were strictly forbidden in the GDR it is possible that the reference was not understood by everyone, even though the *Hammer-Rehwü* audience consisted of many insiders of the *Liedermacher* scene.

[53] Walter Benjamin, "Linke Melancholie" in *Lesezeichen, Schriften zur deutschsprachigen Literatur* (Leipzig: Reclam, 1972), 255. For an analysis of this dispute see also Annette Blühdorn, *Pop and Poetry,* 114–15.

[54] Albert Betz, *Hanns Eisler Political Musician,* translated by Bill Hopkins (Cambridge: Cambridge UP, 1982), 62.

[55] Hanns Eisler, "Unsere Kampfmusik" in *Musik und Politik· Schriften 1924–1948* (Leipzig: VEB Deutscher Verlag für Musik, 1973), 169.

[56] Ernst Busch, "Das Lied der Wohltätigkeit," on CD *Merkt ihr nicht: Ernst Busch singt Tucholsky/Eisler* (Barbarossa, 1997).

[57] Bertolt Brecht, *Gedichte* (Leipzig: Reclam 1976), 112.

[58] See Albrecht Dümling, *Laßt Euch nicht verführen: Brecht und die Musik* (Munich: Kindler, 1985), 391–428.

66   ◆   DAVID ROBB

[59] Karl Siebig, *"Ich geh mit dem Jahrhundert mit." Ernst Busch: Eine Dokumentation* (Reinbek bei Hamburg: Rohwohlt, 1980), 59. Quoted in Dümling *Laßt Euch nicht verführen*, 307).

[60] Siebig, *"Ich geh mit dem Jahrhundert mit,"* 181. Quoted in Dümling, 411.

[61] This section on songs of the Spanish Civil War contains excerpts from David Robb, "Clowns, Songs and Lost Utopias: Reassessment of the Spanish Civil War in Karls Enkel's 'Spanier aller Länder,'" *Debatte: Review of Contemporary German Affairs* 11, 2 (2001): 156–72.

[62] Ernst Busch, ed., *Canciones de las Brigadas Internacionales* (Madrid: Im Auftrag der 11. Internationalen Brigade, 18 July 1937).

[63] Also on CD Ernst Busch, *Lieder der Arbeiterklasse & Lieder aus dem Spanischen Bürgerkrieg* (Pläne, 1967).

[64] Jürgen Schebera, "Ernst Busch auf Schellack," on CD booklet for Ernst Busch, *Der rote Orpheus: In originalaufnahmen aus den dreißiger Jahren* (Edition Barbarossa, 1996).

[65] Wolf Biermann: *Der Sturz des Dädalus* (Cologne: Kiepernheuer & Witsch, 1992), 44.

[66] Otto Riewoldt, "Wir haben jetzt einen Feind mehr" in Arnold, *Wolf Biermann*, 26.

[67] Karls Enkel, "Spanier aller Länder," unpublished manuscript and cassette recording, 1985, collected by Karin Wolf, archive of the Akademie der Künste der DDR, Berlin, Liedertheater-Dokumentation, Forschungsabteilung Musik/Liedzentrum 1985.

[68] See Rolf Tiedemann, ed., in Walter Benjamin, *Das Passagenwerk* (Frankfurt am Main: Suhrkamp, 1983), 20–21.

[69] Unlike Weiss, who had tackled the theme of the Stalinist purges in the International Brigade head-on in his monumental novel *Die Ästhetik des Widerstands*, the three volumes of which had been published in West Germany in 1975, 1978, and 1981. A limited edition came out as a single volume in the GDR in 1983.

[70] See also Steffen Mensching, "Für Peter Weiss," in *Tuchfühlung. Gedichte* (Halle and Leipzig: Mitteldeutscher Verlag, 1987), 20.

[71] Personal interview with Mensching (21 February 1994).

[72] Wenzel, letter to David Robb (12 October 1997).

[15]

Fascist Music from the West: Anti-Rock Campaigns, Problems of National Identity, and Human Rights in the "Closed City" of Soviet Ukraine, 1975-84

Sergei I. Zhuk

In 1991 Igor T., a retired KGB officer, who monitored students' activities in Dniepropetrovsk,[1] a large industrial city in eastern Ukraine, recalled how the local KGB triggered special ideological campaigns against Western popular music. These campaigns were related to the major ideological and political crises in the neighboring socialist countries. (The first and most significant campaign in 1968 was triggered by Prague's spring events in Czechoslovakia. Both Soviet ideologists and KGB operatives feared Soviet youth would imitate Czech cultural developments. The final ideological campaign began in 1981 as a direct reaction to events in Poland and youth involvement in the Solidarity movement.)[2]

According to KGB officers, popular music from the West produced four subsequent waves of Western cultural influence among Soviet youth. The first wave began in the early 1960s, "with Beatlemania and the spread of beat music and hippie fashions among high school and college students." The second wave of Western cultural influence was "Deep Purple mania and the cult of rock opera *Jesus Christ Superstar* which led to the mass popularity of hard rock and triggered an interest in religion among not only students, but also young industrial workers" (author interview with Igor T.) by 1976. After this "hard rock mania," an overwhelming majority of the local youth became obsessed with Western mass culture and "accepted disco dances [sic] as their way of life." That obsession was stimulated by tourism and the entertainment business, which involved both Communist and Komsomol *apparatchiks* who made money on the consumption of Western music by Soviet consumers. This period, from 1976 to 1980 (the third

---

[1] The name of the city is a combination of two words—Dnipro River and Grigorii Petrovskii, a famous Bolshevik and the first President of Soviet Ukraine. After 1991 the spelling became Dnipropetrovs'k.

[2] Igor T., KGB officer. Personal interview with author, May 15, 1991. Compare with the KGB reports in *DADO* (Derzhavnyi arkhiv Dnipropetrovs'koi oblasti [The State Archive of the Dniepropetrovsk Region]), f. 19, op. 52, d. 72, ll. 1-18.

wave of Western mass culture hysteria) was called "disco madness." According to Igor T., it was a direct result of the politics of détente and the relaxation of international tensions. The fourth and the final wave of Western cultural influence was so-called "fascist punk and heavy metal hysteria" which also affected young Communists and Komsomol activists between 1981 and 1984. Fearing that local heavy metal fans would imitate Polish anti-Soviet sentiments, the KGB and Soviet administration tried to suppress this hysteria. As Igor T. noted, all these efforts to protect young people from "Westernization" eventually failed:

> We lost the entire young generation, instead of the loyal Soviet Ukrainian patriots we had now Westernized imbeciles who had forgotten their national roots and who were ready to exchange their Soviet motherland for Western cultural products. Even more dangerous, this Westernization happened in the most strategically important Soviet city, which became a symbol for the entire Brezhnev rule in the USSR. Dniepropetrovsk, that was closed to foreigners, became ideologically polluted by anti-Soviet bourgeois influences as early as the 1970s. (Personal interview with author)

At the end of his interview, this KGB officer complained about "the ridiculous issue of human rights, which the local rock music fanatics raised all the time after 1975." He explained that during the police raids when they were arrested these "Westernized imbeciles" emphasized that according to the international agreements signed by the Soviet government, they had "human rights" to listen to their "weird fascist" music and "express themselves on the dance floor." Soviet police officers discovered that even rock music fans cared about their "human rights" and were ready to defend their rights in public.

Mass rock music consumption among the youth of Dniepropetrovsk created problems for Soviet ideologists and the KGB because this city had a special strategic importance for the entire Soviet regime. This city was officially closed to foreigners in 1959 because it became the location for one of the biggest missile factories in the Soviet Union. At the same time, the city served as a launching ground for the political careers of many Soviet politicians in Moscow because Dniepropetrovsk was always associated with the Brezhnev clan. This city also played an important role in political life in Ukraine. Before 1985, more than 53 percent of all political leaders in Kyiv came from Dniepropetrovsk. By 1996 80 percent of the post-Soviet Ukrainian politicians had begun their career in the closed city.

In 1975, Soviet ideologists sponsored a special discotheque campaign all over the Soviet Union. Their major goal was to organize ideologically reliable dance parties in order to control Western pop music consumption by Soviet youth. This campaign contributed to the spread of rock music throughout Soviet Ukraine, especially in urban industrial cities such as Dniepropetrovsk. By the beginning of 1982, more than 560 youth clubs with 83 officially registered discotheques existed in the region of Dniepropetrovsk.[3] Komsomol ideologists and their KGB supervisors faced a very serious problem: pop music consumers apparently preferred Western music hits to Soviet ones. A majority of rock music enthusiasts rejected completely what they called Soviet *estrada* (pop music). Therefore Komsomol ideologists promoted discotheques that primarily presented Soviet music, including songs from national republics. *Apparatchiks* responsible for the discotheque movement supported themes by the Ukrainian band Vodograi or Byelorussian band Pesniary because these bands represented Soviet traditions instead of the foreign forms of Western pop culture. To show their ideological loyalty and local patriotism many disc jockeys in Dniepropetrovsk included comments about "glorious Ukrainian history" and criticized "capitalist exploitation in the Western countries."[4] Even in their comments about Ukrainian history, they (as loyal Soviet citizens) always emphasized class struggle. Still, their stories were about Ukrainian Cossacks or melodious Ukrainian poetry, which were not popular subjects among the local KGB operatives. Eventually, the KGB supervisors of the discotheque movement had to accept both the stories being told and the national Ukrainian music being played on the local dance floors. For them it was less evil than capitalist music culture from the West.[5]

Discotheques and rock music became an even more dangerous problem for Komsomol officials after the death of Brezhnev, when Yurii Andropov, the new Soviet leader, began his campaign against corruption in the Communist Party and Komsomol. During 1983-84, he declared war on Western pop music as "a dangerous ideological pollution among Soviet youth" (*Pravda*, July 15, 1983, p. 2). Responding to Andropov's directives, the Komsomol introduced special counter-propagandist measures, which affected the discotheque movement. In the Dniepropetrovsk region the local ideologists used a special Komsomol seminar for disco activists, established between October, 1982 and May, 1983 at the prestigious Palace of Culture in downtown Dniepropetrovsk to control music programs and purge those leaders of disco clubs who resisted collaboration. By 1984, more than a half of the 100 discotheques in the region had been closed by

---

[3]   See *DADO*, f. 22, op. 32, d. 1, l. 44.

[4]   *DADO*, f. 17, op. 10, d. 1, ll. 87, 98; op. 11, d. 25, l. 88; op. 12, d. 18, l. 15; f. 22, op. 36, d. 1, ll. 36-37. See also the local periodicals: Chenous'ko, "Disko-klubu—zelionuiu ulitsu," *Dnepr vechernii*, July 1, 1978; L. Titarenko, "Tsikavi tsentry vidpochynku," *Zoria*, August 15, 1978; I. Rodionov, "Vecher v diskoklube," *Dneprovskaia pravda*, January 14, 1979; A. Belkina, "Vechir u dyskotetsi," *Prapor iunosti*, December 11, 1979.

[5]   They especially liked a Ukrainian song about Ukrainian Cossacks that was a cover in Ukrainian of the old hit "Venus" by the Dutch band Shocking Blue. As one police officer noted in 1976, "it is better to have Soviet young people dance to their national song 'Cossacks' than to the American rock and roll" (Personal interview with Mikhail Suvorov, June 1, 1991). For more detail about this song, see Zhuk (2008a, pp. 25-7).

Dniepropetrovsk ideologists for "ideological unreliability."[6] In December, 1983, all college rock bands and disco clubs in the city participated in a special antiwar and anti-American concert organized by the regional Komsomol organization in the Dniepropetrovsk city circus building. Their participation demonstrated their loyalty and ideological reliability. Dniepropetrovsk Komsomol leaders presented this event both as propagandist action in support of the official policy of the Soviet state, and as proof of their efficient ideological work in the discotheque movement.[7]

In Ukraine, Andropov's campaign against rock music converged with another old ideological campaign which targeted so-called "fascist punks." It began in 1980-81 as a result of confusing reports in the central Soviet periodicals where British punks were presented as neo-fascist skinheads. Consequently, all Western music that was associated with the punk movement and used fascist symbols had to be prohibited for mass consumption in the Soviet Union.[8] For many discotheque activists the new anti-punk campaign was a shock. In Dniepropetrovsk the local disc jockeys played the music of British punk rock bands like the Sex Pistols and The Clash as an obligatory, ideological part of their dance programs during 1979 and 1980. This was in accord with a critique of the "political agenda" of progressive rock and punk musicians offered by *Rovesnik*, a central Komsomol magazine. It praised the anti-capitalist spirit of "young English rock musicians" who followed the traditions of legendary, intellectual rock bands like Pink Floyd. Komsomol journalists from Moscow wrote about the collaboration between The Clash and British Communists in their struggle against racism and neo-fascism, and about the criticism of capitalist reality in Pink Floyd's album *The Wall*.[9] KGB officials and Communist ideologists in Dniepropetrovsk followed conflicting ideological recommendations from their Kyiv supervisors: they interfered in local youth clubs and banned the music of any musician who was associated with the word "punk." According to the KGB's taxonomy from Kyiv, the "punk movement" was considered a part of international neo-fascism. Consequently, music by The Clash or the Sex Pistols was forbidden in the region of Dniepropetrovsk as early as 1980.

The first public scandal of the new anti-punk campaign took place at Club Melodia at a dance party on the eve of 1981. As one organizer of this party

---

[6]   On a seminar for disco activists see M. Sukhomlin, "Shkola zaproshue dysk-zhokeiv," *Prapor iunosti*, November 6, 1982, p. 4. On ideological control see Yu. Lystopad, "Ideologichna borot'ba i molod" "(Notatky z oblasnoi naukovo-praktyuchnoi konferentsii)," *Prapor iunosti*, December 17, 1983, p. 2.

[7]   See in F. Sukhonis, "Pisniu druzhby zaspivuie molod," *Prapor iunosti*, December 13, 1983, p. 1.

[8]   See Troitsky (1987, pp. 42-3). He refers to famous images of Sid Vicious wearing a swastika.

[9]   For The Clash, see *Rovesnik*, 1978, No. 6, pp. 13-15; 1980, No. 10, p. 26; 1982, No. 4, pp. 22-3. *Rovesnik* reprinted sheet music and lyrics of two Clash songs: "The Guns of Brixton" in No. 4 for 1982, and "Know Your Rights" in No. 10 for 1983. For Pink Floyd's *The Wall*, see *Rovesnik*, 1981, No. 11, pp. 24-6.

recalled, the program was officially approved by the city Komsomol committee. The ideological part of the program was devoted to the theme "The World Celebrates New Year." A disc jockey began with a summary of the major political and musical events of the last year. He told the audience that three of the most popular musicians among Soviet youth died in 1980: the Russian bard and guitar poet Vladimir Vysotsky; a popular French singer, Joe Dassin; and ex-Beatle John Lennon. After playing their songs a disc jockey mentioned a *Rovesnik* publication on The Clash, and then noted the strange behavior of the Komsomol *apparatchik* who was in charge of the party. In the middle of "London Calling" by The Clash, this *apparatchik* and two KGB officers approached the disc jockeys and ordered them to stop playing "the fascist music." Then one of the Melodia leaders tried to explain that *Rovesnik* had praised The Clash as an anti-capitalist, "leftist" British band:

> The KGB people interrupted our party for one hour. They checked all our tapes of the dance program. Eventually they confiscated all our music records and tapes with recordings of the Sex Pistols, The Clash, AC/DC, Kiss, and 10cc. They punished our Komsomol supervisors for giving us permission to play the music of "fascist punks." One of these Komsomol supervisors tried again to refer to *Rovesnik* publications in his defense. A KGB officer dismissed this as misinformation. "We know better," he told us. "All this music crap you are playing is a part of the fascist anti-Soviet conspiracy. You call this music punk rock, we call this stuff neo-fascism." When one of our discotheque enthusiasts interfered and told the KGB people that AC/DC and Kiss were not punk rock bands, he was arrested by the police and removed from a dance floor. Two organizers of this dance party argued that it was a violation of human rights, and they were also arrested by the KGB. (Igor T., Mikhail Suvorov, and Andrei Vadimov, personal interviews with author, 1991, 1991, 2003)

This was the beginning of a long ideological campaign waged by both Communist Party ideologists and KGB officers. After 1980 nobody tried to play punk rock at dance parties.

According to Professor Vladimir Demchenko, who worked in the 1980s as a Dniepropetrovsk public lecturer for the Communist Party, local ideologists used a description of a British punk from the secret digest of foreign press for Communist propagandists: the main identifying sign of a fascist punk was his shaven head. Apparently, it was a misunderstanding because the author of the original article dealt with British skinheads, and he compared punks and skinheads as the most fashionable trends in Western popular culture. In a confusing translation from English to Russian, a typical punk had shaved temples or, to put it correctly, according to this description, a punk's hair had to be removed from over his ears. When this interpretation was included in an ideological portrait of "fascist punk," Komsomol ideologists were ready to identify as a punk any young man with long hair and a pony tail. As a result, many heavy metal fans from the Dniepropetrovsk region were arrested during 1983-84 because the ignorant policemen were not able to tell one fashionable hairstyle from another or distinguish between "hard rock" and "punk rock" (Vladimir Demchenko and Serhiy Tihipko, personal interviews with author, 1992, 1993). Police and Komsomol activists thought punk and fascist were the same. All Komsomol propagandists and people in charge of discotheques in the Dniepropetrovsk region received special notices about punk ideology with a Russian translation of British punks' phrases. This information was reprinted in many publications by Dniepropetrovsk journalists who covered this anti-punk campaign (personal interviews with Demchenko and Tihipko).[10] Anti-punk hysteria resulted in the prohibition of bands that were tremendously popular among Soviet high school and vocational school students. AC/DC and Kiss had nothing to do with the punk movement at all, yet after 1980, the local Komsomol *apparatchiks* officially considered them "fascist, anti-Soviet bands." Komsomol ideologists in Kyiv "discovered" elements of insignia from Nazi Germany in the names of these bands. The combination "SS" presented as symbols of lightning in the Kiss logo, for example, was interpreted as an expression of the musicians' fascist ideology. Thus Komsomol leaders in Dniepropetrovsk followed the recommendations of the Kyiv "experts" and tried to ban the music of "fascist rock-n-rollers" (Pozdniakov, 1984, p. 3).

By the end of 1982 two British bands had been added to the list of "pro-fascist, anti-Soviet bands": heavy metal icons Iron Maiden and the "art pop" group 10cc, the latter famous for its ironic, intellectual lyrics and interesting melodic arrangements. Komsomol ideologists explained to KGB officers that these bands were especially dangerous because of their "hellish, anti-human imagery, fascist symbols, and anti-Soviet lyrics" (personal interviews with Demchenko and Tihipko). They cited the name "Iron Maiden," derived from the name of a medieval torture device; the group's artistic symbol, or mascot, a ten-foot tall rotting corpse named Eddie; and their 1982 album *The Number of the Beast*, that allegedly contained images of a "fascist satanic cult." The name of the second group was mistakenly re-interpreted as "Ten SS," referring to Hitler's secret police, the SS (Schutz-Staffel). Given that the English letter "c" is the equivalent of the letter "s" in Russian and Ukrainian, cc (cubic centimeters) was pronounced "ess-ess," and local Komsomol ideologists immediately characterized 10cc as a "fascist name." Moreover, the band's 1978 album *Bloody Tourists* included a musical parody of the

---

10   Journalists of youth periodicals quoted the punk slogans: "Live by today's day only! Do not think about tomorrow! Do not give a damn about all these spiritual crutches of religion, utopia and politics! Forget about this. Enjoy your day. You are young, and do not hurry to become a new young corpse" [sic!]. Dniepropetrovsk journalists usually added comments about the anti-human essence of "fascist punk music": "These were slogans of punks, preachers of bestial cynicism and meanness, who were the real spiritual mongrels of the twentieth century." See Gamol'sky et al. (1988, p. 139). Even during *perestroika* local journalists and KGB officials continued to use these materials. Thus, declarations made by British punks were reprinted for the use of Komsomol ideologists.

anti-Soviet hysteria experienced during the Cold War entitled "Reds in My Bed." The refrain of this song shocked the Soviet censors: "I've got Reds in my bed, I'm not easily led to the slaughter, and while the Cold War exists, I'll stay warm with the Commissars daughter ... Let me go home. You're a land full of misery. I don't like your philosophy. You're a cruel and a faceless race." Of course, nobody on a Soviet dance floor cared about these lyrics and nobody understood a word of this song; they just loved the melody. In fact, the major songs from *Bloody Tourists*, including "Reds in My Bed," "Dreadlock Holiday," "For You and I," "Life Line," and "Tokyo," all became hits in discos during 1979-83. Appalled by this "music propaganda" of "anti-Soviet, fascist ideas," Komsomol ideologists asked the police and KGB for help in removing "dangerous" music from the cultural consumption of Soviet youth. In 1981-84 hundreds of the forbidden records were confiscated from young rock fans in the region. An overwhelming majority of these records were albums by AC/DC, Kiss, Iron Maiden, and 10cc.

This anti-punk and anti-fascist hysteria affected even the music of Pink Floyd. This band was traditionally considered by Soviet ideologists an anti-capitalist "progressive" band, and Soviet television and radio occasionally broadcast its music. In the 1970s "One of These Days," from the 1971 album *Meddle*, was constantly heard as the theme song for the political TV show "International Panorama." Moreover, some of the band's more popular songs were included in music compilations produced by the music journal *Krugozor*. "Money" from *Dark Side of the Moon* was praised as "an anti-imperialist anthem" of Western, progressive youth culture. The idealization of Pink Floyd by the Soviet youth media reached a peak with the release of the band's album *The Wall* in 1979, but the official attitude changed in 1983. Its new album, *The Final Cut*, written by Roger Waters, criticized imperialistic aggression all over the world and concentrated mainly on the Falklands War between Argentina and Great Britain. According to Waters's lyrics, three major imperialist powers threatened to destroy the world: the United States, Great Britain, and the Soviet Union. Two tracks, "Get Your Filthy Hands Off My Desert" and "The Fletcher Memorial Home," openly criticized the expansionism of "Mr. Brezhnev and the Party," including the Soviet invasion of Afghanistan. According to KGB officers, the Komsomol experts recognized Brezhnev's name in *The Final Cut* lyrics, and henceforth included Pink Floyd on the list of "forbidden musicians" for discotheques because of their "distortion of Soviet foreign policy." By the end of 1983, all ideological departments of the regional Komsomol organizations in Ukraine had received a complete list of "forbidden music bands" with Pink Floyd at the top.

Soviet cultural consumption of Western products was always very limited and heavily censored. On the one hand, forms of consumption were regulated by various ideological requirements, and, on the other, they were influenced by consumers' demands. The more the ideological experts tried to ban a product, the more desirable it became. Albums by Kiss and AC/DC, for example, became the most profitable items sold on the music market in Dniepropetrovsk.

Both central Komsomol and local periodicals disoriented and confused their readers when they directly connected criminal anti-Soviet and neo-fascist behavior with "forbidden music." The first public scandal, which involved both "fascist music" and the display of "fascist symbols," took place in the closed city during the fall of 1982. The city police arrested two college students, Igor Keivan and Aleksandr Plastun, who had their own collections of Western music records with "fascist symbols" and who demonstrated their "neo-Nazi" behavior in downtown Dniepropetrovsk. These students were dressed in T-shirts bearing images of Kiss and AC/DC which attracted the police who interpreted such images as "fascist." After the arrest of Keivan and Plastun and the confiscation of their "fascist" records, the police sent information about these students' anti-Soviet behavior to their colleges. In December, 1982 the entire city and region of Dniepropetrovsk experienced the beginning of the anti-fascist and anti-punk campaign. The Dniepropetrovsk City Communist Party Committee approached N. Sarana, an old Communist and member of the anti-fascist resistance group during World War II, to write a letter about the dangers of "fascist punks." On December 22, 1982, the Committee staged an open public meeting with participation of all Communist and Komsomol activists in downtown Dniepropetrovsk. During this meeting all activists supported Sarana's letter against punks and "declared war on the punk movement" in the closed city. Later, under KGB pressure, local ideologists organized a special public trial of Keivan, Plastun, and another young punk, Vadim Shmeliov, who were expelled from the Komsomol and their colleges in January, 1983. The KGB officers were especially outraged about an attempt by Keivan and Plastun to "interpret" this punishment as a violation of their human rights. From this time on, all Komsomol organizations of the region began to purge Komsomol members for having unusual enthusiasm for the forbidden music.[11]

Following this scandal, both Communist ideologists and KGB operatives reminded the local Komsomol activists about the ideological danger of Western capitalist culture. They pointed to the case of Polish youth who actively participated in the anti-Soviet movements of the early 1980s. During 1982 and 1983, Dr. Aleksandr Amelchenko, a public lecturer for the regional Communist Party Committee, delivered a series of special lectures about the ideological threat of Western pop music. He visited the major districts and towns of the region and discussed this threat with local activists. In October, 1983, Amelchenko sent some of his material to local periodicals and answered various questions from young rock music fans. In his lectures and publications he emphasized that "the youth was the country's future." For this reason, the ideological enemies of the Soviet

---

[11]   Sarana's letter was titled "We declare war on everybody who interferes in our life and work!" and appeared as "Boi tem, kto meshaet nam stroit' i zhit'!" in *Dnepr vechernii*, December 23, 1982, p. 3. See also A. Liamina and L. Gamol'skii, "Grazhdaninom byt' obiazan," *Dnepr vechernii*, December 23, 1982, about the public trial that took place on December 22, 1982 in Dniepropetrovsk. See also the author's personal interview with Oleksandr Poniezha.

Union tried "to confuse and pollute Soviet youth and undermine the ideological basis of the Soviet Union. Moreover, they tried to distract Soviet audiences with so-called human rights" ("Spetsvypusk 'Politychnogo klubu Plu'," 1983, p. 2). Dniepropetrovsk journalists were so intimidated by the rock music campaign that they rejected any public demonstration of preferences for Western cultural products as an act of betrayal. They even took an active part in a campaign against the Leningrad hard rock band Zemliane during the spring of 1984. The band performed its second concert in the closed city in 1984. Though journalists had lauded the band's first concert in January of that year, the situation changed during the spring. To advertise their concert in Dniepropetrovsk, the Leningrad rock musicians used a photograph of Igor Romanov, their lead guitarist, dressed in a T-shirt bearing a US flag. Moreover, according to the local journalists, during their concert in the closed city, Zemliane played songs by "forbidden fascist and punk bands" (Tishchenko, 1984, p. 4). As a result, the Dniepropetrovsk Komsomol newspaper organized an anti-Zemliane campaign, accusing the Leningrad musicians of "a betrayal of socialist principles of music performance." Despite readers' support for the popular Leningrad band, journalists and local KGB officials insisted on punishing the musicians for their low ideological standards and for promoting "capitalist standards of anti-human mass culture" (Rozumkov and Skoryk, 1984, p. 4). In April, 1984, the administration of "Leningrad Concert," the organization responsible for Zemliane's concert tours, punished the rock musicians by canceling all their concerts and forcing them to rewrite their repertoire. Following this scandal, Dniepropetrovsk officials stopped inviting "suspicious" rock bands from Moscow and Leningrad.

This anti-rock campaign especially affected Dniepropetrovsk heavy metal fans. In 1983, when Dniepropetrovsk police arrested 10 students from a local vocational school for "acts of hooliganism," they discovered that the students had adopted various Nazi and American Ku Klux Klan symbols. As it turned out, Sergei Onushev, Aleksandr Rvachenko, and their friends had made special white robes, put the letters KKK on them, and tried to "imitate acts of this American fascist organization" (Gamol'sky et al., 1988, p. 133). Sergei Onushev, the leader of this "fascist" group, "used to play at home the music tapes of bands which belong to the pro-fascist movement—Kiss, Nazareth, AC/DC, Black Sabbath." Dniepropetrovsk ideologists established direct connections between this music and the fascism of Onushev's group, claiming Kiss provoked the Soviet students to commit inhuman, fascist acts.[12]

Another case that attracted the attention of local journalists concerned Dmitrii Frolin, a student at the Department of Philology at Dniepropetrovsk University.

---

[12]   "What kind of art," a journalist commented, "did the musicians of Kiss represent? They tear apart live chickens and vomit in public during their performances. This band Kiss is a group of four hooligans, who selected the SS Nazi symbol as the symbol of their band. Nevertheless, showbusinessmen transform them into the idols of the contemporary youth and proclaim them 'trendsetters' in popular culture" (Gamol'sky et al., 1988, p. 134).

As a result of the anti-punk and anti-fascist campaign, Frolin was arrested by the police in 1983 and expelled from both the Komsomol and the university in 1985 for "propaganda of fascism." According to the local ideologists, Frolin's activities were the direct result of "intensive listening" to the music of "fascist bands" such as Kiss and AC/DC. As one journalist wrote:

> The musicians of AC/DC, a favorite Frolin band, call themselves the devil's children. Their song "Back in Black" became an anthem of the American Nazi Party. During a Komsomol meeting Dmitrii justified his behavior, "I do not consider my collecting of AC/DC music a crime. As a Soviet citizen and human being, I have my human rights, which are protected by both Soviet and international law. I consider that listening to my favorite music, collecting and listening to music records are part of my private life. And I have a right to protect my privacy according to Soviet and international laws. (Gamol'sky et al., 1988, pp. 135-6)

In December, 1983, a local youth periodical published the results of a sociological analysis of Dniepropetrovsk youth compiled by Komsomol scholars. According to this publication, in many college dorms the special Komsomol raids discovered images of the American band Kiss, "on which any observer could easily find without any difficulty the SS symbols and Nazi signs" (Gamol'sky et al., 1988, pp. 135-6). Indeed, a majority of the student population in Dniepropetrovsk "preferred T-shirts bearing the signs of the US military and insignia of the capitalist countries, the political and military enemies of the Soviet Union." Dniepropetrovsk students bought these T-shirts on the black market and wore them during their college classes.[13]

Komsomol journalists also published translations of the most notorious anti-Soviet songs to become hits in local disco clubs in the late 1970s and early 1980s. As it turned out, the most popular dance songs had obvious or hidden anti-Soviet messages. The journalists drew on publications about various anti-Soviet rock bands issued by Soviet ideologists in Moscow or Kyiv. The range of these bands was wide—from British musicians such as Boy George and Culture Club to West German disco bands such as Genghis Khan. Material about these bands was published under the title: "Beware! Western Poison!" (Dubovyi, 1983, p. 4).

As KGB officers discovered, heavy metal and punk rock music fans also idealized the Ukrainian nationalist leaders of World War II, such as Stepan Bandera. After 1938, Bandera led the radical branch of the Organization of the

---

[13]   Oleksandr Beznosov, a Professor of History at Dniepropetrovsk University, recalled, during a personal interview, how during the same period of time he (an undergraduate history student in 1983) and his roommates were interrogated by the student dorm supervisors because they possessed music records by and posters of Black Sabbath, Iron Maiden, and Kiss. Beznosov was almost expelled from the university. Only interference by his academic mentor saved him.

Ukrainian Nationalists, which became a center of the military resistance to the Soviet Army after 1944 in Western Ukraine. After the suppression of the anti-Soviet activities of the Bandera troops, Bandera became a heroic symbol for many Ukrainian patriots. In 1983 and 1984 the police arrested members of "a fascist Banderite group" who were students of the Dniepropetrovsk agricultural college. These students, Konstantin Shipunov and his five followers, listened to "fascist rock music," organized their own "party," and popularized the ideas of Nazi leaders and the Ukrainian nationalist politicians. They criticized the Russification of cultural life in Ukraine, emphasized the necessity of Ukrainian independence from the Soviet Union, and insisted on protecting the human rights of all Ukrainian patriots. In conversation with a police officer, Shipunov referred to the Final Act of the Conference on Security and Cooperation in Europe signed in Helsinki by the Soviet leaders together with 34 other heads of state on August 1, 1975. According to Shipunov, the Final Act especially emphasized a protection of human rights. By arresting Ukrainian patriots like Shipunov, the local police violated human rights and broke international laws.[14]

Again in December, 1983, the Dniepropetrovsk regional Komsomol committee reported to the Ukrainian Komsomol Central Committee in Kyiv that in February-March, 1983, local ideologists encountered the beginning of a punk movement in the city of Dniepropetrovsk. However, during spring through the fall of that year, they mobilized all activists and "Soviet patriots," organized special counter-propaganda events all over the city and region, and finally stopped this "fascist movement." A secretary of the Dniepropetrovsk regional committee, O. Fedoseiev, concluded this report by saying, "As a result of our anti-punk campaign, there are practically no young people in the region who would imitate 'punks'."[15]

In 1984-85, Dniepropetrovsk police discovered new groups of "fascist-punks" with hundreds of followers. Only a few of them, however, had anything to do with Nazi ideology or fascism. Nonetheless all 10 groups arrested by the police were said to use various fascist symbols and paraphernalia, painted their faces "in punk fashion" and had shaven temples. Because the Komsomol had repeatedly stated that the main sign of punk behavior was "shaven temples of the head," this was enough to be arrested on the streets of Dniepropetrovsk during 1983-85. Hundreds of rock music fans were detained and their music records and audiotapes confiscated in the region of Dniepropetrovsk as a result of the anti-punk and anti-fascist campaign. In addition, a famous discotheque in the cultural center of Dniepropetrovsk University was transformed into a music lecture club called "Dialogue. Music in Ideological Struggle." Instead of dancing, students now listened to lectures about modern music and important issues of

---

[14] Interviews with Oleksandr Poniezha, Andrei Vadimov, and Mikhail Suvorov. Cf. Gamol'sky et al. (1988, p. 137).

[15] See his report in *TDAGOU* (Tsentral'nyi derzhavnyi arkhiv vyshchykh organiv vlady ta upravlinnia, Kyiv, Ukraine [Central State Archive of the High Offices of Power and Management]), f. 7, op. 20, d. 3087, l. 43.

international politics. Local ideologists preferred this kind of cultural consumption to the spontaneous dance parties playing bourgeois music, which were difficult to control. As a result, many talented disc jockeys and music engineers left Komsomol discotheques in 1985-86 and moved to the safer ground of ordinary technician's jobs, far away from the dangers surrounding rock music.

In 1983-84 the police also organized special raids on music markets in downtown Dniepropetrovsk. They were not looking for black marketeers, but for anti-Soviet music products, including records and audiotapes of music by Kiss and AC/DC. Thousands of original Western records were confiscated and hundreds of people were arrested during those two years.[16] Although by the beginning of 1985 the police had destroyed a thriving rock music market in the city, they were unable to halt the consumption. Discos, restaurants, and bars continued to thrive because "fresh" Western popular music was part of a very lucrative business. Indeed, the "disco club enterprise" became the first stable source of significant material profit for the local administration, including Komsomol *apparatchiks*. In 1981-83, according to official records, Club Melodia turned a monthly profit of more than 50,000 roubles. In fact, the organizers of this business earned an additional "nonregistered" 20,000 roubles each month (Rodionov, 1979, p. 4).[17]

As a result of the anti-rock music campaign, those in charge of music entertainment had to find nontraditional—and unofficial—sources of products to satisfy the growing demands of Dniepropetrovsk consumers. International tourism became the major source of new material for rock music consumption during 1983-85. In 1972 only 30 percent of all music records and tapes of Western music came directly through the channels of international tourism to the Dniepropetrovsk music market. By the end of 1984 more than 90 percent came from local tourists who traveled abroad, including those who used the services of the Komsomol travel agency.[18] During the anti-rock music campaign the Komsomol *apparatchiks*

---

[16]   The police released those black marketeers who had no "fascist or punk music products." Those who had AC/DC and Kiss records ("fascist products") were detained in police stations for 15 days (Interviews with Igor T. and Mikhail Suvorov).

[17]   Regarding guest numbers, admission fees, and alcohol beverages in 1982 and 1983, see *Prapor iunosti*, June 24, 1982, and January 15, 1983. Regarding the profits of disco club Melodia, see documents in *DADO*, f. 17, op. 11, d. 1, l. 28; f. 22, op. 36, d. 1, ll. 36, 37, 39, 40.

[18]   Many sources for the banned pop music came to Dniepropetrovsk through representatives of the ruling Soviet elite, who visited foreign countries as the members of local tourist groups. According to discotheque activists, in 1979 KGB supervisors of local tourism brought to Dniepropetrovsk the original rock music albums later banned by Communist ideologists. One tourist returning from a trip to Hungary, another from a trip to Poland, brought the albums *Highway to Hell* by AC/DC and *Dynasty* by Kiss for their own children, who were active participants in the music market in the city. Through these children of KGB officials, recordings of AC/DC and Kiss music became available for thousands of rock music consumers in the region. *DADO*, f. 22, op. 19, d. 2, 143, f. 19,

who had an opportunity to go abroad brought new music records and audiotapes. In 1984, 90 percent of all foreign music material in the central disco club of Dniepropetrovsk came directly from the Komsomol tourists who visited European socialist countries. As the active participants in the Dniepropetrovsk music market recalled, approximately nine out of 10 songs played at a central disco club dance party usually came from material that belonged to tourists. According to contemporaries, anti-rock music campaigns in Dniepropetrovsk did not halt the consumption of Western pop music. To the contrary, the campaigns contributed to the immense popularity of forbidden Western cultural products among young consumers and also among their ideological supervisors who already greatly appreciated and enjoyed these products. The most unpleasant discovery for local KGB officers who supervised student activities in the city was the involvement of political elements in the discussion of forbidden Western cultural products such as rock music. Dniepropetrovsk rock music fans referred to international documents, signed by the Soviet leaders, regarding the protection of human rights and, after 1975, they frequently raised the issue of human rights when police harassed them.

A search for the authentic West became part of the process of identity formation for millions of young Soviet consumers of Western cultural products. These consumers tried to identify themselves only with the West, which as an ideal lost any connections with Soviet Ukrainian culture by the end of the 1970s. In the imagination of these consumers, the official Soviet Ukrainian culture represented all the most conservative, backward, and anti-Western elements in their life. By accepting the real West as a part of their identity, they rejected the official Soviet version of their own ethnic identity. Through consumption of Western pop music, both rock music enthusiasts and young Komsomol activists involved in the disco club business tried to form their own notion of human rights, which became an important part of their self-identity. Eventually, the new cultural activities and tastes resulted in new values and demands for cultural consumption, which gradually replaced and transformed the traditional Soviet values and Communist ideological practices among both ordinary Komsomol members and the young Komsomol elite of the 1980s.

---

op. 60, d. 85, ll. 9-11. See interviews with Oleksandr Beznosov, Oleksandr Poniezha, and Serhiy Tihipko.

Bibliography

Derzhavnyi arkhiv Dnipropetrovs'koi oblasti [The State Archive of the Dnipropetrovs'k Region].

Dubovyi, G., "Oberezhno! Zakhidna otruta!," *Prapor iunosti* (November 24, 1983): 4.

Gamol'sky, Leonid, Nikolai Efremenko, and Vladimir Inshakov, *Na barrikadakh sovesti: Ocherki, razmyshlenia, interviu* (Dniepropetrovsk, 1988).

Pozdniakov, M., "Piraty vid muzyky (v tumani antymystetstva)," *Prapor iunosti* (June 14, 1984): 3.

Rodionov, I., "Vecher v diskoklube," *Dneprovskaia pravda* (January 14, 1979): 4.

Rozumkov, O., and M. Skoryk, "Komu zemliaky "Zemliane"? (Rozdumy pislia kontsertu)," *Prapor iunosti* (March 15, 1984): 4.

"Spetsvypusk 'Politychnogo klubu PIu'," *Prapor iunosti* (October 20, 1983): 2.

Tishchenko, Igor, "Poiot VIA 'Zemliane'," *Dnepr vechernii* (January 21, 1984): 4.

Troitsky, Artemy, *Back in the USSR: The True Story of Rock in Russia* (London: Omnibus Press, 1987).

Tsentral'nyi Derzhavnyi Arkhiv Gromads'kykh Ob'ednan' Ukrainy (*TDAGOU*) [The Central State Archive of Ukrainian Public Organizations], Fond 7, Tsentral'nyi Komitet LKSMU.

Zhuk, Sergei I., "Popular Culture, Identity and Soviet Youth in Dniepropetrovsk, 1959-84," in *The Carl Beck Papers in Russian and East European Studies*, no. 1906 (Pittsburgh: University of Pittsburgh Press, 2008a): 1-68.

Part IV
Local Struggles, Global Impacts

[16]

The Vision of Possibility: Popular Music, Women, and Human Rights

Sheila Whiteley

> Freedom consists of voices that have been broken and blood that has been shed. Freedom tastes of pain ... there is no objectivity ... there is only the vision of possibility.—Sarah Maitland

It is an inexcusable fact that "significant numbers of the world's population are routinely subject to torture, starvation, terrorism, humiliation and even murder simply because they are female ... that women are discriminated against and abused on the basis of gender," that "women's rights and human rights are viewed as distinct" (Bunch, 1990, p. 486). Reports on Human Rights Watch describe how millions of women live in conditions of abject deprivation of, and attacks against, their fundamental human rights for no other reason than that they are women.[1] While it is not unusual to displace such accounts on to the all-encompassing "other" (political, religious, ethnic), it is also evident that female bodily autonomy is not necessarily an unassailable right in Western culture. As such, while the extremes of violence reported daily in the media are largely situated within the context of tribal conflicts and political extremism, as evidenced recently in reports of genocide in Ethiopia, the state-run terror campaign unleashed against supporters of the Movement for Democratic Change in Zimbabwe, and the continuing suicide bombings in Iraq, this chapter shifts the focus on to the UK, southern Ireland, and the United States, exploring women's rights to make reproductive and sexual decisions, and how such issues as pregnancy, domestic violence, rape, and the shaming of the body have been confronted by singer-songwriters.

At the time of writing, two anniversaries have shaped my thinking. On December 10, 1948 the General Assembly of the United Nations adopted and proclaimed a Universal Declaration of Human Rights (UDHR), which enshrined the principles of justice, fairness and equality. Prompted by the atrocities of the Holocaust and the horrors of World War II, it was the first global statement to recognize the inherent dignity and equality of all human beings, and its 30 articles are framed by a concern to support and promote the unalienable rights of all members of the human family, regardless of race, color, sex, language, religion, political or other

---

[1] http://www.hrw.org/en/category/topic/women%E2%80%99s-rights, accessed May 11, 2009.

opinion. The second anniversary commemorated Charles Darwin's birth in a BBC2 program which examined the abuses of his theory of evolution and how it became twisted into eugenics, and then the Nazi's Final Solution, "where bad science and bad politics turned the survival of the fittest into the murder of the weakest" in a perverted interpretation of evolution through natural selection. Six million Jews, together with gypsies, communists, Poles, Slavs, homosexuals, and political and religious dissidents were exterminated as centuries of prejudice were given a scientific gloss: the murder of the weakest (*Darwin's Dangerous Idea*, 2009).

What links the two anniversaries is the way in which the UDHR can be interpreted as a return to and confirmation of Darwinism in its assertion that all human beings are connected by common descent and hence belong to the same species, *homo sapiens*; that difference is due to culture, so placing the emphasis on nurture rather than nature (*Darwin's Dangerous Idea*, 2009). It is this emphasis on cultural difference, and its relationship to family, reproduction, and bodily autonomy that is central to my discussion of women, popular music, and human rights.

In this regard, and returning briefly to the 1948 Universal Declaration of Human Rights, it is relevant to note that its framing of equality and concern for universal dignity and justice includes the identification of the family as the "natural and fundamental group unit of society," and states that men and women are entitled to equal rights when it comes to marriage, during marriage, and at its dissolution.[2] The UDHR's identification of shared responsibility in marital decision-making underpins its concern for equality, but the issues surrounding reproductive rights are problematic.[3] While these relate to "the right to marry and found a family" (UDHR, Article 16), they can also include the right to control one's reproductive functions and to make reproductive choices free from coercion, discrimination,

---

[2]   (1) Men and women of full age, without any limitation due to race, nationality or religion, have the right to marry and to found a family. They are entitled to equal rights as to marriage, during marriage and at its dissolution.

(2) Marriage shall be entered into only with the free and full consent of the intending spouses.

(3) The family is the natural and fundamental group unit of society and is entitled to protection by society and the State (http://www.un.org/en/documents/udhr/, accessed May 12, 2009).

[3]   The General Assembly of the United Nations published its *Declaration of the Elimination of Discrimination* on November 7, 1967. It related to their concern that "despite the Charter of the United Nations, the Universal Declaration of Human Rights, the International Covenants on Human Rights and other instruments of the United Nations and the specialized agencies and despite the progress made in the matter of equality of rights, there continues to exist considerable discrimination against women" (http://www.unhchr.ch/html/menu3/b/21.htm, accessed May 12, 2009). Reproductive Rights were first established as a subset of human rights at the United Nation's 1968 International Conference on Human Rights. The Convention on the Elimination of All Forms of Discrimination against Women (CEDAW) was adopted in 1979 by the United Nations General Assembly and is described as an international bill of rights for women. It came into force on September 3, 1981.

and violence, issues that still remain hotly debated in their relation to bodily autonomy.[4] Two examples provide insights into why this is so important. In 1912, at the first Eugenics Conference, Winston Churchill proposed the sterilization of the feeble-minded so that they could live otherwise normal lives but without "the threat of reproduction." The Feeble-minded Person's Control Bill was thrown out in the UK, but picked up in Scandinavia and the United States, which was alarmed about the influx of refugees and immigrants, and, hence, the continuing strength of American citizens. Between 1904 and 1970, 60,000 "feeble-minded" were sterilized as part of the US Eugenics program. The role of the state in deciding who should and who should not reproduce was also part of the Nazi Eugenics Breeding Program, whereby German officers were instructed to father children by German or Nordic mothers. Ten thousand children were fathered in Norway under Nazi occupation and at the end of the war the mothers were publicly humiliated (*Darwin's Dangerous Idea*, 2009). Most recently, the trafficking of women and girls into forced prostitution, and women being sexually assaulted in war as a way of terrorizing their communities are also being taken into account (Lai and Ralph, 1995, p. 201), but the extent to which existing human rights principles can be applied to protect and promote women's sexual autonomy—including the rights of women to make decisions about when, how, and with whom to conduct their sexual lives—remains contentious, not least in situations where politics are dominated by authoritarian ideologies (such as fascism) and/or religious fundamentalism (for example, Muslim, Jewish, Christian, or tribal).[5]

It is also interesting to note that the Convention on the Elimination of All Forms of Discrimination Against Women (now in its twenty-seventh year) identifies discrimination against women as "… any distinction, exclusion or restriction made on the basis of sex [including] fundamental freedoms in the political, economic, social, cultural, civil or any other field" ("Overview of the Convention"), so highlighting the ways in which cultural self-expression can relate to political, economic, and social circumstances, including the ways in which women represent themselves. As Alice Walker recalls, "It was a punishable crime for a black person to read or write under slavery. What might have been the result if singing, too, had been forbidden by law. Listen to the voices of Bessie Smith, Billie Holiday,

---

[4] Reproductive rights can also refer to education about contraception and sexually transmitted infections, freedom from coerced sterilization, and protection from gender-based practices such as female circumcision.

[5] For example, when the Serbian-Montenegrin forces in the Balkans war cursed the women they raped that they would bear children who would forever be their enemies and fight against their mother and her people, they were behaving according to a particular complex of inherited social beliefs, they were speaking out of commitment to military values, paternal lineage, and a cult of male heroism. See Warner (1994, pp. 28-9).

Nina Simone, Roberta Flack and Aretha Franklin, among others, and imagine these voices muzzled for life" (1983, quoted in Ingram, 1999, p. 173).[6]

The association of "music with lived experience and the broader patterns of culture that it both mirrors and actively produces" (Brett, Wood, and Thomas, 1992, pp. vii-ix) draws attention to female artists who have provided specific insights into subjective experience and the ways in which songs "not only represent to us how things are but also help to construct the very categories of identity through which we experience them" (Middleton, 2000, p. 231). Sonya Aurora Madan's confrontational lyrics on Echobelly's debut CD *Everyone's Got One* (1994), for example, resonate with her self-perception as a strong Asian woman. The album's title creates an acronym (EGO), and its overall mood is challenging, confronting the problems of young Asian and Arab women who are subjected to forced marriage and honor-based brutality ("blame the mother/ sell the sister"), urging them to take control of their lives ("Half the population, one percent of wealth …," "Give Her a Gun"). Madan was acutely aware that her Asian parentage and upbringing could attract adverse attention, and her "I Don't Belong Here" (from the band's 1993 debut EP *Bellyache*) comes across as throwing down the gauntlet and tackling both prejudice and alienation head-on. Her awareness of being "an East-West casualty" was also confronted by wearing a Union Jack T-shirt with "My Country Too" scrawled across it, highlighting the conflicts surrounding identity, tradition, and women's rights. "Father, Ruler, King, Computer," a title inspired by Germaine Greer's *The Female Eunuch*, takes issue with the patriarchal assumptions surrounding marriage ("I was brought up, I've been told, that a husband is the goal,/ What connotations in these loaded words … I am whole all by myself") and is seen by Madan as "a celebration of independence," written at a time when "I was busy trying to discover myself" (quoted in Raphael, 1995, p. 43). Other songs explore sexist exploitation ("Insomniac"), post-abortion denial ("Bellyache"), and the paradox of being abused ("You're the evil world of the nursery rhyme," "Centipede") and loving your abuser ("You're my only friend, don't be cruel to me," "Centipede"). As Madan reflects, an abused woman is an abused woman regardless of her background and religion. "I didn't go into this to represent a minority. I did it for me" (quoted in Raphael, 1995, p. 34).

Despite the UDHR's declaration that "Everyone has the right to freedom of opinion and expression," the freedom for women to represent themselves through the arts as a form of cultural self-expression remains contentious.[7] "Cultural

---

6   It is interesting to note that Billie Holiday's recording company, Columbia, refused to record the anti-lynching song "Strange Fruit." Its powerful lyrics ("the bulging eyes and twisted mouth," the "black bodies swaying in the Southern breeze") were considered too controversial. A deal was made with Columbia, who loaned her to Commodore, and "Strange Fruit" was cut on April 20, 1939 at Brunswick's World Broadcasting Studios with Frankie Newton's Café Society band. See Nicholson (1996, p. 113).

7   Article 19 of the UDHR states, "Everyone has the right to freedom of opinion and expression: this right includes freedom to hold opinions without interference and to seek,

relativism, which argues that there are no universal human rights and that rights are culture-specific and culturally determined, is still a formidable and corrosive challenge to women's rights to equality and dignity in all facets of their lives" (Amnesty International, *Stop Violence Against Women Campaign*). At its most extreme—in the recent murder of singer songwriter Ayman Udas, whose family believed it was sinful for a woman to perform on television[8]—the persecution and sexual abuse of female artists, writers, and musicians in Pakistan and Afghanistan under Shi'ite law is symbolic of the betrayal by the international community to support women's rights.[9] And the recent case of a woman who burnt herself to death on International Women's Day evidences the hopelessness of Afghan women who are desperate to escape abusive marriages yet have no words to express their despair.[10] "Arguments that sustain and excuse these human rights abuses—those of cultural norms, 'appropriate' rights for women, or Western imperialism—barely disguise their true meaning: that women's lives matter less than men's" (Amnesty International, *Stop Violence Against Women Campaign*). The question thus arises as to how to free these silenced voices when they are denied the right to express themselves and to make their distress known.

While the media and the internet offers an opportunity to access information, the struggle against patriarchal religions and the suppression of women's voices— not least the mythologizing of motherhood and its impact on the victimization and repression of the female body—has been given pre-eminence in the flowering of women's writings across and beyond the course of the twentieth century. Virago Press, founded in 1973, was the first British publishing company to highlight the contribution made by women authors, publishing nineteenth- and

---

receive and impart information and ideas through any media and regardless of frontiers" (http://www.un.org/en/documents/udhr/, accessed May 12, 2009).

[8]   As Daud Khattak comments, her murder "has shocked the city's artistic community because it symbolises a backlash against women and cultural freedom in an area that is increasingly dominated by Islamic fundamentalists." She was allegedly shot dead by her own brothers in the conservative city of Peshawar, Pakistan (Khattak, 2009, p. 25).

[9]   President Karzai's signing of the Shia Personal Status Law contradicts both the Afghan Constitution and the Convention of the Elimination of All Forms of Discrimination against Women, to which Afghanistan is a State party. Many activists who have spoken out against the law have received threats. The fears of women activists have been compounded by the killing of a prominent women's rights campaigner and local councilor, Sitara Achakzai, who was shot dead in Kandahar after receiving death threats (Human Rights Watch, April 14, 2009, http://www.hrw.org/en/news/2009/04/14/afghanistan-new-law-threatens-women-s-freedom, accessed May 13, 2009).

[10]   Self-immolation occurs across Afghanistan; its highest incidence is in Herat. The hospital had 81 cases in 2009, almost all women aged 15-25. Fifty-nine died. Attending reading and writing classes has also led to the mutilation and murder of Afghan women, including 25-year-old Nadia Anjuman who was killed by her own husband for her love of poetry (Lamb, 2009).

twentieth-century "classics," and since then there has been a proliferation of ethnically diverse literature (autobiographical, academic, feminist, fact and fiction, prose and poetry) exploring motherhood, bodily autonomy, and identity. The musico-poetic voice has been more constrained; issues such as pregnancy, miscarriage, sexual abuse, the traumas of family life, motherhood, abortion, religion, and racism are not issues usually found on a top-selling album or chart single, and where these do occur, they often tend toward the autobiographical.[11] While it is recognized that such introspection is important in voicing subjective experience, the art of creating a voice for the dead or forgotten draws on the legacy of the story-teller musician who can inhabit the pain and expand our understanding of both the victim(s) and the situation through "direct confronting speech, commingled with imagery and a caustic voice" (Whitesell, 2008, p. 77).[12] As Joni Mitchell recalls,

> In 1996 the Sisters of our Lady of Charity, the Magdalene Laundries in London, sold off 11 half acres to realtors for development and in ploughing it the realtors' tractors unearthed over 100 graves, women just thrown into the ground, named simply Magdalene of the tears, Magdalene of this and that, just anonymously and so the outrage grew ... Most towns had one—a prison for females who committed some crime—but the crimes varied, many of them were just victims, some just pregnant girls, some pregnant by their own father, by their own priest, but the worst crime of all it seems to me was that unmarried women in their late twenties, if men were still looking at them, in some parishes could be deemed jezebels and the town could incarcerate them for life—as scrub women to the nuns.[13]

The Magdalene Laundries, as they came to be known, originated in the nineteenth century as rehabilitation centers for prostitutes and other "fallen" women. Administered by the Roman Catholic Church, and supervised by nuns, the prison-like character of the asylums was justified by the creed of penitence, enforced through hard physical labor (primarily in laundries), corporal punishment, and, commonly, a strict rule of silence. Justified by the religious belief that Mary Magdalene was a reformed sinner (Luke 7: 36-50) and, as such, a good role model for prostitutes, and bolstered by strong conservative values, the Magdalene

---

[11]   See, for example, Tori Amos, "Me and a Gun," Sinead O'Connor, "My Three Babies," and Loretta Lynn, whose song "The Pill" was banned by country stations across the United States.

[12]   Joni Mitchell's encounter with Bob Dylan provided, as she recalls, "an expanded understanding of what pop songs can accomplish. ... I wrote poetry, and I had always wanted to make music. But I never put the two together ... the potential for the song had never occurred to me" (David Wilde, "A Conversation with Joni Mitchell," *Rolling Stone*, May 30, 1991, in Whitesell, 2008, p. 77).

[13]   Joni Mitchell, http://www.youtube.com/watch?v=8S2hv7uVxxY&NR=1, accessed May 15, 2009).

movement spread across southern Ireland, taking under its wing unmarried mothers and other "socially dysfunctional" girls and women.[14] Over its 150-year history it is estimated that 30,000 women were admitted to these institutions, often by family members and parish priests, the last closing in 1996. Southern Ireland was not alone in making profit out of unmarried mothers and other so-termed "social misfits." The Magdalene institutions, under the supervision of the Roman Catholic Church, were also commonplace in Europe, paralleling the practice in state-run asylums in Britain and Ireland where women were stripped of identity and subjected to sexual, psychological, and physical abuse. Little was known about the existence of the Magdalene institutions and the fate of inmates until the remains of female bodies were unearthed by developer's tractors. These were exhumed and, except for one body, cremated and reburied in a mass grave in Glasnevin Cemetery.[15]

Joni Mitchell's response to the "Magdalenes" is one of empathy and outrage, combining character portraits within a statement of social critique. "The Magdalene Laundries" (*Turbulent Indigo*, 1994) adopts an explicit, personalized voice as she takes on the persona of a 27-year-old woman, "cast in shame" into the Magdalene Laundries "for the way men looked at me." Taking on the role of storyteller, she reveals the plight of the "prostitutes and destitutes and temptresses like me ... sentenced into dreamless drudgery," contrasting their status as "fallen women" with the nuns, "these bloodless brides of Jesus," dramatizing the moment when "Peg O'Connell died," reflecting on her own destiny: "One day I'm going to die here too/ And they'll plant me in the dirt/ Like some lame bulb that never blooms ...."

The effectiveness of the song lies in its choice of language and the way in which Mitchell addresses her hypothetical listener. As Lloyd Whitesell writes,

> While in actual terms, Mitchell's songs were all intended for oral performance (either live with an actual audience present or simulated in recorded form with little authorial control over the listening situation), in fictional terms, they present themselves according to four modes of artistic enunciation; dramatic, narrative, lyric, and political. These modes can be distinguished by the different roles they assign the singer as well as to the implied audience. (2008, p. 44)

Mitchell's framing of the political content of the song through the thoughts of an (unnamed) "Magdalene" heightens its communicative power by allowing access to her state of mind and the feelings triggered by the death of Peg O'Connell. In an institutionalized setting characterized by a sense of isolation, the imaginary monologue accesses thoughts normally repressed by the rule of silence—the

[14] There is no reference to Mary Magdalene's association with prostitution or adultery in the New Testament.

[15] For more see Alexander Didden, "Magdalene Laundries: Still No Justice in the World."

certainty of dying, stuffed in a hole like Peg, never to bloom. The use of imagery and simile creates an unspoken sub-text of sterility which is heightened by a pragmatic description of girls who arrived pregnant ("Brigit got that belly by her parish priest"), the brief character sketch of Peg (a cheeky girl, a flirt), and veiled references to the mythology surrounding Mary Magdalene, where the nuns are aligned with the accusers of the anonymous woman "taken in adultery" (John 8: 3-11), stones concealed behind their rosaries. The blend of the ordinary and the poetic resonates with the reflective tone of the narrative. The restrained vocal tone of the opening verse contrasts with the emotional outburst and harsh confrontation of "this heartless place" and its association with "Our Lady of Charity"; the impassioned "Surely to God you'd think at least some bells should ring" subsides into a more muted expression of personal worth ("like some lame bulb that never blooms") before the repetitive lines of the coda ("not any spring") where over-dubbing creates the feel of a subdued chorus of "Magdalenes," a recognition of the shared plight of all the "woe-begotten-daughters."[16]

Unlike many political songs where a verse/chorus structure provides space for group singing (implying both a collective response and an affirmation of shared values), the narrative of "The Magdalene Laundries" "captures the lyric utterance of a single speaker, caught in an identifiable situation at a dramatic moment" (Whitesell, 2008, p. 47). Released in 1994, on the album *Turbulent Indigo*, it can be interpreted as a direct and personalized response to the unearthing of the graves and the silencing of the so-called "fallen women" of the Magdalene Laundries. As Joni Mitchell was only too aware in choosing her central character (identifying what she considered "the worst crime," the unmarried women in their late twenties who, if men were still looking at them, could be incarcerated for life), "There, but for the grace of God ...." As a woman constantly under media scrutiny for her numerous romantic affairs, the 1960s was still a difficult period for women when it came to bodily autonomy, and Mitchell's commitment to personal freedom is given particular poignancy in Christy Moore's cover of "The Magdalene Laundries."[17] Opening with the words, "Joni was an unmarried girl, she'd just turned twenty-seven ...," the naming of the central character creates an additional layer of meaning. Christy, as narrator, tells "Joni's story" (as author of the song, and as imagined character) drawing her into association with the "Magdalenes" and the "dreamless drudgery" of institutional life under the "brides of Christ,"

---

[16] The Catholic Church's dominant image of the Holy Mother and Child as symbolic of nurturing spiritual values within the moral rhetoric of family values provides a religious frame of reference for the relationship between nuns (mothers) and inmates (daughters). Joni Mitchell always performed her own overdubs and here, the effective use of multi-layered voices draws into association the countless women who were lost to the Magdalene Laundries.

[17] "When I went back to my own neighbourhood, I found that I had a provocative image. They thought I was loose because I always liked rowdies ..." (quoted in Whitesell, 2008, p. 92).

while hinting at the existence of her own child, who was given up to adoption in 1963.

The lullaby to "Little Green," on Mitchell's 1971 album, *Blue*, takes the form of a letter of farewell to her daughter, the ambiguity of its final line and the imprecision of its ongoing future tense disguising a very fresh wound in its acceptance of sorrow. Contextualized by songs which explore the cost of self-determination, and a recognition that relationships and prescribed gender roles (housewife, nurturer, submissive partner) constrict and smother personal growth, the thematically linked songs explore the conflict between belonging, freedom, and the emptiness and confusion that can accompany the lonely road of independence.[18] As Tillie Olsen (1978) writes, among the social forces that can lead to the silencing of an author, particularly a female author, including domestic responsibility, poverty, and race, it is motherhood that is the most constraining, and until recently almost all literary achievement came from childless women (Ingham, 1999).[19] Behind the self-exploration of *Blue* lies the reality of the choices Mitchell had to make if she was to achieve her ambitions as a singer-songwriter. As a personalized message to her child, loss is tempered by an underlying mood of resilience: "You're sad and you're sorry but you're not ashamed."

The dramatic focus on personal freedom and prescriptive gender roles have been recurring themes in Mitchell's body of songs,[20] but while religion is frequently at the heart of the moral imperatives surrounding motherhood,[21] violence toward women extends the frame of reference to the domestic sphere. "Not to Blame" (*Turbulent Indigo*, 1994) is, as Philip Martin writes, "an example of Mitchell's willingness to push on into darker channels" (2004, n.p.): "Six hundred thousand doctors are putting on rubber gloves/ And they're poking at the miseries made of love./ That way they're learning how to spot the battered wives/ Among all the women they see bleeding through their lives."

---

[18] For a more detailed discussion see Sheila Whiteley, "The Lonely Road: Joni Mitchell," in Whiteley (2000, pp. 78-94).

[19] Sylvia Plath's suicide has been attributed to the tragic conflict between her art and her responsibility to her two small children against the background of the 1950s and early 1960s ideology of women as homemakers who were meant to assume total responsibility for their children. Margaret Drabble's early 1960s novels stress the difficulties of mothering in a society where to abandon oneself to the needs of one's infant is seen as natural behavior on the mother's part. They depict the problems encountered when highly educated young women find themselves trapped by the expectations of marriage and motherhood.

[20] "Don't Interrupt the Sorrow" (*The Hissing of Summer Lawns*, 1975), for example, exposes the concept of the "natural order as nothing but a cycle of 'sorrow' for women ('Death and birth and death and birth'), the use of religion as a tool for brainwashing ('The good slaves love the good book') and competing theological fictions and their consequences for women's lives" (Whitesell, 2008, p. 83).

[21] "The Sire of Sorrow (Job's Sad Song)" from *Turbulent Indigo* (1994) picks up on the theme of aggressor and abused, justifying chastisement with the reprimand, "God is correcting you."

The stark imagery of the lyrics "your fist marks on her face," and the sense of personal confrontation suggests an accusatory closeness which is heightened by the reference to the husband's "buddies," betting fame and fortune on their assurance that "she was out of line," that "you were not to blame."[22] The impact of these final lines (which act almost like a chorus to the verse) is heightened by their association with blood ("these red words that make a stain on your white-washed claim") and "her lonely little grave" of the third and final verse. As a poet, Mitchell was well aware of the power of rhyme and the broad ā sounds (blame, stain, claim, grave) are drawn into poignant association. They're chilling, and like the repeated lines of "The Sire of Sorrow" (*Turbulent Indigo*, 1994), where she draws blood with repeats of a line that cuts to the emotional bone—"You make everything I dread and everything I fear come true" (Milward, 1994, n.p.)—they have a resonance that extends beyond the boundaries of the song. To paraphrase John Milward, it's irrelevant when Mitchell wrote this song of domestic violence, and its significance isn't tied to a particular time or space. Recent statistics on violence against women is on the rise, and as the Women's Aid website reveals

> at least 1 in 4 women experience domestic violence in their lifetime and between 1 in 8 and 1 in 10 women experience it annually. Viewed as physical, sexual, psychological or financial, violence against women transcends ethnicity, religion, class, age, sexuality, disability or lifestyle and can also occur in a range of relationships, including heterosexual, gay, lesbian, bisexual and transgender. The majority of abusers are men who choose to behave violently to get what they want and gain control. Less than half of all incidents are reported to the police ....[23]

* * *

> ... and when they arrive, they say they can't interfere with domestic affairs.— Tracy Chapman, "Behind The Wall"

---

[22]   The subject matter of the song hints at the indictment of her former friend Jackson Browne who the tabloids had accused of battering his then girlfriend Daryl Hannah. The reference to the three-year-old in the third verse has also been interpreted as a reference to Browne's son Ethan, who was three at the time of his mother's suicide (Browne's first wife, Phyllis). This has been denied by Mitchell. See Martin (2004).

[23]   On one typical day—November 2, 2006—11,310 women and 8,330 children were being supported by domestic violence services in England (both residential and non-residential). This has increased by 50 percent since 2003. On the same day, 3,615 women and 3,580 children were being supported within refuge-based services. Domestic violence accounts for between 16 percent and one quarter of all crime, and on average two women a week are killed by a male partner or former partner (http://www.womensaid.org.uk/domestic_violence_topic.asp?section=0001000100220041&sectionTitle=Domestic+violence+%28general%29, accessed May 26, 2009).

Tracy Chapman's "Behind the Wall" (*Tracy Chapman*, 1988) is still, for me, the most chilling of political songs. Written in the first person singular and sung unaccompanied, she tells of sleepless nights, the "loud voices behind the wall" that precede marital violence, the lyric association of "screaming" with "sleepless," "peace" with "sleep" creating an underlying subtext which situates the triangular relationship between the victim, the narrator/witness, and the police ("here to keep the peace … we could all use some sleep"). The power of the song lies in repetition, with four of the five verses opening with the line "Last night I heard the screaming." The explicit, personalized voice is powerful, recording the narrator's thoughts, giving credibility to her proximity to the violence, and her cynical observation that "it won't do no good to call the police," the extended melisma on "late" creating a sense of resignation before the final phrase, "if they come at all." The structure of the song also reflects the repetitious nature of marital violence, with verse two and the final verse repeating the lyric content and melody line of the opening verse, so effecting a sense of the cyclical nature of abuse: "it never ends."

The everyday language and shaping of the melodic line adds to the impact of the song, reflecting and constructing the mood of the lyrics. Starting on top F (at the upper end of Chapman's vocal range) and ending on the octave below, there is a move from the initial shock of waking to the screams of the abused to a grudging acceptance of police inactivity. Emotional content is heightened by a variation in the melodic line of the fourth verse as "the screaming" is followed by "a silence that chilled my soul." Straining upwards to the very top of her range (the leap from C above middle C to top A on "I prayed"), the slow stepwise fall ("that I was") before the sustained tension on dreaming (top G falling to D) creates a mood of anxious instability that is heightened by the rawness of her vocal tone. Above all, it is the decision to sing alone and unaccompanied that underpins the feeling of vulnerability. Chapman "tells it how it is," without elaboration, the *a cappella* vocal creating a personal and poetic musical language of helpless aloneness in the face of aggression. Not least, the exposed vocal line emphasizes the relationship between vocal delivery and narrative representation. The *a cappella* of "Me and a Gun" (*Little Earthquakes*, 1992) has a similar effect in communicating Tori Amos's personal experience of rape and, like "The Magdalene Laundries" and "Behind the Wall" "captures the lyric utterance of a single speaker, caught in an identifiable situation at a dramatic moment" (Milward, 1994, n.p.).[24] This sense of moment is important. It situates the song in time and place, interpolating the listener into the trauma of the narrative, inviting their response. Genre is thus important in its association with musical identity. It has to speak to the listener.

While the songs so far discussed fall largely within the overarching genre of the singer-songwriter, "Thank You" (2004), by Jamelia, confronts the hopelessness and inertia of the abused women through r&b, combining elements of hip-hop

---

[24] For a detailed discussion of "Me and a Gun" and other songs by Tori Amos see Whiteley (2005, pp. 84-103).

and soul in a catchy pop format.[25] The strength of the narrative lies in its combination of everyday speech and the stylization of its poetic language: "the fights, those nights," "my head, near dead," "my soul, so cold," "so young, so dumb." The explicit use of "I"/"you" creates an accusatory voice, "You hit, you spit, you split every bit of me," drawing the listener into the subjective experience of physical and mental abuse before the revelation "you're such a joke to me" and the realization that the narrator has moved on, "can't believe I stayed with you so long." The lift to an upbeat chorus, "you broke my world, you made me strong, thank you" is, perhaps, surprising within a song about domestic violence, but the success of "Thank You," which peaked at number two on the r&b charts and received the 2004 MOBO (Music of Black Origin) award for best single, has elicited a big response on Jamelia-associated websites. As NelleG, writes on the Thank-you Jamelia website, "there is not a lot of songs that 14 y.o's can relate to but i can relate to this." Other reviewers share their experience: "Fantastic lyric. So real to me. I've been there but now I'm out and laughing," "this song helped me to get over mi xbf john who beat me up and put me in hospital," "thank you explains exactly what I went through." What is apparent is the shared admiration for Jamelia ("great to have artists who write and perform music bout these very real issues such as domestic violence and emotional abuse") and the way in which "this song makes me start believing I actually am strong for everything he put me through." It is interesting that "Jamelia's song also has a meaning to me, not about violence or mental cruelty by a boyfriend, but can only mean a parent, and I can identify with it, as I was once an unhappy child, with a violent parent. Thank you Jamelia," so extending its relevance to the younger listener who has suffered abuse.[26]

Jamelia's popular appeal and the way in which "Thank You" challenges and deflates the often misogynistic representations of sexual violence and sexist power relations inherent in hip-hop ("I understand, to make you feel like a man, you hit, you spit ... you're such a joke to me") provides an insight into cultural self-expression and why it is important for women to represent themselves. As Germaine Greer writes, "Women can be routinely insulted and humiliated for years on end, repeatedly raped and sexually abused and yet keep silence, made to endure a life of kicks and blows ... because they are afraid ... The woman paralysed by terror exists in her own mind as well as that of her abuser to be abused. She can see no way out, no possible rescue, because fear has blinded her" (1999, p. 272). Speaking out, confronting abuse, defusing fear by offering hope and the possibility of personal freedom cannot solve the problem, but it can raise awareness of power and status in relationships by relating music to lived

---

[25]   Contemporary r&b (or urban contemporary) has evolved into a mainstream musical genre which incorporates elements of soul, funk, dance, pop, reggae, calypso, and hip-hop, so assuring both a broad-based appeal and a space for often subversive and left-field music.

[26]   All reviews from http://www.sing365.com/music/lyric.nsf/Thank-You-lyrics-jamelia/, accessed June 6, 2009.

experience, as my brief discussion of web reviews for "Thank You" shows. What is important is not whether the song is the literal truth of personal experience but rather the way Jamelia presents herself as a strong and vibrant woman who has successfully moved on from a sexually abusive relationship ("won't happen again"). It is the way in which she articulates her identity and performance in order to direct her audience to a particular interpretation of her song that is important (Negus, 1997, p. 182).

The "right to freedom of opinion and expression, and the freedom to hold opinions without interference and to seek, receive and impart information and ideas through any media and regardless of frontiers" (UDHR, Article 19) is crucial to politicized music. My choice of case studies was prompted by the ways in which they relate to the abuse and subjugation experienced by women and the contrast between those who are powerless to fight back and those who have a voice. The personal *is* political and the musico-poetic voice is important in questioning power and status, oppression and subordination.[27] Not least, it demonstrates that repression is historical and cultural while drawing attention to the fact that discrimination and exploitation continues to exist. As Germaine Greer tellingly observes, "on every side speechless women endure endless hardship, grief and pain, in a world system that creates billions of losers for every handful of winners" (1999, p. 3). What remains is the vision of possibility.

---

[27]   Joan Baez, for example, provides an unflinching example of commitment to social and political issues not only in her songs, but equally in founding the Institute for the Study of Nonviolence in Carmel, California.

Bibliography

Amnesty International, *Stop Violence Against Women Campaign* <http://www.amnestyusa.org/violence-against-women/stop-violence-against-women-svaw/page.do?id=1108417>, accessed May 15, 2009.

Brett, Philip, Elizabeth Wood, and Gary C. Thomas (eds.), *Queering the Pitch* (New York: Routledge, 1992).

Bunch, Charlotte, "Women's Rights as Human Rights: Towards a Re-Vision of Human Rights," *Human Rights Quarterly*, 12, 4 (1990): 486-98.

Darwin's Dangerous Idea (BBC2, March 5, 2009).

Didden, Alexander, "Magdalene Laundries: Still No Justice in the World," Historytimes.com <http://www.historytimes.com/current-affairs/magdalene-laundries-still-no-justice-in-the-world>, accessed May 27, 2009.

Greer, Chris, *Sex Crime and the Media* (Devon: Willan, 2003).

Greer, Germaine, *The Female Eunuch* (New York: Bantam, 1970).

Greer, Germaine, *The Whole Woman* (London: Transworld, 1999).

Ingram, Heather (ed.), *Mothers and Daughters in the Twentieth Century: A Literary Anthology* (Edinburgh: Edinburgh University Press, 1999).

Khattak, Daud, "Shot by Her Brothers for TV Sin," *The Sunday Times* (May 3, 2009): 25.

Lai, Sara Y., and Regan E. Ralph, "Female Sexual Autonomy and Human Rights," *Harvard Human Rights Journal*, 8 (1995): 201-27.

Lamb, Christina, "The Defiant Poets' Society," *The Sunday Times Magazine* (April 26, 2009): 46-55.

Martin, Philip, "The Genius of Joni," *Arkansas Democrat-Gazette* (September 28, 2004), <http://jonimitchell.com/library/view.cfm?id=1409>, accessed May 26, 2009.

Middleton, Richard (ed.), *Reading Pop: Approaches to Textual Analysis in Popular Music* (Oxford: Oxford University Press, 2000).

Milward, John, Album review of *Turbulent Indigo* by Joni Mitchell, *Rolling Stone* (December 15, 1994) <http://www.rollingstone.com/artists/jonimitchell/albums/album/321631/review/5945724/turbulent_indigo>, accessed May 26, 2008.

Negus, Keith, "My Three Babies," in Sheila Whiteley (ed.), *Sexing the Groove: Popular Music and Gender* (London: Routledge, 1997): 178-90.

Nicholson, Stuart, *Billie Holiday* (London: Indigo, 1996).

Olsen, Tillie, *Silences* [1978] (London: Virago, 1980).

Raphael, Amy, *Never Mind the Bollocks: Women Rewrite Rock* (London: Virago Press, 1995).

172 *POPULAR MUSIC AND HUMAN RIGHTS*

Warner, Marina, *Six Myths of Our Time: Managing Monsters. The Reith Lectures 1994* (London: Vintage, 1994).
Whiteley, Sheila, *Women and Popular Music: Sexuality, Identity and Subjectivity* (London: Routledge, 2000).
Whiteley, Sheila, *Too Much Too Young: Popular Music, Age and Gender* (London: Routledge, 2005).
Whitesell, Lloyd, *The Music of Joni Mitchell* (New York: Oxford University Press, 2008).

Discography

Amos, Tori, *Little Earthquakes* (Atlantic, 1992).
Chapman, Tracy, *Tracy Chapman* (Elektra, 1988).
Echobelly, *Bellyache* EP (Pandemonium, 1993).
Echobelly, "Centipede," *Insomniac* CD single (Fauv, 1994)
Echobelly, *Everyone's Got One* (Rhythm King, 1994).
Mitchell, Joni, *Blue* (Warner, 1971).
Mitchell, Joni, *The Hissing of Summer Lawns* (Warner, 1975).
Mitchell, Joni, *Turbulent Indigo* (Warner, 1994).
Moore, Christy, "The Magdalene Laundries," *Burning Times* (Sony, 2006).

[17]

Rap in Indonesian Youth Music of the 1990s: "Globalization," "Outlaw Genres," and Social Protest[1]

Michael Bodden

Throughout the 1990s, "alternative" musical genres such as rap, punk, and hard rock, derived from North American and European commercial cultures, captured the enthusiasm of large numbers of Indonesian youth, propelling the songs of local Indonesian rock/punk groups such as Slank and rapper Iwa-K to the top of the Indonesian pop charts. Rap music had become popular enough that by January 1995 the Indonesian government, in the person of then minister of research and technology and now former president B. J. Habibie, publicly denounced the genre as crude and alien to Indonesian culture and values (*Kompas* January 8, 10, and 15, 1995). Indeed, in a nation with an astonishingly rich variety of traditional musical forms, it may seem yet another lamentable instance of global commercial culture's erasure of local variety that Indonesian youth were so powerfully attracted to these musical forms.

Yet, I will argue that the appropriation by Indonesian youth of genres like rap and punk actually reveals a far more complex story. It is a story in which particular aspects of global commercial culture, although certainly displacing elements of previous traditions, may also be seized upon and deployed in specifically local struggles. These genres serve as weapons of social protest and/or as expressions of a desire to create a new social space or even identity that flaunts its difference from or rejection of the kinds of social identities and behavior authorized by an authoritarian government and the dominant social groups in society. The possibilities of this deployment are particularly germane to situations, such as that in Indonesia, in which the regime in power seeks to engineer modern culture while also, in order to aid in its pursuit of comprehensive control over all aspects of society, endeavoring to monopolize authority to determine the practice and meaning of "traditional" culture.

2 *Asian Music:* Summer/Fall 2005

Theoretical background

In their introduction to *Articulating the Global and the Local: Globalization and Cultural Studies,* Ann Cvetkovich and Douglas Kellner assert that "global culture" (itself a contested term) is built on the development of consumption-oriented lifestyles and identities, realized through the promotion of particular products, and that this promotion is usually spearheaded by transnational corporations attempting to penetrate local markets. However, they recognize that such market interventions may also provide "new material to rework one's identity . . . [which] can empower people to revolt against traditional forms and styles to create more emancipatory ones" (Cvetkovich and Kellner 1997, 10). This two-part argument coincides with Fredric Jameson's attempt to pinpoint the source of two basic and opposed perceptions of "globalization" through the elaboration of a dialectical model suggesting that whether one sees globalization in a positive or negative light depends upon where one sees the most threatening and oppressive monopolization of power. If the nation state is perceived to be the most immediate site of such a threat, then markets, culture, or federalism may come to be seen as solutions, and "globalization" may offer liberation. Yet if the very system of transnational-led globalization is seen as a threat to differentiated identity, then the nation state may become a space of protection (Jameson 1998, 68–75).

My analysis of Indonesian rap and the brief public debate that flared around it in early 1995 substantiates Jameson's characterization of globalization as offering a form of liberation or a cultural alternative to subjects living in the shadow of an oppressive national state. Further, this example from Indonesia also suggests that such struggles between local actors and a repressive state tend to take root in other processes, such as social conflicts involving class and age. Thus, in order to properly situate Indonesian rap as a locus of resistance against the Indonesian New Order state and its post-Suharto successor, I will begin with a brief description of the Indonesian nation state's attempts to construct particular concepts of politics, society, family, and personal identity, the political system and regime of social organization in response to which rap and other "outlaw" genres of music have been appropriated by segments of middle-class Indonesian youth.

Description of New Order Cultural Dominants

Beginning in the late 1950s, Indonesia's first president, Sukarno, acting in concert with the military and attempting to present himself as preserving (through a process of reformatting) aspects of democracy, established the first stage of a transition to authoritarianism called "guided democracy." This system marked both the advent of a corporatization of much of Indonesian social, political, and cultural life and the "naturalization" of this change through reference to a set of ideas evoking notions of Indonesian tradition and a "national personality." Thus, the beginnings of authoritarianism were justified through the construction of government institutions and ideology partially drawn from hybrid Dutch–Indonesian notions of traditional social relations, structures of hierarchy, rules of conduct, and patterns of leadership (Feith 1963, 358–72). Under General Suharto's New Order Regime (1966–98), this corporatized "traditionalism" included organizations promulgating and enforcing particular concepts of proper familial conduct, organizations governing and regulating civil servants (and their wives), labor unions, and associations of journalists, businessmen, film-industry workers, students, middle peasants, Islamic religious scholars, and Islamic intellectuals.[2] The New Order also attempted to control public discourse and cultural production by various means, including press regulations, film censorship guidelines, and the banning of newspapers, books, and theatrical and musical performances.[3] Further, it endeavored to "guide" and develop traditional art forms and cultural practices both to support its program of economic development and to inculcate "national values."[4]

These dynamics occurred in conjunction with the forced indoctrination in the national ideology, *Pancasila,* of students, civil servants, and members of various other social groups (Morfit 1986; Watson 1987), the mandatory acceptance by all social organizations of *Pancasila* as their sole ideological basis (Morfit 1986), and the simultaneous assertion of a specifically Javanese aristocratic ideology of orderliness, hierarchy, deference to social superiors, and paternalistic familial authority as the code which should govern social conduct.[5] In the second half of the 1980s, the New Order even made a concerted effort to install, as a key part of the official state ideology, a totalitarian, integralist notion of the state which viewed it as one large family with each member of society playing their proper role. This concept was then presented as fitting with the "national personality" (Bourchier 1997).

From this short summary of the New Order's attempts to control society and even social discourse and thought, it should be clear that New Order Indonesia, although unable to eliminate dissent completely, as we shall see, was nonetheless an arena in which notions of control and order, and the sacredness of a particular idea of "Indonesian-ness" came to occupy pervasive and powerfully stifling positions. It was against this background that the appropriation of Western "outlaw" genres of music,[6] dress, and behavior by Indonesian youth, often from the middle classes, occurred.

While Indonesian music may be the least heavily "policed" of a number of

4 *Asian Music:* Summer/Fall 2005

popular mass media (Sen and Hill 2000, 170), nevertheless a history clearly exists of the limitation of certain performers and official criticism of specific styles of music. In particular, the government has been consistent in attempting to limit and eventually co-opt performers like Rhoma Irama and Iwan Fals, whose populist styles, everyday language, and criticism of the government's corruption, human-rights abuses, and the growing social gap between the rich and poor have won them broad popular followings across classes.[7]

The Indonesian government also tried to ban "weepy" songs from television in the late 1980s following the enormous success of one such song, "Hati Yang Luka" (The Wounded heart), which addressed the issue of husbands' abusive behavior toward their wives. According to Minister of Information Harmoko, "weepy" songs appealed to low taste, weakened the spirit of the people, and sapped their commitment to the national effort for progress. Philip Yampolsky argues, however, that one of the reasons for the ban was "Hati Yang Luka"'s frank presentation of a sensitive social problem (Yampolsky 1989, 8–9; Lockhard 1998, 86–7).

Rap and the Habibie Incident

Given the history of governmental intervention in popular music outlined above, it was not completely surprising when, as Minister of Research and Technology, B. J. Habibie launched his attack on rap music in early January 1995. Apparently, having viewed a television program featuring American rap music, Minister Habibie raised objections to a plan to organize an Indonesian national rap festival. Speaking to the media, Habibie blasted rap, claiming that there was no artistry in the genre and that it used disgusting and vulgar language without literary value. Then, as though speaking to an audience whom he feared had gone too far in its adulation of foreign culture, Habibie stated: "not all culture from the advanced countries is of high value. There is also that which brings negative effects" (Raharti and Baskoro 1995, 111).[8] Yudhistira A.N.M. Massardi, reporting for the weekly news magazine *Gatra*, quoted Habibie as remarking:

> The younger generation shouldn't want to be enslaved by an aspect of foreign culture which isn't even liked in its own country. It's not even appropriate over there, much less in Indonesia, it's not suitable. . . . I don't agree with it because it's of no use whatsoever, especially for the young generation (Massardi 1995, 106).[9]

Kompas, Jakarta's highest circulation news daily, even reported that Habibie saw rap as something that ruined the nation's cultural values (*Kompas*, January 10, 1995, 16).

In these statements Habibie tried to present rap as inappropriate to Indo-nesian national culture, thus summoning "national culture and personality" discourses against the genre. His arguments against rap, however, also insisted that the genre is "not even appropriate" or liked in its country of origin, by which he was almost surely referring to criticism of rap surrounding alleged concert violence in the late 1980s and, especially, to vilification of Ice-T's song "Cop Killer" during the 1992 election campaigns in the United States.[10] While Habibie was clearly trying to "police" Indonesian cultural production through his criticism and his efforts to prevent the national rap festival, he was not really arguing against "cultural imperialism" as such, but about being selective in what one allows in the doors. Habibie's tirade sought to cast rap as an illegiti-mate, "outlaw" genre.

Although Habibie's pronouncements attempted to focus attention on the genre's "vulgar" language and "illegimate" reputation internationally, a num-ber of prominent members of the Indonesian music community came forward to defend the music. Their arguments portrayed rap as rhythmically dynamic, offering new possibilities to Indonesian pop music and containing lyrics that could explore a richer array of topics with a more diverse idiom (*Kompas,* Janu-ary 10, 1995, 16; Raharti and Baskoro 1995, 111). Some musicians, including the rapper Denada, sought to explain, quite correctly in fact, that Indonesian rap was generally more polite than American rap and did not use vulgar language (Massardi 1995, 106; *Kompas,* January 8, 1995, 8; *Kompas,* February 8, 1995, 20; Raharti and Baskoro 1995, 111). Other commentators even explained that rather than vulgarity, most rap music contained elements of protest (Massardi 1995, 106), and that leading Indonesian rapper Iwa-K could appropriately be com-pared to Iwan Fals in this respect (Raharti and Baskoro 1995, 111). Most of those from the music community who were interviewed warned against resorting to censorship of musical creations, especially when the person making the accu-sations was a government minister who was not necessarily an expert in the field of music. Some members of the music community went so far as to sug-gest that rather than banning rap, the government should try to understand why youth were attracted to it (Massardi 1995, 106; Roesli 1995, 16; *Kompas,* January 10, 1995).

Eventually, in the face of the defense of rap by local commentators, Minis-ter Habibie sought to moderate his criticism of the genre. The boldness of the music community in defending rap, and even in questioning Minister Habibie's competence to judge it, suggests something of the difficulties the New Order government was having by the mid-1990s in its attempts to control dissent. Ref-erences to rap's protest elements and the critical lyrics of Iwa-K provide clues as to what other issues might have been at stake in this apparently minor skirmish.

Rap, punk, and heavy metal rose to prominence among Indonesian youth beginning in the late 1980s and early 1990s, a time when Indonesia's urban middle classes (business people, professionals, and even the families of the military-officer class) were becoming increasingly critical of, and vocal about, the shortcomings of the New Order (Heryanto 1995, 1996; Bourchier 1997). Circumstantial evidence suggests heavy participation of middle-class youth in creating, performing, and consuming these genres as they were being constituted in Indonesia. In typically middle-class fashion, it has been noted that some punk rockers in Bali end their concerts with trips to a McDonald's at the nearby mall (Baulch 1996, 24).

Reviewing the background of rap performers themselves suggests this connection as well. Iwa-K (Iwa Kusuma), whose breakthrough albums in the early 1990s helped create an explosion of rap and hip-hop culture in Indonesia, rose to fame while taking a degree in social and political sciences at Parahyangan University in Bandung (Raharti and Baskoro 1995). Denada, the best-known woman rapper and daughter of a commercially successful pop singer of the previous generation, recorded her first album while still in high school, and has since gone on to university studies in Australia and Indonesia. Similarly, Budi, of the rap duo Paper Clipp, began his rap career while studying architecture at a Jakarta university (Siagian 1997). A number of rap songs, moreover, feature the accoutrements, attitudes, and activities of life for middle- to upper middle-class youth in Indonesia: going to youth parties (Denada, "Jam Satu Lewat" [Past one A.M.], Neo, "Pesta" [Party]); possessing cell phones and pagers and avoiding going to the office (Sweet Martabak, "Ti Di Dit" [the title imitates the sound of a pager]); hanging out at the malls (Denada, "Hari Ini" [Today], Neo, "Borju" [Bourgeois]); visiting the supermarket (Iwa-K, "Cuma Ulat" [Just a worm]); and the boredom of youth (Neo, "Bosan" [Bored] and "Jalan-Jalan" [Going out for a stroll], Iwa-K, "Kramotak" [Brain cramp] and "Jum'at Malam" [Friday night]).

Anecdotally, university-educated middle-class youths I have gotten to know during my last few trips to Indonesia usually tend to prefer "creative pop," jazz, or the "outlaw" (underground, alternative) genres of Western-derived pop, while industrial workers involved in worker theatre groups generally favor *dangdut, keroncong,* or country-pop/folk à la Iwan Fals. Some alternative and outlaw types of music also seemed better able to hold their own in the market following the onset of the economic crisis in late 1997. The rock/punk band Slank, for example, was able to sell a remarkable 600,000 copies of its album *Mata Hati Reformasi* (Inner soul of reform) in mid-1998 (Harris 1998; Raharti 1999). This suggests that the audience for these kinds of music is relatively well off economically (Raharti, Pareanom, and Budi 1998).

Nonetheless, there are also indications that some of these genres of music have strong cross-class appeals, something which may also make the Indonesian government uneasy. For instance, a 1993 performance by the American band Metallica attracted both middle-class and elite fans able to afford expensive ticket prices, as well as lower class metal and punk fans who, unable to purchase tickets, eventually resorted to frustrated rioting. Tellingly, the New Order government attempted to explain the incident in terms of criminality and disorderliness, warning the public not to use the riot as material for polemics about the glaring social gaps measured in terms of wealth (Thompson 1993, 4–6). Jo Pickles also reports that the underground scene (encompassing punk and several subgenres of metal) aspires to be a community beyond class, one that "is open for all to join and participate in . . . money and education are not barriers" (Pickles 2000, 9).[11]

In light of the proven capacity of these genres to attract the attention of a sizeable number of youth from the increasingly critical and strategic middleclass, as well as their potential to appeal to cross-class audiences, to voice social protest, and possibly to provide occasions—as in Metallica's 1993 concert—where social frustration may erupt in mass violence, it seems likely that the anxiety evident in Minister Habibie's remarks may well have been occasioned by more than vulgar language. In what ways, however, were rap and the other "outlaw" genres specific responses to New Order Indonesia's strict social, ideological, and political regimen?

Subcultures and Noise

Here Dick Hebdige's notion of "subculture" is useful. For Hebdige, the challenge to social hegemony represented by spectacular subcultures is expressed obliquely through styles that interrupt an ongoing process of the "normalization" of the dominant codes, thereby challenging the principles of unity and cohesion operating within society. Further, in the contemporary world the media have come to play a predominant role in defining our experience for us, in providing the most readily available categories for classifying our social world. Subcultures present a kind of "noise" that interferes with this orderly representation of reality in the media, and as such the media and other dominant forces seek either to recuperate them back into the "normal" by reducing them to "ordinary folks" who simply happen to have a different style (which can be commodified), or as deviants who are totally alien, even animals (Hebdige 1979, 13–18, 84–94).

The assertion that subcultures represent a kind of social "noise" disrupting the desired harmony of the normalization of social codes leads us to Jacques

8 *Asian Music:* Summer/Fall 2005

Attali's work on the social history of music. Attali has argued that music, aside from its quality as entertainment or its ability to produce aural pleasure, is also a way of perceiving the world—it is essentially the "organization of noise"—and that both totalitarian and so-called democratic nations all attempt, in different manners, to monopolize the broadcast of messages, to control noise, and to institutionalize the silence of others in order to maintain power. Attali maintains that hegemonic social systems all endeavor to "ban subversive noise because it betokens demands for cultural autonomy, support for difference or marginality" (Attali 1985 [1977], 4–7). A case in point, and one relevant to discussions of "outlaw" genres in Indonesia, is the policing of rap music in the United States during the 1980s and the 1990s. Tricia Rose argues that rap, as a popular articulation of black cultural experience, was itself threatening to institutionalized control of black Americans' mobility, access to public space, and interpretation of their own public expressions. Rose asserts that in the dominant cultural media discourse rap was thus "linked to larger social constructions of black culture as an internal threat to dominant American culture and social order." As such, black rap concerts were stigmatized, blocked, or rigidly policed by American political authorities, media, and music industry promoters (Rose 1996, 252–3).

Still, as Hebdige has observed, subcultures are also capable of recuperation by dominant forces within society, especially to the extent that their clothing styles or music can be commodified (Hebdige 1979, 94–9). Critics of Hebdige have even argued that the fashion and music industries and sympathetic entrepreneurs, as well as figures outside the actual subcultures, may sometimes help produce and shape the styles of those subcultures (see Cohen 1997 [1980]; and McRobbie 1997 [1989]). Thus, social reactions to subcultures are commonly bifurcated, and this seems to be precisely the case with Indonesian rap, punk, and hard rock. For in Indonesia, government concern and criticism mixes with negative stereotyping in the media, but these elements are mirrored by media fascination for the genre, as well as the desires of both the government and the recording industry to incorporate "underground" or "outlaw" groups as soon as they show signs of winning over large popular audiences. I now turn to an examination of these musics and the subcultures surrounding them.

"Outlaw," "Alternative," and "Underground" Subcultures

The main focus of this discussion is rap music, probably the most commercially mainstream of the "outlaw," "alternative," or "underground" genres in Indonesia.[12] I will, however, also draw upon material relating to punk and heavy metal, since these genres and their subcultures share several features with those of rap and all these genres have been grouped together by some commentators as "creative pop" or "alternative/underground," collectively contrasted to the sweetly sentimental and melodious pop so pervasive in Indonesian public space (Siagian 1997).[13]

First, these genres seem to have arisen along with a distinct generational identity. Emma Baulch has asserted that familiarity with "alternative music" (punk, heavy metal, hard rock, and, I would add, rap) has become a crucial aspect of being a modern teen in Indonesia (Baulch 1996, 24). A *Kompas* article dating from January 15, 1995 attributes Habibie's and other negative reactions to rap music to a "generational" difference in taste. An experimental film released in 1998 further underscores this affiliation. The film, *Kuldesak* (Cul-de-sac), not only portrays the frustrated ideals and tragically meaningless lives experienced by many Jakartan youth; it reinforces its themes and images with a soundtrack featuring music by rapper Iwa-K, hard rockers Oppie Andaresta and the group Slank, as well as the more mainstream rock/"creative pop" group Ahmad Band.

A number of themes found in the songs of rappers give additional evidence of the ways in which its youthful creators see the world, as well as how they cast their work to appeal to their peers. For example, Iwa-K's 1996 album *Kramotak* (Brain cramp) features a song about the joy and excitement of playing basketball ("Nombok Dong!"). Even more specific to youth life is his song "Jum'at Malam" (Friday night) which portrays a singer/narrator/rapper who is extremely self-conscious and ashamed of his body, and who feels bored, frustrated, and trapped within his room. Eventually, this narrator leaves the house to meet friends and cruise the city streets. Similarly, Denada's *Ini Album Gue!!!* (This is MY album!!!, 1996) features songs about going to youth parties, hanging out at the mall, and violating her parents' curfew. Several of these same themes can be found in Neo's 1999 release *Borju* (Bourgeois). The theme of "boredom," a youth theme *par excellence*, is also frequently taken up by Indonesian rap artists (see, for example, Iwa-K, "Kramotak" [Brain cramp] and "Jum'at Malam" [Friday night], Neo, "Jalan-jalan" [Go out cruisin'], Blake, "Bosan" [Bored], and Paper Clipp, "Mati Lampu" [Blackout]).

When rap was attacked by then Minister Habibie in 1995, rapper Denada declared that rap was part of the expressive world of youth. Citing Denada, *Kompas* argued that rap provided its fans with a vehicle to channel their abundant energy. The daily quoted Denada: "What kind of music can make you run and jump? Rap can" (*Kompas*, January 15, 1995, 16).[14]

Denada's expression of youthful exuberance not only highlights once again the youth orientation of this music but also suggests a second, more specifically political, impulse behind the emergence of "alternative music" or "outlaw genres." Given the efforts of the Indonesian New Order government to control social organization, discourse, and behavior, Krishna Sen and David Hill (2000, 180–1) have argued that one of the main attractions of punk, heavy metal, and other such genres was primarily that these foreign musical styles themselves were "disorderly." This point becomes much more cogent when such genres are compared to the traditional, highly structured, and frequently meditative Javanese court gamelan music so widely associated with Indonesia, or even the melodious and sweetly sentimental pop love songs that saturate Indonesian radio, television, and public space.

Denada's "Jam Satu Lewat" (Past one A.M.) illustrates this point in a provocative and suggestive manner. Its lyrics reveal both the youth orientation of the music and an accompanying urgent desire to physically and mentally break free of social restraints, rules, and problems. In the song, Denada imagines a party she plans to attend that night, thinking it "will be crazy." Anxious to get going, she can barely stand the wait. When finally she arrives, her language breaks down into breathless, *telegramstil* descriptions of what she sees: happy faces, people "hopping," a riotous party scene. The pulse of the pounding music makes Denada forget herself and all the "orders" her parents gave her, until eventually she realizes that she has stayed out past her designated "curfew" time and must rush home in panic:

> I can't wait imagining the scene at the party
> It'll be crazy no doubt . . . !
> Can't stand it, want to get going
> Almost time
> Want to hurry thing is it's gotta be way cool
> Finally get there where the b-day is
> Faces are happy everything's hopping
> Party, riot, happy
> The music pounds hard heating up
> Everyone's into moving till you forget where you are
> Forget to go home, forget your orders yatta yatta[15]

Most striking about the song is the way in which the lyrics are combined with a hard-driving "wall-of-sound" rap style backed by punk rhythms and punctuated by heavy metal flourishes. This style, in which Denada's rap is divorced from a hip-hop beat and wedded instead to a punk rhythm, and in which her rap frequently seems to be pulled over into punk-style singing, is indicative of the potential for cross-fertilization among the "outlaw" genres in Indonesia. It also constructs a situation in which, although what is narrated is perhaps comical (if excited and panicky by turns), the resulting sound of the song leaves an impression of rage and explosive anger, something not normally condoned in dominant Indonesian ideology and practice. The form and sound of the music, themselves, present another means for the "letting go" of emotion, a kind of "noise" that interferes with the "normalization" of "Indonesian" music typically identified with calmer, more melodious styles and genres.

In fact, the comments of musicians involved in these genres also support Sen and Hill's argument. The drummer in a Balinese punk group, Superman is Dead, told Baulch:

> Our punk is about an anti-establishment attitude that's communicated musically with a letting go, anything goes kind of approach (Baulch 1996, 24).

In relation to the "hollers, screams, and growls" of "alternative music," Pickles has cited the vocalist for a Bandung band as commenting:

> When I'm fed up, this music lets me get out my emotions and become positive (Pickles 2000, 9).

The rhythm guitarist for a Balinese "death metal" band, Behead, further underlines the importance of the nature of the music itself when he told Baulch:

> Most of us are not so much inspired by the themes of death metal lyrics. . . . The attraction is more the music itself, it gives us hope, it's about freedom, it's an expression of our soul (Baulch 1996, 24).

Leading rap singer Iwa-K has stated that what he likes most about rap music is its freedom of expression (Oki and Siagian 1996, 19). He also made this the explicit theme of his most famous song, "Bebas" (Free), from his best-selling and acclaimed second album, 1993's *Topeng* (Mask).[16]

> Let's leave it all behind
> Just leave all your problems behind
> For a moment our time is ours for freeing our thoughts.
> And let them go
> Let them fly till they float up through the clouds.
> For the time being leave behind all the rules
> Which sometimes tie us down too tightly.
> And without reason . . .[17]

The disorderliness of the music leads us to a third feature connected to these genres: subcultural characteristics such as clothing worn by the musicians and their fans. Performers and followers of "alternative" or "outlaw" genres have adopted unique, identifying, and socially "suspect" styles of dress from the already commodified, popular, and visible hip-hop style. These styles have ranged from short baggy pants and baggy shirts, backwards baseball caps, underwear visible above the waistline of the pants, and shaved heads for men—

12 *Asian Music:* Summer/Fall 2005

the shaven-headed style of rappers like Iwa-K and Denada (shaven only on the sides) and Neo's Aldy elicited comments from the media—to spectacular punk styles, with studded jackets, "gravity defying hairstyles and pants patched with angry slogans" (Pickles 2000, 9). Pickles explains punk fashion in Indonesia, like punk in Britain, as "a visual stab at unappetizing social 'norms'" (Pickles 2000, 9–10).

However, Sen and Hill's assertion that disorderliness is the main attraction of these musics[18] reveals only part of what is at work in the appropriation of rap and other "alternative" genres. When I asked the niece of a Jakartan friend why she liked rock, heavy metal, and rap, she replied that these kinds of music took her and her friends out of the boredom and routine of their lives and expressed things they were feeling. Her remarks bring us to a fourth aspect of such genres and the subcultures associated with them. Certainly the "disorderly" quality of the "outlaw genres" of "alternative music" and the subcultures forming around them, as a response to the "orderliness," conformity, and even boredom of life for many Indonesian youth, is itself a powerful component of these youth subcultures. However, the message of much of this music, at least when written and composed by Indonesians themselves, is profoundly expressive, staking out a partial critique of New Order and now, post-New Order Indonesia.

One of the reasons rap music has been appropriated by Indonesian youth, I would argue, is precisely because of its history as a protest genre. Indonesian rappers are perfectly aware of rap's history and context. Eka, half of the rap duo Da' Ricuh, responding to a question about why she likes a genre associated with violence and vulgar lyrics, explains:

> Rap, you know, is identical with social imbalances. Its lyrics contain criticism, but the constructive kind (Siagian 1997, 19).[19]

Denada has also commented on the social side of rap's history:

> Of course the ones coming out with rap music in the past were the blacks. They were treated unequally by their government. So you see, what came out was heavily colored by a tone of protest (Massardi 1995, 107).[20]

These statements foreground the presence, to use Arjun Appadurai's term, of a particular globalized "mediascape" (Appadurai 1990) just as much as the condemnations of then Minister Habibie. Each refers to images and representations of rap and hip-hop generated in the United States, deploying those representations according to specific local needs and contexts. In line with Denada's and Eka's equation of rap with social protest, Iwa-K's comments exemplify the seriousness with which Indonesian rappers view the content of their songs:

> Creating lyrics provides an opportunity to pour out my grudges, so I can't just do it any old way (Oki and Siagian 1996, 19).[21]

Analyzing the appeal of the most popular "alternative music" acts, rapper Iwa-K and rock group Slank (both of which had become best-sellers in the mainstream), a University of Indonesia student explained to me that he felt these groups were popular "because they created songs relevant to the daily experiences and thoughts of the younger generation—both with their protest and social issue songs, and with the images, language, and songs about boredom and other common youth experiences." Indeed, Indonesian rappers consistently critique middle class and elite life, as in songs like Sound Da Clan's "Anak Gedongan" (Rich kid), Black Skin's "Cewek Matre" (Material chick) and "Nyontek Lagi" (Cheating again), or Neo's "Borju" (Bourgeois). In these songs, middle-class and elite subjects are represented as uncreative, always looking for the easy route to success, obsessed with gaining prestige and comfort through consumption, and unaware of vast gaps in social wealth while conspicuously displaying their consumption. A few songs also critique or document the culture of drug and alcohol use that has plagued many Indonesian youth in the past few years (Black Skin, "Sakaw" [Withdrawal], Sound Da Clan, "Anak Gedongan" [Rich kid], and 7 Kurcaci, "Junkeez"). Other themes have also appeared, such as laments about environmental degradation (Iwa-K, "Bumi Hari Ini" [The Earth today]) and condemnations of governmental corruption (Neo, "KKN" [Corruption, collusion, nepotism]).

Some of the most powerful and poetic protest rap songs have been created by Iwa-K. His "DMMT" (an abbreviation for "Dimana . . . Mata . . . Mulut . . . Telinga" or, in English, "Where are . . . your eyes . . . mouth . . . ears") suggests that Indonesian middle-class youth's desire to liberate itself is not simply about a stereotypical younger generation urge to escape from parental control and social rules. Rather, this desire embraces a more politically and socially stimulated liberation from a world in which parental control and social rules of conduct are parts of a system that destroys human feelings of concern for one's fellow citizens. It is a world where human beings refuse to hear the suffering of their hungry compatriots; they go about their lives with empty, vacant eyes and utter lies in the service of greed and personal desire.

> Why is it that today
> Everything everywhere looks so different to me
> I encountered lots of faces
> Which didn't seem to have souls
> Maybe I was dreaming
> Maybe I was hallucinating
> And now I try slapping my cheeks
> But it just hurts a lot,
> Streets with potholes full of saliva

> Bootlickers tongues sticking out
> Licking feet licking pants licking everything
> I'm shoved falling headlong
> Into a space that's divided up
> Subtly and invisibly
> But it feels like it binds us so tightly
> I see human beings with wide ears
> But who never in the least
> Hear the hoarse voices around them
> Which are always screaming out their hunger,
> All eyes gaze at you emptily,
> All mouths speak lies—
> Greedy like the worms who
> Destroy the luxuriant foliage of the trees[22]

This is a social system peopled by grotesque bootlickers and ruled by subtle but binding barriers to full human association. Further, the song's rapper/narratorial voice claims that if a woman is raped, no one hears because the noise of the city is so loud he can't even hear his own conscience: everyone is screaming to sell their products, wearing blinders, simply focusing their gaze on what is directly in front of them—their own concerns. This apocalyptic view of a capitalist city in the developing world receives its proper sequel in "Bom Waktu" (Time bomb) from his 1997 album *Mesin Imajinasi* (Imagination Machine), in which the city is a place where emotions such as frustration, anger at the dangerous and cruel behavior of others, and concern for the poor, who are being evicted from their slum dwellings, become the "time bomb" of the song's title, threatening to explode in an eruption of social rage.

Iwa-K's concerns for the fate of poor and ordinary people highlight a major theme in much Indonesian rap. It appears in rap songs by Denada ("Hari Ini" [Today]), Black Kumuh ("Kaum Kumuh" [The Lower classes]), X-Crew ("Anak Jalanan" [Street kid]), Iwa-K ("Si Kecil Lili" [Little Lili], "DMMT," and "Bom Waktu" [Time bomb]), and Neo ("Borju"). Many rap songs also manifest their populist inclinations in their choice of language: variously, rap songs often combine formal Indonesian with street slang, youth code, regionally colored pronunciations, and even expressions from regional languages (typically Javanese, Sundanese, or Betawi). By diverging from the standard Indonesian so vigorously promoted by the New Order government (Hooker 1993), rap language again positions the genre as a "noise" disruptive of dominant representations of Indonesian culture, as well as giving it a more relaxed, flexible, and populist feel.

This populist bent links rap, and much other rock/punk and "alternative" pop, to earlier populist singers such as Rhoma Irama and Iwan Fals. It is likely no coincidence that Iwa-K and the rock/punk group Slank rose to considerable popularity starting in the mid-1990s, when both earlier singers (and their genres) seemed to have passed the peaks of their creativity and were even being courted by the government. "Globalization" was already evident in both of these earlier Indonesian populist musics. Irama constructed his populist style through the appropriation of Middle Eastern and Indian musical elements combined with Western rock, modern electric instruments and stage effects, Islamic morality, and an exoticized Arabic style of dress. Fals, in turn, drew upon Western folk and country music along with the ethos of the Indonesian *ngamen* (itinerant street singer) tradition. In the 1990s, rap, punk, heavy metal, and hard rock seemed to represent a range of distinct yet connected attempts to create new populist musics that are politically and socially critical and, sometimes, even anti-commercial, announcing disruptively—with stylistic and musical noise—their opposition to the prevailing socio-political order.

The connection with notions of "globalization" is particularly fascinating in this respect, for in order to create disruptive musical and subcultural positions, all of the groups have adapted as their own genres of Western music which represent, in their original cultural location, moment, or subsequent development, parts of "Western" working and lower class or minority subcultures.[23] These types of music are usually viewed as highly suspect by the established authorities on both sides of the Pacific Ocean. Earlier attempts to condemn breakdancing in Indonesia, for example, revealed the Indonesian government's hostility toward hip-hop culture (Dewanto 1995). However, to overestimate the subversive potential of genres such as rap would also be to ignore the specific matrix of Indonesian social, cultural, economic, and political forces with which these genres must contend.

Condemnation, Strategies of Evasion, and Commercial Cooptation

Although socially critical, rappers in Indonesia work within a context in which censorship and other kinds of state pressure have been very real impediments, particularly prior to May 1998. As I have mentioned, rap is possibly the most commercially mainstream of the "alternative" or "outlaw" genres. This makes it more visible, more accessible to wider publics, and also a more likely target for government condemnation (precisely because of its visibility) than other musical forms. During the New Order era, such a position necessitated a number of strategies of evasion. Self-censorship by producers is one possible response. For instance, a song by Eka's Da' Ricuh duo, "Negara Mbeling" (Naughty country), which cited the incident on July 27, 1996, in which then head of the Indonesian Democratic Party and now ex-president Megawati Su-

16 *Asian Music:* Summer/Fall 2005

karnoputri's supporters were violently ousted by government forces from her Indonesian Democratic Party headquarters in downtown Jakarta, was rejected by the producer, who did not want to take the risk of having a cassette banned (Siagian 1997, 19).

In response to Habibie's condemnatory remarks, a number of rappers and commentators pursued different arguments to fend off government opprobrium. Eka's comments cited above demonstrate one such strategy of evasion, an attempt to cast rap's social criticism as "constructive." Similarly, a number of commentators asserted that rap was not simply vulgar and that its social criticism was something to be valued.

Iwa-K pursued a second line of evasion that nonetheless managed to retain considerable defiance while at the same time displaying the "disorderly," "anything goes" attitude of many "alternative" genre musicians. In response to criticism that the lyrics of rap music were at times crude and frightening, he remarked:

> I never think about whether my songs contain social criticism or love. If a lot of the songs are frightening, that's what I see. I don't intend to say this is good, that's bad, because I'm not the judge of that. What's important is that I write what I see and feel (Oki and Siagian 1996, 19; Raharti and Baskoro 1995, 111).[24]

Yet another approach was taken by Denada, who, while acknowledging, as noted previously, that it has been associated with social protest, also declared that Habibie was right to characterize American rap as vulgar. Invoking the notion of a discrete national culture and character, however, Denada went on to argue: "But . . . here you know we have our own culture, our own social life, which isn't the same as over there. So, yeah, it's nothing to be afraid of" (Massardi 1995, 107).[25] This opinion dovetails with the remarks of commentators who maintain that Indonesian rap is more "polite" than American rap. In fact, aside from the absence of expletives, the omission from Indonesian rap/hip-hop of several other features of North American rap lends credence to the suggestion that Indonesian rap is distinct. For example, Indonesian rap and hip-hop rarely use the "sampling" techniques or the boasting[26] so common to much North American rap and hip-hop.

Elsewhere, Denada also struck a chord that echoes Eka's characterization of rap as "constructive" criticism:

> "Sure I like it. Dynamic chattering like that is really fun. We can complain freely, but nobody gets offended, rather they're happy," stated Denada, who admitted that with [rap music] she "channels her talent for complaining," without hurting anyone else, and for that reason it can be called a positive activity (*Kompas,* January 15, 1995, 16).[27]

Thus, as the remarks of Eka, Denada, and Iwa-K demonstrate, although Indonesian rappers have plenty to say in their songs about social problems, during the New Order they were reluctant to claim too openly that they were criticizing the government or social system, or that Indonesian rap was particularly similar to American rap. In this cautious approach we can detect the artists speaking to the perceived all-pervasive ear of the government security apparatus — as well as to more generally negative social perceptions of rap and hip-hop.

Denada's strategy also returns us to discussions of the relationship between "globalization" (understood as North American cultural domination or neo-imperialism) and "national identity." In so doing it broaches a fifth element in rap and other "alternative" genre subcultures. As is obvious by now, many of these groups have taken Western names. A fair number also include entirely or partly English-language songs on their albums. Certainly, much of this reflects the influence of the globalization of North American culture and would appear to confirm the fears of those who see globalization as a one-way process of cultural domination and subordination. In this there is certainly an element of social prestige quite clearly linked to class, wealth, and their attendant opportunities and privileges. Specifically, in this case, the Indonesian middle class is perhaps the group with the greatest access to North American culture through television, travels abroad, and the economic resources to purchase the requisite clothing, musical instruments, and other related accessories. In addition, members of the middle-to-upper classes are most likely to have access to English language lessons and to obtain English-language competence. Indonesian middle-class youth are undoubtedly coming more and more to resemble their counterparts in North America both in terms of style and attitudes.

Yet the appropriation of rap and other genres by such Indonesian youth, and their occasional use of English, as I have demonstrated, is not merely the result of a colonization of passive subjects leading to the production of exact duplicates of North American popular cultural artifacts. The context of rap's appropriation in Indonesia is radically different — here is a genre created chiefly in North America by a racial minority suffering great structural discrimination. Upon immigration to Indonesia, this same genre becomes a vehicle of populist expression and protest for a segment of the youth of a much more privileged social group experiencing no such racial discrimination, yet a group becoming increasingly dissatisfied with authoritarian rule and its own complicity with it.

Furthermore, given the government's promotion of English-language study and the large number of English-language serials and MTV music video clips on Indonesian television, knowledge of the English language, if with varying degrees of competence, has spread quite a bit further socially than might at

18   *Asian Music:* Summer/Fall 2005

first be expected. Nor is Indonesian rap merely part of a two-way dialogue with North America. The inclusion of English-language lyrics in songs by Indonesian rappers (and others) is certainly in part an attempt to "go international,"[28] but going international does not always, perhaps not even in the majority of cases, mean going to North America.

The founding, for example, in Singapore in the early 1990s of an MTV–Asia station, whose language of broadcasting is English, suggested that not only would North American music increasingly be overwhelming Asian households, but that many Asian groups would also be performing for other Asian audiences, sometimes in English. One Indonesian magazine reported that Iwa-K hoped to market his second album (*Topeng*) not only in Indonesia but more widely throughout Asia, since he had a market in Japan, Singapore, and Malaysia (*Popular* Sept. 1994:30). Iwa-K's appearances at the Fukuoka and Tokyo Asian culture and music festivals in late 1995, followed by the release of one of his albums in Japan, were seen as banner moments in the recognition of Indonesian music (and especially rap) on an international stage (Oki and Siagian 1996; Siagian 1997). This success in itself suggests other dimensions to "globalization," other potential circuits of distribution, influence, and consumption.

In line with rap's relatively commercialized status, efforts by producers to self-censor creators' themes, as well as the attempts of music commentators to defend rap, presenting it in turn as acceptable criticism, a more polite Indonesian version of a foreign import, or simply a symptom of a generational difference, indicate not only bids by socially conscious Indonesians within the music industry to defend their right to criticize society, but also expression of the interests of the music industry itself to protect a lucrative subfield of its business. Such arguments allow us to identify attempts to normalize and even co-opt rap in response to regime criticism and pervasive negative social images of the genre.

Still, culture is never easy to control. If recent phenomena have included the co-optative use of rap music in theme songs for television boxing programs and martial arts serials, Denada's increasing turn away from rap/punk toward a softer, more traditional style of pop, Iwa-K's abandonment of the music business altogether, and the antiphonal incorporation of rap lines into the love songs of Indonesian R & B divas like Sania and Imaniar or the even more recent trio, Tofu, other developments suggest that rap-as-protest continues to evade complete social control. Several releases in 2000 announced the commercial mainstream arrival of a rap-metal fusion, tellingly referred to as "hip-metal." Combining rap's rhythmic spoken word delivery of lyrics with a hard-driving metal backing, "hip-metal" music by groups like Red, 7 Kurcaci, and those on the compilation album *Smas Hip* embodied rap's longstanding appropriation into another "alternative" or "outlaw" genre, creating a harder, much more unruly sound than the works of Iwa-K, Neo, and the "Rap Party" albums of an earlier era. Stylistically and musically reminiscent of a number of Denada's earlier songs, "hip-metal" recordings nonetheless cling more tightly than Denada ever did to some of rap's favorite social themes—the drug problem, Indonesian urban society's perceived heartlessness, and concern for the urban poor. However, if anything, the driving metal backing music gives "hip-metal" an even angrier, more urgent sound than most earlier rap protest songs. That such angry "noise" has grown into an explosive rage, almost a cacophony, in a time when democratic reform has stalled in the face of an intransigent military and political elite, may well be no coincidence.

Department of Pacific and Asian Studies, University of Victoria

Notes

[1] I would like to thank Andy Sutton, Jeremy Wallach, Joe Moore, Sailaja Krishna-murti, Bryce Kushnier, Tina Chen, Adam Muller, Martin Roberts, Khoo Gaik-Cheng, and the participants in the October 2001 University of Manitoba Globalization and Popular Culture Conference for various valuable suggestions on how to improve this examination of Indonesian rap.

[2] For analyses of these various developments, see respectively Sullivan 1990, 62–9; Suryakusuma 1996; Hadiz 1994; Sen and Hill 2000, 54–6; MacIntyre 1990; Sen 1994, 55–6; King 1982, 115; and Hefner 1993).

[3] Hill 1987; Hill 1994, 41–51; Sen and Hill 2000; Sen 1994, 66–71; Bodden 1997; *Jakarta Post* 1990; and Pracoyo and Riza 1995 are the sources for this information.

[4] For a sense of the breadth of these efforts, see Bowen 1986; Hatley 1990, 333–5; Hough 1992; Hatley 1994, 229–38, 254–7; Pemberton 1994; Guinness 1994; Widodo 1995; Yampolsky 1995; Sears 1996, 233–65.

[5] See Koentjaraningrat 1985, 460–2; Mahasin 1990, 91–2; Anderson 1990, 125–46; Sur-yakusuma 1996, 96.

[6] What I am labeling "outlaw genres" in this paper are not known by that term in Indonesia, although the point of then Minister Habibie's remarks is precisely to stig-matize them as such. In Indonesian pop music circles they are known as "alternative/underground pop" (Sen and Hill 2000, 177) or "creative pop" (Siagian 1997, 19).

[7] Rhoma Irama, the figure most closely associated with the Arabic-Indian-Malay de-rived pop genre *dangdut*, was prohibited from performing on television during much of the 1980s for the criticism of New Order society contained in his lyrics, as well as for his campaign support for the Islamic opposition party, the PPP (Sen and Hill 200, 175). In addition, Irama's genre, *dangdut*, was long stigmatized by many elite and middle-class Indonesians as vulgar and crude (Lockhard 1998, 101). "Country-pop" super star Iwan Fals (a folk-pop singer à la Bob Dylan) was similarly the target of police interro-

gations because of his critical lyrics, and he also saw his concerts cancelled, possibly because his tour promoter attempted in 1989 to bypass the usual distributional channels for commercial music (Murray 1991, 12–14; Lockhard 1998, 108–12).

Yet equally, if not more important, was the fact that both Irama and Fals had acquired enormous followings through embracing a populist attitude (and in Fals's case, an entire ethos) manifested in both their language—drawn partially from the language of everyday discourse on the streets—and in their themes, which took the point of view of ordinary people left behind by New Order economic development. These features were combined in social protest songs that took up issues of poverty, human-rights abuses, and corruption, issues that were also important to many middle-class youth. Capturing popular disaffection with New Order society across classes, Iwan Fals's concerts occasionally became venues for fans to exhibit antagonism toward police and the wealthy: a concert in Senayan in 1989 designed to kick off Fals's ill-fated tour was followed by a riot. Subsequently, Fals was rarely allowed to perform in concert through much of the early 1990s (Sen and Hill 2000, 182–3).

Still, indicative of the bifurcation of the "system's" responses toward such music, neither performer's cassettes were banned, with Rhoma Irama and *dangdut* being credited by Frederick and Lockhard with playing a large role in creating a modern market for the mass media in Indonesia (Frederick 1982, 103–4; Lockhard 1998, 96). The *dangdut* genre even became the object of elite recuperation in the early 1990s at roughly the same time that the government was trying to more completely co-opt the Muslim community and when even Rhoma Irama himself was persuaded to campaign in national elections for the government party, Golkar. Similarly, although Fals is generally believed to have maintained his personal integrity, by the late 1980s his work had also become big business, and an entrepreneur close to the Suharto family often worked with him on promoting concerts and new albums, eventually leading to several government- and military-sponsored joint concerts (Lockhard 1998, 111–12). Many of his old songs were also repackaged in a number of variations at the beginning of the "reform" movement following Suharto's fall from the presidency.

[8] The passage I am citing reads as follows in Indonesian: Musik rap digugat Menristek BJ Habibie. "Musik rap itu tidak berseni," kata Habibie, awal Januari ini. Menurut dia, yang kebetulan menonton pertunjukan rap di sebuah setasiun televisi swasta pada malam tahun baru lalu, kata-kata dalam lagu rap termasuk kategori jorok, menjijikkan, dan tak bernilai sastra . . . Bukan karena saya terkena kritik. Tapi, tidak semua budaya dari negara maju bernilai tinggi. Ada pula yang membawa dampak negatif.

[9] The Indonesian reads as follows: Generasi muda jangan mau diperbudak unsur budaya asing yang di negaranya sendiri tak disukai . . . di sana saja tidak patut, apalagi di Indonesia, tidak cocok . . . Saya tidak setuju karena tidak ada manfaatnya sama sekali, terutama bagi generasi muda. . . .

[10] Although it was due to be released by Ice-T's "speed metal" band as a metal song, "Cop Killer" was repeatedly labeled a rap song by the U.S. media (Rose 1996, 241).

[11] This would also appear to confirm Sarah Thornton's argument that youthful subcultural capital relies on the fantasy of classlessness to escape the trappings of the parental class (Thornton 1997[1995], 204).

[12] The bridge between the underground and the mainstream was, in the case of rap and several R & B artists like Sania, provided by an independent production studio, Guest Music Productions, founded by three young musicians turned producers. Guest Music Productions actually released Sania's first solo album (*Sania*, 1999) on its own independent label, but in the case of their productions of the Iwa-K and *Pesta Rap* (Rap party) albums, GMP's recordings were marketed under the more commercial, mainstream Musica label (Siagian 1997).

[13] A more detailed and specific differentiation of each genre or subculture is, although necessary and of great interest, unfortunately beyond the scope of this paper.

[14] Rap buat Denada—mungkin juga para penggemar lainnya—adalah musik yang memberi kesempatan buat tersalurnya energi besar yang mereka miliki. "Mana ada musik yang bisa dibuat lari-lari, lompat-lompat. Rap bisa."

[15] Nggak sabar rasanya ngebayangin suasana pesta yang pasti bakal gila . . . ! Nggakkuat pengen berangkat Waktunya semakin dekat Pengen cepat-cepat soalnya pasti asyik berat Akhirnya sampai juga di tempat yang lagi ultah wajah-wajah ceria semua serba meriah Pesta hura-hura, gembira Musik menghentak keras pesta semakin panas Semua asyik bergoyang sampai lupa daratan Lupa pulang lupa pesan keterusan. . . .

[16] *Topeng* sold 100,000 albums in cassette form within the first six months of its release and eventually reached sales of at least 250,000 (Massardi 1995, 107; Raharti and Baskoro 1995, 111), which are very successful sales figures for an Indonesian album.

[17] Sudah tinggalkan, tinggalkan saja semua persoalan, waktu kita sejenak tuk membebaskan pikiran. Dan biarkan, biarkan terbang sampai melayang jauh menembus awan. Sementara tinggalkan semua aturan yang kadang terlalu mengikat. Dan tak beralasan. . . .

[18] And, it could be added, the clothing, attitudes, and scenes that go with them.

[19] Rap itu 'kan identik dengan kesenjangan sosial. Liriknya berisi kritikan, tapi yang membangun.

[20] "Yang ngeluarin musik *rap* itu kan dulu orang kulit hitam. Mereka itu kan diperlakukan secara berbeda oleh pemerintahnya. makanya, yang keluar itu lebih banyak nada protesnya."

[21] The original text reads, "Membuat lirik itu kesempatan buat menuangkan unekunek, makanya tidak boleh asal-asalan." Similarly, underground punk and skinhead bands fill their songs and album covers with social criticism and angry calls to eliminate injustice, oppression, and corruption (Pickles 2000, 10).

[22] Mengapa pada hari ini kulihat semua dimana mana begitu berbeda, banyak kutemukan muka muka, yang seakan tak memiliki jiwa, aku mungkin sedang bermimpi, aku mungkin berhalusinasi dna kini kucoba menampar pipi, namun terasa sakit sekali, jalanan becek tergenang air liur, lidah para penjilat yang selalu terjulur, jilat kaki jilat celana menjilat semuanya, ku terdorong jatuh terjerembab, ke dalam ruang yang bersekat-sekat, halus dan tak terlihat, namun terasa begitu mengikat, kulihat manusia bertelinga lebar, namun tak pernah sedikitpun mendengar suara-suara parau sekitar, yang selalu berteriak lapar, semua mata menatap kosong, semua mulut berkata bohong—rakus seperti ulat yang melumat, dedaunan di pohon yang lebat. . . .

[23] Heavy metal forms a partial exception here. Straw argues that its audience was drawn from suburban and presumably middle-class males. However, during the 1970s and early 1980s, when not being negatively characterized as regressive and uninnovative, heavy metal received little attention from rock critics. By the early 1980s the heavy metal look had come to acquire the connotations of a low socio-economic position, while its audience generally speaking had not moved beyond secondary education and faced diminishing job prospects (Straw 1993).

[24] "Saya nggak pernah mikirin, lagu-lagu saya liriknya mengandung kritik sosial atau cinta. Kalau lagu-lagunya banyak yang seram, itulah yang saya lihat. Saya tidak bermaksud menyampaikan ini bagus, itu jelek, karena saya bukan penilai. Yang penting, saya menulis apa yang saya lihat dan saya rasakan," jawabnya ketika diminta komentarnya soal lirik-lirik lagu rap yang terkadang kasar dan menyeramkan.

[25] "Tapi . . . di sini kan kita punya kebudayaan sendiri, kehidupan sosial sendiri, yang nggak sama dengan di sana. Jadi, ya, aman-aman saja."

[26] This is perhaps a rather odd omission in Indonesia, since a strong element of traditional Malay and, more broadly, traditional Southeast Asian cultures is the verbal poetic jousting that is often, though not always, linked to courtship games. In one song, "Bungaku" (My flower), from Iwa-K's 1997 *Mesin Imajinasi* album, I have noticed the return of some imagery that sounds suspiciously similar to the imagery used in a local, traditional verbal jousting genre, *pantun*. Yet this seems to be a link to tradition not yet explored in depth by Indonesian rap artists.

[27] "Suka aja. Dinamis, merepet-merepetnya itu asyik. Kita bisa ngomel dengan bebas, tapi orang nggak sakit hati malah senang," ujar Denada, yang mengaku dengan itu "menyalurkan bakat mengomel" tanpa merugikan orang lain, dan karena itu boleh disebut kegiatan positif.

[28] In an article on the language and politics of the underground music scene in Indonesia, Jeremy Wallach (2003) argues that there are two main reasons why underground bands use English lyrics in their songs. The first is that English offers links with the outside world while having a certain amount of prestige within Indonesia. Secondly, these groups may use English in order to express strong emotions and political commentary that might be less easily voiced in Indonesian, the official national language. This was anecdotally confirmed in a conversation I had in July 2004 with one member of a Jakarta underground band.

References

Anderson, Benedict
  1990   *Language and Power.* Ithaca: Cornell University Press.
Appadurai, Arjun
  1990   "Disjuncture and Difference in the Global Cultural Economy." In *Global Culture: Nationalism, Globalization and Modernity,* ed. Mike Featherstone, 295–310. London: Sage Press.

Attali, Jacques
   1985 [1977]   *Noise: The Political Economy of Music.* Minneapolis: University of Minnesota Press.

Baulch, Emma
   1996   "Punks, Rastas & Headbangers: Bali's Generation X." *Inside Indonesia* 48: 23–5.

Bodden, Michael
   1997   "Teater Koma's *Suksesi* and Indonesia's New Order." *Asian Theatre Journal* 14.2:259–80.

Bourchier, David
   1997   "Totalitarianism and the 'National Personality': Recent Controversy about the Philosophical Basis of the Indonesian State." In *Imagining Indonesia,* ed. Jim Schiller and Barbara Martin-Schiller, 157–85. Athens: Ohio University Center for International Studies [Southeast Asian Monographs No. 97].

Bowen, John
   1986   "On the Political Construction of Tradition: Gotong Royong in Indonesia." *Journal of Asian Studies* 45:545–61.

Cohen, Stanley
   1997 [1989]   "Symbols of Trouble." In *The Subcultures Reader,* ed. Ken Gelder and Sarah Thornton, 149–62. London: Routledge.

Cvetkovich, Ann, and Douglas Kellner
   1997   "Introduction." In *Articulating the Global and the Local: Globalization and Cultural Studies,* ed. Ann Cvetkovich and Douglas Kellner, 1–30. Boulder: Westview Press.

Dewanto, Nirwan
   1995   "Seni, Birokrasi, Pasar." *Media Kerja Budaya* 2:45–7.

Feith, Herbert
   1963   "The Dynamics of Guided Democracy." In *Indonesia,* ed. Ruth McVey, 309–409. New Haven: Human Relations Area Files, Inc.

Guinness, Patrick
   1994   "Local Society and Culture." In *Indonesia's New Order: The Dynamics of Socio-Economic Transformation,* ed. Hal Hill, 267–304. Honolulu: University of Hawaii Press.

Hadiz, Vedi
   1994   "The Political Significance of Recent Working Class Action." In *Indonesia's Emerging Proletariat,* ed. David Bourchier, 64–73. Clayton, Victoria: Monash University Centre of Southeast Asian Studies [Annual Indonesian Lecture Series No. 17].

Harris
   1998   "Gema Stones dari Gang Potlot." *Popular. Edisi Khusus* Nov.:54–5.

Hatley, Barbara
   1990   "Theatre as Cultural Resistance in Contemporary Indonesia." In *State and*

Civil Society in Indonesia, ed. Arief Budiman, 321–48. Clayton, Victoria: Monash University Centre of Southeast Asian Studies [Papers on Southeast Asia No. 22].

1994   "Culture." In *Indonesia's New Order: The Dynamics of Socio-Economic Transformation,* ed. Hal Hill, 216–66. Honolulu: University of Hawai'i Press.

Hebdige, Dick
1979   *Subculture: The Meaning of Style.* London: Routledge.

Hefner, Robert W.
1993   "Islam, State, and Civil Society: ICMI and the Struggle for the Indonesian Middle Class." *Indonesia* 56:1–35.

Heryanto, Ariel
1995   "What Does Post-Modernism Do in Contemporary Indonesia?" *Sojourn* 10.1: 33–44.

1996   "Indonesian Middle-Class Opposition in the 1990s." In *Political Oppositions in Industrializing Asia,* ed. Gary Rodan, 241–71. London: Routledge.

Hill, David
1987   "Press Challenges, Government Responses: Two Campaigns in *Indonesia Raya.*" In *The Indonesian Press: Its Past, Its People, Its Problems,* ed. Paul Tickell, 21–37. Clayton, Victoria: Monash University Centre of Southeast Asian Studies [Annual Indonesian Lecture Series No. 12].

1994   *The Press in New Order Indonesia.* Perth: University of Western Australia Press and Asia Research Centre of Social, Political, and Economic Change [Asia Paper No. 4].

Hooker, Virginia Matheson
1993   "New Order Language in Context." In *Culture and Society in New Order Indonesia,* ed. Virginia M. Hooker, 272–93. Kuala Lumpur: Oxford University Press.

Hough, Brett
1992   *Contemporary Balinese Dance Spectacles as National Ritual.* Clayton, Victoria: Monash University Centre of Southeast Asian Studies [Working Paper No. 74].

Jameson, Fredric
1998   "Notes on Globalization as a Philosophical Issue." In *The Cultures of Globalization,* ed. Fredric Jameson and Masao Miyoshi, 54–77. Durham: Duke University Press.

King, Dwight
1982   "Indonesia's New Order as a Bureaucratic Polity, a Neopatrimonial Regime or a Bureaucratic Authoritarian Regime: What Difference Does it Make?" In *Interpreting Indonesian Politics: Thirteen Contributions to the Debate, 1964–1981,* ed. Benedict R. Anderson and Audrey Kahin, 104–16. Ithaca: Cornell Southeast Asia Program, Modern Indonesia Project.

Koenjaraningrat
1985   *Javanese Culture.* Singapore: Oxford University Press.

Lockhard, Craig A.
  1998   *Dance of Life.* Honolulu: University of Hawai'i Press.
MacIntyre, Andrew
  1990   "State-Society Relations in New Order Indonesia: The Case of Business." In *State and Civil Society in Indonesia,* ed. Arief Budiman, 369–93. Clayton, Victoria: Monash University Centre of Southeast Asian Studies.
Mahasin, Aswab
  1990   "The Santri Middle Class: An Insider's View." *Prisma* 49:91–6.
Massardi, Yudhistira A.N.M.
  1995   "Si Bawel Kena Omel." *Gatra* 21:106–07.
McRobbie, Angela
  1997 [1989]   "Second Hand Dresses and the Role of the Ragmarket." In *The Subcultures Reader,* ed. Ken Gelder and Sarah Thornton, 191–9. London: Routledge.
Morfit, Michael
  1986   "Pancasila Orthodoxy." In *Central Government and Local Development in Indonesia,* ed. Colin MacAndrews, 42–55. Singapore: Oxford University Press.
Murray, Allison
  1991   "Kampung Culture and Radical Chic in Jakarta." *Review of Indonesian and Malaysian Affairs* 25.1:1–16.
Oki and Tagor Siagian
  1996   "Iwa Kusuma: Pilih Musik Rap Karena Tidak Bisa Menyanyi." *Kompas,* June 5, 19.
Pemberton, John
  1994   *On the Subject of "Java."* Ithaca: Cornell University Press.
Pickles, Jo
  2000   "Punks for Peace." *Inside Indonesia* 64:9–10.
Pracoyo and Riza
  1995   "Diskriminasi bagi Koma." *Forum Keadilan,* 4.18:27.
Raharti, Sri
  1999   "Mari Menjual Reformasi Lewat Lagu." *Forum Keadilan* 8.22:91.
Raharti, Sri and Baskoro
  1995   "Rap: Boleh atau tidak Boleh?" *Forum Keadilan* 3.21:111.
Raharti, Sri, Yusi A. Pareanom, and Johan Budi S.P.
  1998   "Bisnis Kaset Digerus Krisis." *Forum Keadilan* 6.23:63.
Roooli, Harry
  1995   "'Rap' Dan Dosa Sebuah Musik." *Kompas,* January 15, 16.
Rose, Tricia
  1996   "Hidden Politics: Discursive and Institutional Policing of Rap Music." In *Droppin' Science: Critical Essays on Rap Music and Hip Hop Culture,* ed. William Eric Perkins, 236–57. Philadelphia: Temple University Press.
Sears, Laurie J.
  1996   *Shadows of Empire.* Durham: Duke University Press.

26 *Asian Music:* Summer/Fall 2005

Sen, Krishna
    1994   *Indonesian Cinema.* London: Zed.
Sen, Krishna, and David Hill
    2000   *Media, Culture and Politics in Indonesia.* Melbourne: Oxford University Press.
Siagian, Tagor
    1997   "Pesta Rap 2: Menjaring Pengurus Iwa K." *Kompas,* February 13, 19.
Straw, Will
    1993   "Characterizing Rock Music Culture: The Case of Heavy Metal." In *The Cultural Studies Reader,* ed. Simon During, 368-81. London: Routledge.
Sullivan, Norma
    1991   "Gender and Politics in Indonesia." In *Why Gender Matters in Southeast Asian Politics,* ed. Maila Stivens, 61-86. Clayton, Victoria: Monash University Centre of Southeast Asian Studies.
Suryakusuma, Julia
    1996   "The State and Sexuality in New Order Indonesia." In *Fantasizing the Feminine in Indonesia,* ed. Laurie J. Sears, 92-119. Durham: Duke University Press.
"Terobosan Iwa K"
    1994   *Popular* Sept.:30.
Thompson, Edmund
    1993   "Rock and Riots." *Inside Indonesia* 35:4-6.
Thornton, Sarah
    1997 [1995]   "The Social Logic of Subcultural Capital." In *The Subcultures Reader,* ed. Ken Gelder and Sarah Thornton, 200-09. London: Routledge.
Wallach, Jeremy
    2003   " 'Goodbye My Blind Majesty': Music, Language, and Politics in the Indonesian Underground." In *Global Pop, Local Language,* ed. Harris M. Berger and Michael Thomas Carroll, 53-86. Jackson: University Press of Mississippi.
Watson, C. W.
    1987   *State and Society in Indonesia: Three Papers.* Canterbury: University of Kent at Canterbury Centre of Southeast Asian Studies.
Widodo, Amrih
    1995   "The Stages of the State: Arts of the People and Rites of Hegemonization." *Review of Indonesian and Malaysian Affairs* 29.1-2:1-36.
Yampolsky, Philip
    1995   "Forces for Change in the Regional Performing Arts." *Bijdragen tot de Taal-, Land- en Volkenkunde (BKI)* 151.4:700-25.

[18]

The Bitter Wounding:
The Lament as Social Protest
in Rural Greece

ANNA CARAVELI

VERY EARLY on a July morning, with the Cretan village of Dzermiades barely stirring to life after a summer night's sleep, I was led by a boy through the winding cobblestone streets to the house of Anthoula Lyraki, a gifted lament performer who had recently lost her sister in an accident. Hearing of my interest in laments, Mrs. Lyraki had reluctantly consented to talk to me. After several days of negotiation, we agreed that I could record her laments for her dead sister in the privacy of her home on one condition: that it would be done without her husband's knowledge. A boy would be sent to me on the following morning to let me know when Mr. Lyrakis left for his work and to lead me to their home. Mr. Lyrakis was reputed to be particularly strict (*afstiros*) and disapproving of his wife's lament performances, because he feared they would upset her. But frequently during my research into death rituals in the village of Dzermiades in 1978, women lamented for their dead in the company of other women, either despite men's disapproval or without their knowledge.

I conducted fieldwork for this paper in two areas of Greece: four villages in the Zagori area of Epiros and the village of Dzermiades in Crete.[1] Being a woman, Greek-born, and a mother helped me gain access to the female circles of these villages. Motherhood, recovery from an illness, and expatriation (I had been living in the United States for years) enhanced my status as a mature woman. I was considered to have had experience with the griefs caused by "exile" (*tous kaimous tis xenitias*) and, in general, to be knowledgeable about the kind of troubles (*vasana*) that are the subjects of women's informal conversations and formalized narratives such as laments.

By following women to their homes, to the fields, on their visits to the cemetery, and as they did their daily chores, I discovered a universe of female activity outside the realm of men. Although based on the village's larger system of values and interpretations, this universe had its own variants of these, while many of the tasks, social roles, and expressive genres were gender-specific, limited to women only.

At first, when hearing of my interest in laments, many women were surprised. In public conversations, they would laugh and tease me about my desire to record such worthless songs, echoing the general devaluation of lamentation practices that one heard from many nonparticipants in the village. Others were shocked by what they saw as a macabre preoccupation on my part. In time, and in discussions among women that took place in more private surroundings, the conversation would turn to critical appraisals of lament performances and fine lament performers. It was through this type of discussion that the women's high regard for both form and acclaimed performers became evident. Indeed, successful compositions are often passed down through generations, becoming valuable learning tools and prized aesthetic possessions for the traditional women in the village.

An important point, then, is that at least while operating within the world conjured up by the lament performances, women use its participants—other women—as their frame of reference. In his recent book, *The Death Rituals of Rural Greece*, Loring Danforth interprets women's prominence in lament rituals as an attempt to continue their relationship with their male kin beyond death—a relationship that gave them their identity in life (Danforth 1982:136-138). Yet in the villages where I did my fieldwork, narratives about female "heroes" (worthy mothers or wives, skilled midwives or healers, talented singers, storytellers, or craftswomen) constituted a female history of the village, a body of women's expressive genres, and a female line of transmission (Caraveli-Chaves 1980:145).

In Dzermiades, as in the rest of rural Greece, ritual laments for the dead are performed by women.[2] It is important to remember, however, that not all village women performed or approved of laments. Thus the male/female dichotomy is not the only framework for understanding lament practices. A rising village middle class, and those with urban jobs returning to the village for brief visits, frequently were embarrassed by lamenting relatives (Caraveli-Chaves 1980:131). Occasionally, younger family members were unaware of the talent of a lament performer in the family or of the reputation she enjoyed among the traditional women of the village. In the villages where I worked, the lament tradition was, with few exceptions, performed by middle-aged or old women.

The performance of laments, however, creates a symbolic female universe that affects in many ways female activity outside of it (Caraveli-Chaves 1980). This paper examines the intricate dimensions of this universe as they relate to the larger context of the village in which lamentation is performed, and it considers the remarkable aesthetic, ritual, and social elements of lament performances and how they interrelate.

The first part of this study focuses on the performance process, concentrating particularly on three elements: the indigenous system of aesthetics connected with lament composition and performance, as revealed through folk criticism;[3] the role of lament as a type of folk religious expression, separate and often antithetical to institutional religion; and the role of lament performance as a vehicle for affecting social bonding among participants.

The second part of this paper examines the point of convergence between the separate world of women involved in death rituals and the mainstream of public life in the village and beyond. It is through the active choices of the lament performers that creative strategies develop and are handed down traditionally, transforming laments into instruments of protest and social commentary. Thus, while they are engendered by the occasion of death, laments become instruments for voicing the concerns of the living, and although they are created in a separate realm of experience and activity that is exclusive to women, they constitute a dialogue between the performers and the disparate worlds around them.

The Aesthetics of Pain

The death of a beloved person is the catalyst for and focus of women's lamentation and the broader universe of activity and experience generated by it. Yet participation in death rituals also becomes an important expressive avenue for the living. A significant aspect of lament performance is its religious dimensions. While male priests perform rituals in church and interpret official church doctrine, women are the leaders in folk religious events that are principally, but not exclusively, performed in the context of the domestic sphere—events such as calendar holidays, name day celebrations on saint's days, and life cycle rituals.[4]

Ritual lament performances are a significant type of folk religious expression in that they constitute a metaphysical communication outside the official church, relying heavily on an extraordinary state of consciousness or emotional engrossment, with the lamenter acting as the mediator between the living and the dead.[5] Employing the expanded definition of possession offered by Vincent Crapanzano and Vivian Garrison (1977:1-40), which considers "extensions" of posses-

sion to be important phenomena for study since they are "intimately
connected with possession" (1977:10), this paper suggests that there
are at least metaphorical similarities between possession rituals and the
performance of laments.[6] As in some possession rituals, for example,
lamentation uses "a learned idiom" of patterned text and performance
"for articulating a certain range of experience" (Crapanzano and Garrison 1977:10-11) and a state of consciousness removed from that of
ordinary experience (Bourguignon 1976:esp. 5-14). Both lament texts
and folk commentary employ possession-related metaphors, including
an entire system of aesthetics developed around the concept of pain
(*ponos*)[7] and used to connote the state of emotional engrossment of the
performer. In Dzermiades, for example, the consensus regarding the
definition of a lament is that it is a song for the dead, produced when
one is immersed in and inspired by pain. A lament performed by someone who is emotionally disengaged might be considered for its poetic
merit but is not a true lament.

Just as emotional context defines lament aesthetics, a highly refined
system of aesthetics is used to judge the degree and quality of the lamenter's "pain." Criteria include depth, authenticity, and style of delivery. The distinction between "in pain" and "out of pain" (*eine pano
ston pono tis; den eine ston pono tis*) is, in the villages I researched,
among the most significant elements constituting the complex lament
aesthetics. *Den vriskome ston pono mou tora; den boro na po miro-
loyi*, "I am not in pain now; I can't say a lament," was a frequent answer to my request for laments from women in mourning. At times, I
would be urgently referred to a well-known performer because *vriskete
pano ston pono tis tora; tha sou miroloyisi kala*, "she is in her pain
now; she will lament well for you." Moreover, the stronger the pain of
the performer, the more value her composition has as ritual communication with the dead. An interesting parallel is offered in Lauri Honko's
study of Finnish laments. Stating that the best lamenters in Finland are
elderly women, especially widows, Honko cites Volmari Porkka's explanation that older women are considered to "have had time to experience also the shadow sides of life" and thus "do not need to make an
effort to reach a sorrowful state of mind; their hearts are already full of
sorrow" (Honko 1974:26).

Close observation makes clear that *pain* does not refer merely to the
chronological proximity to death, although no one doubts that a recent
death produces more intense pain to the living than a death that occurred long ago. The term as used by lamenters, however, has subtler
and less literal implications. More than just grief produced by a specific
occasion, the "pain" of folk aesthetics refers to an intense and extraor-

dinary emotional state, manifesting itself in specific, structured behavior and achieved by the lamenters either voluntarily or involuntarily.

Artemisia Kapsali, sixty-seven years old in 1978, was born in the village of Asprangeli in Epiros and lived in the city of Ioannina. She was an example of someone who could enter into the state of pain voluntarily. Even though her husband, Yiannis, had been killed in World War II approximately thirty-seven years earlier, she was able to recall, apparently in its original intensity, her grief over his death. The lament she performed in my presence was interrupted by sobbing and displayed the characteristics of laments performed when one is "in pain." The ability to recall effortlessly almost the original intensity of one's grief over the loss of a beloved person who has been dead for a considerable length of time was a situation I encountered repeatedly. A possible explanation might be that bereaved women never completely stop lamenting for their loved ones. Past the prescribed period for mourning (usually the five years between the actual death and the exhumation of the remains—Danforth 1982:148-149), women continue to lament in a variety of contexts. Doing household chores, working in the fields, being present at another funeral—these can all become occasions for the continuation of the dialogue between the living and the beloved dead (Fig. 1). Thus, the channel for symbolic communication and emotional expression is always open.

Performers make use of a variety of methods to induce "pain." First, especially outside the context of funerals, they may use objects that contain rich symbolic associations with the deceased, such as a photograph or personal items that once belonged to him or her. Second, women loosen their black scarves to signal increasing emotional intensity, but also to facilitate it. Finally, narratives about the specific dead person or about topics related to death in general or to vasana—misfortunes or great sorrows—serve to ease participants into the proper frame of mind.

In or out of funeral contexts, the "help" of others is an important factor, contributing to a collectively arrived at emotional climax. Artemisia Kapsali, known as the best lamenter in the area, told me at the end of our recording session, "I could have done it better if I had gathered some women to help me." Each woman's recollection of her own grief serves to remind and intensify the grief of the others. During rituals, a skillful lamenter is judged not only by her talent in poetic composition, but also by her capacity to move others, thus enabling them to reach a charged emotional state.

To move her audience to ponos, and thus, symbolically, to lead the living to the dead, a lamenter skillfully employs the same devices she

Photograph unavailable

1. Women lament at a grave site in the village of Olymbos on the island of Karpathos. (Photograph by Constantine Manos, courtesy of *Magnum*)

uses to bring herself to the state of pain: melodic conventions in conjunction with signs that are associated with sorrow, such as stylized interjections, gestures, and movements of her body; lyrical images and metaphors; manipulations of shared allusions; and repetition of key elements, such as appeals to the dead by name. It is not the poetic language alone, however, but also the style of delivery that is most responsible for inducing emotional intensity.[8] It has often been demonstrated to me that the audience can be deeply moved even when many of the poetic lines are obscured by weeping or interjection which, in the case of the Zagori lament, breaks words in the middle and leaves them incomplete. Singing itself, then, can facilitate the transition from ordinary to extraordinary experience.

There is, in each area I researched and in each culture group within these areas, a set melodic pattern to which laments are sung. In addition to the main melody, stylistic conventions carry emotional associations and can trigger a sense of sorrow in the audience (Caraveli 1982:138-139). The lament melody characteristic of the Zagori province, for instance, uses microtones, stylized interjections of wailing sounds, and leaps of several intervals at the end of each hemistich (half a line) to induce a state of pathos. Lamenters often preferred reciting texts for me rather than performing them. While reciting a text can be relatively unemotional, singing it produces intense emotion on the part of both performer and audience.

Aglaia Hadzopoulou, aged seventy-six, and Alexandra Tsoumani, of approximately the same age, belong to different culture groups. While both live in Tsepelovo, Epiros, Alexandra belongs to the Sarakatsani nomad group, which is presently settling in villages and abandoning its nomadic lifestyle.[9] Although a good deal of tension exists between the established village residents and the more recent settlers, the two women have been friends for years and have shared many trying experiences in the course of their lives. Talking about their personal losses and grievances moved each other deeply. A story about the death of one of Alexandra's children—an event that had been witnessed by Aglaia—produced weeping in both women. Yet when they lamented in their very distinct styles, each woman's performance left the other indifferent. The Sarakatsani lament uses a completely different melody from the Zagori one, and it is sung in a falsetto voice with many artificial breaks in the words that render the text unintelligible to the nonparticipant (Fig. 2). Conversely, on the occasion of the sudden death of a cousin, Xanthippi Papa, aged seventy-six, from the village of Ano Pedina in Epiros, performed a lament in the presence of family members who were unaware of her talent and reputation as a lamenter. Upon the

2. Lament poets in Tsepelovo, Epiros. *Left*: Aglaia Hadzopoulou. *Right*: Alexandra Tsoumani, a Sarakatsani nomad who has settled in the village. They have been lamenting for the death of their children. (Photograph by Jonathan Chaves)

first notes of the lament melody, the entire family burst into sobbing. Such reactions on the part of diverse audiences suggest that responses to specific styles of lament performance are, to some extent, learned. Not only are the texts of laments symbolic languages unto themselves, but performance components also carry symbolic associations, thus triggering "pain" in the participants and facilitating the creation of an extraordinary emotional context.[10]

There are also cases of women who involuntarily experience a "painful state," which signifies more than the mere accidental recollection of a sorrowful event. Alexandra Pateraki, from Dzermiades, performed in a relatively unemotional tone a lament she had heard from her mother. When asked if she could perform a lament "in pain," she chose a lament for her child Pavlos, now dead for over ten years. This time her performance caused her to weep so profusely that her three-year-old granddaughter ran out of the room in fear. In describing the circumstances surrounding the origin of the lament, Alexandra said, "As I was walking to the cemetery once, it suddenly came to me in its entirety." Statements such as "it came to me" (*mou irthe*) also were used by other

lamenters in the region to describe the occasion for the original composition of a lament. Tomais Veringou, also of Dzermiades, whom I recorded performing on her son's grave, related to me how she came to
compose one of her best laments. As she was walking on the public
road at the outskirts of the village, "it" (the pain) came to her (*m'e-
piase*) with such intensity that she could not contain herself. She burst
into a lament so passionate that the few fellow villagers who met her on
the road were startled.

Folk aesthetics, then, define the lament not primarily in terms of its
poetic value but according to its effectiveness as communication with
the dead and its role as a vehicle for an extraordinary experience for the
living participants.[11] Accordingly, laments fall into the following
groups (in ascending order of efficacy and importance):

1. Laments that are simply recited as poetry
2. Laments that are sung, but not on a ritual occasion or in an extraordinary emotional context
3. Laments that are sung in an extraordinary, heightened emotional
context, but in an ordinary setting such as one's home or the fields
4. Laments that are performed both in a heightened emotional context and on a ritual occasion (for example, tending the grave, memorial
services, funerals)

The relationship between aesthetics and heightened emotional context has several implications. It suggests the existence of an intricate
system of folk aesthetics connected to the daily emotional needs of the
performers, such as the need for emotional catharsis and for confrontation with fearful aspects of their world. Moreover, it suggests that the
performance of ritual lamentation, not only as a form of sophisticated
poetic composition but also as an alternative religious expression that
functions outside the official church, is open to women only and bears
similarities to spirit possession.

In addition to the religious dimensions of lament performances, the
social elements they incorporate hold distinct benefits for the living.
The existence of a muted, separate women's world creates the opportunities for strong friendships among women.[12] Rituals of shared grieving reinforce, intensify, and negotiate a great variety of relationships
that often pass into daily narrative as metaphors of and codes for female experiences. The realm of suffering, for example, is believed to be
one in which women dominate over men. Either because of burdens exclusive to women, such as childbirth and child rearing, or because of
women's capacity to experience suffering (especially death) more intensely, villagers believe vasana to be linked especially to women's experiences, and they form a frequent topic of conversation. Both infor-

mal narratives and formalized events, such as laments, echo these themes and reinforce the sense of bonding "in pain" (Caraveli-Chaves 1980:145-146 and passim). In addition, lamentation provides another sphere for female interaction within the extraordinary context of emotional engrossment, as well as a vehicle for shared artistic expression. Finally, the very processes of performance and of providing mutual comfort (especially in the case of laments performed by women for women) enact and negotiate varied significant relationships among women across kinship and generational lines, for example friendships between the old and young and bonds between master performer and apprentice. These relationships are vital to both the women themselves and the larger world of the village that they inhabit.

Ultimately, then, death rituals, both in themselves and in terms of their impact on women's daily lives, constitute an alternative and exclusive sphere of aesthetic, religious, and social interaction, in which participants vent creative impulses, undergo emotional catharsis, and reinforce their individual identity and group membership. Though less accessible to the outsider than the public domain of men, this female realm is equally complex and complete in that it possesses its own criteria for status within it. These criteria include artistry in composition and performance, capacity to experience and transmit ponos, proper performance of rituals, and observance of social relationships associated with death rites.

LAMENTS AND LARGER SOCIAL EXPERIENCE

Women's laments serve not only to create, reflect, reinforce, and negotiate realms of experience and action that are exclusive to women, but also to mediate between the living and the dead and between seemingly disparate or antithetical types of experience: male and female, traditional and modern, sacred and secular, and ideological and actual, as well as between formal institutions and individual or domestic needs not accommodated by them. It is by focusing on the points of overlap between these sets of antithetical experiences that we can gain insight into the lament's use by and for the living and its fluid, continuously adaptive nature.

In the villages where I did my fieldwork, people with "modern" attitudes frown upon the practice of ritual lamentation, but the dichotomy between tradition and change is not as clear-cut as it appears at first glance. Traditional laments can employ textual conventions to comment on a wide range of topics, from the performers' own social roles to practices in modern medicine and the effects of the changing economy on their families. Thus, age-old thematic conventions incorporate modern subjects with relative ease.

Moreover, there is a frequent overlap between the women's realm of lament performance and men's separate sphere of public activities. For instance, while men in the areas of my research often expressed disapproval of their wives' or mothers' participation in laments, and while most of the women I recorded lamented without their husbands' knowledge, closer examination of men's attitudes revealed a complex and ambivalent view of this tradition. Although they expressed disapproval and the fear that such practices might strain their female relatives emotionally, men also displayed open admiration of laments. Professional male folk musicians in Epiros, for example, admitted to their appreciation of the artistic qualities of laments. A clarinet player, Grigoris Kapsalis, told me of his great fondness for the polyphonic laments of the Pogoni area of Epiros. "Whenever I play there," he confessed, "I gather a few women to sing me some laments."

While it is only women who participate actively in ritual laments for the dead, men tend to participate in more passive ways. A man in his sixties, the nephew of a famed lamenter from the village of Kapesovo, told me of his intimate knowledge of lament composition and performance. He described several occasions on which he was alone, when he would burst into lamentation as the only appropriate vehicle for venting his feelings. He spoke of a recent experience, walking through the abandoned fields that he remembered as richly cultivated in his youth, when he spontaneously began lamenting out loud, singing about the changes he saw and the sadness these changes inspired in him.

Finally, while it is women only who perform in rituals such as funerals, men may sing publicly *about* death. The words, however, are often sung to melodies of other folksongs and not to the characteristic lament tunes of the area. Frequently, a *paniyiri*, or village festival, in Zagori opens with such laments before the dance songs begin. I am told that at times the festival may begin at the cemetery where the performance of male *moiroloyia*, "laments," such as the well known Epirotic lament *Mariola*, takes place before the start of the main part of the paniyiri at the village square (Fig. 3).

Another point of convergence between the women's world as created by lament performances and the larger world is the dimension of social protest. Folklorist Ilhan Başgöz explores the notion of a fifth dimension of folklore in discussing its role in heightening rather than resolving tensions that can lead to social change. "Like other art forms such as literature, painting, music and the graphic arts, folklore functions to

3. Musicians in Tsepelovo, Epiros, starting a *paniyiri* (village celebration) with the lament *Mariola*—part of the *epitrapezia* repertory of songs, that is, songs sung while seated around a table.

dramatize conflict, to encourage dissent, to cause disunity, and to rouse people to activism and even to press for revolutionary changes in the social system" (Başgöz 1982:6). His article goes on to document a historical connection between expressive forms and protest, focusing on contemporary performances of the romance and the shadow puppet theater in Turkey.

A historical connection between lament poetry in the Greek tradition and the expression of grievances is evident both in the subject matter and in the various stylistic and thematic conventions of laments. Characteristically, laments have always taken a wide variety of forms, from grievances against death itself and all its metaphorical extensions (which will be discussed below) to social commentary on political events and individual situations. Margaret Alexiou (1974:55-122) lists several categories of laments in the Greek tradition, such as the historical laments for the fall of cities; the laments for "departure from home, change of religion, and marriage"; the ritual laments of women; and the laments for gods and heroes. Thus, since antiquity, laments have commented on, protested against, and affected social change.[13,14]

THE LAMENT AS SOCIAL PROTEST | 181

In addition to the variety of subjects covered in laments, there are thematic conventions that allow the focus of the song to shift from the plight of the deceased to the plight of the mourner. Since the performers of these ritual laments are women, the grievances thus voiced often relate to the social role of women in the context of the androcentric village and to painful situations (child raising, for example) peculiar to women (Caraveli-Chaves 1980:esp. 138, 146).

Widowhood and emigration are regarded in the Greek folk tradition as metaphorical extensions of death, and they can be used interchangeably, as alternative and equivalent forms of death, within one lament, thereby intensifying the impact of the actual death of an individual through inference to its metaphorical dimensions.[15] The subject of widowhood and the loss of social status a widow suffers in rural Greece[16] become frequent topics in laments, forming an entire category that I term "widows' songs." Protest against widows' social isolation and ambiguous status is frequently expressed in these songs. Stavroula Haralambopoulou, forty-nine years of age when ethnomusicologist Sotirios Chianis recorded her in 1959, articulated the theme of widowhood in the following lament.

> The widow stays inside the house—gossip around her all around!
>
> The widow stays inside the house—gossip around her all around!
> (Painful exile!)[17]
>
> She can't gaze out the window, she can't sit by the doorstep.
> (Bitter widow!)
>
> There are fresh breezes by the window, there is gay chatting by the doorstep. (Bitter widow!)
>
> Widow, go change your name, don't let them call you widow!
> (Ah! Bitter widow!)
>
> Widow, night comes on the mountains, yet soon daylight sets in,
> (Bitter widow!)
>
> But so many plumes and feathers as a black hen has,
> (Bitter widow!)
>
> So many times must you sit and wait at your front door, my widow. (Ah, bitter woman!)[18]
>
> Performer: Stavroula Haralambopoulou
> Recorded by Sotirios Chianis,[19]
> Hrysovitsi, Peloponnesos, April 1959

Sometimes protest is expressed more subtly in the poetic voice that recognizes a "sisterhood in pain" among women, a sense of communal victimization inflicted by either social or natural forces (for example, the death of children). Often, this voice takes the form of an invitation to communal grieving.

> Come women! Let you who are still untried, and us, who've known sorrows,
>
> Join together our tears, shape them into a river;
>
> And let the river turn to lake, to seashore, water fountain,
> (Oh, my love, my eyes!)
>
> Where young beauties can come to wash, young men to groom themselves,
>
> And where unmarried children can have their target practice.
>
> Performer: Alexandra Tsoumani
> Recorded by Anna Caraveli,
> Tsepelovo, Epiros, August 15, 1978

At times, protest takes the form of an attack against a vast, all-encompassing category of evils, including war, natural disaster, and death itself. However universal the evil being lamented may be, almost always the point of departure is its effect on the female mourner. In the following lament performed by Artemisia Kapsali of Asprangeli, Epiros, in memory of her husband, Yiannis, who was killed at war, the singer bewails not only war, but also the impotence of women who are powerless over the killing of their children and husbands.

> What's wrong with you, miserable crow, wailing and squealing
> so?   (Oh, I can't bear it, Yianni!)
>
> Are you that thirsty for blood, that hungry for young flesh
> (How awful, my fate!)
>
> Go beyond Gribala mountain, go to Gribala peak
> (I can't bear it, Yianni)
>
> To find proud, young bodies there all bathed in dark blood
> (Oh, I can't bear it, Yianni!)
>
> To find their poor mothers singing laments for them.
> (Oh, my luck is awful!)
>
> How bitter the wound! How poisonous the gunshot! Damned be
> the war! Damn it a thousand times!   (Oh, what horrible fate!)
>
> It takes children away from mothers, brothers away from
> brothers   (Awful, awful fate!)

And it tears man away from wife, though they love each other.
(My fate is awful!)

And on the spot on which they part, no grass can ever grow.

Performer: Artemisia Kapsali
Recorded by Anna Caraveli,
Ioannina, Epiros, August 17, 1978

Ritual laments also protest against a variety of situations that may not be directly connected to the position of women but which are, nonetheless, spoken out against in the voice of the "weak, marginal, or downtrodden." The traditional lament theme of the journey of the deceased often involves an explanation of the manner in which he died—either a mythical account of death (the conventional battle between Charon and the deceased, for instance) or an actual description of his illness. In this portion of a long lament performed by Tomais Veringou on her son's grave, the recounting of her child's treatment for kidney disease clearly conveys her sense of impotence in the face of medical technology, as well as her disapproval of questionable medical practices.

Ah, my beloved child, my only son!

They were practicing their craft on you, my darling!

They were practicing on you and learned their craft, my child.

They learned about medicine my golden, my glad boy.

Oh, they thrust their machinery inside your belly, child,

And more machinery in your hand, my glad son, my king.

They put tubes of oxygen through your nose, my darling,

And fed you blood through the other hand, my king, my good son.

Ah, how can I bear all these now, my child?

Performer: Tomais Veringou
Recorded by Anna Caraveli,
Dzermiades, Crete, July 15, 1978

Indeed, protest against doctors and practices of modern medicine, especially in the case of the death of a small child, as in the following portion of a long lament, is a frequent theme.

Ah, deeply pained child, I have loved you so much!

They tore your belly open with their knives twice,

Looking for the sickness in your guts, my white dove.

184 | ANNA CARAVELI

But the medicines were drained, the healing herbs were lost;

So they left your pain uncured, my small child.

> Performer: Alexandra Pateraki
> Recorded by Anna Caraveli,
> Dzermiades, Crete, July 15, 1978

Implicitly, in terms of subject matter alone, laments comprise a "protest" against the official church and the Christian doctrine of death. The very notion of death expressed in laments is contrary to the Christian views of a rewarding afterlife for the pious. The Hades of the laments is marked by darkness and despair, and it retains its pagan name. Christian attitudes toward death preach patience, acceptance, and perseverance. Laments express despair, fear, and anger toward death and the deceased. The laments that follow convey the physical terror of dying, the despair characterizing the underworld, and the frustration felt, in the first one, by the deceased and, in the second one, by the living.

All lies! All fables you hear in laments!

People don't meet, people don't talk here in the underworld.

They call this "place of rot," where bodies rot away.

I saw them and was frightened. My heart turned to ice.

> Performer: Xanthippi Papa
> Recorded by Anna Caraveli,
> Ano Pedina, Epiros, August 16, 1978

Rise and cast away Charon's sheet.

Wake up to see springtime and people's joy.

I'm left alone again—a desolate bird!—

Singing instead of crying to soothe my bitter pain.

I want to let out a shrill cry and see if you still know me

And see if you can welcome me, my sweet, beloved sister.

Rise on the twenty-first of May! Rise on your name day,

Rise and give out flowers, and give out white lilies—

But slowly, and carefully—body upright with pride;

Oh slowly and carefully—the wound is not yet healed.

A wound is nesting in my heart and when we meet again

I'd like an hour for us to talk, beloved; one short hour!

Up, my love, rise! Rise and talk to me

So I can rest awhile in peace before I come back to you.

> Performer: Anthoula Lyraki
> Recorded by Anna Caraveli,
> Dzermiades, Crete, July 15, 1978

Perhaps in part because of such expressions of protest, a historic antagonism has existed between the church (and, at various times in antiquity, the state as well) and the women's performance of laments (Alexiou 1974:14-24). Alexiou explains the phenomenon of restrictive legislation against laments in antiquity, aimed particularly at women, in terms of the social power inherent in the expressive and symbolic roles of lamentation practices. "If the family, based on father-right, was to be established as the basic unit of society, then the power of women in religious and family affairs must be stopped, and they must be made to apply a more secondary role in funerals" (Alexiou 1974:21).

The use of the lament as an instrument of protest depends greatly on the role of the individual performer as an active manipulator of conventions and as an agent of change. Most studies on the expressive culture of Greece underemphasize the role of the performer. To ignore the lament singer as conscious creator and articulator of the lament tradition would be to lose sight of the lament's use as a creative strategy for coping with change, conflict, and social limitations, as well as to devalue the sophisticated aesthetics of its composition and performance and the skills of its creator. The lament performer's active role, as evidenced by her manipulation of stock poetic units during composition, her use of diverse, often everyday settings for ritual performance, and her incorporation of everyday communication and immediate concerns into the traditional idiom of lamentation, illustrates both the complex skills involved in composition and performance and the superb artistry of actual laments. Clearly, the dynamic nature of the lament in terms of composition, performance setting, and usage endows it with the potential for becoming a potent instrument of protest in the hands of a skillful lament poet.

Laments, like other types of Greek folk poetry, are composed according to formula.[20] Improvisation is possible, depending on the stock patterns of composition and stock individual poetic units, which are dictated by tradition and which vary with the region. In the fluid *mantinades* tradition of the islands, a greater degree of improvisation is possible for the performer. Even with the relatively "set" and less changeable laments of Epiros, however, individual control of traditional poetics is considerable, though more subtle.

In the following lament for the death of her brother Loni, Aglaia Hadzopoulou employed the conventional subject of the encounter and ensuing battle between Charon and the dead man. She was aware of both the mythical dimensions of her subject and the additions that she made. "I heard the lament from my grandmother," she said. "She sang it for someone else, but because my brother was a hunter, I added the line about the sword and gun." She also added the date of his death and the detail of its coincidence with his birthday.

> A young man was roaming on a high mountain slope—
> > (I'll burst with pain, Loni).
> Hunting gun in hand, sword dangling by his waist.
> > (I'll burst with this pain, my soul!)
> And Charon was waiting in a hollow canyon.
> > (Oh, my brother!)
> —Please, Charon, let me through; let me cross this canyon
> > (Ah, poor man!)
> Because I'm young and green, because I'm a young father.
> > (Oh, Loni!)
> And Charon did not let him cross, and Charon snatched him then,
> > (Oh, my brother!)
> On the Virgin's holiday, and on his birthday
> > (I'll burst with this pain!)
>
> > Performer: Aglaia Hadzopoulou
> > Recorded by Anna Caraveli,
> > Tsepelovo, Epiros, August 14, 1978

The state of "pain" does not diminish a singer's control of conventions and compositional techniques. Asked how one could compose such intricate songs when immersed in a seemingly agitated emotional state, Sofia Papakonstadtinou, daughter of the famed Thia Hrysa and a good lamenter in her own right, answered, "It is because the pain concentrates you [*se syngedtroni*]; it does not let your mind wander."

As mentioned earlier and quoted in part above, Tomais Veringou performed a long lament of approximately twenty minutes on the grave of her son who had died a year and a half before of a kidney disease. This lament was part of a weekly ritual for her that involved changing the oil of the oil lamp by the grave, replacing the faded flowers with fresh ones, and censing the grave with incense—all without ceasing to lament for one minute. One day, my husband and I were at the grave site when Tomais entered the cemetery. She made a dramatic entrance—armloads of fresh flowers, black scarf loosened, and already lamenting at the top of her voice, even before leaving the public road to enter the cemetery. During the entire performance, she did not acknowledge our presence once, even when—her grief having driven her to a seemingly uncontrollable state—we tried to raise her from the grave and stop her lamentation. She did, however, acknowledge us within the lament text itself.

Even the strangers grieve for you, child, my only son.

The most obvious difference between this performance and others recorded in more everyday settings was the rapidity and facility of Tomais's composition and delivery. Whereas lamenters who sang relatively "out of pain" paused in an attempt to remember and made mistakes in syllabic count per line, Tomais's lament flowed effortlessly and was metrically flawless, even though it was one of the longest laments I recorded in this area.

Manipulation of textual and performance elements can render a lament applicable to a variety of contexts. Kleoniki Kodtodimou was introduced to me as the greatest living lamenter in the area. She spent her winters in the Epirotic city of Ioannina with her children and her summers in her family home in Kapesovo, which she managed capably by herself for the duration of the season. Though eighty-six years of age, she struck me as a woman in full possession of her intellectual—and even physical—powers. The incidents of her life, which she related to me, were marked by a strong love for life and the desire to survive. In telling me of her husband's death, for instance (he died in his sleep next to her), she said that upon discovering that he was dead, her first thought was for the living, not for the dead. Since her grown son suffered from a heart condition, Kleoniki suppressed her own fright and grief in order to soften the blow for her child. Paralleling the tone and style of her narratives, the lament that follows uses conventional lament subject matter to express, ultimately, Kleoniki's life-affirming message.[21] The usual journey to the underworld taken by the mourner—normally a grim experience—has a different resolution for her. Her dead relatives, both husband and son, receive her kindly but only to heal her and return her to life. She handles the guilt she feels as the bereaved person who is alive when a beloved person is dead by making her own dead loved ones give her permission to rejoin the living. Not only does Kleoniki (through the voice of her dead) allow herself the gift of life, but she also cleverly finds a justification for it: to keep the old family home open and to keep alive what has been left behind.

Listen to that great roar! What is all this confusion

Heard from the earth below, heard from the underworld?

Are they slaying oxen there, or hanging wild beasts?

They're neither slaying oxen, nor hanging wild beasts.

It's only my son, Alcibiades, my husband, Kostakis.

They're waiting for their mother, the mother they had loved.

They're sending servant boys for doctors, servant girls for fresh herbs.

For she must heal and become well, and they must send her back,

So their home won't close down, their old family home.

> Performer: Kleoniki Kodtodimou
> Recorded by Anna Caraveli,
> Kapesovo, Epiros, August 12, 1978

The fact that the lament is considered a communication with the dead by the lamenters themselves enriches the possibilities for conveying everyday grievances to the living and to the dead. When Kleoniki Kodtodimou refused to subject herself to the "pain" of actually performing laments, she merely recited fragments of those laments which she considered her most successful. These informal recitations and discussions of laments revealed the performer's view of laments as communication above all else. Like other lamenters who sang "out of pain," for instance, she would introduce a lament with the words "Then I told him," "This is what I told my mother when she died," or even "This is what I will tell my friend, Victoria, when she dies" (*tha tis po*). Kleoniki said of her husband who died in his sleep, "I remember I turned to him and told him . . . I told him a lot of things, I can't remember them all . . . but I remember I told him":[22]

It was a bitter evening, a heavy winter night

When Charon put me to sleep to take you in secret

Without time for us to talk, without a message from you.

> Performer: Kleoniki Kodtodimou
> Recorded by Anna Caraveli,
> Kapesovo, Epiros, August 12, 1978

Laments also are used to communicate news and other urgent concerns relating to the daily life of the mourner. Tomais Veringou, for example, uses portions of the long lament cited previously to convey all the latest news to her dead son—from his cousin's wedding to Tomais's grievances over the restrictions her family imposes on her visits to the cemetery.

I'm going, child, my young king; evening has come already,

The family will look for me, they'll come here to find me,

And I'll create trouble home, my tender plant, my son.

I'm leaving you now, my boy.

> Performer: Tomais Veringou
> Recorded by Anna Caraveli,
> Dzermiades, Crete, July 15, 1978

These interactive elements in laments allow for links to be created between convention and everyday experience, and they expand the possibilities for the lament's use as an instrument of protest.

CONCLUSION

Most studies of laments tie its performance to a specific setting, mainly cemeteries (for example, see Danforth 1982). My own fieldwork has suggested more diversity in performance contexts and, therefore, this paper offers an expanded definition of lamentation that includes singing, reciting, even silently composing a lament, in contexts as diverse as visiting the cemetery, doing housework, working in the fields, and walking (Fig. 4). Indeed, the laments presented in this paper were recorded in a wide variety of performance situations, in addition to formal funerals. I heard women lament at cemeteries during their weekly visits there, at their homes, in the fields, alone, or in the company of other women. I recorded performances that occurred spontaneously, and I recorded women who performed at my request. The latter were not artificial, in the sense of being emotionally disengaged performances. The women would arrange their weekly visits to the cemetery at a time convenient to both of us, or they would bring themselves, through narrative accounts of the deceased or through the handling of objects that had once belonged to the dead relative, to the heightened emotional state necessary for lament performances. All these performances, in other words, were regularly occurring events in the context of everyday life, but they were occasionally manipulated for the sake of a recording.

Such variety in performance situations and in the motivation of in-

4. Stamatia Biri of Vrisohori, Epiros, one of the best lamenters of her village, performing a lament for all of those recently dead in her family—some of her children and sisters—in a room in her home. (Photograph by Jonathan Chaves)

dividual performers provided important insights into lamentation practices and revealed relatively unexplored aspects of the folk aesthetics associated with laments. Women described to me performances of laments that served them as intimate conversations with their dead and as the means for airing their own grievances. These took place in a great variety of secular settings. An appropriate line for a lament might be conceived and hummed during the performance of household chores, while an entire lament might be performed while walking on the way to an errand or working in the fields—either alone or in the company of other women.

Viewing lamentation beyond formal "genre" categories and performance settings has important implications for our understanding of expressive culture, traditional rural Greece, and gender roles. By examining the continuous interaction between formal event and everyday life, we can understand the process of change and adaptation that gives contemporary meaning and relevance to age-old traditions. Women's sphere of activity and influence is also expanded considerably.

Lamentation, then, is a process that is not defined by its setting but instead symbolically demarcates space as mediating ground between the living and the dead, the ordinary and extraordinary experience. Such extension of performance contexts not only suggests an expanded definition of laments, but also an expanded use of them as instruments for airing grievances on an everyday basis. It is the performer's role as creator and actor that allows her to transform everyday into "extraordinary" space and to utilize conventions as means for personal expression in the same way that she transforms the fact of death into an extraordinary artistic expression and experience of religious significance.

Ritual laments for the dead in rural Greece today, far from being part of a static tradition antithetical to the mainstream culture, are dynamic, ongoing creations that allow for the integration of textual conventions handed down by tradition and topics of immediate relevance to the universe of the performer. Thus, lamentation becomes for the singer an avenue for social commentary on the larger world, rather than an instrument of restriction and isolation.

Performance, as well as the folk aesthetics used to judge performance, suggest still another dimension of protest in the lamentation ritual: its role as a form of folk religion outside, and often in protest against, the practices of official Christianity. In this capacity, laments serve as vehicles for "extraordinary" experience outside both official institutions and the confines of ordinary reality, and they reveal connections between aesthetics and emotional texture.

It is the individual performer who shapes age-old conventions into instruments for the personal expression of grievances, transforms ordinary into extraordinary space, and expands the context and setting of lament performance to suit her everyday needs. Attention to individual performances and their relationship to the performer's life story can illustrate clearly how the singer adapts traditional forms to the immediate concerns of her community, to her personal situation, or to the moment of performance.[23]

Ultimately, it is the role of the individual within the tradition that expands the definition of the lament to include the realm of the living in addition to that of the dead, the everyday experience in addition to the extraordinary experience. It is this interplay between fluid tradition and active performer that enables the lament to serve as a vehicle both for airing grievances and for creating a continuous dialogue between the singer and the larger world. Focus on human dynamics, then, reveals another important dimension in women's role—as creators of coping strategies, artists, critics, articulators, and manipulators of one of Greece's most important verbal arts in continuous existence.

NOTES

1. Fieldwork for this article was conducted mainly during the springs and summers of 1974, 1975, 1978, 1980, and 1981. For my work in the area of Zagori in Epiros, I am deeply indebted to Mrs. Frosso Ioannidi of Tsepelovo. A member of an old, esteemed family, Mrs. Ioannidi has worked relentlessly for over six decades to collect, interpret in public presentations, and write on the folklife of this region. In recognition of these efforts, the Zagori residents have bestowed upon her the honorary title of "Mother of Zagori." Even though she was in her eighties at the time, Mrs. Ioannidi accompanied me to many locations that were nearly inaccessible. Her work and example, as well as her hospitality and support, were of enormous practical and moral value to me. Especially during the summer of 1978, she became a friend, a teacher, and a window to the private world of the Zagori households.

2. See Loukatos (1978:esp. 205-225) for a discussion on rituals and beliefs related to birth, marriage, and death in rural Greece, within the larger context of the history of Greek folklore. Alexiou (1974) provides a comprehensive study of Greek ritual laments, emphasizing continuities between ancient and contemporary traditions. Both books contain rich bibliographies consisting of Greek and non-Greek sources. For examinations of laments in social and performance contexts, see Caraveli-Chaves (1980:129-157) and Danforth (1982). Herzfeld (1981a) discusses Greek laments in relation to taxonomy.

3. For a discussion of Greek folk aesthetics, see Beaton (1980). For studies on the same topic, which consider folk commentary and indigenous interpretive systems, see Herzfeld (1981b:113-141) and Caraveli (1982:129-158).

4. Du Boulay (1974:131-133) discusses the woman's role in the home as both "physical and metaphysical, for it is she who makes of the house a sanctuary for the living and a memorial for the dead" and it is she who "is thought to hold the house together" by overseeing both physical and ritual activity in it.

5. In discussing the beer-drinking ritual among the Iteso people of Africa (near the Kenya-Uganda border), Karp emphasizes the "heightened form of social experience" associated with it (Karp 1980:93). "Increasing engrossment" of the participants in beer-drinking parties was evidence of the success of these events (pp. 105-109) and contributed to the role of beer drinking as "Iteso social theory" and an important social experience (p. 83 and passim). This emotional framework, termed by the Iteso "much understanding," is equivalent to the concept of *ponos* in laments and *kefi* in the ritual *glendia* per-

THE LAMENT AS SOCIAL PROTEST | 193

formed in the Greek village of Olymbos on the island of Karpathos (Caraveli 1982:82 and 1985:263-264, 277-279 and passim).

6. For an important study on the relationship between possession and social marginality, see Lewis (1975). In their study of spirit possession, Karp and Karp (1979:22-25) maintain that the trances encountered in their fieldwork were genuine but served, simultaneously, as strategies for relieving women of responsibility for inappropriate behavior. Kessler (1977:295-331) draws relationships between possession and the low status of widows and divorced women. Danforth (1983) links the expression of submission in a Greek possession ritual to women's strategies for power, while Crapanzano and Garrison (1977:17) link spirit possession and its cure to issues involving identity. This connection between possession and strategies for coping with conflict or ambivalence and, in the more general sense, issues of identity, parallels the central thesis of this paper: the use of lamentation for airing grievances and obtaining power. Thus, the similarites between lament ritual and possession link the two to literal or metaphorical social protest on many levels.

7. Danforth (1982:142-147) cites ponos as an important concept in folk commentary and poetic metaphors, and he notes its desirability and conscious cultivation among lamenters.

8. For an important analysis of the relationships between expressive style and culture and between style and social marginality, see Lomax (1968).

9. See Campbell's (1964) study on the Sarakatsani.

10. For the relationship between style and content and an examination of the role of "meta-textual" factors, such as performance, community world view and history, and symbolic associations contained in music, in the creation of "meaning" surrounding a song, see Caraveli (1982, 1985).

11. In the ritual speech event called the *glendi* (sing.), whose performance in the village of Olymbos and in the Baltimore, Maryland settlement of Olymbos emigrants is especially vibrant, the ritual specialists, or *meraklides*, are judged by criteria similar to those used for lamenters. A good *meraklis* (sing.) is not judged by poetic excellence alone, but rather by a number of social and interactive elements, one of which is his capacity to move the audience to a state of heightened experience, or kefi. A complex set of aesthetics, similar to those defining pain (ponos), differentiates between the various levels of kefi one enters into, while the success of a glendi depends on the existence and quality of kefi in it. See Caraveli (1985).

12. See Kennedy (this volume).

13. See Caraveli (1982:129-157) for an examination of textual conventions in laments and their effect on social action.

14. Alexiou (1974) provides a comprehensive analysis of ritual laments in Greece, including a historical overview and a thematic and stylistic analysis.

15. Danforth (1982) cites emigration both as an important element in shaping the social context of death rituals (for example, pp. 16 and 23) and as partial metaphor for death (pp. 33 and 90-95).

16. For a discussion of widowhood in rural Greece, see du Boulay (1974:122).

194 | ANNA CARAVELI

17. In this paper, the stylized interjections known as *tsakismata* are set apart in parentheses. For a discussion on the stylistic and symbolic meaning of this type of digression in Greek folk song, see Caraveli (1982:129-158).
18. All the translations in this paper are by the author.
19. State University of New York at Binghamton, collection of field recordings by Sotirios Chianis.
20. For an important study of the formulaic nature of epic poetry, see Lord (1965). For varying approaches to the relationship between improvisation and textual conventions in oral poetry, see Finnegan (1977) and, with regard to Greek folk poetry in particular, Beaton (1980) and Caraveli (1982).
21. Danforth (1982:144) observes that "many Greek villagers subscribe to what can be called an indigenous theory of catharsis," and he cites in the same book examples of anthropological interest in "ritual systems of psychotherapy," including Danforth (1978:312ff).
22. Danforth (1982:127) notes that "the social relationship that continues to link the bereaved to the deceased is in effect a conversation between the living and the dead." On a similar note, Danforth observes that "a mother who has lost a child does not say 'I am going to my son's grave.' She says, 'I am going to my son' (*Tha pao sto pedhi mou*)" (p. 133). Also, on lament as communication, see Caraveli (1982:127, 117-152).
23. Başgöz (1982:27, 29) stresses the need for close attention to individual performances and the personality of the performer. He also discusses the process of functional transformation, or changes in the function of the folklore form *during* performance for the purpose of social protest.

Bibliography

Alexiou, Margaret
   1974 The Ritual Lament in Greek Tradition. Cambridge: Cambridge University Press.

Başgöz, Ilhan
   1982 Protest: The Fifth Function of Folklore. Unpublished manuscript.

Beaton, Roderick
   1980 Folk Poetry of Modern Greece. Cambridge: Cambridge University Press.

Bourguignon, Erika
   1976 Possession. San Francisco: Chandler and Sharp Publishers, Inc.

Campbell, J. K.
   1964 Honour, Family and Patronage: A Study of Institutions and Moral Values in a Greek Mountain Community. Oxford: Clarendon Press.

Bibliography

Caraveli, Anna

1982 The Song Beyond the Song: Aesthetics and Social Interaction in Greek Folksong. Journal of American Folklore 95:129-158.

1985 The Symbolic Village: Community Born in Performance. Journal of American Folklore 98:259-286.

Caraveli-Chaves, Anna

1980 Bridge Between Worlds: The Women's Ritual Lament as Communicative Event. Journal of American Folklore 93:129-157.

1977 Case Studies in Spirit Possession. New York: John Wiley and Sons.

Crapanzano, Vincent, and Vivian Garrison, eds.

1977 Case Studies in Spirit Possession. New York: John Wiley and Sons.

Danforth, Loring M.

1978 The Anastenaria: A Study in Greek Ritual Therapy. Ph.D. diss., Princeton University. Ann Arbor, Mich.: University Microfilms.

1983 Power Through Submission in the Anastenaria. Journal of Modern Greek Studies 1(1):203-224.

Danforth, Loring M., and Alexander Tsiaras

1982 The Death Rituals of Rural Greece. Princeton, N.J.: Princeton University Press.

Davis, Nanciellen

1981 Women's Work and Worth in an Acadian Maritime Village. *In*

du Boulay, Juliet

1974 Portrait of a Greek Mountain Village. Oxford: Clarendon Press.

Finnegan, Ruth

1977 Oral Poetry: Its Nature, Significance and Social Context. Cambridge: Cambridge University Press.

Herzfeld, Michael

1981a Performative Categories and Symbols of Passage in Rural Greece. Journal of American Folklore 94:44-57.

1981b An Indigenous Theory of Meaning and its Elicitation in Performative Context. Semiotica 34:113-141.

Honko, Lauri

1974 Balto-Finnic Lament Poetry. Studio Fennica 17:9-61.

Karp, Ivan

1980 Beer Drinking and Social Experience in an African Society. *In* Explorations in African Systems of Thought, I. Karp and C. S. Bird, eds., pp. 83-119. Bloomington, Ind.: Indiana University Press.

Karp, Ivan, and Patricia Karp

1979 Living with Spirits of the Dead. *In* African Therapeutic Systems, Z. A. Ademuwagun et al., eds., pp. 22-25. Boston: Crossroads Press.

Kessler, Clive S.

1977 Conflict and Sovereignty in Kelantanese Malay Spirit Seances. *In* Case Studies in Spirit Possession, V. Crapanzano and V. Garrison, eds., pp. 295-331. New York: John Wiley and Sons.

Bibliography

Lewis, I. M.
  1975 Ecstatic Religion: An Anthropological Study of Spirit Possession and Shamanism. Harmondsworth, England: Penguin. (1st ed. 1971.)
Lomax, Alan
  1968 Folksong Style and Culture. Washington, D.C.: American Association for the Advancement of Science.
Lord, Albert Bates
  1965 The Singer of Tales. New York: Atheneum. (1st ed. Harvard University Press, 1960.)
Loukatos, Dimetrios
  1978 Eisagogi Stin Elleniki Laografia. Athens: Morfotiko Idrima Ellinikis Trapezis.

[19]

Treaty Now: Popular Music and the Indigenous Struggle for Justice in Contemporary Australia

Aaron Corn

I grew up on the Gold Coast in Queensland, Australia's third largest and oldest state, at a most unusual time in my nation's history. In infancy, my mother took me down the road to Miami Beach almost every afternoon before driving north along the strip of local beaches to collect my father from work in Southport. Unbeknown to me and possibly to my parents at that time, forces were afoot that would radically change Australia's sociopolitical terrain and imbue my generation with a vastly different set of cultural assumptions about what it was to be an Australian. Campaigning under the prominent slogan "It's time," December, 1972, saw Gough Whitlam lead the Australian Labor Party back into office for the first time since 1949, and before its controversial dismissal in November, 1975, his government's social reforms were sweeping.

Free tertiary education, free universal health insurance, financial support for single-parent families, the abolition of capital punishment, the lowering of the voting age to 18 years, language support for non-English-speaking residents, equal employment opportunities for women, and an unprecedented platform of self-determination for Indigenous communities were among the many significant reforms introduced under Whitlam's leadership. The White Australia Policy, which had unjustly restricted the entry of non-Europeans to Australia since the federation of the six British Colonies there in 1901, was formally abolished under the Racial Discrimination Act 1975, and the disenfranchised Indigenous peoples of Australia would also find an unprecedented level of protection for their human rights and freedoms under this legislation.

For the earlier part of the twentieth century, governments, missionaries, and pastoralists had systemically subjected these traditional owners of the Australian continent to harsh and degrading treatment and conditions. All but a few entire Indigenous communities were forcibly removed from their homelands into lives of indentured poverty on missions, pastoral stations, and fringe camps, where they were stigmatized and penalized for practicing their own languages and traditions. Children of mixed descent were targets of a brutal policy of assimilation under which they were stolen from their families, and subjected to high incidences of abuse in orphanages and foster homes, and also throughout Australia, Indigenous men in particular were habitually singled out by police for arrest, leading to disproportionately high numbers of Indigenous deaths in custody (McGrath, 1995; Kidd, 1997; Perkins and Langton, 2008).

The overarching aims of these practices had been nothing less than genocidal. They were methodically perpetrated against Indigenous peoples to bring about the complete annihilation of their pre-existing ways of life and their lingering claims of sovereignty over the Australian continent. I entered primary school in the late 1970s, my mother and I made regular trips down the Gold Coast Highway to Burleigh Heads, and each school day we passed right by a traditional Indigenous *bora* "initiation" ring. Although this was the last known ceremony ground of the local Yugambeh people, the Gold Coast's traditional Indigenous owners, to have survived the city's twentieth-century development intact (Bowdler, 1999), it barely registered in my young consciousness. And of the Yugambeh themselves and their rich local heritage (Yugambeh Museum, 2006), I heard nothing but silence from among my circle of adult carers.

The Turning Tide

The Whitlam era also saw the creation of the Australia Council for the Arts in 1973 as a national funding and policy body, and one of its first acts was to convene a National Seminar on Aboriginal Arts in the nation's capital, Canberra (Australia Council, 1973). At this time, the work of Indigenous artists was largely seen by government and industry as a folkloric resource to be plundered freely for political and financial gain. Seeking to end this exploitation, prominent Indigenous elders, such as Wandjuk Marika from Yirrkala, spoke out at this forum for a suite of policy reforms. They called for an independent national network of incorporated Indigenous arts cooperatives, copyright protections for works by Indigenous artists, and an end to all trade in unlicensed reproductions of Indigenous art, and they demanded that all Indigenous artists in Australia receive equal pay for equal work (Marika, 1995, pp. 110-26; Johnston, 1996).

It was on these recommendations that the subsequent Liberal government led by Malcolm Fraser established the Aboriginal Artists Agency in 1976 as a national nonprofit body to protect the legal interests of Indigenous artists, and for the first time in history to ensure that they received royalty payments for their works. This Agency undertook many projects to promote traditional Indigenous artists throughout Australia and overseas. But it also took the unprecedented step of representing emerging Indigenous bands such as No Fixed Address from Adelaide, Coloured Stone from Ceduna, and the Warumpi Band from Papunya. Drawing on a range of globalized popular styles including rock, reggae, and country, their best-known original songs celebrated the strength shown by Indigenous Australians in the face of state oppression, and paved the way for reconciliation with non-Indigenous Australians.

In "We Have Survived" and "Genocide" (both 1981), No Fixed Address, led by singer/drummer Bart Willoughby, recounted the long histories of state oppression suffered by Indigenous Australians. No Fixed Address were formed in 1978 alongside Us Mob at the Centre for Aboriginal Studies in Music, and their music featured in the seminal semi-autobiographical film *Wrong Side of the Road* (Isaac and Lander, prod., 1981), which revealed the endemic racial discrimination, social exclusion, and police harassment still faced by Indigenous youths. "Black Boy" by Coloured Stone (1986), led by singer/drummer Buna Lawrie, railed against the racial mores maintained under the White Australia Policy by encouraging Indigenous Australians to be proud of their dark skins. Similarly, "Blackfella, Whitefella" by the Warumpi Band (1987), led by the flamboyant Yolŋu lead singer George Burarrwaŋa from Arnhem Land,[1] called for an end to the social rift between Indigenous and non-Indigenous Australians and soon became a prominent anthem of the burgeoning movement for Aboriginal Reconciliation in Australia.[2]

By the late 1980s, Labor was again in power under Bob Hawke and I was in my teens. The airwaves bristled with songs by non-Indigenous Australian artists, like "Solid Rock, Sacred Ground" by Goanna (1982), "Beds Are Burning" by Midnight Oil (1987), and "Special Treatment" by Paul Kelly (1989), that had been composed in support of these new ideals, and demonstrated a new yearning among Australians to atone for past injustices against Indigenous peoples. And as I grew into adulthood, even more Indigenous artists joined the chorus.

Songs like "Took the Children Away" by Archie Roach (1992) and "Malcolm Smith" by Tiddas (1994) foreshadowed the damning revelations of the National Inquiry into the Separation of Aboriginal and Torres Strait Islander Children from Their Families, and the Royal Commission into Aboriginal Deaths in Custody (Australian Human Rights Commission, 1997; Council for Aboriginal Reconciliation, 1998). Also popular was "From Little Things, Big Things Grow" on *Comedy* by Paul Kelly and the Messengers (1991). Composed by Paul Kelly and the Indigenous folk balladeer Kev Carmody from southeast Queensland, this song became another prominent anthem of the Aboriginal Reconciliation movement. It celebrated Vincent Lingiari's leadership of the pivotal 1966 strike on the Wave Hill cattle station in the Northern Territory. Sparked by appalling wages and conditions for local Indigenous laborers, this action led to the Whitlam government's eventual handing back of exploited pastoral lands to their traditional Gurindji owners in 1975 (Hardy, 1968; Bird Rose, 1991).

In December, 1991, Prime Minister Hawke was deposed by his former Deputy, Paul Keating, who led Australia into a new era of recognition for Indigenous rights. At Redfern Park in inner Sydney in December, 1992, on the eve of the United Nations International Year for the World's Indigenous People, he gave a moving speech before the media and the local Indigenous community that

---

[1] All spellings of names and words from the Yolŋu languages follow the conventions used today throughout the Yolŋu communities of Arnhem Land (Zorc, 1996).

[2] See <http://www.reconciliation.org.au>, accessed September 7, 2009.

irrevocably acknowledged how Australia's prosperity had come at the terrible expense of systemic injustices against Indigenous peoples (Keating, 1992). In June that same year, the High Court of Australia had ruled to overturn the doctrine of *terra nullius*, the legal fiction that Australia had been unoccupied at the time of British settlement in 1788, which had excluded Indigenous peoples from asserting any rights or controls over their traditional homelands. Known as the historic Mabo judgment (Australia, 1992), this case concerned the Merriam people and their native title over their islands in the Torres Strait, and it was ultimately won under the Racial Discrimination Act 1975 (Sharp, 1996). Keating's government subsequently enshrined this judgment in the Native Title Act 1993, and as the nation celebrated, Indigenous and non-Indigenous artists from all over Australia collaborated on the commemorative album *Our Home, Our Land* (Yothu Yindi et al., 1995). "Mabo," the album's second song by Yothu Yindi (1995) from Arnhem Land, opens with the triumphant declaration, "*Terra nullius* is dead and gone."

Written on a Bark

In another move to mark the United Nations International Year for the World's Indigenous People, Yothu Yindi's engaging lead singer, Mandawuy Yunupiŋu, was named Australian of the Year on Australia Day, January 26, 1993. Mandawuy was a Yolŋu man from the remote Indigenous community of Yirrkala on the northeastern tip of Arnhem Land, which unlike most other Indigenous communities had not been enfranchised into the Commonwealth of Australia until the establishment of a Methodist mission there in 1934. Before embarking on his musical career with Yothu Yindi in 1986, Mandawuy was already recognized as a gifted and influential educator. He was among one of the first Indigenous school teachers from the Northern Territory to earn a bachelors degree in education and be promoted to principal, and for the first time in history his revolutionary ideas about bilingual and bicultural learning made it legitimate for local Indigenous children to be schooled in their own languages as well as English.

In typically Yolŋu fashion, Mandawuy's grand treatise on these ideas came in the form of a song, which he composed while completing his Education degree through Deakin University in 1986. Called "Mainstream" (Yothu Yindi, 1989), it challenged the prevailing assimilationist notion among Australian educators that schools served Indigenous children best by teaching them only in English. It argued that traditional Yolŋu law enshrines a local mainstream of esoteric thought that long predates the transplanted intellectual traditions of Europe, and building on traditional Yolŋu mechanisms for maintaining amicable relations between different clans, it posited a more balanced and equitable way for Indigenous and non-Indigenous Australians to coexist (Corn, 2009, pp. 25-68).

The balance engendered through Mandawuy's ideal of biculturalism was also central to his greater social project for Yothu Yindi (Yunupiŋu, 1994). This kind of balance was constructive. It made space for different views to be exchanged.

It laid foundations for mutual respect among different peoples, and it created new possibilities for different ways of life to coexist. It was also necessary because for the past quarter-century Mandawuy's family had been fighting an entrenched struggle for justice over the unwelcome mining of their traditional homelands around Yirrkala. The state's repeated refusals to recognize Yolŋu sovereignty over this issue is a theme that runs throughout Yothu Yindi's repertoire, and inspired the composition of its most famous song, "Treaty" (1991).

In 1963, the Australian government granted a bauxite lease over the lands surrounding Yirrkala to the mining company Pechiney while ensuring that their Yolŋu owners were locked out of all negotiations. Mandawuy's father, Mangurrawuy Yunupiŋu, was then a senior elder at Yirrkala, and had recently finished collaborating with 15 other elders to paint the "Yirrkala Church Panels" (Marika et al., 1962-63). Spanning two giant bark panels, this extraordinary document was created as a symbol of contemporary Yolŋu solidarity. The panels incorporated the most sacred hereditary designs of nine local Yolŋu clans, and were initially hung on either side of the crucifix inside the Yirrkala Church to demonstrate the equality of the Christian and Yolŋu faiths (Mundine, 1999, pp. 24-5). Mandawuy was a young boy at the time of the panels' production, and Mangurrawuy cut locks of fine hair from his young head to make the delicate paintbrushes required (Corn, 2009, p. 39).

The newfound solidarity of the Yolŋu elders at Yirrkala would soon be tested when the lands to be mined were summarily excised from the Arnhem Land Aboriginal Reserve. They acted swiftly to register an official protest in the form of the "Yirrkala Petition to the House of Representatives" (Marika et al., 1963), which was again spread across two painted bark panels. This second document incorporated a statement in Yolŋu-Matha and English that beseeched the Australian government to spare their lands. Known as the "Yirrkala Bark Petition," it now resides on permanent public display in Parliament House in Canberra, yet did nothing to change the fate of the Yirrkala community.

When the mining company NABALCO obtained Pechiney's lease in 1967, the nearby homeland of Nhulunbuy was instantly bulldozed to make way for a new town to house its miners, and the mine itself went into production in the following year. Heartbroken, the Yirrkala elders issued a writ through the Supreme Court of the Northern Territory in an attempt to halt these developments (Mundine, 1999, p. 22). Their case, *Milirrpum* v. *Nabalco* (Australia, 1968), was heard by Justice Blackburn, who rigorously probed the depths of Yolŋu law and property management provisions among seven resident clans. Mandawuy's father gave evidence for the plaintiffs, while his older brother, Galarrwuy Yunupiŋu, was present throughout the proceedings as a court interpreter, and witnessed their eventual defeat in Canberra in April, 1971, when Blackburn ruled that Yolŋu land ownership had "never formed any part of the law of any part of Australia" (Australia, 1971, pp. 244-5). Mandawuy would later recall his father's disappointment at this loss:

> My father was devastated when we lost that court case, and I saw most of the
> elders, along with my father, saddened. We'll never forget that those aspects of
> our law, our strength and our unity were not seen as part of Australian culture,
> and the Australian way of life in the Yolŋu way. (quoted in Corn, 2009, p. 41)

Further insult to Yolŋu dignity came when Blackburn determined that the plaintiffs
had not proven their descent from the people who had inhabited Yirrkala when
the British First Fleet claimed Australia for the British Crown on January 26,
1788 (Australia, 1971, p. 198). Galarrwuy scathingly satirizes this judgment in
"Luku-Wäŋawuy Manikay 'Sovereignty Song' 1788" (Yothu Yindi, 1989), which
he composed to coincide with Australia's national Bicentennial celebrations in
1988. The song parodies a federal parliament sitting and relates the strange tale of
the Balanda "Anglo-Australians," who claim to have owned the Yolŋu homelands
ever since the British First Fleet landed at Sydney Cove in 1788. That this singular
act of succession took place some 2,500 kilometers away from Yirrkala, and 146
years before the first missionaries arrived there was apparently of no consequence.
The humor of "Luku-Wäŋawuy Manikay 1788" is further underscored by the
offbeat strokes of its acoustic guitar accompaniment, which is reminiscent of the
many Anglo-Australian folk songs that celebrate unbridled pastoral expansion and
colonial conquest (Corn and Gumbula, 2004).

Writing in the Sand

By 1988, Galarrwuy was in his third term as Chair of the Northern Land Council,
which in response to Blackburn's ruling against the Yirrkala elders in 1971 had
been founded under the new Aboriginal Land Rights Act (Northern Territory)
1976 to represent regional Indigenous interests in land. Australia's Bicentennial
celebrations that year presented a high-profile opportunity for Indigenous peoples
to reaffirm the collective sovereignty, and so on the occasion of Prime Minister
Hawke's visit to the Barunga Festival in June, Galarrwuy and fellow Indigenous
leaders from throughout the Northern Territory presented him with the "Barunga
Statement" (Yunupiŋu et al., 1988). This new document took the form of a single
typescript bordered by traditional Yolŋu and central Australian painted designs, and
it called upon the federal government to enter into a formal treaty with Indigenous
Australians in recognition of their prior ownership, continuing occupation, and
sovereignty over their homelands, and in affirmation of their human rights and
freedoms.

Hawke's initial response to the "Barunga Statement" was surprisingly positive.
Yet his promise that the process of negotiating a treaty would commence within
the lifetime of his parliament would never be fulfilled (Aboriginal and Torres
Strait Islander Commission, 2001). By 1991, Hawke's promise of a treaty had all
but faded from public consciousness when Yothu Yindi's first hit song, "Treaty"
(1991), began receiving airplay. The band had teamed up with Bart Willoughby,

Paul Kelly, and Midnight Oil's lead singer, Peter Garrett, to create a rock song that would recapture the public's imagination for this cause. Its lyrics were incisive and its chorus infectiously demanded, "Treaty yeah, Treaty now."

The first verse of "Treaty" recounts how Hawke's promise of action at the 1988 Barunga Festival was broadcast worldwide, but then disappeared "just like writing in the sand," and the song's music video (Yothu Yindi, 1992) presents corroborating evidence. It shows the completion of the "Barunga Statement" onsite at the festival, news reportage of Hawke's visit there, and the ravages of bauxite mining on the Gove Peninsula.

The song's second verse contrasts Hawke's unfulfilled promise against the permanence of Yolŋu law. It asserts that the Yolŋu never sold or ceded their "priceless" homelands to the British Crown, and echoing "Luku-Wäŋawuy Manikay 1788," it declares that "the planting of the Union Jack never changed our [Yolŋu] law at all." The ideal of balance and equity between Indigenous and non-Indigenous Australians first set forth by Mandawuy in "Mainstream" is also referenced in this second verse through the traditional Yolŋu metaphor of "two rivers" flowing together and becoming as "one" (Neuenfeldt, 1993; Corn, 2009, pp. 35-6).

Typical of the compositional style that Mandawuy had been developing since the early 1980s, "Treaty" also incorporated two complete quotations of a traditional Yolŋu song, making it the first hit song in history to feature lyrics in a true Australian language. The old song he selected was of the *djatpaŋarri* style, which had dominated as a popular music among youths at Yirrkala from the 1930s to the 1970s (Knopoff, 1997, p. 603). It had been composed by Rrikin Burarrwaŋa in the 1950s, and its presence in "Treaty" evokes Mandawuy's nostalgia for his early childhood before Yirrkala was ravaged by mining. The exuberant rhythmic drive of the *djatpaŋarri* style sets the mood and tempo heard throughout "Treaty," and the repeated melodic contour of Rrikin's old song, C♯-B-A-G♯-F♯-f♯—generically known in Yolŋu-Matha as a *dämbu* "head"—is stated at the opening of each English verse (Stubington and Dunbar-Hall, 1994, pp. 252-3; Corn and Gumbula, 2007; Corn, 2009, pp. 69-81).

The legacy of mining at Yirrkala is cited in many other songs by Yothu Yindi. "Our Generation" (1993) opens with the couplet, "Someone in the city gets a piece of paper/ Someone in the bush holds the law in their hands," which interrogates the ontological schism between Crown and Yolŋu laws in Australia that underpinned the defeat of the Yirrkala elders' legal case against the mine. "Baywara" and "Gunitjpirr Man" (both 1993) were composed in memory of Mandawuy's uncle, Daḍayŋa Marika, who gave evidence for the plaintiffs. "Homeland Movement" (1989) recounts how after four decades of mission life at Yirrkala, Yolŋu spent the 1970s building outstations on their remote homelands in the aftermath of Blackburn's judgment, and "Lonely Tree" (2000) laments the very last sacred banyan tree left standing in the vicinity of the local bauxite plant. Finally, the fate of the "Yirrkala Bark Petition," displayed behind glass near the "Barunga Statement" in Australia's Parliament House, is remembered in "Written on a

Bark" (1999). Its opening verse evokes contemporary Australia's great failure to recognize the Indigenous rights and freedoms that from 1788 onward, "were taken away in the name of a King," and the grave suffering inflicted upon Yolŋu by the state in recent history.

Treaty Yeah, Treaty Now

Despite the tragedy of Blackburn's ruling against the Yirrkala elders in April, 1971, some good did come from it in the longer term. Upon coming to power in December, 1972, Whitlam's Labor government established the Royal Commission into Aboriginal Land Rights, which led to the creation of Australia's first piece of native title legislation, the Aboriginal Land Rights (Northern Territory) Act 1976, and the formation of the Northern and Central Land Councils to enforce its protections for Indigenous land interests in the Northern Territory (Northern Land Council, 2002; Central Land Council, 2008).

While Prime Minister Hawke's later promise of a treaty in response to the 1988 "Barunga Statement" similarly failed to bear fruit, it too led to his Labor government's establishment of the Aboriginal and Torres Strait Islander Commission (ATSIC) in 1990 as an elected representative body which enfranchised Indigenous Australians into government funding processes that impacted upon their lives (Aboriginal and Torres Strait Islander Commission, 2005). The Council for Aboriginal Reconciliation followed in 1991 (Council for Aboriginal Reconciliation, 2000), and under Prime Minister Keating's leadership of Labor, so too did the pivotal "Redfern Park Speech" (Keating, 1992) and the Native Title Act 1993.

Yet with the election of the Liberals led by John Howard in March, 1996, Australia entered a renewed era of conservatism not seen since Whitlam had come to power, and the nation's Indigenous affairs policies took a series of retrograde steps. In the aftermath of the National Inquiry into the Separation of Aboriginal and Torres Strait Islander Children from Their Families (Australian Human Rights Commission, 1997), Howard refused to offer a national apology to the many Indigenous Australians who had been stolen from their families by government decree in the twentieth century. Sustained public outrage at this refusal was reflected in the Closing Ceremony of the 2000 Olympic Games in Sydney, at which Yothu Yindi performed "Treaty" (1991) and Midnight Oil appeared on stage to perform "Beds Are Burning" (1987) wearing costumes boldly printed with that most elusive of words, "sorry."

In the aftermath of the *Wik Peoples* v. *Queensland* case in 1996, the Howard government successfully introduced the Native Title Amendment Act 1998, which sparked the lengthiest federal Senate debate in Australian history and greatly curtailed the rights enjoyed by Indigenous claimants under the original Native Title Act 1993. In 2005, his government disbanded the Aboriginal and Torres Strait Islander Commission amid allegations of entrenched internal corruption, and in an effort to garner voters' support ahead of the 2007 federal election, it launched the Northern Territory National Emergency Response, which without warning or consultation introduced sweeping mandatory changes to welfare, law enforcement, and land tenure provisions among Indigenous communities of the Northern Territory. Prompted by spurious claims of organized child sexual abuse within these Indigenous communities, the most controversial aspect of this so-called Intervention has been its blanket suspension by the federal government from the Racial Discrimination Act 1975.

Although the election of a new Labor government led by Kevin Rudd in November, 2007, precipitated a long-anticipated Apology to the Stolen Generations of Indigenous Australians on the first sitting day of Parliament in February, 2008, the Northern Territory Intervention continues unabated despite mounting evidence to suggest that it remains a chronically ill-conceived and ineffective infringement of Indigenous human rights (Australian Human Rights Commission, 2007; Northern Territory Emergency Response Review Board, 2008; Anaya, 2009; Rothwell, 2009). Public concerns over this policy have recently been compounded by federal funding cuts to the many hundreds of homelands that sustain Indigenous laws and ways of life throughout the Northern Territory, and the Northern Territory government's rash withdrawal of support for the bilingual school programs that Mandawuy and his contemporaries worked so hard to establish in the 1980s.

Despite these current challenges, many Indigenous peoples throughout Australia continue to observe their laws, languages, and traditions regardless, and from among them, a new generation of popular musicians has arisen in the guise of bands such as Saltwater from Galiwin'ku, Nabarlek from Manmoyi, and Yilila from Numbulwarr (Saltwater Band, 1998, 2004; Nabarlek Band, 1999, 2001, 2005, 2007; Yilila, 2005, 2006; Yunupiŋu, 2008). Following in Yothu Yindi's stead, many of these artists incorporate into their original songs quotations drawn directly from traditional music and dance repertoires that express the ancestral roots of their respective people's continuing sovereignty over their homelands (Corn, 2002, 2009; Corn with Gumbula, 2003, 2005). As Mandawuy explains:

> We're still practicing our law. We're still doing it regardless of our laws being rejected or being trivialised by mainstream Australian law. We don't care. We keep going because it's important to pass our law on to the next generation. It strengthens our identity as Aboriginal people, the First Nations of this country. (Quoted in Corn, 2009, pp. 29-30)

Yet hope for the future, and for a reconciled Australia still remains. As recently as July, 2008, Prime Minister Rudd and his Cabinet travelled to Yirrkala where Galarrwuy led local elders in presenting him with a new "Yirrkala Bark Petition," which called for renewed national leadership toward the full recognition of Indigenous rights and title in Australia through constitutional reform (Yunupiŋu, 2009). Even though Rudd's Cabinet includes the former lead singer of Midnight Oil, Peter Garrett, as Minister for the Environment, Heritage and the Arts, it remains to be seen whether their government will advance Australia toward this end. In the meantime, at least two generations of Australians remember the haunting words of "Treaty," and as sung in its second verse, are "dreaming of a brighter day when the waters will be one."

Bibliography

Aboriginal and Torres Strait Islander Commission, "Everybody's Talking: Treaty," *ATSIC News* (February, 2001): 37.

Aboriginal and Torres Strait Islander Commission, *ATSIC Home* (Canberra: National Library of Australia, 2005) <http://pandora.nla.gov.au/pan/41033/20060106-0000/ATSIC/default.html>, accessed September 7, 2009.

Anaya, James, "Indigenous Intervention Discriminatory: UN," *ABC News* (August 27, 2009) <http://www.abc.net.au/news/stories/2009/08/27/2668915.htm>, accessed September 8, 2009.

Australia, Northern Territory Supreme Court, no. 341, *Milirrpum [Marika] and Others* v. *Nabalco Pty Ltd and the Commonwealth of Australia* (*Milirrpum* v. *Nabalco*), Statement of Claim (Darwin: Australia, 1968).

Australia, *Milirrpum* v. *Nabalco*, Judgment of Justice Blackburn, *Federal Law Reports*, 17 (1971): 141-294.

Australia, High Court of no. 23, *Mabo and Others* v. *Queensland* (*Mabo* v. *Queensland*) (no. 2), Judgment of Chief Justice Mason and Justice McHugh, *Commonwealth Law Reports*, 175 (1992): 1-216.

Australia Council, *Resolutions Carried in the Plenary Meetings of the National Seminar on Aboriginal Arts Held in Canberra from 21-25 May, 1975* (Canberra: Australia Council, 1973).

Australian Human Rights Commission, *Bringing Them Home: Report of the National Inquiry into the Separation of Aboriginal and Torres Strait Islander Children from Their Families* (April, 1997) <http://www.humanrights.gov.au/social_justice/bth_report/report/index.html> (Canberra: Australia, 1997), accessed September 4, 2009.

Australian Human Rights Commission, *Submission of the Human Rights and Equal Opportunity Commission (HREOC) to the Senate Legal and Constitutional Committee on the Northern Territory National Emergency Response Legislation, 10 August 2007* (Canberra: Australia, 2007) <http://www.hreoc.gov.au/legal/submissions/2007/NTNER_Measures20070810.htm>, accessed September 8, 2009.

Bird Rose, Deborah, *Hidden Histories: Black Stories from Victoria River Downs, Humbert River and Wave Hill Stations* (Canberra: Aboriginal Studies Press, 1991).

Bowdler, Sandra, "A Study of Indigenous Ceremonial (*Bora*) Sites in Eastern Australia" (Perth: University of Western Australia, 1999) <http://www. archaeology.arts.uwa.edu.au/about/research/bowdler/a_study_of_indigenous_ ceremonial_(bora)_sites_in_eastern_australia>, accessed September 7, 2009.

Central Land Council, *Central Land Council: The Land is Always Alive* (Alice Springs: Central Land Council, 2008) <http://www.clc.org.au>, accessed September 7, 2009.

Corn, Aaron, "Burr-gi wargugu ngu-ninya rrawa: The Letterstick Band and Hereditary Ties to Estate through Song," *Musicology Australia*, 25 (2002): 76-101.

Corn, Aaron, with Neparrŋa Gumbula, "Djiliwirri ganha dhärranhana, wäŋa limurruŋgu," *Australian Music Research*, 7 (2003): 55-66.

Corn, Aaron, and Neparrŋa Gumbula, "Now Balanda Say We Lost Our Land in 1788: Challenges to the Recognition of Yolŋu Law in Contemporary Australia," in Marcia Langton et al. (eds.), *Honour among Nations? Treaties and Agreements with Indigenous Peoples* (Melbourne: Melbourne University Publishing, 2004): 101-14.

Corn, Aaron, with Neparrŋa Gumbula, "Ancestral Precedent as Creative Inspiration: The Influence of Soft Sands on Popular Song Composition in Arnhem Land," in Graeme Ward and Adrian Muckle (eds.), *The Power of Knowledge, the Resonance of Tradition: Electronic Publication of Papers from the AIATSIS Conference 2001* (Canberra: AIATSIS, 2005): 31-68.

Corn, Aaron, and Neparrŋa Gumbula, "*Buḏutthun ratja wiyinymirri*," *Australian Aboriginal Studies*, 2 (2007): 116-27.

Corn, Aaron, *Reflections and Voices: Exploring the Music of Yothu Yindi with Mandawuy Yunupiŋu* (Sydney: Sydney University Press, 2009).

Council for Aboriginal Reconciliation, "Royal Commission into Aboriginal Deaths in Custody" (Sydney: Australian Legal Information Institute, 1998) <http:// www.austlii.edu.au/au/other/IndigLRes/rciadic>, accessed September 4, 2009.

Council for Aboriginal Reconciliation, *Reconciliation, Australia's Challenge: Final Report of the Council for Aboriginal Reconciliation to the Prime Minister and the Commonwealth Parliament* (Sydney: Australian Legal Information Institute, 2000) <http://www.austlii.edu.au/au/other/IndigLRes/car/2000/16>, accessed September 4, 2009.

Hardy, Frank, *The Unlucky Australians* (Melbourne: Nelson, 1968).

Isaac, Graeme, and Ned Lander (prod.), *Wrong Side of the Road* (Adelaide: Aboriginal Advancement League of South Australia, 1981).

Johnston, Vivien, *Copyrites: Aboriginal Art in the Age of Reproductive Technologies* (Sydney: National Indigenous Arts Advocacy Association, 1996).

Keating, Paul, "Redfern Park Speech," *Aboriginal Law Bulletin*, 3 (1992) <http: //www.austlii.edu.au/au/journals/ILB/2001/57.html>, accessed September 7, 2009.

Kidd, Rosalind, *The Way We Civilise: Aboriginal Affairs, The Untold Story* (Brisbane: University of Queensland Press, 1997).

Knopoff, Steven, "Yolŋu," in Warren Bebbington (ed.), *The Oxford Companion to Australian Music* (Melbourne: Oxford University Press, 1997): 602-3.

Marika, Mawalan, et al., "Yirrkala Petition to the House of Representatives" (Yirrkala: Yirrkala Community, 1963).

Marika, Wandjuk, *Life Story as Told to Jennifer Isaacs* (Brisbane: University of Queensland Press, 1995).

Marika, Wandjuk, et al., "Yirrkala Church Panels" (Yirrkala: Waruki Cooperative, 1962-63).

McGrath, Ann (ed.), *Contested Ground: Australian Aborigines under the British Crown* (Sydney: Allen, 1995).

Mundine, Djon, "Saltwater," in Buku-Larrŋgay Mulka Centre, *Saltwater: Yirrkala Bark Paintings of Sea Country* (Sydney: Isaacs, 1999).

Neuenfeldt, Karl, "Yothu Yindi and *gaṉma*," *Journal of Australian Studies*, 38 (1993): 1-11.

Northern Land Council, *NLC: Northern Land Council* (Darwin: Northern Land Council, 2002) <www.nlc.org.au>, accessed September 7, 2009.

Northern Territory Emergency Response Review Board, *Report of the Northern Territory Emergency Response Review Board, October 2008* <http://www.nterreview.gov.au/docs/report_nter_review/execsumm.htm>, accessed September 8, 2009.

Perkins, Rachel, and Marcia Langton (eds.), *First Australians: An Illustrated History* (Melbourne: Melbourne University Publishing, 2008).

Rothwell, Nicolas, "Sorry State of Affairs," *The Australian* (February 13, 2009) <www.theaustralian.news.com.au/story/0,25197,25046025-5018771,00.html>, accessed September 8, 2009.

Sharp, Nonie, *No Ordinary Judgment: Mabo, the Murray Islanders' Land Case* (Canberra: Aboriginal Studies Press, 1996).

Stubington, Jill, and Peter Dunbar-Hall, "Yothu Yindi's 'Treaty'," *Popular Music*, 13 (1994): 243-59.

Yothu Yindi, "Treaty," Yothu Yindi, *Diṯi Murru* [sic *Diṯimurru*]: *The Videos* (Mushroom, 1992).

Yugambeh Museum, *Yugambeh Museum Language and Heritage Research Centre* (Beenleigh: Yugambeh Museum, 2006) <http://www.yugambeh.com>, accessed September 7, 2009.

Yunupiŋu, Galarrwuy, "Tradition, Truth and Tomorrow," *The Monthly*, 41 (2009): 32-40.

Yunupiŋu, Galarrwuy, et al., "Barunga Statement" (Barunga: Northern Land Council and Central Land Council, 1988).

Yunupiŋu, Mandawuy, "Yothu Yindi," *Race and Class*, 35, 4 (1994): 114-20.

Zorc, R. David, *Yolŋu-Matha Dictionary* (Batchelor, Northern Territory: Batchelor College, 1996).

Discography

Coloured Stone, "Black Boy," *Black Rock from the Red Centre* (RCA, 1986).

Goanna, "Solid Rock, Sacred Ground," *Spirit of Place* (WEA, 1982).

Kelly, Paul, "Special Treatment," Paul Kelly et al., *Building Bridges* (CBS, 1989).

Kelly, Paul, and the Messengers, "From Little Things, Big Things Grow," *Comedy* (Mushroom, 1991).

Midnight Oil, "Beds Are Burning," *Diesel and Dust* (CBS, 1987).

Nabarlek Band, *Munwurrk "Bushfire"* (Skinnyfish Music, 1999).

Nabarlek Band, *Bininj Manborlh "Blackfella Road"* (Skinnyfish Music, 2001).

Nabarlek Band, *Live* (Skinnyfish Music, 2005).

Nabarlek Band, *Manmoyi Radio* (Manmoyi Music, 2007).

No Fixed Address, "We Have Survived," No Fixed Address and Us Mob, *Wrong Side of the Road* (Black Australia Records, 1981).

No Fixed Address, "Genocide," No Fixed Address and Us Mob, *Wrong Side of the Road* (Black Australia Records, 1981).

No Fixed Address and Us Mob, *Wrong Side of the Road* (Black Australia Records, 1981).

Roach, Archie, "Took the Children Away," *Charcoal Lane* (Hightone, 1992).

Saltwater Band, *Gapu Damurruŋ'* (Skinnyfish Music, 1998).

Saltwater Band, *Djarridjarri* [sic *Djärritjarri*] (Skinnyfish Music, 2004).

Tiddas, "Malcolm Smith," *Sing about Life* (Polygram, 1994).

Warumpi Band, "Blackfella, Whitefella," *Go Bush!* (Festival, 1987).

Yilila, *Manilamanila* (Yilila, 2005).

Yilila, *Aeroplane* (Yilila, 2006).

Yothu Yindi, "Mainstream," *Homeland Movement* (Mushroom, 1989).

Yothu Yindi, "Homeland Movement," *Homeland Movement* (Mushroom, 1989).

Yothu Yindi, "Luku-Wäŋawuy Manikay 1788," *Homeland Movement* (Mushroom, 1989).

Yothu Yindi, "Treaty," *Tribal Voice* (Mushroom, 1991).

Yothu Yindi, "Baywara," *Freedom* (Mushroom, 1993).

Yothu Yindi, "Gunitjpirr Man," *Freedom* (Mushroom, 1993).

Yothu Yindi, "Our Generation," *Freedom* (Mushroom, 1993).

Yothu Yindi, "Mabo," Yothu Yindi et al., *Our Home, Our Land ... Something to Sing About* (CAAMA, 1995).

Yothu Yindi, "Written on a Bark," *One Blood* (Mushroom, 1999).

Yothu Yindi, "Lonely Tree," *Garma* (Mushroom, 2000).

Yothu Yindi et al., *Our Home, Our Land ... Something to Sing About* (CAAMA, 1995).

Yunupiŋu, Gurrumul, *Gurrumul* (Skinnyfish Music, 2008).

[20]

"My Dirty Stream": Pete Seeger, American Folk Music, and Environmental Protest

David Ingram

God Bless the Grass *(1966) was the first album dedicated to songs of environmental protest. Pete Seeger and Malvina Reynolds placed environmental issues within the tradition of proletarian realism, while revising its celebrations of the heroic industrial worker. Seeger became involved in environmentalism, notably the* Clearwater *project, when he felt marginalized within the Civil Rights movement.* God Bless the Grass *was recorded a month before the Newport Folk Festival in July 1965, when Bob Dylan's performance of his new electric repertoire indicated that Seeger's turn to conservationism coincided with what, to the new rock audience, was artistic conservatism.*

In the aftermath of the Second World War, American folk music began to engage with topical concerns over the health of the environment. The nuclear arms race was the most immediately pressing focus for the protest song. Stephen O'Leary observes that the American nuclear bombing of Japan in 1945 marked an epochal division in history, in that for the first time fear of planetary destruction appeared to be matched by the technical means to carry it out. "The rationalist world view of scientism," he writes, "seemed to have reached its limit with an invention that threatened the ultimate negation of the dreams of technological progress" (O'Leary 209). West coast journalist Vern Partlow wrote "Talking Atomic Blues" (or "Old Man Atom") in 1946, using black humor to register both this distrust of scientists and the fear that human history was on an irrational course. Recorded by Sam Hinton in 1950, and later by the Sons of the Pioneers, the song questions the undemocratic Faustian power of the "science boys," who have "hitched up the power of the goldurned Sun" and "put a harness on old Sol." The world faces a stark choice: either we "stick together" or "All men/Could be cremated equal" (Hinton; Sons of the Pioneers).

After scientists discovered the presence of Strontium-90 in cows' milk in 1959, anxieties over nuclear war began to focus in particular on the environmental effects of atomic bomb testing (Boyer 352). In 1963, Pete Seeger sang "Mack the Bomb," a parody of Kurt Weill by Nancy Schimmel, in which the threat of invisible nuclear fallout is matched by the secrecy of the Atomic Energy Commission. Compared to a shark, whose threatening nature is at least visible in its white teeth and in the blood of its victim, Strontium 90 "leaves no trace," while the AEC "has figures/but they keep them out of sight" (*The Best of Broadside*). In the same year, Malvina Reynolds published "What Have They Done to the Rain," which pictures a boy standing in the "gentle rain," until, because of the invisible and deadly threat concealed within it, the "grass is gone" and the "boy disappears," and the song ends on an unresolved chord (*The Best of Broadside*; Reynolds).

Ralph Lutts observes that when Rachel Carson published *Silent Spring* in 1962, she adopted the tropes of invisibility and contagion familiar in such popular discourses about nuclear fallout to describe the newly perceived threat of chemical pollution (Lutts). By the late 1950s, pollution was one of a number of concerns over the effects of industrial development that began to feature as subjects for the topical folk song.

Katie Lee began to write protest songs about the construction of the Glen Canyon Dam in 1953. As a raftswoman and river guide, her close involvement in the life of the Colorado River fuelled a lasting sense of outrage at what she saw as its sacrilegious violation. "The Wreck the Nation Bureau Song" gave "three jeers" to the "freeloaders with souls so pure-o" who wiped out the "good Lord's work" while standing "at their drawing boards with cotton in the ears." A few years later, Los Angeles smog provided Ernie Marrs with the subject matter for "Talking Smog Bowl" and "Smoggy Old Smog," the latter set to the tune of Woody Guthrie's "So Long, It's Been Good to Know You." Written in 1959, the song pointed the finger of blame at the rich: when "some big shot" chokes on the smog, at least it "did some good for the people at last" (Seeger *Sing Out!* 1959, 41).

Pete Seeger's *God Bless the Grass*, released in January 1966, became the first album in history wholly dedicated to songs about environmental issues. For Seeger and Malvina Reynolds, who contributed several songs to the album, environmentalist advocacy was an extension of their earlier involvement in the Civil Rights movement, and, before that, the Popular Front during the Second World War. The Popular Front was created in 1935, when the Seventh World Congress of the Communist Party called for the workers and the bourgeoisie to unite across class lines against the greater, common enemy of fascism. The Popular Front continued the aesthetic values of socialist realism that had influenced left-wing folk music in the United States since it was adopted as the official policy of the Communist International in 1928. Socialist realism, or "proletarian realism" as it was called in the United States, had the direct social purpose of supporting the working class in its struggle against the bourgeoisie. Lenin had decreed that art must "penetrate with its deepest roots into the very midst of the laboring masses. It must be *intelligible* to these masses and be loved by them. It must unite the feeling, thought, and will of these masses; it must elevate them" (emphasis in original). For Lenin, art should be a weapon: classical music only soothed the masses, he said, whereas art should "hit them on the head" (qtd in Denisoff 15). Under the influence of Lenin, many members of the American Communist Party chose folk music as the people's art form. Party member Mike Gold wrote that art should be for "lumberjacks, hoboes, clerks, sectionhands, machinists, harvesthands, waiters—the people should count more than the paid scribblers" (Denisoff 15).

Folk "songs of persuasion" were thus works of agitation-propaganda, in which artistic form was considered secondary to content, and language was intended to be a transparent means of communication. The musicologist Charles Seeger, father of folksingers Pete, Mike, and Peggy, played a key role in promoting proletarian realism in classical music in the 1930s. His son Pete did the same for folk (Davis; Reuss).

As already mentioned, when Pete Seeger and Malvina Reynolds became involved in environmental advocacy in the early 1960s, their politics were informed by the same ideologies of nationalism, populism, and criticism of big business as their earlier Popular Front commitments. The song collection that Seeger put together with Woody Guthrie in 1940, *Hard Hitting Songs for Hard Hit People*, contained songs such as "Mister Farmer," written in support of a strike by dairy farm workers over the low prices given by the corporate owners for their milk (Greenway 214). Yet advocacy of conservationism potentially conflicted with the celebration of the industrial worker that was central to the proletarian realist folk tradition. This celebration had a long history in American folk music, from the Industrial Workers of the World to Woody Guthrie. In the early decades of the twentieth century, the Wobblies popularized political folk song particularly through union organizer Joe Hill. These proletarian realist songs celebrated male struggles in heavy industries such as mining. Aunt Molly Jackson, a coal miner's wife from Appalachia, sang "Which Side Are You On," written during a coal strike in Harlan County, Kentucky, in 1932, to protest conditions in the mining industry and to call for the unionization of mine workers (Greenway 169). As Georgina Boyes observes of the similar repertoire of British folksingers Ewan MacColl and A. L. Lloyd in the 1950s, the industries worth researching and writing about "were never catering or nursing, hairdressing or office work, and only the heroic was celebrated" (Boyes 240).

At the center of Woody Guthrie's songs in the 1930s, however, was a rural nostalgia that partly distanced them from these materialist tendencies in the Left. As Robert Cantwell writes:

> Whereas the leftist program was essentially secular and historical, grounded in economic theory and tending toward more or less radical reform, Guthrie's vision—or, rather, the vision around which he and the other cultural seekers and idealists converged—was essentially pastoral and mythical, echoing Christian eschatology and rooted in the Gospel according to Matthew. (Cantwell 137)

Nevertheless, Guthrie believed that his pastoral vision of "Pastures of Plenty" would be brought about by industrialization and modernization. America was a land of material plenty and democratic potential prevented only by an artificial scarcity that industrial development would remove. Guthrie's songs thus celebrated the big public works of President Roosevelt's New Deal, such as the building of the Grand Coulee Dam on the Columbia River. In the early 1940s, Guthrie was hired by the Bonneville Power Administration to write songs celebrating these new construction projects.

The folk revival of the late 1950s continued this workerist tradition. Phil Ochs's 1964 "Automation Song" returned to John Henry's protest against the replacement of human labor by the machine. The male worker, with "the muscles on my arm and

24   *D. Ingram*

the sweat upon my back," is left walking down the road, jobless and with nowhere to go. Gordon Friesen, in the liner notes to Ochs's album *All the News That's Fit to Sing*, commented that the "same feeling expressed here has led Phil to write songs for, and several times visit, the impoverished mining families in eastern Kentucky made jobless by automation."

Both Pete Seeger and Malvina Reynolds inherited this proletarian realist celebration of the heroic industrial worker. Seeger's first group, the Almanac Singers, formed in December 1940, did benefits for strikers at which they sang such songs as "Talking Union," about the struggles for unionization of industrial workers such as miners and automobile workers. Reynolds had also been involved in socialist causes. Yet by the early 1960s, both singers had managed an uneasy reconciliation of their Old Left notions of authenticity through manual labor with their turn to environmentalist advocacy. Reynolds thus continued to write protest songs in support of the rights of industrial workers at the same time that she voiced her concerns on environmental matters. In 1963, Seeger recorded "Mrs. Clara Sullivan's Letter," which Reynolds had written in support of miners in Scuddy, Kentucky, who were striking, as the song put it, "for jobs at decent pay." The chorus noted that "there's no better man than a mining man" (*The Best of Broadside*; Seeger *Where Have All the Flowers Gone* 110). Here, allegiance to the working class was predicated on a denial of the wider environmental effects of the mining industry. In contrast, the last verse of "Cement Octopus," which Reynolds wrote for the protests against the proposed construction of a freeway through Golden Gate Park, San Francisco, in 1964, took a more environmentalist line, recognizing that constraints on development may cause unemployment, and suggesting a solution in the redeployment of workers into more environmentally sound jobs: "The men on the highways need those jobs, we know/Let's put them to work planting new trees to grow" (*God Bless the Grass*). In this way, Reynolds's song negotiated the problem of reconciling the new environmentalism with traditional Leftist workerism.

For both Reynolds and Seeger, this growing environmentalist concern for the destructive effects of industrialism came in spite of their membership in the American Communist Party, with its faith in progress though industrial development. Yet their allegiance to Communist Party orthodoxies had always been loose. Reynolds left the Party in the late 1940s, because, as she commented in 1977, its leadership "had no concept of what I was doing or of what effect it would have" (Lieberman 78). Although Seeger continued to be a member of the Party, his group the Almanac Singers, as Cantwell writes, were not driven by the artistic agenda of the Communist Party, but by a "sheer love of a dreamed-of folk America, or more precisely of American folks, whom few in the group had ever known up close" (Cantwell 131). Seeger described his next group, the Weavers, which he founded in 1948, as:

> political in the broad sense—we weren't Progressive Party, Communist Party, or even Peace Party singers, but we realized that the human race was in a bad situation, and looked on music as part of the on-going struggle to get the human

race together, banish war for ever more, bring peace, justice and jobs for all, and all those nice-sounding things. (Denselow 13)

Speaking in 1963, Seeger again qualified his allegiance to Communism, writing that it derived not from his reading of Marx and Lenin, but from his childhood interest in Ernest Thompson Seton. The Canadian naturalist, he wrote, "held up the Indian as an ideal, for strength and morality and selflessness, and in tune with all of nature. Anthropologists call this period of human history 'tribal communism.' I think next time some character asks me, 'Are you a communist?' I'll answer, 'Oh, about as much as the average American Indian'" (Seeger Summer 1963, 67). Like Woody Guthrie, then, Seeger's political values were informed more by pastoral nostalgia and American nationalism than by the dogmatic economic materialism of the Communist Party. His pseudonym for his regular column in *Sing Out!* magazine was Johnny Appleseed, the legendary patron of American agriculture and horticulture who dispersed apple seeds as he moved westwards across the North American continent. It was this sentimental adherence to a pastoral ideal of America that smoothed Seeger's transition into environmentalism.

The muscular Christianity of Guthrie and Seton was another important factor in Seeger's adoption of environmental causes. "As a kid," he wrote in 1993:

> I'd been a nature nut. Age 15 and 16, I put all that behind me, figuring the main job to do was to help the meek inherit the earth, assuming that when they did the foolishness of the private profit system would be put to an end. But in the early '60s, I realized that the world was being turned into a poisonous garbage dump. By the time the meek inherited it, it might not be worth inheriting. I became an econik. (Seeger *Where Have All the Flowers Gone* 201)

For Seeger, then, environmentalism, by mitigating the damage inflicted on the world by the capitalist system, was a necessary prerequisite for a future socialist society that would itself be a fulfillment of Christ's humanist, egalitarian vision.

Seeger first made public his environmentalist concerns as early as 1958, when he told a radio interviewer in Cleveland, Ohio: "Look at the waste we make of our rivers, beautiful clear streams like the Hudson which flows past my door—an open sewer!....A river which was once clean and clear—Indians speared fish twenty feet down—is now an open sore. Nobody swims in it; you go on a boating trip, you just don't look down" (Dunaway 285). In the same year, he wrote "Oh, Had I a Golden Thread," in which he sang of "a land of parks/Where people can be at peace." His concern for pollution could be seen in his wish that "the land will be sparkling clean" (*Strangers and Cousins*).

In October 1963, Seeger mentioned his environmentalist views for the first time in his Johnny Appleseed column in *Sing Out!* While chopping firewood, he wrote, he had made up new verses to "Take This Hammer": "I don't want no s..t [*sic*] filled river; past my door, no, past my door. I don't want your litterbug highway, through my land, no, through my land. I don't want no d..n [*sic*] fool strontium, in my sky, no, in my sky." These verses, he added, were "irrelevant, I suppose, to all but me" (Oct. 1963, 65). The diffident, apologetic tone Seeger showed here had disappeared completely by June 1965, when he recorded *God Bless the Grass*.

26   *D. Ingram*

When the album was released in January 1966, the freedom and topical song movement was declining in popularity, due, culturally, to the rise of rock music and, politically, to the growing schism within the Left over race. *God Bless the Grass* marked a new social and political cause for Seeger at a time when he was beginning to feel marginalized by the leadership of the Civil Rights movement. He and his wife Tochi had taken part in the protest march from Selma to Montgomery in March 1965 at the direct invitation of Dr Martin Luther King, Jr. However, Seeger sensed the new direction that African-American politics were taking. Late in the same year, the Student Non-Violent Co-ordinating Committee had begun to purge itself of its white, northern, middle-class elements to become an organization led by African Americans for African Americans. Seeger's prominent role in the Civil Rights movement was at an end (Dunaway 236ff.). Biographer David Dunaway notes that Seeger was stung by criticisms that African-American organizers had made of his role as a paternalistic outsider in the southern struggle for Civil Rights. Moreover, he suggests that political despair over the failure of his integrationist dreams and his exclusion from the movement with the rise of black separatism were important motives behind Seeger's adoption of environmental causes. He began to spend more time on building the *Clearwater*, the replica of a nineteenth-century sloop which, since its launch in May 1969, has been used by the Clearwater organization to campaign for cleaning up the Hudson River (Wilkie).

More positively, environmentalism was for Seeger a cause which, as Dunaway puts it, was "closer to home, one he had understood instinctively as a child" (280). Indeed, it was the first cause that Seeger had adopted that was located in his own personal experience. Seeger's involvement in environmentalism thus confirmed the shift in leftist activism at this time towards working in one's own community. As the sleeve notes to the 1974 *Clearwater* album observed, "At some point in the mid-sixties, he decided that it was time to stay home…to fight for his ideals in a somewhat smaller sphere." But Seeger's turn to local conservationism in 1965 was not a retreat from global politics in that it also coincided with his joining the newly formed protest movement against the Vietnam War. Indeed, a year after *God Bless the Grass* he released his famous anti-Vietnam War protest song "Waist Deep in the Big Muddy" (*Waist Deep in the Big Muddy*). Crucially, Seeger saw the Vietnam War as the murderous product of the same military industrial complex that was responsible for polluting the Hudson River near his home. Dunaway records an incident in which a conservative board member asked Seeger not to sing "Big Muddy" at a *Clearwater*-sponsored event, saying to him, "We're singing about the water. Can't you stay away from all that Vietnam stuff?" Seeger replied that "all these subjects are tied together. You know why we don't have money to clean up this river? Guess who takes the big bite out of the tax dollar?" (292). For Seeger, then, the global and the local coincided.

The main environmental concerns of *God Bless the Grass* were with pollution, over-development, and resource wastage. This focus on "quality-of-life" issues was mainly anthropocentric: human happiness and well-being were under threat from these destructive forces. The new environmental protest songs thus reflected the main areas of social concern for those mainly white, middle-class Americans who made up the emerging environmental movement. Environmental hazards were seen as threats to a pastoral America whose imperiled green spaces were natural resources that existed to fulfill human needs for leisure and recreation. However, in a handful of songs, a more biocentric perspective also began to emerge, as we shall see (Eckersley 57; Pepper 48–53).

Malvina Reynolds wrote the four consecutive tracks on side one that establish the album's environmentalist theme: "70 Miles" (co-written with Seeger), "The Faucets Are Dripping" (published as early as 1959), "Cement Octopus," and "God Bless the Grass" itself. The album embodies the proletarian realist aesthetic of clarity and accessibility in form, and optimism in content. "Seventy Miles" uses bathos to make its point: "Seventy miles of open bay—it's a garbage dump." "Cement Octopus" develops its extended metaphor for highway construction with wit and sardonic humor. The refrain is a direct appeal for collective action: "Oh, stand by me and protect that tree/From the freeway misery."

The liner notes to the album were written by liberal Supreme Court Justice William O. Douglas, proponent of the Wilderness Act, which had been passed in 1964. Douglas's essay asserts the value of wilderness for American national identity, and argues that wilderness areas should not be overdeveloped to serve recreational uses. "There are dollar values in our mountains to be exploited," he wrote. "But a tree is measurable not only by its board feet or its cellulose content, but by its beauty, the wildlife it shelters, the biotic community it nourishes, and the watershed protection it gives" (*God Bless the Grass*) This acknowledgment of the need to conserve wilderness for reasons other than its commercial value suggests an extension of environmentalist concerns beyond an exclusively anthropocentric focus on human welfare. Two songs on the album reflect this direction. Seeger wrote of "Coyote, My Little Brother," written by Native American folksinger Peter LaFarge: "Pete told me that the Indian name for the coyote was 'Little Brother'. His song used the fate of the coyote to symbolize what modern man was doing to all of nature (whereas the Indian lived in harmony with nature)" (Seeger *Sing Out!* 1967, 54). This quietly understated lament for the declining coyote thus shows a biocentric sensibility growing out of Seeger's sympathy for American Indian cultures.

A similar perspective was also developed in "The People Are Scratching," a witty ballad written by Seeger, Ernie Marrs, and Harold Martin about pollution of the food chain, which shows the influence of Rachel Carson's *Silent Spring*. Its nine verses tell a story of complex ecological interrelationships: a cold winter kills the grass, so rabbits start eating the bark off the trees. The farmers poison the rabbits; the hawks and owls die from eating them, so the field mice multiply and spread to the town; city people poison the mice, and their cats die from eating the poisoned mice, leaving the people scratching from the fleas, which multiply in the absence of their natural predator. The moral of the story is for all small creatures to "Stay clear of the man with the poisonous hand." Even though the factor that initiates the environmental collapse is a natural one, it is human stupidity that escalates a problem that could have been solved, not by poison, but simply by feeding "a few bales of hay" to the starving rabbits.

In the winter of 1965, after recording *God Bless the Grass*, Seeger began to concentrate his energies on building the *Clearwater*. "My Dirty Stream (The Hudson River Song)" thus highlighted the cause of river conservation that was to be the focus of his political activism for the next decade. The song, first published in 1961, is an elegy for the lost perfections of an Edenic nature. In *The Machine in the Garden*, Leo Marx defined the "complex pastoral" as a mode which works "to qualify, or call into question, or bring irony to bear against the illusion of peace and harmony in a green pasture" (25). In "My Dirty Stream," as the narrator sails down the dirty Hudson, the lilting melody and gently swinging rhythm of the banjo, suggesting the "tacking to and fro" of the boat, evoke a pastoral ideal ruined by what Marx calls the "counterforce" of industrial pollution. The river is "crystal clear" at its source in the northern mountains, but downstream is polluted by chewing gum wrappers dropped "by some hikers to warn of things to come." Retaining the optimism of the proletarian realist tradition, however, Seeger keeps the dream that some day the river will "once again run clear."

Seeger's use of the pastoral is not merely a late Romantic nostalgic yearning for an impossibly utopian relationship with nature. Instead, it is future-oriented and radicalized by his socialist politics. As ecocritic Lawrence Buell argues, the pastoral mode can take on a reformist or revolutionary political agenda when the act of valuing a pastoral landscape implies opposition to industrial development (*The Environmental Imagination 42–4*). "My Dirty Stream" reconciles this criticism of industrialism with a generalized sympathy for the working class reminiscent of Seeger's Popular Front politics of the 1940s. The workers at the Consolidated Paper Plant have "honest hands," he sings. But the song singles out neither the bosses nor middle-class consumers for blame. Instead, it takes a more liberal view, using the first person plural to attribute collective responsibility for, and complicity in, environmental degradation: "Five million gallons of waste a day/Why should we do it any other way?"

As we will see later in this essay, the political stance taken by Seeger in "My Dirty Stream" can also be seen in the contradictory environmental politics of his *Clearwater* project. In contrast to "My Dirty Stream," Malvina Reynolds's songs on *God Bless the Grass* take a more orthodox leftist view of political responsibility for environmental degradation: "The Faucets Are Dripping" blames absentee landlords for the wasted water that leads to dry reservoirs; the "cement octopus" of California highway construction emerges from the state capital Sacramento; in "Seventy Miles," permission to dump garbage in San Francisco Bay is granted by the "city fathers."

As already mentioned, Seeger's involvement in river conservation can be seen as part of a general shift in left-wing activism at this time towards working in one's local community. But while the autobiographical element in "My Dirty Stream" ("But I live right at Beacon here") is unusual for Seeger, the notion of self that the song constructs is typically outward looking and social. When the song was published in *Sing Out!* in July 1969, it was described as Seeger "sharing a private dream warmly and intimately" (1). The private dream had become a public, political concern.

Popular Music and Society   29

Newport 1965 and the Limitations of Proletarian Realism

In July 1965, one month after he recorded *God Bless the Grass*, Seeger, with fellow organizers Alan Lomax and Theodore Bikel, was outraged when Bob Dylan, dressed in a black leather motorcycle jacket, gave a concert of loud, electric rock music with the Paul Butterfield Blues Band on the closing night of the Newport Folk Festival. Within a year of Dylan's ground-breaking performance, writes Greil Marcus, "what had been understood as folk music would as a cultural force have all but ceased to exist" (13).

The new rock music challenged many of the long-held proletarian realist values of the topical folk song tradition, those values embodied in *God Bless the Grass*. Most importantly, in folk circles, the collective response of the audience was considered more important than the artistic demands of the individual performer. Communal singing established a shared identity around a political cause. Dunaway describes the relationship between Seeger and his audience as being like a concave mirror: he "focused his listeners' admiration back out into the balconies, inspiring people with an image of themselves as better (more tolerant, compassionate, international) than they were. He kindled their hopes" (Dunaway 228). Seeger himself revealed his aesthetic principles in a letter to a festival organizer in Japan, in which he wrote that "we need songs with strength to make cowards stop fleeing, turn around, and face the future with a breath of courage." His songs, he said, "must be so good that they reach out to 190 million Americans" (Dunaway 270).

Questions of artistic quality were thus paramount in Seeger's mind. In his introduction to Woody Guthrie's *California to the New York Island* (1960), he elaborated on his artistic aims by listing the three qualities that singers could learn from Guthrie's performance style. The first was his "matter-of-fact, unmelodramatic, understatement throughout." The second was "simplicity above all—and getting the words out clearly. They are the most important part of the song." The third quality was "irregularity." He explained: "to avoid a sing-song effect, from repeating the same simple melody many times, Woody, like all American ballad singers, held out long notes in unexpected places, although his guitar strumming maintained an even tempo. Thus no two verses sounded alike. Extra beats were often added to measures" (Heylin 82).

Proletarian realism was not lacking in artistry, then. Nevertheless, the form had its aesthetic limitations. Dunaway notes that that, in the late 1960s, Seeger continued to maintain his optimistic public persona even when privately he became more somber and pessimistic as the Vietnam War intensified. "He had endured and persisted," Dunaway writes, "even when his optimism weakened, for revolutionists have to say they will overcome, even when they know they may not" (Dunaway 272). It was the repressive limits of this official optimism, however, that Dylan's new repertoire exposed.

Dylan himself had written topical protest songs between January 1962 and June 1963, but then began to rethink his involvement in the movement. Discussing *Another Side of Bob Dylan*, he told journalist Nat Hentoff in June 1964, "There aren't any finger-pointin' songs in here....You know—pointing to all the things that are wrong. I don't want to write for people anymore. You know—be a spokesman.... From now on, I want to write from inside me" (Heylin 160).

Dylan's rejection of the protest song in this period may be seen as part of a growing body of dissent within folk music circles about the political efficacy of proletarian realism. In particular, the suggestion was that listeners to topical protest songs, rather than having their consciousnesses raised, might only be having their consciences salved. When *The Freewheelin' Bob Dylan* was released in May 1963, critic Paul Nelson criticized the aesthetics of the topical protest song movement as practiced by singers like Dylan and Phil Ochs. He commented later : "We were sort of the anti-topical-song people, not because we disagreed with it politically but just because we thought it was such shitty art, y'know. These songs were like fish in the barrel stuff....It's like patting yourself on the back music, it just seemed so obvious and not particularly well done" (Heylin 123).

By 1966, Julius Lester, an African-American songwriter friend of Seeger's, had also come to doubt the political efficacy of the topical folk song movement. The church bombing in Birmingham, Alabama, in September 1963, which killed four black children less than a month after the March on Washington, was for him a political turning point. In an article in *Sing Out!* entitled "The Angry Children of Malcolm X," Lester wrote:

> Those northern protest rallies where Freedom Songs were sung and speeches speeched and applause applauded and afterwards telegrams and letters sent to the President and Congress—they began to look more and more like moral exercises. See, my hands are clean. I do not condone such a foul deed, they said, going back to their magazines and newspapers, feeling purged because they had made their moral witness. (Lester 24–5)

For Lester, then, as for Paul Nelson, protest folk music had come merely to promote a complacent listening position.

The 1965 Newport Folk Festival saw Dylan's new aesthetics of noise, provocation, and interiority clash with the proletarian realism of Pete Seeger and *God Bless the Grass*. Seeger did not object to Dylan's use of electric guitars *per se*, as Johnny Cash had used electric guitar accompaniment at the previous year's festival. Rather, he thought that the volume was too loud, and it was difficult to hear Dylan's words. As he commented later, "It wasn't a real sound check. They were tinkering around with it and all they knew was, 'Turn the sound up! Turn the sound up!' They wanted to get volume" (Heylin 211). As a result, when Dylan performed "Maggie's Farm," said Seeger, "you couldn't understand a word, because of the distortion" (Seeger *Where Have All the Flowers Gone* 173). Joe Boyd, who engineered Dylan's sound at Newport, acknowledged that the volume was high, but pointed out that the sound mix was deliberate. By the standards of the day, he said, "it was the loudest thing anybody had heard. The volume. That was the thing, the volume....It was powerfully, ballsy-mixed, expertly done rock and roll" (Heylin 211).

Newport 1965 can thus be seen as a clash between the old Apollonian folk and the new Dionysian rock: the wordy and the ballsy. Seeger's music was genteel, ascetic, and emotionally contained; appealing to the superego rather than the id, it was rational message rather than disruptive noise. In contrast, Dylan's new music and performance style signified rebellious individualism, the pursuit of pleasure, and the division of society into the hip and the square, the young and the old. Moreover, in rock music, as Joe Boyd understood, the voice is part of the mix, the music's affect deriving from the overall sound rather than from the foregrounding of lyrical content. In this sense, Dylan's new music was a threat to the entire social and political project of the topical song movement, his performance at Newport in 1965 the symbolic moment in which the Puritanism and populist certainties of the folk movement began to give way to the new, hybrid forms of 1960s rock music and counter-cultural protest.

The ways in which Dylan was reinventing popular music may be sensed in the positive reaction of reviewer Jim Rooney, a member of the Cambridge, Massachusetts, folk scene and later a record producer. He described how, at the start of the day, Pete Seeger had played a tape of a newborn baby, and asked the audience to sing to it, and "tell it what kind of a world it would be growing up into." Rooney commented that Seeger "already knew what he wanted others to sing. They were going to sing that it was a world of pollution, bombs, hunger, and injustice, but that PEOPLE would OVERCOME." Rooney compared this attitude to the new direction in which Dylan was taking popular music, and asked: "can there be no songs as violent as the age? Must a folk song be of mountains, valleys, and love between my brother and my sister all over this land? Do we allow for despair only in the blues?...[That's all] very comfortable and safe." Dylan was, for Rooney, the only performer at the festival who "questioned our position" and "shook us" (McGregor 31–2). For Rooney, the new rock aesthetic was urban rather than rural ("mountains, valleys"), and rejected the sentimental Popular Front insistence on optimism, collective solidarity, and predigested dogma (Seeger "already knew what he wanted others to sing").

Greil Marcus elaborates on the way Dylan's music allowed for an exploration of individual subjectivity prohibited by the folk revival's insistence on collectivism and ideological orthodoxy. Protest songs such as the ones Dylan wrote in his early career were, Marcus writes, "pageants of righteousness" in which there was no room "for the selfish, confused, desirous individual who might suspect that his or her own story could fit no particular cause or even purpose" (Marcus 27).

After what he saw as the personal humiliation of Newport, Seeger resigned from the board of directors of the festival, and temporarily dropped his *Sing Out!* column, before resuming it in December 1966. The new rock culture was rejecting as outmoded and restrictive the Puritanism that underlay Seeger's musical aesthetics. In *God Bless the Grass*, then, Seeger's new-found conservationism had been expressed through what for the newly emerging rock audience of the time appeared to be artistic conservatism.

The opposition between Seeger and Dylan should not, however, be overstated. By 1967, Dylan had returned to acoustic folk music with *John Wesley Harding*, and subsequently wrote topical protest songs such as "George Jackson" (1971) and "Hurricane" (1976), as well as more general political songs such as "Political World" (1989). Nevertheless, for Seeger, the debacle of the 1965 Newport Folk Festival had the immediate effect of giving him further impetus to dedicate himself to his *Clearwater* project, which, as we will see in the following section, was a practical engagement with the environmental concerns raised in *God Bless the Grass*.

The Environmental Politics of the *Clearwater*

The *Clearwater* organization founded by Seeger in 1969 has won advances in sewage treatment and the disposal of industrial wastes into the Hudson River. In 1975, chemists hired by the organization discovered contamination from PCB (polychlorinated biphenyl), a colorless, odorless carcinogen, which General Electric had dumped in the river. Seeger warned: "The people of America must realize we've got to organize a defense against these chemical companies—they're getting away with literal murder." The organization took General Electric to court and eventually won one of the largest environmental penalties ever awarded (Dunaway 301–02).

As we saw earlier, if there were some negative motives behind Seeger's embrace of conservationism, this does not mean that he had abandoned his earlier political concerns. He was, however, accused of exactly that by many of his erstwhile comrades in the Old Left, who criticized his involvement as a betrayal of the class war. Dunaway quotes a former friend of Seeger's who described the *Clearwater* as "probably the closest thing in recent years to Don Quixote tilting at the windmills. It's a diversion. Pete's a playboy with a yacht" (Dunaway 287).

Such comments proved unfair, however, as the boat became a democratic, community resource that challenged the element of class privilege usually associated with sailing. Seeger believed that conservationism was a consensus issue that could unite people across classes and create a new Popular Front at a local level. He spoke of the *Clearwater* uniting "wealthy yachtsmen and kids from the ghettoes, church members and atheists." It was this appeal to consensus that particularly alienated his Marxist friends, who disapproved of his decision to approach the rich financiers who traditionally underwrite conservationist causes for financial backing. Irwin Silber, one time editor of *Sing Out!*, told Seeger that he was "capable of wasting a huge amount of effort, energy, time, and funds on hare-brained, diversionary projects." "I wish I could believe that these undertakings and the philosophy behind them were leading us to fundamental change," he went on. "But I don't believe it. And if you think they are, I think you're kidding yourself. Perhaps it's easier that way" (Dunaway 290).

But Silber underestimated the extent to which Seeger explicitly linked his new environmental politics both with his older Civil Rights agenda and with the newly emerging anti-Vietnam War movement. Indeed, that Silber should deem local, environmental politics "diversionary" reveals the narrowness of Marxist dogma at this time (this was before attempts in the 1970s to produce a "Green" version of Marx and Engels). In fact, Seeger elsewhere analyzed the causes of the pollution of the Hudson River in Marxist-Leninist terms, linking environmental pollution at the local level with the destructive power of the military-industrial complex that at the same time was fighting the war in Vietnam.

Dunaway tells the story of a Hudson Valley millionaire who had reservations about the *Clearwater* project. "It's a beautiful boat all right", he told Seeger. "But why do you want to sail the Hudson for? I do my sailing around the Virgin Islands." Seeger responded: "I felt my fingers clenching in anger, but I didn't say anything. Unwittingly, he had given us our best reason for building the boat....We had allowed some people to make a good profit along the Hudson, and then go somewhere else to enjoy clear water" (Dunaway 285–6).

In Seeger's hands, then, conservationism was not a retreat from class politics. He wrote:

> There's as much of a relation between the *Clearwater* and socialism as there is in putting out a book on how to play the banjo. [Both] are part of a continual struggle to oppose the inhumanity of the technology which capitalism foists on people: "Don't do anything creative yourself, just do your job, and let the machine do the rest for you." But you play a little music yourself, you start making up songs for yourself, and next thing you know, you'll be thinking for yourself. Maybe voting right. (Dunaway 290)

In an article in *Audubon* magazine in March 1971, Jack Hope quoted a speech that Seeger gave on stage during a concert, in which he placed responsibility for environmental degradation squarely with the power elite rather than with the ordinary citizen. Although we are all guilty to an extent, he told his audience, a black man from Harlem should be considered less guilty than the president of Consolidated Edison or General Motors.

> "After all," said Seeger, "the man from Harlem is probably demoralized, unable to get a job. And it's simply unrealistic to expect people to be concerned over the environment when they're having trouble holding their own lives together. For that matter, anyone who is poor isn't much of a drain on the environment, because he isn't consuming many resources. But the officers of these big industrial concerns are personally wealthy. They're educated and influential. And they head up companies that are wholesale polluters. Now, if *they* would speak up for the sake of the environment, people would listen. But they don't speak up." (Hope 6)

Seeger's appeal to Marxist notions of class conflict in this concert speech contradicted the appeal to liberal consensus politics we saw earlier in his stated desire for the *Clearwater* to unite wealthy yachtsmen and kids from the ghettoes, an attitude also evident in "My Dirty Stream." But the speech also demonstrates that Seeger's move into environmental politics, rather than abandoning his earlier Civil Rights agenda of racial equality and social justice, was in fact an extension of it. *God Bless the Grass* remains an understated expression of such focused political intelligence.

Afterword: Folk Music and Environmental Protest since the 1960s

Like the tradition of topical folk song of which it was a part, the folk music of environmental protest did not disappear with the rise of rock music in 1965, even if folk music as a whole had lost some of the cultural prestige it had enjoyed during the folk revival. Songs were an integral part of the *Clearwater* project, and Seeger carried on voicing his concerns in songs such as Bill Steele's "Garbage" (1969) and "Throw Away That Shad Net" (1975), otherwise known as "The PCB Song" (Seeger *Where Have All the Flowers Gone* 211). Don McLean was also a member of the *Clearwater* crew in the early 1970s. His "Tapestry" (1970) combined a sense of environmental apocalypse with an ecocentric celebration of the web of life that recalls Seeger and Maars's "The People Are Scratching" or LaFarge's "Coyote, My Brother" on *God Bless the Grass*: "every thread of creation is held in position/By still other strands of things living." In contrast to this delicate beauty, the "smoldering cities" are "so gray and so vulgar": industrialism and urban living are unnatural impositions on the web of life (*Clearwater*).

Tom Paxton wrote "Whose Garden Was This" for the first ecological teach-in at Northwestern University in 1970 (*The Best of Tom Paxton*). The song refers to a world in which nature has been totally destroyed. All that remain are simulacra: the speaker has seen "pictures of flowers" and heard "records of breezes," but longs to experience the real thing. Minor chords evoke a melancholy decorated with recorders and delicate strings, as, like Seeger's "My Dirty Stream," the song concisely states the conservationist cause in the mode of Leo Marx's complex pastoral.

John Prine's "Paradise" (1971) explored the sense of place achieved by Seeger in "My Dirty Stream," by relishing the specificity of place names. His childhood haunt, the Green River in Muhlenberg County, has been destroyed by coal mining interests and the song names names: "Mister Peabody's coal train has hauled it away" (*John Prine*). Lawrence Buell writes that environmental awareness and action develop from a sense of "critically aware place-connectedness" (*Writing for an Endangered World* 66). The use of concrete detail by songwriters like Prine, Seeger, and Reynolds can create this sense of place which is a vital early step in developing an ethics of care for one's environment. Buell also notes that indignation and betrayal are key tropes in narratives of wilderness preservation.

Earth First! supporter Walkin' Jim Stoltz began to write songs that celebrate wild rivers, mountain trails, and wild animals, based on walks in the back-country west he began in 1974. Stoltz's voice is a warm, slurring bass vibrato; set to dobro, fiddle, and female harmony vocals, it makes for a nurturing, uplifting folk music. Like John Prine, Stoltz records the involvement of ordinary people in the history of a place, particularly where the spirit of the place has been irretrievably lost. "The Ballad of Willie and Millie" is about a couple who meet at a dance in the Columbia Gardens in Butte, Montana, in the 1930s, before it is burned down and strip mined in the early 1970s. Stoltz adds ruefully in his notes: "The motherlode the mining company expected to find was never located" (*Listen to the Earth*).

Stoltz's environmental advocacy emerges from a sense of nationalistic attachment to the landscape of the American west as a scene of future potentiality. Yet his songs celebrate not the solitary man in nature or rugged male individualist, but sociability, generosity of spirit, and the optimism of the proletarian realist tradition, as his notes on *Spirit Is Still on the Run* indicate: "It's still out there. You can hear it in the mountain wind, feel it in the stillness of the desert, and taste it in the freshness of the wild places still left. Get out and experience it. Take a friend. The Spirit will never die as long as there are those who love and respect the Earth."

In the 1970s, under the continuing influence of Bob Dylan, many folk singers aspired to be rock musicians, and "going electric" seemed the best option, both artistically and commercially, for many singers who began in the acoustic folk tradition. But acoustic music and the intimacy of the singer-songwriter mode that goes with it underwent a revival with the emergence of "Americana" as a radio format in 1995. This cultural development has led to the increased visibility of environmental protest music. One of the most prolific writers in this vein is David Rovics, whose grasp of the drama and pithiness of the topical song recalls Phil Ochs. Of the many environmental songs Rovics has made available to download for free on the Internet, "Here at the End of the World" (2004) illustrates well his revival of the art of plain speaking. His demotic, unaffected voice runs through a familiar list of environmental and political horrors: rising sea levels, the soil erosion and pollution caused by industrial agriculture, globalized trade, polluted cities, and the cause of it all, class inequality. Rovics animates his language with rhetoric familiar to the protest song: the intimacy of direct address, the turning around of colloquial expressions ("Let them eat coffee/Sugar, coca and flowers"), playful alliteration ("political pundits and corporate crooks"), and visual and metonymic details ("they sit in their mansions/On their plush leather chairs"). He builds up dramatic tension by varying the dynamic range of his simple guitar strumming, based around a repeated minor chord, and releases it at the end of each refrain with a descending riff. In David Rovics, among others, the tradition of folk music as environmental protest lives on, continuing the work begun by Pete Seeger and Malvina Reynolds in the early 1960s.

Works Cited

Boyer, Paul. *By the Bomb's Early Light: American Thought at the Dawn of the Atomic Age.* Chapel Hill, NC, and London: U of North Carolina P, 1994.

Boyes, Georgina. *The Imagined Village: Culture, Ideology and the English Folk Revival.* Manchester and New York: Manchester UP, 1993.

Buell, Lawrence. *The Environmental Imagination: Thoreau, Nature Writing, and the Formation of American Culture.* Cambridge, MA, and London: The Belknap Press of Harvard UP, 1995.

———. *Writing for an Endangered World: Literature, Culture, and Environment in the U.S. and Beyond.* Cambridge, MA, and London: The Belknap Press of Harvard UP, 2001.

Cantwell, Robert. *When We Were Good: The Folk Revival.* Cambridge, MA, and London: Harvard UP, 1996.

Carson, Rachel. *Silent Spring.* Harmondsworth: Penguin, 1991.

Davis R. G. "Music from the Left." <http://www.usoperaweb.com/2002/jan/left.htm>, 5 Oct. 2004.

Denisoff, R. Serge. *Great Day Coming: Folk Music and the American Left.* Urbana, IL: U of Illinois P, 1971.

Denselow, Robin. *When the Music's Over: The Story of Political Pop.* London and Boston, MA: Faber, 1989.

Douglas, William O. "Justice Douglas on Conservationism." Sleeve notes. *God Bless the Grass.* Pete Seeger, 1998.

Dunaway, David King. *How Can I Keep From Singing: Pete Seeger.* London: Harrap, 1985.

Eckersley, Robyn. *Environmentalism and Political Theory: Toward an Ecocentric Approach.* London: UCL Press, 1992.

Greenway, John. *American Folksongs of Protest*. New York: A. S. Barnes, 1960.

Heylin, Clinton. *Bob Dylan Behind the Shades: The Biography Take Two*. London: Viking, 2000.

Hope, Jack."A Man, a Boat, a River, a Dream." *Audubon* March 1971 <http://home.earthlink.net/~jimcapaldi/audobon.htm>, 5 Aug. 2002.

Lester, Julius. "The Angry Children of Malcolm X." *Sing Out!* 16.5 (Oct. 1966): 24–5 .

Lieberman, Robbie. *"My Song Is My Weapon": People's Songs, American Communism, and the Politics of Culture, 1930–1950*. Urbana and Chicago, IL: U of Illinois P, 1989.

Lutts, Ralph. "Chemical Fallout and the Environmental Movement." *The Recent Past: Readings on America since World War Two*. Ed. Allan M. Winkler. New York: Harper & Row, 1989.

McGregor, Craig. *Bob Dylan: A Retrospective*. London: Angus & Robertson, 1973.

Marcus, Greil. *Invisible Republic: Bob Dylan's Basement Tapes*. New York: Picador, 1997.

Marx, Leo. *The Machine in the Garden: Technology and the Pastoral Ideal in America*. Oxford: Oxford UP, 2000.

"My Hudson River (My Dirty Stream)." *Sing Out!*. 19.2 (July 1969): 1.

O'Leary, Stephen D. *Arguing the Apocalypse: A Theory of Millennial Rhetoric*. New York and Oxford: Oxford UP, 1994.

Pepper, David. *Modern Environmentalism: An Introduction*. London and New York: Routledge, 1996.

Reuss, Richard A. with Reuss, JoAnne C. *American Folk Music and Left-Politics, 1927–1957*. Lanham, MD, and London: Scarecrow Press, 2000.

Seeger, Pete (as Johnny Appleseed, Jr.), *Sing Out!*. 9.2 (Fall 1959): 41.

———. *Sing Out!* 13.3 (Summer 1963): 67.

———. *Sing Out!* 13.4 (Oct. 1963): 65.

———. *Sing Out!* 16.6 (Dec. 1967): 54.

Seeger, Pete. *Where Have All The Flowers Gone? A Singer's Stories, Songs, Seeds, Robberies*. Bethlehem, PA: Sing Out Corporation, 1993.

Wilkie, Richard W. "The Hudson River Sloop Restoration." *Sing Out!* 19.2 (July 1969): 2–3.

Discography

The Best of Broadside 1962–1988: Anthems of the American Underground from the Pages of Broadside Magazine. Produced, compiled and annotated by Jeff Place and Ronald D. Cohen. Smithsonian Folkways Recordings SFWCD40130, 2000.

Clearwater, Sound House Records PS1001, 1974.

Hinton, Sam. "Talking Atomic Blues." *Newport Broadside*. Vanguard VSD79144, 1963.

Lee, Katie. *Colorado River Songs*. Folkways FH5333, 1980.

Ochs, Phil. *All the News That's Fit to Sing*. Hannibal HNCD4427, 1964.

Paxton, Tom. *The Best of Tom Paxton*. Elektra 8122-73515-2, 1999.

Prine, John. *John Prine*. Atlantic-WEA ATL-001, 1990.

Reynolds, Malvina. *Ear to the Ground*. Smithsonian Folkways Recordings FW 40124, 2000.

Rovics, David. "Here at the End of the World." 5 July 2006 <http://www.davidrovics.com>.

Seeger, Pete. *God Bless the Grass*. Columbia/Legacy CK 65287, 1998.

———. *Strangers and Cousins*. Columbia CL2334/CS9134, 1965.

———. *Waist Deep in the Big Muddy*. Columbia CL2705/CS9505, 1967.

Sons of the Pioneers. "Old Man Atom." *Atomic Café: Radioactive Rock 'n Roll, Blues, Country and Gospel*. Rounder Records 1034, 1984.

Stoltz, Walkin' Jim. *Listen to the Earth*. Wild Wind Records WW001, 1989.

———. *Spirit Is Still on the Run*. Wild Wind Records, 1984.

[21]

Hybridity, Arabness and Cultural Legitimacy in *Rock Métis*

Barbara Lebrun

Rock métis is another offshoot of *rock alternatif* that grew in parallel with *chanson néo-réaliste* during the 1990s. It has, like *chanson néo-réaliste*, been characterized by its commitment to left-wing causes and rejection of mainstream music codes, but it differs in the music style chosen to convey this. *Rock métis* (the phrase was coined in 1987 by the journalist Paul Moreira) is a genre fusing rock music with instruments, rhythms and languages drawn from non-Western, non-white genres, and often performed by French artists of migrant origin, whose parents usually, but not exclusively, hailed from France's ex-colonies. This genre is versed in musical and linguistic hybridity, a technique which the French term *métissage*, and this chapter examines the ways in which *métissage* has been used as a vehicle of protest by *rock métis* artists, at once against the dominant format of pop, and more specifically against the dominant discourse that insists on a neutral, non-ethnically marked definition of national identity.

This chapter examines the protest value of *rock métis* with specific reference to French North African, 'Arab' performers, often referred to, in many ways problematically, as *beurs*.[1] We shall see that, on the one hand, these *rock métis* artists have managed to move away from the connotations of exoticism that previously characterized an 'Arab' presence in French popular music, using the genre to mix together Western and Maghrebi influences in a critically acclaimed and innovative whole, which also appears to contest, more or less radically, the universalist understanding of French republicanism. On the other hand, *rock métis* has, spurred by the growth of so-called world music, become an increasingly popular genre over the last two decades, and its success has problematized its

---

1 I am using the word 'Arab' here, as Ursula Mathis-Moser (2003, p. 131) does, with caution, because of its multiple meanings. In the French context, 'Arab' is a catch-all term used to refer almost exclusively to Maghrebis and French Maghrebis of non-Jewish extraction. The term is thus at once specific and indiscriminate, bypassing the ethnic diversity of the North African population (Berber, Kabyl, Arab, but also Muslim, Jew, Christian, and so on). Because it reveals the prejudice of the dominant white French population, and is the usage prevalent in the French language, 'Arab' will be used here, with inverted commas. The notion of Arabness will also be used in the sense of those cultural elements that connote, both for Maghrebis and non-Maghrebi French, an origin in North Africa. The term *beur*, explained below, refers to the descendants of the (ex-)colonial migrants from North Africa, usually born in France (French Maghrebis). See Tarr (2005).

claims of radicality. Significantly, this success also paralleled the expansion of *métissage* as a catchphrase in left-wing discourse, the term referring to cultural and ethnic mixing in what the French believe to be a politically correct way, without having to mention the word 'ethnicity'.

In order to examine these tensions, and their role in shaping a *métis* form of protest in French popular music, this chapter provides a summary of the conceptual debates surrounding notions of identity in post-colonial France, introduces the development of *rock métis* in general terms, and charts the dominant representations of Arabness prevalent in French popular music up to the 1980s. The innovative yet fragile power of *rock métis* is then treated in greater detail with reference to Zebda (1988–2003), a group led by *beur* artists. While the main tendency in French popular music studies is to insist on rap music and its role in providing a meaningful platform for the cultural expression of French Maghrebis, this case-study challenges this consensus by locating Zebda firmly within France's rock and post-*rock alternatif* culture. However, as will be shown, gaining access to the more privileged rock milieu, with its politically active and anti-mainstream ethos, has thrown up its own problems for ethnic-minority youth.

Republicanism, *Métissage* and *Rock Métis*

In 1987, Paul Moreira published *Rock métis en France*, a book surveying the birth of a new music genre characterized by French rock groups singing primarily in French, but mixing Anglo-American rock music with North African, Latin and Afro-Caribbean influences. This was innovative in the French soundscape of the 1980s but, equally importantly, all the artists in this genre came from an immigrant and often post-colonial background. While it may sound reductive to locate an artist's process of artistic creation in their parental background, the fact remains that this new generation of artists was intentionally borrowing the rhythms, melodies, instruments and languages prevalent in the cultures of their migrant parents. In so doing, they explored the ambiguity of their own hybrid identities, being at once French nationals and visible 'others', projecting onto their music their special 'doubleness' (Gilroy, 1993, p. 30). Harlem Désir, the then-president of the anti-racist organization SOS Racisme, prefaced Moreira's book, and identified *rock métis* as 'an unheard-of hybrid that is radically original' (in Moreira, 1987, p. 9).[2] The radical power of the genre, it seemed to him, came from the artists' ability to reflect the contemporary multi-ethnicity of French society, and through this to challenge the official ideology of republicanism.

It is worth summarizing some of the tenets of republicanism, the prevailing political and structural system that channels and, in many ways, controls, national cohesion in France. French republicanism is based on the fundamental idea that the nation is 'one and indivisible', and that all individuals must be integrated within it,

---

2   'Un alliage inédit radicalement original' (Harlem Désir in Moreira, 1987, p. 9).

regardless of personal differences (sex, religion, language, skin colour, etc.). This principle seeks to guarantee democratic equality by distinguishing, artificially as it turns out, between the so-called 'private' and 'public' spheres. Only in the private sphere can social, sexual, racial or cultural characteristics be referred to, as the state considers that the public claiming of such individual differences can only lead to an atomization of identities (Silverman, 1995; Hargreaves, 1997). Dreading the fragmentation of national unity, into what the French call *le communautarisme*, the state considers that being 'French' is the sole admissible formulation of identity within the public sphere, where particularisms do not feature, individuals are purely citizens, and the democratic objective of equality is achieved. Although this understanding of what constitutes French national identity is relatively recent (it was only in 1905 that the separation between Church and State was officialized, and republicanism suffered a serious set-back during the Vichy regime), it is now indisputably dominant (Cole, 1998, p. 225). Of course, the relationship between republicanism and the expression of ethnicity is highly problematic, given the former's normative and rather inflexible insistence that national identity can only be an abstract, neutral and exclusively legal definition. Indeed, republicanism dismisses the ways in which one's sense of sexual, geographical, linguistic or ethnic belonging affects allegiance to the nation, and social behaviours more generally. Thus, especially since decolonization and the gradual realization that 'the end of colonialism presents the colonizer as much as the colonized with a problem of identity' (Dirlik, 1994, p. 337), debates have arisen in France around the relevance or otherwise of republicanism as a model of unity for a post-colonial society.

Métissage has been one of the most useful linguistic and conceptual tools for mediating this questioning of universalism. The noun 'métis' in French refers to the child of a mixed-race relationship. As an adjective, applied to music as in *rock métis*, it identifies the fusion of elements previously thought of as disparate. *Métissage* is the process through which this fusion takes place: it is a multicultural encounter, a cross-fertilization. From the first coining of the term in the 1830s in scientific circles, where biologists argued about the supposed 'degeneration' arising from racial mixing, to the present, when it mainly applies to the cultural domain and generally carries positive overtones, the meaning of *métissage* has evolved dramatically (Yee, 2003). Since the 1970s and 1980s, and partly thanks to the rise of the Parti Socialiste as an anti-conservative force in government, *métissage* has emerged as a notion challenging the shortcomings of republican universalism precisely because it signalled hybridity (Hargreaves, 1997, p. 192). Sometimes formulated as the 'right to difference', and basically functioning as a French form of multiculturalism, *métissage* recognizes the possibility of plural identities, and welcomes the visibility of particularisms as well as the merging of private 'differences' with the public sphere.

In *rock métis*, the enthusiasm for hybridity was immediately obvious in the artists' chosen pseudonyms, which all emphasized particularisms that connected their identities with (post-colonial) migration and non-Western 'otherness'. In the mid-1980s, when Moreira was researching *rock métis* acts, he identified two types of band, 'Arab' and 'Latin' respectively, and these two, often overlapping, articulations of 'otherness' would also dominate French popular music in the 1990s. In the 'Latin' camp were the Hispanic-sounding Mano Negra, Massilia Sound System, Lo'Jo, La Ruda Salska, Sinsémilia, Général Alcazar and Sergent Garcia among others. In the 'Arab' camp, the bands Zebda, Gnawa or Zen Zila all favoured the use of Arabic-inspired names. Gnawa payed homage to the ritual music of nomadic Maghrebi tribes, Zen Zila translated as 'earthquake', and Zebda meant 'butter', a pun on the French word *beur* explained below. These foreign or pluri-lingual *noms de scène* echoed the artists' desire to reach beyond the confines of the French language, and by extension those of French national identity. This process of self-othering, however, is far from rare in French popular music, the vogue of Anglo-American pseudonyms having been a regular feature of the twentieth century, from Max Dearly and his impersonations of English gentlemen in the 1900s, to Mistinguett' ('la Miss') in the 1920s, and, most notoriously perhaps since the 1960s, Johnny Hallyday, the alias of Jean-Philippe Smet. With *rock métis*, however, there were identifiable borrowings from Hispanic and North African cultural systems, which is to say from implicitly 'Third World' and ex-colonial locations. The sheer number of French bands ready to claim these influences, and to take them out of their previously 'exotic' confines, signalled a shift in mentalities. In relation to Arabness, these artists marked an evolution in French culture, from the silence or reticence vis-à-vis the North African 'other' throughout the twentieth century, to its integration and celebration in the 1980s and 1990s.

The enthusiasm of *rock métis* artists for hybridity was also evident in their music, and in the terms used to describe it. Overall, artists used electric guitars, bass and drums as in any rock music package, but fused that well-known punk-rock sound with influences from the Maghreb (châabi, gnawa, raï...), Latin America (salsa, cha-cha, tango, mambo, bossa...) and the Caribbean (ska, reggae and raggamuffin). Moreira's term of *rock métis* was a convenient umbrella for identifying like-minded artists, yet the phrase never really caught on in French discourse. Instead, journalists, producers and artists preferred to use lengthy, convoluted compounds, which precisely detailed the innovative qualities of the fusion realized by each band, and implied, by the impossibility or refusal to name the music in a simple, definite way, the ideological tensions at stake in its creation. For instance, one of the precursors of this style, Négresses Vertes, were described as playing 'popular waltzing tunes, java and world-music' (H.M., 1992b, p. 79). Mano Negra mixed 'rap, reggae, 1960s rock, Hispanic musics, Hendrix-like feedback, ska and Middle-Eastern song' (Saka and Plougastel, 1999, p. 315). Other groups were presented as playing 'French-rock-oriental-groove compositions' (Zen Zila), and as having 'an original sound, mixing ragga, rock, and Arab singing' (Gnawa).[3] Zebda was a 'grooving machine swinging between oriental tones, Occitan reggae and post-Négresses Vertes accordion' (Renault, 1999, p. 31). The band Lo'Jo

---

3   *Libération*, 19 February 2000, p. 41; *Dauphiné Libéré*, January 1999.

was introduced as 'chanson, ballade, châabi, accordian lunacy and dub fusionists from France'.[4] Occasionally, neologisms were forged to qualify these new results. Manu Chao, the lead singer of Mano Negra, invented the term 'patchanka' to describe his band's music, a mix of 'electric musette, Apache [Parisian] lyrics and a chorizo spirit' (in Barbot and Sorg, 2001, p. 72). The band Sergent Garcia, led by an ex-member of the *rock alternatif* group Ludwig Von 88, proclaimed itself as a 'salsamuffin' group, mixing salsa with raggamuffin.

Rock Métis and Protest Identities

Not only was *rock métis* a new music genre in the late 1980s and 1990s, but by also showcasing ethnic difference and cultural diversity in post-colonial France, it posed a stylistic and political challenge to the status quo. Firstly, in a manner akin to the development of world music (itself a contested term) in the 1980s, *rock métis* evolved around 'the tactic of deliberately and provocatively disrupting the commercial compartmentalizing that ... has seen world music confined to a musical and ethnic ghetto' (Warne, 1997, p. 147). As a product that was not inscribed in any single musical or linguistic tradition, it asserted its non-mainstream identity. Mano Negra was admired for its intentional 'scrambling' of genres ['brouiller les pistes'] (H.M., 1991b, p. 42). In their song 'Toulouse' (1995), Zebda claimed that living from their fusion of 'raï, rock and musette' allowed them to stand, proudly, on the periphery of mainstream TV success (this was before their hugely successful hit of 1999).[5] A journalist agreed that Zebda's force resided in their ability to bridge the previously separated genres of rock, rap and *chanson* (H.M., 1992d, p. 33). The band P18, featuring an ex-member of Mano Negra, was introduced as a lively answer to the 'deadly nothingness of mainstream radio pap'.[6] In a special issue of *Les Inrockuptibles* on French music (July 1999), almost every article referred to a need to go beyond the apparent simplifications of single definitions. Critics in general were concerned with disrupting the conventional and all-too-frequent compartmentalization of genres (Norot, 1999, p. 42).[7] It is clear, then, that musical hybridity was highly regarded by the profession as a welcome challenge to traditional conventions, in contrast to the supposed standardization of *variété*. Of course, these declarations were rather out of touch with the more complex workings of the music industry, since the majors have always thrived on originality to a certain extent, and even 'mainstream' acts regularly incorporate 'foreign' influences (Negus, 1999, pp. 152–72). Nonetheless, they helped those

---

4 Flyer announcing Lo'Jo's concert at Queen Elizabeth Hall, London, 14 November 2001.

5 '... à la périphérie des succès cathodiques'.

6 '... la dissolution mortifère dans la grande marmite FM', Von Badaboum (1999).

7 '... tordre le cou à ces a-priori qui cloisonnent encore trop souvent les genres'.

who made them to assert their own alternative identity, and authenticate their personal rebellion against perceived conventions.

Secondly, *rock métis* achieved a seemingly radical and long-awaited repositioning of national identity by taking French music outside its usual confines of a white, Western European ethnicity. For the journalist of *Rock & Folk* (H.M., 1992a and 1992b), Négresses Vertes represented a 'colourful touch of vibrant colour in the French musical landscape', and Mano Negra brought a welcome degree of originality and cosmopolitan warmth to the French scene. His positive descriptions implied that, roughly until the mid-1980s, French popular music had seemed disappointingly bland and cold, unable to engage dynamically with 'others', a view that was widespread among French critics at the time (Yonnet, 1985, p. 193; Looseley, 2003b, p. 38). Following the colour analogy, Paul Garapon (1999, p. 112) considered that the many *rock métis* bands of the 1990s reconfigured what it meant to compose and play French music: 'Now parts of our common language, African music, raï and rap contribute, alongside all the other colours of the world's musical palette now possessed by the artist, to shaping the new face of French popular music'.[8] In their song 'Le mélange sans appel' (1999), Zen Zila eulogized cultural inter-mixing ('I always recommend a cultural melting-pot'), while using diglossia in French and Arabic to home in on the idea that 'mixing' ['le mélange'] was a good way forward.

These positive appreciations of *métissage*, coming from artists and journalists alike, fitted into the broader context of a celebration of mixity in popular culture. In film, literature and political discourse, *métissage* was, throughout the 1980s and 1990s, hailed as a new definition of national cohesion, especially on the left, and potentially as the panacea to racism and segregation. From the Ministry of Culture under the Socialists, which was particularly ready to sponsor works of art that seemed to present a form of unexpected hybridity, to the conservative President of the Republic Jacques Chirac who, in 1998, praised the victory of a multiracial 'black, blanc, beur' football team at the World Cup, a consensus emerged that enthusiastically anticipated the collapse of traditional republicanism, or at least welcomed its 'mellowing' (Pinto, 1988). Indeed, these enthusiastic comments about *rock métis* were due to the critics' perception that *métissage* was new to France, constituted a radical change from past attitudes and could only lead towards greater tolerance. They also implied that France had well and truly shed its unease vis-à-vis ethnic difference and its paternalist aura as a colonial power. Ironically, by taking France outside of its traditional self, *métissage* gave reasons to be proud of being French.

Another aspect of the high value attributed to *métissage* in relation to national identity was the way in which it was systematically seen as a means of opposition to the rise of the Front National (FN), which was achieving its strongest electoral

---

8 'Devenues parties du langage commun, musique africaine, raï, rap contribuent, avec toutes les autres couleurs de la palette musicale planétaire dont dispose désormais le chanteur, à façonner le nouveau visage de la chanson française' (Garapon, 1999, p. 112).

results at this time. Openly racist, the FN was the first party in the 1980s to engage in debates about a redefinition of republicanism and national identity, albeit recommending greater separatism between 'native' French and foreigners, rather than less partitioning between private and public spheres. The fact that the FN vocally appropriated the concept of 'national identity', giving it connotations of racial exclusion, apparently made it difficult for mainstream parties to tackle the same topic (McMurray, 1997, p. 35). For Peter Fysh (1998, p. 21), this hesitation on the part of the left to confront the FN on this issue was 'rather specious', but the fact remains that anti-racist movements in late twentieth-century France, in and outside established parties, stopped short of questioning republicanism's assimilationist core, reverting instead to the catch-all term of *métissage* to praise the multi-cultural reality of society.

As a notion describing and accepting the inter-mingling of different elements, *métissage* thus stood out as a cultural, rather than political, possibility, and the term in fact became something of a buzzword, hiding the profound social dissatisfactions affecting ethnic minorities in France. As right-wing and centre-right parties moved towards an increasingly exclusionary understanding of national identity during this period (see below), so praising cultural *métissage* could imply the questioning of the status quo – if not its total rejection. The release of Négresses Vertes's first album (*Mlah*, 1987), for instance, was greeted as a powerful message of resistance to Le Pen: 'the real java, the popular java of the streets, threatens Le Pen more than any political discourse' (Vandel and Rambali, 1988, p. 105).[9] This being said, targeting the FN in songs was never the preserve of left-wing 'protest' artists. Many mainstream singers with prime-time exposure have also attacked racism, even if this was done in less hybrid music genres or with less vindictive lyrics (Vignol, 2007). For this reason, the notion of *métissage* is by no means a guarantee of radical protest, and equating it with a dramatic reconfiguration of inter-ethnic relationships in French society is idealist and naïve. In fact, *métissage* is a highly problematic notion that demands further qualification.

The Limits of *Métissage*

A contradiction sits at the heart of its formulation, since *métissage* seeks to reach beyond the 'archaism' of national confines, while at the same time hoping to establish new roots in a specific geographical and cultural space (Wolton, 2003, p. 31). This was the dilemma facing *rock métis*, a genre apparently taking France and French music beyond traditional confines, while relocating a sense of pride within national boundaries. When Garapon enthused, in his celebration of *rock métis* quoted above, about the 'new face' of French music, he certainly referred to a new, multicultural identity, yet this identity was also single, specific and

---

9 '... la vraie java, la java populo et gouailleuse, menace plus Le Pen que tous les discours politiques'.

ultimately French rather than trans- or non-national. Touring with Négresses
Vertes in Switzerland, the journalist H.M. (1992b, p. 57) remarked that, for the
Swiss, Italians and Germans who composed their foreign audience, the band
epitomized France, and the French capacity to achieve a musical melting-pot.[10]
Carte de Séjour, similarly, found that when touring abroad, foreigners would
think of them as French ('we were French rockers, at least we were introduced
as such. We might be denied this here, but outside it's quite clear', in Moreira,
1987, p. 32).[11] Stéphane Jarno (1999), a *Télérama* rock critic, considered that
the 'salsamuffin' of Sergent Garcia demonstrated the innovative approach and
remarkable skills of French artists, who could compose a believable salsa and
make a foreign genre 'truly' theirs ('the French rockers have a secret recipe').[12]
Jarno dubbed Sergent Garcia and P18 'Parisian *gringos*' ['les gringos parigots'],
a playful rhyming of French slang with Hispanic connotations that went along
the same lines as the description of Manu Chao, the lead singer of Mano Negra,
as 'our smart little Spanish guy' ['notre titi espingouin'] (Barbot and Sorg, 2001,
p. 72). Both appellations signalled the journalists' pleasure at realizing that some
French artists could sing credibly in Spanish, and compose what they deemed to
be good music influenced by Latin sounds. A certain sense of national pride seeped
through, with the ultimate and affectionate grounding of the artists' prowess in a
Parisian location (a 'titi' is a Parisian street urchin).

If the success of 'world' and *métis* forms of music in France, in the 1980s and
1990s, can be read as the enthusiastic projection of France as 'modern, dynamic
and multicultural' and, importantly, as providing a welcoming ground for foreign
music professionals (Looseley, 2003, p. 54), then championing *rock métis* also
reproduces, in many ways, a series of traditional expectations of what constitutes
national identity. These journalists still wanted to pin down the national identity of
the musicians, and to fix them in a specific (French) territorial system. In another
way, too, praising France's assimilation of, and tolerance towards, non-Western
'differences' is far from disruptive of republicanism, since it follows the aim of
transnational fraternity that republicanism holds at its core. Having gone full circle
therefore, *métissage* is as much a mode of national authentification as it is a means
of national disruption (Looseley, 2003, p. 53).

Another limitation of *métissage* lies in its insistently upbeat joyfulness.
Mano Negra were described as playing a 'happily *métis* alternative rock' ['un
rock alternatif joyeusement métissé'] (Loupias, 2001, p. 124), Zebda embodied
'joyous contestation' ['la contestation festive'] (Leclère, 1999, p. 31), Sergent
Garcia and P18 showed their 'celebratory ethos' ['un credo festif'] (Jarno, 1999),

---

10 'Les Négresses Vertes, c'est la France ... car ils renvoient une certaine image
mythique de l'Hexagone ... le brassage musical' (H.M., 1992e, p. 57).

11 'Cette année on a tourné dans toute l'Europe. ... Nous étions des rockers français.
En tous cas présentés comme tels. Ici on nous le nie, mais à l'extérieur c'est très clair'
(Rachid Taha of Carte de Séjour).

12 '... les french [sic] rockers ont leur recette'.

with a widespread use of the French adjective 'festif/ve'. The assignation of 'fun' feelings to musical *métissage* was extremely widespread in the 1990s but, for several critics, would constitute the notion's main shortcoming. By celebrating inter-ethnic encounters through the central emotion of joy, cultural *métissage* grew at the expense of a consciousness of the real and unpleasant inequalities that develop, in France as elsewhere, along racial lines (Bhattacharyya, Gabriel and Small, 2002). Focusing on France, Hargreaves and McKinney (1997, p. 15) noticed 'the tendency to indiscriminately celebrate the post-modern play of hybrid difference', and underlined that *métissage* could never be a 'real' force of social transformation. Jennifer Yee (2003, p. 422) warned against the enthusiastic mixophilia of the 1980s and 1990s in France, precisely because of the ambiguous colonialist antecedents of the term, and its false promise of an end to race conflicts. A few music professionals also noted how *métissage* had become a new orthodoxy. For H.M. (1992d, p. 33), the first success of Zebda's music was down to the widespread fashion for an 'ethnic mix' in the early 1990s. For Fred Chichin, the late composer of the rock duo Rita Mitsouko, the 1990s were a period of dictatorial 'musical correctness', as artists, including himself, felt the pressure to compose with previously 'distant' genres. Interestingly, Chichin dismissed the material that his band released in that period, believing that he was always at his best as a composer when he followed his first passion for 'pure' rock music (in Cassavetti, 2007a, p. 14).

If *métissage* is at once a radical possibility and a type of musical correctness, an anti-racist statement and a form of neo-universalism, an expression of meaningful festivity and a naive celebration, then the ambivalence of the term becomes most salient when observed in relation to the place of Arabness within French society. 'Arab' music and the Arabic language compose one facet of *rock métis*'s hybridity. This is perhaps one of its most original and transgressive declarations of identity, yet one that also reveals most brutally the limits of *métissage* as a positive recasting of Frenchness. Basically, if *métissage* became a celebrated notion during the 1980s and 1990s, this was most certainly not the case for the presence of Arabness in France, and for *beur* identities in particular. The analysis of the rise to success of the group Zebda, as well as their rather bitter split, illustrates this point. Before this, however, it will be useful to survey the dominant representations of Arabness in French popular music in the twentieth century, as a backdrop for the innovative inclusion of 'Arab' elements in *rock métis* later on.

'Arabs' and Representations of Arabness in French Popular Music

Despite the view expressed by some that France has, in the twentieth century, enjoyed 'a century of mixed French music' (Hakem, 1999, p. 40), and that there is 'an extraordinary plenitude of all things Arab in French popular culture' (McMurray, 1997, 33), expressing Arabness in France has always been a problematic proposition. In fact, since 1830 and the first 'modern' contacts between

France and Algeria, courtesy of the French invasion, representations of 'Arabs' in French popular music have been virtually non-existent (Liauzu and Liauzu, 2002, p. 25; Mathis-Moser, 2003, p. 133). In the nineteenth century, the conquest of Algeria was mainly referred to in popular song from the perspective of conscripts and settlers, lamenting their exile or boasting of their good fortune overseas. Between 1880 and 1930, when the French colonial project was in full swing and song-making was becoming an increasingly popular form of entertainment, the colonies and the colonized were treated overall in a comical and/or exoticizing mode (Liauzu and Liauzu, 2002, p. 85). It was, however, the many Asiatic and black African characters of songs who were the butt of openly racist jokes, and not 'Arabs' (Liauzu and Liauzu, p. 97).[13]

This makes popular music rather unrepresentative of broader tendencies in French popular culture at the time, since many illustrations, postcards and, later, films, stereotyped the 'Arab' as a threatening colonial subject (Rosello, 1998b). While there is no scope to explain this difference of treatment here, the very absence of the 'Arab' from French song is noteworthy for it signifies a certain unease towards the depiction of North Africans. This unease carried on after 1962, with the independence of Algeria (the last French colony), although a few songs started to reflect the new economic relations between the ex-colonial power, France, and her ex-colonial subjects, many of whom were now migrant workers resident in mainland France. In the 1970s, some white French (metropolitan) artists, usually situated on the political far-left, composed songs sympathetic to what they saw as the plight of North African immigrants, and attacked the prevalent representations of 'Arabs' in the French media at the time.[14] Nonetheless, even when they were well intentioned and respectful of 'Arabs', these non-Arabs (the *chanson* artists Serge Reggiani, Renaud and Colette Magny for instance) would often represent Maghrebis as male immigrants, vulnerable yet aggressively proud, thereby forging a new kind of stereotype (Mathis-Moser, 2003, p. 139).

In parallel to this, throughout colonization and until the 1980s, no 'Arab' music performers in France reached any significant degree of recognition. There were, after the First World War, a handful of Maghrebi musicians in Paris, who followed the first wave of emigration and played in the cafés of immigrant districts, notably Barbès, for an 'Arab' clientele (Gastaut, 2006, p. 108). Despite evidence of some success, especially after the Second World War when the Maghrebi population increased, and the creation of a distinct 'Arab popular music' section in the catalogue of France's largest record label (Gastaut, 2006, p. 111), these artists

---

13   Liauzu and Liauzu (2002, p. 27) note three exceptions in a corpus of over 1,000 songs, all to do with the figure of Abd-el-Kader, the leader of Algerian resistance in the 1830s, and praising his military exploits.

14   Chris Tinker (2005, pp. 155–7) notes that Léo Ferré, with his support for the petitioners against France's conduct during the Algeria war, provides a rare yet distant engagement with anti-colonial criticism, in keeping with 'the long tradition of writing songs that oppose nationalism and militarism' only in general, symbolic terms.

never reached a mainstream audience. After the independence of Algeria, around 1 million French settlers, or *pieds-noirs*, were repatriated, and this set the scene for the success of non-'Arab' artists from North Africa, including many Maghrebi Jews. Most famously, the singer-songwriter Enrico Macias, born in 1938 in Constantine (Algeria), would provide early examples of a *métissage* between French lyrics and evocations of North Africa. His songs, however, mostly lamented the uprooting of Algerian colonists, and enthused about fraternity beyond racial divides (Dicale, 2006, p. 638), two themes that guaranteed his success among the large *pied-noir* community, and more generally among a French audience nostalgic for the loss of Algeria as a French possession, or indifferent to questions of the moral status of colonialism (Saka and Plougastel, 1999, p. 312). During the 1960s and 1970s, then, it was mainly Algerian Jews who carried echoes of Maghrebi music for the French audience, while many *pieds-noirs* threw themselves into the mainstream pop wave of *yéyé* music, in groups such as the highly successful Les Chaussettes Noires, whose four musicians were born in Algeria and Tunisia (Dicale, 2006, p. 193; Verlant, 2000, p. 54). Overall, the absence of any successful 'Arab' artists in France at that time signalled, quite dramatically, the lack of avenues for artists from this minority to reach a large audience.[15]

This brief overview is necessary to understand the shift that *rock métis* represented from the mid-1980s onwards, giving as it did a voice to a generation of, by then, *beur* artists, and allowing them to evoke, in more complex and personalized ways in their songs, the place of 'Arabs' and Maghrebi minorities in France. The term *beur* has often been contested, especially by those it denotes, yet its permanence in the French language and in academic studies of post-colonial France justifies its use here. The *beurs* are the descendants of 'Arab' (non-Jewish) North African immigrants who, by right of birth and/or residency on French soil, have French nationality. Given that the main wave of 'Arab' emigration occurred after the Second World War, the first generation of *beurs* reached adulthood at the turn of the 1980s, and this period marked the beginning of a conflictual relationship between French republicanism and the hybrid identity of these individuals, who were at once French nationals and 'visible' others (Cole, 1998, p. 226). The *beurs* are arguably 'the most visible, the most stigmatised and the most dynamic ethnic minority in postcolonial France' (Tarr, 2005, p. 3). Unfortunately, they became associated in the media and public consciousness with aggression, as a series of urban riots erupted in 1981 in the *banlieue* of Lyons, and in which some *beurs* took part. The image of the *beur* as unassimilable delinquent became widespread

---

15   Dalida, perhaps the most successful female performer of the 1970s in France, was born in Egypt, but only her Italian origins were emphasized in her early songs ('Ciao ciao bambina', 'Romantica', 'Bambino'). Besides, it was only in the late 1970s and early 1980s that she gradually recorded a few songs in vernacular Egyptian and Lebanese, taking diction lessons to 're-learn' a language she never fully mastered (Barnel, 2005, p. 166 and p. 194), and the success of her Arabic output was mainly limited to the Arabic-speaking world. She is not, in that sense, an example of a French 'Arab' performer.

(Rosello, 1998b, p. 2), and as the far-right seized on these events to advance its own racist agenda, even mainstream parties focused their efforts on reinforcing 'security' and facilitating exclusion.

This led, for instance, to a proposal for the limitation of access to nationality for French-born foreigners in 1986–8, and to the official recommendation after the first 'Headscarf Affair' (1989) that the secular, neutral and supposedly universal values of the Enlightenment should be upheld against the perceived threat of multiculturalism (Hargreaves, 1997, pp. 184–5). This culminated in 2004 in the highly idiosyncratic exclusion of 'ostensible religious signs' from state-run schools, a ban which sought to re-affirm the importance of republican universalism, but was particularly detrimental to, and some have argued intentionally discriminatory against, France's Muslim minority (Hargreaves, 2007, p. 111). Other instances of political unease with the presence of ethnic 'difference' in France characterized the 1990s, with the official denunciation of the dangers of *communautarisme*, and the violent expulsion of illegal immigrants (*sans-papiers*) throughout the decade (Cole, 1998; Balibar et al., 1999). In November 2005, new riots in French suburbs shook the country and triggered yet more antagonism between the expression of ethnic particularism on the one hand, and the supposed cohesion of republican universalism on the other (Mucchielli, 2006).

This dishearteningly repetitive history of social exclusion, from the early 1980s to the 2000s, forms the backdrop to the rise of *métissage* as a possibly radical, and hopefully more tolerant, way to envisage allegiance to French identity. It was also the context in which 'Arabs' in France, most of them *beurs* and French nationals by then, became successful musicians and performers for the first time. The extent to which their success led to durable changes in the perceptions and representations of 'Arabs' and French Maghrebis is debatable, however, and examining the rise and fall from grace of Zebda in the 1990s and early 2000s will help to build a picture of the ambivalence of French society towards *beurs* in that period, and of the role that *rock métis* played in channelling their attempts to establish a hybrid and 'protest' identity.

Zebda: *Métissage* and Success in the 1990s

Zebda was a *rock métis* band of the 1990s (they split in 2003), from Toulouse, which gained a high degree of commercial success and critical acclaim. Despite being composed of a majority of non-*beurs*, and in spite of the conflicts that arose within the group about whether or not to project Arabness (Marx-Scouras, 2005, p. 117), Zebda did construct their identity around a *beur* specificity. The three frontmen, Magyd Cherfi (lead singer, lyricist) and the Amokrane brothers, Hakim and Moustapha (chorists and dancers), were of Algerian origin, and it was Cherfi and Moustapha Amokrane who most frequently gave interviews. Zebda's *beur* members were therefore the band's main spokepersons, and the band's name played on the Arabic for 'butter' (زبدة), the French word for butter being *beurre*, which is an exact homophone of *beur*. This inter-linguistic pun expressed the group's concern with post-colonial identities, and many of their songs' protagonists were North African migrants and second-generation *beurs* ('Arabadub', 1992; 'Toulouse', 1995; 'Ça va pas être possible', 1998; 'J'y suis, j'y reste', 1998).

This 'Arab' element has led a number of critics to compare Zebda with an earlier *beur* band, Carte de Séjour. Carte de Séjour, a rock band formed in 1981 in Lyons by three musicians of Algerian origin, the most famous being the band's lead singer Rachid Taha, is often held as the first example of a French-Arab rock group, representative of a vibrant, empowered *beur* identity (Liperi, 1988, p. 248; Meouak and Aguadé, 1996; Breatnach and Sterenfeld, 2000, p. 253; Looseley, 2003, pp. 51–2; Howarth and Varouxakis, 2003, p. 150; Huq, 2006, p. 76). For the *Télérama* rock critic Philippe Barbot (2002, p. 30), Carte de Séjour paved the way for the possibility of Zebda's success in the 1990s, allowing *beur* artists to participate in the genre of protest rock music, and triggered a degree of enthusiasm among the public for their kind of musical hybridity. The major Universal Music, which still produces the solo music of Rachid Taha, connects the two groups on its website, with Taha's page offering a link to that of Zebda (also produced by Barclay/ Universal).[16] Nonetheless, Carte de Séjour did not make a lasting impression on French culture. They rose to national fame in 1986 with a controversial cover version of Charles Trenet's 'Douce France', and split, largely unnoticed, in 1989. Carte de Séjour's expressions of Arabness were often brash and boastful, in line with Taha's own belligerent personality (Moreira, 1987, p. 34), and the brevity of their success signalled the presence of obstacles to the full acceptance of *beurs* as 'authentic' artists in the cultural sphere in the 1980s.

By contrast, Zebda presented a tentative, more despondent articulation of Arabness, befitting the introspective style of the lyricist Magyd Cherfi, and their active participation in left-wing activism earned them the praise of the elite press, as we shall see. Zebda first became famous in 1995 with 'Le bruit et l'odeur', a song targeting the racism of Jacques Chirac, and later reached media omnipresence in 1998–9 with 'Tomber la chemise', an inoffensive piece of fun which was the best-selling single of 1999. Generally speaking, the band benefited from a much longer 'shelf life' than Carte de Séjour, being together from 1988 to 2003 and releasing four studio albums, one live double album, two side projects under the names of 100% Collègues and Motivés, and taking part in various tribute albums and compilations. This larger output suggests that, in the 1990s, a *beur* group could achieve greater economic success than had been possible in the previous decade. Zebda also became culturally integrated, indeed an exponent of 'high' culture. They took part in all three of the tribute albums paying homage to the holy trinity of 'authentic' *chanson* artists, Jacques Brel (*Aux suivants*, 1999), Georges Brassens (*Les oiseaux de passage*, 2001) and Léo Ferré (*Avec Léo*, 2003). The only *beur* band alongside white artists, including the 'alternative' rock groups

---

16 www.universalmusic.fr/servlet/FrontCreatorServlet?action=biography&artiste_ id=3784, last accessed 21 March 2009.

Têtes Raides and Noir Désir, Zebda proved that French Maghrebis could, at the turn of the twenty-first century, be constituent elements of France's national and musical heritage. Unlike Carte de Séjour's pastiche of Trenet, these cover versions were intentional homages to older, established singer-songwriters. Over the years, Zebda also became the object of several academic studies, articles and books published in English and French, testament to a recognition of their significant contribution to French popular music (Seery, 2001; Lin, 2001; Lebrun 2002 and 2007; Marx-Scouras, 2004 and 2005; Ervine, 2008).

Zebda's success raises the question of the place of Arabness in French popular music, since it would seem that only by appearing to follow the cultural norm (paying homage to *chanson*, participating in right-on political events), and thus assimilating into the model of left-wing 'authenticity', could French Maghrebis hope to gain artistic recognition. However, departing from the argument prevalent in most accounts of Zebda's career, namely that their success heralded the articulation of a 'vibrant and dynamic' *beur* identity (e.g. Ervine, 2008, p. 200), It is important to focus instead on the fragility of the process of cultural validation, and examine the contradictions in the group's trajectory towards success and cultural legitimacy as a *rock métis* act. Indeed, the evolution of Zebda from *beur* outcasts in Toulouse, to the status of national superstars from 1999 onwards, was as much a story of bitterness and compromise as it was a story of empowerment. As the word 'integration' suggests, becoming part of dominant society is imbued with inner conflicts as personal characteristics get lost along the way. As we shall see, Zebda shed the most obvious signs of their Arabness when they became a 'national' group, and lost some of their credentials as a protest group when they found commercial mediatization and fame.

Reluctant Arabness and bitter-sweet métissage

Magyd Cherfi, the lead singer and lyricist for the group, was born in Toulouse in 1963. Unlike Rachid Taha of Carte de Séjour, who wrote and sung mostly in Arabic, Cherfi primarily wrote his lyrics in French, although the occasional Arabic words cropped up ('Oulalaradime', 1998; 'Sheitan', 2002). From a purely linguistic perspective, then, Zebda would appear more 'integrated' than Carte de Séjour, and less ready, or less able, to contest the dominant model of linguistic integration. This conformist aspect of their identity was also evident in most of Zebda's songs, which emphasized the legal Frenchness of *beurs* in lyrics such as: 'I'm French, I've got the documents to prove it, I'm well integrated, I stand within the French norm', or 'I am secular and republican'.[17] In interviews, Cherfi often elaborated on the profound soundness of the republican principle separating the private and public spheres of identity, considering that the future of Arabness

---

17 '... moi je suis Français, j'ai tous mes papiers, je suis bien intégré, je suis dans la norme française' ('France 2', 1995); 'je suis laïc et républicain' ('Le Bruit et l'odeur', 1995).

was to disappear as a term of self-identification as it would as a term of othering: '*Beur* is a rather nice word ... . A transition. We were Arab, then *beurs* before becoming French. That's the positive evolution of society' (Aubel, 1999, p. 64).[18] These declarations contrasted with Taha's rejection of 'beur' as a meaningless compartmentalization (Moreira, 1987, p. 51). Moreover, when he worked as a social worker, Cherfi always tried to convince second-generation immigrants of the suitability of the French identity model: 'we kept repeating to the lads that they should integrate into a democratic framework, a French identity, their identity' (Aubel, p. 65).[19] As a teenager, Cherfi was ashamed of his working-class Algerian family and illiterate mother, and retrospectively considered that acculturation was the best thing that had happened to him, going to school, meeting French friends and having 'enlightened' role-models (Sorgue, 1998; Renault, 1999, p. 32). For Cherfi, mastering the French language brought refinement to his intellectual thought, coherence to his political beliefs, and general access to French culture (Marx-Scouras, 2005, p. 116; also Lebrun, 2007). Taha would probably identify this desire to 'fit in' as compliance, and Cherfi's declarations contrasted with the fact that he and his band derived credibility from being presented as outcasts, as social, ethnic and even regional marginals.

Similarly, in declarations the group often seemed to exemplify a certain strand of officially sanctioned republicanism. In interviews and song lyrics, Cherfi always extolled the virtues of the Enlightenment, stressing the theoretical righteousness of republicanism and the validity of its humanist foundations. In the face of reactionary tendencies and anti-Arab prejudice, for instance, he considered that '[liberty, equality, fraternity], that's the real driving anger, the real struggle, that of maturity' (Sorgue, 1998, p. 15).[20] Nonetheless, Zebda's desire for Frenchness and 'normalcy' was always contextualized in the existence of widespread prejudice against *beurs* in France, and Cherfi found that the centring of republicanism on abstract citizenship was not only one of the fairest political ideas, but also the perfect radical discourse with which to oppose the French state's day-to-day detachment from its own morally irreproachable objective.

As a result, Cherfi's affirmations of Frenchness in interviews, such as 'we are French, secular and republican' (Leclère, 1999, 32), or in songs as in 'Le bruit et l'odeur' ('I am secular and republican'), were not simple signs of compliance with the system, because the system simply did not work. Instead, they were in equal part provocations against France's hypocrisy and injustice, and appeals for the revival of France's philosophical tradition of human justice. Consequently, rather than being unequivocal expressions of empowerment and pride (Marx-Scouras, 2004;

---

18   'Beur, c'est un mot sympa .... Une transition. Nous étions arabes, puis beurs avant de devenir français. C'est l'aspect positif de la société'.

19   '... on se crevait à dire aux mômes d'intégrer un repère démocratique, une identité française, la leur'.

20   '[Liberté, égalité, fraternité] voilà la vraie colère, le vrai combat, celui de la maturité', Sorgue (1998).

Ervine, 2008), Zebda's declarations of identity often reached an ideological impasse, as *beurs* found themselves at a destabilizing crossroads between self-assertion, rejection and integration. In 'Je suis' (1999), one line goes 'I wasn't born the day I was born / I became myself when I realized I was different',[21] which conveys the idea that being a French 'Arab' in France is a tiresome process of self-awareness, due to the white population's tendency to other the 'visible' offspring of post-colonial migrants.[22] In 'Le bruit et l'odeur' (1995), this distress is also expressed: 'When I understood the law, I understood I was lost. "Integrate", it said, but that was already done'.[23] And again in 'Quinze ans' (1999), the following line becomes a repetitive chant: 'I am integrated, where's the solution? I am integrated, where's the solution?'[24] Such calls for help showed the gap between the theory of equality and the practice of discrimination in France, and were certainly not affirmative expressions of identity.

Although avoiding miserabilism (Seery, 2001, 22), Zebda's songs expressed Cherfi's ambivalence towards *beur* identity by portraying *beurs* as at once powerful protest figures, and victims of socio-economic constraints and racial prejudice. The song 'Toulouse' (1995) epitomizes this duality. A self-introductory song, opening the band's second album *Le bruit et l'odeur*, 'Toulouse' presents the mixed identity of the group by stressing their French origins, implanted in Toulouse, and praising the virtues of a 'vie métisse' ['hybrid life']. The lyrics talk of mixing spices, eating tagine and cassoulet, having roots at once in France, in a Mediterranean culture and further afield. Musically, it starts with a sample of a slow Arabic prayer, before kicking off with a fast raggamuffin beat, played with the usual instruments of rock music while acoustic percussions sustain the North African feel. Cherfi sings rapidly in French while the backing singers intervene one after the other on every other line, with a strong Toulouse accent. This fast delivery of words and music gives the song something of a confused air, conveying the idea that *métissage* challenges received wisdoms about the stability and tranquillity of national identity, and introduces Zebda as a lively band, hard to pin down.

This message is reinforced by the intentional contrast of this 'Toulouse' with the version, more famous in France, by Claude Nougaro (1929–2004), a singer-songwriter born in Toulouse who released, in 1966, a song of the same title. Nougaro carved out a career as an exponent of musical *métissage*, his inspirations coming from Afro-American and Brazilian music. He was famous for French cover versions of blues and samba numbers, including 'Armstrong' (1965) after a traditional gospel, and 'Bidonville' (1965), a cover of Baden Powell's 'Berimbau' (1963).

---

21   'Je suis pas né le jour de ma naissance / je suis né lorsque j'ai compris ma différence'.

22   On the 'oriental other' as non-assimilable, and Islam as the ongoing threat to Christian Europe, see Hargreaves and McKinney (1997, p. 17).

23   'Quand j'ai compris la loi j'ai compris ma défaite: "intégrez-vous" disait-elle, mais c'était chose faite'.

24   '... intégré je le suis où est la solution, intégré je le suis où est la solution...?'

Nougaro always encouraged the experience of 'difference', and the lyrics of his 'Toulouse' referred to the town's Spanish diaspora with delight. Nonetheless, Nougaro's 'Toulouse' was a slow-paced, oratorio-like song, accompanied by a symphonic orchestra and sprinkled with the jazz accents of a piano and horn section. The dominant tone was nostalgic, the narrator proclaiming his love for his hometown and retracing his happy childhood in a warm community. Not unlike Carte de Séjour's cover version of 'Douce France', therefore, Zebda's 'Toulouse' contrasted with this initial and well-known song. The first stanza nodded to Nougaro ('mon cher Claude'), but the whole song turned against his pleasant account of the city by depicting it as socially and geographically segregated, with the tramps clustering around the train station, North Africans bustling about in the poorer districts, and middle-class engineers relaxing in the city-centre cafés. In Zebda's representation of Toulouse, ethnic pluralism did not lead to joyfulness, and musical *métissage* accompanied a rather perplexed understanding of identity. Equally, the singers' quick-fire vocal delivery, and the splintering of identities via the three voices, brought dynamism as much as confusion. With their 'Toulouse', Zebda introduced themselves as disruptive towards national heritage (the supposed unity of Toulouse, the cultural prestige of Nougaro), but also problematized the situation of *beurs* and post-colonial migrants in France by refusing to use *métissage* as a straightforward expression of happiness.

In all their albums, Zebda have developed a rather embittered criticism of the habitually 'fun' connotations of *métissage*. In 'Le bruit et l'odeur' ['The Noise and the Smell'] (1995), Cherfi reformulated a line from Nougaro's song 'Armstrong', in which he wished to be black and sing like Louis Armstrong. Speaking this time from the standpoint of post-colonial migrants who had experienced racial prejudice, Zebda attacked the absurdity of this wish: 'to those who regret not being black, there's only one answer, guys, and that's you're bloody lucky'.[25] This statement was highlighted by a break in the music, and turned Nougaro's rather racialist argument around, suggesting that belonging to an ethnic minority was rarely an opportunity to be proud, at least as long as anti-Arab and anti-Black racism existed. This criticism of Western fondness for non-Western difference echoed theoretical debates on post-colonialism (Gilroy, 1993) and cosmopolitanism (Wolton, 2002), and revealed Zebda's complex, slightly defeatist account of hybridity in France, at the same time as their music resulted in inter-ethnic cross-encounters.

The imbrication of *métissage* within a deeper questioning of the global conditions of mass-migration has extended to Zebda's visual presentation. The cover of their last album, *Utopie d'occase* [Second-Hand Utopia] (2002), is a mise-en-scène of the group's concerns with worldwide economic disparities. In the outdoor setting of an African village, a young black child is photographed wearing the black cape, mask and hat of Zorro, the legendary Mexican righter of wrongs. The juxtaposition of Africa with Mexico sets the tone for a denunciation

---

25 '... si certains regrettent de ne pas être noir de peau / je n'ai qu'une réponse, les gars, vous avez du pot!'

of poverty in African and Latin American countries, an idea reinforced by the small print across the picture which describes the functioning of Human Development Indicators (HDIs). HDIs are a calculation system accepted by the UN to measure a country's level of development, using criteria of life expectancy, literacy and standard of living. As Zebda's record sleeve implies, at the time of this release in 2002, the bottom ten countries in this classification were all in Africa, while none of the Central or Latin American countries featured in the 30 wealthiest countries.[26] This awareness of global inequalities underlines Zebda's participation in the anti-globalization movement (the relationship of this international coalition with French popular music is analyzed in the next chapter, through the involvement of fellow *rock métis* performer Manu Chao). It also, via the presence of the large letter 'Z' on the child's cape (Z for Zorro and Zebda), asserts the group's protest identity, as they themselves adopt the role of dispensers of justice. The band's recourse to children's stories and to utopianism could elicit accusations of naivety, and in interviews Cherfi has often appeared something of a dreamer, considering music as the means to realize a 'society [that would be] just, fraternal' (in Barbot, 2002, p. 30). The band's projection of themselves as Zorro figures also contrasts with Taha's refusal to act as spokesperson for general unfairness (Moreira, 1987, p. 39). Nonetheless, Zebda have grounded their political discourse in a concrete, evidence-based knowledge of world migration, and showed their ability to discern between the illusions of *métissage* and the socio-economic reality of displacement.

Political and national integration

The level of intellectual sophistication shown by Zebda is one reason behind the band's important place in France's national culture, but another is their systematic and intentional political commitment, usually taken to be an outward sign of 'authenticity' in France. Carte de Séjour only had irregular and somewhat chaotic relationships with various anti-racist organizations in the 1980s, and Rachid Taha sharply rejected what he considered to be the moroseness and strictness of left-wing militants (Moreira, 1987, p. 51; Pascaud, 2007, p. 16). By contrast, Zebda have frequently and systematically supported left-wing organizations, parties and causes, ultimately appearing as some of the most 'committed' artists of the period. For example, Zebda created Tactikollectif, an anti-fascist organization aiming to help disaffected Maghrebi youths (Reijasse, 2002, p. 83). In 1997, they released an album of 'protest songs' with the sponsor of the radical far-left party, the Ligue Communiste Révolutionnaire, which covered well-known French and foreign revolutionary hymns, including 'La Cucaracha', 'Bella Ciao' and the Resistance song 'Le Chant des Partisans'.[27] In 2001, during the Toulouse municipal elections, some

---

26   'Human Development Reports', http://hdr.undp/org/en/statistics, last accessed 24 March 2009.

27   In this album, Zebda covered 'Hasta siempre', Carlos Puebla's 1965 homage to Che Guevara. At exactly the same time (Winter 1997–8), the French actress Nathalie

members of the band launched a 'citizen-centred' electoral roll, the Motivé-e-s, which won 12 per cent of votes in the first round. Zebda have also played in support of José Bové, the leader of the Confédération Paysanne, are vocal opponents of globalization, and have participated in various charity concerts, supporting factory strikers in Toulouse, illegal immigrants (*sans-papiers*), and taking part in actions against the repatriation of foreign convicts (*double peine*). Engaged in local and global politics, then, and always taking the side of the 'oppressed', Zebda have, more systematically than Carte de Séjour, demonstrated their rigorous 'protest' identity and strong left-wing allegiance.

As a result, Zebda have been recognized as a 'French' group by critics. They were held to be 'real representatives of French rock' ['une réalité du rock français'] (H.M., 1992d, p. 32), and considered to have composed, with 'Tomber la chemise', 'a song to which the whole French population danced during the summer of 1999' (Marx-Scouras, 2005, p. 96).[28] They have been compared to a winning goal by Zidane, the Tour de France and 14 July, all symbols of national pride, for their capacity to unite the French population (Monnin, 2000). In the press, the dominant approach in assessing Zebda's place in French popular music has been to acknowledge their role as an authentic rebel group, with such qualifiers as 'honest', 'useful', 'brave', 'radical', 'refined' and 'impeccable'.[29] This all-round positive appreciation suggests that Zebda have acquired the cultural credibility

---

Cardone also released a version of this song (arr. by Laurent Boutonnat, collaborator of Mylène Farmer), which she interpreted in a less politicized manner. The video of the song showed Nathalie wandering in a sun-drenched landscape, in a floaty and slightly ripped dress, sweat pearling down her cleavage and her long black hair sexily tousled. In the chorus, she danced in the mud, under heavy rain, her dress totally torn, while photos of Che were interspersed. This rather raunchy pop video was broadcast on prime-time TV, where Cardone also made several appearances, and her single sold 500,000 copies (http://nathaliecardone.malibuprod.com, last accessed 24 March 2009), therefore faring much better than Zebda's album (150,000 according to Reijasse, 2002, 61). There was no video for the Motivés, no prime-time TV exposure, and their 'non-mainstream' identity, which had 'nothing to do with M6's prime-time TV Che' ['rien à voir avec le Che sauce M6'] (Aubel, 1999, p. 65) was asserted at the time in contrast to this other product.

28   '... cette chanson sur laquelle toute la France a dansé pendant l'été 1999'.

29   See the highly positive reviews by Mortaigne (1998), Renault (1999), Leclère (1999), Monnin (2000), Verlant (2000, 161), Barbot (2002) and Santolaria (2002). By contrast, one disparaging review is worth mentioning, even if it comes from the unreliable source of www.amazon.com, and takes the form of a message posted by a certain Austin C. Beeman from Ohio, USA (6 June 2001). Beeman considers that *Essence Ordinaire* was only worth buying for 'Tomber la chemise', the best-selling single: 'The rest of the album is awful Arab rap with depressing lyrics and unimaginative rhythms. Zebda is completely a one-hit wonder.' His remark interestingly goes against the grain of French reviews, which considered that this song remained an embarrassing, out-of-character foray into purely 'fun' and mainstream pop.

that Carte de Séjour never possessed and, by extension, become a 'legitimate' national product worthy of, and validated by, the intellectual (left-wing) elite.

Indeed, Zebda's ambivalent positioning vis-à-vis republicanism associated them with 'authentic' left-wing protest artists. The band's utopianism, its attachment to universalism, its political commitment and calls for electoral participation, were all features of a typical protest discourse *à la française*, strictly in line with the evolution of the left. Zebda clearly asserted their broad left-wing support: 'from the Socialists to the far-left, there is a lot of scope for us to get involved'.[30] Asked to elaborate on the meanings of his participation in the Toulouse electoral list, Cherfi explained that his aspiration was to 'revive politics, seriousness and commitment', while the main route to achieving this was to 'stir things up'.[31] His insistence on maturity and seriousness reflected the French tendency to consider intellectual reflection as the best way to achieve political destabilization. The leap from seriousness to unruliness is characteristic of the modalities of existence of the French Republic, which originated in revolutionary upheavals, yet owes its resilience to order and control. In France, the Revolution, and by extension any idea of transformation and contestation, has remained 'a constant inspiration and call to action wherever injustice and exploitation were present' (Gildea, 1994, p. 16). Seeking to disrupt the Republic, in order to attain yet more justice, is exactly what republicanism seeks. If, in France, to transgress is somehow to fit in, then Zebda proved that they were French to the core, as they combined dissidence, in their criticism of injustice, with assent, in their validation of the Republic's foundations.

Cultural Integration and Exclusion

Finally, if Zebda's commercial success and enthusiasm for republicanism made them French, their intellectual and cultural sophistication also associated them with the French cultural elite. Cherfi never hid his aspiration to belong to the more articulate and educated segment of the French population, and often sought to use his politicized songs as a means to attain recognition in this area (Marx-Scouras, 2005, p. 74; Lebrun, 2007, p. 334). His lyrics, for instance, showed off his 'high' cultural capital by their frequent references to France's most revered novelists (Voltaire, Hugo, Saint-Exupéry), even paying homage to that most emblematic of French books, the *Robert* dictionary (Seery, 2001, p. 22). Unlike Rachid Taha, who parodied *chanson* artists, Zebda willingly paid homage to 'quality' singer-songwriters, including Georges Brassens and Nougaro. Although Cherfi disagreed with Nougaro on certain points (see above), he referred to him as the artist he

---

30   '... des socialistes à l'extrême-gauche, il y a un vaste terrain sur lequel on peut s'impliquer' (in Cyran, 2000, p. 11).

31   '... renouer avec la politique, le sérieux et l'engagement' and 'foutre le bordel', interviewed by Daniel Mermet for 'Là-bas si j'y suis', *France Inter*, 5 December 2000.

would most like to emulate, as the epitome of musical and poetic refinement (Aubel, 1999, p. 64). Nougaro himself sought to use poetry to 'open up people's intelligence', and his song lyrics were published in the same 'Today's Poets' collection as Brassens, by the editor Seghers in 1974.[32] This, as Looseley (2003, p. 38) demonstrated, was one of the most evident signs of the inclusion of French music artists within an 'authentic' and prestigious national cannon. Zebda pursued this traditional form of legitimation, and certainly since releasing solo albums and publishing collections of short stories, Cherfi has become considered as a serious, successful poet (Jordana, 2004; Dahan, 2004).

The access of Zebda to an established form of popular culture was also evident in their choice of playing, and affirmation that they played, rock music ('we're evolving within a rock culture, ... I am not a rapper', Cherfi in H.M., 1992d, 33).[33] As we will demonstrate later (Chapter 5), a taste for rock music is, in France, typically the prerogative of a well-educated middle class, and *beurs* playing rock music are something of an anomaly. Because *beurs* tend to come from the least educated, least privileged sections of society, only a few of them actually developed a taste for or the inclination towards playing this music – and when they did, this was usually through friendships with non-*beurs*, as was the case for Cherfi. In the 1980s, it was common for *beurs* to be refused entry to white nightclubs, where pop and rock music were predominantly played, so they would attend 'alternative' clubs run by blacks and Antillais, where funk music, disco and later rap music, were played (Moreira, 1987, p. 40). As a result, many ethnic minority French ended up playing in rap groups, while only a few *beurs* 'integrated' into France's rock music culture. Taha and Cherfi both epitomized the exception to this tendency, their participation in a rock rather than raï or rap music culture signalling their access to the cultural tastes of the ethnic majority.

There is obviously no harm in this as such, and this trajectory is in fact typical of the most 'successful' cases of post-colonial integration in contemporary France. However, the problem here is that, in joining the club of French rockers, the group became caught up in the 'messiness' of maintaining a sense of authenticity, which was doubly complicated by their desire to also maintain a sense of ethnic difference. This ambiguity was harshly felt with the success of the single 'Tomber la chemise' ('Take your shirt off') in 1999. This song, by far Zebda's least political track, and originally appearing on a generally gloomy album (Marx-Scouras, 2005, p. 95), was a rock-steady number about dancing and having simple, physical fun. It was released as a single just before the summer, with the agreement of the artists, and its repetitive music and simple lyrics were excellently timed for a summer hit. To promote it, Zebda appeared on many prime-time TV shows, the song was broadcast on commercial radio, and it very quickly became number one,

---

32   Froissart and de Gaudemar (2004).
33   'On évolue dans le circuit rock, ... je ne suis pas un rapper'.

selling over 1.5 million copies (Santolaria, 2002, p. 9) and receiving the NRJ Music Award for Best Francophone Single in 2000.[34]

Rock music, as we have seen, thrives on its opposition to mainstream mediatization and 'pure' entertainment (Chapter 1), and Zebda's conflictual relationship with this code was demonstrated in their handling of the success of 'Tomber la chemise'. By contrast to the 'popular' authenticity sought by *néo-réaliste* artists, the kind of popularity Zebda achieved from 1999 onwards was not associated with working-class fraternity, cultural 'authenticity' or protest politics. Rather, since it resulted from an entertaining, non-political song, in which the group's habitual questioning of the place of ethnicity in France was markedly absent, and was broadcast relentlessly on all commercial media, the group lost their credibility for their existing 'serious' fans. Zebda's success suddenly affiliated them with 'mere' entertainers of *variété*, with conservative pop music. For the left-wing press that had, up until then, enthused about the political credentials of Zebda, the widespread success of 'Tomber la chemise' suddenly marked their downfall as serious artists, and commentators gradually rejected the group as 'chavvy' ['beaufisant'] (Renault, 1999, p. 31), narrow-minded and populist ['franchouillard'] (Barbot, 2002, p. 30).

Reluctantly, the members of Zebda were drawn into a debate about the potential loss of their 'authenticity'. The satirical radical-left weekly *Charlie Hebdo* ran a whole interview premised on the idea that mainstream exposure corrupted political integrity (Cyran, 2000). Elsewhere, the artists were asked to explain how they dealt with this misrepresentation of their protest identity on a mainstream and national scale (Renault, 1999, p. 32; Santolaria, 2002, p. 14; Barbot, 2002, p. 30). If, in these interviews, the journalists revealed their cultural prejudices as members of an intellectual elite, the artists' answers to these questions were interestingly subtle. On the one hand, they agreed that finding fame had crowned their aspiration to 'make it' and was a recompense for the many years spent struggling financially (Cyran, 2000, p. 10; Barbot, 2002, p. 30). They also considered that inflexible positions against mediatization were untenable, given that they had chosen to become professional musicians: 'As soon as one decides to play music within a commercial framework, it would be incoherent to reject all forms of television advertising' (Cherfi in Cyran, 2000, p. 10).[35] On the other hand, they sought to re-establish their original, broader political credentials, admitting for instance that their commitment in this song was 'not very far-reaching' (Renault, 1999, p. 32).[36] They also commented on its unrepresentative genesis: 'This song, we almost didn't record it. We didn't

---

34   The album from which it was taken, *Essence Ordinaire*, also fared well with over 600,000 copies sold (Barbot, 2002, p. 30), and Zebda received the Victoires de la Musique Award for Best Group in 2000.

35   'Dès lors qu'on accepte de faire de la musique dans un cadre marchand, ce serait incohérent de refuser la télé en bloc'.

36   'Sur cette chanson, notre démarche ne va pas très loin'.

like it', said the keyboard player Rémi Sanchez (Barbot, 2002, p. 30).[37] Zebda also insisted that the rest of their album was much darker, and found solace in the fact that it also sold well (Renault, 1999, p. 32; Barbot, 2002, p. 30). These remarks, elicited by journalists who implied that Zebda's authenticity had become diluted by fame, sounded like apologies at times, and revealed that Zebda suffered from rock culture's dominant, purist belief that commerce corrupts thought.

At the same time, the way Zebda dealt with their *beur* ethnicity also became problematic, since the group's only large-scale national success had been a song in which ethnicity was irrelevant. The unproblematic insistence of 'Tomber la chemise' on singing and dancing, delivered with a heavy Toulouse accent, now followed the superficial celebration of *métissage*, as the perception of ethnic minority for the public was now only present, and unquestioned, in the name of the band and the faces of its singers. This also confirmed Cherfi's dreaded perception that 'Arabs' could only be tolerated and successfully mediatized in France if they 'sang about the desert and exoticism' (Sorgue, 1998).[38] By contrast, all the other politicized songs of Zebda, which reflected on integration and Arabness in sophisticated terms, had failed to reach no.1 and to make a profound impact on France's mainstream culture. In a 2002 interview for the state-sponsored radio station France Inter, Cherfi and Moustapha Amokrane explained that they had aspired to be at once 'popular and refined' ['large et fin'], and to stand at the junction between 'consensus and anger' ['consensus et colère'].[39] This subtle approach to popular music, however, had proven impossible to achieve. Managing mainstream success ultimately proved impossible for Zebda, and a few months later they split.

Zebda's access to national success is thus a complex story, and not simply a symbol of empowerment. On the one hand, the group demonstrated that French mentalities had changed since, at last, at the very end of the twentieth century, 'Arab' artists could achieve visibility in the media and commercial success on a large scale. Their success was certainly noteworthy in the sense that it went beyond that afforded to *beur* artists within rap music. None of the biggest stars of French rap in the 1990s, including MC Solaar, NTM or the frontmen of IAM, were *beurs*.[40] On the other hand, it sadly confirmed the ossified state of cultural and political conventions in the country. Zebda's mainstream success of 1999 only

---

37   'Cette chanson, on a failli ne jamais l'enregistrer ... . Elle ne nous plaisait pas'.

38   '... un pays qui tolère les Arabes lorsqu'ils chantent le désert et l'exotisme'.

39   Interview by Pascale Clark for 'Tam Tam Etcetera', *France Inter*, 2 October 2002.

40   The mainstream success of raï stars in France, such as Khaled, Cheb Mami and Faudel, only serves to confirm Cherfi's perception that 'Arabs' are only tolerated if they sing 'Arab' (in this case, Algerian) music, thereby reinforcing existing cultural stereotypes. Faudel's endorsement of conservative politics was also evident in 2007, when he attended the concert organized in support of the election of the new right-wing President Sarkozy (see Chapter 5).

seemed possible because this was a group of *beur* artists showing their compliance with republicanism's general rule of assimilationism. In the group's only number one hit, 'Tomber la chemise', their Arabness had become completely invisible. Besides, their sudden access to mainstream mediatization also revealed the sharp intransigence of the rock music sector, for whom a momentary lapse in the group's commitment to politically conscious music, through the release of just one 'fun' song, constituted an unforgivable transgression. Zebda were certainly a longer-lasting group than Carte de Séjour, although not on account of their hybridity, Arabness or contestatory power, and participation in France's 'authentic' popular music culture was denied to them in the long-term. The following chapter continues the examination of these difficulties, this time looking at what happens when French 'protest' music encounters commercial success abroad.

Bibliography

Aubel, François (1999), 'Zebda: le chant des partisans', *L'Evénement du jeudi*, 15 April, 62–5.

Balibar, Etienne, Monique Chemillier-Gendreau, Jacqueline Costa-Lacoux and Emmanuel Terray (eds) (1999), *Sans-papiers: l'archaïsme fatal* (Paris: La Découverte).

Barbot, Philippe (2002), 'Zebda: "Pas des rebelles à trois sous"', *Télérama*, 2744, 16 August, 30–2.

Barbot, Philippe and Christian Sorg (2001), 'L'été sera Chao', *Télérama*, 2681, 30 May, 72–4.

Barnel, Jeff (2005), *Dalida, la femme de cœur* (Paris: Editions du Rocher).

Bhattacharyya, Gargi, with John Gabriel and Steven Small (2002), *Race and Power: Global Racism in the Twenty-First Century* (London and New York: Routledge).

Breatnach, Mary and Eric Sterenfeld (2000), 'From Messiaen to MC Solaar: music in France in the Second Half of the 20th Century', in William Kidd and Siân Reynolds (eds), *Contemporary French Cultural Studies* (London: Arnold), 244–56.

Cassavetti, Hugo (2007a), 'Les Rita Mitsouko', *Télérama*, 2986, 4 April, 14–18.

Cole, Alistair (1998), *French Politics and Society* (Hemel Hempstead: Prentice Hall).

Cyran, Olivier (2000), 'Zebda: "Y'a pas d'arrangements avec la télé"', *Charlie Hebdo*, 397, 26 January, 10–11.

Dahan, Béatrice (2004), 'Livret de famille (suite)', *Empan*, 56 (4), 170–71.

Dicale, Bertrand (2006), *La chanson française pour les nuls* (Paris: First Editions).

Dirlik, Arif (1994), 'The Post-Colonial Aura: Third World Criticism in the Age of Global Capitalism', *Critical Inquiry*, 20, 328–56.

Ervine, Jonathan (2008), 'Citizenship and Belonging in Suburban France: The Music of Zebda', *ACME. An International E-journal for Critical Geographies*, 7 (2), May, 199–213.

Froissart, Alain and Antoine de Gaudemar (2004 [1974]), 'Nougaro: "Je suis un négro-grec"', *Libération Hors-Série*, 'Chanson française, 1973–2006: paroles, musiques et polémiques', 6–9.

Fysh, Peter (1998), 'The Failure of Anti-Racist Movements in France, 1981–1995', in Mairi McLean (ed.), *The Mitterrand Years. Legacy and Evaluation* (Basingstoke: Macmillan), 198–214.

Garapon, Paul (1999), 'Métamorphoses de la chanson française, 1945–99', *Esprit*, July, 89–118.

Gastaut, Yvan (2006), 'Chansons et chanteurs maghrébins en France (1920–1986)', *Migrations Société*, 18 (103), 105–15.

Gildea, Robert (1994), *The Past in French History* (New Haven and London: Yale University Press).

Gilroy, Paul (1993), *The Black Atlantic. Modernity and Double Consciousness* (London: Verso).

H.M. (1991b), 'Mano deluxe', *Rock & Folk*, 290, October, 42–3.

H.M. (1992a), 'La Mano Negra. Amerika Perdida', *Rock & Folk*, 293, January, 78.

H.M. (1992b), 'Les Négresses Vertes. Famille nombreuse', *Rock & Folk*, 293, January, 79.

H.M. (1992d), '7 à Toulouse (Zebda)', *Rock & Folk*, 302, October, 32–3.

H.M. (1992e), 'Négresses with Attitude', *Rock & Folk*, 303, November, 56–9.

Hakem, Tewfik (1999), 'Métèque et mat', *Les Inrockuptibles*, 206, 7 July, 40–41.

Hargreaves, Alec (1997), 'Multiculturalism', in Christopher Flood and Laurence Bell (eds), *Political Ideologies in Contemporary France* (London and Washington: Pinter), 180–99.

Hargreaves, Alec (2007), *Multi-Ethnic France. Immigration, Politics, Culture and Society* (London and New York: Routledge).

Hargreaves, Alec and Mark McKinney (1997), 'Introduction', in Hargreaves and McKinney (eds), *Post-Colonial Cultures in France* (London and New York: Routledge), 3–27.

Howarth, David and Georgios Varouxakis (2003), *Contemporary France. An Introduction to French Politics and Society* (London: Arnold).

Huq, Rupa (2006), *Beyond Subculture. Pop, Youth and Identity in a Postcolonial World* (London and New York: Routledge).

Jarno, Stéphane (1999), 'Les gringos parigots', *Télérama*, 2567, 24 March, 66.

Jordana, Huguette (2004), 'Livret de famille', *Empan*, 56 (4), 169–70.

Lebrun, Barbara (2002), 'A Case Study of Zebda: Republicanism, *Métissage* and Authenticity in Contemporary France', *Volume!*, 1 (2), 59–69.

Lebrun, Barbara (2007), 'Le bruit et l'odeur… du succès? Contestation et contradictions dans le rock métis de Zebda', *Modern and Contemporary France*, 15 (3), August, 325–37.

Leclère, Thierry (1999), 'Zebda, les chanteurs de la contestation festive', *Télérama*
    2566, 17 March, 31–2.

Liauzu, Claude and Josette Liauzu (2002), *Quand on chantait les colonies.
    Colonisation et culture populaire de 1830 à nos jours* (Paris: Editions
    Syllepse).

Lin, Zoé (2001), *Zebda 100% Motivés* (Paris: Agnès Vienot Editions).

Liperi, Felice (1988), 'Sound Waves from the Edges of the Empire: The Ethno-
    Wave', *Cultural Studies*, 2 (2), May, 247–50.

Looseley, David (2003), *Popular Music in Contemporary France: Authenticity,
    Politics, Debate* (Oxford and New York: Berg).

Loupias, Bernard (2001), 'Le retour du clandestino', *Le Nouvel Observateur*,
    31 May, 124–6.

Marx-Scouras, Danielle (2004), 'Rock the Hexagon', *Contemporary French and
    Francophone Studies*, 8 (1), January, 51–61.

Marx-Scouras, Danielle (2005), *La France de Zebda, 1981–2004. Faire de la
    musique un acte politique* (Paris: Editions Autrement).

Mathis-Moser, Ursula (2003), 'L'image de "l'Arabe" dans la chanson française
    contemporaine', *Volume!*, 2 (2), 129–43.

McMurray, David A. (1997), 'La France arabe', in Alec Hargreaves and Mark
    McKinney (eds), *Post-Colonial Cultures in France* (London and New York:
    Routledge), 26–39.

Meouak, Mohamed and Jordi Aguadé (1996), 'La Rhorhomanie et les Beurs:
    l'exemple de deux langues en contact', *Estudios de dialectología norteafricana
    y andalusí* (EDNA), 1, 157–66.

Monnin, Isabelle (2000), 'Zebda: la colère en chantant', *Le Nouvel Observateur*,
    23 March, 10.

Moreira, Paul (1987), *Rock métis en France* (Paris: Souffles).

Mortaigne, Véronique (1998), 'Toulouse, capitale de la résistance musicale des
    quartiers', *Le Monde*, 8 November, 27.

Mucchielli, Laurent (2006), 'Les émeutes urbaines', in Xavier Crettiez and Isabelle
    Sommier (eds), *La France rebelle* (Paris: Michalon).

Negus, Keith (1999), *Music Genres and Corporate Cultures* (London and New
    York: Routledge).

Norot, Anne-Claire (1999), 'L'un dans l'autre', *Les Inrockuptibles*, 206, 7 July,
    42–5.

Pascaud, Fabienne (2007), 'Rachid Taha: "La France est un pays de plus en plus
    féminin"', *Télérama*, 2977, 31 January, 14–18.

Pinto, Diana (1988), 'The Atlantic Influence and the Mellowing of French Identity',
    in Jolyon Howorth and George Ross (eds), *Contemporary France: A Review of
    Interdisciplinary Studies*, vol. 2 (London: Pinter), 116–33.

Reijasse, Jérôme (2002), *Zebda, Guide Musicbook* (Paris: Prélude et Fugue).

Renault, Gilles (1999), 'Mouiller la chemise', *Libération*, 6 September, 31–2.

Rosello, Mireille (1998b), *Declining the Stereotype. Ethnicity and Representation in French Cultures* (Hanover and London: Dartmouth College/University Press of New England).

Saka, Pierre and Yann Plougastel (eds) (1999), *La chanson française et francophone* (Paris: Larousse/HER).

Santolaria, Nicolas (2002), 'Zebda. Les agités du vocal', *Epok*, 28, July–August, 9–14.

Seery, Mairéad (2001), 'Essence ordinaire de Zebda: carburant pour une République en panne', *The Irish Journal of French Studies*, 1, 15–24.

Silverman, Max (1995), 'Rights and Difference: Questions of Citizenship in France', in Alec G. Hargreaves and Jeremy Leaman (eds), *Racism, Ethnicity and Politics in Contemporary France* (Aldershot: Edward Elgar), 253–64.

Sorgue, Pierre (1998), 'Liberté, égalité, fraternité!', *Télérama*, 2548, 14 November, 15.

Tarr, Carrie (2005), *Reframing Difference. Beurs and banlieue Film-making in France* (Manchester: Manchester University Press).

Tinker, Chris (2005), *Georges Brassens and Jacques Brel. Personal and Social Narratives in Post-war Chanson* (Liverpool: Liverpool University Press).

Vandel, Philippe and Paul Rambali (1988), 'La java contre Le Pen', *Actuel*, 108, June, 105–15.

Verlant, Gilles (ed.) (2000), *L'encyclopédie du rock français* (Paris: Editions Hors Collection).

Vignol, Baptiste (2007), *Cette chanson qui emmerde le Front National* (Paris: Editions de Tournon).

Von Badaboum, Hermann (1999), 'Hasta siempre la techno', *Charlie Hebdo*, 350, March, 10.

Warne, Chris (1997), 'The Impact of World Music in France', in Alec Hargreaves and Mark McKinney (eds), *Post-Colonial Cultures in France* (London and New York: Routledge), 133–49.

Wolton, Dominique (2003), *L'autre mondialisation* (Paris: Flammarion).

Yee, Jennifer (2003), '*Métissage* in France: A Postmodern Fantasy and Its Forgotten Precedents', *Modern and Contemporary France*, 11 (4), November, 411–26.

Yonnet, Paul (1985), *Jeux, Modes et Masses* (Paris: Gallimard).

[22]

Don' Go Down Waikiki

Social Protest and Popular Music in Hawaii

George H. Lewis

"Hey brah," Israel Kamakawiwaole waves his arm in the hot dusky air. His huge brown fist, clenched with the thumb and little finger sticking out at right angles, looks like a smoked ham with horns as he wags it up and down in the Hawaiian-pidgin symbol of greeting.

A bearded man in a red T-shirt and jeans smiles and waves from the back of the club.

Israel settles his 350 pounds back in his chair on stage, picks up an electric ukelele in a fist that nearly swallows the instrument, and announces: "Dis song tell how them stu-u-pid *baoles* fight ovah land, when it not theirs to fight ovah. It ours, yeah!" Strumming quickly, and amazingly lightly on the instrument he holds captive in his huge hands, Israel leads his group, the Makaha Sons of Ni'i'hau, in his own pidgin-clever version of "Waimanalo Blues." The four voices blend sweet as a choir in the dark smoky air of the rough-cut Honolulu club.

The cultural counterattack, spearheaded by popular music and dance, is in earnest in Hawaii. Local people are teasing out and uncovering their cultural roots while, at the same time, they are emphatically rejecting the artificial "tourist culture" that has been developed, packaged, and sold on the Islands by outside (mainland American and, increasingly, Japanese) concerns, and has all but swallowed up Hawaiians in its implications.

Haunai-Kay Trask, a local Hawaiian rights activist, has explained: "Hawaiians look to the land as something to feed them. Westerners look at land as a commodity, to be exchanged for something else, for money, for profit-making. When you take the land away from Hawaiians, you've cut them off from who they are. What's the alternative? You want us to go dance in the hotels and keep prostituting our culture? Is that being Hawaiian? Don't talk to me about the aloha spirit. That was an invention of Arthur Godfrey."[1]

172/Rockin' the Boat

The last two decades have seen, in Hawaii, the cultural and political rebirth of native Hawaiians. No longer content to dance in the hotels of the tourist industry or to act like mainland-created caricatures of themselves, Hawaiians have rekindled a pride in their heritage and have sought out their own cultural traditions, from a revival of their ancient forms of dance—*hula kahiko*—to the renewed popularity of slack key guitar and traditional chanting styles in Hawaiian songs.

Reacting against the commercial gloss of the tourist industry and the expectations it has created in the Waikiki audience for artificial Hawaiian songs and dances, Island musicians in the past two decades have forged a musical movement in search of their own traditional roots and culture, reaching back to encourage and embrace the few ethnic artists still alive and performing—merging this material with their own pressing social and cultural concerns to create a new type of music—part contemporary, part traditional, and all layered with social protest critical of non-natives who Hawaiians see as having nearly destroyed their culture, their self-identity, and their sacred land.

The lyrics of one of these newly constructed popular songs, "Hawaiian Awakening," reveals the tone and thrust of this concern:

> Deep in this tortured land all alone
> Hear the winds cry, the mountains moan...
> We followed their rules much too long
> Our protests are heard in our music and song...[2]

Kaona: Social Protest and Hidden Meanings

Social protest has always been a part of Hawaiian music, but—as with many oppressed peoples—this social protest has been hidden from the ears of outsiders. In January 1893, *"Mele Ai Pohaku"* was written in protest of the contrived annexation of Hawaii to the United States. The song, considered sacred when it was written, affirms the Hawaiian intent not to sign the papers of annexation—"We will not sign the *haole's* [whites'] paper, but will be satisfied with all that is left to us, the stones, the mystic food of our native land."[3]

The song's title, translated from the Hawaiian, means "Stone Eating Song," and the lyrics speak of the "children (flowers) of Hawaii, ever loyal to the land," who will back Lili'u-lani as queen monarch—"she will be crowned again"—lyrics quite bitter and subversive in nature, if one considers the context of their creation. And yet the song—because it was written and sung in Hawaiian—could be understood by almost no English-speaking American in Hawaii. In addition, its message was disguised with a bright and gay melody. It could, therefore, be sung in most public places without much fear of *haoles* deciphering its content.

As the song became a popular staple of Hawaiian singers at the turn of the century, its name was changed to *"Kaulana Na Pua"* (Famous Are the Flowers).[4] This change meant the song's title could be translated for non-Hawaiians, and the whole thing could be passed off as a gay musical tribute to tropical flowers, produced, sung, and enjoyed by "happy-go-lucky" Hawaiians—even as its deep political meaning continued to be understood by native people.

This disguising of meaning is called *kaona* in Hawaiian, and is a traditional element of the culture, found to as great an extent in the new, pop-oriented music of today as it was in these turn-of-the-century songs. The *kaona* style is also evident in *"Ku'u Pua I Paokalani,"* a song written by Queen Lili'u-o-Ka-lani herself during her imprisonment by the Americans in the 'Io lani Palace, and which has been revived by the new singers of today. The song title translates as "My Flower At Paokalani," which was the name of the Queen's home and garden. In Hawaiian, *paokalani* means "fragrance of the royal chief——the first layer of hidden meaning to the song. Also, this is a name song *(mel inoa),* a traditional form in Hawaiian culture, that is said to have been dedicated to the son of Evelyn Townsend Wilson (though this was never admitted to), an intimate of the Queen who voluntarily went into imprisonment with her. Her son, John Wilson, smuggled to the Queen newspapers, which were banned, by wrapping flowers picked from her gardens in them and delivering them to the palace. And yet the lyrics to this quietly beautiful song literally refer only to "the gentle breeze" that "blows to me the fragrance of my gentle flower."[5]

Finally, today, the site of Paokalani is occupied by the concrete parking lot and high-rise form of a Holiday Inn—a fact not lost on local audiences, nor on the artists, such as George Helm, who have revived the song.

Such songs of social protest have been kept alive among the people and sung in community gatherings throughout this century. They have become the touchstone upon which a fragile thread of musical dissent has stretched—connecting people and generations—from that earlier time of oppression until the current musical explosion in Hawaii that has brought these themes out, vividly, into the open.

Tourism and the Invention of Commercial Hawaiian Music

As the United States took over formal power in the Islands via annexation, interest on the mainland in things Hawaiian began to catch fire. In 1912, the Broadway production of "Bird of Paradise," with its Hawaiian theme and pseudo-Hawaiian music, was the talk of the nation. And when a group of Hawaiian musicians, singers, and dancers—featuring George E.K. Awai's Royal Hawaiian Quartet—were headline acts at the Panama-

174/Rockin' the Boat

Pacific International Exposition in San Francisco in 1913, a musical craze
was born that was to sweep the United States and, later, Western Europe
as well.[6]

The early Hawaiian musicians—Awai, Frank Ferara, and Sol Hoopii
(who played background music for many Paramount movies)—inspired
mainland music composers, the Tin Pan Alley people, to begin writing this
sort of material for mass consumption. The result was a series of "phony"
Hawaiian songs, many with nonsense lyrics that were supposed to "sound"
like the Hawaiian language, such as "Oh, How She Could Yacki Hacki
Wicki Wacki Woo (That's Love in Honolulu)," a big hit across mainland
America in 1919.

The sexual suggestiveness of "Wicki Wacki Woo" was amplified in
songs that were pointedly degrading to the Hawaiian, such as Harry Owens'
"Princess Poo-Poo-Ly Has Plenty Papaya," which is not only racist and
demeaning to Hawaiian women, but also mocks the recently overthrown
Hawaiian monarchy in lyrics such as:

> The Princess Poo-Poo-Ly has plenty papaya
> She loves to give them away
> For all the neighbors, they say…
> Oh me, oh my, you really should try
> A little piece of the Princess Poo-Poo-Ly's papaya
> Ssa, sasa, sasa, sasa, say.
> She may give you the fruit
> But she holds on to the root
> Sasa, sasa, sasa, sasa say.[7]

At the time he wrote this song, Owens was band leader at the ballroom
of the newly opened Royal Hawaiian Hotel (the "Pink Palace") in Waikiki.[8]
Phony songs such as these, many of them written a continent and an ocean
away from Hawaii in New York City, only added fuel to the emerging
stereotype of native Hawaiians as lazy, happy-go-lucky, music-loving,
sexually promiscuous primitives who were only too happy to perform for
the civilized white mainlanders. Now, with Owens and others, these songs
were coming "home" to Hawaii, to entertain the growing number of
around-the-world cruise line tourists, and others, who were stopping
off—and staying—in the newly constructed Island hotels.

The first of these hotels, the Moana, was built in 1901 in the Waikiki
area, then primarily a marshy farmland where rice was grown and where
a few people had beach homes.[9] The Moana, a grand, five-story structure,
could be seen from all over Honolulu—the first of what was to become, by
mid-century, an urban nightmare of high rises catering to the mainland
tourist industry.

In its time, the Moana was a grand dame—tourists arriving by ship on
the Matson Line could stroll on the beach or be entertained in the hotel's

outdoor courtyard, shaded by an immense banyan tree. The tourists expected Hawaiian song and dance in the hotel, and they got it. Local entertainers, such as Frank Ferara and Pali Lua and his Bird of Paradise Trio would sing and strum gentle versions of Hawaiian tunes—as likely as not following arrangements made popular on mainland America, rather than in Hawaii.

In the early 1920s, an immense dredging and land-fill project in Waikiki displaced local rice growers and obscured several native religious sites, as it announced the conscious development of tourism as a major industry in Hawaii. Farms and rice paddies were replaced with white coral chip acreage. Later, sand would be hauled in and dumped, to create the famous beaches of Waikiki. In 1927, the Royal Hawaiian Hotel opened its doors—the first "resort concept" hotel of its kind—and tourists, traveling on world-cruise steamers, voted it "The World's Most Beautiful Hotel."[10]

As more hotels opened in Waikiki, commercial "Hawaiian" music seemed the natural sound for the stage shows and dance bands that sprang up with the tourist industry. Ragtime, jazz, blues, foxtrot—all were used in creating songs with Hawaiian themes, but with English lyrics and sensibilities. These *hapa haole* songs, played live in Waikiki and across the United States by touring bands, were broadcast throughout the world on radio programs such as the famous Webley Edwards-hosted "Hawaii Calls," as well as being featured in films such as Bing Crosby's 1937 *Waikiki Wedding,* (filmed entirely in southern California), from which the Harry Owens song "Sweet Leilani" won the Oscar for best song.[11]

This music, much of it commercially produced by non-Hawaiians, came to be defined as authentic Hawaiian music and was mistakenly assumed to represent and reflect the cultural identity of the people. Although the fragile tradition of authentic Hawaiian music was kept alive by some—mainly in the rural areas of the Islands—it was true, sadly, that even among Hawaiians themselves, many took on this "false culture" and the impact of its negative images of Hawaiians as part of their heritage. From 1930 and on into the 1950s, this "Hawaiian Sound" flourished commercially both on the American mainland (especially in the 1930s and 1940s) and in the lounges and supper clubs of Waikiki.

In 1959, the incorporation of Hawaii into the United States as a state and the increased ease of reaching the Islands via mass air travel intensified mainland interest in Hawaii. Middle-class tourist trade to the Islands heated up and was reflected throughout U.S. popular culture, in television programs such as *Hawaiian Eye,* books such as James Michner's *Hawaii,* and the infamous hula hoop craze. This new mainland interest was also reflected in the commercial music of the time, which added the "exotic" Island sounds of Martin Denny and Arthur Lyman (and Elvis Presley's "Blue Hawaii") to the commercial *hapa haole* standards of the 1930s and 1940s.

176/Rockin' the Boat

Completing the musical mix by incorporating into it the mainstream easy listening pop and country sound of the early 1960s, Don Ho and the Aliis, performing nightly at Duke Kahanamoku's, rapidly became the most popular act in Waikiki, playing such songs as "I'll Remember You," and the ever requested "Tiny Bubbles." With a mainland recording contract and hit songs that swept the easy listening American music market, Don Ho *was,* in the 1960s, Hawaiian music to most Americans. As the Don Ho Show became increasingly bloated with hoax and hype—middle-aged tourist women stepping on stage to be kissed by the entertainer and staying there to be taught, and dance, the "traditional" hula—many Hawaiians began to distance themselves from this spectacle that commercial Hawaiian music and culture had become. As Charles K.L. Davis, a noted traditional performer, said: "Hawaiian music is going right down the drain as far as Waikiki goes...it's a shame. Have you seen [Don Ho's] show lately? Awwwe! It's the most frightening thing I've ever seen...It was just dismal. God, it was awful! It's absolute amateur hour."[12]

Don Ho, in his turn, defended the show and its content and intentions: "I do it because people pay me a lot of money to do it...So what if the show's for tourists? What's wrong with tourists? I mean, why are local people so prejudiced against tourists?"[13]

The Creation of Popular Protest Music in Hawaii

That there was something new beginning to happen culturally and musically in Hawaii was evidenced by the decision, in November 1966, of a local radio station—KCCN—to broadcast Hawaiian music exclusively, 24 hours a day. Although a good deal of the available music was of the commercial, tourist variety, some of it was authentic, traditional, and "grassroots." This music was being made by a few artists, people like Genoa Keawe, Maki Beamer, Gabby Pahinui and the Sons of Hawaii, who were performing in the old styles and keeping alive a tenuous and fragile musical tradition—one that was supported mostly in rural and working-class, blue-collar Hawaiian areas and venues. This music, much of it programmed at first in order to fill the demands of 24 hours a day of programming, became, upon its exposure, increasingly popular with the more urban-oriented, socially conscious, and dissatisfied young Hawaiians who listened to this local station. As the station received feedback from this highly vocal audience, traditional Hawaiian music began to make up more and more of the playlist.

Due to pressure from the owners, in 1969 the station briefly entertained the idea of dropping the all-Hawaiian format, but abandoned its plans when it received 4,200 letters of opposition in one week's time.[14] In April 1971, KCCN sponsored a four-hour concert at the Waikiki Shell that featured over 50 local musicians, many of whom played traditional music in the old styles. The concert was a sell-out and a symbolic watershed in the resurgence of interest in authentic Hawaiian music.

Much of this interest from young Hawaiians who were searching for some sort of cultural roots resulted not only in their increasingly strong support of the few traditionalists who were still performing, but also in their own desire to play this music, to be a part of this tradition, and, soon following from this, to create new music within the old traditional forms. As Krash Kealoha, then station manager of KCCN, explained it in 1973:

> Up until that point [1970], we were playing old Hawaiian music and hapa haole tunes. Then several kids started talking to me, and it turned out they were disappointed because they were writing their own music and coming up with their own style, and some were even going into the studios and spending their own money—$5,000 or whatever it cost to produce a record. But when the record came out, it wouldn't get on any radio stations...At first there was a lot of resistance from our steady listeners [to us playing this new music], some of the older people who felt anything that wasn't sung in Hawaiian was rock and roll.[15]

KCCN, with its exclusive focus, became a key in dissemination and popularization of the new Hawaiian music, as well as a source of information about the music and the people who were creating it.

A second key to the launching of the new music was the interaction between an aging traditional singer from the poor town of Waimanalo, Phillip Pahinui (who died of a heart attack in 1980), and two young musicians, Peter Moon and Palani Vaughn. Pahinui, better known as "Gabby" or "Pops," had been active musically in the 1930s, '40s, and early '50s, playing mostly traditional music, though he was, at times, heavily influenced by mainland jazz and did play in the lounges of the tourist hotels early in his career. But his music had not been popular enough to base a career around, and he made his living working on street crews for the city of Honolulu. By the 1960s, he remembered: "I had just about given up, was working with the City and County then. The only time we'd play music was when we'd finish work on the road and sit down under a tree and strum."[16]

Peter Moon and others, attracted by Gabby's knowledge of the old songs and the techniques of slack key guitar playing, haunted him for lessons. As Moon said:

> Gabby is the truth master, the real thing. The old man down in Waimanalo with the chickens...He's just uncanny, he baffles us four or five times a year. He'll play slack key in these real old tunings, then smile at Cyril [his son] and me as if to say, "See, you didn't think I had it, did you."[17]

178/Rockin' the Boat

At the same time that Peter Moon was learning slack key guitar from
Gabby Pahinui, Palani Vaughn was seriously researching Hawaii's musical
past, looking for material upon which to build a career. Vaughn met Peter
Moon in a course on Hawaiian art history at the University of Hawaii, and
soon the two of them formed a band.

The Sunday Manoa, first recorded in 1969 and the most influential of
the new Hawaiian groups, originally consisted of Moon, Vaughn, Baby
Kalima, and two of Gabby Pahinui's sons, Cyril and Bla. Not only did all
these young musicians have a strong interest and grounding in traditional
Hawaiian music, they also had been extensively exposed to the popular
traditions of 1960s youth music and politics, from Bob Dylan to the Beatles.
Prior to his involvement with Pahinui, Peter Moon himself had gone to
school in the early- and mid-1960s on the American mainland, where he
soaked up the sounds of social change that were being created in American
and British music of the time.[18]

Adding some amplification and increasing the number of instruments
used, while experimenting harmonically, the Sunday Manoa developed a
style of playing that pleased most of the purists, but still attracted the
interests of the younger, pop-oriented listeners. Within a month of organizing in a garage in Waimanalo, the band landed a local recording contract
and was playing regularly in the Kahala area, in many of the same clubs
that were keeping Gabby Pahinui and other traditionally oriented singers
afloat. In addition, their recordings began to be aired on KCCN, and the
band began to attract a following. Their album *Cracked Seed,* recorded in
the early 1970s, sold nearly 30,000 copies in one year in Hawaii—a huge
number for a local band on a local label—showing that a band could remain
faithful to traditional music and also be an economic success in the Islands.

But, having said that, it is important to note that the music of the
Sunday Manoa was *not* traditional, acoustic Hawaiian folk music. It was
electric, with a jazz/rock thrust that put the group in the mainstream of pop.
As Peter Moon told an interviewer in 1972, who asked him why, when so
much traditional Hawaiian music was written to be played as ballads or at
hula tempo, did the Sunday Manoa play so many fast, up-tempo numbers.
Moon replied: "It was because we were in a club 75 to 80 percent of the
time. You've gotta sell drinks, you've gotta get the people going. We're pop
music, no matter what people say."[19]

With the success of the Sunday Manoa, there quickly came other bands,
intent on creating a new music of pop/rock through the late 1970s and 1980s
that touched both the dissatisfied urban youth of Hawaii and, hopefully, their
rural elders, who had kept alive the tradition of social protest against the *haole*
outsider that they were drawing upon for inspiration.

The new musical groups of this movement refused to continue the
tradition of "cute" group names of the hotel performers of the past, like the

Royal Hawaiian Serenaders or the Waikiki Beachboys—names that conjured up images of happy-go-lucky brown lackies of the Hawaiian films and nightclubs. Instead, they named themselves after Hawaii, the land: the Sunday Manoa, Ma Kapu'u Sand Band, Hui Ohana, Hokule'a, the Makaha Sons of Ni'i'hau.

This last group's name cleverly makes all the cultural connections of the new music. Makaha is an area near Honolulu that is poor, blue collar, and overwhelmingly native Hawaiian. Ni'i'hau is a small island that has resisted the cultural onslaught of the 20th century. The few native Hawaiian families who live there work the land in the old ways. There is no electricity, no running water. No one, not even the governor of the state, is allowed on Ni'i'hau without an invitation. Being "sons of" this island (which two of the group actually are) links them with the past and, at the same time, the land that means so much to Hawaiians.

The Sound of Social Change

This new music has had much in common with the music of many emergent social and cultural movements, performing ideological, motivational, and integrative functions for those who perform and listen to it. It is nationalistic and, above all, celebrates the traditions of native Hawaiians, in opposition and reaction to the cultural domination of the mainland United States and the entertainment needs of the booming tourist industry of the 1970s and 1980s.

An ongoing concern with the land is a theme strongly reflected in the lyrics of the new songs (such as *"E Kuu* Morning Dew," and *"Nanakuli* Blues")which celebrate the beauty of various Island places and lament their destruction by contemporary off-Island concerns, or the fact that the land—once Hawaiian—is now owned by foreigners who refuse to treat it with the care and reverence it demands. George Helm, a singer and activist who was lost at sea in 1977 while protesting against the U.S. military use of Kahoolawe Island as a practice bombing range, said in description of these new songs:

> Hawaiian views on nature are the subject of many songs and contain a true respect for nature. Many of the songs now openly express, if one understands the words, the language—pain, revolution; it's expressing the emotional reaction the Hawaiians are feeling to the subversion of their lifestyle—without the *aine* [land] and without the *aloha aina* [love of the land], we have nothing.[20]

The second major topic addressed in the lyrics of the new music is hostility toward the tourists and the U.S. military, and criticism of their impact on Hawaii in terms of land use, real estate development, and

180/Rockin' the Boat

bastardization and cooptation of traditional Hawaiian culture. Walter Ritte articulated this feeling in a 1982 interview:

> We have no control over the tourist industry. It's like a giant malignant cancer and it's eating up all our beaches, all the places that are profound for our culture. It's grabbing them. They take the best. You know, at least Captain Cook gave us a nail—one nail for three pigs and caskets of water. They're not even giving us the nail back.[21]

Songs dealing with tourism and its impact include Chip Hatlelid's "Fujumina Store," which chronicles the tearing down of an old landmark business to build a shopping complex, and Olomana's songs about the re-zoning of Kawela Bay and Turtle Bay in order that new resort hotels could be built. As Olomana's Jerry Santos said: "Nobody even knew about it…but if you sing a song…all kinds of people will know."[22]

A third strong theme in this new music is that of an urgent concern for preserving the traditional ways of Hawaii, and even the Hawaiian race itself. Songs such as "All Hawaii Stands Together" and *"E Na Hawai'i"* are eloquent in addressing this theme. As Palani Vaughn, who has written a number of these sorts of songs, has said of his work: "By the third album, the content got rather political, saying things like 'the race is dying, but we must survive.' In fact I've been called a racist, but my answer is the Hawaiian race is a dying one and I don't find it a crime to foster its survival."[23]

Finally, these songs—in their messages and in the traditional instruments that are many times used in playing them—consciously attempt to connect themselves to that thin and fragile line of social protest in Hawaiian music that, since the time of annexation, had been kept alive mainly in the rural areas by a handful of respected artists. George Helm would always begin his concerts with the Hawaiian phrase *He punahele no 'e na Ka makua,* which translates to "You are the favorite of the generation before." In his choice of material, Helm (who, after his death, was elevated to the status of martyr by the movement) relied heavily on songs written in the first half of this century by native Hawaiians—songs that, in their fragile, rural voices, spoke out against the destruction of Hawaiian culture. He called these songs Hawaiian soul. As his close friend 'Ilimia Pi'ianai'a observed:

> George came to understand the political activism, the crying hurt and the unspoken dignity of the Hawaiians of the 1920s, the 1930s and the 1940s through these songs, which were very dear to him…a connection that flowered in his generation, in the movement he was a big part of.[24]

The Music, the Movement, and the Tourist Industry

From the mid-1970s on, this new, politically aware Hawaiian popular music was heard—not only on radio stations such as KCCN, but also at meetings and gatherings of the people. When the Hawaii Coalition for Native Claims held fundraising concerts on the 'Iolani Palace lawn, Hawaiian musicians, singers, and dancers performed from nine in the morning, non-stop, until dusk. When there were skirmishes with land developers, when demands were made for long-promised Hawaiian homestead lands, when the H-3 freeway drew fire from environmentalists, when protesters occupied the small island of Kahoolawe to protest its use as a bombing target by the U.S. military, the music was there, articulating an ideology of protest and opposition to the dominant, mainland controlled political and economic culture of the state.

By 1978, the movement—and its music—had brought enough pressure to bear that the Office of Hawaiian Affairs was created and official attention was paid to issues of education and land tenure at the State Constitutional Convention. The leader of that convention, John Waihee, called the new music of the movement the "glue that held this package together." In addition, Hawaiian was officially recognized, along with English, as a language of the state.

And yet, even as it proved effective in mobilizing cultural and social protest in Hawaii, this new music was popular far beyond the boundaries of these social movements. Peter Moon and the Sunday Manoa could sell 30,000 to 40,000 copies of their albums in this relatively tiny consumer market, sandwiched as it is between the world's two largest music markets—those of the United States and Japan. Songs such as Moon's reggae-tinged "Guava Jelly" and the wildly exciting "Cane Fire" (which documents with indelible Vietnam-tinged images the irresponsible burning of the cane fields—dark smoke obscuring the sun, poor native kids running to escape the flames, the helicopters of the establishment roaring above the inferno) shot to the top of the pop charts in Hawaii, and were clearly heard—and purchased—by some of the tourist trade, as well as by many local people who were not at all directly involved in the activist part of the movement. In fact, as contradictory as it may sound, there are those who speculate that without the tourist industry and the market it created in Hawaii, there could likely have arisen no strong musical and cultural movement to oppose it.

KCCN, the radio station that first aired the new music, did so in order to fill air space—space that was sold commercially primarily because of the tourist population of Honolulu and Waikiki. In addition, the studios and recording technology necessary to record the new music was already available and in place because of the on-going and lucrative business of recording tourist-oriented music for souvenir-type albums and cassette tapes.

182/Rockin' the Boat

As far as exposure of new acts goes, Peter Moon and the Sunday Manoa first broke into the urban Honolulu scene (from the more rural club dates they had been playing) at Chuck's Cellar, located underneath Don Ho's Polynesian Palace in the glittering heart of the tourist district. And Millie Fujinaga, a Japanese hotel manager who ran a Waikiki nightclub called The Noodle Shop, is generally credited by the new music community as having done as much, or more, than anyone in first bringing local Hawaiian musicians together. Moe Keale, a musician of the movement, said of Fujinaga: "Besides bringing Hawaiians together, she also keep us Hawaiians working."[25]

George Kanahele of the Hawaiian Music Foundation has claimed:

> Tourism has been good to Hawaiian music. It has created a vast new market; it has helped to discover and encourage new talent; it has inspired new songs and new styles of playing; and, above all, it has provided jobs to Hawaiian musicians. In a sense, the tourist industry is the grand patron, albeit a very impersonal one, of Hawaiian music.[26]

And, although they do not like a lot of what they have to do, a good number of the musicians of the movement do play some gigs in the tourist centers, in order to keep food on the table and also to stay in the music business.[27] Gabby Pahinui spoke of the feeling when "you have the right atmosphere with some old folks dancing. But when you go into a place with chandeliers and candles, you…have to play songs like 'Blue Lei,' and 'Sweet Leilani.'"[28] And Peter Moon has pointed out that "Hawaiian musicians adopt these other styles because they have to, in order to make a living. But you can only compromise so much."[29]

As Hawaiian music and culture moves into the 1990s, the compromises have taken on still another twist. As could have been predicted, by becoming as popular and as visible as it did in the 1980s, the new Hawaiian music has also become marketable in the tourist industry, especially to the younger professional mainland crowd who remember the 1960s and musical protest, and are in the market for consuming "authentic" culture. As Peter Moon has said, "People are interested now more in the real, the grass roots. And the recording industry is a very powerful media…A lot of people are looking at us…at slack key…like people are looking at reggae. The industry's always looking for something new, every hour of the day."[30] The Brothers Cazimero, originally a part of the Sunday Manoa, have been lured to the Monarch Room of the Royal Hawaiian Hotel, where they perform their "authentic" Hawaiian music for those tourists who want to experience the *real* Hawaii. Tickets for the annual concert of traditional Hawaiian music, *kanikapila,* are obtainable in the tourist agencies of Waikiki and in the major hotels. Hui Ohana, a popular movement band that had broken up, reunited in 1987 for a Waikiki Shell concert and reunion album that won them a *Ma Hoku Hanohano* Award—an honor created in 1977 by

KCCN radio and awarded annually by the Hawaii Academy of Recording Arts. Traditional slack key guitar styles, resurrected by movement musicians were fused with U.S. mainstream pop by Keola and Kapono Beamer to create the hit, "Honolulu City Lights," a bouncy tune that became the most popular Island song of the 1980s.

As the 1990s dawn, reggae-inspired Island music has become the latest "new" sound—likely inspired by Peter Moon's 1982 hit "Guava Jelly," which mixed Jamaican rhythms and Hawaiian images. Moon himself recently has reached back to Tin Pan Alley to record "Stardust," although he has not given up his commitment to songs of social protest. "Chinatown," on the same album as "Stardust" looks at what has happened to that area of Honolulu. "You can smell hell burnin' in times like these," he sings, as he paints pictures of gang wars, run-down tenements, and old men "living from a tin can."[31]

Conclusion

And yet, no matter how hard the culture industry tries to co-opt Hawaii's new music, the fact remains that change—political, social, and cultural—occurred in Hawaii in the 1980s in no small part due to the efforts of these artists and the effects of their music. The motivating force of any cultural renewal is stronger identity, greater self-esteem, pride, and dignity. Ultimately, these qualities become goals that can only be fully realized in the market place and in the arena of political power. Some of this is difficult to measure, but, in Hawaii, it does exist.

As George Kanehele saw beginning to happen in the late 1970s, Hawaiians are coming together far more now than they ever did before the advent of the movement—at hula competitions, musical concerns, political gatherings, and church meetings. The specific political gains made—such as the declaration of Hawaiian as an official language of the state, and changes in the allocation and tenure of Hawaiian land for native Hawaiians—are tangible and hard-won. But, in addition, this coming together has led to a spirit of awareness, of self-identity and pride—which, in turn, is reflected in the new music. This feeling of social solidarity and ethnic and cultural pride, awakened by the movement and nurtured by the music, is a force that now has to be taken seriously in the politics and culture of Hawaii.

Israel Kamakawiwaole finishes the smoky blues, sung in Hawaiian, with a flourish. "Someone tell me some *haoles* in dis place," he says with a grin, rolling his eyes. There's a laugh from the audience. "Poor *haoles,* don' unnerstan' dose Hawaiian words," Israel shakes his head sadly, "Hey, I got it," he says brightly. "You guys, you go down Waikiki. You unnerstan' *all* the words down there, yeah!" As the audience claps and whistles its appreciation, Israel says softly, "You unnerstan' us soon enough."

Notes

1. Hauni-Kay Trask, "Interview," *Honolulu Star Bulletin*. November 7, 1982. P. C-9. Arthur Godfrey was well-known for his 1930-1940s radio shows that featured artificial, tourist-orientated "Hawaiian" music and his own ukulele playing.

2. Debbie Maxwell, "Hawaiian Awakening." Caleb Music, 1976. Translated from the Hawaiian, as are several other lyrics of the "new" Hawaiian music that are quoted in this essay.

3. Ethel Damon, *Sanford Ballard Dole and His Hawaii*. Palo Alto, CA: Pacific Books, 1957. p.317.

4. Samuel Elbert and Noelani Mahoe, *Na Mele o Hawai'i Nei*. Honolulu: University of Hawaii Press, 1970. p.63.

5. Ibid. p.72.

6. George Awai, "Interview," *Ha 'Ilono Mele*, Volume 3, No. 8. 1977. pp.5-6.

7. Harry Owens, "Princess Poo-Poo-Ly," Royal Music Publishers, 1935.

8. Harry Owens, *Sweet Leilani*. Pacific Palisades, CA: Hula House, 1970.

9. De Soto Brown, Hawaii Recalls: Selling Romance to America. Honolulu: Editions Limited, 1982. p.96.

10. Ibid. p.99.

11. Interestingly, Crosby felt that "Sweet Leilani" (named for Harry Owens' little daughter) was the *only* authentic song in the film. Crosby had met Owens while on vacation in Hawaii and had learned the song from him. When he came back to Hollywood to do *Waikiki Wedding*, all the songs had been written by mainland composers and were ready for him to sing. He insisted on inserting "Sweet Leilani" and was at first turned down. Only by threatening to walk out on the production did he force the producer to include Owens' song.

12. Charles E.K. Davis, "Interview," in Robert Kamohalu and Burt Burlingame, Eds., *Da Kine Sound*. Honolulu: Press Pacifica, 1978. p. 93.

13. Don Ho, "Interview." *Honolulu*, Volume 15, No. 9. 1982. p.50

14. Krash Kealoha, "Krash Kealoha Tells Why He Left KCCN." *Ha 'Ilono Mele*, Volume 7, No. 4. 1981. pp.1, 6-8.

15. Ibid. p.7.

16. Gabby Pahinui, "Interview," in Robert Kamohalu and Burt Burlingame, 1978. p.21.

17. Peter Moon, "Moon Bridges Gap." *Ha 'Ilono Mele*, Volume 3, No. 2. 1977. p.7.

18. Jerry Hopkins, "Slack Key and Other Notes." *Hawaii Observer*, No. 123. 1978. p.22.

19. Peter Moon, "Interview." *Ha 'Ilono Mele*, Volume 3, No. 3. 1977. p.2.

20. George Helm, "Language-Pain Revolution." *Ha 'Ilono Mele*, Volume 3, No. 6. 1976. p.3.

21. Walter Ritte, "Interview," *Honolulu*, Volume 15, 1982. p.68.

22. Jerry Santos, "Olomana Interview," *Da Kine Sound*. Honolulu: Press Pacifica, 1978. p.47.

23. Palani Vaughan, "Interview," *Honolulu*, Volume 12, 1979. p.149.

24. 'Ilimia Pi'ianai'a, "Liner Notes," on *Music of George Helm*. Honolulu: Gold Coin Records # G.C. 1001.

25. Hopkins, 1978. p.21.

26. George Kanahele, "Hawaiian Renaissance Grips, Changes Island History." *Ha 'Ilono Mele*, Volume 5, No. 7. 1979. pp.3-4.

27. George H. Lewis, "Beyond The Reef: Role Conflict and the Professional Musician in Hawaii," *Popular Music* 5. Cambridge: Cambridge University Press 1985. pp.189-198.

28. Pahinui, 1978. p.21.

29. Peter Moon, "Interview," in Kamohalu and Burlingame, 1978. p.22.

30. Ibid. p.42. moon knew what he was talking about in 1978. In 1982, he experimented with reggae rhythms on songs like "Guava Jelly," and by 1991, the Hawaiian/Reggae sound had become the "new hot thing" on the Hawaiian pop charts.

31. Peter Moon, *Chinatown*. Kanikapila Record #KC 1003, 1986.

[23]

MUSIC AS PROTEST STRATEGY: THE EXAMPLE OF TIANANMEN SQUARE, 1989[1]

Valerie Samson

During the spring of 1989, the capital city of the People's Republic of China became paralyzed by demonstrations that brought the nation to the brink of civil war.[2] At that time I was studying at the Central Conservatory of Music in Beijing, only a fifteen-minute bicycle ride from Tiananmen Square. The music students and I were able to participate in, observe, and document the events as they unfolded. My role as both an American and a student enhanced my status with demonstrators, enabling me to spend many hours in the square and on the streets of Beijing recording extensively with a video camera. Until the invasion on June 4, I enjoyed unprecedented freedom of movement, even under martial law at the end of May, but my activities were more noticeable because I was a foreigner. This put me at risk, eventually resulting in my arrest and the confiscation of my camera as well as two videotapes.

The speed at which the population became politically activated astonished even veteran China-watchers. The period from the catalytic event of Hu Yaobang's death[3] on April 15 to the military invasion of Beijing on the night of June 3 was only seven weeks. As a major feature of the demonstrations in Beijing, music contributed to this dramatic transformation. Singing or chanting could be heard wherever people congregated in large groups. Protesters sang children's songs, Communist party songs, folk songs, popular songs, and at least one theme song from a television program.

In spite of the ubiquitous use of music, its importance to the protest movement during this time was not obvious to many observers. One reporter wrote that the demonstrators in April appeared to be out on the streets simply enjoying a holiday rather than protesting (Shapiro 1989a:74). Even student leader Wuer Kaixi remarked later that the students were more interested in their

[1]This paper was written as a special studies project with Professor Ali Jihad Racy at the University of California, Los Angeles. Generous funding for research in Beijing, 1988–1989, was provided by the Committee for Scholarly Communications with the People's Republic of China. I thank the students and people of Beijing for their encouragement and help. I also thank Professor Bonnie Wade at the University of California, Berkeley for her advice in preparing a shortened version for presentation at the meeting of the Association for Chinese Music Research in Chicago, 1991.

[2]According to Consul General Zheng Wanzhen, in a statement to the U.S.–China Peoples' Friendship Association, March 18, 1990, in San Francisco. The last name is given first according to Chinese practice.

[3]Hu Yaobang, formerly the general secretary of the Chinese Communist Party, was respected as sympathetic to intellectuals.

popular music than in the ideas of reformist intellectuals (Feigon 1990:186).

Yet music was a significant factor in politically arousing protesters to such a degree that they increasingly engaged in risky behavior. By the beginning of June, protesters openly printed political fliers in the square, affixed posters in broad daylight, and broadcast propaganda to the soldiers. It was not only the young men in the "Dare To Die" squad who became willing to sacrifice their lives, but also countless ordinary citizens of all ages.

The role of music in political protest has been studied in a number of world contexts and interpreted in many ways. Many of these studies have focused on song texts or musical style. Marty (1988), Greenway (1960), and Watson (1983) have shown that textual content contributes to the political value of songs, expressing political sentiments either directly or indirectly through symbolic language. In her study of revolutionary song in China, Ferguson demonstrates that musical style contributes to political value. For example, the use of dotted rhythms, melodies based on chordal harmonies, and loud dynamics helps ensure that songs are motivational and memorable (Ferguson 1979:51).

However, the political impact of music heard in Beijing during the spring of 1989 was far greater than what one might expect from examining either musical style or textual content alone. There was no obvious connection between the musical or textual content of some songs and the ongoing struggle. It appeared that almost any kind of music could have value as political protest depending on the circumstances of performance. The effectiveness of music as a protest strategy appeared to depend on aspects beyond musical and textual content.

Blacking makes several observations concerning the political value of music in South African churches that relate to the situation in Beijing. He notes that singing promoted a black collective consciousness that church members could not express in words. "Music is non-referential and sensuous, and no claim can be made that it is directly political. But some music can become and be used as a symbol of group identity, regardless of its structure" (Blacking 1981: 35). Of great political importance is the ability of the performer to adapt to the context of performance: "Singing required constantly creative decision-making, as congregations adapted their model for performance to the unique character of every social situation, and...it enhanced rather than anesthetized political consciousness" (Blacking 1981:51).

This paper describes some of the many contextual and performance factors that contributed to the efficacy of music as a protest medium in Beijing, 1989. My observations at Tiananmen Square suggest that Blacking's statements have validity when applied to other political struggles around the world and that creative adaptation in performance enhances the political value of many kinds of music. Indeed, performance process and context are critical in establishing the power of music as a protest strategy.

Because of the dramatic growth of the political movement over a short period of time, I present my observations in roughly chronological order. My discussion focuses primarily on the chanting and singing of student demonstrators; the struggle for control of the sound-space at Tiananmen Square; music and the Goddess of Democracy; the invasion of Beijing on June 3 and 4, 1989; and the use of the "Internationale."

THE CHANTING AND SINGING OF THE EARLY DEMONSTRATIONS (APRIL 23 TO APRIL 30)

On the morning of Hu Yaobang's funeral, April 23, a thousand or so students sat and chanted in Tiananmen Square so that the officials at the Great Hall of the People would hear them. They had marched for hours during the night and had waited patiently all morning without access to bathrooms or drinking water. The area had been sealed off by more than a hundred police at 7 A.M. to keep people away from the funeral service, but the students had already installed themselves in Tiananmen Square. As the officials climbed the steps to the hall around 10 A.M., the students chanted: *"Aiguo wu zui"* ("Patriotism is no crime"), and *"Li Peng duihua!"* ("Li Peng talk with us!"). The chanting generated a momentum of its own, like the steady lapping of waves on a shore. The chanting consisted of short phrases of texts, recited rhythmically but without specific pitches, usually delivered in a call-and-response format. Using a bullhorn or simply cupping a hand and yelling, the leader would chant the first half of a phrase, pause for the group to repeat it, then continue with the second half. The chanting was well-coordinated and clearly audible, but once the government-controlled loudspeakers started emitting funeral music, it was virtually impossible for the students to make themselves heard. The repeated dirge forced the students to stop chanting and effectively told them that the officials would not listen to them.

On April 27, the university students staged their first daytime march in Beijing. Leaving their campuses early in the morning, students literally walked all day, circulating around town, sporadically chanting and singing. The authorities inadvertently gave a great boost to the movement by refusing the students access to Tiananmen Square that day. By continuing to march around the city, the students disseminated their ideas to a wider audience than if they had settled in the square.

Most chants consisted of a phrase divided into two parts of four syllables each. Some rhymed: *"Fandui ponei, aiguo wu zui"* ("Oppose internal persecution, patriotism is no crime"); others did

not: *"Guojia xing wang, pifu you zi"* ("The common man is responsible for the rise and fall of the country"). Where the chant consisted
of only four syllables, it was recited in its entirety, for example, *"Li
Peng wan sui"* ("Long live Li Peng"),[4] and *"Renmin wan sui"*
("Long live the people"). Sometimes longer chants were performed.
The leader decided whether the completed chant would be repeated
before the introduction of a new phrase, or whether it would be repeated at a later time.

The streets were lined with people who had come out to observe
and encourage the marchers. Naturally the students directed their
chants at these bystanders, especially the press. At the beginning of
the march and again at several places along the way, the students
encountered uniformed police and soldiers. Wherever there were
soldiers present, the students directed their chanting at them. On
the west side of town I heard the chant *"Renmin jundui ai renmin,
renmin jundui baohu renmin"* ("The people's army loves the people, the people's army protects the people"). Just east of Tiananmen
Square, along the Avenue of Eternal Peace, the students cheered,
waved, and broke into song when they saw the large groups of soldiers there. They explained to me that the song they sang was from
a popular television program about an undercover policeman who
followed his conscience rather than his orders.

Each group of marchers consisted of students from one school or
one department within a school. The identity of each group was
clearly displayed on banners, and members of the group had strict
control over who could march with them. In order to keep a digni-
fied front, the students in the first row of a group usually linked
their arms or held onto a long school banner. The sides of the group
were maintained by students holding hands, creating a human wall
that kept out intruders. Chant leaders were normally situated in the
protected area within this human wall. In the early days of the
demonstrations, most women marched within the protected area as
well. On later marches more women maintained the edges of their
groups. Eventually few groups bothered with the protective hand-
holding.

The students took the advice of their university teachers, who
had warned them to stick together while demonstrating. Chant unified groups of students, reinforcing audibly what was evident visually. Everyone present in a group participated. Only the chant leaders were responsible for the content of chants, and because they often composed these chants in advance, erratic interjections were
kept to a minimum. Through uniformity of expression, group
chanting provided safety. At the same time, the call-and-response
format encouraged the more timid students to find their voices by

---

[4]Li Peng, protégé of respected former premier Chou Enlai, currently serves as
premier of the People's Republic of China. On this early march, students solicited
his support.

giving them words to repeat. Both men and women initiated and led chants.

At the beginning of the movement, chant leaders avoided expressing strong, impulsive feelings, but as the conflict intensified, the chants became more daring, such as those calling for Premier Li Peng's resignation. The stronger the solidarity with the citizens of Beijing, the more the student groups dared to chant criticism of the government, yet this criticism was mild in comparison with the speeches and interjections made by individuals. In the absence of group chant, individuals expressed a much broader range of content and feeling.

Throughout the demonstrations singing was a common group activity. A conscious effort was made to insure that participants knew how to sing a few important songs. By the end of April, several scores with words to political songs had been posted outdoors on the walls of buildings at Beijing Normal Teachers College. One poster listed the titles of four important songs: the "Internationale"; the National Anthem by Nie Er;[5] "Tuanjie Jiushi Liliang" ("Unity is Strength");[6] and "Gong, Nong, Bing Lianhe Qilai" ("Workers, Farmers, and Soldiers Unite").[7] The scores in cipher notation and the lyrics, often including several verses, were written out on other posters. In addition, there were scores and lyrics of a few other songs: "Zhengqi zhi Ge" ("Song of Healthy Atmosphere"); "Ru Huo Gui Qingchun" ("Like Fire, Youth Returns"); and even "Blowing in the Wind" with lyrics in both Chinese and English. Scores like these, along with a plethora of political writings and cartoons, were posted on the walls of buildings at various local colleges. All day students copied these works into their notebooks, photographed them, or read them into tape recorders. By night, new material was posted.

In cases where there was more than one version of the text of a Communist song, demonstrators typically sang the earlier version. Most song lyrics that were changed during the Cultural Revolution were restored after the deaths of Chairman Mao and Zhou Enlai (Ferguson Rebollo-Sporgi, pers. com. 1992) so this preference was not unusual. To my knowledge, no one questioned the choice of the older texts, yet, as in the case of the National Anthem, the difference between the newer and older text was sometimes significant. The original version of the National Anthem, written by Nie Er as the theme song for a movie in 1932 and adopted as the national anthem in 1949, made no mention of the Communist party:

---

[5]The National Anthem is published in *Chairman Mao, You are the Unsetting Red Sun in Our Hearts* (Anon. 1977:1–2,4).

[6]There are two settings of this text: One uses the melody of "Glory, Glory, Hallelujah" from "The Battle Hymn of the Republic" and simply repeats the words of the title. The second setting uses additional text by Mu Hong with music by Lu Su, composed in 1944 (Wang 1986: 494 , 651).

[7]This song is published in 1956 (Wang 1986: 115).

> Arise, people unwilling to be slaves! With our blood and flesh, con-
> struct our new Great Wall. The Chinese people have arrived at the
> most perilous time, each person must urgently give his last cry!
> Arise! Arise! Arise! Ten thousand as one mind, risk the enemy's fire,
> advance! Risk the enemy's fire, advance! Advance! Advance![8]

The lyrics published in 1978 mention both the Communist party
and Chairman Mao, and delete the reference to the threat of slavery:

> March on, brave people of our nation! Our Communist party leads us
> on a new Long March. Million as one, march on, towards the
> Communist goal! Build our country, guard our country! We will work
> and fight. March on, march on, march on! For ever and ever, raising
> Mao Tse-tung's banner, march on! (Reed 1985: 112)

By singing the original version of the National Anthem,
protesters projected a strong plea for action without making a direct
statement against the Communist leaders.   According to one
Chinese student, the National Anthem "got resonance from the
people" (Zhou, pers. com. 1991) because of its call to defend the nation and its historical importance during the Japanese invasion.

The obvious high spirits of the students on their first daytime
march of April 27 did not detract from the effectiveness of the
demonstrations. Many young women wore their best clothes in order to make a good impression. Even if the protesters' good sports-
manship and ready sense of humor masked their seriousness of
purpose, their audacity in demonstrating at all acted as a vital stimu-
lant to the people of Beijing. Within a few weeks, at least a million
people a day would demonstrate on the streets of Beijing. The early
marches thus had political consequences far greater than the actions
and attitudes of the students seemed to warrant.

THE CHANTING AND SINGING AT TIANANMEN SQUARE AND AROUND THE CITY DURING THE HUNGER STRIKE (MAY 13 TO 19)

From May 13 through May 19, both the students and the general
population of Beijing became extraordinarily vocal. The hunger
strikers sang, chanted, and played instruments, while visitors to
Tiananmen Square sang to entertain them. Several different cho-
ruses performed special programs to crowds seated in the square.
Accompanied by an accordion, two women circulated among the
buses housing the fasters, singing for each small group in an intimate setting. As the fast continued, sympathetic city people chanted,
sang, beat out rhythms, and played recorded music as they

---

[8]My translation from *Kangri Zhanzheng Gequ Xuanji (Selected Songs from the War
of Resistance against Japan)* (Anon. 1957:12).

demonstrated on the streets. Most supporters were young, but many older workers also marched, chanted, and sang.

It seemed to me that certain songs were performed only by particular groups of students and workers. For example, only artists, musicians, and dancers sang the song "Women Dou Shi Meishujia" ("We Are All Artists"). Art and music students seemed to gloat aloud in their rendition of this song, making up their own lyrics but always ending in "*Bu huijia*" ("We won't go home"). Some students smiled when they sang this song, others could not keep from laughing. They seemed to derive great satisfaction from proclaiming their unity and defying the authorities to make them go home.

May 19, 1989, Beijing: "Artists are sick and tired of performing the disgraceful schemes of the officials" ("Qiong yishujia yan jin taishang qun chou tu").

While sitting in Tiananmen Square on May 15, the art students sang "San Da Jilu Ba Xiang Zhuyi"[9] ("The Three Main Rules of Discipline and the Eight Points for Attention"), appearing highly amused by the politically-correct lyrics of this People's Liberation Army song: "We must be polite when we're speaking to the masses, Respect the people, don't be arrogant...Get rid of all habits decadent" (Ferguson 1979:93). This text outlined exactly what the protesters were criticizing in the current regime.

Students from the Traditional Music Conservatory often sang a hilarious and lively rendition of the call-and-response song "Ho! Hei!" Originally a Gansu folk song, it was transformed into an

---

[9]This is the third song in the book *Zhandi Xin Ge* (Anon. 1972). For a translation, see Ferguson 1979:93.

Eighth Route Army song in support of the War of Resistance against Japan. Instead of singing the army's verses, the students made up their own: "For freedom, let's *ho! hei!* For democracy, let's *ho! hei!* We all arise, so *ho! hei!* We're not afraid, so *ho! hei!*" The refrain *"ho! hei!"* was accented as if accompanying the motions of work, reflecting the original folk song (Wong, pers. com. 1990). During the hunger strike, the students who sang this song always included a verse thanking the fasters. Sometimes verses were made up on the spur of the moment in response to a particular event. With the arrival of dancers at the square on May 15 the artists sang: "For the dancers, let's *ho! hei!* Let them in, so *ho! hei!*" This verse caused an outburst of laughter. Leaders sometimes repeated a phrase of the song. While entertaining the fasters on May 16, one student leader rhythmically shouted the phrase *"jiu shengli!"* ("victory!") in the song "Ho! Hei!" until the crowd of participants had worked up to a frenzied state of excitement. Repeated over and over, it elicited pulsating body-motion in the crowd and an outburst of cheers and applause afterwards.

At Tiananmen Square, and elsewhere around the city, people often used well-known tunes as carriers of new texts. The tune of "Frère Jacques," for example, was given the new words *"Dadao guandao"* ("Fight for the fall of the government"). The origin of the music did not seem to be as important as the familiarity of the melody. Well-known melodies could be adapted with new words and quickly taught to demonstrators.

Protesters usually limited their musical material to familiar melodies, including some recent songs, although newly composed songs were not considered to have the impact of older, more established material. Newer songs such as "Hand in Hand We Stand" and "Blood-Stained Glory" had clear political associations, and to my knowledge, no new texts were sung to the melodies of these songs.

By May 18 even school-aged children were participating in the demonstrations around Beijing. The youngsters I observed asserted their independence without disrespect for their elders. The children from the Central Conservatory of Music would not chant what their elders suggested they chant, showing independence from any authority regardless of political orientation. They insisted on complete control over the form and contents of their chants, which differed from those of the older students in several ways. The chants were in shorter fragments. The leader would give the first two syllables and the group would answer with the last two or three. For example, a boy about 10 years old might start with *"Gongren"* ("Workers") followed by the group with *"Wan sui!"* ("Long live!") This lack of repetition made the chants seem shorter. The young leaders generally could not keep the attention of the group for more than a few chants and the orderliness of the group easily deteriorated into noise-making.

Children showed less restraint than adults in expressing themselves in chant. The thrill of self-expression seemed to outweigh
their intent to communicate the textual meanings of their chants.
These 8-to-12-year-olds were the only demonstrators I heard who
dared name Deng Xiaoping in a chant, and they did so with reckless
humor. Despite the occasional daring content of their chants, their
purpose was less to shock than to please their audience, and they
maintained respect for the bounds set for them by their elders.
When their teachers forbade them to march, they complied.

THE STRUGGLE FOR CONTROL OF TIANANMEN SQUARE (MAY 13 TO JUNE 2)

With the beginning of the hunger strike and continuous occupation of Tiananmen Square on May 13, conflict between demonstrators and officials escalated, manifesting itself as a struggle for control
of the sound-space at the square. The fact that both sides wanted to
use the sound-space for their own ends suggests that both sides recognized the importance of auditory communications in achieving
political goals.

When I arrived at the square at 5:20 A.M. on May 15, patriotic
Mao-era band music was already emanating from the official loud-
speakers. It was still dark, but even at this hour, small groups of
fasters were marching around the square for their morning exercise.
Instead of listening to the broadcast, the students sang as they
walked. One tired-looking group sang the "Internationale," a
Communist anthem that appeared to be the most popular song in
Beijing during this period. A group of students from the
Traditional Music Conservatory sang a folk song with new words.
Often more than one group of students would sing simultaneously,
either different songs or unsynchronized renditions of the same
song.

The students attached loudspeakers to poles to amplify announcements, speeches, and live performances of songs.
Microphones helped singers lead call-and-response songs involving
the participation of large crowds and helped them compete with the
official broadcasts. Eventually the students disabled many official
loudspeakers and the People's Liberation Army reportedly shot out
the student loudspeakers.

Judging by volume, one reporter concluded at the end of May
that the students were overpowered by the government broadcasts
(Bernstein 1989). Another reporter pointed out that superiority in
volume was not a measure of success because the students ignored
these broadcasts:

> The sound of Tiananmen Square was not like any other sound. It was
> a mix of oppressive government loudspeakers that never stopped

> blaring and as many as a million human voices speaking individu-
> ally and freely. Often the government loudspeakers were louder,
> but people no more cared that the propaganda was so loud than
> they cared that the afternoon sun was so hot. In the midst of all
> that blare you could hear people laughing and singing. Very
> clearly, way over on the other side of the square, you could hear a
> little megaphone emitting Beethoven's *Ode to Joy*. (Allman
> 1989:230)

Most people, young and old, expected the broadcasts and performances at Tiananmen Square to be important to them. They
brought cassette tape recorders to the square to record speeches, live
performances, and even other people's private conversations. Their
desire to document the aural and visual environment of the square
was sometimes passionate. When pop singer Hou Dejian and three
other celebrities began their fast on the afternoon of June 2, many
amateur photographers held cameras high over their heads and
clicked their shutters without even looking through the viewfind-
ers. At their peril, crowds climbed whatever was available as they
jockeyed for good viewing positions.

Since Tiananmen Square held up to a million people during the
demonstrations, the occurrence of multiple, simultaneous events
was common. In the latter part of May, the result resembled a performance of John Cage's multi-media performance piece *Circus*, in
which the audience wanders around a space defined by booths of
various events lined up side by side. In this case the events unfolded at each tent, and the sounds from many loudspeakers mixed
and spread over the crowds. While chaotic, the effect was highly
stimulating. Students were not always aware of whether broadcasts
were official or not, and moreover, did not always seem to care. If
they felt the broadcasts were important, they would ask each other to
quiet down.

The audience and the performers were mobile, often changing
places. We heard a variety of instruments, including the *dizi*
(Chinese flute), an amplified plucked instrument resembling a
yueqin (short-necked lute), guitars, and accordions. Battery-powered
bullhorns were used to play simple tunes, by pressing different but-
tons for different pitches. During the latter part of the hunger strike,
ambulance sirens sounded sporadically day and night.

The environment in the square was also visually saturated with
banners, posters, drawings, and many kinds of art works. Students
wrote on and wore costumes made from cloth, paper, plastic, and
straw.

Activity was everywhere. Long chains of students holding hands
rapidly crossed the square; young men climbed high on each other's
shoulders to adjust banners on poles. Shortly after the beginning of
martial law, students flew balloons and a Mickey Mouse kite over
Tiananmen Square in an attempt to discourage attack by helicopter.
Tents were continuously being put up, repaired, or improved. Large

groups marched; food and beverage delivery wagons inched through the crowds. The net result was a kind of hum:

> The sound of Tiananmen Square periodically would change pitch in such a way that from a hundred yards you could tell something new was happening. Most of the time it was a soprano hum that, even through closed windows, said, Everything is still O.K. Then the pitch would drop and you'd know immediately to rush to the balcony. Sometimes the pitch would change in a way you didn't so much hear as feel, and on those occasions you didn't run to the balcony. You ran right out of the room, out of the Beijing Hotel, up Chang'an, so as to get to Tiananmen Square as fast as possible. (Allman 1989:230)

The stimulating aural and visual environment promoted intense feelings. Greater risk-taking behavior was observable at this time. Crowds gathered in front of the official residence at Zhongnanhai to kick symbolically towards the main gate during their morning exercises, and commentators speaking to large crowds on the square made scathing remarks, no longer wishing Li Peng a long life. In addition to risk-taking, there were many manifestations of generosity, trust, and kindness between strangers. The Chinese press noted that pickpockets must have gone on holiday because crime was practically non-existent. Vendors no longer tripled their prices when they saw me coming and housewives pressed homemade dumplings into my hand. On the night of May 19, I heard reports of a wedding ceremony in the square.

THE DEMONSTRATIONS DURING MARTIAL LAW (MAY 20 TO JUNE 3)

Singing and chanting continued in a wide variety of contexts during the period of martial law. Around 1 A.M. on the first night of martial law, I arrived at Gongzhufen, on the west side of the city, to find a huge, impromptu chorus sitting in front of a convoy of parked military vehicles. The group was so large that three conductors were coordinating its singing of the "Internationale." A full moon and the floodlights of television cameramen provided the necessary lighting. The soldiers on duty had no choice but to listen to the songs being sung to them by protesters.

In Tiananmen Square itself, large crowds coordinated their singing by broadcasting with microphones and loudspeakers. This was especially useful at night when visibility was poor. Choral groups both at Tiananmen Square and on the streets of Beijing often used multiple conductors, regardless of musical need. Many wanted to conduct not only music, but also traffic. Volunteers sometimes claimed an intersection or a stretch of road and gave hand signals well into the night.[10]

When I visited the square later in the day on May 20, a group of sports students who had just ended their hunger strike beckoned me to their bus. Smiling broadly, they immediately sang "Wo Ai Beijing Tiananmen." The text of this well-known children's song expressed the common cultural and political experience the students shared: "I love Beijing, Tiananmen, the sun always rises on Tiananmen, our great leader Chairman Mao leads us forward." The ironic circumstance of performance appeared to give these students great satisfaction. By singing the Communist doctrine they had been taught as children while physically present in Tiananmen Square, the students validated their defiance of the current regime.

Another group of sports students sang a popular song with lyrics that seemed to reflect their plight: "Stay awhile, there's too much I haven't said." The leader smiled as he sang and put his arms around a classmate. During the period of martial law, people often sang and chanted with their arms around one another. Following the song, the leader gave a short speech denouncing Premier Li Peng. He continued smiling as if no political topic could erase the good feelings he had just experienced in singing with his peers.

During martial law, the students sang several songs important in the history of the Chinese Communists. Accompanied by a guitar, youngsters atop a bus at Tiananmen sang "Nan Ni Wan," from the period when the Communists were establishing themselves in Yunnan Province (Zhou, pers. com. 1991). While marching into Tiananmen Square at dawn on May 22, the group of young men calling themselves the "City People's Dare To Die Squad" sang the National Anthem. Within the human wall formed by the men holding hands, one young man raised his arms high over his head and, smiling as if amazed by his own confidence, jubilantly proclaimed that he was not afraid.

On the afternoon of May 18, demonstrators drove a large truck displaying a huge likeness of Mao Zedong very slowly past the square while broadcasting a stately instrumental rendition of the "Internationale." In keeping with many other references to Chairman Mao during this political movement, the slow tempo afforded respect and honor to the immortalized leader whose embalmed remains rest in a mausoleum in Tiananmen Square itself. The students were ambivalent about Mao's status, but some of the older workers clearly cherished his memory. On May 19 a sign on the side of a truck full of demonstrating workers stated "Chairman Mao lives forever in the hearts of the people."

---

[10]The increase in traffic directing may have been an attempt to prove that the demonstrators were orderly: "It was obvious to even casual observers that the municipal government had ordered traffic police withdrawn from the center of the city, in what seemed a deliberate effort to show that the demonstrators were bringing disorder to the city" (Barmé 1991: 42).

Each night for about a week the students expected a military invasion of the square before dawn. Because it was difficult to sleep under the threat of violence, they intermittently sang patriotic songs, performed slowly and with emotion. The paced renditions of the "Internationale" in the darkness seemed to be a way of confirming vows and praying for justice. They seemed to calm nerves and fortify resolve, maintaining the spirits of the protesters, just as afternoon naps helped maintain their bodies.

THE GODDESS OF DEMOCRACY (MAY 29 TO JUNE 3)

On the evening of May 29, students from the Central Academy of Art ceremoniously erected a ten-meter plaster statue of a woman holding a torch in the north part of Tiananmen Square. They named her the "Goddess of Democracy." The event was solemnized by music and spectacle. By the time I arrived in the square around 7 P.M., student guards had sectioned off a large area. They controlled the pressing crowds by chanting "*Yi, er, zuo xia!*" ("One, two, sit down!"). As the students erected the scaffold in preparation for the arrival of the segments of the statue, their broadcast system played J. S. Bach's chorale *A Mighty Fortress* and a choral piece by Handel. Once the scaffold was in place, a student climbed to the highest horizontal pole to hang a basket of flowers. Then the young men raised school flags and the national flag to fly at the top. With the arrival of the four statue segments after midnight, the crowd cheered victoriously and a group of young people burst into song. Barely audible above the cheering, it was the "Internationale." The students continued to broadcast the Bach chorale from a small tent well into the night as the men on the scaffold labored to raise the segments of the statue without the help of machines. To coordinate their pulling and pushing, the men chanted together. By the time the first segment of the statue, the head, was in place, many people in the crowd were in tears.

The repetition of the Bach chorale during the raising of the statue accented the seriousness of the event by giving it a solemn aura. The rhythmically unified chorale style seemed to proclaim the unity and strength of the people, while the "mighty fortress" reference may have symbolized the indomitable will of the Chinese masses. While I did not speak directly with the person who chose this music to discuss its intended effect, it seemed to me that through music the people claimed the mandate of heaven to self-rule, and with the raising of the statue, they inaugurated themselves. This was a very emotional experience for observers and participants alike.

According to a report by participant Tsao Hsingyuan, the unveiling ceremony the next day was accompanied by music:

> As these "veils" fell the crowd burst into cheers, there were shouts
> of "Long live democracy!" and other slogans, and some began to sing
> the "Internationale." A musical performance was given by students
> from the Central Academy of Music: choral renditions of the "Hymn
> to Joy" from Beethoven's Ninth Symphony, another foreign song and
> one Chinese, and finally the "Internationale" again. (Han 1990:
> 347-8)

Celebrations continued day and night at the foot of the statue
with a wide variety of performances, both planned and unplanned.
All performances took place facing north towards Mao Zedong's
portrait on Tiananmen Gate, with the statue also facing north and
serving as a backdrop. I observed many kinds of vocal and instrumental music; drama, in the form of story-telling and comedy;
dance; and martial arts. Performers were mostly young, ranging in
age from kindergartners to men in their forties.

Among the planned musical performances were traditional instrumental pieces, Communist songs, children's songs, Western and
popular songs, and songs with new lyrics written especially for the
occasion. One child sang a song with lyrics in English: "Happy New
Year!" A mixed chorus singing in unison rehearsed off to the side
of the statue, then took up a position in front of it to perform.
Unplanned performances involved audience participation. Anyone
present might be asked to get up and perform, regardless of ability to
sing or play. Like the flowers and plants that had been offered to the
Goddess at her base, the performances appeared to be offered with
love and respect.

Their faces glowing with pleasure, audiences at the statue responded enthusiastically to all the performances, including the
Communist songs. Mistakes and imperfections sometimes elicited
laughter, but never derision. The children's musical contributions
seemed especially effective. One listener mentioned that he fer-
vently wanted the demonstrators to succeed for the benefit of the
children.

During the time the Goddess of Democracy reigned over the
square, the students named one of their loudspeaker systems the
"Goddess of Democracy Broadcast Station." This was controlled by
young women in a small red tent near the statue. In the quiet early-
morning hours of June 2, the Goddess of Democracy Broadcast
Station played the Largo movement of Handel's *Xerxes* and other
Western classical music as swallows chirped and soared above
Tiananmen Gate. The square seemed bathed in a calm serenity detached from time and place.

Besides confronting Mao Zedong's portrait, the strategic place-
ment of the Goddess facing north allowed all traffic on the Avenue
of Eternal Peace to pass under her gaze and receive her symbolic
blessing. Those who performed at her feet not only received her
blessing, but temporarily became her voice.

By modeling the statue of the Goddess of Democracy somewhat after the Statue of Liberty,[11] the young students implied that their ideals were rooted in the long history of another civilization. The repetition of the Bach chorale and the Handel piece enhanced the link to the West. At the same time, the Goddess of Democracy was distinctive enough to show that the students were not simply mimicking Western concepts of democracy. Many observers have remarked on the statue's use of both arms to hold up her torch. Besides the obvious implications of fragility, this variation from the Statue of Liberty was a statement of individuality, demonstrating that her creators were fully prepared to make their own decisions.

By allowing diverse people to perform, the student organizers showed that they were willing to cooperate with others outside their immediate group. This acceptance of a wide variety of musical styles echoed the attitudes of participants in the black South African churches:

> Performance of their church music was the chief sign of their commitment to the Zionist way of life, and it occupied much of their spare time, but their appreciation and performance of other musical styles reflected their view that they were not an exclusive in-group so much as a community that encompassed all walks of black African life. (Blacking 1981:51)

In Beijing, the performance of patriotic music was often a clear sign of commitment to the student movement, but protesters also appreciated and used many other kinds of music. By accepting songs of diverse origins, including the Communist songs, the protesters showed that the Goddess of Democracy accepted the voices of all who came to her. Enhanced by audience participation, these performances were auditory realizations of the abstract concept of democracy.

Even though the morale of the people was already high after the statue was completed, the performances raised it even higher. They helped create a celebratory mood at the statue, counteracting the pall of anxiety that had hung over the square since the beginning of martial law on May 20. Live performances and broadcasts added to the fragile illusion of peace and security around the Goddess, providing relief to the many city people who visited the square, as well as to the students who had written their wills and night after night risked violent eviction from their encampments.

Besides raising morale, performing and attending performances at the statue channeled energy that otherwise might have caused trouble during the tense period of martial law. Participation in these activities was a harmless way to pass the time while waiting

---

[11]According to Tsao Hsingyuan, the Goddess of Democracy was modeled after the statue *A Worker and Collective Farm Woman*, by Russian revolutionary realist Vera Mukhjina (Tsao 1989:16), yet the resemblance to the Statue of Liberty was unmistakable.

for a resolution to the brewing conflict. On the other hand, many students had tired of the demonstrations by the end of May. If the statue and the events at the statue had not given them a focus of interest, many more might have given up and gone home.

The Military Invasion of Beijing (June 3 and 4) and the Aftermath

Although martial law went into effect on May 20, applying only to the inner districts of the city of Beijing, it was not until the night of June 3 that the army made a determined assault on the city. Many people at different locations around Beijing used music and chant as a way of coping with the crisis of this military invasion. People of all ages, from infants to the elderly, both male and female, were on the streets that night. At first, people had difficulty believing that the army was shooting its way into Beijing and joked about it. They argued about which gunshots were blank and which were real bullets and scrambled to collect spent shells as souvenirs. They applauded when the windows popped out of their burning buses at Fuxingmen and yelled *"Hao!"* ("Good!") when tires exploded with a bang. These buses had been set on fire by the city people to block the road. As the severity of the situation became more apparent, some young men yelled insults at the soldiers or threw bricks or Molotov cocktails. In an effort to maintain order and reduce the danger to individuals, an older man at Fuxingmen, west of Tiananmen Square, instructed the agitated crowds to chant as one voice. Shortly after midnight a great number of male and female voices rose up together out of the darkness and repeated the question: *"Ni shi shenma jundui?"* ("Whose army are you?") to the soldiers as they passed by. This amorphous group thus reminded the soldiers that the People's Liberation Army was never intended to be used against the people. The call-and-response pattern of chanting was still employed, but the leader's role seemed less prominent. Probably for safety reasons, the leader's voice was loud enough for only those in the immediate vicinity to hear. Chanting like this allowed people to address the soldiers without drawing attention to themselves as individuals. Under cover of darkness, the disembodied sound seemed to float up from many directions. Anonymity was complete. I heard one man chant an earlier favorite, "The people's army loves the people, the people's army protects the people," but he did so quietly and to himself.

Around two o'clock in the morning just east of Fuxingmen, a group of young and middle-aged men walking their bicycles followed a battalion of foot soldiers eastward down the Avenue of Eternal Peace towards Tiananmen Square. Sometimes they sang; sometimes they chanted. Normally they ducked behind their bicycles when the soldiers turned around to shoot, but on one blood-chilling occasion they were in the midst of vigorously singing the "Internationale" when the soldiers began shooting. Instead of duck-ing, the men held their ground and kept singing in spite of the ma-chine gun fire. The song continued as if nothing could stop it, trans-fixing the listeners standing on the sidewalk, myself included. Nobody retreated. After this incident was over, the crowd contin-ued towards Tiananmen Square, putting itself at risk regardless of the violent tendencies of the soldiers. I learned later that this was not an isolated event, but that others witnessed similar singing. According to Shapiro's report in the *New Yorker*, which quotes ob-server Peter Thompson:

> "I think the most awful moment came when [the confrontation] reached a point a couple of blocks west of the square, just north of our building, and we could hear really large groups of people singing 'The East is Red'—an old Maoist anthem—and the 'Internationale,' and then we could hear the machine guns, and then the crowd would begin singing again." The "Internationale" was sung by Beijing Normal Teachers College students, who linked arms and marched forward in an insane and terribly courageous attempt to block the armored column at Xi Dan. Two hundred were later reported killed. (Shapiro 1989b: 84)

Patrick Finley quoted Tsao Hsingyuan in *The Monthly*: "We held each other's hands and sang the 'Internationale' and walked toward the soldiers. I forgot who I was. I forgot where I was. I followed the people" (Finley 1989: 21).

According to excerpts of a report by student leader Chai Ling, there was singing in the Square that night:

> At this time, megaphones inside the headquarters tent and loud-speakers outside played the song, "The Descendents of the Dragon" [a popular song about the Chinese race by Hou Dejian]. Our class-mates sang along with the music, their eyes welling up with tears. Everybody hugged each other and held hands, for each person knew the last moment of his or her life had arrived, the moment had come to sacrifice our lives for the Chinese people....The students be-gan singing the "Internationale"; over and over they sang it, hands clasped tightly together. (Han 1990: 363-4)

The "Internationale" and a few other songs helped the people meet their most urgent needs during this time of crisis. The value of singing the "Internationale" was so great that many protesters took no further measures besides singing this song to save their lives during gunfire or while approaching the soldiers. Through song, the protesters dramatically demonstrated the strength of their faith in non-violent methods.

Immediately after June 4, all public performances of music, dance, and drama in Beijing were canceled by authorities, reducing opportunities for self-expression. Even three weeks after the inva-sion professional dancers and musicians still could not perform in public. A dancer explained to me that for safety reasons no one wanted to be out at night anyway. Yet even daytime performances were temporarily discontinued. Elderly Peking Opera musicians who usually gathered at a small grassy spot west of Fuxingmen dispersed during the time soldiers were camping on the north side of the street. On the other hand, some outdoor performances of music still took place. While soldiers kept vigil nearby on the evening of June 24, an informal band played tango music outdoors in Binhe Park on the west side of Beijing. Anyone who wanted to dance could do so, and many did, although the students in my group just sat on a retaining wall and watched. After June 4, individuals generally refrained from singing while out in the street. Humming a patriotic song while approaching a military roadblock at night was considered to be far more dangerous than allowing small children to point their toy guns at the soldiers.

On June 5 a clock tower on the Avenue of Eternal Peace continued to chime out the melody of "The East is Red" even as the avenue lay quiet in ruins below. Army vehicles had torn up some of the ornamental trees, the tanks had chewed up the pavement and crushed the cement lane dividers, many vehicles were still burning, and the rubble of destruction brought all but military traffic to a halt. As if this scene were not painful enough, a reminder of the lyrics of the third verse of this song added insult to injury: "the Communist Party is like the sun/Bringing light wherever it shines/Where there's the Communist Party...there the people win liberation."

THE "INTERNATIONALE"

More than any other song, the "Internationale" characterized the protest movement in 1989. It was heard so often and in so many different contexts that it seemed to fill every possible role. The "Internationale" originated in France after the fall of the Paris Commune. The text was written by Eugene Pottier in 1871; Pierre Degeyter composed the music in 1888. Sung by the proletariat of the late nineteenth century, it then served as the national anthem of the Soviet Union from 1917 to 1944. Translated into Chinese first in 1920 in France, and then again in 1923 in Beijing, the "Internationale" was revised by the People's Republic in 1962 for the following role:

> To unite in struggle the world's proletariat and revolutionary people, to overthrow the system of exploitation, to use one's own strength to liberate one's self, and to be the bugle call for the struggle to realize Communist theory. (Wang 1985:137, my translation)

It survived the Cultural Revolution's purge of European music because of its role as "the emblem of the rise of proletarian music"
(Kraus 1989:173).

The "Internationale" strengthened the fragile position of the
protesters by referring to past Communist struggles around the
world. Used by the Chinese Communist Party for more than half a
century, the "Internationale" was given the most prominent position in a book of more than one hundred political songs in 1977.[12]
By singing a song with such high political status among the
Communists, the people suggested that they were the true inheri-
tors of the revolutionary spirit, and that their actions were patriotic
and reasonable. This helped validate their purpose.

The lyrics of the "Internationale" promoted solidarity. The first
verse and refrain translate roughly as:

> Arise, poverty-stricken slaves; Arise, suffering people of the world;
> Full of seething hot blood, struggle for the truth! The old world
> passes like falling flowers and flowing water; slaves arise, arise!
> Don't say we have nothing, we can become the masters of the world.
> [refrain] This is the ultimate struggle, unite and arise until tomor-
> row. Heroes calling forth endurance will definitely succeed. (My
> translation)

The Chinese characters "*Yingtenaxiongna*," transliterated from
the title "Internationale" in the last phrase of the refrain, can also be
loosely interpreted to mean "International Communist theory will
definitely become a reality throughout the world" (Anon. 1972: 2).
On the other hand, a middle-aged Chinese-born composer (Wong,
pers. com. 1990) told me later that the lyrics "*Yingtenaxiongna*" referred only to the name of the song and had no other meaning. It is
possible that the words in this phrase were less important than the
allusion to the early days of struggle.

The importance of the "Internationale" during the crisis of June
3 and 4 can be explained in many ways. Its performance had an impact on both singers and audience. It is almost certain that the soldiers heard and recognized the "Internationale," although what
meaning it had for them is not clear. In any case, the song did serve
to identify the people to the soldiers, letting them know that the
"*baotu*" ("hooligans") their officers had warned them against were
in fact citizens with ideals inherited from the Chinese Communist
Party founders. The protesters apparently had confidence that the
soldiers would not want to hurt their own people. This confidence
was still evident in the first weeks after the invasion when mothers
held up their babies for soldiers to admire and middle-aged men

---

[12]*Mao Zhuxi Nin Shi Women Xinzhong Bu Luo de Hong Taiyang (Chairman Mao,
You are the Unsetting Red Sun in Our Hearts)* (Anon. 1977). The high status of the
"Internationale" has not been continuous. There is no mention of it in *China's
Patriots Sing*, a collection of 22 patriotic songs published in 1944.

brought them orange sodas. I observed one soldier kindly repairing a woman's bicycle.

By singing behind the backs of the soldiers as well as to their faces, the people indicated that they were not planning to commit acts of violence. To my knowledge, no one engaged in acts of violence while singing. Since fear increased the likelihood that some skittish young soldiers would shoot, anything that helped reduce fear would also have helped reduce chaos and bloodshed. Throughout the uprising protesters showed a distaste for chaos. According to Blacking, the black nationalists in the churches of South Africa also shunned chaos (Blacking 1981:46).

The act of singing the "Internationale" also promoted solidarity among the singers themselves. The circumstances of performance along with its historical associations and its text enhanced the feeling of solidarity to such a degree that the sense of individual importance seemed to vanish. John Fraser sums up the strength of the "Internationale" in his story of the Democracy Wall in 1978:

> Finally, after about fifteen minutes, the organizers restored discipline, and everyone relaxed after a very inspired bit of crowd control: a man simply started singing the "Internationale," the stirring anthem of the world's working classes....Everyone sang lustily. I have never heard such singing, never heard a song so moving. I saw what had first seemed a ragtag, disorderly mob transformed into a melded whole, and I got a vision of what "the masses" really meant. The force of their singing was a symbol of the force of their power. (Fraser 1980: 244)

Besides promoting solidarity, singing the "Internationale" also helped demonstrators maintain a positive self-concept in spite of the dehumanizing treatment they received during the invasion on the night of June 3. Like the *sefela* songs of South Africa described by Coplan, the "Internationale" and other patriotic songs were powerful vehicles in establishing self-identity (Coplan 1987: 419). Feelings of solidarity and a secure self-identity gave individuals the courage to face perilous conditions on behalf of their group.

Coplan has suggested that war anthems sung by black South Africans served the role of preparing participants for death rather than victory (Coplan 1987: 416). It is possible that singing in Tiananmen Square at this time served a similar purpose. According to student leader Chai Ling, those in the square on the night of the invasion were preparing to sacrifice themselves. The sound of the "Internationale" radiated like a beacon of conviction that left no doubt about the worthiness of the cause. It seemed to represent a moral commitment that was not negotiable even in the face of death. Encouraged by the lyrics "struggle for the truth," the people may have felt that moral victory was theirs regardless of military outcome, and that at worst, the song would provide an honorable context in which to fall. The singers represented not only themselves, but their fellow countrymen as well. Those who sang assumed the voices of those who fell, demonstrating to the soldiers that their ideals were not easily dispatched. The song would continue even if the individuals did not. The desire for honor was apparent in the actions of the students as they began to leave Tiananmen Square shortly before 5 A.M. on June 4.[13] Holding their banners high, they marched out as if in victory for some invincible power.

Singing the "Internationale" during the military invasion may have helped neutralize the horror of violence, enabling protesters to focus their thoughts enough to continue forward in difficult circumstances. Together with the National Anthem, it helped suppress fear, both during martial law and during the invasion. The jubilant boasting of fearlessness by the member of the "Dare-to-Die" squad mentioned above suggested to me that overcoming fear had been difficult. With the help of a few important songs, protesters reduced the probability that fear would prevent them from committing heroic acts. The people on the streets of Beijing during the military invasion succeeded well enough to convince one reporter that there was a total lack of fear in their faces (Allman 1989:231).

By singing in the face of imminent danger during the military invasion, the people showed how important the "Internationale" was to them in all its different strategic roles. Liu Liang-mo observed in 1945 that the mass-singing movement in China had reached phenomenal heights and that it had a tremendous effect on China's ability to resist the Japanese invasion (Liu 1945). In 1989 singing neither halted the invading army nor gained protesters a voice in the government, yet it formed a fundamental strategy used by the Chinese people to gather their political strength. Singing enhanced the protesters' ability to resist internal oppression and helped establish such a strong network of social bonds that the foundation for subsequent political agitation was firmly established.

MUSIC AS A "DANGER ZONE"

All public performances in Beijing were cancelled immediately after the invasion. This phenomenon was in keeping with what Zhou Fangyang encountered as chairman of the Shanghai Radio and Television Bureau:

> In 1960 I came to work at the radio station (in Shanghai). At that time, music was a "danger zone." Music was called "the sacred sensor of class struggle" and was considered a sensitive area. Every time there was political turbulence, music was always the first area

---

[13]My ability to observe was severely curtailed after 5:15 A.M., June 4, 1989, when soldiers took me into custody, confiscated my video camera and tape, and detained me all day.

> to be affected. The time allotted for music programs was cut time
> and again, many programs were banned. (Zhou 1988, quoted in
> Hamm 1991:24)

In 1989 music was still considered to be a "danger zone," with
live performances having more subversive potential than broadcast
ones. Before the invasion of Beijing on June 4, dissidents sang
songs together in public while soldiers typically listened to popular
music on their truck radios. Even though I observed soldiers daily
on the streets of Beijing from May 20 to July 8, and spent the whole
day of June 4 surrounded by soldiers in their temporary stronghold
at the Workers' Cultural Palace, I never heard them sing anything.
After the invasion I did hear groups of soldiers chanting together
while exercising. In Beijing, not only was the performance of patriotic music a chief sign of commitment to the student movement,
but the public performance of music in general was seen as a clear
sign of political activism. Blacking's observation that the performance of church music in South Africa was a chief sign of commitment to the Zionist way of life is a specialized example of the
general theory that any music can play a political role. If music-
making in general is politically dangerous, then Tiananmen Square
was a hotbed of upheaval during the few weeks of spring in 1989.
The phenomenal rise of political and social feelings in such a short
span of time attests to the potency of the methods used.

Part of the "danger" of music was due to the potential of singing
and chanting to bridge the physical space between people. During
times of threatened invasion, protesters often held hands or hugged
each other while singing. Physical contact was not limited to the
young. Older scientists also put their arms around each other while
chanting. Physical contact during singing or chanting generally enhanced feelings of solidarity, and sometimes continued after performances.

The combination of activity in Tiananmen Square had significance beyond the details of its content in the same way that the early
daytime marches had political consequences beyond the implications of the students' individual actions. A look at the chanting of
the elementary-school children helps explain this phenomenon.
The act of chanting itself was exhilarating, regardless of what was being chanted. Temporarily and within prescribed bounds, the youngsters freely expressed themselves, usually imitating the older students, but never forced to do so. Moreover, their audience gave
them immediate, positive feedback. The demonstrators passing by
either on foot or in their decorated vehicles provided a steady
stream of appreciative responses. This feedback was an exciting re-
ward for the young demonstrators because it proved that they were
able to achieve solidarity with other protesters on their own terms.
Politics and patriotism, though important, were secondary to the establishment of strength in numbers and the feeling of empowerment that accompanied it. To establish the broadest popular

support, the basis for solidarity was quite general and echoed the desire for empowerment: *"renmin wansui"* ("long live the people"). Many chants were variations on this theme. With the supremacy of the people foremost in importance, it was assumed that a responsive and responsible government would follow.

The quest for solidarity with others cut across social strata and divisions by occupation, education, and age. The city people cheered the police and the police cheered back. Older workers marched in support of the student hunger strikers. Communist party members and non-members helped each other demonstrate. Businesses donated goods and funds while workers volunteered services. To safeguard the health of demonstrators at Tiananmen Square, farmers' families distributed garlic and doctors dispensed free medication and advice on how to avoid catching cold while sleeping outdoors. The university students had even hoped to achieve solidarity with foreigners, preparing a warm welcome for Soviet Premier Gorbachev on his May 15 visit. Although prevented from seeing Gorbachev, they were nevertheless successful in forging solidarity with many other people using a variety of means.

The act of chanting was one of the means of establishing strength in numbers. Protesters of all ages became audible and intelligible to onlookers by uniting their voices in chant. Sheer volume was not the goal—a solitary chanter could easily have been amplified with the use of a bullhorn. Numbers of participants were as important as volume in achieving and expressing solidarity. The more endorsement ideas got, the more acceptable they became.[14] Group chanting was therefore an effective way of presenting ideas.

Music was not simply a reflection of the conflict between protesters and officials, it was a central part of the struggle. By accepting each others' singing and chanting, demonstrators accepted each others' freedom of expression. This freedom of expression was a threat to party leaders, especially since the solidarity that resulted from it led to feelings of empowerment, encouraging further independence. Beyond the control of the authorities, music in this context was clearly a "danger zone." The usually silent masses united their voices group by group and delivered their very audible messages. On the most fundamental level, the cacophony on the streets of Beijing and at Tiananmen Square was the emergence of the sound of self-determination and feelings of solidarity made possible by its realization.

---

[14]The value of endorsement was nowhere more prominent than in Tiananmen Square itself during the hunger strike when the students spent many hours soliciting signatures and statements of support from visitors and other hunger strikers. They invited people to write on their clothing, their hats, their school identification cards, and even on their bodies. Heavily "endorsed," these youngsters endured their self-imposed starvation.

CREATIVE ADAPTATION, CULTURAL AUTHORITY, AND SYMBOLISM

The rationale of music as a "danger zone" becomes clearer upon examining the role of creative adaptation in performance and the invocation of cultural authority through historical reference and symbolism. According to an observer in Xi'An, the demonstrators followed a tradition of ritual and political theater, which they manipulated to assert their own identities:

> Whenever students are brought together for a ceremonial occasion, they will try to transform the ritual into an opportunity to affirm their own identities and express their own views. The "Internationale" was the most important anthem of 1989, and it will remain the anthem of the students. It is very hard to ban the "Internationale" as a symbol of bourgeois liberalism.

> The problem goes beyond a specific song. Ritual has always been central to Chinese governance, especially given the Confucian preference for ritual over law. In the Twentieth century, when Confucian ritual began to lose force in the political realm, politicians tried to substitute political theatre....the spring of 1989 has shown us that young people schooled in a politics of theatre will adapt the official repertoire to scripts of their own making. Once they bring their theatre to the streets, they are strikingly creative in devising new repertoires of symbolic protest....the creative potential of China's young actors was proved beyond a doubt. (Esherick 1991: 104-5)

Creative adaptation in performance is an essential ingredient of successful political protest. Contextual factors such as the location and timing of performances were as important as the selection of songs and texts. The call-and-response format of chanting involving large numbers of people might appear to demand little creativity, and yet the interaction between leaders, followers, and audience allowed for considerable creative adaptation. Individual phrases could be added, repeated, or emphasized. Gestures, tone of voice, and shifts from singing to chanting within a song all allowed leaders to shape expression in order to maximize impact on listeners and performers alike. This flexibility in performance heightened the political consciousness of the people of Beijing in the same way that it heightened the political consciousness of church members in South Africa, as noted by Blacking. In addition, the creative manipulation of performance elements helps explain why a wide range of music had political value at Tiananmen Square in 1989. Similarly, Caraveli notes that laments could be used in a variety of contexts in rural Greece: "The manipulation of textual and performance elements can render a lament applicable to a variety of contexts" (1986:187).

Partly through creative adaptation, older songs acquired new meaning in the context of the struggle at Tiananmen Square, contradicting arguments by Greenway and Watson that political songs rarely outlive their composers: "most are occasional songs that lose their meaning when the events for which they were composed are forgotten, or displaced by greater crises" (Greenway 1960:5). The "Internationale" outlived its composer to become the most frequently heard song of the 1989 demonstrations in Beijing, possessing greater political value than the newer songs. Whether or not songs retain political value over time appears to depend on the ability of performers to adapt them to new contexts.

History and tradition furnished a rich and important source of material to be creatively manipulated in performance. In China, the performing arts and popular culture are strongly linked with the traditional heritage:

> The cultural scene as a whole consists of a wide variety of genres and forms. When performing arts are studied alongside written literature, and popular arts are given the same depth of analysis as elite forms, phenomena such as the strength of the traditional heritage in contemporary Chinese culture become more apparent. (McDougall 1984: xiii)

The activities of the students drew upon these connections. The use of human walls to keep out strangers echoed the Great Wall, the all-day march echoed the Long March of Mao's supporters, and the call-and-response format in political chanting echoed protests of the 1930s.[15] Many of the songs heard in 1989 had folk origins, and banners made reference to the demonstrations of 1919.

Besides the practicality of using well-known melodies and songs, references to the past bestowed cultural authority on performers. According to Coplan, historical references are important in legitimizing political criticism by establishing the cultural authority of the performer. The use of metaphors, symbolism, and traditional imagery in creative self-expression helped confirm the cultural authority of the performers, enhancing their status in the eyes of viewers, who often loudly and enthusiastically expressed their admiration. This cultural authority strengthened the identity of the demonstrators, encouraging them to develop heroic self-concepts and entitling them to express dissatisfaction with the current leadership (Coplan 1987:415).

Often ironic or humorous, historical references established the cultural authority of protesters and enhanced group identity while delighting both performers and audiences. When the authorities promised to pay 30 *renminbi*, the equivalent of an average city worker's weekly salary, to each person demonstrating in favor of the government, protesters accepted the offer but circumvented the government's intent by symbolically evoking historical references. Participants on this march of June 2 donned historic masks or hats, some of which referred to the Ming Dynasty, and recited slogans

---

[15]In 1930, workers sang a call-and-response song when reminded of their recent strike for a 10-hour day in a silk factory (Smedley 1943: 92).

taken from feudal ideology, ironically espousing conservative, deliberately anti-modern sentiment, as they marched to Tiananmen Square. Thrilled onlookers ran up to them laughing, yelling, and applauding. By associating the current leadership with Ming Dynasty feudalism, participants in this government-sponsored demonstration were able to make a very effective, ironic statement supporting reform.

Barmé suggests that the protests were especially powerful because they "used the symbols and emotions created by years of government propaganda to oppose the government itself" (Barmé 1991: 52–3). The "Internationale" had greater political value to protesters because of its origins as a Communist song. Likewise Mao-era songs that originated as government propaganda, such as "I Love Beijing, Tiananmen" and "The Three Main Rules of Discipline and the Eight Points for Attention," were particularly effective as protest. This "subversion of symbols" was a powerful tool in the hands of demonstrators.

Referential meaning was not always essential to a song's political impact. The common use of vocables, such as "e-i-o," "fa la la," and "*ho! hei!*" in some songs suggests that participants sought to free themselves from the restrictions of words. Even the "Internationale" contained transliterated syllables whose meaning was obscure. The use of these syllables indicates that other aspects of the songs' performance, such as mood, historical association, or accompanying physical motions, may have been as significant as referential content. The frequent use of non-lexical syllables also suggests that self-expression was important in itself, independent of referential meanings in the texts.

SUMMARY AND CONCLUSION

During the seven weeks of demonstrations in the spring of 1989, music served as a multi-faceted protest strategy in Beijing. It helped maintain order, both on the streets and in Tiananmen Square, and strengthened bonds between people while also distinguishing insiders from outsiders. Chanting unified groups of people, provided safety in numbers, promoted participation of the more timid demonstrators while checking the behavior of the more daring ones, and enhanced the intelligibility of groups to observers. By establishing strength in numbers, chanting promoted solidarity and feelings of empowerment.

Singing and chanting were important in maintaining high morale during the hunger strike, dispelling doubt and fear, and channeling energy for constructive purposes. They assisted in validating the protesters' actions as legal and patriotic, and helped disseminate information, raise money, and minimize danger. Music, as well as other arts, such as literature, calligraphy, painting, drawing, fashion, and even food, were essential in meeting these critical needs during the uprising.

Demonstrators at Tiananmen Square were expected to be able to sing a few patriotic songs such as the "Internationale" and the National Anthem. In addition, individuals and small groups performed a wide variety of music including folk, popular, and classical songs. Sometimes new verses were written or improvised, and phrases were repeated or modified to fit the circumstances of performance. Instrumental music played or broadcast as part of the demonstrations showed a similar breadth of styles and origins. The context of performance or broadcast contributed significantly to the meaning of this music.

The struggle for control of the sound-space at Tiananmen Square enhanced the political consciousness of those on the square and ultimately increased their willingness to act. The sheer bulk of sound-mass at Tiananmen had a stimulating effect on listeners irrespective of the details of its content, indicating that self-expression was as important as the content of what was being expressed. Music not only reflected the conflict between students and government officials, it was itself part of the struggle.

Music played a major role at the Goddess of Democracy statue. It added to the sense of ritual during her construction. The choice of Western classical music helped to validate the project by evoking strong historical and ideological connections. The continuous performances at the statue had symbolic value not only as offerings to the Goddess, but also as representations of her voice. By actively seeking audience participation in performances at the Goddess's base and welcoming a wide variety of music, student organizers indicated a desire not only to be democratic, but also to cultivate solidarity. By accepting all kinds of self-expression, organizers and participants "endorsed" one another, forging strong solidarity regardless of political orientation.

During the invasion of Beijing, singing served as a means of non-violent protest. By singing, the people were able to identify themselves and their non-violent intentions to the soldiers. The act of singing together, as well as the lyrics of the songs, promoted solidarity, enabling people to focus their attention on facing the army and helping them counteract the impact of violence on their ability to respond. Thanks to its high status among the Communists, the "Internationale" provided singers with historical validity and honor regardless of military outcome.

My observations support Blacking's theories concerning the importance of context in music as a protest strategy. The act of singing together at the square and on the streets of Beijing enhanced a collective consciousness. As both Blacking and Caraveli have observed, creative decision-making in performance heightens the political feelings of the performers. In Beijing, singers accentuated timely ideas in their verses and adapted their performances to immediate ‿ circumstances.   My observations firmly support McDougall's theories about the importance of traditional heritage, and also support Coplan's interpretation that historical references strengthen the cultural authority of demonstrators, validating their right to self-expression. As a vehicle for self-expression, music was an integral part of the struggle at Tiananmen Square in 1989, and its remarkable strength as protest strategy depended significantly on contextual factors.

By examining and comparing political protests around the world, we can reach a better understanding of how music affects the development of uprisings. The strength of music as a protest strategy in Beijing illustrates the important position the arts may play in world political events, and suggests that further study in this area will yield valuable results.

REFERENCES

Allman, T.D.
    1989   "The Crushing Wheel of China." *Vanity Fair* 52:10.
Anonymous
    1957   *Kangri Zhanzheng Gequ Xuanji (Selected Songs from the War of
            Resistance against Japan)*. Vol. 1. Beijing: The China Youth Publishing
            Company
    1972   *Zhandi Xin Ge (New Songs of the Battleground)*. Beijing: People's
            Literary Publishing Society.
    1977   *Mao Zhuxi Nin Shi Women Xinzhong Bu Luo de Hong Taiyang
            (Chairman Mao, You are the Unsetting Red Sun in Our Hearts)*. Beijing:
            The People's Music Publishing Company.
Barmé, Geremie
    1991   "Beijing Days, Beijing Nights." *The Pro-Democracy Protests in China:
            Reports from the Provinces*. Jonathan Unger, ed. Armonk, New York:
            M.E. Sharpe.
Bernstein, Richard
    1989   "In a Beijing Shouting Match, the Students Are Loud but Are
            Overpowered." *New York Times International* May 30:4A.
Blacking, John
    1979   "The Power of Ideas in Social Change: The Growth of the Africanist
            Idea in South Africa." *The Conceptualisation and Explanation of
            Processes of Social Change*. David Riches, ed. Belfast: Queen's
            University, Department of Social Anthropology.
    1981   "Political and Musical Function in the Music of Some Black South
            African Churches." *The Structure of Folk Models*. Ladislav Holy and
            Milen Stuchlik. A.S.A. Monograph 20. New York: Academic Press.
Caraveli, Anna
    1986   "The Bitter Wounding: The Lament as Social Protest in Rural Greece."
            Gender and Power in Rural Greece. Jill Dubisch, ed. Princeton: Princeton
            University Press.
Coplan, David B.
    1987   "Eloquent Knowledge: Lesotho Migrant's Song and the Anthropology of
            Experience." *American Ethnologist* 14(3):413–433.

Esherick, Joseph W.
  1991   "Xi'An Spring." *The Pro-Democracy Protests in China: Reports from the
          Provinces.* Jonathan Unger, ed. Armonk, New York: M.E. Sharpe.
Feigon, Lee
  1990   *China Rising: The Meaning of Tiananmen.* Chicago: I. R. Dee.
Ferguson, Francesca
  1979   *A Socio-aesthetic Analysis of Revolutionary Song in the People's
          Republic of China: 1930–1979.* M.A. Thesis, University of California,
          Los Angeles.
Ferguson Rebollo-Sporgi, Francesca
  1992   Personal communication.
Finley, Patrick
  1989   "Beyond the Square: the Roots of Tiananmen." *The
          Monthly.* 19(2):19–39.
Fraser, John
  1980   *The Chinese, Portrait of a People.* New York: Summit Books.
Greenway, John
  1960   *American Folksongs of Protest.* New York: A.S. Barnes.
Hamm, Charles
  1991   "Music and Radio in the People's Republic of China." *Asian Music* 22(2).
Han, Minzhu (pseudonym) and Hua Sheng, eds.
  1990   *Cries for Democracy: Writings and Speeches from the 1989 Chinese
          Democracy Movement.* Princeton: Princeton University Press.
Kraus, Richard Curt
  1989   *Pianos and Politics in China: Middle-Class Ambitions and the Struggle
          over Western Music.* New York: Oxford University Press.
Lee, Pao-chen
  1944   *China's Patriots Sing.* Calcutta: The Chinese Ministry of Information.
Liu, Liang-mo
  1945   *Folk Songs and Fighting Songs of China Collected by Liu Liang-mo.*
          Arranged and translated by Evelyn Modoi. New York: Carl Fischer.
Marty, Ginette and Georges
  1988   *Dictionnaire des Chansons de la Revolution 1787–1799.* Paris:
          Tallandier.
McDougall, Bonnie S., ed.
  1984   *Popular Chinese Literature and Performing Arts in the People's
          Republic of China 1949–1979.* Berkeley: University of California Press.
Reed, W. L. and M.J. Bristow, eds.
  1985   *National Anthems of the World.* 6th edition. Poole, U.K.: Blandford
          Press.
Shapiro, Fred C.
  1989a "Letter from Beijing." *The New Yorker* May 26:13
  1989b "Letter from Beijing." *The New Yorker* June 9:84
Smedley, Agnes
  1943   *Battle Hymn of China.* New York: A.A. Knopf.
Tsao, Hsingyuan
  1989   "The Birth of the Goddess of Democracy." *California Monthly.*
          September.
Wang, Fengqi, ed.
  1985   *Zhongguo Yinyue Cidian (Dictionary of Chinese Music).* Beijing:
          People's Music Publishing Company.
Wong, Ren-Liang
  1990   Personal communication.
Wang, Yuhe, et al., eds.
  1986   *Zhongguo Jin Xiandai Yinyue Shi Jiaoxue Cankao Ziliao (Educational
          Reference Materials in the History of Modern Chinese Music).* Beijing:
          The Central Conservatory of Music.

64 • PACIFIC REVIEW OF ETHNOMUSICOLOGY   **1991**

Watson, Ian
    1983   *Song and Democratic Culture in Britain.* New York: St. Martin's Press.
Zhou, Fangyang
    1988   *From "Radio Friends" to "Stereo Friends."* Shanghai: Radio Shanghai.
Zhou, Qinru
    1991   Personal communication.

Name Index